# Violence Against Women

## New Canadian Perspectives

Edited by
Katherine M. J. McKenna
and
June Larkin



Inanna Publications and Education Inc.
Toronto, Canada

Published by:
Inanna Publications and Education Inc.
operating as *Canadian Woman Studies/les cahiers de la femme*
212 Founders College, York University
4700 Keele Street
Toronto, Ontario M3J 1P3
Telephone: (416) 736-5356 Fax (416) 736-5765
Email: cws/cf@yorku.ca Web site: www.yorku.ca/cwscf

Printed and Bound in Canada.

Cover Design/Interior Design: Luciana Ricciutelli
Cover Art: Rochelle Rubinstein
"The Fall," handpainted woodblock print, draped over artist and photographed, 55" x 42", 2001

The anthology was prepared with the assistance of Health Canada. The opinions expressed in this text are those of the authors and do not necessarily reflect the views of Health Canada.
We acknowledge the support of the Family Violence Prevention Unit and the Women's Health Bureau.

National Library of Canada Cataloguing in Publication Data
Main entry under title:

Violence against women : new Canadian perspectives / edited by Katherine M. J. McKenna and June Larkin

ISBN 0-9681290-6-4
1. Women–crimes against–Canada. 2. Women–Abusde of–Canada. I. McKenna, Katherine Mary Jean, 1955– II. Larkin, June, 1952–

HV6250.4.W6V5352 2002 362.88'082'0971 C2002-9301647-9

# CONTENTS

**Section II**
**Violence and Women's Health**

**Section III**
**Structural Forms of Violence Against Women**

# ACKNOWLEDGEMENTS

The authors would like to thank Holly Johnson (Chief of Research and Analysis, Canadian Centre for Justice Statistics, Statistics Canada) for her helpful comments on an early outline of this book. We have also benefitted from the assistance of two bright young students: Tammy Coleman and Jennifer Shaw. This book was published with generous funding from Health Canada. We would particularly like to express our appreciation for the support of Katalin Kennedy, Issues Expert on Women and Family Violence Prevention with Health Canada. Of course, our tireless editor, Luciana Ricciutelli, was a constant source of encouragement, reminding us tactfully about deadlines and doing all the endless behind-the-scenes work necessary to bring a book into being.

# INTRODUCTION

JUNE LARKIN AND KATHERINE M. J. McKENNA

This book is a reader on violence against women, comprised of articles written by Canadians about multiple aspects of our experience with this critical issue. Though the context is Canadian, the themes are international in scope. Indeed, for a small country, Canada has led the way in many areas of work to end gender-based violence. For example, it has now been more than 25 years since the first shelters for battered women and their children were opened across Canada, and today there is a network of 422 refuges for women fleeing domestic violence (Statistics Canada 44). The inspiration for these services, along with many others such as sexual assault crisis centres, came from the hard work of grassroots feminist activists, who started with little or no funds, and were ultimately successful in convincing government and charitable agencies to support this important work in their communities. Research, writing and publishing on the issue of male violence against women came in the wake of these very practical achievements. A major impetus to this was given in December 1989 by the most tragic of events—the Montreal Massacre—where 14 young women engineering students were rounded up in their university classrooms and shot dead by a man who hated feminists. If nothing else, this moved the issue of systemic violence against women to the forefront of the Canadian public consciousness. Several developments followed this in the early 1990s. The Canadian Panel on Violence Against Women published its groundbreaking report in 1993. In response to public concern, the federal government established the Family Violence Prevention Unit and allocated $2.5 million to establish five centres for research on family violence and violence against women and children across Canada. Health Canada decided that it could no longer ignore this pressing social issue and contracted with Statistics Canada to undertake the 1993 Violence Against Women Survey (VAWS), which was a first in the world and is still a uniquely comprehensive national data source on all forms of violence against women. The consequence of this was a growth in research on violence, fueled by increased funding, public interest, and the continued pressure of those activists who had worked for many years in the front lines of the anti-violence movement.

This book, then, looks at some of the results of that surge in research about male violence against women. All of the articles chosen were originally published since 1995, and they represent some of the latest thinking on these issues in Canada. As editors, we felt that the time was ripe to gather these together in an easy to access single volume that could be a resource for the interested general reader, and would also serve as a text for university undergraduate courses.

Violence against women is undeniably pervasive in Canadian society. The VAWS reported that, "51 per cent of all women had experienced at least one incident of physical or sexual violence since turning the age of 16" (Johnson 92). Although most of these incidents were with men the women knew, and only seven per cent of Canadian women experienced a serious stranger assault, the fear of random violence dominates women's lives. In fact, 42 per cent reported feeling very or somewhat unsafe walking alone after dark in their own neighbourhoods (Johnson 63). This is not the ordinary fear of criminal behaviour felt by all Canadians; this is a gender-based and generalized fear that controls and shapes a woman's life in multiple ways. For this reason, we understand violence against women to be a form of social control that operates to regulate female behaviour.

Our definition of violence is one that encompasses physical, psychological and structural forms of abuse. From this perspective, systems that produce inadequate health care, economic vulnerability, cultural racism and other discriminatory processes are factored into the violence equation. In agreement with O'Toole and Schiffman, our concept of violence, "extends from individual relationships, to the arrangement of power and authority in organizations, to the relations among countries of the world" (vii). At each level, we are concerned with the ways violence functions to preserve inequities in gender relations. The authors included in this volume offer various and sometimes conflicting perspectives on the construction of gender relation—positions we attribute to the complexity of the very notion of gender in a contemporary and globalized world.

In thinking about violence, we are drawn to theorists such as Himani Bannerji who takes an intersectional approach that considers the way gender, race, class, and other forms of oppression interact to mutually construct and reinforce each other. We agree with her that the conceptualization of "intersectionality" is an analytical challenge that has yet to be worked out, but it is a challenge that we see as foundational to understanding the processes that support violence. Yet this book is not solely about theory. We have tried throughout this volume to include articles that link theory and practice and not to lose sight of the lived realities of real women who experience violence.

This book has been organized into three sections. The first examines the nature and prevalence of violence against women. We start with Holly Johnson of

Statistics Canada, who was responsible for the 1993 VAWS. In her article, "Methods of Measurement," she looks critically at various means of gathering evidence about the prevalence of violence against women, including police statistics, clinical samples, population surveys, and the VAWS. The VAWS improved upon previous surveys by adding detailed questions on the forms of violence more common for women and extending the reference period for violent incidents, allowing it to capture incidents of violence that would otherwise not have been detected. Johnson concludes her discussion by commenting on the Conflict Tactics Scale (CTS), the most commonly used instrument to measure family violence. The CTS has been widely criticized by feminists as a research tool that conflates types of abuse, takes violence out of context, ignores gender-based power relations and differences in the reporting of rates of violence between men and women. Wherever the CTS is used, men and women are shown to have nearly identical rates of domestic violence. The VAWS did not interview men, and its higher reported rates of violence were seen by a small but vocal group as being proof that the survey was deeply flawed and biased.

Anthony Doob addresses this backlash in "Understanding the Attacks on Statistics Canada's Violence Against Women Survey." He points out that "the issue of violence against women is, quite simply, a different question from violence against men" (57-58) and one that requires a specifically tailored screening approach. Because it is well documented that the rates of gender violence are higher for women than for men, Doob claims that the survey's focus on women makes sense from both a research and a policy perspective. This was clearly shown, Yasmin Jiwani contends, by the only follow up that has been done to the 1993 VAWS. In 1999, questions only about domestic violence, asked of both men and women, were added to the General Social Survey (GSS) carried out by Statistics Canada. The questions asked, she observes, have much in common with the CTS in their lack of context. For example, an act of self-defence would be classified as being the same as an unprovoked attack, if the same type of violence was used. The result was that a superficial examination of the GSS results would seem to support the conclusion that men and women are almost equally violent. At the time this resulted in front-page headlines which, she observes, "[have] contributed to the growing gap between the realities of wife abuse that women and front line workers know first-hand, and the popular myths that permeate society about women's aggression and tendencies to violence" (63). Yet, a closer examination of the results shows an entirely different picture, with women being subject to much more severe forms of abuse with a far greater impact on them than men. Jiwani also notes that the full spectrum of violence against women is not captured in the survey and questions the validity of the results when women who do not speak English or French, homeless women (many of whom are escaping violence), Aboriginal women on reserves, and women without access to phones were excluded from the study. Both Jiwani and Doob provide evidence to dispute claims that violence within gender relations is symmetrical and express concerns that such assertions can be used to dismiss the reality of women's experiences.

Aysan Sev'er shares this concern, that the media reports violence against women in a distorted, partially understood, and sensationalized manner which hides the fact that violence against women is endemic in our society. In "Exploring the Continuum: Sexualized Violence by Men and Male Youth Against Women and Girls," she contends that we have to look at the systemic nature of violence against women, seeing it within a general climate of misogyny as manifested in the rise in sexual harassment, terrorist activities against abortion providers, and instances of femicide. Expressing doubts about the effectiveness of punitive measures on individuals who commit acts of violence, Sev'er proposes that we consider how the continuum of misogyny operates on a broad social scale.

At one end of Sev'er's continuum, there is femicide, which is the subject of Rosemary Gartner's, Myrna Dawson's, and Maria Crawford's article, "Woman Killing: Intimate Femicide in Ontario, 1974-1994." At the other end, we have the more mundane and everyday realities of abuse within dating relationships, discussed by Walter DeKeseredy and Martin D. Schwartz in "The Incidence and Prevalence of Woman Abuse in Canadian Courtship."

DeKeseredy and Schwartz examine woman abuse in college dating relationships and find that it has roots in earlier dating experiences. They suggest that the lower disclosure rates in elementary and high school may be a consequence of the victims spending less time with the victimizers than they do in the university setting where they are often living away from home. In comparing statistics, the authors conclude that college dating abuse is just as prevalent in Canada as it is in the United States and that women have more to fear from dating partners than strangers. These findings provide evidence to challenge the popular construction of violence against women as a problem of women's vulnerability in public places. In reality, women are more likely to be abused in the private sphere by males with whom they have an intimate connection.

At its worst, such intimate relationships may lead to the most extreme form of violence against women, femicide. Gartner, Dawson and Crawford echo the points made by earlier authors in contending that the portrayal of the murder of women by their partners within a general rubric of "spousal violence" obscures that there are significant gender differences involved. They observe that male proprietariness and sexual jealously are common issues in female homicide. The authors caution, however, that the statistics on intimate femicide which show that almost two thirds of women who are killed are victims of their intimate male partners, is almost certainly an underestimate because the research included marital partners but not estranged, common-law, and current and former boyfriends.

Gartner and her colleagues suggest that the rates of femicide are particularly high among Aboriginal populations. Emma D. LaRocque stresses the importance of examining current statistics on violence in a larger historical context. In "Violence in Aboriginal Communities," she considers how the legacy of violent colonialism and the internalization of racism by the colonized group have led to "staggering" rates of violence, particularly against Aboriginal women. Considering the problems associated with being a victim of sexual assault in a small community, as well as the racial biases of the judicial system, LaRocque is particularly concerned with justice for the victim. She recommends that violence be taken up as a social issue by Aboriginal leaders and that training workshops and conferences are needed for agencies working with this problem.

The unique problems experienced by abused women in small communities are also addressed by Diane J. Forsdick Martz and Deborah Bryson Saraurer in "Domestic Violence and the Experiences of Rural Women in East-Central Saskatchewan." Based on interviews with rural women who were survivors of abuse, they discuss the specific challenges such women face in situations of domestic violence. In rural settings, there are fewer, if any, services for abused women and many are unable to get to an urban area where shelters and other services are more available.

Returning to the less extreme end of the violence continuum, Himani Bannerji looks at the issue of sexual harassment. In her article, "In the Matter of 'X': Building Race into Sexual Harassment," Bannerji shares with LaRocque a desire to show how the particular historic and cultural realities of a community work to make violence a more complex and even more harmful reality. She examines this "intersectionality" of race, class, and gender in the experience of one black woman in a hostile workplace. Bannerji argues that the way sexual harassment is constructed with regard to women is limited because women are differently sexed in a racist society. Considering that the conceptualization of sexual harassment begins with an undifferentiated notion of "woman" that is neither raced nor classed, Bannerji questions how we make the transition from "woman" to "black woman" in our understanding of sexual harassment. According to Bannerji, racist sexism, which is the foundation of racist sexual harassment, "codes a gender-'race' organization of the western societies ... historically connected to colonialism and slavery and presently to an imperialist form of capital" (201). Bannerji argues that racist sexual harassment in the workplace needs to be considered in the larger context of the gender, race and class organization of Canadian society.

Taken together, the readings in the first section show that the way, and in what context, we examine violence are just as important as the facts that we report. Violence affects all women to different degrees depending on their various locations or intersectionalities, yet the experience of fear of male violence is pervasive. Increasingly, many who have studied violence against women have found that a useful frame in which to place it is that of quality of life, a woman's right to live in peace and security, in a safe and healthy environment free of all kinds of violence. Looked at from this perspective, violence against women is perhaps best constructed as an issue of public health, a concern that is systemic and not just a matter of individual victims and oppressors. Accordingly, the second section of this book examines "Violence and Women's Health."

Building upon concepts closely related to Bannerji's "intersectionality," Yasmin Jiwani looks at "Race, Gender, Violence, and Health Care." She argues that the violence immigrant women of colour experience at the juncture of these intersecting systems of domination is compounded by their subordinate status within their own communities. This, in turn, is the result of patriarchal forces heightened by state immigration policies, isolation, cultural racism, and the fear of exclusion from their community if violence is reported. She cautions against the promotion of culturally appropriate services which foreground "culture" and obscure structural issues such as racism, economic exploitation, the privileging of western scientific medicine over indigenous knowledge and fears about legal status. These are just some of the factors that create additional health risks for immigrant women of colour. In general, she observes, the health care system has not been hospitable to women victims of violence, and "the medical encounter is a hierarchical one in which power inequalities between the patient and the physician are asserted and reinforced" (234).

This hierarchical dynamic, combined with a lack of understanding of the particular needs of women who have suffered abuse is the subject of Sari Tudiver's, Lynn McClure's, Tuula Heinonen's, Christine Kreklewitz's and Carol Scurfield's article, "Remembrance of Things Past: The Legacy of Childhood Sexual Abuse in Midlife Women." At a time of their life when they are most likely to need medical aid, some women may avoid seeking it due to a past history of abuse which makes the physical invasiveness of medical procedures very difficult to deal with. Medical practitioners need to be educated about child sexual abuse (CSA) and ways to identify and respond appropriately to these women's issues. The authors point out that, "Women with disabilities, a large proportion of whom have CSA histories, and immigrant and refugee women who may be fearful to speak of their past, encounter particular obstacles in accessing services" (261).

The trauma of early violent experiences can manifest itself in many ways. Jenny Horsman in "Literacy Learning for Survivors of Trauma: Acting 'Normal'" explores the impact of abuse on women's literacy learning and critiques the notion that healing from trauma is simply a process of moving from abnormal to normal responses. Her claim that the pressure to act "normal" can slow or block learning for survivors of violence is also evident in Mary Nyquist's moving account of the ways trauma can hinder learning in a traditional educational setting. Nyquist's first person stream of consciousness account of a traumatized teen, "Struck Dumb," shows vividly how difficult it can be to cope when under severe stress. Horsman concludes that women who have experienced trauma may bring survival strategies to their learning situations which should be acknowledged in educational programs.

Elizabeth Comack is also concerned about the pathologizing of women's trauma. In "Do We Need To Syndromize Women's Experiences? The Limitations of the 'Battered Woman Syndrome'" she argues for a cautious reading of the Lavelle case, the landmark judgment in Canadian jurisprudence that marks the legal recognition of the Battered Women's Syndrome (BWS) in cases involving women who kill their abusive partners. The authors argue that BWS appeals to psychological discourse so that abused women's experiences are individualized, medicalized, and depoliticized with little attention to the social and economic conditions that promote male violence against women. As a result, women are seen more as victims of their dysfunctional personalities than they are of their male abusers.

The politics of examining violence and health is the subject of Katherine M. J. McKenna's and Dawn G. Blessing's work "Mapping the Politics of a Research Journey: Violence Against Women as a Public Health Issue." They argue that the hierarchical medical model of treatment might best be replaced by a more community-oriented public health focus on wellness and prevention of violence against women. The authors trace a research project designed to put violence against women on the public health agenda and describe the obstacles they encountered in an attempt to take a community coalition approach to research. Ultimately, the authors conclude that it is a patriarchal system that privileges theorizing and professionalism over community activism.

June Larkin, in her article, "Women, Poverty, and HIV Infection," also takes a broad systemic view of women's health. Noting that, worldwide, the rates of HIV infection for women are on the rise, Larkin examines poverty as a form of structural violence that operates as a conduit for the gender transmission of AIDS. With a particular focus on sexual violence, she explores the local and global factors that put women at HIV risk and discusses the ways structural inequities are ignored in the discourse on women and HIV/AIDS.

The concluding article in this section, by Tanis Day and Katherine M. J. McKenna, "The Health-Related Economic Costs of Violence Against Women in Canada: The Tip of the Iceberg," examines how the health burden of violence is felt, not just by those who experience the violence, but by all of us in society. This is a good example of a study which only became possible because of the data made available by the 1993 VAWS. Using conservative estimates, and acknowledging that there are many gaps in the data that mean that only the "tip of the iceberg" of violence against women can be costed, the final calculation of health-related economic costs to Canadian society in one year alone are still in excess of 1.5 billion dollars for 1993.

The authors in our final section, Structural Forms of Violence Against Women, consider the ways institutional forces create or reinforce conditions of inequity that increase women's vulnerability to abuse.

To understand violence against women in South Asian communities in, "A Question of Silence: Reflections on Violence Against Women in Communities of Colour," Himani Bannerji argues that we must extend our analysis beyond a critique of patriarchal and gendered social organization. When communities are constructed politically from the outside through forces related to imperialism, immigration, and the sexism and racism of the host country, Bannerji notes that internal sources of division related to class, gender and other power relations can be suppressed. As a form of resistance to assimilation, communities may embrace the so-called "cultural differences" the state uses to differentiate them from the dominant group. According to Bannerji, such differences, often framed as "tradition," are commonly expressed through religious practices and moral regulation that are oppressive to women and increase their vulnerability to violence.

From both a local and global perspective, Helene Moussa considers the systems contributing to gender-related violence against refugee women. As she discusses in her article, "Violence Against Refugee Women: Gender Oppression, Canadian Policy, and the International Struggle for Human Rights," the horrific physical conditions of refugee camps have a reality for women that is actually far worse than what we see every night on North American television news. She offers an analysis of the context in which refugee women experience sexual violence and oppression in their home countries and how militarization and war adds to it. Moussa considers, as well, refugee women's vulnerability to violence in transition and in the asylum country. Based on a discussion of the ways international and Canadian policies can both help and hinder refugee women, Moussa outlines gender factors that should be considered in decisions about refugee claims.

Refugee and immigrant women face numerous systemic obstacles in Canadian society as do those who suffer from poverty and homelessness. Suzanne Lenon points to other risk factors for violence in "Living on the Edge: Women, Poverty, and Homelessness in Canada." For Lenon, the dynamics of violence in women's lives and the ways they cope can also challenge conventional notions of "homelessness." She points out that homelessness is a problem for women but may also be a strategy for escaping violence. In cases of abuse, for example, homelessness may be considered a solution to a lack of safety in the home, particularly when cuts to social services have limited women's ability to escape violent situations.

The connection between violence against women and economic vulnerability described by Lenon is highlighted in two articles that focus on the devastating effects of the cutbacks to social services for abused women in Ontario. In the first article, "Before and After: A Woman's Story With Two Endings," the Metro Woman Abuse Council examines a Spanish-speaking woman's experience of spousal abuse. One story offers an ending in which a woman was able to escape the violence in her own home by accessing services available to her. In the second story, a woman is forced to return to the abusive situation because these services have been eliminated by the Harris government. A second article written by The Ontario Association of Interval and Transition Houses (OAITH), "Locked In, Left Out: Impacts of the Budget Cuts on Abused Women and their Children," also considers the impact of budget cuts on abused women. In listing the services affected by the cuts, the authors paint a vivid picture of a crumbling safety net of programs and policies that had provided essential support for women in violent situations. The end result is "the blocking of escape routes abused women and women's advocates have struggled to open for over 20 years" (421).

In contrast, in "Men at Work to End Wife Abuse in Quebec: A Case Study in Claims-Making," authors Juergen Dankwort and Rudolph Rausch detail how in Quebec, services for abusive men have been allocated significant resources. They argue that these men's groups have developed based on male identity politics, with little evidence of collaborative work, consultation and accountability to women's groups and shelters. Yet the authors feel that there should be a significant role for men in eliminating violence against women and that there is real potential to further the efforts started by the battered women's movement. To ensure that victims of violence are not ignored, the authors conclude that the institutionalized privilege of males should be a focus of men's groups.

In the next two articles, the authors focus on the connection between violence and the ways particular institutions reproduce systems of domination through processes of cultural representation, exclusion, and the construction of marginalized groups as deviant or inferior. In "Erasing Race: The Story of Reena Virk," Yasmin Jiwani critically analyzes the media coverage of the brutal murder of Reena Virk, a 14 year old girl of South Asian origin. She argues that framing the murder as a crime of girl-on-girl violence overshadows the larger problem of male violence and ignores critical issues that increase the risk of violence in the lives of racialized girls. By focusing on weight and height as the reason Virk did not "fit in," Jiwani argues that normative standards of beauty were not examined and issues of racism and assimilation were overlooked.

Kim Pate, in "Labelling Young Women as Violent: Vilification of the Most Vulnerable," is also concerned about distorted media coverage which sensationalizes and wildly exaggerates "girl violence." In her discussion of the criminal justice system and youth, Pate provides evidence to counter these inaccurate claims of increased violence by girls and explores the factors contributing to poor, young racialized women and girls becoming the fastest growing prison population worldwide. For Pate, the criminalization of what can also be seen as girls' survival strategies is one example of the way gender bias in the law can compromise girls' safety. She concludes that the legal system "reinforces sexist, racist and classist stereotypes of women while simultaneously legitimizing patriarchal notions of the need to socially control women" (468).

Taking a broader perspective on the justice system, Elizabeth Sheehy's "Legal Responses to Violence Against Women in Canada" chronicles the history of the women's movement and its relationship to the law. She demonstrates the ways in which formal equality approaches to the law have failed women and argues that violence against women must be conceptualized as an issue of substantive equality which takes account of the inequalities women face and challenges power relations and beliefs. Stressing the importance of the women's movement, Sheehy argues that, although the law is an important tool, violence against women will not be eliminated until equality for all women is fully realized.

We agree with Sheehy that ending violence against women is really a question of ending all forms of power abuse, structural inequality, unfairness and discrimination in Canadian society. We offer this volume as one small contribution toward achieving that ultimate goal.

## References

Canadian Panel on Violence Against Women. *Changing the Landscape: Ending Violence, Achieving Equality, Final Report*. Ottawa, 1993.

Johnson, Holly. *Dangerous Domains: Violence Against Women in Canada*. Toronto: Nelson Canada, 1996.

O'Toole L. L., and J. R. Schiffman. *Gender Violence: Interdisciplinary Perspectives*. New York: New York University Press, 1997.

Statistics Canada. *Family Violence in Canada: A Statistical Profile 2001*. Ottawa: Minister of Industry, 2001.

# I. THE PREVALENCE AND NATURE OF VIOLENCE AGAINST WOMEN IN CANADA

# Methods of Measurement

Holly Johnson

In studying violence against women, researchers frequently begin with questions such as "How many women are affected?" "How often?" "Who is affected?" and "What are the consequences?" Answers to these questions are important for determining the seriousness or magnitude of the problem and to attract the attention of other researchers, policy-makers, and legislators. But the answers are not altogether straightforward.

The most common and longstanding source of statistical information about violent crime is the Uniform Crime Reporting (UCR) Survey, which records criminal incidents that come to the attention of the police (Canadian Centre for Justice Statistics 1993). Police statistics are problematic because, for a variety of reasons, a very significant proportion of all types of crimes are not reported to the police, many of which involve serious harm to victims. In order to get around the shortcomings of police statistics, early researchers began using the testimonies of victims in counselling or offenders in treatment to examine the impact of violence on victims and the motives behind these offences. From the testimony of these subjects, researchers began to understand that incidents of sexual assault and wife battering were not rare, sadistic acts of a few psychotic men but were much more prevalent than available statistics or popular belief would suggest. But these approaches also had their limitations. Like police statistics, the samples of women and men used in these studies were extreme cases and not representative of all incidents.

Random sample surveys of the population emerged as a social science tool in the late 1970s, and criminal justice researchers began exploring the "dark figure" of crime that is not reported to the police. One purpose of these surveys was to estimate the prevalence of criminal victimization in the general population. Specialized surveys of family violence and violence against women followed as researchers attempted to address some of the shortcomings demonstrated by traditional crime victim surveys in measuring these events. Statistics Canada's national survey on violence against women is one such special survey that is based on the random sample method of surveying. It provides representative data on the nature and the extent of a wide range of violent events reported by women and is referred to extensively throughout this text.

Thi article explores the various methods that have been used to measure the dimensions and the nature of male violence against women, including police statistics, clinical samples, and population surveys, as well as a detailed description of the methodology of the National Violence Against Women Survey. The advantages and limitations of each approach are discussed.

## Police Statistics

For decades, information collected by police and entered into the UCR Survey has formed the basis for official crime rates and criminal justice policies. Yet students of criminology and criminal justice practitioners know that police statistics have certain limitations as a measurement of crime, including the fact that many serious acts of violence are never reported to the police and so will not appear in their records. Another limitation relates to the high degree of discretion that accompanies the police officer's role. While discretion and professional judgement are essential components of effective policing, both can have a profound effect on what is eventually recorded as a crime in police statistics.

Police officers on patrol act as gatekeepers through which complaints from citizens must pass before becoming part of the official crime count. When officers are dispatched to answer calls for assistance, they take with them a personal set of values and beliefs about what constitutes a criminal assault by a man against his wife and what is merely a "domestic dispute." They generally know what kinds of cases Crown prosecutors have set as priorities and which are likely to be dismissed before they get to court; they know from experience what kind of evidence is required to secure a conviction at a criminal trial, and they know before they respond to a call what priorities have been established by their own departments. Dispatchers may be under many of the same directives, and so some calls for assistance may not even be forwarded to a police officer for action (Jaffe, Hastings, Reitzel and Austin).

But the filtering process begins even before a call is made to the police. A labelling process takes place in which the victim defines the incident as a crime and something that is appropriate for the police to know about. A number of factors influence this process and her eventual decision to call the police or not: the seriousness of the event for her; her relationship to the offender; her age, education, and social standing; the circumstances surrounding the incident; her past experiences with the same offender and the same type of incident; and her past experiences with the police. Her relationship to the offender is a critical factor influencing the labelling process and her eventual decision to involve the police or other outsiders. If she or others around her minimize, excuse, or accept a certain amount of violence in the context of marriage, she is unlikely to feel it is appropriate to call the police when her husband assaults her.

All of these factors combine to influence the discretion of both the victim and the individual officer who responds to a complaint. Each can have a significant impact on the official rates of violence recorded by the police, and each may vary among different communities and within the same community over a period of time. Changes in the levels of sexual assault or wife assault over time may reflect real changes in the number of these crimes committed, or they may reflect changes in the willingness of women to report to the police, changes in policies set by individual departments, increases in resources dedicated to responding to certain types of crimes, or even improvements in technology and the ability of the police to detect and record incidents that are reported to them. The way the police record certain crimes, such as wife assault, can also be affected by perceptions of the seriousness of violence among family members and the extent of harm done, perceptions that have undergone dramatic change in recent years. One research study in Newfoundland found that many calls to the police involving violence by men against their wives were recorded by the police as "drunk and disorderly in the home" or "weapons offences" rather than some type of assault, categories that were not even counted as violent crimes (O'Grady).

When interpreting police statistics, it is also important to note that the UCR Survey covers crimes that have been reported to and substantiated by the police. If, after a preliminary investigation, the police officer determines that an offence did not occur, it becomes "unfounded" and is subtracted from the number of reported incidents to produce a figure that represents the "actual" number of incidents. Lorenne Clark and Debra Lewis, in an examination of rape cases in Toronto police files from 1970, discovered that "unfounding" did not always mean that an incident of rape did not take place. The criteria used by the police in unfounding a case included no injury to the victim; no weapon present; an offender who was known to the victim; a woman who had been drinking; an incident that was not reported immediately; a woman who was separated, divorced, or living common-law; and a woman who was unemployed or living on welfare. In many unfounded cases, there was factual evidence that a rape did take place. The reasons for designating a case as "unfounded" seemed more to do with the police officer's perception of the victim's character and the probability that the case would be successfully prosecuted than whether a rape had actually occurred.

## The Laws on Assault and Sexual Assault

In the early 1980s, Parliament undertook a review of the Criminal Code provisions related to assault, and in 1983 three offences of assault and three parallel offences of sexual assault came into effect. The definition of assault in Section 265 of the *Criminal Code* is as follows:

(1) A person commits an assault when

(a) without the consent of another person, he applies force intentionally to that other person, directly or indirectly;
(b) he attempts or threatens, by an act or gesture, to apply force to another person, if he has, or causes that other person to believe on reasonable grounds that he has, present ability to effect his purpose; or
(c) while openly wearing or carrying a weapon or an imitation thereof, he accosts or impedes another person or begs.

Physical violence is not necessary for an assault to occur, but there must be a threatening act or gesture that causes the other person to believe the perpetrator has the ability to carry out an assault.

Assaults are categorized according to the degree of injury or harm done. Simple assault, commonly known as Level I assault, is punishable by a maximum prison term of five years. A threatened assault, or an actual assault that did not result in serious physical injury, would both be categorized as Level I assault. Level II assault involves the presence of a weapon or bodily harm to the victim such as broken bones, cuts, or bruises and is punishable by up to ten years in prison. Level III, or aggravated assault, results in wounding, maiming, or endangering the victim's life and can result in a maximum prison term of 14 years.

One important component of these legislative changes, from the perspective of crimes against women, is the manner in which police can now lay assault charges. Under the new law, police officers can lay a charge against someone they suspect of committing an assault if there is "reasonable and probable cause" for believing that an assault has occurred. This is a dramatic and important change from the pre-1983 legislation, which stated that, in the absence of physical evidence such as injuries, there had to be a witness to the assault before a charge could be laid. This was a significant problem in cases of wife assault, where there were seldom witnesses other than the woman herself. Police officers often had to leave the home knowing that further assaults were likely to happen and that they were unable to protect the woman. The new law enables police to offer greater protection to women by laying charges, removing the man from the home, and decreasing the immediate risk of further violence.

Closely following these legal changes, police departments across the country issued directives to police officers to lay charges in cases of domestic violence in which there were reasonable and probable grounds to believe that an assault had occurred. These directives were intended to encourage women to report incidents of wife assault, to demonstrate to the public that these assaults were treated seriously by the criminal justice system, and to change norms and attitudes among many in the justice system who treated assaults on wives as less serious offences. These directives were accompanied by special training for most police officers in the appropriate handling of domestic assaults, and some of the larger police departments have established special units to deal exclusively with these types of calls. Special training, and in some cases special units, have also been developed for Crown prosecutors to improve the treatment of victims prior to and during court and improve conviction rates.

The legislative changes of 1983 also abolished the offences of rape, attempted rape, sexual intercourse with the feeble-minded, and indecent assault on males and females, and replaced them with three levels of a new offence of sexual assault that parallel the assault provisions. While many of the biases against rape victims that were popular at the time of the Clark and Lewis study have faded substantially over the past 20 years, the new law did nothing to restrict the decree of discretion open to police officers. Sexual assault is undefined by the Criminal Code, except that the general definition of assault described in Section 265(l) (on the previous page) also applies to all forms of sexual assault. This left a great deal of uncertainty among police and discretion as to what differentiated an assault from a *sexual* assault and how these events would be classified in official statistics.

Section 271 simply sets out the penalty for Level I sexual assaults as follows:

Every one who commits a sexual assault is guilty of

(a) an indictable offence and is liable to imprisonment for a term not exceeding ten years; or
(b) an offence punishable on summary conviction by 18 months imprisonment and/or a fine of $2,000.

Section 272 describes Level II sexual assaults as follows:

Every one who, in committing a sexual assault,

(a) carries, uses or threatens to use a weapon or an imitation thereof,
(b) threatens to cause bodily harm to a person other than the complainant,
(e) causes bodily harm to the complainant, or
(d) is a party to the offence with any other person,

is guilty of an indictable offence and liable to imprisonment for a term not exceeding 14 years.

In defining Level III sexual assaults, Section 273 states:

(1) Every one commits an aggravated sexual assault who, in committing a sexual assault, wounds, maims, disfigures or endangers the life of the complainant.

(2) Every one who commits an aggravated sexual assault is guilty of an indictable offence and liable to imprisonment for life.

It was not until 1987, in the Supreme Court case of *R.* v. *Chase*, that the top court provided guidelines as to what constitutes a sexual assault. In this case, a New Brunswick man had been found not guilty of sexual assault after grabbing a 15-year-old girl's breasts. He was originally found guilty after a trial in provincial court, and when he appealed to the New Brunswick Court of Appeal, a conviction for common assault was substituted for the sexual assault conviction. The appeal court argued that "sexual" should be taken to refer to genitalia and that a broader definition could lead to "absurd results" if it encompassed other parts of the body such as secondary sex characteristics. The Supreme Court rejected this argument, noting that appeal courts in Ontario, Alberta, and British Columbia had also done so. In their judgement, the Justices of the Supreme Court ruled that the test for the sexual nature of an assault does not depend solely on contact with specific areas of the body but on circumstances of a sexual nature such that the sexual integrity of the victim is violated. The court established certain factors that are relevant in considering whether the conduct is sexual, including the part of the body touched, the nature of the contact the situation in which the conduct occurred, the words and gestures accompanying the act, and all other circumstances surrounding the conduct, including threats.

## Trends in Assault and Sexual Assault Statistics

Recent trends in the official rates of sexual and nonsexual assault in Canada paint a picture of rapidly rising rates of violent crime. There have been clear increases in the rates of both sexual and nonsexual assault since the passage of the reform legislation in 1983: in 1993, a total of 34,764 incidents of sexual assault were reported to the police in Canada, a figure that can be calculated as 121 incidents for every 100,000 people in the population, up from 11,932 incidents reported in 1983 (48 per 100,000 population) (Figure 1 and Table 1). This is an increase of 152 per cent in the rate over the ten-year period. In the five years prior to the 1983 law reform, rates of rape and indecent assault increased only 18 per cent, from 38 to 45 per 100,000 (Figure 1).

Although the number of nonsexual assaults reported to the police each year is much higher than the number of sexual assaults, they follow a similar pattern. The rate of nonsexual assaults increased only 14 per cent in the five years prior to 1983, from 427 to 487 per 100,000. Following the enactment of the new legislation, the rate of assaults recorded by the police increased 62 per cent, from 498 to 805 per 100,000. Like sexual assaults, rates of nonsexual assault have levelled off in recent years (Figure 2).

The historical UCR Survey that dates back to 1962 does not differentiate incidents of wife assaults, and so it is not clear what percentage of the increase in assaults can be traced to increases in reported wife assaults and what percentage

**TABLE I**
**Number and Rate of Incidents of Sexual Assault[1] and Nonsexual[2] Assault Reported to the Police in Canada, 1978-1993**

| | Sexual Assault | | Nonsexual Assault | |
|---|---|---|---|---|
| Year | Number | Rates per 100 000 Population | Number | Rates per 100 000 Population |
| 1978 | 8, 961 | 38 | 100, 512 | 427 |
| 1979 | 9, 754 | 42 | 107, 082 | 451 |
| 1980 | 10, 164 | 42 | 110, 991 | 461 |
| 1981 | 10, 550 | 44 | 114, 748 | 471 |
| 1982 | 10, 990 | 45 | 119, 869 | 487 |
| 1983 | 11, 932 | 48 | 123, 611 | 498 |
| 1984 | 14, 793 | 59 | 129, 613 | 509 |
| 1985 | 18, 248 | 73 | 137, 726 | 547 |
| 1986 | 20, 530 | 82 | 149, 982 | 592 |
| 1987 | 22, 369 | 88 | 163, 005 | 637 |
| 1988 | 24, 898 | 96 | 171, 734 | 662 |
| 1989 | 26, 795 | 101 | 183, 265 | 690 |
| 1990 | 27, 843 | 104 | 199, 377 | 741 |
| 1991 | 30, 351 | 113 | 218, 762 | 799 |
| 1992 | 34, 355 | 121 | 226, 350 | 796 |
| 1993 | 34, 764 | 121 | 231, 699 | 805 |

[1]Includes rape and indecent assault in the years 1978 to 1982 and sexual assault Levels I, II, and III in the years 1983 to 1993.
[2]Includes wounding, causing bodily harm and other assaults in the years 1978 to 1982 and assault Levels I, II, and III, causing bodily harm, discharging a firearm with intent, and other assaults in the years 1983 to 1993.

Source: Canadian Centre for Justice Statistics, 1993.

are due to other types of assault. Revisions to the UCR Survey began in the 1980s to expand it from a summary survey to a micro-database survey with details about victims, offenders, and incidents that can be cross-tabulated and linked in various ways. Until this revision, the UCR Survey did not contain information about the gender of victims or the relationship between victim and offenders that could identify incidents of violence against women. Although the number of assaults of

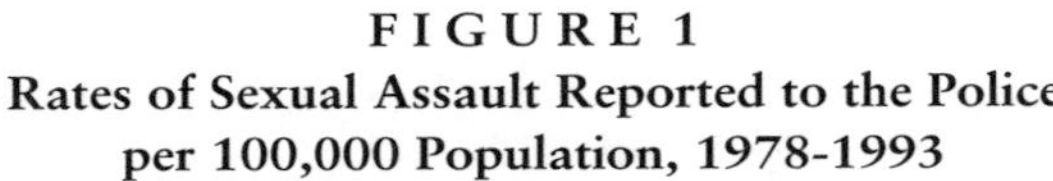
FIGURE 1
Rates of Sexual Assault Reported to the Police per 100,000 Population, 1978-1993

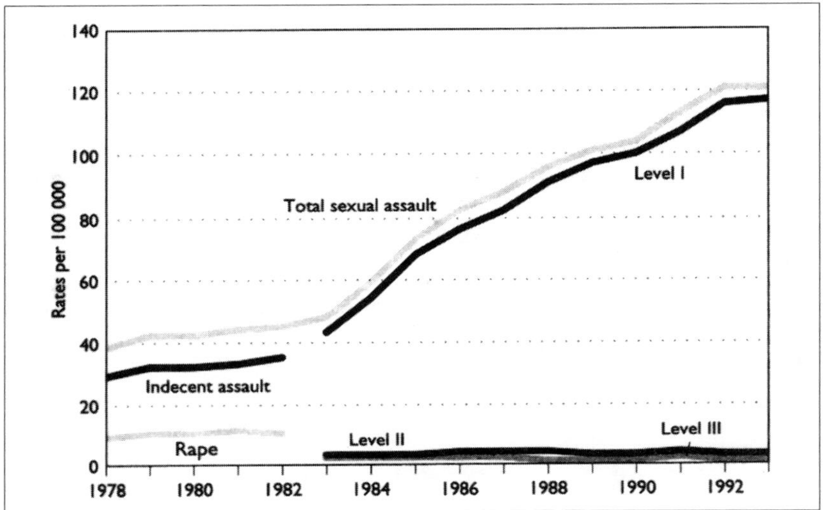


Source: Canadian Centre for Justice Statistics, UCR, 1993.
Note: Legal reform in 1983 abolished the offences of rape, attempted rape, and indecent assault and replaced them with three levels of a new offence—sexual assault.

varying degrees of seriousness were recorded by the police each year, there was no way of telling how many were committed by a man against his wife. A sample of the revised survey indicates that 21 per cent of all assaults in 1993 involved assaults against women by their husbands or common-law partners (Canadian Centre for Justice Statistics 1993).

It also indicates that over half of all sexual assaults (Levels I, II, and III were committed against young people under 18 years of age, an important detail unavailable until recent revisions to this survey.

How can we explain the dramatic increase in rates of sexual and nonsexual assault since 1983? It is unlikely that the passage of the new legislation would have coincided with a real increase in sexual aggression and other acts of violence. It would appear on the surface that the legal reforms, and the publicity surrounding them, have had the desired effect of encouraging victims of sexual and nonsexual assault to come forward to seek redress through the criminal justice system and that confidence in the justice system continues to rise. On the other hand, increases in rates of these offences could have been caused by gradual increases in the numbers of suspects apprehended or charged as police attitudes and charging policies continue to influence the attention these cases are given (recall that these

FIGURE 2
**Rates of Nonsexual Assault Reported to the Police per 100,000 Population, 1978-1993**

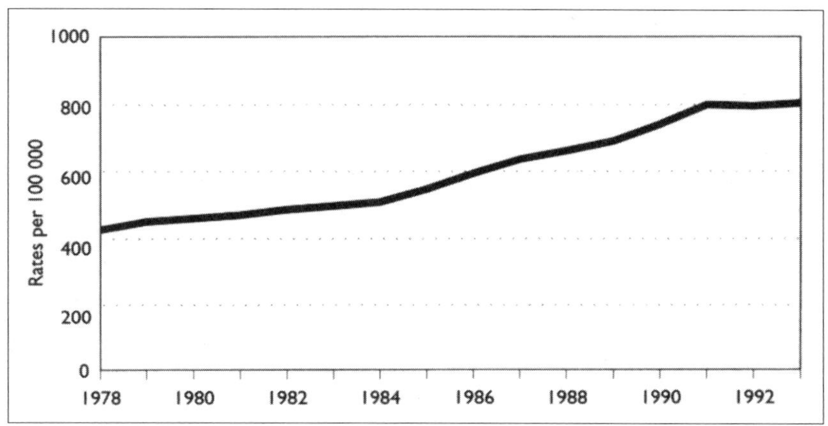


Source: Canadian Centre for Justice Statistics, UCR, 1993.

statistics represent cases substantiated by police). An alternative explanation is that both victims and police have interpreted the new laws to include a wider range of behaviours that were not included under the previous offences of assault and sexual assault (Roberts and Gebotys; Roberts and Grossman; Johnson).

Investigations undertaken by the Department of Justice in the evaluation of the reform legislation relating to sexual assault suggest that these factors alone are not sufficient to have caused the sharp increase in reported cases of sexual assault. This research found that incidents now recorded by the police as sexual assault do not differ greatly from the kinds of incidents formerly recorded as rape or indecent assault. Furthermore, legal reform tends not to precede public opinion but to be an expression of it. That is, legal reform generally comes about as a result of widespread dissatisfaction with existing legal codes, intensive lobbying on the part of interest groups, and lengthy public debate. Scott Clark and Dorothy Hepworth (117) cite a number of historical factors that coincided with or preceded the change in the law on sexual assault that must be taken into account when evaluating the impact of legal reform. These factors apply equally to wife assault:

1. The changing social, economic, and political status of women;
2. Increased media scrutiny on the treatment of women in the courts;
3. Heightened awareness of and focus on victims of crime, particularly female victims, accompanied by government initiatives and services;
4. The growth in specialized investigation units in police departments

across the country where expertise has developed regarding the investigation of complaints, the gathering of evidence, and the treatment of victims;
5. The expansion of sexual assault support centres;
6. The growth in specialized treatment teams in hospitals to deal sensitively with victims of sexual assault;
7. The intensive lobbying by women's groups that long preceded the passage of the rape reform legislation.

In view of these important social changes, it would be a mistake to attribute the dramatic and steady increase in the reporting of assaults and sexual assaults entirely to the success of law reform. While important changes were brought about by the law, police statistics cannot be divorced from the context in which the legal reform took place. Significant social changes, of which legal reform was but one, have brought about growing efforts to eradicate the biases that have confronted complaints of sexual assault and wife assault in the justice system and to provide better treatment and services for victims. All of these factors may have had an effect on victims' willingness to report sexual assault, even in the absence of law reform.

In summary, the advantage of police statistics is that they provide a standard measure that can be used with some confidence to track changes in the number of criminal incidents that come to the attention of the police over time. However, increases or decreases in the rates of violent crime must be interpreted within the context of other social factors. Fluctuations in rates of wife assault and sexual assault may be due to changes in reporting practices, changes in legislation, changing social mores, declining tolerance toward these offences on the part of women, and improved response on the part of the justice system.

Police statistics can also be useful for studying the effects of changes in legislation or criminal justice policies or for studying how the police handle cases of wife assault or sexual assault. If one wants to understand the characteristics and needs of women who seek assistance from the criminal justice system in order to develop training materials for the police, for example, then police statistics are a good place to start. If, on the other hand, the objectives of the research are to develop estimates of the prevalence of violent victimization among women in the general population, or to understand factors that may put women at risk of violent victimization, then police statistics will almost certainly misrepresent the breadth and the nature of violent incidents that women experience.

## Clinical Samples

The earliest attempts to study rape and wife battering involved case studies of female victims who had been in contact with a helping agency, such as a rape crisis centre or a shelter for battered women or case studies of men who had been tried and convicted of such offences. These "clinical" or "convenience" samples were drawn primarily from medical or counselling caseloads or jail populations.

Clinical caseloads of women and men have the advantage to researchers of being readily available, inexpensive to acquire, and not biased (in the case of female victims) by having to first report to the police. However, they are biased in other important ways. Like women who report wife assault or sexual assault to the police, women who use shelters or other services are unrepresentative of all battered or sexually assaulted women. Most women who seek help from an agency have endured the most severe forms of violence, some for many years, and in the case of shelter users, most are economically destitute with few other options open to them.

The earliest studies of violent men attempted to pinpoint how rapists differ from normal men so that therapies could be developed for them. Most described rapists as having psychological defects that caused uncontrollable violent impulses. The conclusions drawn from this research were largely a function of the sample of men who were studied—very violent men, many psychologically disturbed, who were unable to escape police detection, arrest, and conviction. As few rapes are reported to the police and fewer result in conviction, clinical samples represented only the very extreme examples of men who rape.

The early focus on clinical samples was in part a response to assumptions by therapists and researchers that wife assault and sexual assault were rare and the acts of a few mentally deranged men. And for the most part, the results of these studies helped reinforce these beliefs. But despite significant limitations to clinical samples, some clinicians such as American psychologist Nicholas Groth and his colleagues (1977; 1979), in their work with convicted sex offenders, developed a broader explanation that took into account social factors. Their work was instrumental in dispelling certain myths about rape and increasing our understanding of the motivation of offenders. They identified three components to a rape situation: power, anger, and sexuality (Groth and Birnbaum 12). These authors argued that feelings of power and anger dominate; sex is merely the weapon through which power and conquest, anger and contempt are expressed.

The growing attention of feminist scholars to issues related to violence against women caused a shift in focus from offenders to victims and to the study of clinical samples of women using shelters for battered women, rape crisis centres, or hospitals. There are obvious problems of bias associated with this method of selecting samples, and for the most part, the way the sample is selected will determine the characteristics of the women who respond. Women who use shelters, for example, are likely to be poor, to have had their lives or the lives of their children threatened by the most serious types of violence, and to have few other options available to them. These studies seldom include a control group of non-battered women to indicate how they compare with the clinical sample. As a result, there is no way of knowing from clinical samples how representative these women are of all victims of wife assault, and researchers must be careful not to generalize the characteristics of these women or their experiences to all battered women.

The way in which the clinical or convenience sample is selected can also affect the results of the study and the extent to which the findings can be generalized to other populations. Typically, the researcher has limited funds available and must judiciously select a readily available sample of women to interview about their experiences. Some researchers have attracted subjects through notices posted in magazines or newspapers or on university campuses. This method is called "self-selection" as respondents make the decision to select themselves as subjects. While it may be the least costly method of selecting a sample and does not carry with it the same problems inherent in samples of shelters or police statistics, the biases are clearly unknown as the researcher will not know the criteria the subjects have used to decide to participate in the study. There may be a tendency for women who have already reported their experiences to the police or a crisis centre to come forward, or there may be certain class or education factors at play. The types of magazines or newspapers in which the notice is posted will also have a strong bearing on who responds. For example, subjects recruited from a university will differ in important ways from women responding to an advertisement in a public housing project. The important point is that there is bias in the selection for these studies and the direction of the bias is largely unknown to the researcher.

Despite the limitations of clinical studies, the case study information that has emerged from clinical research has provided much-needed insight into the contexts in which sexual assault and battering occur and the motivations of both victims and offenders. Qualitative information adds richness and meaning to the purely quantitative estimates tallied from police statistics and other sources and reminds us of the human drama and suffering behind the statistics. Unstructured interviews can capture the nuances of context, meaning, and culture, and the enduring nature of violent relationships, in a way that statistics cannot. Perhaps as importantly, clinical studies were early catalysts for change. In the beginning of the battered women's movement, the real-life accounts of women seeking refuge in shelters caught the attention of the public, governments, and academics. This was instrumental in putting the issue on the public policy agenda and illustrating the need for more services and resources for abused women, as well as for more in-depth research.

## Population Surveys

In an ideal world, the most accurate and reliable method of measuring the prevalence of violent victimization in the female population would be to interview all women about their experiences. This approach is called a census survey and a prime example is the Census of the Population conducted by Statistics Canada every five years.

It is obviously not feasible, or necessary, to conduct census surveys of the entire Canadian population in order to measure changes in or patterns of various phenomena in society. A sample of the population, so long as the sample is selected randomly from among all eligible subjects, will suffice to produce estimates of social phenomena that are accurate within a measurable range. Sampling essentially involves selecting a segment of the population and attempting to make inferences about the population based on analysis of the sample. Random selection helps ensure that those who respond are statistically representative of everyone in the population and that the results can be generalized to the population at large.

Crime victimization surveys are sample surveys that are based on this model. A number of households are selected at random for these surveys from among all households within a geographic area, and usually one person is selected as the respondents for that household. The first large-scale crime victimization survey undertaken in Canada was the Canadian Urban Victimization Survey (CUVS) in 1982, in which 61,000 people 16 years of age and over were interviewed by telephone about their perceptions of crime and the criminal justice system and about their experiences of victimization (Statistics Canada, 1982). Eight crime types were addressed, including sexual and nonsexual assault, and seven urban centres were included in the sample frame.

Statistics Canada has incorporated a cycle on crime victimization into the General Social Survey (GSS) program (Statistics Canada, 1988; 1993b). This survey interviews approximately 10,000 people 15 years of age and over in the ten provinces with each cycle running every five years. The first crime victimization component ran in 1988 and the second in 1993. These surveys provide information that is complementary to police statistics as they include incidents that were reported to the police and those that were not reported. They have the added advantage of providing detailed information about victims' experiences with crime and the criminal justice system, the impact of the experience on them, their reasons for contacting or not contacting the police, their perceptions of their personal safety, and other details not available from official police records.

Canada's crime victimization surveys were modelled on the National Crime Victimization Survey (NCVS) conducted every six months by the Bureau of Justice Statistics in the United States (Bachman; Bachman and Taylor). The methods used to conduct these surveys have been refined over the past two decades, and the NCVS has served as a prototype for crime victim surveys in many other countries as well as an International Crime Survey that operates in several countries simultaneously. These surveys are not without certain limitations, however. They have been criticized for reducing human suffering to a set of numbers and for failing to account for the context and the meaning of events, particularly in the case of violent interactions. Like the criticisms directed at police statistics, victim surveys are accused of taking single incidents out of the context of what may be ongoing violent relationships.

The accuracy of the information collected in crime victim surveys depends to a greater extent than in clinical studies or police statistics on candid and honest answers from the respondents. In clinical settings and situations in which a victim has called on the police for help, the victim's participation in the interaction is typically initiated by her, whereas in an interview setting, the respondent is selected 'out of the blue' and is not prepared for the questions to come. The clinician and the police officer also have physical evidence and witnesses to draw on in their interpretation of the events that are not available to survey researchers. American criminologist Wesley Skogan (1986), who has worked extensively with the NCVS, cites a number of factors that can influence the accuracy of responses provided in crime victim surveys:

1. People may forget about certain things that have happened to them, especially if they seemed unimportant at the time or happened some time ago.
2. They may fail to report incidents that they perceive to be embarrassing or shameful.
3. They may deliberately choose not to tell the interviewer about an incident if they perceive the interview to be an intrusion or a waste of time.
4. They may not perceive certain experiences to be "crimes' worthy of reporting to a crime survey.
5. They may intentionally or unintentionally report incidents that happened outside the reference period of the survey.
6. Questions may be so poorly worded or ambiguous that respondents may be confused about how to interpret them.

## Measuring Sensitive Experiences

The accuracy of reports of very sensitive or personal experiences is of particular concern to survey researchers. Reverse-record checks, in which people who report incidents to police are later interviewed in a telephone survey about the same experiences to test for honesty of disclosure, have found that many of these incidents are withheld. The magnitude of non-reporting increases with the intimacy of the relationship between the victim and the perpetrator. One such study by Statistics Canada found that 71 per cent of assaults committed by strangers were recalled to survey interviewers but only 56 per cent of assaults by someone known to the victim and only 29 per cent of those involving someone related to the victim (Catlin and Murray).

Very often, the willingness of victims to disclose personal or sensitive experiences to interviewers is influenced by the wording of the questions used and the context in which the questions are placed. Omnibus surveys like the CUVS, the GSS, the NCVS, and the British Crime Survey, with a wide-ranging focus on a variety of crimes, were not designed specifically to measure the very sensitive experiences of violence that primarily affect women. As researchers have gained experience and knowledge about the capabilities and shortcomings of crime victim surveys, many have begun to question the ability of these surveys to accurately and reliably measure sexual assault and assault by intimate partners (Skogan 1984; Hough and Mayhew; Koss, 1992; 1989). As evidence, crime victim surveys consistently portray wife assault and sexual assault as far less prevalent than other research suggests.

Some of the limitations of these surveys can be addressed by the manner in which the questionnaires are constructed, the order and structure of the questions asked, the training interviewers receive, and how the interview is conducted. For example, respondents typically are not asked directly if they have been assaulted, raped, or sexually assaulted. Rather, they are asked a series of highly explicit questions about acts that have happened to them to avoid having people respond on the basis of preconceived notions of certain offences. How these questions are asked has a significant impact on how people respond to them.

Attempts have been made to address the shortcomings of crime victim surveys in recent years by improving the wording of questions relating to sexual assault and assault by family members. For example, respondents to the 1982 CUVS were first asked if they had been attacked, beaten up, hit or kicked, or had something thrown at them, or if anyone had threatened to beat them up or threatened them with a weapon. In a separate question, they were asked if anyone had attacked or molested them, or tried to attack or molest them, while they were "in a car, in a public place, at home or anywhere else." Those who said they had been attacked, threatened, or molested in some way were then asked how they were attacked, at which point they could reply that the attack was a rape, an attempted rape, a molesting, or an attempted molesting. All respondents were asked a question about the relationship of the attacker to them. As a result of these questions, less than one per cent of women reported experiencing violence by a spouse in the year preceding the survey and a similar percentage reported a sexual assault (Solicitor General of Canada).

The 1988 GSS, which was modelled on the CUVS, attempted to clarify the wording of questions concerning sexual assault and assaults by spouses. The phrase "including members of your own household" was added to questions about attacks and threats. Respondents who said they had been attacked or threatened were then asked how they were attacked, at which point they could reply that the attack was a rape, an attempted rape, a molesting, or an attempted molesting (all one category). The number of women assaulted by a partner was one per cent. There were too few cases of sexual assault reported to produce statistically reliable estimates (Sacco and Johnson).

The 1993 GSS attempted to clarify questions about family attacks even further and completely changed the questions relating to sexual assaults. The initial question about attacks asks respondents to "please remember to include acts committed by family and non-family." Two questions about sexual assault were included. The first reads as follows: "Has anyone forced you or attempted to force you into any sexual activity when you did not want to, by threatening you, holding you down or hurting you in some way? Remember this includes acts by family and non-family and that all information provided is strictly confidential." The second sexual assault question reads: "Has anyone touched you against your will in any sexual way? By this I mean anything from unwanted touching or grabbing to kissing or fondling." Those who said they had been sexually assaulted in these ways were later asked how they were attacked, at which point responses were categorized as sexually assaulted, molested, or attempted sexual assault or molesting (one combined category). These questions had the effect of raising the overall rate of violence against women to be higher than that of men; the rate of violent victimization in 1993 (including robbery, assault, and sexual assault) was 84 per 1,000 women (Wright). The wording of the questions had relatively little effect on the rate of wife assault (from 15 to 19), but sexual assaults increased from a negligible number to a rate of 29 per 1,000 women. In all three of these surveys, too few spousal assaults and sexual assaults were reported by men to permit statistically reliable estimates to be made.

The NCVS in the United States has also undergone major revisions to the wording of questions concerning rape and domestic assault (Bachman and Taylor). Prior to 1993, the NCVS did not ask specific questions about attacks involving relatives or other offenders known to the respondents, nor did it specifically ask about rape or sexual assault. Like the Canadian surveys, questions simply asked about attacks, attempted attacks, and threats. If respondents volunteered information about attacks by known offenders, rape, or attempted rape, they were categorized as such. Respondents were not asked directly whether they had been victims of attempted or completed rape, and no definition of rape was ever given. In 1993, questions were added that broadened the type of attack or threat that could be chosen and that encouraged respondents to include events they were not certain would be considered crimes. In addition, respondents were told that, "incidents involving forced or unwanted sexual acts are often difficult to talk about," and were specifically asked about such incidents involving strangers, acquaintances, and well-known offenders. Respondents who replied that they had experienced forced or unwanted sexual acts were then asked to clarify what type of sexual activity had occurred. Incidents could be categorized as completed or attempted rape, verbal threat of rape, sexual attack (grabbing, fondling, etc.), verbal threat of sexual attack, unwanted sexual contact, and verbal harassment (such as abusive language) (see Bachman and Taylor).

One-year incident rates of sexual assault and wife assault produced by Canadian and American crime victimization surveys are presented in Table 2. It is evident from the increases in rates of these crimes with improvements to the wording of questions how important this wording can be to the results. Questions must be very specific in order to orient respondents toward thinking about these acts as crimes, and they must be sensitively worded in order for victims to feel comfortable reporting their experiences.

The differences in the rates presented in Table 2 also indicate the problems in comparing rates of violence produced by seemingly similar surveys. One must be cautious in making comparisons about the level of violence against women in Canada and the United States and over different time periods, even though the methodologies are similar. Comparability among surveys is affected by a number of factors in addition to the wording of questions including:

1. Definitions of violence (strict definitions of rape were used in the CUVS and in the 1972-92 version of the NCVS);

**TABLE 2**
**One-Year Victimization Rates of Sexual Assault and Wife Assault per 1,000 Adult Female Population, Produced by Crime Victim Surveys**

| Survey | Year | Sexual Assault | Wife Assault |
|---|---|---|---|
| | | Rate per 1,000 female population | |
| Canadian Urban Victimization Survey | 1982 | 6[1] | 4 |
| General Social Survey | 1988 | —[2] | 15 |
| General Social Survey | 1993 | 29[3] | 19 |
| U.S. National Crime Victimization Survey | 1987-92 | 1[4] | 5 |
| U.S. National Crime Victimization Survey | 1992-93 | 5[5] | 9 |

— Not statistically reliable
[1]Includes rape, molesting, and attempts against women age 16 and older.
[2]Includes, rape, molesting, and attempts against women age 15 and older.
[3]Includes sexual assault, molesting, and attempts against women age 15 and older.
[4]Includes rape and attempts against women age 12 and older.
[5]Includes rape, attempted rape, sexual attacks, and unwanted sexual acts against women age 12 and older.

Sources: Solicitor General of Canada, 1985; Canadian Centre for Justice Statistics, 1990; Statistics Canada, GSS, 1993; Ronet Bachman, *Violence Against Women: A National Crime Victimization Survey Report*, 1994; Ronet Bachman and Linda Saltzman, *Violence Against Women: Estimates from the Redesigned Survey*, 1995.

2. Precise question wording and placement of these questions relative to others in the questionnaire;
3. How the purpose of the survey was explained to respondents;
4. The definition of "spouse" (whether it includes ex-spouses and common-law partners);
5. The method of counting, i.e., whether victims or individual incidents are counted;
6. Whether incidents over one year or the woman's lifetime are counted;
7. Whether rates are based on all women or only those who have ever been married or lived with a man in a common-law relationship; and,
8. Characteristics of the sample, for instance, age cutoffs and geographic area.

All of these factors are important to interpreting the findings of different surveys and trends over time.

## The Violence Against Women Survey

Despite gradual improvements to national crime victim surveys, it became evident to policymakers that a large-scale survey dedicated entirely to women's experiences of male violence was needed in order to obtain the kind of detailed data required to understand the issue more fully. Canada's Federal Department of Health responded to this need by commissioning a national population survey on male violence against women. This survey was conducted by Statistics Canada in 1993 and interviewed 12,300 women by telephone about their adult experiences with sexual and physical assault by marital partners, dates, boyfriends, other men known to them, and strangers. The survey also included questions about non-criminal forms of sexual harassment and detailed questions about women's fear of violence in public places. The technique used for the VAWS was the crime victim survey approach of interviewing people about their experiences as crime victims.

An entire survey dedicated to asking women about their experiences of violence over their adult lifetime has several advantages (Johnson and Sacco). First, a great many women are not comfortable relating these occurrences on traditional crime victim surveys, perhaps because of the lack of sensitive lead-in questions, lack of special training for interviews, and the use, in some cases, of male interviewers. Second, in their attempt to measure a wide variety of both personal and crimes, victim surveys cannot address the issue of violence against women in its complexity or in the detail necessary to test theories or devise prevention strategies. Traditional crime victim surveys typically orient respondents to think about crime in their own neighbourhood, which may dissuade some women from reporting certain types of violence.

The third advantage to a focused survey is the added information about threats, intimidation, and sexual harassment that help to place women's experiences of sexual assault and wife battering into a broader social context and can significantly enhance discussions about the correlates of women's fear. It is common for women to be threatened and intimidated through acts of sexual harassment, but because these acts are not considered "criminal" in the legal sense, they typically are not considered in victim surveys or analyses of women's fear. The effect of these experiences is to remind women that they are targets for sexual violence and to undermine their feelings of security.

Finally, the one-year reference period used by most crime victim surveys is problematic. It does an artificial boundary around certain experiences while discounting others. This practice may avoid problems of memory recall and may be useful for tracking trends over time, but it can undercount the rate of victimization in the population and obscure the scope of the problem.

The need to rethink this practice is underscored by the fact that 80 per cent of violent incidents reported to Statistics Canada's Violence Against Women Survey occurred before the twelve months leading up to the survey (Statistics Canada 1994a).

## Constructing Definitions of Violence

Definitions of violence against women in the research literature vary widely. Some include psychological and emotional abuse, financial abuse, and sexual coercion, as well as physical and sexual assault as legally defined (see DeKeseredy and Kelly; Koss and Gidycz). The prevalence of "violence" was restricted in the Violence Against Women Survey to legal definitions of physical and sexual assault as contained in the Canadian Criminal Code in view of the fact that respondents would be asked questions about the actions they took to get help, including reporting to the police, whether the incident resulted in an offender appearing in court, and satisfaction with actions taken by the police and the courts. However, the scope of the questions extended beyond those contained in traditional crime victim surveys that yielded very low rates of disclosure.

Questions inquiring about sexual assaults by men other than spouses are shown in Box 1. These are the same questions used in the 1993 GSS, although in the VAWS, the questions were repeated for different categories of relationships. Physical violence outside marriage was measured through responses to the two questions shown in Box 2. Incidents that had both a sexual and a physical component were counted only once as sexual assaults.

An important distinction was made when questioning women about sexual violence involving intimate partners. With respect to dating and marital relationships, women were asked about violent sexual attacks but not about unwanted sexual touching. While unwanted sexual touching does technically fall under the legal definition of sexual assault, when the questionnaire was tested the majority of respondents found the concept of unwanted sexual touching by intimate partners to be ambiguous and confusing. They were excluded because of a concern among the survey designers that the results of these questions would not

**Sexual Assault**

Under Canadian law, a very broad range of acts qualify as **sexual assaults,** from unwanted sexual touching to sexual violence resulting in wounding, maiming, or endangering the life of the victim. Rape is included but is not an essential component of sexual assault.

The number of women who have experienced **unwanted sexual touching** by a stranger was estimated by responses to the following question:

*Has a (male stranger, other known man) ever touched you against your will in any sexual way, such as unwanted touching, grabbing, kissing or fondling?*

The number of women who have been **sexually attacked** by a stranger were those who said yes to the following question:

*Has a (male stranger, date or boyfriend, other known man) ever forced you or attempted to force you into any sexual activity by threatening you, holding you down or hurting you in some way?*

Source: Statistics Canada, Violence Against Women Survey, 1994b: 10-14.

**Box 1 Sexual Assault Outside Marriage**

**Physical Assault**

Experiences of nonsexual assault were estimated by responses to the following questions:

*Now, I'm going to ask you some questions about physical attacks you may have had since the age of 16. By this I mean any use of force such as being hit, slapped, kicked or grabbed to being beaten, knifed or shot. Has a male stranger, date or boyfriend, other known man ever physically attacked you?*

The Criminal Code also considers a threat of physical violence to be an assault if it is a face-to-face threat and the victim has a reasonable expectation that it will be carried out. Responses to the following questions were counted as physical assaults:

*The next few questions are about face-to-face threats you may have experienced. By threats I mean any time you have been threatened with physical harm, since you were 16. Has a (male stranger, date or boyfriend, other known man) ever threatened to harm you? Did you believe he would do it?*

Source: Statistics Canada, Violence Against Women Survey, 1994b: 16-22.

**Box 2 Physical Assault Outside Marriage**

be reliable or valid.

The method used by the VAWS to derive estimates of wife assault differs substantially from the single-question methods used in crime victim surveys. Ten specific questions were used to measure violence by a spouse ranging from threats of physical harm to use of a gun or knife. This method is intended to take account of the advice of Smith and others to offer many opportunities for disclosure in order to counteract a reluctance to disclose painful or embarrassing experiences. Obtaining details about specific types of violent acts also adds important information about the dimensions and the nature of wife assaults. These ten items, in the order in which they were asked, appear in Box 3.

## The Prevalence of Violence Against Women

An advantage of random sample surveys such as the VAWS and crime victim surveys is that, by interviewing a relatively small sample, the responses can be weighted to represent all women in the general population. The responses of the 12,300 women who participated in this survey were each given a weighting factor that represents all other women in the geographic region of the respondent who were not interviewed. Responses total the approximately 10.5 million women (18 years of age and over) in the Canadian population in 1993. National estimates are expected to be within 1.2 per cent of the true population at the 95.0 per cent confidence interval. Estimates of subgroups of the population have wider confidence intervals.

According to the Violence Against Women Survey, 51 per cent of Canadian women have experienced at least one incident of physical or sexual assault since the age of 16 and 10 per cent had been victims of violence in the 12-month period preceding the survey (Table 3). Sixteen per cent have been assaulted by a date or boyfriend, 23 per cent by a stranger or other non-intimate, and 29 per cent of ever-married women have been assaulted by a spouse (this includes common-law marriages). As other research has suggested, women reported higher rates of violence by men they know than by strangers. Grouping together all known men and comparing them with strangers, almost half of all women (45 per cent) have been victimized by men known to them (spouses, dates, boyfriends, friends, neighbours, acquaintances, etc.) compared with 23 per cent who reported violence by a stranger.

Sexual assault was somewhat more common than physical assault, with four out of ten (39 per cent) women reporting this type of experience (Figure 3). The less serious forms of unwanted sexual touching and violent sexual attacks occurred with almost equal frequency (25 per cent and 24 per cent, respectively). A smaller proportion of women reported sexual attacks by spouses (eight per cent). Approximately 34 per cent of women have experienced a non-sexual assault, and the majority of these involved spouses. Less common were physical assaults by men other than spouses.

The Violence Against Women Survey estimates that a total of 572,000 women experienced at least one incident of sexual assault in the one-year period preceding

**Violence by Spouses**

Violence by husbands and common-law partners was measured by response to the following:

*We are particularly interested in learning more about women's experiences of violence in their homes. I would like you to tell me if your husband/partner has every done any of the following to you. This includes incidents that may have occurred while you were dating.*

- *Threatened to hit you with his fist or anything else that could hurt you*
- *Threw something at you that could hurt you*
- *Pushed, grabbed or shoved you*
- *Slapped you*
- *Kicked, bit or hit you with his fist*
- *Hit you with something that could hurt you*
- *Beat you up*
- *Choked you*
- *Threatened to or used a gun or knife on you*
- *Forced you into any sexual activity when you did not want to, by threatening you, holding you down, or hurting you in some way*

Source: Statistics Canada, Violence Against Women Survey, 1994b: 31-43.

**Box 3 Violence by Spouses**

the survey, and 201,000 women experienced violence by a spouse. Figures 4 and 5 illustrate the differences in the number of women who reported these experiences to the VAWS, the GSS, and the police in 1993. The VAWS captures almost twice as many incidents as the GSS, three times as many cases of wife assault as are reported to the police, and about 38 times as many cases of sexual assault as police statistics. This graphically illustrates the extent to which victim surveys more completely represent the population of assaulted women than police records. Equally important, these surveys provide information about victims' perceptions of these experiences, how they were affected, what the consequences were for them, and how they reacted. These surveys are founded on the belief that, in may ways, victims are the best source of information about their own experiences and that they are experts on what has happened to them, how it has affected them, and the decisions they made in response to the experiences.

## Ethical Considerations in Survey Research

**TABLE 3**
**Number and Percentage of Women 18 Years of Age and Over Who Have Experienced Violence, by Relationship to Perpetrator**

| Relationship | Number in Millions | Per Cent Adult Lifetime | Per Cent 12 Months |
|---|---|---|---|
| Total women victimized | 5.38 | 51 | 10 |
| Spouse or ex-spouse | 2.65 | 29[1] | 3[1] |
| Date/boyfriend | 1.72 | 16 | 2 |
| Other known man | 2.46 | 23 | 4 |
| Stranger | 2.46 | 23 | 4 |

Figures do not add to totals because of multiple responses.
[1]Based on the number of women who have ever been married or lived with a man in a common-law relationship.

Source: Holly Johnson and Vincent Sacco, "Researching Violence Against Women: Statistics Canada's National Survey," 1995: 294.

The sensitivity of the subject matter of the VAWS presented a number of complex methodological and ethical issues in the survey design. A survey of this nature asks the respondents to disclose the most intimate and perhaps the most troubling details of their lives to a stranger over the telephone. Survey designers must be cognizant of the fact that questions asking respondents to relive these very troubling memories have the potential to cause serious emotional trauma. Perhaps even more importantly, from an ethical point of view, researchers must never lose sight of the possibility that with every telephone call the respondent could be living with an abusive man and that her safety could be jeopardized should he learn of the content of the survey (Johnson and Sacco).

In the design phase of the Violence Against Women Survey, solutions to these issues were found through an extensive consultation process with a wide variety of experts, including academics, federal and provincial government representa-

## FIGURE 3
## Types of Violence Reported by Canadian Women

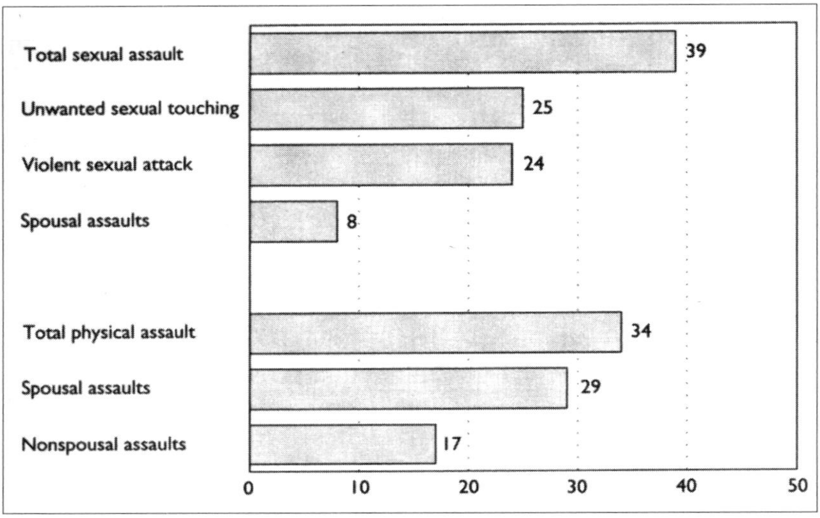

Figures do not add to totals because of multiple responses.

Source: Statistics Canada, Violence Against Women Survey, Microdata File, 1994a.

tives, a police advisory group, shelter workers, crisis counsellors, as well as victims of violence seeking support from these agencies. These groups offered suggestions about the content of the questionnaire, the wording of the questions, and innovative approaches that would give respondents options as to when and where they would participate. At the outset of the interview, every respondent was provided with a toll-free telephone number that she could use to call back to resume the interview in the event that she had to hang up suddenly. No call-backs were made to respondents' households, which gave them control over their participation. Many women took advantage of the call-back option. A total of 1,000 calls were received on the toll-free line over the five-month period of interviewing; 150 of these were from women who wanted to continue an uncompleted interview that they had had to interrupt or who were calling to add additional information to a completed interview. Over half of all calls were from women wanting to verify the legitimacy of the survey, many at the point of sensitive questions about violence in their lives. This response signals the level of emotional commitment that this line of questioning can provoke and to which survey researchers must respond.

A common concern among survey researchers is that results will be biased if a large proportion of respondents refuse to participate in the survey or refuse to answer specific questions. A number of reasons why a woman may not wish to

FIGURE 4
**Number of Sexual Assaults Against Adult Women in 1993 Recorded by Police, the General Social Survey, and the Violence Against Women Survey**

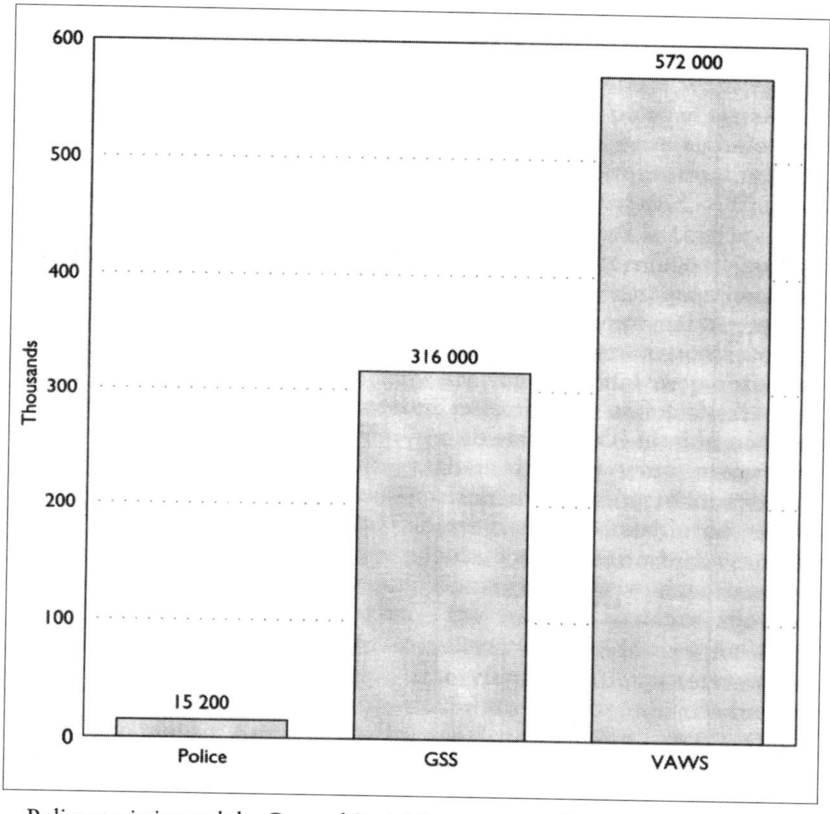


Police statistics and the General Social Survey count the number of incidents of sexual assault. The Violence Against Women Survey counts the number of women who have been sexually assaulted.

Sources: Canadian Centre for Justice Statistics, Revised Uniform Crime Reporting Survey, 1994a; 1993 General Social Survey, Microdata File; Statistics Canada, Violence Against Women Survey, Microdata File.

reveal her experiences to an interviewer over the telephone were articulated by Smith: she may feel they are too personal or painful to discuss, she may be embarrassed or ashamed about them, she may fear further violence from her abuser should he find out, or she may have forgotten about them if they were minor or happened a long time ago. The selection and training of interviewers

FIGURE 5
Number of Wife Assaults in 1993
Recorded by Police, the General Social Survey,
and the Violence Against Women Survey

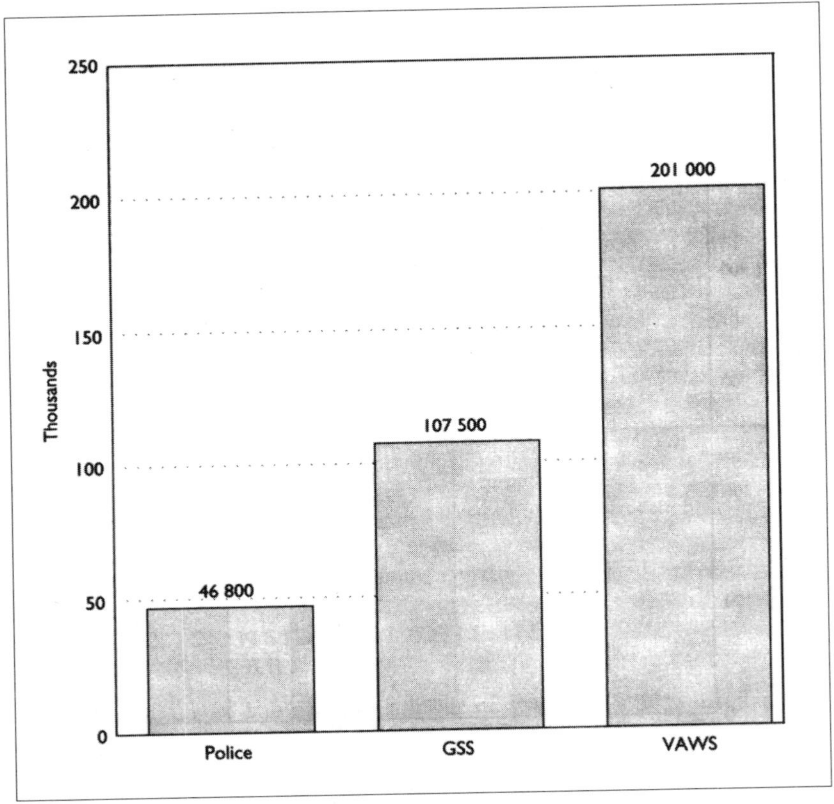


Police statistics and the General Social Survey count the number of incidents of assault. The Violence Against Women Survey counts the number of women who have been assaulted.

Sources: Canadian Centre for Justice Statistics, Revised Uniform Crime Reporting Survey, 1994a; 1993 General Social Survey, Microdata File; Statistics Canada, Violence Against Women Survey, Microdata File.

were critical factors in fostering a relationship of trust between interviewers and respondents and a climate in which respondents would feel comfortable discussing their experiences. Knowledge and sensitivity about the issue of violence against women were central criteria in selecting interviewers for this survey, in addition to standard interviewing skills, interviewing experience, and keyboard skills, as the survey would be conducted using Computer Assisted Telephone Interviewing (CATI). Only women were considered for the job of interviewing because of the concern that many respondents would refuse to discuss their personal experiences with male interviewers. Through training and experience, interviewers became skilled at detecting whether respondents had privacy and were able to speak freely. Women who disclosed abuse in a current relationship were asked if they were able to continue the conversation freely, and interviews were rescheduled if they were unable to proceed at that time.

In a survey of this sensitivity, survey managers have a responsibility to respond to emotional trauma. This applies to respondents, but it also applies to interviewers who may be distressed by the personal stories they hear. Distress can occur as a result of a particular interview, or it can be cumulative, building up over the course of many weeks or months of hearing about experiences of violence and feeling powerless to help.

A clinical psychologist became part of the survey team for the purpose of providing support to Interviewers. It was her responsibility to help in selecting appropriate interviewers by assessing each candidate's level of knowledge and sensitivity toward the issue of violence against women, as well as the ability of each to handle the kinds of stress anticipated through participation in the survey. The psychologist took part in training sessions and conducted regular debriefing sessions with interviewers where they could discuss stress management techniques and other issues that arose as a result of their work on the survey.

To enable them to react effectively to respondents' emotional trauma, interviewers had available to them an automated list of shelters and other services for abused and sexually assaulted women across the country. When the interviewer activated a special computer key, services in the respondent's geographic area appeared on the screen, linked to the area code and prefix of her telephone number (this was facilitated by the CATI system). Using this system, interviewers were able to offer support to respondents who either reported current or recent cases of abuse or who appeared to be in distress. It was emphasized throughout the training sessions that interviewers must not undertake to counsel respondents, no matter how upset a respondent might be. Referring respondents to support services in the community addressed the need to respond to their distress without compromising the role of the interviewer or the collection of objective statistical data.

## A Word on The Conflict Tactics Scale

The Conflict Tactics Scale (CTS) is the most commonly used instrument in family violence surveys (Straus). Using the "family conflict" approach, the CTS consists of 18 items intended to measure ways of handling interpersonal conflict in family relationships. The items range from "verbal reasoning" (from discussing the issue calmly to bringing in someone to help settle things) to "verbal aggression" (ranging from insults and swearing to throwing, smashing, hitting, or kicking something) and "physical aggression" (from throwing something at the other person to using a knife or gun). Respondents are asked how frequently they had perpetrated each act in the course of settling a disagreement with a spouse, a child, or a sibling, and how frequently they had been the victim of these acts. Estimates of rates of violence and victimization for both men and women are tallied from these self- reports. Sexual assault is absent from the scale.

Studies using the Conflict Tactics Scale consistently produce equivalent rates of wife battering and husband battering on both minor and severe types of violence (Brinkerhoff and Lupri; Kennedy and Dutton; Lupri; Steinmetz; Stets; Szinovacz). However, research that is designed to test the reliability of responses given to the CTS has established large discrepancies in the reports of violence given by men and women as to the occurrence and frequency of violence committed between them (Dobash, Dobash, Wilson, and Daly; Brush; Szinovacz; Edleson and Brygger). In clinical studies of counselling groups for violent men using the CTS to assess violent behaviour, the female partners of these men reported higher levels of violence committed by their husbands than the men reported themselves (Browning and Dutton; Edleson and Brygger), and men frequently ignored the fact that their actions caused severe injury to or hospitalization of their wives (Browning and Dutton; Brush; Makepeace).

This discrepancy in reporting is not surprising, since many men who inflict violence and injury on their wives will feel remorseful and guilty and will deny their actions. Others may rationalize their actions as a way of maintaining an image of themselves as good people. Many therapists working with abusive men have found denial to be a typical response of those confronted about their behaviour. In other cases, batterers may honestly have difficulty recalling events or not realize the consequences of their actions for their female partners if they were intoxicated at the time. And some victims may conceal their injuries from their partners in an attempt to smooth over the incident (Makepeace). Further qualitative work is needed to more fully understand the differences between men's and women's perceptions and responses to questions about their own use of violence and their partners' use of violence against them.

The way the CTS is traditionally applied has been criticized on the grounds that it ignores the gendered power imbalances that exist within marriage and society and excludes crucial details about motives, intentions, and consequences (Dobash *et al*; Brush; Browning and Dutton; Saunders; DeKeseredy and MacLean). This scale rests on the assumption that a level playing field exists in families and society whereby men and women enjoy equal power, authority, and resources. The CTS overlooks the unique social roles of men and women within marriage that cause them to assign different meanings to similar acts and to suffer different consequences of acts that appear similar when measured without context. Treating a slap by a man and the same act by a woman as equivalent ignores the damage that can be inflicted, as well as victims' ability to restrain assailants or to retaliate. The meaning of a violent act also differs significantly for male and female victims. Men begin as the dominant partners in marriage, and one episode of violence, or even the threat of violence, has the potential to change the dynamics of the relationship, reinforcing his dominance and her passivity (Walker 1984). A woman's violence against her husband seldom has such an effect.

Murray Straus, the architect of the CTS, acknowledges the need to give primary attention to wife battering as the more pressing social policy issue on the basis that men tend to under-report their own violence, men are more likely to use very dangerous and injurious forms of violence (such as beating and using a knife or gun), men use more repetitive violence against their wives, women very often must endure beatings by their husbands because of economic and social constraints to terminating the relationship, and much of women's violence is committed in defence against their husbands' assaults (Straus; Gelles and Straus; see also Browne; Saunders; Dobash and Dobash 1988; Makepeace). Straus concedes that it is "advisable to base analyses of violence by men on data provided by women" (Stets and Straus 162).

The manner in which the CTS is typically introduced to respondents, as a list of ways of "settling differences," is also problematic. It reads as follows:

> No matter how well a couple get along, there are times when they disagree, get annoyed with the other person or just have spats or fights because they're in a bad mood or tired or for some other reason. They also use many different ways of trying to settle their differences. I'm going to read some things that you and your spouse might do when you have an argument. I would like you to tell me how many times in the past 12 months you have (done any of the following). Thinking back over the last 12 months you've been together, was there ever an occasion when your spouse (did the following)? Tell me how often. (Straus 33)

Introductions are crucial components of sample surveys. They establish the context of the survey at the outset and ensure that respondents have a common understanding of the focus of the questions to follow. One reason that traditional crime victimization surveys have had difficulty eliciting responses about sexual assault and wife assault is that respondents are told that the survey is interested in experiences of crime, and the wording leading up to questions about victimization reinforce this. Reliability of sample surveys will be badly affected if there is ambiguity in the wording of the questions and if respondents are likely to attach significantly different meaning to the same questions. Validity is affected by questions that poorly represent what the researcher is attempting to measure.

Both of these problems are present in the above introduction. The wording is potentially ambiguous and is inappropriate for orienting respondents toward thinking about violence they have suffered at the hands of their partners. While some respondents may think about experiences of violence as ways of settling differences, a great many may not. This brings into question the reliability and validity of a scale to measure violence that is, in fact, designed to address ways of settling differences. There can be little doubt that most violent relationships are conflict-ridden; however, there is substantial evidence that many acts of aggression by men against their wives are not precipitated by an argument or disagreement between them, and it is questionable whether respondents would think these acts appropriate to include (Dobash and Dobash 1984; Browne).

The Violence Against Women Survey departs from the conflict tactics approach in the extensive lead-up it has to questions about spousal violence, through detailed questions about fear of violence in public places and precautions taken to protect oneself, sexual harassment, and sexual and physical violence by strangers, dates and boy-friends, and other known men. The VAWS does not use the "verbal reasoning" scale or the "verbal aggression" scale to ease respondents into questions about violence. Moreover, the introduction to the section inquiring about wife assault states very directly that "We are particularly interested in learning more about women's experiences of *violence* in their homes. I'd like to ask you to tell me if your husband/partner has ever done any of the following to you" (Statistics Canada 1994b: 35). This survey is concerned not with ways of settling differences but with violence against women, and this context is established at this point.

The ten items of the VAWS used to measure acts of wife assault are similar to those used in the CTS; however, a number of modifications were made to the original items during the testing phase in order to correct ambiguity in the question wording. The CTS item "threatened to hit or throw something at you" was altered to read "threatened to hit you *with his fist or anything else that could hurt you.*" Similarly, the item "threw something at you" has been clarified to read "thrown anything at you *that could hurt you.*" The item "hit you with something" now reads "hit you with something *that could hurt you.*" These modifications were made following focus-group testing and field-testing, in which some respondents were clearly confused about whether to include incidents in which they were threatened or hit in a playful way with harmless objects that could not possibly hurt them. The addition of an item on sexual attacks takes into account sexual violence in marriage and the links between wife battering and marital rape.

## Summary

The growing awareness of sexual violence and wife battering over the past two decades has been accompanied by significant improvements to the methods used to study these issues. Researchers have moved from an early reliance on police records and clinical samples, which tap only a small proportion of cases, to wide-scale sample surveys that are capable of capturing the broad range of experiences, the consequences for the woman involved, her reactions to the incident, the reactions of others around her, her decisions to involve the police or other services, and the way she is treated by the police and the court process. While sample surveys offer the best hope for the most comprehensive information about violence against women, the estimates produced almost certainly undercount the true prevalence of violence. Survey researchers can do their best to ensure a sensitive approach with valid measures of violence, but it is almost certain that some women will refuse to reveal their experiences to an interviewer. The issue of under-reporting or non-response can be addressed by special attention to the difficult situation many abused women find themselves in when responding to survey questions. However, it is clear that victim surveys, like other data sources, are imperfect tools and that researchers must continue to strive for better and improved methods of measuring the physical and sexual abuse of women.

## References

Bachman Ronet. *Violence Against Women: A National Crime Victimization Survey Report.* Washington, DC: Bureau of Justice Statistics, 1994.

Bachmen, Ronet, and Bruce Taylor. "The Measurement of Family Violence and Rape by the Redesigned National Crime Victimization Survey." *Justice Quarterly* 11 (3) (1994): 499-512.

Bachman, Ronet, and Linda Saltzman. *Violence Against Women: Estimates from the Redesigned Survey.* Washington, DC.: Bureau of Justice Statistics, 1995.

Brinkerhoff, Merline, and Eugen Lupri. "Interspousal Violence." *Canadian Journal of Sociology* 13 (4) (1988): 407-34.

Browne, Angela. *When Battered Women Kill.* New York: Free Press, 1987.

Browning, James, and Donald Dutton. "Assessment of Wife Assault with the Conflict Tactics Scale: Using Couple Data to Quantify the Differential Reporting Effect." *Journal of Marriage and the Family* 48 (1986): 375-79.

Brush, Lisa. "Violent Acts and Injurious Outcomes in Married Couples: Methodological Issues in the National Survey of Families and Households." *Gender and Society* 4 (1990): 56-67.

Canadian Centre for Justice Statistics. "Revised Uniform Crime Reporting Survey." Unpublished data. 1993.

Canadian Centre for Justice Statistics. "Conjugal Violence Against Women." *Juristat Service Bulletin* 10 (7) (1990).

Catlin, Gary, and Susan Murray. *Report on Canadian Victimization Survey Methodological Protests.* Ottawa: Statistics Canada, 1979.

Clark, Lorenne, and Debra Lewis. *Rape: The Price of Coercive Sexuality.* Toronto: The Women's Press, 1977.

Clark, Scott, and Dorothy Hepworth. "Effects of Reform Legislation on the Processing of Sexual Assault Cases." *Confronting Sexual Assault: A Decade of Legal and Social Change.* Eds. J. Roberts and R. Mohr. Toronto: University of Toronto Press, 1994. 113-35.

DeKeseredy, Walter, and Katharine Kelly. "The Incidence and Prevalence of Woman Abuse in Canadian University and College Dating Relationships." *Canadian Journal of Sociology* 18 (2) (1993): 137-59.

DeKeseredy, Walter, and Brian Maclean. "Researching Woman Abuse in Canada: A Realistic Critique of the Conflict Tactics Scale." *Canadian Review of Social*

*Policy* 25 (1990): 19-27.

Dobash, Russell, and Rebecca Emerson Dobash. "Research as Social Action: The Struggle for Battered Women." *Feminist Perspectives on Wife Abuse.* Eds. K. Yllo and M. Bograd. Newbury Park, CA: Sage, 1988. 51-74.

Dobash, Russell, and Rebecca Emerson Dobash. "The Nature and Antecedents of Violent Events." *British Journal of Criminology* 24 (1984): 269-88.

Dobash, Russell, Rebecca Emerson Dobash, Margo Wilson, and Martin Daly. "The Myth of Sexual Symmetry in Marital Violence." *Social Problems* 39 (1) (1992): 71-91.

Edleson, Jeffrey, and Mary Pat Brygger. "Gender Differences in Reporting of Battering Incidences." *Family Relations* 35 (1986): 377-82.

Gelles, Richard, and Murray Straus. *Intimate Violence: The Causes and Consequences of Abuse in the American Family.* New York: Simon & Schuster, 1988.

Groth, A. N., A. W. Burgess, and L. L. Holmstrom. "Rape: Power, Anger and Sexuality." *American Journal of Pyschiatry* 134 (11) (1977): 1239-43.

Groth, Nicholas, and J. Birnbaum. *Men Who Rape.* New York: Plenum Press, 1979.

Hough, Michael, and Patricia Mayhew. *The British Crime Survey.* Home Office Research Study No. 76. London: Her Majesty's Stationery Office, 1983.

Jaffe, Peter, Elaine Hastings, Deborah Reitzel, and Gary Austin. "The Impact of Police Laying Charges." *Legal Responses to Wife Assault: Current Trends and Evaluation.* Ed. Zoe Hilton. Newbury Park, CA: Sage, 1993. 62-95.

Johnson, Holly. "Sexual Assault." *Crime Counts.* Eds. Leslie W. Kennedy and Vincent F. Sacco. Scarborough, ON: Nelson, 1996. 133-49.

Johnson, Holly and Vincent F. Sacco. "Researching Violence Against Women: Statistics Canada's National Survey." *Canadian Journal of Criminology* 37 (3) (1995): 281-304.

Kennedy, Leslie, and Donald Dutton. "The Incidence of Wife Assault in Alberta." *Canadian Journal of Behavioural Science* 21 (1989): 40-54.

Koss, Mary. "The Underdetection of Rape: Methodological Choices Influence Incidence Estimates." *Journal of Social Issues* 48 (1) (1992): 61-75.

Koss, Mary. "Hidden Rape: Sexual Aggression and Victimization in a National Sample of Students in Higher Education." *Violence in Dating Relationships: Emerging Social Issues.* Eds. Maureen Pirog-Good and Jan Stets. New York: Praeger, 1989. 145-68.

Koss, Mary, and Christine Gidycz. "Sexual Experiences Survey: Reliability and Validity." *Journal of Consulting and Clinical Psychology* 53 (1985): 422-23.

Lupri, Eugen. "Male Violence in the Canadian Home: A Re-examination." *Canadian Social Trends* 14 (1989): 19-21.

Makepeace, James. "Gender Differences in Courtship Violence Victimization." *Violence in Dating Relationships: Emerging Social Issues.* Eds. Maureen Pirog-Good and Jan Stets. New York: Praeger, 1989. 94-107.

O'Grady, B. "Crime, Violence and Victimization: A Newfoundland Case." *Crime in Canadian Society.* Eds. Robert A. Silverman, James J. Teevan, Jr. and Vincent

F. Sacco. Toronto: Butterworths, 1991. 79-91.

*R.* v. *Chase.* 37 C.C.C. (3d) 97 (S.C.C.) [1997].

Roberts, Julian V., and Robert Gebotys. "Reforming Rape Laws." *Law and Human Behaviour* 16 (5) (1992): 555-73.

Roberts, Julian V., and Michelle Grossman. "Changing Definitions of Sexual Assault: An Analysis of Police Statistics." *Confronting Sexual Assault: A Decade of Legal and Social Change.* Eds. J. Roberts and R. Mohr. Toronto: University of Toronto Press, 1994. 57-83.

Sacco, Vincent P., and Holly Johnson. *Patterns of Criminal Victimization in Canada.* Ottawa: Minister of Supply and Services, 1990.

Saunders, Daniel. "Wife Abuse, Husband Abuse or Mutual Combat: A Feminist Perspective on the Empirical Findings." *Feminist Perspectives on Wife Abuse.* Eds. K. Yllo and M. Bograd. Newbury Park, CA: Sage, 1988. 90-113.

Skogan, Wesley. "Methodological Issues in the Study of Victimization." *From Crime Policy to Victim Policy: Reorienting the Justice System.* Ed. Ezat Fattah. London: Macmillan, 1986. 80-116.

Skogan, Wesley. "Reporting Crimes to the Police: The Status of World Research." *Journal of Research in Crime and Delinquency* 21 (2) (1984): 113-37.

Smith, Michael D. "Enhancing the Quality of Survey Data on Violence Against Women: A Feminist Approach." *Gender and Society* 8 (1) (1994): 109-27.

Solicitor General of Canada. *Female Victims of Crime.* Canadian Urban Victimization Survey, Bulletin 4. 1985.

Statistics Canada. *Violence Against Women Survey.* Microdata file. Ottawa, 1994a.

Statistics Canada. *Violence Against Women Survey: Questionnaire Package.* Ottawa, 1994b.

Statistics Canada. "The Violence Against Women Survey." *The Daily* November 18, 1993a.

Statistics Canada. *General Social Survey.* Microdata file. Ottawa, 1993b.

Statistics Canada. *General Social Survey.* Microdata file. Ottawa, 1988.

Statistics Canada. *Canadian Urban Victimization Survey.* Microdata file. Ottawa, 1982.

Steinmetz, Suzanne. "A Cross-Cultural Comparison of Marital Abuse." *Journal of Sociology and Social Welfare.* 8 (1981): 404-14.

Stets, Jan. "Verbal and Physical Aggression in Marriage." *Journal of Marriage and the Family* 52 (1990): 501-14.

Stets, Jan, and Murray Strauss. "Gender Differences in Reporting Marital Violence and Its Medical and Pyschological Consequences." *Physical Violence in American Families: Risk Factors and Adaptationsto Violence in 8,145 Families.* Eds. Murray Strauss and Richard Gelles. New Brunswick: NJ Transaction, 1990. 151-65.

Straus, Murray. "Measuring Intrafamily Conflict and Violence: The Conflict Tactics (CTS) Scales." *Physical Violence in American Families: Risk Factors and Adaptations to Violence in 8, 145 Families.* Eds. Murray Strauss and

Richard Gelles. New Brunswick: NJ Transaction, 1990. 29-47.
Szinovacz, Maximiliane. "Using Couple Data as a Methodological Tool: The Case of Marital Violence." *Journal of Marriage and the Family* 45 (1983): 633-44.
Walker, Lenore. *The Battered Woman Syndrome*. New York: Springer, 1984.
Wright, Christine. "Risk of Personal and Household Victimization: Canada, 1993." *Juristat Service Bulletin* 15 (2) (1995).

# Understanding the Attacks on Statistics Canada's Violence Against Women Survey

Anthony N. Doob

When I first heard that Statistics Canada was going to be carrying out a survey on violence against women, I didn't think much about it. I had tried, on a few occasions over the past ten years, to find out something about the prevalence of certain kinds of spousal violence. With the exception of homicide data, however, it was very difficult. My search of the Canadian literature turned up two types of data: some small scale surveys of Canadian women that suggested that the rates were quite high, and data such as those from the 1988 General Social Survey which did not address the issue directly and suggested much lower rates. As a social scientist, I was not very surprised by the variability of the findings: one does not need to be a survey researcher to realize that if one wants to get information about a phenomenon in a survey, one has to ask questions about it. Thus, hearing that a survey of women's experience with violence was being carried out seemed completely unsurprising and sensible. I didn't think much more about it.

Some months later, Holly Johnson, project manager for Statistics Canada on this survey, sent me a draft questionnaire for comment. It was clear from this early draft that this was to be a serious study where women would be probed about different kinds of violence they had experienced. This is a very different approach from that used in most "general" victimization surveys, such as the 1988 and 1993 General Social Surveys that Statistics Canada carried out. In the General Social Survey, women and men were asked very general "screening" questions about their victimizations. Then if they indicated that they had been victimized, more specific questions were asked. In contrast, the Violence Against Women survey was asking detailed questions. Women were to be asked separate sets of questions about violence perpetrated by strangers, dates, boyfriends, known men (other than husbands and partners), and husbands and partners (in current relationships and, separately, in previous relationships). A wide range of other questions were also being asked.

Holly Johnson's "Response to Allegations about the Violence Against Women Survey" lists those who, like me, were contacted. I am sure that the project team that Holly Johnson headed received a lot of advice from all of us. Undoubtedly some of this advice was useful and some was not: Some was probably followed; other advice was probably not followed. Large surveys involve compromises: one can never ask all the questions one would like to. One can never get as large a sample as one would want, and judgements have to be made about how best to ask questions or structure an interview. People will differ on how these compromises should be made. Had I thought about it, I probably would have assumed that there might subsequently have been some methodological critiques of the survey suggesting that some of these difficult questions should have been answered differently. That would not have been surprising nor would it have been disturbing. To a large extent, it goes with the territory.

However, there were some rather unexpected criticisms of the survey that surfaced during this consultation period. The Yukon and the Northwest Territories were excluded from the survey largely for practical reasons. This decision was not welcomed by those with particular interests in the territories. More fundamental was the criticism that the survey would not allow generalizations to be made at the local level. Those involved in the providing of services to abused women would not, therefore, be able to use the survey to provide information that was specific to their jurisdictions. The reason that "local" inferences could not be made is simple. Even though the survey involved questioning over 12,000 women, the sample size of women in any particular location who were recent victims of a particular kind of violence would be small.

Some women expressed the view that a survey such as this would not be very helpful since everyone knew that women experienced a large amount of violence within marital relationships. Their view was that funds would be better spent on providing services rather than doing research. Such views miss an important finding. As Holly Johnson pointed out in a *Globe and Mail* response to critics,

> more than one fifth of all incidents of violence were known to no one, not even the closest friends or relatives, let alone the police, before the women disclosed them to an anonymous Statistics Canada interviewer. From this we can draw two important observations: One is about the very hidden nature of violence in women's lives, even today; the other is about the critical importance of this type of survey which, carefully designed and implemented...gives a statistically reliable portrait of the population that cannot be acquired in any other way. (A17)

## The Release of the Findings

The first set of results of the survey was released on November 18, 1993. Data collection had been completed in June 1993. From my perspective, as an academic, a five month "delay" between the end of data collection and the release of the first set of findings, qualifies as lightning speed. A number of processes have to be carried out before the data can be properly analyzed and understood. Data such as these are a bit different from simplistic questions typically asked on public opinion polls. It is easy to tabulate the answers to a simple set of questions such as "If the election were to be held today, how would you vote?" or "Does the *Globe and Mail* women's column do an adequate job of addressing women's issues—yes or no?" But if you want to understand the answers to either of these questions, or if you want to understand the relationships among questions, it takes a bit more time.

The printed form of the English language questionnaire used in the Violence Against Women survey is 72 pages long, but since some questions are contingent upon particular answers to other questions, all respondents were not asked to respond to every question. Nevertheless, an enormous amount of data was collected. The first release of the data dealt with only a tiny proportion of what is possible to find out from this survey. Whether the November 1993 release dealt with those findings that all readers might think are the most important is impossible to know. However, the English language version of first release of findings consisted of nine pages of text and tables in the Statistics Canada *Daily*. In addition, as part of the formal release, Statistics Canada made available, as they often do, a set of "shelf tables." In this case, 25 such tables were released. It would be hard to argue that important facts were withheld from the public.

The first set of findings included some of the more dramatic findings about the incidence of violence against women. The data demonstrated that most violence aimed at women came from men known to the victim. The data showed, not surprisingly, that the type of violence perpetrated against married women by their partners varied considerably and the frequency of different types of violence also varied. In terms of the distribution of violence, the data demonstrated that household income was not very highly correlated with the prevalence of violence, although young women appeared to be much more highly at risk than any other age group. A wide range of findings were released that day, most of which were not, of course, reported in the public press.

## What About Violence Against Men?

From time to time, in the context of discussions of violence against women, the issue of violence against men is raised. In the context of this survey, I heard the question: "Why didn't Statistics Canada survey men at the same time that they did this survey?" There appeared to me to be a subtext of these questions: "Isn't this an instance of Statistics Canada attempting to be politically correct?" or "Isn't this just another instance of women hijacking the public research agenda?"

"Why not survey men?" is a very peculiar question, in this context, particularly when it comes from within the research community. It appears to me that the issue of violence against women is, quite simply, a different question from violence against men. For example, research has shown that:

•Female homicide victims are much more likely to have been killed by their spouses than are male homicide victims.

•The nature of violent victimizations vary: women are much more likely to be sexually assaulted than are men; men are more likely than women to be robbed; and men and women are equally likely to be assaulted.

•Women, overall, are more likely to be victims of violent victimizations than are men, particularly if they are separated or divorced.

•Women in marital relationships are considerably more likely to be victims of violence perpetrated by their partners than are men in such relationships.[1]

But data such as these focus on victimizations only; violence against women has other harmful effects on women. And these effects differ from the effects on men. These differences also serve as important justifications for a research focus on violence against women:

•Men and women differ dramatically in how safe they feel walking alone in their neighbourhoods at night. In the 1993 General Social Survey, for example, 42 per cent of women indicated that they feel unsafe, as compared to ten per cent of men.

•Thirty-seven per cent of women, but only 12 per cent of men indicated (on the same survey) that they were worried when home alone in the evening or at night. Young women were particularly likely to be frightened. Among men, it was the oldest group (age 65 or over) who indicated highest level of fear.

•Having been a victim—particularly of sexual assault—tends to lead to higher levels of fear.

It is hard to imagine that anyone in our society could believe that the impact of crime on men and women is the same. And, if it is not the same, one wouldn't, as a researcher, consider using the same approach to understand a different phenomenon. A study of violence against men, if it were to be carried out, would have to start from the beginning, identifying the issues and concerns identified by men as being important.

From a research perspective, the question—"why not simply extend the survey to include violence against men?"—makes no sense. Since we know that violence against women is different from violence against men—and, presumably, its effects are different—it makes sense to address different questions to men and women. Questions about "unwanted attention" from male (or female) strangers or questions about whether "a man you knew ever made you feel uncomfortable by making inappropriate comments about your body or your sex life" or whether a man (or a woman, for that matter) has ever "leaned over you unnecessarily, got close or cornered you" simply have different meanings for men and women. More to the point, they do not on the surface appear to be questions which address issues that are as salient for men as they are for women. Similarly, it is unlikely that the following questions could be adapted to address an issue that is a salient concern for many men: "Excluding husbands or common-law partners, has a date or boyfriend ever forced you or attempted to force you into any sexual activity by threatening you, holding you down or hurting you in some way?" Certainly one could ask questions such as: "Has your wife/partner ever thrown anything at you that could hurt you?" But, as a researcher, I do not think it would be hard to find data to suggest that such violence—or even more serious forms of violence—affects women's lives more than men's.

Violence against men certainly is an issue, but the available data suggest that the effects of violence are more of an issue for women—both in terms of their own victimizations and, at least as importantly, in terms of their adaptations and concerns about possible victimizations. Focusing on violence against women, then, appeared to be sensible from a policy perspective and necessary from a research perspective. Clearly, then, nobody could seriously complain about a survey of violence against women being carried out with taxpayers' money.

## Violence Against the Survey

I was wrong. The survey findings were released in November, 1993. Five months later another set of findings focusing on wife assault was released as a Statistics Canada *Juristat* (Rodgers). The first press reports were rather straightforward stories and commentaries on the findings. There were occasional rumblings of concern about the "political" issues surrounding the survey. The most direct and public attack on the survey did not occur, however, until November, 1994—a full year after the first findings had been released. In two columns in the *Globe and Mail*, Margaret Wente, the *Globe and Mail's* columnist on women, attacked the survey under the rather provocative titles, "A serious case of statistics abuse," (1994a: A2) and "Why the Statscan tale needs debunking" (1994b: A2). They are extraordinary columns. The open question, of course, is what the subtext might be.

There were two official replies published in the *Globe and Mail.* A letter from Sange de Silva, Executive Director of the Canadian for Justice Statistics, Statistics Canada, corrected in a very matter-of-fact fashion some of the more glaring mistakes that Ms. Wente had made in the first column. De Silva's letter was published on the same day as Ms. Wente's second column, which attacked the survey on somewhat different grounds from those in the first column.

On the Monday before Christmas—rather than on a Saturday, the day Ms.

Wente's column normally appears—the *Globe* also published a more pointed critique of Ms. Wente's column, written by Holly Johnson. Finally, in late December, 1994, and early January, 1995, three more letters were published in the *Globe and Mail.* All three letters were from men,and all of them highly critical of the survey.[2]

Some of the criticisms of the survey contained in Ms. Wente's column, though refuted by Sange de Silva's letter and by Holly Johnson's article, were repeated in the letters *subsequently* published by the *Globe and Mail.* For example, the final letter suggests that:

> the study's failure to emphasize the enormous difference between sharp (even vicious) contentions and criminally abusive behaviour—as Ms. Wente argued—leaves it open to both misinterpretation and attack. By failing to distinguish not very good behaviour from really bad behaviour, the study concluded that a majority of males in our society are guilty of violence against females. (Roddick A18)[3]

It is true that one of Ms. Wente's contentions was that:

> the Statscan report painted a false picture of the world because it failed to make any distinction between the transient and insignificant conflicts of everyday life and truly violent behaviour as it is commonly understood by most people. (1994b: A2)

It is, however, true that Sange de Silva pointed out in his letter that the survey, in fact, *does* allow one to look at the range of different levels of seriousness of marital violence women experience.

Both Sange de Silva and Holly Johnson were a bit too polite when responding to Ms. Wente. Neither of them pointed out that Ms. Wente appeared not to have read any or all of the report she was criticizing. Had she read the straightforward and short (nine page) report, and had she successfully processed what she read, she would have found, on page five of the November 18, 1993, Statistics Canada *Daily*, a table indicating the proportion of "ever-married women" who reported each of ten different kinds of violence. This showed, for example, that 25 per cent of ever-married women reported being "pushed, grabbed or shoved" (presumably, in Ms. Wente's eyes, some of the "transient and insignificant conflicts of everyday life"). It also showed that 15 per cent of ever-married women reported having been slapped, but "only" seven per cent reported having been choked by a current or previous partner. I obviously cannot speak for Ms. Wente, but I, personally, as a man, would put "being choked" in the category of "truly violent behaviour."

If one were interested in assessing Ms. Wente's skills as a critic of social science research, one only has to read a few lines of her column in the *Globe and Mail* of December 3, 1994:

> But, if [those responsible for the survey] had drawn a more reasonable conclusion from the violence data—"Rates of spouse abuse probably haven't changed much in the past 30 years, and most wives with abusive husbands get a divorce"—there would be no headlines and not much justification for their existence. (A2)

This is an extraordinary statement and is quite revealing of her own criticisms of the survey and perhaps others' criticisms as well. The statement clearly implies that, in her view, wife assault isn't really a problem. Months after reading this sentence, I am still trying to figure out how Ms. Wente would suggest that the published Statistics Canada survey data—which were collected only at one point in time—would support the inference that the size of the problem had not changed much in the past 30 years. On the other hand, whether "most wives with an abusive husbands get a divorce," is, of course, an empirical question that my be answerable from the data.

Holly Johnson has responded in detail to the criticisms that have been leveled at this quite remarkable survey. Two conclusions are clear to me from the responses to the survey:

- The findings of high levels of violence directed at women not only are disturbing for anyone concerned about violence, but also appear to disturb those who would prefer to believe that violence against women is not a problem.

- Criticisms of the survey—couched often in "technical" or methodological language—appear to be motivated primarily by political and social attitudes, rather than by concerns about the actual methodology.

Finally, the findings from this survey are just beginning to be known. Although some of the results have been published, it is clear that there is an enormous amount of interesting and important information contained in this survey. A large number of Canadian researchers are now working with these data. We will all know an enormous amount more about women's experience with violence at the end of this process.

## Notes

[1]Surprisingly, statements such as this have been challenged by some writers. For a thoughtful and detailed analysis of the data, demonstrating quite conclusively that violence within marital relationships is not symmetrical, see Dobash *et al.*
[2]These were the only letters we were able to find. We are aware of two other letters—both authored or co-authored by men—which were highly critical of Ms. Wente's columns. Neither of these were published. One can draw one's own

inferences about the *Globe and Mail's* reasons for not publishing letters which were critical of one of its own columnists.

[3]The study did not, of course, address the question of the distribution of violent behaviour among men and, therefore, did not conclude that "a majority of males in our society are guilty of violence against females" (Roddick A18).

## References

Dobash, Russell P., R. Emerson Dobash, Margo Wilson, and Martin Daly. "The Myth of Sexual Symmetry in Marital V iolence." *Social Problems* 39(1) (1992): 71-79.

Johnson, Holly. "The reality of violence against women." *The Globe and Mail.* 19 December 1994: A17.

Rodgers, Karen. "Wife assault: The findings of a national survey." *Juristat* 14 (9): (March 1994).

Roddick, Paul M."Statistical violence." [Letter to the Editor] *Globe and Mail* 5 January 1995: A18.

de Silva, Sange. "Dimensions of violence against women." [Letter to the Editor] *Globe and Mail* 3 December 1994: D7.

Wente, Margaret. "A serious case of statistics abuse." *The Globe and Mail* 26 November 1994a: A2.

Wente, Margaret. "Why the Statscan tale needs debunking." *The Globe and Mail* 3 December 1994b: A2.

# The 1999 General Social Survey on Spousal Violence

## An Analysis

Yasmin Jiwani

Against a backdrop of headline murders of women and children by their abusive partners, the unveiling of Statistics Canada's 1999 General Social Survey on Spousal Violence has contributed to the growing gap between the realities of wife abuse that women and front line workers know first-hand and the popular myths that permeate society about women's aggression and tendencies to violence. The General Social Survey (GSS) on Spousal Violence was released as part of Statistics Canada's annual publication on *Family Violence in Canada: A Statistical Profile, 2000*. Already, journalists and men's rights proponents are publicizing these results in support of their claims about women's violence. The danger lies in policy-makers taking the survey results at face-value and using them as a rationale for further reducing the already scarce resources allocated to rape crisis centres, shelters, and services for battered women.

In a country where 3.4 wives are murdered for every one husband killed (Locke), and where previous statistics reveal that 98 per cent of sexual assaults and 86 per cent of violent crimes are committed by men (Johnson 1996); where women constitute 98 per cent of spousal violence victims of sexual assault, kidnapping, or hostage taking (Fitzgerald); and where 80 per cent of victims of criminal harassment are women while 90 per cent of the accused are men (Kong), the GSS findings are startling. The GSS findings reveal that the rates of spousal violence experienced by men and women were only slightly different—eight per cent for women, seven per cent for men in relationships five years prior, and four per cent for both women and men in their current relationships. At a superficial level, the findings suggest that women and men are equally violent, thus feeding the backlash against the experiences and observations of front line workers, academics, and policy-makers who have long argued about the widespread prevalence of male violence.

Could it be that these findings reflect an accurate portrait of the declining levels of violence and/or that women have now achieved gender parity in violence when they have not been able to achieve this in other domains of social life? Or are we to completely negate everything we hear about the growing levels of violence—from road rage to stalking, date rape, sexual harassment, workplace harassment and the murder of women in their homes and on the streets? Or are we to discount all the other statistics that Statistics Canada has published beginning with the decisive 1993 Violence Against Women Survey to the 1999 statistical profile on *Family Violence in Canada*? If violence is about power and dominance, have women become increasingly powerful and dominant?

The GSS survey results were derived from telephone interviews with a sample of 26,000 respondents aged 15 years or more, and located in ten provinces. The total number of respondents included 14,269 women and 11,607 men. Respondents were asked ten questions which were derived from the Violence Against Women Survey (VAWS) and subsequently modified. The questions focused on violence, ranging from threats to sexual assault, that had occurred in the twelve-month or five-year period prior to the interview. The definition of violence used in the GSS was derived from acts of violence as defined and described in the *Criminal Code*.

The following sections outline some of the problematic aspects of the GSS and how they could be used to minimize the reality of the overwhelming prevalence of male violence against women. The GSS findings should be used cautiously as they do not capture the full extent of violence against women. In fact, in comparing the 1993 GSS results with the findings of the 1993 VAWS, the GSS results captured approximately half the actual percentage of cases of wife assaults that were reported by women who participated in the Violence Against Women Survey (Johnson 1996: 54). Further, unlike the VAWS, the GSS does not take into consideration sexual harassment and emotional abuse in its reported rates of violence. Nor does it track the increase in violence directed against pregnant women or women who are vulnerable because of their social class, disability, race, or sexual orientation. The GSS, unlike the VAWS, only focuses on experiences of violence within a confined time period (twelve months and five years), and in the context of a spousal relationship, whereas previous surveys have focused on women's experiences of violence from age 16 and up, and have considered numerous forms of violence.

Finally, the GSS relies on self-reports by respondents. This in itself can limit how much women who are in current or have had previous abusive relationships, may wish to reveal. There is still an aura of shame surrounding violence in intimate relationships, and, for many women, self-disclosure may be influenced by feelings of guilt, embarrassment, sense of personal failure, and fear of trusting an interviewer, particularly one representing what is a government agency (i.e., Statistics Canada). Further, it can take a long time before a woman is able to disclose the violence she has experienced.

Violence is about power and control. Women who are in violent relationships tend to experience low self-esteem (as revealed by the GSS), and, in the context of being isolated from the support of others, the abuser and his perceptions become the referent. The low self-esteem itself is perpetuated by the abuser and enhanced by the social messages that women receive about their status as women and their powerlessness as victims of abuse. These women may respond to an interviewer in a manner that not only minimizes their abuse but also mistakenly communicates that they did something to merit the abuse. Women tend to take on the responsibility for the relationship and are often blamed for the failure of a relationship. Front line workers are well aware of these dynamics, but survey research tends not to capture them.

## The GSS and Who It Excludes

The GSS, unlike the Uniform Crime Reporting Survey, which is based on police reported incidents, collects data based on individual experiences of victimization. In the GSS survey released on July 25, 2000, respondents in same-sex relationships constituted only one per cent of the total sample surveyed. The GSS only includes English- and French-speaking individuals living in households that have a telephone. In terms of the exclusion of non-English or non-French speakers, the GSS findings are limited particularly in light of the number of women who may be caught in abusive relationships and who, for reasons of safety, immigration criteria, and dependency on their sponsoring spouse, are not able to speak the official language and reveal their experiences of violence.

In addition, the survey's criteria for respondents—that they live in households equipped with telephones—effectively excludes homeless women, women in transition, women who are escaping abuse, and women who by virtue of their social class, poverty, and homelessness are more vulnerable to violence. In fact, many homeless women may have become homeless as a result of the violence they experienced in their relationship. Aboriginal women living on reserves and homes without access to household telephones are also excluded. Telephones are also not the preferred medium of communication for those with hearing or speech disabilities. Hence, these potential respondents are also excluded, despite research which suggests that women with disabilities are more vulnerable to violence (Roeher Institute).

## Questions Asked

The GSS asked respondents the following questions about violence, which were defined according to the *Criminal Code* as constituting offences that could be reported to the police or elicit police intervention. The overall rates of spousal abuse reported in the GSS do not include emotional abuse although these are presented within the context of Statistics Canada's profile on family violence in Canada.

The module of questions and the preamble that preceded them used in the GSS is presented below:

> It is important to hear from people themselves if we are to understand the serious problem of violence in the home. I'm going to ask ten short questions and I'd like you to tell me whether, in the past five years, your spouse/partner has done any of the following to you. Your responses are important whether or not you have had any of these experiences. Remember that all information provided is strictly confidential.
>
> During the past five years, has your partner:
>
> 1. Threatened to hit you with his/her fist or anything else that could have hurt you?
> 2. Thrown anything at you that could have hurt you?
> 3. Pushed, grabbed or shoved you in a way that could have hurt you?
> 4. Slapped you?
> 5. Kicked, bit, or hit you with his/her fist?
> 6. Hit you with something that could have hurt you?
> 7. Beaten you?
> 8. Choked you?
> 9. Used or threatened to use a gun or knife on you?
> 10. Forced you into any unwanted sexual activity by threatening you, holding you down, or hurting you in some way? (Canadian Centre for Justice Statistics 13)

On the surface, these questions appear to be common-sensical and direct in their focus. However, the crucial element that is missing is the context of the violent incident. There is no indication whether a respondent slapped, kicked, or bit her/his partner in retaliation or self-defence. It is known that women who have been abused are often forced to retaliate against the abuser in self-defence. The number of high profile cases of women who endured abuse and battering and who have acted in self-defence is a well-known issue which Statistics Canada could have considered when composing the module of questions asked of respondents. There are no questions about the intent of the abuser, e.g., "Why did he hit or threaten you?" Similarly, there are no other forms of violence included, e.g., "Did he ever sit on you?" Although the questions asked make reference to the use of a gun or knife, there are many other weapons of violence, such as a baseball bat, that are used against women.

The GSS questions equalize all forms of violence. Not only are extreme forms ranked with less extreme acts of violence, but when decontextualized (i.e., without asking for a context or tapping into the power dynamics inherent in the situation), the questions imply that one form of violence is like another and that the intent of an action equals the outcome. So a statement like: "thrown anything at you that could have hurt you" may elicit an answer that does not take the outcome of an action into consideration (i.e., "it could have hurt me") as opposed to the reality, which is that there was no injury involved or none that merited medical attention. Within a framework which denies that women's response to violence with violence is often predicated on self-defence, the above response would be meaningless at the least and dangerous if taken at face-value. Throwing something at an abuser in order to impede his violent actions allows the abuser, if he is the respondent to these questions, to shift the responsibility of his actions and to claim that he could have been hurt.

In analyzing the set of questions that respondents were asked, it is clear that there are several problematic assumptions at work. The first is the assumption that a woman would have had only one intimate relationship—there are no questions pertaining to the possibility that multiple abusers might have been involved. The question could have been phrased as "Has any person with whom you have had an intimate relationship, done the following to you?" Such a question might then have included dating violence.

Although the GSS includes a component on emotional abuse, the specific questions it asks could well have fitted within the above module of questions. Thus, one of the common ways by which abusers harass their victims is by threatening to hurt their loved ones (children, other family members, and/or pets). This is a measure of violence and should have been included here particularly because the final figures for spousal violence do not take into consideration the figures derived from the module assessing the impact of emotional abuse. These two modules and results are separated. Similarly, although isolation as a variable is measured by the emotional abuse module, it should have been asked in the spousal abuse module outlined above based on the reality that abusers will begin by isolating their victims from family, friends, and acquaintances, and, through isolation, make their victims more vulnerable to violence. Research demonstrates that the impact of emotional abuse is far greater than that resulting from physical violence. Since violence in intimate relationships is about power and control, the most powerful way in which power and control are imposed is through emotional abuse and fear. Separating the physical violence from emotional abuse fails to take into consideration the ways in which violence is used in intimate relationships.

## The Findings

Even though the GSS results reveal a similar rate of spousal abuse among women and men, a closer reading divulges interesting and symbolic differences. For instance, women not only experience more severe forms of abuse, but the impact of the abuse is far greater on them as compared to men who report experiences of violence.

What is most clear from the data presented is that the severity of woman abuse outweighs the kinds of violence experienced by male spouses. If we focus on the responses to questions 7 to 10, the differences in results are dramatic. More than twice as many women as men reported being beaten, five times as many women as men reported being choked, almost twice as many women as men reported having a gun or knife used against them, and, finally, more than six times as many women as men reported being sexually assaulted. These findings are similar for women and men in their current relationships.

That women may end up using less severe forms of violence in retaliation or self-defence is evident in the kinds of violence reported by men. These included being slapped, having something thrown at them, or being kicked, bitten or hit by their spouses. Women tend to be smaller than men, have less physical strength, and tend to use violence for purposes of self-defence (Duffy and Momirov 36). This is not to imply that there are no violent women but that violence directed by women against men is very different in social meaning and outcome than the violence directed by men against women. This is especially significant when we take into consideration the unequal status of women and the historic entrenchment of gender-based discrimination.

Drawing from the work of Lenore Walker, Johnson notes that:

> ...the meaning of a violent act also differs significantly for male and female victims. Men begin as the dominant partners in marriage, and one episode of violence, or even the threat of violence, has the potential to change the dynamics of the relationship, reinforcing his dominance and her passivity. A woman's violence against her husband seldom has such an effect. (1996: 58)

The GSS also reveals that women are victimized more frequently than men, and end up being physically injured as a result of the violence. The results underline the severity of violence experienced by women. Some 65 per cent of the women were assaulted more than once, and 26 per cent reported being assaulted more than ten times. Forty per cent of women compared to 13 per cent of men reported being physically injured as a result of the violence in the five years preceding the interview and women were five times more likely to require medical attention as a result of the violence (Canadian Centre for Justice Statistics 14). Four out of ten women are afraid for their lives, as compared to one out of ten men. Age is also a relevant factor indicating a heightened vulnerability to violence for women under 25 years, as compared to women who are 45 years and older.

## Emotional Abuse

While the findings of the differential rates of emotional abuse experienced by both women and men were not included in the rates of spousal violence, the GSS measures of emotional abuse are again indicative of how women are more severely impacted by violence and rendered more vulnerable to violence as a result of the psychological abuse they experience.

Interestingly, the GSS results indicate that men and women are equally jealous and possessive. What this finding does not capture is how jealousy and possessiveness are part of the dynamics of abuse. More specifically, qualitative studies indicate that jealousy and possessiveness are often invoked in a violent relationship and stem from the isolation, control, and coercion exercised by the dominant partner. In this regard, it is worth viewing the jealousy and possessiveness percentages in the context of the other kinds of emotional abuse that are measured by the GSS.

For instance, women reported a larger incidence of being isolated (in response to the question: "He/She tried to limit contact with family and friends"). Similarly women also reported a significantly higher rate of being called names and being put down. Four times as many women as men reported being threatened, harmed, or having someone close to them being threatened or harmed; more than twice as many women reported having their property damaged or their possessions destroyed as compared to men; and four times as many women as men reported being denied access to family income.

All of these measures indicate a level of emotional abuse that far outweighs that experienced by men. They also indicate the deliberateness with which women are rendered dependent on men. This is especially the case with access to family income and hence financial independence.

Many studies indicate that women who are in violent relationships often do not leave these relationships because of their fear for their children, isolation from networks of support, financial dependence on the spouse, and low self-esteem (Duffy and Momirov; Jiwani and Buhagiar; DeKeseredy and MacLeod). The GSS results illustrate the extent to which these dynamics of abuse are still prevalent. What they do not capture is the range of violence that women experience—from the initial period in a relationship, to the violence they experience during pregnancy (21 per cent of women reported this in a previous survey, see, for example, Fitzgerald), to the escalation of violence upon leaving a relationship—an escalation that can lead to stalking and other forms of criminal harassment. The GSS only captures the more overt forms of this. More than this, the GSS fails to underscore the reality and extent of male violence against women.

## Consequence of Violence

The severity and multiple consequences of violence for women are clearly identified in the GSS results. Women, more than men, report being more fearful, experiencing problems sleeping, and suffering from depression, anxiety attacks and low self-esteem.

## Discussion

The high rates of violence reported by men in the GSS results may be indicative of the popularization of the issue of violence and its decontextualization as a phenomenon divorced from power and power imbalances. The similar levels of violence reported by both women and men would seem to suggest that men and women are equally violent. Without including questions about the contextual elements that may have precipitated the violence or how violence was used as an instrument of power and control, the GSS results do not tell us anything new. In fact, the overall GSS results match those obtained in other surveys using the Conflict Tactic Scale. The latter instrument has been criticized by social scientists for not taking into consideration the unequal power relations between men and women (DeKeseredy and MacLeod; Johnson 1996), an inequality that may be even more pronounced and potent within the context of intimate relations. As DeKeseredy and MacLeod observe with regard to the Conflict Tactic Scale (CTS):

> The CTS simply counts the number of violent acts committed by people and thus cannot tell us why people use violence. Even though CTS data almost always show that men and women are equally violent, the fact is they use violence for different reasons, with women using violence primarily to defend themselves and men using violence mainly to control their female partners. ... The CTS overlooks the broader social forces (e.g. patriarchy) that motivate men to victimize their female partners. (63)

While the GSS is different from the Conflict Tactic Scale, it shares the same refusal to acknowledge the contextual factors that underpin and increase women's vulnerability to gender-based violence and how that violence is used to maintain inequality. According to the commentary concluding the GSS results, Holly Johnson (2000) posits that the statistics indicate a significant decline in wife assault and a decline in the severity of violence directed against women. She does note, however, that women are slightly more fearful now than before. Fear of violence or the threat of violence results from the use of violence as a tool of power and control which is used to maintain women's unequal status.

In contrast to the 1993 Violence Against Women Survey, the GSS does not examine the full spectrum of violence against women including such factors as sexual harassment. In fact, while the GSS attempts to capture the rates of emotional abuse, it does not take into consideration all the different forms of violence (from harassment, sexualization, objectification, and institutional forms of violence) that serve to "keep women in their place."

If the reported rates of violence against women are on the decline, it may be, as Holly Johnson (2000) suggests, a result of the successful struggles of front line workers, advocates, and policy-makers. On the other hand, the reported decline may be due to the normalization of violence, which the GSS tries to address through the specific formulation of its questions but may only be capturing in a limited way (as for example in the "equal" rates of violence reported for men and women). Alternatively, the decline may be due to what Johnson (2000) refers to as the different reference periods in which the 1993 VAW survey and the current GSS were conducted. Qualitative studies of women's experiences of violence based on frontline workers' perceptions (e.g. Chambers; Jiwani and Buhagiar) suggest that although official rates of violence reflect a decline, the numbers of women who are victimized by violence have not decreased significantly. Rather, women have learned not to rely on institutions to protect them and to use other ways and means of protecting themselves from violence.

The GSS on violence only captures a small section of the continuum of violence experienced by women every day. It does not take into consideration the socio-economic and political context in which women live—a context symbolized by the pervasive objectification, sexualization, and devaluation of women as it occurs in the media, within the labour force, and in the increasing numbers of women who are made poor. Neither does it capture the full range of violence meted out to those women who cross normative boundaries, or who are at the intersections of various kinds of oppressions. The GSS cannot erase the reality of male violence against women.

*The author would like to acknowlege Fatima Jaffer, Nancy Janovichek, and Agnes Huang for their valuable feedback.*

**References**

Bunge, Valerie Pottie. "Spousal Violence." *Family Violence in Canada: A Statistical Profile.* Ottawa: Statistics Canada, 2000. 11-20.

Canadian Centre for Justice Statistics. *Family Violence in Canada: A Statistical Profile, 2000.* Ottawa: Statistics Canada, 2000.

Chambers, Susan. *An Analysis of Trends Concerning Violence against Women: A Preliminary Case Study of Vancouver.* Vancouver: FREDA Centre for Research on Violence Against Women and Children, 1998.

DeKeseredy, Walter S. and Linda MacLeod. *Woman Abuse: A Sociological Story.* Toronto: Harcourt Brace and Company, 1997.

Duffy, Ann and Julianne Momirov. *Family Violence: A Canadian Introduction.* Toronto: James Lorimer and Company, 1997.

Fitzgerald, Robin. *Family Violence in Canada: A Statistical Profile.* Ottawa: Statistics Canada, 1999.

Jiwani, Yasmin and Lawrence Buhagiar. *Policing Violence against Women in Relationships: An Examination of Police Response to Violence Against Women in British Columbia.* Vancouver: FREDA Centre for Research on Violence Against Women and Children, 1997.

Johnson, Holly. *Dangerous Domains: Violence Against Women in Canada.* Scarborough, ON: Nelson Canada, 1996.

Johnson, Holly. "Trends in Victim-Reported Wife Assault." *Family Violence in Canada: A Statistical Profile.* Ottawa: Statistics Canada, 2000. 20-21.

Johnson, Holly and Vincent Sacco. "Researching Violence against Women: Statistics Canada's National Survey." *Canadian Journal of Criminology* 37 (3) (July 1995): 281-304.

Kong, Rebecca. "Criminal Harassment." *Juristat* 16 (6) Ottawa: Canadian Centre for Justice Statistics, 1996.

Locke, Daisy. "Family Homicide." *Family Violence in Canada: A Statistical Profile, 2000.* Ottawa: Statistics Canada, 2000. 39-44.

Marshall, Pat Freeman and Marthe Asselin Vaillancourt. *Changing the Landscape: Ending Violence, Achieving Equality*. Final Report of the Canadian Panel on Violence Against Women. Ottawa: Minister of Supply and Services, 1993.

Roeher Institute. *Harm's Way: The Many Faces of Violence and Abuse Against Persons with Disabilities*. North York, ON: Roeher Institute, 1995.

# Exploring The Continuum

## Sexualized Violence by Men and Male Youth Against Women and Girls

Aysan Sev'er

In the last few decades, interest in violence against women has been on the rise. Whether one reads or watches the news media, or scrolls down popular or academic journals or books, coverage of violence against women abound. Two recent national surveys clearly reflect this rising interest (the Violence Against Women Survey and the Canadian Panel on Violence Against Women). Nevertheless, specialization on narrow topics (like sexual harassment or female partner abuse or date rape), or coverage exclusive to geographic locations (the U.S. or Canada or the Third World, etc.) often glosses over a continuum of violence. Moreover, exclusive coverage of extreme cases (i.e., wife killings) often fails to emphasize a climate of misogyny within which these events take place.

The goal of this article is to bring the continuum of violence to the foreground. To this end, I will first review theories of violence against women, then provide selected examples. The examples are drawn from general risk of violence for women, subtle forms of violence such as sexual harassment, terrorist activities against abortion service providers, and instances of femicide. These dimensions may at first seem unrelated to one another. However, I will explore their widespread existence and their resilience to change as part of the web of gendered violence.

I will also explore the cross-border nature of gendered troubles. Despite the often justified attempts to dissociate Canada from the much more crimogenic social patterns that exist in the Unites States, this paper will show that the continuum of gendered violence may be a more widespread phenomenon that subsumes Canada. To trace the web among different patterns of violence against women, I will provide news reports from the *Toronto Star, Globe and Mail, Ottawa Citizen,* and *Montreal Gazette*. I will attempt to buttress the non-random media coverage with findings from relevant surveys and theoretical research.

Finally within a social responsibility framework, I will call upon individual, social, as well as structural change as a possible way out.

## A Recent Example of Violence Against Women and Girls

On March the 24, 1998, two youngsters, aged 11 and 13, gunned down four of their school mates and a teacher in Jonesboro, Arkansas. Aside from the natural disbelief and dismay about this disturbing news (Bensman and Egerton), what was glaring was that the killers were boys and the victims were all girls and a woman. Shortly after the initial horror, reports suggested that this may not have been a random incident of violence after all. Despite their youthful ages, both boys were avid gun-users and hunters. At least one of the two was meticulously trained in target practice and shooting at "pop-up targets" in a military style (Dyer). Readers were also told that one of the slaughtered girls was an estranged "girlfriend." Before the shooting, one of the killers had sworn revenge on her and her friends who had snubbed him (Bensman and Egerton). An issue which never got adequate media coverage, but which was easily deducible from a CNN report on the day of the funerals, was that at least 15 of the 16 wounded people in the same incident had distinctly female names. This rampage was against women.

In attempts to make sense of such a "senseless" act, some were tempted to blame teenage hormones, the unruliness of kids, or the ever increasing levels of violence in schools. Some argued for individual pathology. Others regurgitated the negative and almost always reductionist arguments about the faults of single or working (read: female) parents, or passed on moralistic judgements about the decline of "the family" (read: the traditional nuclear family). Moreover, there were muted insinuations about how one of the killers (Johnson) may have been compromised by his mother's "broken marriage" and work schedules (Booth, Schwartz and Mencimer). Perhaps the only common denominator behind such diffused justifications was the need to impose some kind of cognitive distance between "them" and "us" to overcome the feelings of one's own vulnerability. Of course, the definition of "them" or "us" was different according to who invoked the cognitive distancing process.

It was also tempting to interpret the Jonesboro disaster as a reflection of the overall violence of our southern neighbours (see Dyer). After all, everyone from the most insightful social analyst to the people on the street, know that the United States carried the ignominious distinction of being the most violent developed nation in the world (Crawford and Gartner). Indeed, Canada has a political system with more common sense about gun-control legislation, a much weaker gun-lobby than the powerful National Rifle Association (NRA), and tougher laws to regulate the use and ownership of firearms. Canadian laws are still being improved ("Gun law would raise alarms"). As Canadians who do not enthusiastically aspire to the guns-for-all mentality/politics of our southern ally, it was all too easy for us to separate what happened to "them" from what happened to "us."[1] However, despite the apparent differences in crime statistics, and despite

Canadians' undying belief in their "kinder and gentler society," I believe that it will be a mistake to interpret the Jonesboro slaughter as part of a uniquely U.S. plague. Rather, this incident might be better conceptualized as one that feeds on and reflects a continuum of violence against women. Within this continuum some of the factors at play are a culture of machismo, wide spread misogyny, and the troubling natures of work and intimate relations all over North America.

I am going to focus on a power, control, and sexuality triangulation which often sets men/boys against women/girls at the interpersonal, social and structural levels. Moreover, I am going to demonstrate how violence by males towards women and female partners often engulfs people who are family and friends of the target.

## Theories of Intimate Violence Against Women

Intimate violence is the physical, psychological, or sexual degradation and harm that one member of an exceptionally bound group inflicts upon one or more members of the same group. Unique aspects of intimate violence are that it is repetitive, malicious, intentional, and not random. Another aspect of intimate violence is that it is often inflicted by an individual who has more resources (very often men) against those who are weaker and lack resources (very often women and children; see Johnson for a discussion of risk factors). Intimate femicide is an extreme point in the continuum of intimate violence, where women are killed by their current or former partners (Bean; Block and Christakos; Crawford and Gartner; Daly). Killing one's own or step-children and hurting friends or colleagues who get in the way are other extreme manifestations.

Although no theory can claim full explanatory power over the complexity of intimate violence, there are numerous general violence theory applications to this area. These applications can be grouped under individual pathology, social learning/general culture of violence, and feminist orientations (for examples see Bart and Moran; DeKeseredy and MacLeod; Gelles and Loseke; Sev'er 1997a, 1997b; Viano). Since this paper is on interpersonal, social and structural aspects of violence, individual pathology theories fall outside of the immediate focus. Moreover, research shows that most men who repeatedly abuse or even kill their female partners or hurt their children do not fit into the individual pathology models (Gelles and Straus). Finally, most men do not randomly beat up on their bosses, friends, and neighbours which shows that they selectively target their victims (Bograd). Therefore, I will briefly review the two models which are more helpful in understanding the continuum of gendered violence addressed in this paper: namely the social learning/general culture of violence and feminist orientations.

Social learning and, by extension, general culture of violence theories, assert that violence is learned through observation, modelling, reward systems, or lack of punishment, and thus highlight the inter- or intra-generational transmission of violence. Inter-generational transmission is extremely important when one considers the fact that children witness violence against their mothers in 40 per cent of violent marriages (Ney; Rodgers; Wolfe, Zak and Wilson), and women whose fathers-in-law are violent report more frequent and more severe abuse than women with non-violent fathers-in-law (see Egeland for history of abuse as a risk factor; Rodgers; VAWS). Moreover children, especially (but not exclusively) female children, themselves experience violence. For example, in a recent national Canadian survey, 50 per cent of the female respondents reported that they have experienced at least one incident of sexual molestation before they reached the age of 16 (Canadian Panel). Reppucci and Haugaard conservatively estimate that ten per cent of America's female children are subjected to some form of sexual assault and abuse. Such transmission of violence could be vertical (such as violent fathers/sons; Levinson). Expanded versions of learning theories also highlight the intra-generational, or horizontal transmission of violence (violent peers, subcultures of violence; DeKeseredy 1988). There is substantial support for the role of learning in violent interactions.

There are also feminist explanations of men's violence towards women in general and towards their intimate partners (Dobash and Dobash; Okun; Yllö). Although a detailed review of the variations among feminist theories falls outside the modest goals of this paper (i.e. liberal, socialist, and radical), these theories converge on seeking the roots of violence in social structures without disregarding the confounding role of inter- or intra-personal processes. What is emphasized is the central role of unequal and gendered distribution of power and resources, a differentially valued division of labour and a general patriarchal system which fuels and protects these inequalities. Feminists underscore the fact that even men who do not directly harass, abuse or otherwise subjugate women benefit from the status quo where women's chances and choices are compromised. Thus, in feminist explanations, gender, power and control triangulation determines work, as well as institutions of politics, law, health and education.

What is also emphasized is that the structural inequalities that exist also colour and shape intimate relations. Even women's right to their own bodies, their freedom of thought or action becomes contested grounds. Radical feminists emphasize the role of sexualized power and discuss who is most likely to benefit and who is most likely to be subjugated in such power-imbalanced relationships (Firestone). Women and children, especially female children, frequently fall into the latter category.

Although all men are not "all powerful" and all women are not "all powerless," and all men are certainly not abusers, what is noted is that men abuse and kill while women and children get abused and die in disproportionate numbers (Crawford and Gartner; Daly 1; Jones 1994; Wilson and Daly). The patterns of abuse and violence are not confined to adults alone, since dating relationships among teens are also infested with violence (DeKeseredy 1989; Dekeserdy and Kelly). In addition, leaving abusive relationships is particularly dangerous for the female partner and her children (Ellis 1992; Ellis and DeKeserdy; Sev'er 1997a, 1997b; *WAC Stats* 1993). It has been shown that violence during and shortly after the dissolution of a relationship can be particularly vicious and may easily spread outside the immediate couple (Sev'er 1997a, 1997b). Aside from those who are the direct targets (women/girlfriends), family and friends, children, new partners and even altruistic passers-by can find themselves in the midst of violence.

It goes without saying that no theory can adequately explain a complex social structural phenomenon such as intimate violence against women and girls. However, as the previous review indicates, learning theories which highlight the transmission of violence through different combinations of rewards, lack of punishment, and negative modelling and feminist theories that locate abuse within gendered power differentials and a climate of misogyny, offer compelling insights. Moreover, these theories suggest that remedies to interpersonal violence are complex; requiring personal, social, and structural efforts. For example, learning type theories show the necessity of altering reward outcomes for violent behaviour, while at the same time emphasizing positive role-modelling for both men and women to make non-violence a valued aspect of life. Feminist theories suggest the need for equity in the allocation of resources, a stronger voice and representation for women and children, and an equal concern for women's issues in the private as well as public spheres. What I consider the sum total of these approaches is a social responsibility model against violence (Eichler).[2]

## Methods

As stated earlier, this article is an exploration. In that sense, it does not have valid and reliable results to report from a carefully conducted study. Instead, media coverage is generously used to show that violence against women is rampant and occurs in multiple forms and thus mirrors a climate of misogyny. The sources of media articles are the *Toronto Star, Globe and Mail, Ottawa Citizen* and *Montreal Gazette.* As can be expected, the media reports are sometimes a little sensational and not necessarily free of bias. In addition, these newspapers are from a very concentrated area in the Southeastern part of Canada and definitely not generalizable in and of themselves. However, despite these obvious shortcomings, the sum total will show a continuum of violence against women as the discussed theoretical models assert. The careful testing of some of the assertions awaits future exploration.

## The Climate of Misogyny

It goes without saying that North American women have made significant gains since the 1970s. One of the most noteworthy is the increase in labour force participation and the closing (yet not closed) wage gap (Baker and Lero; Hamilton). Also, attitudes and behaviour of a sizeable percentage of men towards women have changed for the better (see Stancu).[3] However, these positive changes do not negate that fact that women have not been able to eradicate the thinly disguised misogyny in our midst. Moreover, we have barely scratched the surface of rampant violence against women at home or in the workplace. In the following section, I am going to review types of misogyny which are on the rise. These are risk of violence, sexual harassment, violent demonstrations against abortion service providers and intimate femicide.

Of course, there are numerous other examples of misogyny such as the current political milieu where social safety nets are being dismantled, often keeping women in abusive relationships (see "Cuts prolong abuse, shelters say"; Colin; and Mitterstaedt for the effects of cuts to women's shelters).[4] However, it is my contention that the four examples I have chosen are sufficient to clearly establish a continuum that structurally traps many women and puts their careers, and sometimes lives, at risk.

## Increased Risk of Violence

In 1992, a Statistics Canada survey showed that the risk of violence women face has increased. According to the findings, which were widely publicised in the mass media, women were victims in 49 per cent of all violent crimes ranging from assault to rape and murder ("Women facing more risk of violence"). Two subsequent national surveys showed that one of four adult women had experienced violence at the hands of a current or former partner (Canadian Panel; VAWS) and the reported frequency of victimization was much higher for previous than for current partners. Moreover, one of two Canadian women have experienced at least one incident of violence since the age of 16 (Canadian Panel). Although a subsequent Statistics Canada report showed an 18 per cent decline in spousal assaults (8), the latter finding has been received with much scepticism.

The argument is that get-tough policies towards the abusers introduced since the early 1990s may have backfired by making victims more reluctant to lay formal complaints against their abusers "especially if they have children and he is the provider" (Hess A8). These women still live in terror and continue to seek shelter in ever increasing numbers, without laying charges or involving all enforcement agencies (Carey). Unfortunately, the same era also coincides with severe government cut-backs to services for women and shelter closures ("Women's shelters feel cuts"; Wright).

According to the 1996 Canadian Crime Statistics, crime rates against the person are on the decline (Statistics Canada 8). However, this positive trend lacks a positive mirror-image when one looks at violent acts committed against wives and ex-wives. One third of the 84 women killed in 1996 were killed by their spouses or ex-spouses. In addition, spouses and ex-spouses of women perpetrated 41 per cent of the 42,005 non-sexual assaults against them (53). According to recently introduced stalking legislation, there was a sharp increase in reports of criminal harassment by husbands or ex-husbands (2,480 in 1994 but 3,313 in 1996; *Juristat*). During a spousal abuse and murder inquiry of Arlene May by her long-time abusive partner Randy Iles, expert witness Dr. Peter Jaffe (the director of the London Family Court and clinical psychology at the University of Western Ontario) testified that even the streets are safer for women than their own homes (Darroch 1998a, 1998d; Duffy and Momirov; see DeKeseredy and MacLeod for the effects of seeing the home as "private" and thus hidden from public scrutiny).

Children are also routinely victimized. A recent Statistics Canada report found that children were victims in 22 per cent of all assault cases reported to the police, and of these, girls suffered 56 per cent of the physical and 80 per cent of the sexual assaults (*Juristat*).

## Instances of Sexual Harassment

Other instances of misogyny are more subtle but nevertheless recurrent. In fact, one can argue that in the 1990s, there is a particularly callous attitude about the indiscretions of men against women, while younger women may erroneously believe that the gender battles are won. A case in point is the increasing number of sexual harassment complaints, and what appears to be the simultaneously increasing leniency towards those who have crossed boundaries of acceptability. Even in positions of utmost visibility and trust, men who should serve as role-models are failing to do so by allowing or instigating embarrassing situations and finding ways to put the whole blame on women.[5]

Sexual harassment examples are many. Both in the U.S. and Canada, the reported rates of sexual harassment can be as high as 90 per cent in non-random samples (Brooks and Perot) and about 50 per cent in more generalizable surveys (Canadian Human Rights Commission). Most of us still recall the U.S. Senate hearings against Judge Clarence Thomas in the early 1990s. We remember how the all-male senate committee rushed to the aid of their accused brother, despite the impeccable track-record of his accuser, law professor Anita Hill. More recently, the Ford Motor Company paid $1.5 million (U.S.) to settle a sexual harassment and hostile work environment suit out of court ("Ford Motor Co. has paid out about 1.5 million U.S...."). In two difference contexts, a 1997 survey of athletes and coaches showed that 12.6 per cent reported first-hand experience of sexual harassment (Aubry).

A recent Amnesty International report strongly criticized the U.S. correctional system, charging that female inmates routinely face sexual abuse and harassment from male guards (*Toronto Star* March 4, 1999: A14). Not surprisingly, men's sexualized transgressions are not confined to incarcerated women. A psychiatrist recently received a six-year jail term for sexually harassing and assaulting his female patients (Bourrie). Even a senior Vatican envoy has been charged with sexual harassment, leading to discussions about whether the Vatican should seek diplomatic immunity in the case (Harper).

The army remains one of the most entrenched bastions of male-domination. Recently, Sergeant Major Gene McKinney was acquitted on all charges of sexual harassment against him, which translated to the dismissal of 19 charges by women on one man's word ("Accuser tells court-martial of raunchy come-on"). Ironically, McKinney was convicted and demoted on a single obstruction charge, not as justice for any of his victims ("Disgraced soldiers to quit U.S. army"). In Canada, after long silences and repeated denials, even Defence Minister Art Eggleton and Chief of Defence Staff, General Maurice Baril publicly admitted that "sexual abuse exists in the military" (Thompson 1998a: A3). Since publicity began, numerous cases have been brought to light, some involving harassment allegations against top ranking officials (Thompson 1998b:). Is it any wonder that women are avoiding the army like a plague, and is it any wonder that the Canadian Army is desperately trying to recruit women in order to clear its image (Murray 1998)?

On the other hand, what job or occupation is perfectly safe? Recently, a 17-year-old young woman was sexually assaulted during a job interview, despite the fact that she had said "no" at least three times. Yet an Alberta lower court judge (John McClung) acquitted the assailant claiming that the teen did not "present herself in a bonnet and crinolines" ("Supreme Court makes an enlightened judgment"). McClung also engaged in a personalized attack against one of the female Supreme Court judges, Madame Clair L'Heureux-Dubé, even though the Supreme Court decision to overturn McClung's earlier judgement was unanimous (MacCharles 1999a).

## Violence Related to Abortion Issues

Perhaps one of the most profound forms of oppression women suffer is when their fundamental rights over their own bodies are taken away or threatened. In the United States, this right was debated at the Supreme Court level and legally entrenched with the *Roe* v. *Wade* case (1973). Canadian legislation soon followed, and under the dedicated leadership of Dr. Henry Morgentaler, Canadian women began to exercise their choice over unwanted pregnancies. Nevertheless, the battles over women's bodies are not over. In fact, as it has been argued in the media,"the intimidation, torment and murderous violence" may be on the rise (*Toronto Star* 1997: A1).

Within the last few years, there were shooting murders of abortion clinic doctors and staff in Birmingham, Alabama (Sniffen; *Toronto Star* 1998) and Miami, Florida (*Ottawa Citizen* 1994a, 1994b). Even more recently, a New York doctor was murdered in his own home (Rankin 1998). There have been arson and bombings in Atlanta ("Army of God claims it set Atlanta bombs") and in suburban Boston and Brooklin, New York (*Montreal Gazette* ). Extremist anti-choice organizations have launched a guerilla campaign not only against women but people who defend women's choice. A Presbyterian minister, Paul Hill, has lead anti-choice demonstrations with a sign that read "execute murderers, abortionists, and accessories." He eventually killed two people and maimed a third (Clarey A4). In fact, between 1982 and 1994, there have been 146 incidents involving bombing and arson against abortion clinics in 31 U.S. states (Handleman

B3). Since 1994, there have been five more attempted murders and two murders of doctors that provide abortion services (Rankin 1998).

According to a Montreal newspaper, Canadian clinics are extremely wary about the influx of A2merican anti-abortion protesters and the spread of U.S.-type violence. Already there has been an escalation in intimidation tactics, such as cutting phone and power lines, stalking and threatening doctors and staff, harassing patients, break-ins and vandalism (Cornacchia). The Morgentaler clinic in Toronto was bombed in 1992 and a gynecologist in British Columbia was shot in 1994 after receiving numerous death threats. Extremist right-to-life groups, which give themselves names like "Army of God" or "Operation Rescue," are distributing literature against women's choice. Some of these pamphlets have been found to include instructions for making plastic explosives (Cornacchia). Investigation of the recent murder of Dr. Barnett Slepian also showed that the violent segments of the anti-choice movement have moved their attack strategies into cyberspace. These electronic hate-sites contain pictures and detailed information about doctors who provide abortion services and immediately put an X-mark on the pictures of those who are murdered (Rankin 1998; "Anti-abortion web site 'a hit list for terrrorists'").

## Examples of Femicide and Intimate Femicide

Fortunately, blatant hunting and killing of women is rare. It is often confined to pathological serial killers and rape/kill campaigns in ethnic wars (Albanese). Nevertheless, there are shocking cases where revenge against one or hatred of all women seem to be the only motive in mass murders. For instances, the 1989 killing of the 14 college women in Montreal is a notorious example of generalized woman hatred. Although the tender ages of the Jonesboro killers (13 and 11) may make such a comparison unpalatable for many, there is an eerie resemblance between the gunning-down of 14 university women and the massacre of five and wounding of more than a dozen girls/women in the 1998 shootout.

While the 13 and 11 year-old killers are extraordinarily young, the Jonesboro massacre is yet another example of violence by men of all ages towards their intimate female partners and friends/family. A much publicized Canadian example of how revenge against one woman spreads was the 1996 shooting murders of nine members of a British Columbia family. Mr. Chahal, the estranged husband of one of the daughters, killed nine family members of his estranged wife and also killed himself (Mallar). The news media is littered with similar reports, where violence against women partners has consumed numerous other lives. For example, Mark Clark detonated a bomb in his estranged wife's car, killing himself, her, and her three children ("Man kills his family in car bomb suicide"). He had lured his ex-wife and the children to a mall with the promise of buying school clothes. Helen Kirec and her four children were killed by her estranged husband, who also killed himself ("Family farewell'"). Michael Stevens sent parcel-bombs to close friends and family of his estranged lover, killing five and maiming two others (Edwards). Dean Roberts strangled his wife and their 13-month-old twin boys, then set the house on fire (Farries). Ken McLeod stabbed his girlfriend, her three-year-old daughter, and 18-month-old niece to death. There were 40 to 50 stab wounds on each victim ("Woman, kids stabbed with kitchen knife"). David J. Gorton bludgeoned to death his common-law-wife and her four children ("British Columbia family killer sought"). The slaying of Nicole Brown and her friend (Ronald Goldman) became one of the most widely publicized events of the 1990s. Although her former husband O. J. Simpson managed to get a "not guilty" verdict in the criminal trial, he was found guilty in the civil trial of the wrongful death of Ms. Brown and Mr. Goldman (Rutten and Weinstein; Deutsch).

In line with the feminist interpretations of intimate violence, the rage fueled by possessiveness and need to control one's wife/girlfriend and the total disregard for her wish/right to terminate a relationship are similar, time after time (Campbell). Even in Canada, tougher measures have not barred the likes of Randy Iles from obtaining a gun permit and murdering his estranged lover despite multiple outstanding charges of stalking, threatening, and confinement against him (Darroch 1998b, 1998c). When guns are not available, kitchen knives, ice picks, or bludgeons are used ("Family slain, man held").

What is additionally worrisome is the youthful ages of some of these killers and their victims. Vincent Gray was 29 when he stomped his girlfriend (19) to death while in a jealous rage (Oakes). Roderick Ballentino Brown (28) beat his girlfriend (22) to death (Rankin 1995). Twenty-six-year-old Gilles Loubier shot and killed his girlfriend and her five-year-old daughter and wounded another daughter ("Man charged after woman, girl, 5, killed ). Joan Heimbeck was shot four times and killed by her 25-year-old former boyfriend (Andrus). Bac Quong Lu (24) smashed his girlfriend's head with a four-pound wrench ("Man charged in woman's beating death"). Laurie White (20) was found hanged in her bedroom and her 24-year-old estranged boyfriend was charged with murder (Irish). Patrick Deocharran was 21 when he repeatedly stabbed his ex-girlfriend in the heart (Gombu). John Breen was only 21 when he stabbed and killed his wife, mother, and cousin in 1993 ("Man gets life in killings of wife, mom and cousin"). Rohan Ranger (20) faced two first-degree murder charges for the stabbing deaths of his ex-girlfriend (Marsha Ottey, 19) and her sister (Vincent). Perhaps most telling of all, Brian Tackett killed himself and his 21-year-old lover in a hotel room when he was only *fourteen-years-old*. He had incessantly talked to his friends about his murderous intentions, but none had taken him seriously ("Friendly family looking for clues to murder-suicide"). Thus, the difference between the Jonesboro case and other countless examples is a slight difference in age, not in the deed.

The young killers and their older predecessors that occupy the North American news chillingly demonstrate how early these violent patterns are learned. The events also demonstrate how young boys/men can and do transgress against women/girls. Recently, a "little boy predator" has been stalking and sexually molesting girls in his school by sticking his finger "right up inside" their bodies. What is alarming about this news is that the predator is eight-years-old and thus exempt from the intervention of the criminal justice system (see DiManno). The victims' parents were advised to move their children out of the classroom, leaving the predator untouched (and possibly in the position to prey on other girls).

### Some Ways Out and Conclusions

I believe that events such as the Jonesboro slaughter can lead to self-reflection in order to make sure that they are less likely to happen again. An easy (although questionable) response is to toughen up legislation to deal with "young criminals." In an early U.S. news program following the killings, there were discussions about changing Arkansas laws to deal with young offenders. In the wake of the slaughter, many voices wanted to dismantle the existing leniency towards very young offenders (protection from being tried as adults and protection from long-term sentences). The Canadian government also wants to get tough with young offenders (Walker and Ferguson). Just recently, Justice Anne McLellan introduced tougher legislation called the *Youth Criminal Justice Act* (MacCharles 1999b).

Some may even try to establish the death penalty where it does not currently exist and/or widen its scope where already in use. In their social anguish, many Americans want revenge and some U.S. politicians are eager to oblige the electorate. For example, despite a worldwide outrage, Karla Fay Tucker was recently executed in Texas, and the state gloated in its notoriety of never having pardoned any of the 76 appellants in the last ten years (Caplan and Laxer). However, there are serious doubts about the effectiveness of such punitive measures in dealing with the social ills they are meant to ameliorate (see Hodge, McMurray and Holin for insightful analyses about deterrence; Murray 1997; Shonebaum; and also West for high recidivism rates among young offenders despite punitive measures).

I believe that the Jonesboro disaster should not be dismissed as another violent fluke that is exclusive to the U.S. Instead, a more constructive approach would be to honestly and openly re-evaluate the continuum of misogyny and violence in our homes and work lives. Also, each of us, man or woman, victim or perpetrator, must take responsibility for the role we play in its perseverance. The two words I want to underscore here are "continuum" and "responsibility." As lovers or friends, as families and parents, as workmates, as teachers, as law-enforcers or politicians, we must recognize and be willing to stand up to all types of violence as well as gendered transgressions, rather than wait for the worst possible scenario before showing our dismay.

Can most of us can honestly say that we never witnessed controlling pushes and shoves, heard demeaning and degrading jokes, belittled a woman's voice, weight, dress, performance, or outright achievements or stayed impartial in the face of such belittlement?[6] How many men can say that they did not openly or covertly root for another male colleague during hirings, evaluations, or promotions? How many of us put down women for demonstrating the exact drive, perseverance, and type of leadership that we admire in men? How many of us know a sexual predator at work or an abuser at home, but choose to turn a blind eye just because he is a good friend, a good worker, a fun guy, a good provider, an available golf partner, too young, too old, too powerful, etc. etc.? How many of us can claim that we did something about any transgression, whether we were the butt of demeaning jokes, loser in an unfairly resolved dispute, or endured an unwanted hug or wandering hands? How many of us still think that these things are none of our business and thus contribute to the conspiracy of silence?

It would also be misleading to deflect the whole burden of troubled gender relations to men, despite the unacceptable conduct of some famous recent examples. Clarence Thomas, Bill Clinton, Gene McKinney, O.J. Simpson, Tommy Lee, Charlie Sheen, Mickey Rourke, and their unfamous but equally oppressive counterparts that harass and abuse their mates or co-workers. Women also need to ask themselves about their own role in the continuation of the status quo, as socializers of young children, as workers, as mates, as teachers, lawyers, and politicians, and most importantly as role models. This is not to blame the victim, but to reclaim the resilience and agency of women in initiating much needed social change. It is to encourage women to stand united in their demand for social accountability and justice in the face of gendered transgressions against them.

In sum, the two boys in Jonesboro, Arkansas did not just wake up one day, arm themselves to the teeth, and hunt down and kill four girls and a woman, and wound more than a dozen other females. They are a part of a violent continuum. Like their older predecessors, they are products of a society where subtle as well as overt violence against women is rampant. They are a product of a society where women still get paid less, are still disproportionally poor, are continuously saddled with the crushing responsibilities of single-parenthood with little or no help from the state or their former partners (Sev'er 1992). They form a part of society where laws of equity are still not entrenched, where law enforcement still fails to protect those who are in danger. They form a part of society where judges and juries still acquit abusers and even murderers on the basis of sexist myths, and where some politicians and high-paid lawyers still cater to the rich and the powerful whose needs rarely coincide with the everyday safety of women (see Pence for an in-depth analysis of safety of women in not woman-friendly social contexts). The Jonesboro killers live in a society where men in positions of power still do and say things which degrade all women. From early years onward, these two boys, along with millions of others, may have been inundated by the overlapping images of love, passion, control, exploitation, and violence through films, video-games, music, and television commercials. More recently, every North American household has been subjected to the almost pornographic sex content of even the most sombre news reports due to the poor judgement and equally poor behaviour of the U.S. president (Letters to the Editor). Undoubtedly, these young killers have seen women and girls repeatedly put down by men and boys. They may have seen violence against women in their own homes or in the homes of their best friends. They may have seen their heroes, whether actors, sports figures, musicians or politicians, hurt women. What is more, they may have learned that not much happens to men who transgress. Their behaviour then, as abhorrent as it is, is nothing more than a peak of the gargantuan iceberg.

In conclusion, I do not mean to suggest that there is or will ever be an epidemic of gun-toting 13- and 11-year-olds hunting down women and girls. It is also true that most boys and men remain non-violent despite exposure to the sexist and misogynist stimuli that our culture provides. Nevertheless, given the stubborn resilience of gendered inequalities in work and all-too-common violence in intimate relations, it would be naïve to assume that the Jonesboro slaughter is a singular case. I take exception to those who throw up their hands and say they do not understand how this could have happened. I also take exception to those who suggest that a particular family (read the divorced mother) failed. This mass murder, like its predecessors, is clearly understandable within the misogyny and gendered violence that already plagues North American society. Similar shocking events have happened before, both in Canada and in the U.S. The question is, are we going to put aside our differences in creed, colour, status, religion, and political affiliation and demand an end to all gendered transgressions and violence? After all, the next time (and there will be others, if the status quo remains), it could be our own daughters, sisters, mothers, nieces or ourselves who are harassed or stalked. The next time, a woman who decides to exercise control over her own body may not find a doctor who can help her with her choice. The next time, it could be one of us who is paid less than we deserve, or gets overlooked in a new appointment or a promotion. The next time, it could be "us" rather than "them" in the line of fire of a disgruntled man or a teenaged boy, or it could be our own lovers, fathers, nephews, or sons who thrust the knife or pull the trigger.

*The author thanks the Social Sciences and Humanities research Council of Canada (SSHRC) for generously funding my work with victims of interpersonal violence which also includes a time-consuming content analysis of media reports on violence. She also thanks the two anonymous reviewers who made extensive and insightful comments on an earlier version of this paper.*

## Notes

[1]Since the original version of this paper was written, Ontario passed a revised gun law which now permits 12-year-olds to use firearms for "hunting" purposes. The controversial legislation was partially justified with comments such as: "In British Columbia 10-year-olds can get junior hunting licences"; "children are going

hunting anyway"; and "families can now spend 'quality time' with their children during a hunt" (Gillespie A2; Gillespie and Girard A2). A representative poll conducted by the *Toronto Star* showed that 76 per cent of respondents were opposed to 12-year-olds having legal access to guns (Gillespie).

[2]Margrit Eichler has developed her social responsibility model specifically for the understanding of families and family policy. However, her insight about seeing gendered relationships not as "isolated microcosms" but as "organizational structures" which "interact with society at large" (122) can also shed light on violence of men by women. For more details on this model, see Eichler, especially chapter 7).

[3]I acknowledge that some men are also victimized by other men (e.g. sexual molestation of male children and youth by fathers, step-fathers, other male relatives, teachers, coaches, male clergy, etc.), or even by some women (e.g., rare instances where male children are molested by mothers, step-mothers, female baby-sitters or teachers, or when men are abused by their female partners; see Straus). Although any one of these may constitute a criminal offence as well as a moral transgression, this article exclusively concentrates on abuse perpetrated by men and male youth.

[4]Another area of increased misogyny can be found in vociferous fathers' rights groups (Bertoia and Drakich) who are demanding extended rights after a separation or divorce and/or automatic joint custody decisions. If legislated, these changes can drastically curb the decision-making power and the freedom of movement of the custodial mothers. Another example of misogyny can be found in the militant suppression of the production and wide distribution of RU-468 (the-morning-after pill) which includes death threats to its developers, manufacturers, and distributors (Hurst).

[5]The original version of this paper, which was written before the historic impeachment trial of President Clinton, had a section on how the most powerful political figure in the world short-changed women. After the over-publicized Senate decision to leave him in office, I no longer wish to belabour this point except to say that his treatment of and relations with female workers in his employ, and his highly questionable words and deeds which caused endless embarrassment to his colleagues, party supporters, co-workers, including his wife and daughter, have been less than exemplary.

[6]Recently, a Toronto city councillor was reported to shriek at his female colleague "shut up, you fat slut" during a council session. Although a security officer had recorded this gendered insult, the offender claimed that he had said something else, like "fat slub" (Lakey B3). With the exception of a few headlines, *nothing happened*.

## References

"Accuser tells court-martial of raunchy come-on." *Toronto Star* February 12, 1998: A11.

Albenese, Patricia. "New Nations: Old Oppressions." *Frontiers in Women's Studies: Canadian and German Perspectives*. Ed. A. Sev'er. Toronto: Canadian Scholars' Press, 1998. 113-34.

Andus, Rob. "Ex-boyfriend jailed for life in killing." *Toronto Star* May 24, 1996: A16.

"Anti-abortion web site 'a hit list for terrorists'." *Toronto Star* February 3, 1999: A14.

"Army of God claims it set Atlanta bombs." *Ottawa Citizen* February 25, 1997: A6.

Aubry, Jack. "Guide will help fight harassment, abuse in sports." *Ottawa Citizen* January 22, 1998: D1.

Baker, Maureen and Donna Lero. "Division of Labour: Paid Work and Family Structure." *Families: Changing Trends in Canada*. Ed. M. Baker. Toronto: McGraw, 1996. 78-103.

Bart, Pauline B. and Eileen Geil Moran. *Violence Against Women: The Bloody Footprints*. Newbury Park, CA: Sage, 1993.

Bean, Constance. *Women Murdered by the Men They Loved*. New York: Hayworth, 1992.

Benson, Todd and Brocks Egerton. "Slaughter of children in schoolyard." *Toronto Star* March 25, 1998: A1.

Bertoia, Carl and Janice Drakich. "The Fathers' Rights Movement: Contradictions in Rhetoric and Practice." *Journal of Family Issues* 14 (1993): 592-615.

Block, Carolyn R. and Antigone Christakos. "Intimate Partner Homicide and Chicago Over 29 Years." *Crime and Deliquency* 41 (4) (1995): 496-526.

Bograd, Michelle. "Feminist Perspectives of Wife Abuse: An Introduction." *Feminist Perspectives on Wife Abuse*. Eds. K. Yllö and M. Bograd. Newbury Park, California: Sage, 1988.

Booth, William, John Schwartz, and Stepanie Mencimer. "The 'good boy' outsider didn't fit in." *Toronto Star* April 6, 1998: A4.

Bourrie, Mark. "Psychiatrist jailed 6 years for assaults on patients." *Toronto Star* May 30, 1998: A22.

"British Columbia family killer sought." *Toronto Star* September 20, 1997: A8.

Brooks, L. and A. R. Perot. "Reporting Sexual Harassment: Exploring a Predictive Model." *Psychology of Women Quarterly* 15 (1991): 31-47.

Campbell, Jacquelyn C. "If I Can't Have You, No One Can: Power and Control in Homicide of Female Partners." *Femicide*. Eds. J. Radford and D. E. H. Russell. Toronto: Maxwell Macmillian, 1992. 99-113.

Canadian Human Rights Commission. *Unwanted Sexual Attention and Sexual Harassment: Results of a Survey of Canadians*. Ottawa: Minister of Supply and Services, 1983.

Canadian Panel of Violence Against Women (Canadian Panel). *Changing the Landscape: Ending Violence, Achieving Equality*. Eds. M. P. Freeman and M. A. Vaillancourt. Ottawa: Minister of Supply and Services, 1993.

Caplan, Gerald and James Laxer. "Executions good politics in U.S." *Toronto*

*Star* February 5, 1998: A24.

Carey, Elaine. "8500 moms, kids in shelters last year." *Toronto Star* December 8, 1995: A3.

Clary, Mike. "Ex-minister guilty of abortion murders." *Ottawa Citizen* November 3, 1994: A4.

Cornacchia, Cheryl. "Will U.S. violence come to Canada?" *Montreal Gazzette* February 6, 1995: D1.

Crawford, Marla and Rosemary Gartner. *Women Killing: Intimate Femicide in Ontario, 1974-1990.* Toronto: Women We Honour Action Committee, 1992.

"Cuts prolong abuse, shelters say." *Toronto Star* November 19, 1996: A10.

Daly, Martin. "Till Death Us Do Part." *Femicide*. Eds. J. Radford and D. E. H. Russell. Toronto: Maxwell Macmillian, 1992. 83-98.

Darroch, Wendy. "Streets safer than home inquest told. Domestic assaults 13 times more likely." *Toronto Star* February 19, 1998a: E1.

Darroch, Wendy. "Fearful victim was sobbing on the day she died, jury told." *Toronto Star* March 24, 1998b: F3.

Darroch, Wendy. "Iles was not asked to surrender gun permit." *Toronto Star* March 26, 1998c: B4.

Darroch, Wendy. "Violence has emotional toll, experts warn." *Toronto Star* May 26, 1998d: B3.

DeKeseredy, Walter. *Woman Abuse in Dating Relationships: The Role of Male Support.* Toronto: Canadian Scholars' Press, 1988.

DeKeseredy, Walter. "Woman Abuse in Dating Relationships: An Exploratory Study." *Atlantis* 14 (2) (1989): 55-62.

DeKeseredy, Walter and Katharine Kelly. "The Incidence and Prevalence of Women Abuse in Canadian University and College Dating Relationships." *Canadian Journal of Sociology* 18 (1993): 137-59.

DeKeseredy, Walter and Linda MacLeod. *Women Abuse: A Sociological Story.* Toronto: Harcourt-Brace, 1997.

Deutsch, Linda. "Jury rules O.J. liable." *Toronto Star* February 5, 1997: A1.

"Disgraced soldiers to quit U.S. Army." *Toronto Star* March 24, 1998: A11.

Dimanno, Rosie. "Little boy predator stalks girls." *Toronto Star* May 15, 1998: F1.

Dobash, Emerson R., and Russell Dobash. *Violence Against Wives: A Case Against Patriarchy.* New York: Free Press, 1979.

Duffy, Ann and Julianne Momirow. *Family Violence: A Canadian Introduction.* Toronto: Lorimer, 1997.

Dyer, Gwynne. "American culture ensures more killings by guns." *Toronto Star* March 30, 1998: A15.

Egeland, Bryon. "A History of Abuse is a Major Risk Factor for Abusing the Next Generation." *Current Controversies in Family Violence.* Eds. R. J. Gelles and D. R. Loseke. Newbury Park, CA: Sage: 1993. 197-208.

Eichler, Margrit. *Family Shifts: Families, Policies and Gender Equality.* Toronto: Oxford, 1997.

Edwards, Peter. "Gilted lover held in 5 deaths. Victims were just 'average' quiet people." *Toronto Star* December 30, 1993: A1.

Ellis, Desmond. "Woman Abuse Among Separated and Divorced Women: The Relevance of Social Support." *Intimate Violence: Interdisciplinary Perspectives*. Eds. E. C. Viano. Bristol: Taylor and Francis, 1992. 177-88.

Ellis, Desmond and Walter DeKeseredy. "Rethinking Estrangement, Interventions and Intimate Femicide." *Violence Against Women* 3 (6) (1997): 590-609.

"Family slain, man held." *Toronto Star* September 20, 1997: A8.

Farries, Anne. "B.C. man guilty of killing wife, twin baby boys." *Toronto Star* November 3, 1995: A30.

Firestone, Shulamith. *The Dialectic of Sex: The Case for Feminist Revolution.* New York: Bantam. 1970.

"Family farewell."*Globe and Mail* April 22, 1997: A1.

"Ford Motor Co. has paid about 1.5 million U.S...." *Ottawa Citizen* January 30, 1998: C12.

"Friendly family looking for clues to murder-suicide." *Globe and Mail* August 18, 1997: A5.

Gelles, Richard J. and Donileen R. Loseke. Eds. *Current Controversies on Family Violence*. Newbury Park, CA: Sage, 1993.

Gelles, Richard J. and Murray A. Straus. *Intimate Violence: The Causes and Consequences of Abuse in the American Family.* New York: Touchstone Book, 1988.

Gillespie, Kerry. "Father of 4 happy to see new gun law." *Toronto Star* September 16, 1998: A2.

Gillespie, Kerry and Daniel Girard. "Young hunters anxious for 'quality' bush time." *Toronto Star* September 6, 1998: A2.

Gombo, Phinjo. "Slaying linked to break-up." *Toronto Star* February 6, 1993: A4.

"Gun laws would raise alarms." *Toronto Star* March 13, 1998: E3.

Hamilton, Roberta. *Gendering the Vertical Mosaic.* Toronto: Copp Clark, 1996.

Handelman, Stephen. "The deadly solution to 'sin' in the U.S."*Ottawa Citizen* August 20 1994: B3.

Harper, Tim. "Harassment charges laid against envoy." *Toronto Star* January 2, 1999: A22.

Hess, Henry. "Findings on wife assaults challenged." *Globe and Mail* August 7, 1997: A8.

Hodge, John E., Murray McMurray, and Clive R. Holin. Eds. *Addicted to Crime?* New York: Wiley, 1997.

Hurst, Lynda. Untitled. *Toronto Star* July 20, 1997: A1.

Johnson, Holly. "Risk factors Associated with Non-lethal Violence Against Women by Marital Partners." *Trends, Risks and Interventions in Lethal Violence. Volume III*. Eds. C. R. Block and R. Block. Washington D.C.:

National Institute of Justice, 1995. 151-68.

Jones, Ann. *Next Time, She'll be Dead: Battering and How to Stop It.* Boston: Beacon Press, 1994.

*Juristat.* Canadian Centre for Justice Statistics: Ottawa [Cat. 85-002-XPE], 17 (8 and 11) (1996).

Irish, Paul. "Ex-boyfriend faces charges in 'suicide'. Durham woman found hanging in her bedroom." *Toronto Star* May 8, 1997: A6.

Lakey, Jack. "Insult sparks call for conduct code." *Toronto Star* September 17, 1998: B3.

Letters to the Editor, *Toronto Star* December 30, 1998: A25.

Leslie, Colin. "Growth areas hit hardest in the year of the cuts. Social services already lagging outside Toronto." *Toronto Star* December 7, 1995: N11.

Levinson, D. *Family Violence in Cross-Cultural Perspective.* Newbury Park, CA: Sage, 1989.

MacCharles, Tonda. "Judge 'sorry' for outburst." *Toronto Star* March 2, 1999a: A5, A21.

MacCharles, Tonda. "New law gets tough on youth." *Toronto Star* March 11, 1999b: A1.

Mallar, Caroline. "White wreaths mark city's mourning." *Toronto Star* April 7, 1996: A1.

"Man charged after woman, girl, 5, killed."*Toronto Star* November 28, 1994: A10.

"Man charged in woman's beating death."*Toronto Star* October 17, 1992: A18.

"Man gets life in killings of wife, mom and cousin." *Toronto Star* July 28, 1995: A10.

"Man kills his family in car bomb suicide." *Toronto Star* September 13, 1995: A17.

Mitterstaedt, Martin. "Ontario's cutbacks trapping battered women, group says." *Globe and Mail* November 19, 1996: A8.

*Montreal Gazette* February 6, 1995: D1.

Murray, Charles A. *Does Prison Work?* London: IEA Health and Welfare Report, 1997.

Murray, Maureen. "Army's recruiters targetting women." *Toronto Star* March 25, 1998: A9.

Ney, Philip G. "Transgenerational Triangles of Abuse: A Model of Family Violence." *Intimate Violence: Interdisciplinary Perspectives.* Ed. E. C. Viano. Bristol: Taylor and Francis, 1992. 15-26.

Oakes, Gary. "Boyfriend jailed in stomping death." *Toronto Star* January 20, 1995: A18.

Okun, Lewis. *Woman Abuse: Facts Replacing Myths.* New York: State University of New York Press, 1986.

*Ottawa Citizen* August 20, 1994a: B3

*Ottawa Citizen* November 3, 1994b: A4.

Pence, Ellen. "Safety for Battered Women in a Textually Mediated Legal System." Toronto: OISE/University of Toronto. Unpublished Ph.D. dissertation, 1996.

Rankin, Jim. "Slain woman had been upset, co-workers say." *Toronto Star* October 11, 1995: A4.

Rankin, Jim. "The sniper with a mission." *Toronto Star* October 31, 1998: A2.

Reppucci, N. Dickon and J. Jeffrey Haugaard. "Problems with Child Sexual Abuse: Prevention Programs." Eds. R. J. Gelles and D.R. Loseke. *Current Controversies in Family Violence*. Newbury Park, CA: Sage, 1993. 306-22.

Rodgers, Karen. "Wife Assault in Canada," *Canadian Social Trends*. Ottawa: Canadian Centre for Justice Statistics, 1994.

Rutten, Tim and Henry Weinstein. "Nicole Simpson diaries tell sordid tale. O.J. confronted with excerpts in law suit hearing." *Toronto Star* March 3, 1996: A12.

Sev'er, Aysan."Recent or Imminent Separation and Intimate Violence Against Women: A Conceptual and Some Canadian Examples." *Violence Against Women* 3 (6) (1997a): 566-589.

Sev'er, Aysan. Ed. *A Cross-Cultural Exploration of Wife Abuse: Problems and Prospects*. New Jersey, Edwin Ellen, 1997b.

Sev'er, Aysan. *Women and Divorce in Canada: A Sociological Analysis*. Toronto: Canadian Scholars' Press, 1992.

Shonebaum, Stephen E. Ed. *Does Capital Punishment Deter Crime?* San Diego, California: Greenhaven Press, 1998.

Sniffen, Michael J. "Links sought between bombings." *Ottawa Citizen* February 28, 1998: A8.

Stancu, Henry. "Men march to help women. Labour joins efforts to quell spousal abuse." *Toronto Star* May 5, 1998: A7.

Statistics Canada. *Canadian Crime Statistics*. Minister of Industry: Ottawa [Cat. 85-205-XPE], 1997.

Straus, Murray. "Physical Assaults by Wives: A Major Social Problem." *Current Controversies in Family Violence*. Eds. R. J. Gelles and D. R Loseke. Newbury Park, CA: Sage, 1993. 67-87.

"Supreme court makes enlightened judgment." *Toronto Star* March 5, 1999: A5, A21.

Thompson, Allan. "Colonel under fire in new sexual harassment case; 2 top military officers probed." *Toronto Star* June 18, 1998a: A1.

Thompson, Allan. "General admits sexual abuse exists in military." *Toronto Star* May 20, 1998b: A3.

*Toronto Star* March 4, 1999: A14.

*Toronto Star* January 30, 1998: A3.

*Toronto* Star July 20, 1997: A1.

Violence Against Women Survey (VAWS). Ottawa: The Daily Statistics Canada [cat.11-001], November 18, 1993.

Viano, Emilio C. Ed. *Intimate Violence: Interdisciplinary Perspective*. Washington: Taylor and Francis, 1992.

Vincent, Donovan. "Ottey killing accused is denied bail." *Toronto Star* June 12, 1996: A11.

*WAC Stats: The Facts About Women.* New York: Women's Action Coalition, 1993.

Walker, Wilham and Derek Ferguson. "Tougher law soon on young offenders." *Toronto Star* May, 12, 1998: A7.

West, Gordon W. *Young Offenders and the State: A Canadian Perspective of Delinquency.* Toronto: Butterworths, 1984.

Wilson, Margo I. and Martin Daly. "Spousal Homicide Risk and Estrangement." *Violence and Victims* 8 (1993): 3-16.

Wilson, Margo I. and Martin Daly. "Who Kills Whom im Spousal Killings?" *Criminology* 30 (2) (1992): 189-215.

"Woman, kids stabbed with kitchen knife." *Toronto Star* March 4, 1996: A8.

"Women facing more risk of violence." *Toronto Star* November 19, 1992: A14.

"Women's shelters feel cuts" *Toronto Star* December 7, 1995: SC2.

Wolfe, D., L. Zak, and S. Wilson. "Child Witness to Violence Between Parents: Critical Issues in Behaviour and Social Adjustment." *Journal of Abnormal Child Psychology* 14 (1) (1986): 95-102.

Wright, Lisa. "Cuts force some women back to abuse, group says."*Toronto Star* November 19, 1996: A10.

Yllö, Kersti and Michelle Bograd. Eds. *Feminist Perspectives on Wife Abuse.* Newbury Park, CA: Sage, 1988.

# The Incidence and Prevalence of Woman Abuse in Canadian Courtship

Walter DeKeseredy and Martin D. Schwartz

> I went to the drive-through window at the bank to cash a check and he followed me in his car. He got out and started telling me what a cunt I was and how nobody would ever love me. I was really embarrassed. Everyone was watching me through the bank window. When they sent my money out, he took it and my driver's license. We argued, and he called me names. I grabbed my driver's license as he started to crack it, and I turned to run. He grabbed me by the hair and slammed my head into the top of his car. A bunch of my hair ripped out. I fell back against the car. Everything was blurry. He shook me, saying, "Why do you make me hurt you." (Stone 30)

Each of us has been extensively involved in the profeminist male movement on woman abuse for many years, both as activists and as scholars. Having written more than two dozen pieces on courtship violence, together and separately, we view some of the research presented in this chapter as a logical extension of our evolving views that students do not come to college or universities as "clean slates" but, too often, as highly experienced abusers of females. For example, the vicious and extremely injurious behaviours described in the quote above were committed by a high school student.

The word evolving is important because, prior to analyzing data generated by the Canadian National Survey (CNS), most of our theoretical and empirical work was in the area of male peer support for woman abuse among college-aged men.[1] We originally (as does much of the literature) saw certain college institutions as key factors in the development of such abuse. However, we heard from many people interested in the topics addressed in this book—students, parents, colleagues, and others—who suggested that pro-abuse attitudes start much earlier than college.

For example, it was a subject of great derision and joking that in 1996 two elementary school boys were in trouble for allegedly sexually harassing their female schoolmates. It was an illegitimate use of the legal system to deal with the typical boyhood behaviour of children, the argument generally went. Now, we have no facts on the specifics of these cases, and an argument can certainly be made that there are other venues than the courtroom to deal with these problems. However, the real problem was the ready tendency to dismiss the seriousness of such events simply because the participants were children.

It is interesting that people seem to think that most views are rooted in childhood behaviour but have a blind eye when it comes to violence against women. We force children to go to church and Bible study against their will, so that they will learn the habit early. We do what we can to make them respect their elders, keep their language clean, study hard, and in general start to develop the habits we wish to see in them as adults. When they beat up girls, denigrate them, devalue them, make fun of them, exclude them, make them cry, play pranks on them, scare them, and chase them home, however, they are just boys being boys. Why is it that we would not assume that boys would learn lessons from their own behaviours?

These behaviours may even be taught to little boys. Fine, for example, studied Little League baseball and found that this organization was particularly detrimental to boys who might wish to develop normal relations with girls. To be less than a star was to be like a girl. Actually, quite a number of approved organizations and outlets provide the same messages: men must be sexually aggressive as girls love it that way; boys cannot show emotion; any failure (especially at sports) is girl-like, if not homosexual. The media generally, the military, a wide variety of sports outlets, and even a great number of parents pass on these messages.

Nelson points out that a large number of coaches make fun of athletes who may not have performed at the approved level of aggression by putting bras, tampons, or sanitary napkins in their lockers. What is it about not only colleges but society in general that would demand a coach be fired immediately for using the word *nigger* but allows coaches across the country to refer regularly to their male players as *cunts*? What does it tell us about our attitudes about women and girls?

What we then find is that boys do engage in sexual harassment of girls from a very early age, certainly starting in elementary school. It may start as gender harassment (nothing sexual about it, just constant harassment of girls), combined with the lessons boys are learning long before they get out of elementary school about the importance of avoiding close relationships with girls and about portraying oneself as sexually aggressive.

Thus, in addition to presenting data on the incidence and prevalence of woman abuse in Canadian college and university courtship in this chapter, we present data showing that identified woman abuse in college relationships has some roots in earlier dating relationships.

## Locating a History of Some Canadian Woman Abuse in Elementary and High School Dating Relationships

Again, woman abuse in dating does not start only after high school. In some ways, few people have argued this specific point. However, most of the literature on the subject takes this view. The most reprinted articles in the field are those that suggest that fraternities and sports teams are to blame for campus sexual assault. Presumably, if fraternities and sports teams are to blame, then in the absence of these organizations, campus sexual assault would not take place or would not be as widespread. The opposite argument is that high school boys can be as violent or more than college men and may in fact be headed off to college looking for mechanisms that will facilitate their abusive behaviours. As pointed out in our earlier work (see Schwartz and DeKeseredy 1997), momma's perfectly innocent little alter boys don't go to college and just happen to come under the influence of aggressive fraternity men, who teach these new students a brand-new set of college values based on the exploitation and victimization of women. For example, in Charlotte Rae's study, a middle school boy told her what society had taught him: "One of the big messages, [and] I don't think it's a visible message, like nobody gets up and *says* it, is that men rule and all men are leaders and men have to be violent, like soldiers and stuff" (70).

What several small-scale surveys, summarized in Table 1, show is that many Canadian men while in high school have also physically, sexually, and psychologically abused their female dating partners. Moreover, the patterns usually associated with wife abuse appear in high school dating relationships and often for similar reasons. For example, Shirley Litch Mercer argues that there is great pressure among adolescent girls to "get" a boyfriend. These girls often internalize ideologies that assign relationships as "women's work" and blame women for the failures of men. Thus, it is understandable that there are many young women who are under intense pressure to "think positively and to forgive him," even if he is physically violent. Still, while we knew much about such behaviour locally, there were no national estimates of the extent of such behaviour either in Canada or in the United States.

So far we have talked about the need for national high school data. The same can be said about reliable estimates of the extent of woman abuse in North American elementary and middle school dating relationships (grades 1 to 8). Because many elementary school girls date heterosexual boys (Holmes and Silverman), albeit to a much lesser extent than their high school and college counterparts, it is fair to hypothesize that some of them are abused. Even at young ages, boys have been found to have developed strong masculinist and pro-woman-abuse attitudes (Connell; Hobbs). They are heavily influenced by the ideology of familial patriarchy, which has been found to be a key determinant of woman abuse in later dating contexts. According to Mercer:

> Adolescence is clearly not a period when young people reject the traditional

> gender roles for which they have been groomed. It is characteristically a time when they act them out—sometimes to their worst extremes. The alarming revelations about this process testify to the grave personal implications that male power has for females long before they become adults. (16)

For example, Davis, Peck, and Storment found that 60 per cent of surveyed high school boys approved of forcing sexual activities on a girl at least in some circumstances. Unfortunately, one of the disadvantages of this sort of research is that it does not let us know for sure whether those who hold such attitudes would ever act them out. One of the problems of much experimental research into such things as the effect of pornography on behaviour is that we do not know whether these attitudes ever leave the laboratory settings (Schwartz 1987).

Still, there is a great deal of reason to worry about such findings. First, an unknown number of these boys might indeed be currently engaging in forcing girls into sexual activity. Or they might be willing under certain future circumstances to force a woman physically. Second, boys who hold these attitudes often provide the atmosphere that encourages and gives permission to others to engage in sexual aggression, even if they themselves never move beyond verbal support for such behaviour (Schwartz and DeKeseredy 1997).

Some researchers have commented that the injurious behaviours described here as taking place in elementary and high school dating relationships will continue in subsequent intimate relationships (Girshick; Roscoe and Callahan). However, such conclusions have been based on comparing completely different college and high school samples. This means that the data are not directly relevant to their arguments. Using CNS data, we tried to overcome this and other methodological problems related to empirical work on woman abuse in elementary and high school courtship. Before we describe our findings, however, it is first necessary to discuss the ways in which the CNS generated these data.

## Definition and Measurement of Woman Abuse in Elementary and High School Courtship

The CNS used a broad definition of woman abuse, one that refers to this problem as any intentional, physical, or psychological assault on a female by a male dating partner. Four measures were used to measure the prevalence of this problem in elementary school courtship (grades 1 to 8), and different wording was used for male and female respondents. For example, men were asked to report their abusive behaviour, while women were asked to disclose victimization. Below are the female questions; for each one, respondents were asked to circle "yes" or "no":

In elementary school, did a male dating partner and/or boyfriend ever...

•threaten to use physical force to make you engage in sexual activities?

## TABLE 1
**Description of Surveys of Woman Abuse in Canadian High School Dating**

| *Survey* | *Survey Location* | *Sample Description* | *Interview Mode* | *Prevalence Rates* |
|---|---|---|---|---|
| Mercer (1988) | 4 Metropolitan Toronto high schools | 217 female and 87 male high school students | Self-administered questionnaires | Of the total number of female respondents, 11% stated that they were physically abused, 17% reported having been verbally abused, and 20% disclosed having been sexually abused |
| Jaffe, Sudermann, Reitzel and Killip (1992) | 4 London, Ontario high schools | 358 female and 379 male high school students | Self-administered questionnaires | 23.6% of the females and 16.4% of the males experienced verbal abuse* |
| Sudermann and Jaffe (1993) | 2 London, Ontario high schools | 790 female and 757 male high school students | Self-administered questionnaires | Of the female respondents, 44.5% stated that they experienced verbal abuse, 13.5% disclosed experiencing physical abuse, and 14.2% indicated having experienced sexual abuse; 25.3% of the males reported having experienced verbal abuse, 4.4% disclosed experiencing physical abuse, and 3.7% stated that they experienced sexual abuse* |

*There is no way of determining how many of these respondents were victims or offenders because they were not asked to provide such information. Rather, they were only asked to disclose having "experienced" abuse.

•use physical force in an attempt to make you engage in sexual activities, whether this attempt was successful or not?
•intentionally emotional hurt you (i.e., insult, say something to spite you)?
•intentionally physically hurt you?

The same questions were asked about woman abuse in secondary school courtship, except the words "high school (grades 9 to 13)" were included in the preamble.

Abuse that occurred in college and university dating relationships was measured through the use of modified relevant questions from Koss, Gidycz, and Wisniewski's Sexual Experiences Survey (SES) and Straus and Gelles's Conflict Tactics Scale (CTS). The items included in these measures are described later in this chapter.

## Results

### *The Prevalence of Woman Abuse in Elementary School Courtship*

Of the men who answered the elementary school questions (and said that they dated before the ninth grade),

•1.7% (*N*=12) stated that they threatened to physically force their partners to engaged in sexual activities,
•1.5% (*N*=11) disclosed having physically forced women to engage in sexual activities,
•18.6% (*N*=133) reported having been emotionally abusive and
•3.6% (*N*=26) admitted to having been physically abusive.

As we anticipated, women reported higher rates of victimization:

•3% (*N*=25) stated that their partners threatened to physically force them to engaged in sexual activities,
•4.3% (*N*=36) revealed that they were physically forced to engage in sexual acts,
•23.7% (*N*= 98) said their partners emotionally hurt them, and
•7.2% (*N*=60) disclosed having been physically hurt.

Are Canadian women more likely to be abused in elementary school courtship than their U.S. counterparts? Unfortunately, because the above findings, are, to the best of our knowledge, the first of their kind, this question cannot be answered. However, some Canadian-U.S. comparisons can be made with the figures described below.

### *The Prevalence of Women Abuse in High School Courtship*

Given that high school students spend more time dating than those in elementary school, we anticipated higher rates of disclosure from both men and women because they spend greater "time at risk" of abuse (Ellis and DeKeseredy). For the women, 89 per cent said they dated in high school, while 38.2 per cent said they dated in elementary school. For the men, the equivalent figures are 87.1 per cent in high school and 48.3 per cent in elementary school. However, this increased rate in dating did not result in an increased rate of self-reported abuse, except for an 80 per cent increase in reported emotional abuse:

•1% (*N*=11) stated that they threatened to use physical force to make their partners engage in sexual activities,
•2.3% (*N*=25) reported having used physical force to make women engage in sexual activities,
•33.4% (*N*=362) disclosed having emotionally hurt their dates, and
•1.4% (*N*=15) admitted to having physically hurt their dates.

On the other hand, all of the estimates from females support the hypothesis that the more time at risk, the more likely women were to have been the objects of violence in dating high school. In the first three questions, the high school rates are significantly higher than the elementary school rates, while the rate is slightly higher in the fourth area (physical harm):

•8.3% (*N*=13) stated that their partners threatened to physically force them to engage in sexual activities.
•14.5% (*N*=228) revealed that their dates physically force them to engage in sex acts,
•49.7% (*N*=780) reported having been emotionally hurt, and
•9.1% (*N*=143) stated that their partners physically hurt them.

Table 2 shows that the above statistics are markedly lower than the U.S. physical and sexual violence data uncovered by Bergman—although her questions are much broader in their scope—and approximate those generated by Henton, Cate, Koval, Lloyd, and Christopher. Comparisons with Roscoe and Callahan's U.S. study cannot be made because the authors do not present data on gender variations in acts committed by and against men and women.

Trying to make comparisons of these findings with previous U.S. and Canadian high school prevalence data is problematic for at least three reasons. First, different measures of abuse were used. This actually makes it almost impossible to compare statistics from study to study. For example, U.S. researchers Henton *et al.* and Roscoe and Callahan used modified versions of Straus's Conflict Tactics Scale. Another U.S. scholar, Bergman, employed four closed-ended questions that are more specific but broader in scope than those used in the CNS,[2] and she used one open-ended question. Second, the samples in the studies reviewed in Tables 1 and 2 are all local, rather than being national, representative samples. Further, the questions are less well crafted than those used in the study described in this

## TABLE 2
### Description of Surveys of Woman Abuse in U.S. High School Dating

| *Survey* | *Survey Location* | *Sample Description* | *Interview Mode* | *Prevalence Rates* |
|---|---|---|---|---|
| Henton, Cate, Koval, Lloyd, and Christopher (1983) | 5 Oregon high schools | 351 male and 293 female high school students | Self-administered questionnaires | Of all respondents, 12.1% reported that they were involved in a violent dating relationship. In 71.4% of the violent relationships, each partner had been both a victim and an offender at some point in time. Of the remaining 28.6% of those involved in violent relationships, 12.9% were victimized women, 1.4% were male offenders, 8.6% were male victims, and 5.7% were female abusers.* |
| Roscoe and Callahan (1985) | 1 midwestern senior high school | 96 male and 108 female high school students | Self-administered questionnaires | Of all participants, 9% stated that they experienced violence in a dating relationship: 5% disclosed having been violent to a dating partner and 4% stated that they had been in a relationship in which both partners were violent to each other. Females were more likely (65%) to experience violence than were males (35%),** and female were more likely to be victims of violence.*** |
| Bergman (1992) | 3 midwestern high schools | 337 female and 294 male high school students | Self-administered questionnaires | 15.7% of the girls and 4.4% of the boys stated that they were victims of sexual violence; 15.7% of the girls and 7.8% of the boys disclosed having been victimized by physical violence; 24.6% of the females and 9.9% of the males stated that they were targets of "severe violence" (a combined category of sexual and physical violence); 32% of the females and 23.5% of the males reported being victimized by any violence (verbal, sexual, and physical violence). |

*It is unclear whether these women acted in self-defence or out of fear of being attacked. **The researchers do not define the term *experience*; therefore, it is unclear whether they are referring to offenders, victims, or both. ***The researchers do not present data in support of this assertion.

book. Finally, because all of the participants described in the other studies summarized in Tables 1 and 2 were not told to focus only on heterosexual dating abuse, it is possible that a considerable number of them reported acts that occurred in gay or lesbian relationships. This is not to discount the harm from these abusive acts but only to point out that the studies may be measuring different things.

Although they involve different samples and measures, three previous Canadian surveys on high school abuse have been conducted (see Table 1). It is difficult to compare our CNS findings to any of the three. First of all, the other studies ask questions directly of high school students. Later, we will discuss the methodological advantages and disadvantages of this approach, but here it is important to note that the CNS asked university and community college students about their experiences in high school. Obviously, then, students who did not go on to tertiary education are eliminated from the CNS sampling frame.

Jaffe, Suderman, Reitzel, and Killip did not ask respondents to report whether they were victimized by or engaged in physically or sexually abusive behaviours, and Sudermann and Jaffe only asked high school students to indicate whether they had "experienced" these two types of behaviours and verbal or emotional abuse, leaving open the possibility for each individual respondent that they were either an offender or a victim. Jaffe, Sudermann, Reitzel and Killip however, did ask their respondents if they used "verbal force" on a dating partner and if their partner had victimized them in such ways. A substantially lower number of their male respondents (14.1 per cent) reported using verbal force, and a much smaller number of women reported being victimized by this conduct (23.6) per cent.

It is unclear how Mercer measures abuse because she does not report her questions. Even so, a review of her findings described in Table 1 reveals the following differences:

- A markedly higher percentage of her high school male respondents admit to having been sexually abusive (12 per cent), while 16.4 per cent of CNS female respondents report being sexually abused in high school, a bit lower than Mercer's 20 per cent.
- Mercer's male and female physical abuse figures are very similar to those produced by the CNS.
- CNS male (33.3 per cent) and female (49.7 per cent) psychological abuse self-reports are markedly higher than Mercer's (17 per cent male, 13 per cent female). This could be because she seems to have limited psychological abuse to something called "verbal" abuse, although we cannot be sure because the question is not reported or discussed by Mercer.

### *The Relationship Between Postsecondary School Dating Abuse and Elementary and Secondary School Dating Abuse*

Although the number of men who admit to the physical, sexual, and psychological victimization of women in elementary and high school dating is fairly small, it is large enough for us at least to look to see if these are the same people who admit to similar victimization in college and university dating relationships. In other words, do men establish these patterns early? Do men begin patterns of victimization in elmentary and high school and bring them to college?

*Additional measures.* To speak to these questions, we must first explain how the questions asked about college and university experiences differed from those explained above that discussed elementary and high school experiences. Because the main purpose of the CNS was to obtain data on postsecondary dating experiences, the questions here are deeper and more complex.

Physical and psychological abuse were measured using a modified version of Straus and Gelles's Conflict Tactics Scale (CTS). The psychological abuse component of the CTS consisted of six items, four of which are part of the Straus and Gelles verbal aggression subscale: "insulted or swore at her"; "did or said something to spite her"; "threatened to hit or throw something at her"; and "threw, smashed, or kicked something." Two new items were added to this subscale that were used in Statistics Canada's pretest for the national Violence Against Women Survey.[3] These measures are "put her down in front of friends and family" and "accused her of having affairs or flirting with other men." Previous research shows that these items are related to male-to-female violence in marital contexts (Smith 1990), so there was some reason to investigate whether they were also related to such violence in dating violence.

The physical abuse component of the CTS consisted of nine items used by Straus and Gelles: "threw something at her"; "grabbed or shoved her"; "slapped her"; "kicked, bit, or hit her with your fist"; "hit or tried to hit her with something"; "beat her up"; "choked her"; "threatened her with a knife or a gun"; and "used a knife or a gun on her." The last six items in this subscale constitute Straus, Gelles and Steinmetz operational definition of "severe violence."

It should be noted in passing that one version of the CTS used in the CNS was tailored to elicit women's reports of their victimization, and the other was designed to elicit men's accounts of their abusive behaviour. In other words, different wording was used for male and female respondents.

Sexual abuse was operationalized using a slightly reworded version of Koss, Gidycz, and Wisniewski's Sexual Experiences Survey (SES), and different wording was used for male and female respondents (e.g., men were asked to report abusive behaviour and women were asked about their victimization). In designing the CNS, DeKeseredy and Kelly chose the SES because it has been used widely in the field as a standard instrument for sexual victimization on campus both in the United States and in Canada. The ten items in the CNS version of the SES can be examined in their totality, for one measure of sexual abuse. Or, following Koss, Gidycz, and Wisniewski, they can be subdivided into four types of sexual abuse:

- *Sexual contact* includes unwanted sex play (fondling, kissing, or petting) arising form menacing verbal pressure, misuse of authority, threats of harm,

or actual physical force.
- *Sexual coercion* includes unwanted sexual intercourse arising from the use of menacing verbal pressure or the misuse of authority.
- *Attempted rape* includes attempted unwanted sexual intercourse arising from the use of or threats of force or from the use of drugs or alcohol.
- *Rape* includes unwanted sexual intercourse arising from the use of or threats of force and other unwanted sex acts (anal or oral intercourse or penetration by objects other than the penis) arising from the use of or threat of force or from the use of drugs or alcohol.

*Making the comparison.* There are some indicators that a pattern exists showing that men who are admitted victimizers often have some earlier experience as precollege victimizers in each of the three areas of physical, sexual, and emotional abuse.[4] Table 3 and subsequent tables only look at that part of the sample that began dating in elementary school, because that is the group relevant to the question being discussed here. Although most physical abuse obviously takes place after high school, of the 31 men who claim that they were intentionally physically abusive in elementary and high school dating relationships, 17 (54.8 per cent) also admit to similar acts after high school. Earlier, we had predicted that the increased rate of dating in college and university life would increase the time at risk for being abusive. On the other hand, it is worth pointing out that two thirds of these men were in the autumn term of their first year (39.2 per cent) or second year (27.9 per cent) at the time of the survey. Thus, the time at risk as college or university students (measured in months) is not very long for some of these students.

A similar pattern can be seen in Table 4 with the small number of men who admit the use of force to make a dating partner engage in sexual activities. When those who admit to using such force in high school and/or elementary school are compared with those who admit to using such force after high school, eight (32 per cent) of the 25 elementary and/or high school admitters also disclose similar forced sexual behaviour in college. If one takes a retrospective look, eight (34.85 per cent) of the 23 men who admit to using force in college also admit to having used it in the elementary and/or high school dating relationships.

Finally, Table 5 shows the strongest pattern, and the one where the admitted behaviour of male offenders most approximates the reported victimization of women. A bit less than half of all the men (48.1 per cent) admit to abusing women emotionally in any of the ways covered by the survey questions. However, virtually all of the men who admit such abuse in elementary and high school also admit similar abuse after high school (96.1 per cent). Perhaps most interesting of all, especially considering that a strong majority of the men are first-and second-year students, is that 85.3 per cent of all the men who had dated since elementary school admit being emotional abusers since high school.

Of course, as we pointed out earlier, women in this survey and in many others report much more victimization than men report being victimizers. Whether this

## TABLE 3
### Physical Abuse: Comparison of Precollege With College Men

| | | Admitted Abuse Precollege | |
|---|---|---|---|
| | | yes | no |
| Admitted Abuse After High School | yes | 17<br>54.8% | 109<br>17.4% |
| | no | 14<br>45.2% | 516<br>82.6% |
| | Total | 31<br>100% | 625<br>100% |

NOTE: $x^2 = 26.62$; $df = 1$; $p = .0000$; phi = .201; gamma = .704.

## TABLE 4
### Sexual Abuse: Comparison of Precollege With College Men

| | | Admitted Abuse Precollege | |
|---|---|---|---|
| | | yes | no |
| Admitted Abuse After High School | yes | 8<br>32% | 15<br>2.4% |
| | no | 17<br>68% | 607<br>97.6% |
| | Total | 25<br>100% | 622<br>100% |

NOTE: $x^2 = 61.37$; $df = 1$; $p = .0000$; phi = .308; gamma = .900.

is because women, or victims, are most likely to disclose or whether it is because there is a small number of men who victimize many women each is impossible to tell from this methodology (or any other methodology currently in use).

Women not only report more victimization than men, but the patterns are also the same. Table 6 shows that, retrospectively, 31.6 per cent of those women who report being sexually assaulted since high school had a similar experience

**TABLE 5**
**Emotional Abuse: Comparison of Precollege With College Men**

| | | Admitted Abuse Precollege | |
|---|---|---|---|
| | | yes | no |
| Admitted Abuse After High School | yes | 273<br>96.1% | 294<br>77.2% |
| | no | 11<br>3.9% | 87<br>22.8% |
| | Total | 284<br>100% | 381<br>100% |

NOTE: $x^2 = 46.56$; $df = 1$; $p = .0000$; phi = .265; gamma = .760.

**TABLE 6**
**Sexual Assault by Force: Comparison of Precollege With College Women**

| | | High School or Elementary Victimization | |
|---|---|---|---|
| | | yes | no |
| Victimized After High School | yes | 50<br>31.6% | 82<br>13.2% |
| | no | 108<br>68.4% | 537<br>86.8% |
| | Total | 158<br>100% | 619<br>100% |

NOTE: $x^2 = 30.21$; $df = 1$; $p = .0000$; phi = .197; gamma = .504.

earlier. Due to space constraints, we have not reproduced the similar tables here for physical and emotional abuse. But of those women who were physically harmed in college, 25.4 per cent report similar episodes in high school. The pattern on emotional abuse matches that for male admitted offenders. Slightly less than two thirds of all college and university women (64.5 per cent) report being emotionally abused in some way since high school. However, virtually all

(95.7 per cent) of the women who report abuse in high school or elementary school report that it happened again after high school.

## Summary of Precollege Information

The above statistics add to the small amount of data on woman abuse in North American high school dating relationships and mark the start of the development of a numerical database on the physical, sexual, and psychological victimization of females in elementary school courtship. The data presented here also constitute an exploratory attempt to determine whether abuse in these two educational contexts persists into university and college dating relationships.

We know that high school boys, even more than college men, believe in rape myths and assign blame to sexual assault victims (Blumberg and Lester). It is generally accepted that these myths permeate virtually all levels of society (Schwartz and DeKeseredy 1997). Of interest, Metz argues that white, upper-middle-class girls are particularly at risk of sexual assault on dates. In other words, looking to isolate the causes of the abuse of women in one segment of society is not useful. Further, these data suggest that many men come to college with the full armory of ideology and behaviours necessary to engage in sexual, physical, and emotional harm of women.

As we have suggested, this idea is important because there is a literature centering on fraternities that leaves the impression that men learn to abuse women after arriving at college (e.g., Martin and Hummer; Sanday). Although such learning patterns may be true in many cases, it may also be true that many other men arrive at college fully prepared to abuse women with no additional learning required.

It appears that men are much less likely to report having been abusive and women are much less likely to report having been abused in Canadian elementary and high school dating relationships. We would suggest that there are several reasons for this difference.

First, younger students spend more time at home with their parents and thus their contacts with dating partners are less frequent. In other words, their routine activities place them at lower risk of offending or being victimized. In comparison, many college and university students live away from their parents in residences, houses and apartments, which criminologists have sometimes termed "hot spots" of female victimization (Ellis and DeKeseredy).

Perhaps the relatively low rates of assault in elementary and high school courtship uncovered by the CNS are functions of the methodological pitfalls.[5] Again, some of the major factors that contribute to under-reporting are

- embarrassment
- fear of reprisal
- deception
- the belief that some events are too trivial or inconsequential to mention

- "reverse telescoping," and
- the reluctance to recall traumatic events (Kennedy and Dutton; Smith, 1987, 1994; Straus *et al.*).

Another factor that may contribute to low disclosure rates is the absence of multiple measures, such as those used to generate data on abuse in university and college dating.[6] Unfortunately, because the main objective of the CNS was to elicit rich data on college and university students' experiences, time and financial constraints meant that we could not include additional open- and closed-ended questions on abuse in elementary and high school courtship. Perhaps future surveys will attempt to do so.

Under-reporting also could have been minimized by administering the questionnaire to high school and elementary school students. This strategy might have decreased the chance of memory error. As Bradburn correctly points out, the longer the time period examined, the greater the chance that people will forget various life events. This argument is well taken. However, it is extremely difficult, if not impossible, to administer well-worded questionnaires on sexual abuse to these students because few, if any, Canadian school boards are amenable to such research (Lenskyj; Marlies Sudermann, personal communication). In the United States, human subjects research boards typically require that academic researchers obtain written permission from the parents of each students under 18 years old before the questionnaire can be administered. Obviously, it would be impossible to obtain an adequate sample for questionnaires. As a result of such restrictions, other researchers have decided not to ask direct questions on sexual behaviour, which are the ones that could most easily be compared with the data now being gathered on college campuses. For example, rather than ask high school students in London, Ontario, to report abusive acts committed by or committed against them, Sudermann and Jaffe asked them if they had "experienced" abuse in teen dating relationships.

To obtain a better understanding of woman abuse in elementary as well as high school courtship, and to prevent and control injurious behaviours, more than just accurate prevalence data are inquired. Future representative sample surveys need to discover the major factors associated with male-to-female assaults in elementary and high school dating, such as attachment to dominant ideologies, male peer support, level of intimacy, educational status, or many others. This type of analysis can provide information on who is at risk of being abused or of being abusive. Such correlational research also assists the development of theories and practical, progressive policies that might keep men from becoming abusive in university/college dating relationships (DeKeseredy and Kelly 1993a).

### *Jealousy*

Although Canadian researchers Gagné and Lavoie did not measure the incidence and prevalence of violence in adolescent dating relationships, their nonprobability survey of young people's views on the causes of this problem warrants some brief attention here. In April 1992, they administered a questionnaire to 151 grade-11 students in a private secondary school in Quebec City, Quebec and found that the majority of their male and female respondents consider jealousy to be the most important cause of psychologically and physically abusive behaviour among couples of their age. Moreover, one quarter of the female respondents believed that violent boys are motivated by a desire to intimidate their partners. Similarly, in the United States, two small-scale high school surveys found that most of the respondents view jealousy as the most common cause of dating violence (Roscoe and Callahan; Roscoe and Kelsey).

Many adolescents view jealousy as a sign of love (Lavoie, Vezina, Piche, and Boivin). However, the story described in Box 1 as well as a growing body of research show that jealousy is often an expression of domination, control, and psychological abuse (Gagné and Lavoie). For example, according to Gamache,

> An abusive boyfriend seeks greater and greater control over his victim in the name of love. He loves her so much that he can't stand for her to spend time with others, especially other guys. He's jealous of her friends and her family; he wants to have her all to himself. Teens often feel flattered by these demands and view them as proof of passion, a view reinforced in our society. Jealousy is often accepted as an excuse for abusive behaviour in relationship. In cases involving so-called crimes of passion, sympathy and sometimes leniency are accorded to the perpetrators, particularly when victims, usually females, have engaged in behaviour likely to arouse sexual jealousy. (77)

## The Incidence and Prevalence of Woman Abuse in Canadian University and College Dating

Unlike fine wine, some things don't improve with age, and the incidence and prevalence data reported in the next few sections of this article support this assertion. *Incidence* refers here to the percentage of women who stated that they were abused and the percentage of men who indicated that they were abusive in the past 12 months. *Prevalence* is, since they left high school, the percentage of men who reported having been abusive and the percentage of women who indicated having been abused.

## Results

Prior to the CNS, many Canadian people thought that the phenomenon of high rates of woman abuse in dating was unique to the United States, that the U.S. violent crime rate (much higher than Canada's) in some way influenced the rate of sexual assault and other variants of woman abuse in courtship on campus (Schwartz and DeKeseredy 1997). This perception is due in part to Canada's

**Box 1**
**The Brutal Nature of Jealousy and Possessiveness**

I was sure that he loved me. He often showed it through displays of extreme jealousy and possessiveness. I couldn't talk to another boy. In fact, David wanted me all to himself, to the point that he resented my girlfriends and family. All we needed was each other, he said. He did a lot of subtle things to discourage me from spending time with anyone else. And if he chose to go out with his friends or not bother to call me, I was still to sit home alone and wait by the phone for his call. If I wasn't there, I was interrogated about where I was, who I talked to, even what I wore. The hassle wasn't worth it. I became more and more isolated, more dependent on David as my sole source of support. Actually, I was a little frightened of David's temper if I didn't do what he wanted me to do. The confusing part was that his expectations frequently changed.... It seemed that I could do nothing to please him. The more I failed to please him, the more I felt like a failure myself.

I felt it was up to me to make this relationship work. You see, we had become sexually involved by this time. To me, that meant commitment. I had to protect my image of myself as a "nice girl." Our sexual intimacy seemed to create a strong bond of ownership. I was now "his" to control and to use as he wished. My boundaries began to disintegrate as I reliniquished my self-identity to become a part of David.

We began to fight a lot. That is, David fought. He was often very angry for little or no reason at all. I'd try to calm him down. He'd smash his fist into a wall or destroy something. That also frightened me. Sometimes he'd swear at me or call me names. That hurt a lot. I'd cry. Then he'd cry and hold me close, begging me to forgive him. He promised not to act that way again. I was the only one who could help him change, he always said. He needed me so much, and he was so afraid of losing me. That was why he acted the way he did. So I forgave him ... and tried to forget.

We played the "if only ... " game. *If only* we could get married and be together all the time, we'd be happy and wouldn't fight. *If only* his dad wasn't so abusive, David wouldn't be so angry. *If only* I was more loving and caring, he wouldn't feel so bad. The game went on and on. The cycle of abuse had begun, although we were both too entrenched in denial to see the reality of it all. I needed to deny what was happening to protect my shaky self-esteem. He needed to deny his actions to avoid taking responsibility for changing his behaviour.

Source: Jenson 45-49

proximity to the United States. For example, approximately 90 per cent of the Canadian population lives within 200 miles of the U.S. border, so that the U.S. media are influential in shaping concern about crimes in the street and private domains (MacLean; Surette). Although the precise number is unknown, it is fair to state that a substantial portion of the Canadian population watch popular television shows such as *Oprah, America's Most Wanted,* and *Top Cops* that feature stories abut woman abuse and other highly injurious behaviours (DeKeseredy and MacLean 1993). As Taylor correctly points out:

> Day in and day out, these programs portray an image of urban life in North America as a dangerous human jungle, where the prospect of criminal assault and homicide is almost random and immediate. Human life is seen to be threatened in particular, by the presence (especially "on the street" but also in everyday business and personal relationships) of psychopathic individuals intent on murder and general mayhem. (92)

The CTS and SES data generated by the CNS and analyzed by DeKeseredy and Kelly (1993a) show that woman abuse in post-secondary school courtship in not restricted to the United States. Further, the findings support the United Nations's view of Canada as a country where many heterosexual women experience a substantial amount of physical and psychological pain in a variety of intimate and domestic relationships.

### *The Incidence and Prevalence of Sexual Abuse*

The responses to each of the items in the SES are presented in Tables 7 and 8. DeKeseredy and Kelly (1993a) found the following:

- Of the female participants, 28 per cent stated that they were sexually abused in the past year, while 11 per cent of the males reported having sexually victimized a female dating partner during the same time period.
- As was expected, the prevalence estimates are significantly higher, with 45.1 per cent of the women stating that they had been abused since leaving high school and 19.5 per cent of the men reporting at least one incident at the same time period.
- Except for the male prevalence figure, these data approximate DeKeseredy, Kelly, and Baklid pre-test estimates.
- Despite some methodological differences, the data presented in Tables 7 and 8 are consistent with Koss *et al.*'s U.S. national data.

These findings yield several conclusions. Perhaps the most important one is that a substantial number of Canadian women are sexually abused by their university/college male dating partners. There are, however, large gender differences in reporting the incidence of sexual abuse, and the reporting gap widens for the prevalence data. What accounts for these discrepancies? In Box 2, we provide

**Box 2**
**What Accounts for Gender Discrepancies in Reporting Sexual Assault in Postsecondary School Dating?**

One argument popular in conservative men's quarters is that the data here are wrong: "Women do lie about sexual assault, and do so for personal advantage or some other personal reason, which is pretty well why anybody lies" (Fekete 54). The problem is that such critics almost never have any evidence to offer on this score, other than a deep-seated mistrust of women generally. The debate is similar to earlier ones on marital rape, where large numbers of men without any evidence argued that the law should not allow a husband to be prosecuted for raping his wife, because women are natural liars (Schwartz 1982). It is similar to debates over rape law itself, which until fairly recently made it almost impossible to obtain a rape conviction in most jurisdictions because the state had to overcome a presumption written into law that women lie (Schwartz and Clear; Tong). In each of these cases, rape law was changed virtually everywhere in North America to remove the presumption that all women are liars. On the college campus, however, and in the backlash literature, this presumption continues to exist.

In fact, there is no reason to believe that survey data generated by measures such as the SES exaggerate the extent of sexual assault on college campuses. Rather, it is much more likely that such surveys underestimate the problem. Many survey participants do not report incidents because of embarrassment, fear of reprisal, reluctance to recall traumatic memories, deception, memory error, and many other factors (Kennedy and Dutton, 1989; Smith, 1994). A great number of women report on such surveys that they have lived for years without telling a single person about their victimization and are revealing the fact for the first time on an anonymous questionnaire. It would be naive not to believe that there are additional women (how many is, of course, unknown) who continue to keep their secret, even when given this questionnaire opportunity.

Thus, it is unlikely that men and women report differently because large numbers of women are lying. Some researchers have argued that a more likely explanation is that social desirability plays a key role in shaping male responses (Arias and Beach; DeKeseredy and Kelly, 1993a; Dutton and Hemphill). It is already difficult to obtain honest and complete responses from male perpetrators (Smith 1987). One worry is that to the extent that we become successful in getting the message out that sexual assault in college settings is illegitimate and illegal, it will become less likely that men will admit to doing it, even when researchers guarantee anonymity and confidentiality.

## TABLE 7: Sexual Abuse Incidence Rates

| | Men (N =1,307) | | Women (N = 1,835) | |
|---|---|---|---|---|
| *Types of Abuse* | % | N | % | N |
| Have you given in to sex play (fondling, kissing, or petting, but not intercourse) when you didn't want to because you were overwhelmed by a man's continual arguments and pressure? | 7.8 | 95 | 18.2 | 318 |
| Have you engaged in sex play (fondling, kissing, or petting, but not intercourse) when you didn't want to because a man used his position of authority (boss, supervisor, etc.) to make you? | .9 | 10 | 1.3 | 21 |
| Have you had sex play (fondling, kissing, or petting, but not intercourse) when you didn't want to because a man threatened or used some degree of physical force (twisting your arm, holding you down, etc.) to make you? | 1.1 | 13 | 3.3 | 54 |
| Has a man attempted sexual intercourse (getting on top of you, attempting to insert his penis) when you didn't want to by threatening or using some degree of physical force (twisting your arm, holding you down, etc.), but intercourse did not occur? | .6 | 7 | 3.9 | 67 |
| Has a man attempted sexual intercourse (getting on top of you, attempting to insert his penis) when you didn't want to because you were drunk or high, but intercourse did not occur? | 2.5 | 29 | 6.6 | 121 |
| Have you given in to sexual intercourse when you didn't want to because you were overwhelmed by a man's continual arguments and pressure? | 4.8 | 55 | 11.9 | 198 |
| Have you had sexual intercourse when you didn't want to because a man used his position of authority (boss, supervisor, etc.) to make you? | .8 | 9 | .5 | 8 |
| Have you had sexual intercourse when you didn't want to because you were drunk or high? | 2.2 | 25 | 7.6 | 129 |
| Have you had sexual intercourse when you didn't want to because a man threatened or used some degree of physical force (twisting your arm, holding you down, etc.) to make you? | .7 | 8 | 2.0 | 34 |
| Have you engaged in sex acts (anal or oral intercourse or penetration by objects other than the penis) when you didn't want to because a man threatened or used some degree of physical force (twisting your arm, holding you down, etc.) to make you? | .3 | 3 | 1.8 | 29 |

**TABLE 8: Sexual Abuse Prevalence Rates**

| | *Men (N =1,307)* | | *Women (N = 1,835)* | |
|---|---|---|---|---|
| *Types of Abuse* | % | N | % | N |
| Have you given in to sex play (fondling, kissing, or petting, but not intercourse) when you didn't want to because you were overwhelmed by a man's continual arguments and pressure? | 14.9 | 172 | 31.8 | 553 |
| Have you engaged in sex play (fondling, kissing, or petting, but not intercourse) when you didn't want to because a man used his position of authority (boss, supervisor, etc.) to make you? | 1.8 | 24 | 4.0 | 66 |
| Have you had sex play (fondling, kissing, or petting, but not intercourse) when you didn't want to because a man threatened or used some degree of physical force (twisting your arm, holding you down, etc.) to make you? | 2.2 | 25 | 9.4 | 154 |
| Has a man attempted sexual intercourse (getting on top of you, attempting to insert his penis) when you didn't want to by threatening or using some degree of physical force (twisting your arm, holding you down, etc.), but intercourse did not occur? | 1.6 | 19 | 8.5 | 151 |
| Has a man attempted sexual intercourse (getting on top of you, attempting to insert his penis) when you didn't want to because you were drunk or high, but intercourse did not occur? | 5.5 | 6.3 | 13.6 | 244 |
| Have you given in to sexual intercourse when you didn't want to because you were overwhelmed by a man's continual arguments and pressure? | 8.3 | 96 | 20.2 | 349 |
| Have you had sexual intercourse when you didn't want to because a man used his position of authority (boss, supervisor, etc.) to make you? | 1.4 | 17 | 1.5 | 24 |
| Have you had sexual intercourse when you didn't want to because you were drunk or high? | 4.7 | 55 | 14.6 | 257 |
| Have you had sexual intercourse when you didn't want to because a man threatened or used some degree of physical force (twisting your arm, holding you down, etc.) to make you? | 1.5 | 18 | 6.6 | 112 |
| Have you engaged in sex acts (anal or oral intercourse or penetration by objects other than the penis) when you didn't want to because a man threatened or used some degree of physical force (twisting your arm, holding you down, etc.) to make you? | 1.4 | 16 | 3.2 | 51 |

some answers to this question.

### *The Incidence and Prevalence of Physcial Abuse*

The CNS physical abuse data summarized below and in Tables 9 and 10 are alarming examples of "when 'I love you' turns violent" (Johnson, S.). For example, DeKeseredy and Kelly (1993a) found that the male physical abuse incidence rate (13.7 per cent) approximates those generated by previous Canadian and U.S. incidence studies that employed similar measures (DeKeseredy; DeKeseredy *et al.;* Makepeace ). Even so, this estimate is considerably lower than the CTS incidence rate (37 per cent) uncovered by White and Koss's national survey of college students. The CNS female estimate (22.3 per cent) is also markedly lower than that of White and Koss (32 per cent). These differences may be the result of using different psychological abuse measures.

Table 9 shows that every type of violence was reported by at least one respondent; however, what many people regard as "less lethal" forms of physical abuse apparently occurred more often. This is consistent with most of the earlier North American research (see Sugarman and Hotaling).

As expected, the prevalence data presented in Table 10 also show that "less severe" types of violence occur more often. For example, almost 3.5 per cent of the women reported having been physically abused and 17.8 of the men stated that they were violent since leaving high school. These prevalence estimates are similar to the pre-test results (DeKeseredy *et al.*). Even so, the male figure is much lower than Barnes, Greenwood and Sommer's rate (42 per cent). This inconsistency probably reflects differences between the versions of the CTS employed by the other two Canadian studies. For example, Barnes *et al.*'s version included a sexual assault item, and several other items were distinct from those used in the CNS version. National representative sample survey data on the *prevalence* of physical abuse were not gathered by White and Koss. Therefore, at this point in time, it is extremely difficult to make Canadian-U.S. comparisons using similar samples.

Again, we find gender variations in reporting. In our opinion, the reasons for these discrepancies are found in Box 2.

### *The Incidence and Prevalence of Psychological Abuse*

Men and women provided similar incidence rates. For example, 74.1 per cent of the men stated that they were psychologically abusive, and 79.1 per cent of the women stated that they were abused this way in the past year. The mail incidence figure is higher than other Canadian estimates produced by DeKeseredy (1988) and DeKeseredy *et al.* The women's estimate is also higher than DeKeseredy *et al.*'s. However, White and Koss obtained higher male (81 per cent) and female (88 per cent) figures. Furthermore, the CNS male prevalence statistic is 12 per cent lower than that reported by Barnes *et al.*'s Canadian male respondents (92.6 per cent). These differences possibly reflect the use of different measures.

The reponses to the pyschological abuse items presented in Tables 9 and 10 show that there is considerable congruency in male and female reporting. This is particularly true of "insults to swearing"; "throwing, smashing, or kicking something"; and "doing something to spite a partner." However, there were inconsistent responses to the following items: "threatening to throw something at her"; "putting her down in front of friends and family"; and "accusing her of having affairs or flirting with other men."

## Summary of the College and University Data

The incidence and prevalence data described here show that for many Canadian women, college and university dating relationships are indeed "dangerous domains"(Johnson, H.). Furthermore, based on the assumption that most of the students who participated in the CNS come from the more affluent sectors of Canadian society, these data challenge the popular notion that those who engage in woman abuse are economically disadvantaged—an inaccurate perception unfortunately supported by flawed police statistics (Hinch). Although these figures are high, as is the case with *all* survey statistics on woman abuse, they should be read as underestimates. The problem of under-reporting affects *all* woman abuse surveys; however, the CNS, like other Canadian surveys (e.g., Johnson, H.; Smith 1987), included methods specifically designed to overcome or minimize this shortcoming.

The CNS data described here yield two more important conclusions. First, a comparison of the incidence and prevalence figures with those reviewed by Sugarman and Hotaling show that the problem of college dating abuse is just as serious in Canada as it is in the United States. Second, like their U.S. counterparts, while Canadian female undergraduates have a "well-founded fear" of being attacked by strangers in public places (Hanmer and Saunders; Kelly and DeKeseredy), they have more to fear from their male dating partners. In fact, as Gibbs correctly points out, "What people think of as 'real rape'—the assault by a monstrous stranger lurking in the shadows—accounts for only 1 out of 5 attacks" (206). Unfortunately, many people's ideas of what constitutes woman abuse are based on the myths and stereotypes transmitted by the media (e.g., pornography, feature films, and rock videos) and sexist male social networks (DeKeseredy and Schwartz 1993; Koss and Cook; Schwartz and DeKeseredy 1997).

## Conclusion

In this article, we presented data on the unknown or "dark side" of courtship. Unfortunately, the estimates of women's pain and suffering desribed here probably constitute only tip of the iceberg. Even so, these statistics suggest that male pyschological, physical, and sexual assault on female dating partners "happen with alarming regularity" (Lloyd).

Some of the research reported here also adds to the small amount of data

**TABLE 9: Psychological and Physical Abuse Incidence Rates**

| | *Men (N =1,307)* | | *Women (N = 1,835)* | |
|---|---|---|---|---|
| *Types of Abuse* | % | N | % | N |
| Psychological: | | | | |
| •insults or swearing | 52.7 | 623 | 52.5 | 857 |
| •put her (you) down in front of friends or family | 18.9 | 233 | 30.7 | 491 |
| •accused her (you) of having affairs or flirting with other men | 29.3 | 350 | 37.2 | 614 |
| •did or said something to spite her (you) | 57.7 | 350 | 37.2 | 614 |
| •threatened to hit or throw something at her (you) | 6.1 | 71 | 10.6 | 174 |
| •threw, smashed, or kicked something | 25.4 | 304 | 25.5 | 433 |
| Physical: | | | | |
| •threw something at her (you) | 3.5 | 40 | 5.1 | 85 |
| •pushed, grabbed, or shoved her (you) | 11.7 | 132 | 19.6 | 319 |
| •slapped her (you) | 2.9 | 30 | 5.5 | 85 |
| •kicked, bit, or hit her (you) with your (his) fist | 1.7 | 16 | 3.9 | 61 |
| •hit or tried to hit her (you) with something | 1.9 | 20 | 3.3 | 54 |
| •beat her (you) up | .9 | 7 | 1.4 | 21 |
| •choked her (you) | 1.0 | 10 | 2.1 | 32 |
| •threatened her (you) with a knife or gun | .9 | 9 | .5 | 9 |
| •used a knife or gun on her (you) | 1.0 | 8 | .1 | 2 |

accumulated on woman abuse in North America high school dating relationships and marks the start of the development of a numerical database on the physical, sexual, and pyschological victimization of females in elementary school dating. Furthermore, the CNS constitutes an exploratory attempt to determine whether abuse in these two educational contexts persists into university/college dating relationships.

Some conservative critics, however, contend that the CNS is an example of a "serious case of distorted science in Canada" (Christensen). Similarly, others, such as Fekete, one of Canada's premier "media darlings of the anti-feminist backlash" (Renzetti), contend that by labelling some of the acts listed in the CNS and SES, the CNS research team has "disrespected and discounted" respondents' interpretations of these events. Fekete asserts that the CNS would have generated considerably lower estimates if respondents were asked to describe their interpretations of their own experiences. In his opinion, the CNS research team has learned that if women are explicitly asked if they have been abused, the incidence and prevalence estimates described in this article would be much lower than those generated by the CTS and SES.

We and others who were involved in the development and administration of the CNS do not derive any pleasure from eliciting alarmingly high rates of abuse, and the CNS research team did not manipulate the questionnaires to guarantee the

**TABLE 10: Psychological and Physical Abuse Prevalence Rates**

| Types of Abuse | *Men (N =1,307)* % | *Men (N =1,307)* N | *Women (N = 1,835)* % | *Women (N = 1,835)* N |
|---|---|---|---|---|
| Psychological: | | | | |
| •insults or swearing | 62.4 | 747 | 65.1 | 1105 |
| •put her (you) down in front of friends or family | 25.9 | 322 | 44.2 | 742 |
| •accused her (you) of having affairs or flirting with other men | 40.9 | 495 | 52.6 | 901 |
| •did or said something to spite her (you) | 65.2 | 773 | 72.2 | 1216 |
| •threatened to hit or throw something at her (you) | 8.0 | 97 | 20.6 | 346 |
| •threw, smashed, or kicked something | 30.6 | 373 | 37.3 | 652 |
| Physical: | | | | |
| •threw something at her (you) | 4.3 | 50 | 10.6 | 185 |
| •pushed, grabbed, or shoved her (you) | 15.8 | 182 | 31.3 | 529 |
| •slapped her (you) | 4.9 | 53 | 11.1 | 186 |
| •kicked, bit, or hit her (you) with your (his) fist | 2.8 | 28 | 8.0 | 135 |
| •hit or tried to hit her (you) with something | 2.9 | 33 | 8.0 | 136 |
| •beat her (you) up | 1.0 | 8 | 3.9 | 63 |
| •choked her (you) | 1.0 | 9 | 4.6 | 80 |
| •threatened her (you) with a knife or gun | .9 | 9 | 2.4 | 41 |
| •used a knife or gun on her (you) | 1.0 | 9 | .5 | 8 |

generation of "big numbers." Rather, like other survey researchers, the CNS team was well aware of the fact that most female and male members of the general public do not identify intimate forms of victimization as "rape," "abuse," or "violence." Unlike most crimes in which right and wrong are reasonably clear to most people (e.g., armed robbery), date rape and other examples of intimate abuse are problems that often "muddy the normative waters" (Fenstermaker).

What Fekete and other conservative critics of the CNS fail to recognize is that the bulk of the abusive events listed in the CNS instruments are violations of the Canadian *Criminal Code*. Simply because many women who experience these behaviours do not realize that their dating partners have committed a crime does not mean that they view the outcome of their partners' behaviours positively or even neutrally (Koss and Cook). In fact, 50 per cent of the rape victims in Koss *et al.*'s national sample of college students defined their experiences as rape or some crime similar to rape, and only ten per cent stated that they did not feel harmed by this experience (Koss and Cook). In addition, several studies show that many women who did not initially view their experiences as rape contacted researchers later on to disclose events they now define as rape after the legal criteria were explained to them (Koss and Cook; Russell; Wyatt).

Feketer, Christensen, and other conservative "people without data" have also tried to discredit CNS findings by saying "but women do it too" (DeKeseredy and

MacLean 1977; Stanko). Of course, there has never been any question that women strike their male dating partners, sometime with the intent to injure. That there are battered male dating partners should not be a subject for disagreement (Schwartz and DeKeseredy 1993). The points of contention between conservative critics of the CNS and us are whether female dating partners *primarily* use violence as a means of self-defence and whether the presence of some male victims mitigates or changes the meaning of the conclusion that women are overwhelmingly predominant victims of dating abuse. This debate played a central role in the developments of the CNS.

## Notes

[1]See Schwartz and DeKeseredy (1997) for a comprehensive review of our work on this topic.
[2]Bergman provides examples of injurious behaviours in each question.
[3]In all cases of the data analysis that follows, definitions of physical, sexual, and emotional abuse in university and college dating relationships follow those used by DeKeseredy and Kelly (1993a, 1993b).
[4]There are several comparisons that could be made here, because college sexual victimization was measured using the Sexual Experiences Survey (SES). Much of the victimization uncovered by the ses comes from questions about unwanted sex while the woman is drunk or high. Although we are clear that this constitutes sexual assault (see Schwartz and Pitts), in this case the decision was made to limit the table to cases in which the question clearly asks whether or not physical force was used.
[5]Refer to Chapter 1 of DeKeseredy and Schwartz (1998) for a discussion of methodological pitfalls of CNS.
[6]See Chapter 1 of DeKeseredy and Schwartz (1998).

## References

Arias, I., and S. Beach. "Validity of Self-Reports of Marital Violence." *Journal of Family Violence* 2 (1987): 139-149.

Barnes, G., L. Greenwood, and R. Sommer. "Courtship Violence in a Canadian Sample of Male College Students." *Family Relations* 40 (1991): 37-44.

Bergman, L. "Dating Violence Among High School Students." *Social Work* 37 (1992): 21-27.

Blumberg, M., and D. Lester. "High School and College Students' Attitudes Toward Rape." *Adolescence* 26 (1991): 721-729.

Bradburn, N. "Response Effects." *Handbook of Survey Research*. Eds. P. Rossi, J. Wright, and A. Anderson. New York: Academic Press, 1983. 289-238.

Christensen, F. "A Serious Case of Distorted Science in Canada." Unpublished manuscript. Department of Philosophy, University of Alberta, Edmonton,

Alberta, 1995.

Connell, R. *Maculinities.* Berkeley: University of California Press, 1995.

Davis, T., G. Peck, and J. Storment. "Acquaintance Rape and the High School Student." *Journal of Adolescent Health* 14 (1993): 220-224.

DeKeseredy, W. *Woman Abuse in Dating Relationships: The Role of Male Peer Support.* Toronto: Canadian Scholars Press, 1988.

DeKeseredy, W., and K. Kelly. "The Incidence and Prevalence of Woman Abuse in Canadian University and College Dating Relationships." *Canadian Journal of Sociology* 18 (1993a): 157-159.

DeKeseredy, W., and K. Kelly. "Woman Abuse in University and College Dating Relationships: The Contribution of the Ideology of Familial Patriarchy." *Journal of Human Justice* 4 (1993b): 25-52.

DeKeseredy, W., and B. MacLean. "Critical Criminological Pedagogy in Canada: Strengths, Limitations, and Recommendations for Improvement." *Journal of Criminal Justice Education* 4 (1993): 361-376.

DeKeseredy, W., and B. MacLean. "But Women Do It Too: The Contexts and Nature of Female-to-Male Violence in Canadian Heterosexual Dating Relationships." *Battered Women: Law, State and Contemporary Research in Canada.* Eds. K. Bonneycastle and G. Rigakos. Vancouver: Collective Press, 1997.

DeKeseredy, W., and M. Schwartz. "Male Peer Support and Woman Abuse: An Expansion of DeKeseredy's Model." *Sociological Spectrum* 13 (1993): 393-414.

DeKeseredy, W., and M. Schwartz. *Woman Abuse on Campus: Results from the Canadian National Survey.* Thousand Oaks, CA: Sage, 1998.

DeKeseredy, W., K. Kelly, and B. Baklid. "The Physical, Sexual, and Psychological Abuse of Women in Dating Relationships: Results from a Pretest for a National Study." Paper presented at the annual meeting of the American Society of Criminology, New Orleans. November, 1992.

Dutton, D., and K. Hemphill. "Patterns of Socially Desirable Responding Among Perpetrators and Victims of Wife Assault." *Violence and Victims* 7 (1992): 29-40.

Ellis, D., and W. DeKeseredy. *The Wrong Stuff: An Introduction to the Sociological Study of Deviance.* (2nd Ed.).Toronto: Allyn and Bacon, 1996.

Fekete, J. *Moral Panic: Biopolitics Rising.* Montreal: Robert Davies, 1994.

Fenstermaker, S. "Acquaintance Rape on Campus: Responsibilities and Attributions of Crime." *Violence in Dating Relationships: Emerging Issues.* Eds. M. Pirog-Good and J. Stets. New York: Praeger, 1989. 257-271.

Fine, G. *With the Boys: Little League Baseball and Preadolescent Culture.* Chicago: University of Chicago Press, 1987.

Gagné, M., and F. Lavoie. "Young People's Views on the Causes of Violence in Adolescents' Romantic Relationships." *Canada's Mental Health* 41 (1993): 11-15.

Gamache, D. "Domination and Control: The Social Context of Dating Violence." *Dating Violence: Young Women in Danger.* Ed. B. Levy. Seattle: Seal, 1991. 69-

83.

Gibbs, N. "The Incidence of Rape: An Overview." *Violence Against Women.* Eds. K. Swisher and C. Wekesser. San Diego, CA: Greenhaven, 1994. 206-211.

Girshick, L. "Teen Dating Violence." *Violence Update.* 1993: 1-6.

Hanmer, J., and S. Saunders. *Well-Founded Fear: A Community Study of Violence to Women.* London: Hutchinson, 1984.

Henton, J., and R. Case, J. Koval, S. Lloyd and S. Christopher. "Romance and Violence in Dating Relationships." *Journal of Family Issues* 4 (1983): 467-482.

Hinch, R. "Sexual Violence and Social Control." *Social Control in Canada: Issues in the Social Construction of Deviance.* Eds. L. Schissel and L. Mahood. Toronto: Oxford University Press, 1996.

Hobbs, D. "Mannish Boys: Danny, Chris, Crime, Masculinity and Business." *Just Boys Doing Business? Men, Masculinities and Crime.* Eds. T. Newburn and E. Stanko. New York: Routledge, 1994. 118-134.

Holmes, J., and E. Silverman. *We're Here, Listen to Us!* Ottawa: Canadian Advisory Council to the Status of Women, 1992.

Jaffe, P., M. Sudermann, D. Reitzel, and S. Killip. "An Evaluation of a Secondary School Primary Prevention Program on Violence in Intimate Relationships." *Violence and Victims* 7 (1992): 129-146.

Jenson, J. "If Only...." *Dating Violence: Young Women in Danger.* Ed. B. Levy. Seattle: Seal, 1991. 45-49.

Johnson, H. *Dangerous Domains: Violence Against Women in Canada.* Toronto: Nelson, 1996.

Johnson, S. *When "I Love You" Turns Violent: Emotional and Physical Abuse in Dating Relationships.* Far Hills, NJ: New Horizon, 1993.

Kelly, K. and W. DeKeseredy. "Women's Fear of Crime and Abuse in College and University Dating Relationships." *Violence and Victims* 9 (1994): 17-30.

Kennedy, L., and D. Dutton. "The Incidence of Wife Assault in Alberta." *Canadian Journal of Behavioural Science* 2 (1989): 40-54.

Koss, M., and S. Cook. "Facing the Facts: Date and Acquaintance Rape are Significant Factors for Women." *Current Controversies on Family Violence.* Eds. R. Gelles and D. Loseke. Newbury Park, CA: Sage, 1993. 104-119.

Koss, M., C. Gidycz, and N. Wisniewski. "The Scope of Rape: Incidence and Prevalence in a National Sample of Higher Education Students." *Journal of Consulting and Clinical Psychology* 55 (1987): 162-170.

Lavoie, F., L. Vezina, C. Piche, and M. Boivin. "Devélopment et évaluation formative d'un programme de promotion voulant contrer le problème de la violence dans les relations intimes des jeunes." Research Report. Quebec City: Conseil Québecoise de la Recherche Social, 1993.

Lenskyj, H. "Beyond Plumbing and Prevention: Feminist Approaches to Sex Education." *Gender and Education* 2 (1990): 217-230.

Lloyd. S. "The Dark Side of Courtship: Violence and Sexual Exploitation." *Family Relations* 40 (1991): 14-20.

Maclean, B. "The Emergence of Critical Justice Studies in Canada." *Humanity and Society* 16 (1992): 414-426.

Makepeace, J. "Life Events Stress and Courtship Violence." *Family Relations* 32 (1983): 383-388.

Martin, P. and R. Hummer. "Fraternities and Rape on Campus." *Violence Against Women: The Bloody Footprints.* Newbury Park, CA: Sage, 1993. 114-131.

Mercer, S. "Not a Pretty Picture: An Exploratory Study of Violence Against Women in High School Dating Relationships." *Resources for Feminist Research* 17 (1988): 15-23.

Metz, E. "The Camouflaged At-Risk Student: White and Wealthy." *Momentum* 24 (1993): 40-44.

Nelson, M. *The Stronger Women Get, the More Men Love Football: Sexism and the American Culture of Sports.* New York: Harcourt Brace, 1994.

Rae, C. "That Macho Thing: Social Supports of Violence Against Women." Unpublished doctoral dissertation, Ohio University, 1995.

Renzetti, C. "Forward." *Sexual Assault on the College Campus: The Role of Male Peer Support.* Eds. M. Schwartz and W. DeKeseredy. Thousand Oaks, CA: Sage, 1997. vii-xiii.

Roscoe, B., and J. Callahan. "Adolescents' Self-Reports of Violence in Families and Dating Relationships." *Adolescence* 20 (1985): 545-553.

Roscoe, B., and T. Kelsey. "Dating Violence Among High School Students." *Psychology* 23 (1986): 53-59.

Russell, D. *Rape in Marriage.* (2nd Ed.). Bloomington: Indiana University Press, 1990.

Sanday, P. *Fraternity Gang Rape.* New York: New York University Press, 1990.

Schwartz, M. "The Spousal Exemption for Criminal Rape Prosecution." *Vermont Law Review* 7 (1982): 33-57.

Schwartz, M. "Censorship of Sexual Violence: Is the Problem Sex or Violence?" *Humanity and Society* 11 (1987): 212-243.

Schwartz, M., and T. Clear. "Toward a New Law on Rape." *Crime and Delinquency* 26 (1980): 129-151.

Schwartz, M., and W. DeKeseredy. "The Return of the 'Battered Husband Syndrome' Through the Typification of Women as Violent." *Crime, Law and Social Change* 20 (1993): 249-265.

Schwartz, M., and W. DeKeseredy. Eds. *Sexual Assault on the College Campus: The Role of Male Peer Support.* Thousand Oaks, CA: Sage, 1997.

Schwartz, M., and V. Pitts. "Exploring a Feminist Routine Activities Approach to Explaining Sexual Assault." *Justice Quarterly* 12 (1995): 9-31.

Smith, M. "The Incidence and Prevalence of Woman Abuse in Toronto." *Violence and Victims* 2 (1987): 173-187.

Smith, M. "Patriarchal Ideology and Wife Beating: A Test of a Feminist Hypothesis." *Violence and Victims* 5 (1990): 257-273.

Smith, M. "Enhancing the Quality of Survey Data on Violence Against Women: A Feminist Approach." *Gender and Society* 18 (1994): 109-127.

Stanko, E. "The Struggle Over Commonsense Feminism, Violence and Confronting the Backlash." *Proceedings of the Fifth Symposium on Violence and Aggression.* Eds. B. Gillies and G. James. Saskatoon, Saskatchewan: University Extension Press, University of Saskatchewan, 1995.

Stone, S. "They Said I Was 'Young and Immature.'" *Dating Violence: Young Women in Danger*. Ed. B. Levy. Seattle: Seal, 1991. 28-32.

Strauss, M. "Measuring Intrafamily Conflict and Violence: The Conflict Tactics (CTS) Scales." *Journal of Marriage and Family* 41 (1979): 75-88.

Strauss, M., and R. Gelles. "Societal Change and Change in Family Violence from 1975 to 1985 as Revealed by Two National Surveys." *Journal of Marriage and Family* 48 (1986): 465-479.

Strauss, M., R. Gelles, and S. Steinmetz. *Behind Closed Doors: Violence in the American Family*. New York: Anchor, 1981.

Sudermann, M., and P. Jaffe. "Violence in Teen Dating Relationships: Evaluation of a Large Scale Primary Prevention Program." Paper presented at the annual meeting of the American Psychological Association, Toronto, August, 1993.

Sugarman, D. and C. Hotaling. "Dating Violence: Prevalence, Context, and Risk Markers. *Violence in Dating Relationships: Emerging Issues*. Eds. M. Pirog-Good and J. Stets. New York: Praeger, 1989. 3-32.

Surrette, R. *Media, Crime and Criminal Justice: Images and Realities*. Pacific Grove, CA: Brooks/Cole, 1992.

Taylor, I. *Crime, Capitalism and Community: Three Essays in Socialist Criminology*. Toronto: Butterworth, 1983.

Tong, R. *Women, Sex, and the Law*. Totawa, NJ: Rowan and Allanheld, 1984.

United Nations. *Human Development Report of 1995*. Toronto: Oxford University Press, 1995.

White, J., and M. Koss. "Courtship Violence: Incidence in a National Sample of Higher Education Students." *Violence and Victims* 6 (1991): 247-256.

Wyatt, G. "The Sociological Context of African American and White American Women's Rape." *Journal of Social Issues* 48 (1992): 77-91.

# Woman Killing

## Intimate Femicide in Ontario 1974-1994

Rosemary Gartner, Myrna Dawson, and Maria Crawford

In March 1988, a young mother of two was killed by her estranged husband in a northern Ontario town. The killer had been visiting his wife who was staying in a shelter for abused women. Convinced that she was not going to return to him, he shot her twice at close range. Later that year, in a small town outside of Edmonton, a woman was shot dead in her home by her estranged husband who then shot and killed himself. Miraculously, the woman's three-year-old girl, who she was holding in her arms when she was shot, was not wounded. These women were two of the 202 female victims of homicide in Canada in 1988. They shared with 68 other female victims a marital relationship with their killers. These two women also shared the experience of having been clients and friends of women who worked in shelters for abused women in Ontario.

In response to these and other killings of women they had worked with, eight women met in January 1989 to share their experiences and provide each other emotional support. Within a few months the group had named itself the Women We Honour Action Committee, setting itself the task of learning more about the phenomenon of women killed by their intimate partners. With the support of a grant from the Ontario Women's Directorate, they conducted a literature review on women killed by their intimate partners, or intimate femicide.

The literature review (Women We Honour Action Committee and Gartner) lead to a number of conclusions about the then-existing state of knowledge about intimate femicide. First, obtaining an accurate estimate of the number of such killings in Canada or in Ontario from statistics in official publications was not possible because official publications restricted their classifications to "spouse" killings, which excluded killings by estranged common-law partners and current or former boyfriends. Second, information on the nature of intimate femicide—its dynamics as well as its structural and cultural sources—was incomplete. In part this reflected researchers' reliance on small, highly-select samples, on offenders' recollections of their crimes, and on traditional psychological and psychiatric concepts and classifications. Third, much of the research had been conducted in the United States which is atypical in both the quantity and quality of its homicides. That is, spousal homicides make up a much smaller proportion of total homicides in the US compared to many other nations. Moreover, the ratio of female to male victims of spouse killings is more balanced in the U.S. than in other countries (about 1.3:1 compared to about 3:1 in Canada, Australia, Denmark, the UK and other countries).[1]

It was to address these limitations that the Women We Honour Action Committee approached the Ontario Women's Directorate for funding to conduct their study of intimate femicide in Ontario. The study had three goals: to document for Ontario the incidence of killings of women by intimate partners, including legal spouses, common-law partners, and boyfriends, both current and estranged; to describe the characteristics of the people involved and the circumstances surrounding these killings; and to present the stories of a small number of women who had been killed by their intimate partners. That study, completed in 1992, compiled and analyzed data on all intimate femicides known to authorities in Ontario from 1974 to 1990 (Crawford, Gartner and Women We Honour Action Committee). A second study, designed to update the data through 1994, was completed in April 1997 (Crawford, Gartner and Dawson).

In this article, we describe the major findings of these two studies of intimate femicide. Our purpose is two-fold: first, to provide an overview and statistical picture of intimate femicide in Ontario for the 21 years from 1974 to 1994 and, second, to locate this statistical picture in what is now a substantially larger and more sophisticated literature on violence against women by intimate partners. That literature encompasses studies similar in many ways to ours—that is, studies of the incidence and characteristics of relatively large numbers of femicides—as well as work designed to provide a theoretical and conceptual framework for understanding intimate femicide. We draw on that literature below in discussing our findings.

## Framing the Issue of Intimate Femicide

After completing our literature review in 1989, we concluded that intimate femicide is a phenomenon distinct in important ways both from the killing of men by their intimate partners and from non-lethal violence against women; and, hence, that it requires analysis in its own right. This view was in contrast to much of the existing literature which treated "spousal violence" as a relatively undifferentiated phenomenon arising out of the intense emotions, stresses, and conflicts that often characterize marital relations (Blinder; Chimbos; Boudoris; Goode). These analyses tended to locate the sources of "spousal violence" in patterns of learning early in life, in the disinhibitory effects of alcohol consumption, and in dysfunctional patterns of communication between marital partners. Much of this early work also tended to devote limited attention and analysis to gender differences in spousal violence.

In response to this neglect of gender, a number of analysts have made gender a central feature of their accounts of spousal violence. Sex role theorists highlight gender differences in socialization which teach males to view toughness, power, and control as masculine attributes. Evolutionary theorists argue that violence is an adaptive strategy for males facing the loss of status and control over their partners. Resource theorists view violence as the ultimate resource available to men when other means of exerting control over their partners are exhausted. General systems theorists argue that for men the rewards of violence against their wives are greater than the costs, because of society's failure to adequately sanction such violence. The arguments of these more gender-sensitive analyses resonated with the experiences of members of the Women We Honour Action Committee. Power, control, and domination were themes that they encountered daily in talking with abused women and that they detected in relationships ending in intimate femicide.

In recent work specifically focussed on women killed by their intimate partners, these themes have been elaborated and, in the case of feminist analyses, placed in a historical and institutional context (Campbell 1992; Kelkar; Mahoney; Marcus). For example, Wilson and Daly (1992b) cite "male sexual proprietariness" as the predominant motive in the killing of wives across cultures and historical epochs.

> Men exhibit a tendency to think of women as sexual and reproductive "property" that they can own and exchange.... Proprietary entitlements in people have been conceived and institutionalized as identical proprietary entitlements in land, chattels, and other economic resources. (85)

They go on to note, "that men take a proprietary view of female sexuality and reproductive capacity is manifested in various cultural practices," including claustration practices, asymmetrical adultery laws, and bride-prices (Wilson and Daly 1992b: 85). From this perspective, an extreme, if apparently incongruous manifestation of male proprietariness is intimate femicide. If unable to control or coerce his partner through other means, a man may exert the ultimate control over her by killing her.

Thus, male proprietariness, or male sexual jealousy, has been placed at the centre of many empirical and theoretical analyses of intimate femicide. For example, research on intimate femicide and spousal homicide in Canada, Australia, Great Britain, and the United States (see Dobash and Dobash; Wallace; Polk; Daly and Wilson; Eastel) has identified a common core in these killings of "masculine control, where women become viewed as the possessions of men, and the violence reflects steps taken by males to assert their domination over 'their' women" (Polk 56). This empirical work challenged many of the popular notions about the characteristics of such crimes, for example, the belief that they are explosive, unplanned, and unpredictable acts of passion. At the same time, it contests the validity and coherence of the concept "spousal homicide" with its connotations of sexual symmetry in violence by revealing distinct differences between intimate partner killings by men and those by women. As Dobash and Dobash note:

> Men often kill wives after lengthy periods of prolonged physical violence accompanied by other forms of abuse and coercion; the roles in such cases are seldom if ever reversed. Men perpetrate familicidal massacres, killing spouses and children together; women do not. Men commonly hunt down and kill wives who have left them; women hardly ever behave similarly. Men kill wives as part of planned murder-suicides; analogous acts by women are almost unheard of. Men kill in response to revelations of wifely infidelity; women almost never respond similarly. (cited in Wilson and Daly 1992a: 81)

In sum, there have seen significant advances in both empirical and conceptual analyses of lethal violence against women by their partners since the literature review that served as the impetus for our research. Those advances have not, however, filled all of the gaps identified in our earlier review. In particular, empirical research in Canada has continued to rely largely on official statistics from police sources, which exclude from their classification of spousal homicides killings by men of their estranged common-law partners and girlfriends. Relying on these official statistics also restricts analyses to the information and coding schemes employed by police agencies and personnel. Because of our concerns about the potential for lost information and for the introduction of unknown biases, we relied on a wider range of information sources than typically used in previous research. In this way, our study is unusual in the comprehensiveness of its data. As we see below, it is not however unique in its findings about the nature of intimate femicide.

## Data Sources

We began our data collection by searching death records kept by the Office of the Chief Coroner for Ontario. Coroner's records provide a centralized source of information on all death in Ontario and a means of identifying and accessing records for death identified by the Coroner's Office as homicides. These files frequently contain copies of police reports as well as medical reports on the condition of the body, the way in which the woman was killed and the violence she suffered—details often not available from other sources. However, coroner's records, like all official sources of information on homicide, are imperfect measures of the actual number of deaths due to homicide. For example, cases of homicide in which no body has been found will not typically appear in coroner's records. As a consequence, we expect our estimates of the incidence of intimate femicide to undercount the true incidence, an issue we discuss in more depth below.[2]

We were able to cross-check and supplement data from coroner's records by reviewing police homicide investigation files for many of our cases.[3] In the second study, we were also able to review data from Crown Attorney files on many of the cases in which charges were laid between 1991 and 1994. In both studies, we supplemented our data from official sources with information from newspaper and magazine articles on some of the killings and on trials of some of the alleged offenders.

We compiled this information so that it could be used in both quantitative and qualitative analyses. Our final data collection instrument was designed to provide codes for approximately 52 variables, as well as space to record a narrative of the case where further information was available.[4]

## The Incidence of Intimate Femicide in Ontario, 1974-1994

Between 1974 and 1994, 1206 women aged 15 and older[5] were killed in Ontario, according to official records. In 1120 (93 per cent) of these cases, the crimes were solved and the killers were identified. In 705 (63 per cent) of the solved cases, the killers were the current or former legal spouses, common-law partners, or boyfriends of their victims. Thus, in Ontario over this 21-year period, intimate partners were responsible for the majority of all woman killings and an average of 34 women were victims of intimate femicide each year. These data indicate that the focus in official publications and some academic research on "spousal homicides" of women provides an incomplete picture of the more general phenomenon of intimate femicide: excluding killings of women by their estranged common-law partners and current and former boyfriends underestimates the total number of intimate femicides by about 25 per cent.

The actual number of intimate femicides in Ontario during these years is undoubtedly higher than this. Intimate partners were certainly responsible for some portion of the cases in which no offender was identified or in which we had too little information to determine the precise nature of the relationship between victim and offender.[6] Adjusting for excluded cases, we estimate that intimate femicides may have accounted for as many as 76 per cent of all femicides in Ontario between 1974 and 1994. However, since it is impossible to know the number and characteristics of excluded cases, the analyses that follow focus only on those 705 cases in which the offender was officially identified as the current or former intimate partner of the victim.

## Trends in Intimate Femicide

Between 1974 and 1994, the rate of intimate femicide (i.e., the number of victims of intimate femicide per 100,000 women in the general populations) ranged from a low of .55 in 1978 to a high of 1.26 in 1991 but appears to follow

Figure 1
Trends in Rates of Lethal Violence, Ontario 1974-1994

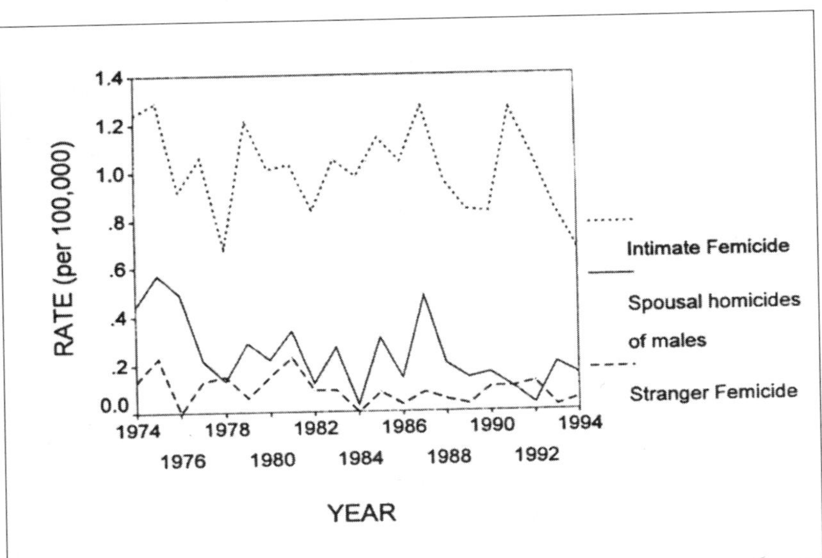


no particular trend over time (see Figure 1).[7] Dividing the 21-year period in half suggests otherwise, however: the average annual rate for the second half of the period (1.02 per 100,000) was slightly higher than the rate for the first half (.92 per 100,000).

On its own, this difference is insignificant statistically and, it might appear, substantively, however, when compared to the slightly higher rate of intimate femicide in the latter period, takes on great importance. The annual rate at which women were killed by strangers or unknown assailants declined significantly from an average of .27 between 1974 and 1983 to .16 between 1984 and 1994. Moreover, the annual rate at which men were killed by their spouses also declined significantly, from an average rate of .31 between 1974 and 1983 to .18 between 1984 and 1994. In other words, during a period when women's risks from strangers and men's risks from spouses decreased, women's risks from their intimate partners increased slightly. Put another way, after 1984—a period of substantial expansion in services for abused women—men's risk of being killed by intimate partners decreased significantly whereas women's risk did not.

Without further analysis of these patterns, which is beyond the scope of this article, we can only speculate as to the reasons for this apparently counter-intuitive finding. One possible explanation is that while the expansion of services for abused women may have resulted in the protection of abusive men from defensive violence by their intimate partners, these same services did not necessarily protect women from their male partners' violence. Research shows that women are most likely to kill their intimate partners after prolonged abuse and when they fear continued or more serious violence against themselves or their children (Browne). Where services for abused women are available, women in abusive relationships have an alternative to killing their partners. As Browne and Williams note, "By offering threatened women protectionism escape and aid, [legal and extra-legal] resources can engender an awareness that there are alternatives to remaining at risk" and thus prevent "killings that occur in desperation" (91). Their analysis of U.S. data lends support to this interpretation: states with higher levels of services to abused women had lower rates of spouse killings of males but not lower rates of spouse killings of females.

## Characteristics of the Victims and their Killers

In many respects, the women killed by their intimate partners and the men who killed them[8] are very similar to women and men in the general population of Ontario, as can be seen from the data in Table 1. For example, women killed by their intimate partners were, on average, about 37 years old; 51 per cent were employed; 80 per cent had children; and 76 per cent were born in Canada. These characteristics do not distinguish the victims from other women in Ontario.

In some other respects, however, victims of intimate femicide and their killers differed from women and men in the general population.[9] We can think of these differences as risk markers for intimate femicide because they tell us that some types of women and men face disproportionately high risks of intimate victimization of offending.[10] Each of the markers we discuss below has also been associated with increased risks of lethal violence against women in other research.

### *Relationship Status*

Research based on data on spouse killings from Great Britain, Australia, the U.S. and Canada shows that two indicators of the relationship—estrangement and common-law status—are associated with a higher risk of spouse killings of women (Wallace; Campbell 1992; Wilson and Daly 1993; Johnson). We find similar patterns in our intimate femicide data, although the limited availability of data on marital separation and common-law unions within the general population restricts our analysis somewhat.

Census Canada collects information on marital separations, but only for registered marriages. According to census figures, during the years of our study, three per cent of women in Ontario were separated form their legal spouses. According to our data, among the victims of intimate femicide, 16 per cent were separated form their legal spouses. Separation, then appears to be a risk factor for intimate femicide, since women who were separated from their partners were greatly over-represented among victims of intimate femicide. However, exactly how much greater the risks are for separated women cannot be determined from

**TABLE 1**
**Characteristics of Victims of Intimate Femicide and their Killers, Ontario, 1974-1994**

| Characteristics | Victims | | Offenders |
|---|---|---|---|
| Total number | 705 | | 705 |
| Average age | 37 | | 41 |
| % born in Canada | 76% | | 70% |
| % with children | 80% | | 77% |
| **Employment Status** | | | |
| % employed | 51% | | 64% |
| % unemployed | 17% | | 21% |
| % homemakers | 18% | | 0% |
| % students | 5% | | 2% |
| % retired or on disability pension | 9% | | 13% |
| **Relationship of Victim to Offender** | | | |
| % legal spouse, cohabiting | | 39% | |
| % legal spouse, separated | | 16% | |
| % common-law partner, cohabiting | | 18% | |
| % common-law partner, separated | | 7% | |
| % divorced spouse | | <1% | |
| % current girlfriend | | 12% | |
| % estranged girlfriend | | 8% | |
| %Aboriginal | 6% | | 6% |

our data. This is because our measure of separation and the census measure of separation are not precisely comparable: the census measure captures largely long-term and relatively well-established separations, whereas our measure is more sensitive and captures short-term as well as long-term separations. Thus our measure will yield a higher estimate of separated couples. Nevertheless, we expect that even correcting for this difference, we would find separation to be associated with higher risks of intimate femicide.

Data on the prevalence of common-law unions in the general population have been collected only since 1991, so we can estimate the risks to women living in common-law relationships only for the most recent years of our research. According to census data, four per cent of women were living in common-law unions in 1991 in Ontario. According to our data, during 1991-1994, 21 per cent of the victims of intimate femicide were killed by common-law partners with whom they were living. Based on our calculations, the rate of intimate femicide for women in common-law unions was approximately six times greater than the average rate of intimate femicide in Ontario in the early 1990s.[11] Clearly, then, women in common-law unions were greatly over-represented among victims of intimate femicide during the early 1990s and perhaps in earlier years as well.

The higher risks associated with common-law status and estrangement have been interpreted in various ways. Compared to couples in registered marriages, common-law partners are more likely to be poor, young, unemployed, and childless—all factors associated with higher homicide rates. Compared to co-residing couples, estranged couples are more likely to have a history of domestic violence (Rodgers; Johnson and Sacco). This violence may be associated both with women's decisions to leave their relationships and with their greater risks of intimate femicide. In other words, "the fact that separated couples constitute a subset of marriages with a history of discord could explain their higher homicide rates" (Wilson and Daly 1994: 8).

Male sexual proprietariness could also play a role in the higher risks for common-law and estranged relationships. If, as some have speculated, "husbands may be less secure in their proprietary claims over wives in common-law unions than in registered unions"(Wilson, Johnson and Daly 343), they may be more likely to resort to serious violence to enforce those claims or to lethal violence when those claims are challenged. Echoing a similar theme, several studies that have found elevated risks at separation have cited the male's inability to accept termination of the relationships and obsessional desires to maintain control over his sexual partner: "He would destroy his intimate 'possession' rather than let her fall into the hands of competitor male"(Polk 29; see also Rasche; Campbell 1992; Wilson and Daly 1993).

### *Ethnicity*

Women in certain ethnic groups have risks of intimate femicide disproportionate to their representation in the population, according to several studies. For example, in the United States African-American women face unusually high risks of intimate femicide. In Canada, such research is more difficult because of restrictions on the collection of crime statistics by race and ethnicity. However, Statistics Canada has collected data on Aboriginal victims of spousal homicides which indicate that Aboriginal women's rates of spousal homicide are between five and ten times higher than the rates for non-Aboriginal women (Kennedy, Forde and Silverman; Silverman and Kennedy).

We had initially hoped to explore ethnic and cultural differences in the risk of intimate femicide in our research. Our community advisory group,[12] which was composed of women from various ethnic backgrounds active in community organizations, encouraged us to do so. However, our research agreement with the Ministry of the Solicitor General prevented us from compiling "statistics based upon social, cultural, regional, linguistic, racial or ethnic group" from the coroners' records. Nevertheless, we were able to document the number of Aboriginal victims of intimate femicide during these years by relying on other sources of data.[13]

We estimate that at least 6 per cent of the victims of intimate femicide in Ontario between 1974 and 1994 were Aboriginal women. Census data for these years indicate that just under one per cent of all women living in Ontario classified themselves as Aboriginal. Thus, Aboriginal women in Ontario appear to be over-represented among the victims of intimate femicide. Conversely, Aboriginal men are over-represented as offenders, since all but four of the Aboriginal victims were killed by Aboriginal men.

A number of factors might explain the disproportionate risks of intimate femicide faced by Aboriginal women. Aboriginal Canadians, similar to African-Americans, are an economically impoverished and politically disenfranchised ethnic minority. Considerable research has shown that economic, social, and political disadvantages are associated with higher homicide rates generally, as well as higher rates of serious spousal violence. In addition, Aboriginal Canadian heterosexual couples also have disproportionate rates of other risk makers for intimate partner violence, such as common-law marital status, low income, bouts of male unemployment, exposure to violence in childhood, alcohol abuse, overcrowded housing conditions, and social isolation—all of which have been cited as reasons for the higher rates of family violence in Aboriginal communities (Health and Welfare Canada; Long). Some analysts situate these risk factors within a structural approach that views them as consequences of internal colonialism: "the conditions of colonialism [are] directly related to aboriginal acts of political violence as well as rates of suicide, homicide, and family violence among the aboriginal peoples" (Long 42; see also Frank; Bachmann).

### *Employment*

Men's unemployment is commonly cited as a risk factor for wife assaults and is also associated with elevated risks of spousal homicide. Women's employment status, on the other hand, does not appear to be consistently associated with their risks of violence from their partners (Hotaling and Sugarman; Brinkerhoff and Lupri; Johnson; Macmillan and Gartner). The association between men's unemployment and violence against their female partners has been attributed to the stresses produced by unemployment and limited economic resources. But if this were the case, one would expect to find more evidence that women's unemployment is also associated with spousal violence, which is not the case. For those who see male violence against their partners as one resource for demonstrating power and control, the gender-specificity of the effects of unemployment is not surprising: men who lack more traditional resources (such as economic success) may "forge a particular type of masculinity that centers on ultimate control of the domestic setting through the use of violence"(Messerchmidt 149).

Our data on intimate femicide are consistent with this interpretation. For women, employment status is not associated with differential risks of intimate femicide: 51 per cent of women in both the victim population and the general population were employed during the period of our study. For men, however, employment status is associated with differential risks. Among intimate femicide offenders, 64 per cent were employed, whereas among males in the general population, 73 per cent were employed. In Ontario, then, male unemployment appears to be associated with higher risks of intimate femicide offending.

### *Offenders' Violent Histories*

Several studies have shown that men who kill their spouses frequently have histories of violent behaviour, both in and outside of their marital relationships.[14] As Johnson notes, "[a]lthough some wife killings are the result of sudden, unforeseeable attacks by depressed or mentally unstable husbands and are unrelated to a history of violence in family, most do not seem to fit this description" (183). Because of this, risk assessment tools designed to assess battered women's risk of lethal violence typically include measures of their partners' violence against their children and outside of the home, as well as threats of serious violence against their wives or others (Campbell 1995).

We also found evidence of unusual levels of violence in the backgrounds of the offenders in our sample. At least 31 per cent of them had an arrest record for a violent offence.[15] At least 53 per cent of them were known to have been violent in the past toward the women they ultimately killed. This corresponds to data for Canada as a whole which indicates that in 53 per cent of spousal homicides of women between 1991 and 1993, police were aware of previous violent incidents between the spouses (Canadian Centre for Justice Statistics). In addition, in at least 34 per cent of the cases of intimate femicide, the offenders were known to have previously threatened their victims with violence.[16] At least ten per cent of the killings occurred while the offender was on probation or parole, or under a restraining order.

It is important to emphasize that these are *minimum* estimate of the number of offenders with violent and criminal histories. In over 200 of the 705 cases of intimate femicide we did not have enough information to determine if previous violence or police contact had occurred. Nevertheless, the information we were able to find clearly challenged the view that intimate femicides are typically momentary rages or heat-of-passion killings by otherwise non-violent men driven to act out of character by extreme circumstances.

### *A Summary of Risk Markers for Intimate Femicide*

Women killed by their intimate male partners and the men who kill them are drawn from all classes, and all age groups, all cultural and ethnic backgrounds. However, the victims of intimate femicide and their killers in our study did differ from other women and men in Ontario in some important respects: they were more likely than women and men in the general population to be separated from their partners, to be in common-law relationships, and to be Aboriginal. In addition, men who killed their intimate partners were also more likely to be unemployed and to have histories of criminal violence.

These risk markers for intimate femicide have been noted in other research on spousal homicides and have been interpreted from within various theoretical frameworks. We suggest that they are perhaps most consistent with a framework which views intimate femicide as the manifestation of extreme (if ultimately self-defeating) controlling and proprietary attitudes and behaviours by men toward their female partners.

## Characteristics of the Killings

An adequate understanding of the sources of intimate femicide will need to take account of the particular characteristics of these killings. Prior research has devoted much less attention to these characteristics than to the characteristics of the individuals involved in the killings.[17] As a consequence, we are limited in both the comparisons we can draw between our findings and the findings from other research and in the interpretations we can offer of these findings.

Intimate femicides are typically very private acts: three quarters of the victims were killed in their own homes and, in almost half of these cases, in their own bedrooms. Less than 20 per cent occurred in public places, such as streets, parks, workplaces or public buildings. The most typical method was shooting: one-third of the victims were killed with firearms. Virtually all the other methods required direct and often prolonged physical contact between offenders and their victims: about two-thirds of the offenders stabbed, bludgeoned, beat, strangled, or slashed the throats of their victims.

One of the distinguishing features of intimate femicide is the extent and nature of the violence done to the victim. Unlike killings by women of their intimate partners,[18] intimate femicides often involve multiple methods or far more violence than is necessary to kill the victim. For example, in over half of the stabbings, offenders inflicted four or more stab wounds—leading some coroners to use the term "over-kill" to describe them. In about 20 per cent of the cases, offenders used multiple methods against their victims, such as stabbing and strangling or beating and slashing. In about 10 per cent of the cases, we also found evidence that the victim's body had been mutilated or dismembered.

The violence in these killings is much more likely to be sexualized than when women kill their intimate partners.[19] Records of approximately half of the cases in our study provided sufficient information for us to determine whether sexual violence was present. In 27 per cent of these cases we found evidence that the victims had been raped, sodomized, or sexually mutilated; in another 22 per cent of the cases the victim's body was found partially or completely unclothed.

Consumption of alcohol by offenders and/or victims was no more common in intimate femicides than in other killings: 39 per cent of the offenders and 32 per cent of the victims had been drinking immediately prior to the killing. In only three per cent of the cases was there evidence of drug use by offenders or victims immediately prior to the killing.

Establishing the motives in these killings is fraught with difficulties, as suggested earlier. We made our own determination of the motive after reviewing all the information available to us. In about one-fourth of the cases we felt we had insufficient information to make a judgement about the offender's motive. In the remaining cases, one motive clearly predominated: the offender's rage or despair over the actual or impending estrangement from his partner. This motive characterized 45 per cent of the killings in which we identified a motive. In contrast, women who kill their intimate partners only rarely kill out of anger over an estrangement (Browne; Daly and Wilson).

Suspected or actual infidelity of the victim was the motive in another 15 per cent of the intimate femicide. In ten per cent of the cases the killing appears to have been the final act of violence in a relationship characterized by serial abuse.[20] In only five per cent of the cases did stressful life circumstances—such as bankruptcy, job loss, or serious illness—appear to motivate the killer,[21] and in only three per cent of the cases was there evidence that the killer was mentally ill.

Another feature that distinguishes intimate femicide from intimate partner killings by women is the number of people who die as a result of these crimes. The 705 cases of intimate femicide resulted in the deaths of 977 persons. Most of these additional deaths were suicides by the offenders: 31 per cent of the offenders killed themselves after killing their female partners.[22] But offenders killed an additional 74 persons, most of whom were children of the victims. In addition, over 100 children witnessed their mothers' deaths; thus, while they may have escaped physical harm, they obviously suffered inestimable psychological harm.

Our documentation of these characteristics of intimate femicide cannot sufficiently convey the complexity and context surrounding these crimes. Nevertheless, it serves important purposes. Comparing characteristics of intimate partner killings by males and females shows the distinctiveness of these two types of killings—a distinctiveness that is, in fact, obscured in studies that treat intimate partner killings by men and women as instances of a single phenomenon. Compared to killings of men by intimate female partners, intimate femicides are much more likely to involve extreme and sexualized violence, to be motivated by anger over separation, to be followed by the suicide of the offender, and to be accompanied by the killing of additional victims. These features highlight the gender-specificity of intimate partner killings and are consistent with a perspective on intimate femicide which views it as based in a larger system of gender[ed] inequality and stratification which perpetuates male control over women's sexuality, labour, and, at times, lives and death.

## The Criminal Justice Response to Intimate Femicide

In our initial study of intimate femicide, we had not intended to collect and analyze data on the criminal justice responses to men who killed their intimate partners—in part because our primary interest was in the victims of intimate femicide and in part because we did not expect information on criminal justice responses to be consistently reported in coroners' and police records. However, contrary to our expectations, we were able to obtain information on charges laid, convictions, and sentencing in a substantial number of the cases. In 90 per cent of the 490 cases in which we were able to establish that offenders did not commit suicide, we found at least some information on criminal justice processing.

In 94 per cent of these cases, the offenders were charged with either first- or second-degree murder.[23] The proportion charged with first-degree murder increased over time, from 34 per cent of the cases in the first half of the period to 52 per cent in the second half. Of the 346 cases for which we found information on dispositions, ten per cent were convicted of first-degree murder, 35 per cent of second-degree murder, and 38 per cent of manslaughter. Murder convictions increased over time: from 32 per cent of the dispositions in the first half of the period to 56 per cent in the second half. Acquittals accounted for a total of 13 per cent of the cases: eleven per cent were verdicts of not guilty by reason of insanity and two per cent were straight acquittals.

Sentencing information, available for 302 of the men convicted of killing their partners, also indicates that criminal justice response to intimate femicide increased in severity over time. Prior to 1984, seven per cent of convicted offenders received no jail time, 14 per cent were sent to secure mental institutions for indefinite periods, 25 per cent were sentenced to less than five years in prison, 38 per cent were sentenced to between five and ten years, and 15 per cent received sentences of more than ten years. After 1983, four per cent of convicted offenders received no jail time, seven per cent were sent to secure mental institutions, ten per cent received sentences of less than five years, 37 per cent received sentences of between five and ten years, and 41 per cent were sentenced to prison for more than ten years.

This evidence clearly shows that criminal justice responses to intimate femicide became increasingly punitive over the 21 years of our study. How much of this trend reflects increasing punitiveness towards all violent criminals and how much reflects growing public awareness and intolerance of violence against women is an issue requiring further research.[24]

## The Gender-Specific Nature of Intimate Femicide

We have alluded to the gender-specific nature of intimate femicide at various points in our analysis. Here, we develop our ideas about this gender specificity by considering what is known about gender differences in homicide more generally. We base this discussion on a large body of criminological research on homicide, as well as on data on over 7,000 homicides collected by Rosemary Gartner and Bill McCarthy as part of a separate research project.

Among those who study homicide, it is well known that women and men are killed in different numbers, by different types of people, and in different circumstances. Women are less likely to be victims of homicide than men in virtually all societies. Canada and Ontario are no different; men outnumber women as victims of homicide by a ratio of approximately two: one in Canada and in Ontario between 1974 and 1994.

This may appear to indicate that women have a sort of protective advantage over men—that, at least in this sphere of social life, women are not disadvantaged relative to men. However, if we consider gender differences in offending, a different picture emerges. Men accounted for 87 per cent of all homicide offenders in Ontario during these years; and males outnumbered females as offenders by a ratio of almost seven to one. When women were involved in homicides, then, they were almost three times more likely to be victims than offenders; when men were involved in homicides they were more likely to be offenders than victims. In other words, women are over-represented among victims and under-represented among offenders, for men the opposite is true.

Women were also much more likely than men to be killed by someone of the opposite sex, as these figures imply. Fully 98 per cent of all women killed in Ontario between 1974 and 1994 were killed by men. Only 17 per cent of adult male victims were killed by women. Thus, man killing appears to be primarily a reflection of relations *within* a gender, whereas woman killing appears to be primarily a reflection of relations *between* genders. Because women are the majority of victims in opposite-sex killings, such killings can be seen as one of the high costs to women of male dominance and desire for control in heterosexual relationships.

It is in intimate relationships between women and men that male dominance and control are most likely to erupt into physical violence. Women accounted for about 75 per cent of all victims of spouse killings in Ontario during the last two decades.[25] So women outnumber men among victims of spouse killings by a ratio of about 3:1. Moreover, spousal homicides accounted for over 50 per cent of all killings of women but less than 10 per cent of all killings of men.

If males, unlike females, are not killed primarily by their intimate partners, who are they killed by and under what circumstances? In Ontario, about 60 per cent of male victims are killed by acquaintances and strangers; another 20 per cent are killed by unknown assailants. Most male-male homicides are the result of arguments or disputes that escalate to killings. In many cases, both victim and offender have been drinking, and who becomes the victim and who the offender is a matter of happenstance.[26] One classic study of homicide (Wolfgang 1958) concluded that male-male homicides, as an instance of the more generally physically aggressive behaviour of males, converge with notions of masculine identity.

When males kill their intimate female partners, their methods of and motives for killing take on a character distinctive from male-male killings—a character that denotes the gender specificity of intimate femicide. As noted above, a substantial number of intimate femicides involved multiple methods, excessive force, and continued violence even after the woman's death would have been apparent.[27] The violence in intimate femicides also frequently involves some form of sexual assault, a very rare occurrence in killings of men.

The motives in intimate femicide also point to its gender-specificity. The predominance of men's rage over separation as a motive in intimate femicides has no obvious counterpart in killings of men—even killings of men by their intimate female partners. We agree with others who see this motive as a reflection of the sexual proprietariness of males towards their intimate female partners.

In sum, our analysis of intimate femicide and our review of other research and data on gender differences in homicide suggest that woman killing in general and intimate femicide in particular are uniquely gendered acts. By this we mean these killings reflect important dimensions of gender stratification, such as power differences in intimate relations and the construction of women as sexual objects generally and as sexual property in particular contexts. Intimate femicide—indeed, probably most femicide—is not simply violence against a person who happens to be female. It is violence that occurs and takes particular forms because its target is a woman, a woman who has been intimately involved with her killer.

## Conclusion

Our purpose in this article has been to document the incidence and provide a description of the phenomenon of intimate femicide. For some, our approach may be unsatisfying because we have not proposed a systematic explanation of, nor outlined a detailed strategy for preventing, these killings. Obviously explaining and preventing intimate femicides are critical tasks, but both require comprehensive knowledge of the phenomenon. The statistical data we have gathered and analyzed are intended to contribute to this knowledge.

Nevertheless, we recognize that our overview of the extent and character of intimate femicide in Ontario between 1974 and 1994 has raised at least as many questions as it has answered. Why, for example, did women's risks of intimate femicide increase slightly when public concern over and resources available to abused women were also increasing; when other forms of lethal violence were decreasing; and when criminal justice responses to intimate femicide were becoming more punitive? Why did some women—such as those in common-law relationships and Aboriginal women—face disproportionately high risks of intimate femicide? Were there other types of women with elevated risks of intimate femicide—for example, immigrant women or women with disabilities—whom we couldn't identify because of the limitations of our data? Why are intimate partner killings by men and women so distinctively different? All of these questions deserve answers, but the answers will require research that goes beyond the data and analysis we have been able to present in this paper.

There are other types of questions raised by our research that are more immediately pressing, questions about how to prevent intimate femicides. Our research has shown that intimate femicides are not the isolated and unpredictable acts of passion they are often believed to be. Most of the killers in our study had acted violently toward their partners or other persons in the past and many had prior contact with the police as a consequence. Many of the victims had sought help from a variety of sources. In a substantial portion of these intimate femicides, then, there were clear signs of danger preceding the killing, signs that were available to people who might have been able to intervene to prevent the crime. We believe this information could be combined with what we know about the risk factors of intimate femicide—such as estrangement—to develop interventions that would save women's lives.

This is the question that has been at the core of our research and the recommendation that we tabled at the conclusion of both of our studies. We urged the establishment of a joint forced initiative that would include police, coroners, researchers, experts working in the field, as well as survivors of intimate violence, who would be charged with developing a system to respond more effectively to men when they are at a greater risk of intimate femicide. Such response would need to be swift and focused on ensuring the victim's safety and deterring the offender from further violence or threats.

Of course, this kind of intervention must be coupled with efforts to address the underlying sources of intimate femicide. If, as we and others have argued, the sources lie at least in part in attitudes and behaviours that have been supported for centuries by patriarchal systems of power and privilege, those attitudes and behaviours, as well as the systems supporting them, must be confronted and contested. Some feminists argue that one means of doing this is through refining and reformulating law as a weapon against men's intimate violence against women. Isabel Marcus, for example, argues for identifying domestic violence as terrorism and, as such, a violation of international human rights accords (Marcus). Elizabeth Schneider suggests redeploying the concepts of privacy, not to keep the state out of intimate relationships as the concept has been used in the past, but to emphasize individuals' autonomy and independence. She argues this affirmative aspect of privacy could frame a new feminist agenda against woman abuse.

As these and other analyses emphasize, preventing intimate femicides will require that the public as well as those working in fields relevant to the prevention of violence begin to see intimate femicide as a preventable crime. From our own and others' research on intimate violence, it should be apparent that these crimes are patterned and predictable. The danger lies in maintaining the view that violence in inevitable, unavoidable, and inherent in intimate relationships. Such fatalism must be challenged, so that women's safety in and outside their homes is seen as an achievable and preeminent goal.

*Major funding for the studies in this paper was provided by the Ontario Women's Directorate. The Ministry of Community and Social Services and the School of Graduate Studies at the University of Toronto each provided additional funding for one of the studies. The analyses and opinions in the paper are those of the authors and do not necessarily represent the views of any of these funders.*

## Notes

[1]For efforts to analyze the source of these variations in the sex ratio of spouse killing, see Wilson and Daly 1992c; Regoeczi and Silverman.

[2]Coroner's records are limited in another obvious and unavoidable way: they are observations removed in time and space from the actual killing. As a consequence, the descriptions in the records will be shaped by the interests and perspectives of the observer. A coroner's perspective is that of an investigator after the fact , and his/her primary interest is in determining the cause and means of death. Thus, the information recorded by coroners is intended to serve these purposes, not the interests of researchers.

[3]Different procedures were used in the two studies to obtain access to municipal police and Ontario Provincial Police (OPP) records. These records are not centrally compiled and it was impossible to contact and obtain cooperation from all forces around Ontario which investigate and keep records on cases of homicide.

[4]Obviously, the coded data provide only a partial and, in some respects, an incomplete portrayal of intimate femicide. The lives and deaths of the women represented in these statistics cannot be sufficiently understood from counts and categorizations. For this reason, we devoted a considerable portion of our first study to reconstructing the stories of some of the women who died, through interviews with their family and friends.

[5]Our research has looked only at killings of females aged 15 and older because the killing of children differs in distinctive ways from the killing of adults.

[6]The number of intimate femicides is undercounted in official records for other reasons as well. For example, in some cases of intimate femicide, the woman's death may be incorrectly classified as due to suicide, accident, or natural causes. Among the intimate femicides in our study, at least eight were not initially classified as homicides and only re-classified after further investigation. Another example of this occurred while this article was being written: the body of a Southern Ontario woman who died by hanging was exhumed and an investigation revealed she had not killed herself, as originally determined, but had been killed by her boyfriend.

[7]Although there are no statistics on the rate of intimate femicide for Canada as a whole, there are statistics on the rate of spousal killings of women. Since the mid-1970s, trends in Ontario's rate have paralleled those for Canada as a whole; and

the mean rate for Ontario (.77) is very close to the mean rate for Canada (.83).

[8]Of the cases of intimate femicides between 1974 and 1994, we found only three in which the offender was a woman.

[9]Identifying differences between victims or offenders and women and men in the general population requires establishing the proportion of victims (or offenders) with the particular characteristic and comparing this to the proportion of women (or men ) in the general population of Ontario during the years 1974-1994 with the same characteristic. If the former proportion is larger than the latter proportion, this indicates that women with that particular characteristic are over-represented among victims of intimate femicide. Tests for statistically significant differences are not appropriate here because the data are based on populations, not samples. Because we used information from census reports to determine the characteristics of women in the general population of Ontario, we were limited in our search for risk markers of intimate femicide to characteristics which are measured in the census.

[10]By highlighting these characteristics, we do not mean to obscure the fact that women from all types of backgrounds and in all types of relationships are victims of intimate femicide; nor do we mean to imply that certain characteristics of women make then likely targets for intimate violence. Rather, we would suggest that certain groups of women may be more vulnerable to intimate violence because they share characteristics that have isolated them, limited their access to resources for protection, or prevented them from obtaining a level of personal security that many Canadians take for granted.

[11]The average annual intimate femicide (per 100,000 women aged 15 and older) for the years 1991-1994 was calculated by: (1) dividing the number of victims during those years(159) by the number of women aged 15and older in the Ontario population in 1991 (4,130,450); (2) multiplying this figure by 100,000; and (3) dividing this figure by four. This yields an average annual rate of .96 per 100,000 women aged 15 and older. The average annual rate of intimate femicides of women living in common-law unions was calculated by: (1) dividing the number of victims living in common-law during those years (45) by the number of women aged 15 and older in Ontario living in common-law unions in 1991 (182,155); (2) multiplying this figure by 100,000; and (3) dividing this figure by four. This yields an annual average rate of 6.18 per 100,000 women aged 15 and older in common-law unions.

[12]This group was formed at the beginning of our first study and met with the principal researchers regularly to review the research for cultural sensitivity and validity. At the completion of the first study, its members also reviewed and made contributions to the final report.

[13]The final report for our first study (pp.67-76) documents the problems with collecting information on race and cultural backgrounds of crime victims and offenders, as well as the procedures we followed to gather the data on Aboriginal victims.

[14]See, for example, the review in Johnson (183-186).

[15]Another 30 per cent had been arrested and charged with non-violent criminal offences.

[16]In contrast, in only six per cent of the cases were the victims known to have been violent toward their killers in the past; and in only two per cent of the cases were the victims known to have previously threatened their partners with violence.

[17]What researchers can describe about homicide and femicide is largely determined by the types of information collected by officials. This means that many details about the events leading up to the killing, the dynamics of the interaction immediately preceding the killing, or the states of mind of victim and offender are absent or at most only hinted at in official reports. Some characteristics of intimate femicide can be easily and reliably determined, such as where they occurred or whether weapons were involved. Other characteristics –such as the offender's motivation—are more susceptible to post hoc reconstructions that introduce the inevitable biases of observers and officials. When we collected and coded information we reviewed all the information available to us and made our own best judgments about these characteristics. We recognize, however, that our judgments are necessarily based on limited information about extremely complex events. Our discussion of the characteristics of the killings therefore should be viewed with these limitations in mind.

[18]We base this and other conclusions about the characteristics of intimate partner killings by women on data from an on-going study by the first author of over 7,000 homicides in two Canadian cities and two U.S. cities over the twentieth century.

[19]Indeed, none of the data or research with which we are familiar indicates that women who kill their intimate partners exact sexual violence against their victims.

[20]This does not mean that offenders who appeared to act for other motives had not engaged in systematic abuse of the women they killed. Rather, it indicates that in 10 per cent of the cases, the only motive we could identify was systematic, serial abuse that ultimately lead to the woman's death.

[21]Typically, offenders who kill under these circumstances are characterized as extremely depressed and are more likely than other offenders to commit or attempt suicide after the killing. Nevertheless, some have argued that sexual proprietariness can still be seen in killings apparently motivated by stressful life circumstances (e.g., Daly and Wilson). According to this view, when men kill their wives (and often their children as well) because they feel they can no longer provide for them, their acts suggest that they see their wives as possessions to dispose of as they see fit and/or that they cannot conceive of their wives having an existence separate from their own.

[22]Other research has noted the high rates at which offenders commit suicide after intimate femicides, and has contrasted this to the rarity of suicides by women who kill their intimate partners (see, e.g., Block and Christakos). Daly and Wilson have suggested that this pattern is grounded in males' feelings of possessiveness and ownership over their partners.

[23]Murder is first degree when the killing is planned and deliberate, when the victim

is an officer of the law, or when a death is caused while committing or attempting to commit another offense, such as kidnapping. Any murder that does not fall within these categories is second-degree murder. According to the courts, the distinguish between first and second-degree murder is made solely for sentencing purposes. While anyone convicted of murder is sentenced to imprisonment for life, the parole ineligibility period varies between first and second- degree murder.

[24]Some analysts (e.g., Rapaport) have speculated that the killing of a woman by her intimate male partner is treated more leniently by the criminal justice system than other types of homicides, such as killings of men by female intimate partners. However, empirical evidence in this area is sparse and not conclusive.

[25]We use the category "spouse killings" here because we could find no statistics on the number of men killed by intimate partners, only statistics on men killed by spouses. To be comparable, we compare these figures to the number of women killed by spouses—a subset of all intimate femicides.

[26]Marvin Wolfgang has noted in *Studies in Homicide* (1967) that where males are victims of homicide, victim-participation of the violence is fairly common.

[27]Marvin Wolfgang (1967) found a similar pattern in his study of homicides in Philadelphia.

## References

Bachmann, Ronet. *Death and Violence on the Reservation: Homicide, Family Violence, and Suicide in American Indian Populations*. New York: Auburn House, 1993.

Blinder, Martin. *Lovers, Killers, Husbands, and Wives*. New York: St. Martin's Press, 1985.

Block, Carolyn R. and A. Christakos. "Intimate Partner Homicide in Chicago over 29 Years." *Crime and Delinquency* 41 (1995): 496-526.

Boudoris, James. "Homicide and the Family." *Journal of Marriage and the Family* 32 (1971): 667-676.

Brinkerhoff, Merlin and Eugene Lupri. "Interspousal Violence." *Canadian Journal of Sociology* 13 (1988): 407-434.

Browne, Angela. *When Battered Women Kill*. New York: The Free Press, 1987.

Browne, Angela and Kirk Williams. "Exploring the Effect of Resource Availability on the Likelihood of Female-Perpetrated Homicides." *Law and Society Review* 23 (1989): 78-94.

Campbell, Jacquelyn C. "'If I Can't Have You No One Else Can': Power and Control in Homicide of Female Partners." *Femicide: The Politics of Woman Killings*. Eds. J. Radford and D. E. H. Russell. New York: Twayne, 1992. 99-113.

Campbell, Jacquelyn. "Prediction of Homicide of and by Battered Women." *Assessing Dangerousness: Violence by Sexual Offenders, Batterers, and Child Abusers*. Thousand Oaks, CA: Sage, 1995. 96-113.

Canadian Center for Justice Statistics. "Homicide Survey." Unpublished statistics, 1993.

Chimbos, Peter D. *Marital Violence: A Study of Interspousal Homicide.* San Francisco: R & E Associates, 1978.

Crawford, Maria and Rosemary Gartner and the Women We honour Action Committee. *Woman Killing: Intimate Femicide in Ontario, 1974-1990.* Toronto: Women We Honour Committee, 1992.

Crawford, Maria, Rosemary Gartner, and Myrna Dawson, in collaboration with the Women We Honour Action Committee. *Woman Killing: Intimate Femicide in Ontario, 1974-1990.* Toronto: Women We Honour Committee, 1997.

Daly, Martin and Margo Wilson. *Homicide.* New York: Aldine de Gruyter, 1988.

Dobash, R. Emerson and Russell P. Dobash, "The Nature and Antecedents of Violent Events." *British Journal of Criminology* 24(1984): 269-288.

Easteal, P. W. *Killing the Beloved: Homicide Between Adult Sexual Intimates.* Canberra: Australian Institute of Criminology, 1993.

Frank, Sharlene. *Family Violence in Aboriginal Communities: A First Nations Report.* Vancouver: Report to the Government of British Columbia,1993.

Goode, William. "Violence Among Intimates." *Crimes of Violence* [Vol. 13]. Eds. D. Mulvihill and M. Tumin. Washington, DC: USGPO, 1969. 941-977.

Health and Welfare Canada. *Reaching for Solutions: Report of the Special Advisor to the Minister of National Health and Welfare on Child Sexual Abuse in Canada.* Ottawa: Supply and Services, 1990.

Hotaling, Gerald and David Sugarman. "An Analysis of Risk Markers in Husband to Wife Violence: The Current State Of Knowledge." *Violence and Victims* (1986): 101-124.

Johnson, Holly. *Dangerous Domains: Violence Against Women in Canada.* Toronto: Nelson Canada, 1996.

Johnson, Holly and Vincent Sacco. " Researching Violence Against Women: Statistics Canada's National Survey." *Canadian Journal of Criminology* 3 (1995): 281-304.

Kelkar, Govind. "Women and Structural Violence in India." *Femicide: The Politics of Woman Killings.* Eds. J. Radford and D. E. H. Russell. New York: Twayne, 1992. 117-123.

Kennedy, Leslie W., David R. Forde, and Robert A. Silverman. "Understanding Homicide Trends :Issues in Disaggregating for National and Cross-National Comparisons." *Canadian Journal of Sociology* 14 (1989): 479-486.

Long, David A. " On Violence and Healing: Aboriginal Healing, Aboriginal Experiences, 1960-1993." *Violence in Canada: Sociopolitical Perspectives.* Ed. J. I. Ross. Don Mills, ON: Oxford University Press, 1995. 40-77.

Macmillan, Ross and Rosemary Gartner. "Labour Force Participation and the Risk of Spousal Violence Against Women." Paper presented at the Annual Meetings of the American Society of Criminology, 1996.

Mahoney, Martha A. "Victimization or Oppression? Women's Lives, Violence and Agency." *The Pubilc Nature of Private Violence: The Discovery of*

*Domestic Abuse*. Eds. M. A. Fineman and R. Mykitiuk. New York: Routledge, 1994. 59-92.

Marcus, Isabel. "Reframing 'Domestic' Violence: Terrorism in the Home." *The Public Nature of Private Violence: The Discovery of Domestic Abuse*. Eds. M. A. Finerman and R. Mykitiuk. New York: Routledge, 1994. 11-35.

Messerchmidt, James W. *Masculinities and Crime: Critique and Conceptualization of Theory*. Lanham, MD: Rowman and Littlefield, 1993.

Polk, Kenneth. *When Men Kill: Scenarios of Masculine Violence*. Cambridge: Cambridge University Press, 1994.

Rapaport, Elizabeth. "The Death Penalty and the Domestic Discount." *The Public Nature of Private Violence: The Discovery of Domestic Abuse*. Eds. M. Fineman and R. Mykitiuk. New York: Routledge, 1994. 224-251.

Regoeczi, Wendy and Robert Silverman. "Spousal Homicide in Canada: Exploring the Issue of Racial Variations in Risk." Paper presented at the Annual Meetings of the American Society of Criminology, 1997.

Rodgers, Karen. *Wife Assault: The Findings of a National Survey*. Ottawa: Canadian Center for Justice Statistics,1994.

Rasche, Christine. "Stated and Attributed Motives for Lethal Violence in Intimate Relationships." Paper presented at the Annual Meetings of the American Society of Criminology, 1989.

Schneider, Elizabeth. "The Violence of Privacy." *The Public Nature of Private Violence: The Discovery of Domestic Abuse*. Eds. M. Fineman and R. Mykitiuk. New York: Routledge, 1994. 36-58.

Silverman, Robert and Leslie Kennedy. *Deadly Deeds: Murder in Canada*. Toronto: Nelson Canada, 1993.

Wallace, Allison. *Homicide: The Social Reality*. New South Wales: New South Wales Bureau of Crime Statistics and Research, 1986.

Wilson, Margo and Martin Daly. "The Myth of Sexual Symmetry in Martial Violence." *Social Problems* 39 (1992a): 81.

Wilson, Margo and Martin Daly. "Till Death Do Us Part." *Femicide: The Politics of Woman Killing*. Eds. J. Radford and D. E. H Russell. New York: Twayne, 1992b.

Wilson, Margo and Martin Daly. "Who Kills Whom in Spouse Killings? On the Exceptional Sex Ratio of Spousal Homicides in the United States." *Criminology* 30 (1992c): 189-215.

Wilson, Margo and Martin Daly. "Spousal Homicide Risk and Estrangement." *Violence and Victims* 8 (1993): 3-16.

Wilson, Margo and Martin Daly. "Spousal Homicide." *Juristat Service Bulletin* 14 (8) (1994): 1-15.

Wilson, Margo, Holly Johnson, and Martin Daly, "Lethal and Non-Lethal Violence Against Wives." *Canadian Journal of Criminology* 37 (1995): 331-361.

Wolfgang, Marvin. *Patterns in Criminal Homicide*. Philadelphia: University of Pennsylvania Press, 1958.

Wolfgang, Marvin. *Studies in Homicide*. New York: Harper and Row, 1967.

Women We Honour Action Committee and Rosemary Gartner. *Annotated Bibliography of Works Reviewed for Project on Intimate Femicide*. Toronto: Women We Honour Action Committee, 1990.

# Violence in Aboriginal Communities

Emma D. LaRocque

The issue of domestic violence in First Nations and Métis communities is one that demands urgent study and action. There is every indication that violence has escalated dramatically. For example, studies show that among First Nations "the single most important group of health problems in terms of both mortality and morbidity is accidents and violence" (Young 54). The goal of this paper is not to comment on family violence generally, though it does require further comment. This paper will focus on family violence as it affects Aboriginal women, teenagers and children. And since much family violence involves sexual assault, special attention is given to sexual violence within Aboriginal communities.

While domestic or family violence clearly affects all members within a family, the most obvious victims are women and children. A 1989 study by the Ontario Native Women's Association reported that eight out of ten Aboriginal women were abused. While this study focused on northern Ontario, it is statistically representative of other communities across the country. There is growing documentation that Aboriginal female adults, adolescents, and children are experiencing abuse, battering and/or sexual assault to a staggering degree. A 1987 report by the Child Protection Centre of Winnipeg stated that there is "an apparent epidemic of child sexual abuse on reserves." And just recently, it was reported by the press that on one reserve in Manitoba, 30 adults were charged with having sexually abused 50 persons, many of them children.

Since it is considerably more difficult to get precise statistics on Métis people, it is virtually impossible to say with any exactness the extent of sexual violence on Métis families or communities. However, as more victims are beginning to report, there is every indication that violence, including sexual violence, is just as problematic, and just as extensive as it is on reserves. In November 1992, the Women of the Métis Nation of Alberta organized an historic conference near

Edmonton dealing specifically with sexual violence against Métis women. The interest shown by Métis women from across Canada was overwhelming. The stories shared by the 150 or so conference participants indicated that Métis women, no less than Indian women from reserves, have been suffering enormously—and silently—from violence including rape and child sexual abuse.

This paper will address the following: (1) women's perspectives on factors that generate and perpetuate domestic violence and (2) strategies proposed to reduce and eliminate violence. Barriers to implementing these strategies are implied within this discussion.

## Colonization

Colonization refers to that process of encroachment and subsequent subjugation of Aboriginal peoples since the arrival of Europeans. From the Aboriginal perspective, it refers to a loss of lands, resources, and self-direction and to the severe disturbance of cultural ways and values. Colonization has taken its toll on all Aboriginal peoples, but it has taken perhaps its greatest toll on women. Prior to colonization, Aboriginal women enjoyed comparative honour, equality, and even political power in a way European women did not at the same time of history. We can trace the diminishing status of Aboriginal women with the progression of colonialism. Many, if not the majority, of Aboriginal cultures were originally matriarchal or semi-matriarchal. European patriarchy was initially imposed upon Aboriginal societies in Canada through the fur trade, missionary Christianity and government policies. Because of white intrusion, the matriarchal character of Aboriginal spiritual, economic, kinship, and political institutions was drastically altered.

## Racism, Sexism, and the Problem of Internalization

Colonization and racism go hand in hand. Racism has provided justification for the subjugation of Aboriginal peoples. While all Aboriginal people are subjected to racism, women further suffer from sexism. Racism breeds hatred of Aboriginal peoples; sexism breeds hatred of women. For Aboriginal women, racism and sexism constitute a package experience. We cannot speak of sexual violence without at once addressing the effects of racism/sexism. Sexual violence is related to racism in that racism sets up or strengthens a situation where Aboriginal women are viewed and treated as sex objects. The objectification of women perpetuates sexual violence. Aboriginal women have been objectified not only as women but also as Indian women. The term used to indicate this double objectification was and is "squaw."

A complex of white North American cultural myths, as expressed in literature and popular culture, has perpetuated racist/sexist stereotypes about Aboriginal women. A direct relationship between racist/sexist stereotypes and violence can be seen, for example, in the dehumanizing portrayal of Aboriginal women as "squaws," which renders all Aboriginal female persons vulnerable to physical, verbal and sexual violence.

One of the many consequences of racism is that, over time, racial stereotypes and societal rejection may be internalized by the colonized group. The internalization process is one of the most problematic legacies of long-term colonization. It is not well understood, but it is certainly indicated by various oppressed or minority groups in North America. Many Black, Chicano and Aboriginal writers have pointed to this problem. Understanding the complex workings of the internalization process may be the key to the beginnings of understanding the behaviour of the oppressed and the oppressive in our communities.

In his book *Prison of Grass*, Howard Adams referred to the problem of "internalization." By this he meant that as a result of disintegrative processes inherent in colonization, Aboriginal peoples have subconsciously judged themselves against the standards of white society, often adopting what he called the White Idea. Part of this process entails internalizing or believing—swallowing the standards, judgements, expectations, and portrayals of the dominant white world. Many other Aboriginal writers have pointed to the causes and consequences of having struggled with externally imposed images about themselves and the policies that resulted from them. The results was/is often shame and rejection not only of the self but also of the similar other, i.e., other Aboriginal people.

A lot has changed in Aboriginal communities since Adams wrote *Prison of Grass*. A lot more Aboriginal people are aware of the whys and wherefores of their position in Canadian society. As more Aboriginal people grow in political awareness, they are less prone to judge themselves or act by outside standards. However, the damage has been extensive, and the problem of internalization of racist/sexist stereotypes may be at work in the area of violence.

One of the central questions we need to address is this: we know there has been violence by white men against Aboriginal women, but what do we make of the violence by Aboriginal men against Aboriginal women and children?

Too often the standard answer or reason given is that Aboriginal "offenders" were themselves abused and/or victims of society. There is no question that this answer may be partly true for some of the abusers, especially the young. However, it is hardly a complete answer and certainly should not be treated as the only or final answer to this problem.

There are indications of violence against women in Aboriginal societies prior to European contact. Many early European observations as well as original Indian legends (e.g., Wehschkehcha stories) point to the pre-existence of male violence against women. It should not be assumed that matriarchies necessarily prevented men from exhibiting oppressive behaviour toward women. There were individuals who acted against the best ideals of their cultures. Even today, all the emphasis on Mother Earth has not translated into full equality and safety of women.

There is little question, however, that European invasion exacerbated whatever the extent, nature or potential violence there was in original cultures. Neither is there much question that Aboriginal men have internalized white male devaluation of women. As one scholar observes:

> Deprived of their ancestral roles...men began to move into areas that had previously been the province of women, adopting some of the white attitudes toward women and treating them as inferiors rather than equals. (Fisher 13)

How might this internalization work with respect to violence generally and sexual violence specifically? Consider this: what happens to Aboriginal males who are exposed not only to pornography but also to the racist/sexist views of the "Indian" male as a violent "savage" and the Aboriginal female as a debased, sexually loose "squaw"?

Pornography in popular culture is affecting sexual attitudes and behaviour within Aboriginal communities. And given the lengthy and unrestricted mass media projection and objectification of "Indians" as violence-crazed savages, the problem of internalization should come as no surprise.

But it is disturbing. Aboriginal internalization of racist/macho views of Aboriginal men and women has contributed to violence generally and to sexual abuse specifically.

## Defense of Offenders Perpetuates Violence

It is difficult to say whether there is more sexual violence in Aboriginal communities than in white ones, for we know that sexual assault is also prevalent in white homes and neighborhoods. But I don't think we should defend either community in this regard. Rather, we should expend our energies in showing categorical disapproval appropriate to the crime and seeking solutions to what is an intolerable situation.

I have been troubled by a number of things relevant to the discussion on sexual violence. It is distressing to observe apathy by both Aboriginal and non-Aboriginal populations concerning sexual violence. The Aboriginal leadership in particular, must be called on to address this issue. Nor should the general public or governments walk away. The onus for change cannot rest solely on Aboriginal shoulders. White people in positions of power must share the burdens of finding answers, as they have been part of the problems.

I have also been concerned about the popularity of offering "cultural differences" as an explanation for sexual violence. When the horrifying story of the Lac Brochet teenager came out in the late 1980s, I was stunned by comments and attempted explanations around me. The numerous males who had attacked this 14-year-old girl (who had been repatriated against her will in the name of "culture" to begin with) were being defended with tortured and distorted notions of Aboriginal culture.

Erroneous cultural explanations have created enormous confusion in many people and on many issues. Besides the problem of typecasting Aboriginal cultures into a status list of "traits," 500 years of colonial history are being whitewashed into mere "cultural differences." Social conditions arising from societal negligence and policies have been explained away as "cultural." Problems having to do with racism and sexism have been blamed on Aboriginal culture. When cultural justifications are used on behalf of the sexually violent, we are seeing a gross distortion of the notion of culture and Aboriginal peoples. Men assault; cultures do not. Rape and violence against women were met with quick justice in original cultures. And if there is any culture that condones the oppression of women, it should be confronted to change. But sexual violence should never be associated with Aboriginal culture! It is an insult to healthy, functioning Aboriginal cultures to suggest so. Would one entertain using "racial differences" as an explanation for sexual assaults? Is it any less racist to resort to "cultural" ones?

As long as offenders are defended in the name of culture, they will continue to avoid taking personal responsibility for their actions. And this will only perpetuate the problem.

Equally troubling in the defense of offenders is popular advancement of the notion that men rape or assault because they were abused or are victims of society themselves. The implication is that as "victims," rapists and child molesters are not responsible for their actions and that therefore they should not be punished—or, if punished, "rehabilitation" and their "victimization" must take precedence over any consideration of the suffering or devastation they wreak on the real victims! Political oppression does not preclude the mandate to live with personal and moral responsibility within human communities. And if individuals are not capable of personal responsibility and moral choices (the things that make us human), then they are not fit for normal societal engagement and should be treated accordingly.

## Obstacles Facing Real Victims

And what do victims of sexual assault face within Aboriginal and mainstream communities? The following is a brief but realistic scenario. Aboriginal victims face obstacles that come with all small communities. There is a lack of privacy. Fear of further humiliation through community gossip and fear of ostracism and intimidation from supporters of the perpetrator may all be at work. Often a victim is confronted with disbelief, anger, and family denial or betrayal. Secrecy is expected and enforced. There is, in effect, censorship against those who would report sexual assault or even other forms of violence.

But if a victim does proceed with reporting, who will want to hear? And if she goes out of the community, she faces racism/sexism in the form of judgement, indifference or disbelief. Many non-Aboriginals in positions of social service or power either have little knowledge of what circumstances confront the victim or they do not take complainants seriously. The stereotype that Aboriginal women are sexually promiscuous is still quite prevalent. Also in many communities women cannot trust policemen since some policemen, especially in previous generation, were also doing the attacking! This is not to mention that the entire process of reporting is itself a formidable challenge.

If the victim goes as far as the courts, a whole new set of problems emerges. It is well-known that even for white middle-class women, rape trials are torturous with no guarantee of justice at the end of it all. If only ten per cent of white women report sexual assault, then considerably less than ten per cent of Aboriginal victims report. And of course, the conviction rate is dismal.

The other problem, a problem I believe perpetuates sexual violence, is the fact that the courts are wantonly lenient with regard to sentencing. As a rule, thieves and minor drug dealers receive stiffer penalties than do child molesters, rapists or even rapist-murders. This in itself is a chilling message regarding societal devaluation of human dignity. Many Aboriginal communities have expressed concern that courts are especially lenient with Aboriginal offenders who assault other Aboriginal people. The easy parole system, along with lenient sentencing, further sets up Aboriginal victims.

If the victim succeeds in sending her assailant to prison, she may expect quick retaliation. Sexual offenders may come out of prison within three weeks, perhaps six months. These men usually go straight back to their small settlements and proceed to wreak further violence and intimidation.

When all is said and done, what of the victim? Where is the help for her? Where is the concern for *her* rehabilitation?

The whole judicial process reflects privileged, white male definitions and experience. It also reflects tremendous naïveté—naïveté often found in white liberal social workers, criminologists and justices. These lenient sentences are consistent with the growing heroification of rapists and child molesters as "victims." Today there is persistent sympathy for sexual offenders with little, if any, corresponding concern for the real victims. It is a bizarre situation.

## Questions About the Causes of Sexual Violence

Given the popularity of presenting rapists as victims, and that such a notion has not in any way resolved the problem—and in fact may be perpetuating sexual violence—is it not time for new and hard questions here? While it is sociologically apparent that poverty and marginalization can play havoc in a community, it is difficult to accept without question that being a so-called victim causes one to be a victimizer. If that were true, millions of women would take to victimizing. Further, if poor social conditions necessarily breed "offenders," this raises more questions than it answers. Why, when the chips are down, do men turn on women and children? What are we saying here about the nature of man? What are we saying of Aboriginal men—that when conditions of oppression, poverty or abuse exist, they cannot think of anything else but to turn on innocent women and children? And this should then be met with sympathy? And what about the other statistics—what about, all the poor men and abused men who do not turn to violence?

Sexual violence is global and universal. Men of all backgrounds, cultures, classes and economic status assault women. Indeed, history is replete with examples of rich, powerful, and privileged men who abused women and children. This suggests that the origin of sexual violence is considerably more disturbing than we might like to admit. Maybe it is not as mysterious as we make it out to be.

Most adults who violate others do so from a place of awareness and choice. As one article on child sexual abuse, written by a group of concerned Aboriginal women, state: "Offenders are aware of what they are doing and they know it is wrong" (Aboriginal Women's Council of Saskatchewan 90). I believe sexual violence is best explained by sexism and misogyny, which are nurtured in our society. North American popular culture feeds off the objectification and degradation of women. Women are presented as sexual playthings who must conform to male needs. Stereotypes of female sexuality are concocted as a rationalization for violence. It is about male maintenance of power, but it is a conscious and deliberate form of power, not one that is necessarily caused by "abuse" or other traumas. Obviously power brings all sorts of advantages. It has been in the interests of men to keep women down. Society supports all this with its tolerance of violence against women. The criminal justice system reflects its bias through its laws and judgements.

Rape in any culture and by any standards is warfare against women. And the degree to which any community tolerates sexual violence is an indication of concurrence in this warfare against women.

The point is, we may never know for certain what exactly causes sexual violence. But whether we know or not, we should never use an "explanation"—be it psychological, personal, or political—as absolution for the offender. We should never justify or tolerate sexual violence. The criminal justice system must do its duty and serve "justice" not only because justice is essential to a victim's healing but also because a message must be given that sexual violence is insupportable. Justice and concern for rehabilitation must not be seen as mutually exclusive.

The other point, which is perhaps more to the point, is this: Why all this concern with finding reasons or explanation for what causes men to be rapists and child molesters? Given that we may never know, should we not turn our attention to the real victims?

## Towards Prevention

Strategies to reduce and eliminate violence would, of course, include addressing the issues that contribute to violence. Perhaps we can approach the strategies under three headings: prevention, services for victims, and judicial action with respect to offenders.

I believe a preventive approach is necessary. How can we ever stem the tide of all this violence? It surely will not happen overnight. Meanwhile, we have young people to attend to. If we can reach the Aboriginal youth, we may see some improvement on a number of fronts. The first set of recommendations concerns young people. Obviously a multifaceted, comprehensive approach is required. Socio-economic revitalization is a must. Human beings need to have meaning in their lives; one of the avenues for meaning lies in economic bases/activities. This issue of the economy is crucial to young people who are caught within a socio-cultural vacuum. They are looking for vocational opportunities in a world that has stolen their land-based ways yet has not prepared them for urbanization and industrialization.

The miseducation of Aboriginal youth must be address. One of the enduring legacies of colonization is the mistreatment of Aboriginal history and issues in schools. Schools must stop presenting Aboriginal history, cultures, peoples and issues in biased, ethnocentric or racist ways. Along with correcting the social studies aspect of the curriculum, schools must make every effort to stop alienating Aboriginal youths by providing skills and knowledge relevant to both cultures. Also, attitudes toward Aboriginal culture itself must change. Aboriginal cultures should not be presented only in terms of the past (often stereotyped at that). Young people often feel paralyzed: how can they move toward the future if their culture is defined in terms of the past? Young people need help in clarifying what is heritage and what is culture. They also need to be reassured that it is within Aboriginal cultural definitions to change and to make bridges from the past to the future. Aboriginal young people should not have to feel that in order to be loyal to their personal identities they have to sacrifice vocational choices of the future.

Another large problem in many Aboriginal communities is that of boredom. It is a problem that has not received the attention it should. Boredom is often the cause of a lot of difficulties young people get into including drugs, alcohol, and sexual experimentation, mob behaviour, violence, and suicide. Community leaders must make every effort to provide quality recreation for young people. Funding and resources must be made available for the development of recreation facilities, sports programs, and other projects. I have often wondered, what is everybody waiting for? Why haven't there been massive efforts to provide recreation facilities for youth in Aboriginal communities? There is so much untapped potential for excellence in our youth. Every time I watch any national or international sports event, I think of all the Aboriginal youths who could be participating. Is it not time to move in that direction?

With respect to sex and violence, education and sexual enlightenment may be our best hope for the future. One of the biggest problems in Aboriginal homes and communities is lack of quality sex education. As a rule, parents and other adults are not providing sex education to their young. Children and adolescents are left to their own devices and to the influences of popular cultures, misguided peers, or even abusers to learn about sex. In this sense, sexual problems are recycled. Aboriginal children and teenagers are desperately in need of solid sex education. Schools (preferably in cooperation with community initiatives and programs) should step in by providing qualitative sex education to children and teenagers. Such education must include not only the physiological aspects of sex and sexuality but must also promote respect for persons. There must be special emphasis on respect to female persons, respect for each other's sexuality, and self-respect. There must also be education about safe sex, birth control, pregnancy, reproductive choice, and sexual responsibility. Schools must also provide education on drugs, alcohol, smoking, glue-sniffing, etc.

A special word needs to be said about Aboriginal teenage girls. Little has been documented thus far, but many of the stories of sexual abuse reveal that Aboriginal women were often attacked as teenagers. Teenage girls with little or no sex education in an environment conducive to alcohol abuse and violence are particularly vulnerable to adult male sexual seductions or attacks. Rape can devastate teenagers. There is growing documentation that following sexual assault, teenagers turn to substance abuse, prostitution, self-mutilation and/or suicide. They can also get pregnant and/or contract sexually tran-smitted diseases. The suicide rate is five times the national average in the 15 to 24 age group among Aboriginal youth. One book analyzing the death of an Ojibwa community in northwestern Ontario links female suicide with sexual assaults (Shkilnyk 46-48).

Teenagers are perhaps among the most susceptible to sexual assault. They are sexually sensitive yet immature; they are often unmindful of what adults are capable of doing to them. This is another reason why silence must end. Often, adults who know who the offenders are keep such information from others. If there could be disclosure, exposure, and open discussion between victims and other youth, it would help protect the unsuspecting. Adults such as parents, grandparents, teachers, ministers, counselors and so forth must take special care to protect, educate, and prepare teenagers about sex and sexual violence. And if violence takes place, there must be emotional, psychological, medical, and legal support services in place. All Aboriginal youth should also have access to counselling services. They also need safe houses for those times when their homes or communities do not feel safe. Some youth may be in need of psychological or psychiatric services—these too should be made accessible to them. There should also be some attention to young people's spiritual needs. Aboriginal young men and women have dreams and hopes for their futures and their wellbeing. Every effort must be made by all parties concerned to protect these young people and to facilitate their aspirations. I think Aboriginal communities could organize conferences, guest speakers, and seminars that could address their needs as well as present role models.

If young people enjoy their daily existence, and if they can have dreams that are attainable, I do believe their daily activities would change substantially. I believe they would respond to a creative environment and move away from destructive influences and destructive behaviours. If we wish to eliminate violence, we have to substitute it with constructive, creative, and meaningful alternatives. Our children deserve nothing less.

## Better Responses for Victims

The silent suffering of girls and women who have been subjected to rape and other assaults demands immediate attention. Silence must end. Support systems must be created. Aboriginal victims of violence need safe houses, rape crisis centres, counseLling services and clinics. They need family and institutional support. They need therapists who are skilled in dealing with post-traumatic stress syndrome. They need a society that cares about them and that values their safety, their dignity and their rehabilitation. Laws must be changed and enforced. The whole judicial process of dealing with complaints of violence must be changed.[1]

It cannot be emphasized enough how very desperately longterm qualitative counselling/therapy and community programs are needed. Rape and early childhood abuse cause lifetime devastation. As concerned Aboriginal women put it, "sexual abuse is a reality and a hell that must no longer be ignored.... We have felt the pain and anger ... for damaging a child's life forever" (Aboriginal Women's Council of Saskatchewan 90). An indication that Aboriginal women are suffering from post-traumatic stress syndrome can be seen in the level of female violence, alcoholism and extent of incarceration.

Studies show that rural Aboriginal women move to urban centres to escape family or community problems. Most Aboriginal communities are small, making the situation that much more difficult for victims. Apathy and lack of leadership or family support effectively chase victims from their own communities. This should not have to happen. No one should ever have to leave home in order to feel safe!

The Aboriginal leadership at the federal, provincial, and regional levels must take a strong stand against violence, and certainly against sexual violence. The message and modeling must be clear and firm that sexual violence against women, teenagers, and children is inexcusable, intolerable, and insupportable. In effect, the Aboriginal leadership must take the initiative in raising the consciousness of communities about the destructiveness inherent in violence. Violence must be raised as the social problem it is, a problem requiring urgent attention. Forums for discussion, education, and information must be set up to facilitate awareness and social concern. Every effort must be made by the leadership to prevent abuse and to help those who have been abused.

All Aboriginal and non-Aboriginal agencies involved with Aboriginal family problems (like hospitals, police, lawyers, judges, social workers, therapists, child care organizations, etc.) should be required to attend workshops and/or conferences geared to addressing the issue of sexual violence. Again, the Aboriginal leadership must initiate such forums; the government must provide the resources.

Aboriginal women must be free to address unwieldy and unpopular issues such as violence, equality, patriarchy, political leadership, etc. They also must receive support to create forums through which they can gather to discuss issues of mutual concern. But there must be recognition of issues/concerns that pertain to First Nations women and those that pertain to Métis women.

To these ends, Aboriginal women need their own organizations and must be funded separately from the larger, umbrella organization.

As discussed earlier, a large portion of the root of our problems lies with our colonization. Again, Aboriginal leaders and educators must make every effort to facilitate forums for discussions on the legacies of colonization in our lives, in our homes and communities. Perhaps Paulo Freire's ideas on the "pedagogy of the oppressed" could be adopted. Raising the consciousness of the Aboriginal grassroots is one of the important tasks in moving toward wholeness and can be seen as "service" to victims of violence. People need to understand the disintegrative process of colonization; they need to know the consequences of having been defined outside of themselves, of being powerless. Aboriginal people need to understand the institutional forces of invasion in their worlds and what that has done to their lands and economies, their relationships, their cultural values and symbols, their self-determination and self-confidence. They also need to believe that restoration is possible. They need to believe that they can act to make changes and that by acting on issues they are empowering themselves. People may best be able to make changes once they can articulate the places of invasion in their lives and in their histories.

We may need years to help Aboriginal peoples understand and resolve the violence; meanwhile, we must deal with the everyday realities of it. Even if we agree about what causes sexual violence, we could not immediately, if ever, end it. Besides the social, economic and educational programs we can pursue, we are forced to look at the criminal justice system with respect to protection and justice.

## Victims, the "Offender," and the Criminal Justice System

In terms of change in the judicial process, it would be redundant to repeat the extensive and generally excellent recommendations offered in the Manitoba *Aboriginal Justice Inquiry Report* (1991). Anyone working in this area must consult this report. I also recommend the handbook *The Spirit Weeps*, published by the Nechi Institute (Martens), which offers useful information on the characteristics and dynamics of incest and child sexual abuse with an Aboriginal perspective.

The criminal justice system is, of course, a whole field of study. I wish only to emphasize certain (and to me more bothersome) aspects of it, namely, its sympathetic posture toward sexual offenders and other hardcore violent criminals. Since the mid-1960s, the criminal justice system has increasingly exhibited wanton leniency in the trying and sentencing of sexual offenders. Such leniency amounts to negligence. What feeble laws exist regarding sexual assault are routinely diluted by the judicial process and decisions. In the case of Aboriginal people against Aboriginal people, victims of aggravated sexual assault (the majority being female, a great number being teenagers) are set up to live lives of silent pain, fear and continual victimization. For example, the leader of those gang rapes against the Lac Brochet girl received only four years—with virtual apologies from the judge! I believe such an irresponsible sentence makes a mockery of all women and certainly of the girl's trauma and what will surely be her lifelong post-traumatic stress syndrome.

Obviously, there are no easy answers. Nor am I suggesting any simplistic solutions, but I do believe that we have so over-complicated the issues surrounding violence that the laws and the exercising of these laws have become absurd and have played into the hands of child molesters, rapists, and calculating murderers. This has resulted in the devaluation of human dignity in the whole system. Property and liquor/drug offences mean more to the system than violation of one's person.

I do suggest the corrections system, be it Aboriginal or mainstream, take the following direction. A dual structure should be set up to accommodate the types of crimes and criminals being addressed. Distinctions must be made between non-violent and violent offences. There is a world of difference, say, stealing a VCR and brutalizing a human being.

People committing certain non-violent crimes could become involved in community-oriented programs instead of jails to compensate for their offenses. Here, "meet-the-victim" models might apply. Also, we must draw on alternative-to-jail programs that are in existence in Canada, the United States and elsewhere.

There are also various degrees and forms of violence, and the system of punishment must make a distinction between a slap, a minor brawl, and gross violence such as battering, stabbing, and shooting, or willful and callous violence such as sexual assault and premeditated murder.

Those involved in minor scuffles should receive help via community-based education and renewal programs. Personal, family, and community counseling with an educational and/or therapeutic focus might be considered.

Those involved in gross violence should receive stiff custody penalties along with strong education/therapy programs.

Those involved in gross and willful crimes should receive very lengthy jail sentences and, in specific cases, should also be permanently removed from their communities. In cases of brutalization, rape, and ruthless murder, removal may be the only effective measure of protection for victims and their families, especially in small and/or remote settlements. Indeed, many northern communities have requested removal and stronger penalties.

All forms of sexual assault are on a continuum of violence; therefore, most forms must fall under the category of violence. Those, including boys, who commit "minor" sexual offences must be considered potentially dangerous.

Those who commit violence and plead no-sentencing on the basis of insanity, drunkenness, youthfulness, or even poverty, must be placed in custody away from their victims. The law must also change from "not guilty by reason of insanity" to "guilty but insane" and proceed to sentence such parties to custody appropriate to their crime and condition.

As well, the *Young Offenders Act* must be changed. I think it is atrocious that a 13-year-old can brutally kill two women and be sentenced to only three years.[2] There is no question that our colonial, negligent, violence-crazed, misogynist popular culture is culpable for violent (usually male) children; still, innocent people should not be sitting ducks for such violence.

There are degrees of youth and knowledge. There are large differences even between two 12-year-olds. Surely, the law (and psychiatrists) must profile and reflect these differences. The law must also reflect the changing times—children today are must more street-wise than those of yesteryear.

On every level of sentencing, whether in the non-violent or violent category, there must, of course, be extensive efforts towards rehabilitation. A word again must be said about rehabilitation. Often, lenient sentences have been promoted on this basis. The problem here is that there has been a blanket assumption that justice and rehabilitation are mutually exclusive. Yet statistics show that sexual offenders, for example, are rarely "rehabilitated."

But the point that seems to be missed in this discussion is this: primary consideration as to sentencing should not be whether the offender is going to be rehabilitated. Rather, the primary consideration should be justice on behalf of the victim. Interrelated with concern for justice must be an unequivocal message to the offender and to society that sexual violence is not acceptable and that it is punishable by law.

While I support the ideals of rehabilitation, I believe that it is incumbent upon any criminal justice system first to dispense justice, then to concern itself with rehabilitation. But rehabilitation must never be at the expense of justice.All ancient cultures have had traditions of justice, and Aboriginal cultures no less so. Aboriginal cultures used a range of penalties, depending on the nature of the offence; ridicule, shunning, payment, or violence in kind (in the tradition of "an eye for an eye"). We may disagree with some ancient measure, but we cannot deny that justice is essential to the human psyche. There is no peace or healing without justice. Simply on the basis of providing therapeutic service to victims, offenders must be made accountable.

But places of confinement/custody should have extensive and mandatory rehabilitation programs. Such programs should incorporate not only personal therapy but education with respect to decolonization and spiritual/cultural renewal and a sociological grasp of sexism and its relationship to violence against women. And, of course, there should be longterm rehabilitation programs for victims and their families and communities. The destruction inherent in any violence ripples widely into the families and communities of victims.

I am aware that a number of community programs have been developed that promote offender-victim reconciliation. I have read with careful interest the Aboriginal Justice Inquiry's report on the Hollow Water Resource Group of Manitoba. As the Aboriginal Justice Inquiry describes it:

> Not only does it provide rehabilitation to the offender, and support and comfort to the victim, but it provides a mechanism to heal and restore harmony to the families and the community.... The Hollow Water model was created to protect people against repetition of the offence and to prevent any new incidents of abuse. (495)

I have to admit, on paper it sounds promising. And those who developed it must be commended for their initiative, courage and vision. But since it is so new and does seem to operate on assumptions of rehabilitation, some further questions are raised. It is perhaps too early to tell whether it is as constructive as it sounds. A number of questions come to mind: Are victims in small communities really free to become part of these meet-the-offender programs? How young are the victims? What is the nature of the violence? Are victims agreeing to these models as a result of social pressure and lack of other choices? How are they being affected by all this? Do they have enough political and social awareness to be able to make a choice with such programs? Are offenders really being "rehabilitated"? And should this be the primary goal for helpers, families of victims, justices and communities? Is it possible that offenders use such programs to get out of sentencing and other responsibilities? I have some difficulty with the attention given to sexual offenders. Might there be other programs besides having to meet their assailants that would be perhaps more healing and less stressful for victims?

Calls for services for women often contain the phrase "culturally appropriate." While the principle behind this phrase is supportable, there is a need for clearer definitions of what is meant. I am afraid that there is some notion in society at large that it is "cultural" for Aboriginal women to tolerate violence at all costs in the name of "family" or "tradition." This is reminiscent of some churches that admonish women never to leave "the sanctity of marriage," even if the women and children are being battered and/or sexually assaulted. Care must be taken that violence of women and children never be advanced in the name of "culture."

Family counselling must be encouraged but women must not be made to feel they have to tolerate violence in the name of family or culture. Family means that men must take responsibility and get involved in counselling.

Questions remain as to notions of healing, notions of rehabilitation, and the value of emphasizing family and community unity at the possible expense of victims, many of them children. Studies on abuse of children show that families can be the most dangerous places for them to be. We must take care that we do not advance notions about the unity of families in any formulaic way because we know, unfortunately, that families are not inherently safe. Each situation must be carefully screened.

## Room for Research Questions and Answers

No one has the final answers; we barely have embryonic suggestions. The subject of violence, and particularly sexual violence, is extremely difficult, and made more so because it goes to the heart of personal, family, and societal politics. It is also a subject of emotional intensity. While we are beginning to have access to more information and beginning to gain better understanding of the causes and effects of violence, there is room for continued research at all levels.

I think, though, that the focus should move toward prevention, comprehension, support and protection on behalf of the victims. Research monies and energy should be spent there. Services, programs, counseling and longterm therapy for victims should be addressed.

Several times I have referred to post-traumatic stress syndrome. We know that sexual violence causes lifetime problems. Research on the longterm effects of sexual violence must be pursued.

On this note, I wish to caution about some standard usage of terms and notions. Words such as "healing," "counseling," and "family violence" are used a lot. The cumulative effect of using such terms gives the impression that sexual violence causes no great harm and that it is easy to fix. Just go for counseling and that pain will go away. "Healing" is used so often that it risks promoting the idea that victims of sexual violence can be easily healed. There is every indication that sexual violence is extremely traumatic and destructive and that these effects are long-term. Indeed, is it possible to "heal" sexual violence? This is not to suggest we should not try, but it is to question the all too hasty use of such terms. We run the risk of trivializing sexual violence by using descriptions and terms that couch and soften the impact.

Words like "offender," rather than rapist or child molester, serve to minimize the calculated nature of sexual attacks. Phrases like "family" or "domestic violence" also serve to twist the issue: women and children are experiencing brutality to a staggering degree, but it is being reduced and ignored as "domestic" or "family" violence. In relation to this, the word "incest" is also often misused. Incest means that there is consensual sexual intercourse between two people who are too closely related to be married. Sexual attacks on children by male relatives is not incest; it is rape and child molestation. Children, teenagers, and women are not consenting to have sex with their relatives; they are being attacked or in some way coerced into unwanted sexual activity.

I believe research would show that as long as softened, couched terms continue to be used, steps to address this monstrous problem will continue to be slow.

Research specific to Métis families, concerns and data is very much needed. There is such a dearth of specific data on Métis people that no one can even agree as to the population of Métis. How are we going to strategize to eliminate violence unless we have more precise information to work from?

With respect to justice and "offenders," research into the viability of old notions in new models is also required. We need to follow up on projects such as the Hollow Water Resource Group.

## Conclusion

As most of us know, violence has long been rampant in many Aboriginal communities. I know too that we have shied away from dealing with the issue partly because we have had to fend off racism and stereotypes. But given the seriousness of the situation we must confront the problem(s). If we do not, there will be self-government without selves to govern, for people are leaving their places of birth to escape the violence. And it is possible to deal with these issues in an intelligent manner, without having to resort to racist stereotypes.

Finally, lest I be misunderstood, I must emphasize that I am painfully aware of the criminal justice system's dismal record with respect to Aboriginal peoples! I grew up watching police abuse my parents' generation. I saw police rough up and pick up my mother, aunts, and uncles for no reason whatsoever. This generation could not defend itself in the courts because of language differences, discrimination, and/or poverty. But I also saw or heard of police and courts neglecting Aboriginal victims of Aboriginal violence. This is the ultimate form of racism. It is this latter fact that must be addressed as much as the former. It is not time for us to take a stand against violence in our midst?

In my community, we were all victims of colonization but we did not all turn to violence. Further, why should Aboriginal victims of Aboriginal violence bear the ultimate brunt of colonization/racism and negligence of the criminal justice system? My hope, of course, is that our communities will be renewed, that people will find support and restoration.

### Notes

[1]For recommendations on these, see the *Report of the Aboriginal Justice Inquiry of Manitoba*.

[2]A Manitoba case several years ago.

### References

Aboriginal Women's Council of Saskatchewan. "Child Sexual Abuse: Words from Concerned Women." *Canadian Woman Studies/les cahiers de la femme* 10 (2,3) (Summer/Fall 1989): 90-91.

Adams, Howard. *Prison of Grass: Canada from a Native Point of View*. Toronto: New Press, 1975.

Martens, Tony. *Characteristics and Dynamics of Incest and Child Sexual Abuse: The Spirit Weeps*. Edmonton: Nechi Institute, 1988.

Child Protection Centre. Winnipeg, 1987.

Fisher, Dexter. Ed. *The Third Woman: Minority Women Writers of the U.S.* Boston: Houghton Mifflin, 1980.

Freire, Paolo. *Pedagogy of the Oppressed*. New York: Continuum, 1993.

Ontario Women's Native Association. *Breaking Free: A Proposal For Change to Aboriginal Family Violence*. Thunder Bay, December 1989.

*Report of the Aboriginal Justice Inquiry of Manitoba*. Winnipeg: Public Inquiry into the Administration of Justice and Aboriginal People, 1991.

Shkilnyk, Anastasia M. *A Poison Stronger than Love: The Destruction of the Ojibway Community*. New Haven: Yale University Press, 1985.

Young, T .Kue. *Health Care and Cultural Change: The Indian Experience in the Central Sub-Arctic*. Toronto: University of Toronto, 1988.

# Domestic Violence and the Experiences of Rural Women in East Central Saskatchewan

Diane J. Forsdick Martz
and Deborah Bryson Saraurer

The roots of this study begin in 1998 with one woman's voice on the other end of a Mental Health Office telephone line. She insisted that there must be a group in our health district for survivors of domestic violence. Each agency that she called told her that the closest group for survivors was in Saskatoon, 100 kilometers away. She did not own a car, she could not afford to take the bus and, as a result, the services in the city were of no value to her.

She kept running into a brick wall, but she kept on calling. She met with a mental health therapist who pronounced her free of any mental illness but in need of support from other women who had experienced domestic violence. This was exactly what the woman had been insisting all along. Her determination spurred a mental health therapist to call the Saskatoon Family Support Centre and, with their help, a support group for women who had survived domestic violence was offered in our community.

The response was overwhelming. Thirteen women registered in the first group within three hours. Women needed to talk to each other, they wanted to learn, and they wanted to stop violence.

Mental health workers were the catalyst that brought other interested people together to form the Partners for Rural Family Support. The Partners consist of professionals, private citizens, and survivors themselves who are committed to finding innovative ways to provide services for the families who are experiencing domestic violence. The formation of this group was the first public acknowledgement that domestic violence was a problem in the Centre Plains Health District.

Family violence and women abuse moved into the public policy sphere in the 1980s (McLaughlin and Church). In Saskatchewan, "safe shelter staff in the larger urban areas were at the fore-front of establishing services for abused women, creating residences, providing counselling services, educating the public and the government about these issues and pressing for recognition and response to the needs of spousal assault victims" (Turner 188-189).

Although services are now much more available in urban centres, this availability often has little benefit for women in rural Saskatchewan. Counselling in a large centre 100 kilometers away is not useful to a woman who cannot reach that centre, because she has no vehicle, no money for gas or the bus, and/or no childcare.

Similarly, a safe shelter 100 kilometers away may not be of much help to an abused woman on a farm in a rural area. Women from rural Saskatchewan who try to access these shelters are often turned away because they are full. Existing services are stretched to the limit serving the needs of urban women. As a result rural women have limited access to services in urban centres.

During the past decades government agencies have centralized services in urban centres and as a consequence reduced the level of service available to rural people. For example, the Department of Social Services has office hours in our rural area only one day a week. The Family Protection Worker comes to rural areas when reports are made. Social Service workers are not a visible presence in rural areas. Legal Aid is located in larger urban centres and phone calls to the RCMP after office hours and on weekends are routed through Regina.

There is also dissonance between geographic boundary lines used by various government departments. This can cause survivors of domestic violence great stress as they try to sort out the system. Police boundaries differ from Social Service boundaries which differ from Health District boundaries which differ from Legal Aid boundaries. It can all be very confusing to women who are trying to navigate a system so that they can create a new and safe life for themselves and their children.

Over and over again we hear from rural women that existing services are not adequate. They want services that are close to home, immediate and will allow them to maintain a stable existence for themselves and their children. It is a full time job for women to deal with all of the different agencies and services. It is always a costly process both economically and emotionally.

Women choose to live in rural Saskatchewan because their support systems are here. Family, schools, careers and friends are important to the meaning of women's lives. Women have a right to live free from fear or violence in their own communities. To isolate women from their support systems, however frail they may be, is to disregard their experiences and their voices once again.

There are many myths that sustain gender identities in rural society. One of these myths is that domestic violence does not happen in a close knit rural community. Studies show lower rates of domestic violence in rural areas than in urban areas. However, rural women report that that they believe women abuse to be as common in rural areas as in urban areas (McLaughlin and Church). Fear and isolation may reduce reported incidences of violence in rural areas.

Until recently, many rural communities were reluctant to acknowledge that domestic violence exists in their communities. Rural attitudes are seen as conservative and slow to change. These attitudes often involve very traditional views of the appropriate roles of women and men. As a result, women who seek support in dealing with violence in their lives must break with community norms (McLaughlin and Church).

Bringing an adequate level of support to rural areas for victims and survivors of domestic violence is a challenge. Existing programs often have an urban bias and must meet criteria of cost effectiveness usually based on numbers served. A new paradigm of service delivery needs to be developed for rural areas.

Programming offered in rural areas must consider the lower population densities, the lack of centralized communication systems, and rural value systems. Programming for rural women can also build on the strengths of rural areas. Easier access to informal support networks, pride in self-sufficiency, and community cohesiveness all offer opportunities for communities to plan and implement new services. Programs in rural areas are more highly visible and the smaller scale of these services may make it easier for agencies and interested groups to co-operate to design new and innovative types of programs (McLaughlin and Church).

The Partners for Rural Family Support are working together to advocate with women who stand up for rural families as they challenge the myths around violence in rural areas. This research project, Domestic Violence and the Experiences of Rural Women in East Central Saskatchewan is one of the first steps in honouring rural women's experiences and their hard won knowledge about domestic violence in rural communities. This project is an important step in telling the truth about domestic violence and the impact that it has in rural society.

In this research project, rural women told us about their experiences of domestic violence and their successes and frustrations trying to deal with the abuse. The women also told us how they would like to see things change and offered many excellent ideas on how to make those changes happen. The information from this study will be used to create an action plan to put in place a much higher level of service for rural women and their families.

## Methodology

This study was conducted in East Central Saskatchewan in an area centresed around Humboldt located 100 kilometers east of Saskatoon, Saskatchewan. The women interviewed lived in the area at the time they were experiencing domestic violence. Seventeen of the women interviewed lived in the Central Plains Health District, whose head office is in Humboldt. Two of the women lived in the Living Sky Health District, whose head office is in Lanigan, Saskatchewan. At the time of the interview, some of the women had left the region to live in other centres where they would be safe. Central Plains Health District and Living Sky Health District are both rural areas. The largest centre is Humboldt with a population of 5000 people. The dominant economic activity in the region is agriculture and agriculture-related industry.

The Health Districts deliver hospital, health care and mental health services to their regions. Social Services are delivered to the region from Saskatoon and Yorkton, 100 kilometers and 270 kilometers away, respectively. The boundary between the social services districts is located ten kilometers east of Humboldt, splitting a historic cultural region and confounding the delivery of services to women who are dealing with spousal abuse.

## Research Design

The research was structured as participatory action research. The research problem was identified by the Partners for Rural Family Support (PRFS). PRFS, a group of service providers, concerned citizens and survivors of domestic violence, was formed to provide services for women in the Humboldt region who had experienced domestic violence.

Participatory action research is intended to create change (Weber), and PRFS, is committed to changing the way the community deals with domestic violence. The outcomes of this research will form the basis for action by the Partners for Rural Family Support as they work to develop innovative services and programs to support families in rural Saskatchewan.

The research design was based on two methodologies: a semi-structured interview of 19 survivors of domestic violence and three focus groups, two with survivors of domestic violence and one with service providers in the region. The interviews addressed the experiences of this group of women as they attempted to cope with their abusive relationships and sought services and support to enable them to free themselves of the violence.

## Sampling

The participants in this study were self-selected. Potential participants were contacted in three ways: 30 women were approached directly, letters were sent to Living Sky Health District, doctor's offices and the George Bailey Centre (a drug and alcohol abuse facility) and the research was publicized in regional newspaper articles. Sixteen women who were directly contacted agreed to participate, two women came forward after the contact with Living Sky Health District and one woman volunteered after reading about the research in the newspaper. The women who were interviewed were also given the opportunity to participate in the focus groups. Ten women participated in two focus groups.

One criteria for inclusion in this study was that the women had to be safe from violence. Fifteen of the nineteen women had left their abusive relationships. One women was in the process of leaving, but was in no danger, and three women were living with their formerly abusive partners. The women ranged in age from their late 20s to mid-50s. There were no Aboriginal women or recent immigrant women represented. The focus group of service providers was drawn from the Partners for Rural Family Support Group. Six service providers participated.

Each woman participated in a qualitative, unstructured interview based on a schedule of questions.[1] The questions were developed by a committee consisting of the two principal researchers and three survivors of domestic violence. This qualitative methodology allows the researcher to develop a much deeper understanding of the experience of spousal abuse and the subsequent experience of making the transition out of the abusive relationship.

Interviews were conducted by a mental health therapist with extensive counselling experience with women who have been abused. The initial interview lasted between 1.5 and 2.5 hours. These interviews were transcribed and the women met with the interviewer a second time to edit, correct or add information to the transcript. Interestingly, the second interview often lasted as long as the first interview and in one case it was longer.

In a number of cases, women found the interviews very difficult. The interviews brought back experiences and feelings the women thought they had dealt with. For many women, the process of reading the transcripts of their interviews was very difficult and took a long time. Some women had to read them over a period of days. Some felt the transcripts didn't convey how bad things really were.

As a precautionary measure, Mental Health Services in Humboldt agreed to immediately see any women who encountered problems as a result of the interviews. A number of the women chose to re-enter counselling.

The women who chose to participate were hopeful that their experiences would bring some benefits for other women who were experiencing family violence. One woman stated that being part of the research project was a big turning point in her life. She could now turn the pages and finally move on. Many women expressed their desire to get involved so they could help others.

## Domestic Violence Definitions

Domestic violence in this study is defined as violence against women and children by intimate partners and other family members (UNICEF). In this study, the term domestic violence is used interchangeably with the term spousal abuse.

Domestic violence is usually associated with physical violence, however it can manifest itself in many types of abuse including psychological and verbal abuse, financial abuse, sexual abuse and spiritual abuse or it may result from neglect. The definitions of the various types of abuse are extracted from Walter DeKeseredy and Linda MacLeod.

- *Psychological abuse* includes behaviour that intends to intimidate and control women. It may mean withdrawing affection, keeping track of everything a person does, making harassing phone calls or visits, uttering threats, destroying prized possessions, hurting or killing pets and making suicide threats. *Verbal abuse* is a form of psychological abuse. It often includes constant criticism and name-calling. It also includes unjust blaming, false accusations about loyalties or sexual actions and repeated threats of violence against another person—the victim's friends, relatives and/or pets.

•*Physical abuse* includes slapping, punching, kicking, biting, shoving, choking, or using a weapon to threaten or injure. These behaviours can result in death.

•*Sexual abuse* means forcing someone against their will to perform sexual acts or to endure pain or injury during sex. Sexual abuse can also occur when an infected person infects his or her partner with a sexually transmitted disease such as HIV.

•*Financial or economic abuse* occurs when the abused person is denied access to the family's money, and say in what will be bought and money for her or his own use. It may also involve denial of access to health care or employment.

•*Spiritual abuse* means the imposition of beliefs on others in order to control them. Spiritual abuse includes belittling or attacking someone's spiritual beliefs or preventing them from practicing their religion. Spiritual abuse can also include ritual abuse.

•*Neglect* is a form of abuse most commonly experienced by young children, elderly people and disabled persons. It can include long-term neglect that may result in physical ailments as well as sporadic neglect used as punishment. Neglect by a husband or partner is a real and ongoing threat for some elderly or disabled women. In addition, women have reported neglect when they were recovering from an illness or when they were pregnant or had recently given birth.

Domestic violence is usually but not exclusively carried out by males who are in positions of trust, intimacy and power. At the beginning of the interview, the women were asked to describe the abuse they had experienced. Women described abuse by their husbands, boyfriends, fathers, fathers-in-law, sons, mothers, and in one case, by their mother-in-law. A small number described themselves as abusers as well.

In this study all 19 women interviewed identified verbal and psychological abuse in their relationships. Sixteen out of the 19 described occasions of physical abuse and six described incidents of sexual abuse. Most women experienced multiple types of the abuse described above.

### *Verbal Abuse*

The women in the study reported that the sequence of abuse started with verbal abuse and escalated into other types of abuse. Verbal abuse started early in the relationship. In many cases it was present right from the beginning and happened every day. It is an insidious form of abuse because it leaves no obvious marks and it is hard to define and report, leaving the woman feeling mentally destabilized and powerless (UNICEF). For some, ongoing psychological violence may be more unbearable than physical brutality (UNICEF) and leaves scars that require long-term treatment.

The constant humiliation encountered by victims of psychological abuse destroys the victim's sense of self worth and reduces her ability to resist control by the abuser (Wallace). As part of the humiliation, many women endured constant criticism and name calling.

*I can't tell you how many times a day I was called a stupid bitch, I never did anything right.*

*One day he would say the house was such a mess that he was embarrassed to bring people over, then the next day when I'd be busy cleaning ... it wasn't right because I should be spending more time with him.*

*Every time something went wrong ... it was my fault. I wasn't a good enough wife, everybody else had a good wife around and I was supposed to know absolutely everything and be able to respond to all needs.*

Verbal abuse also meant criticism of the women's personal appearance.

*His idea of making things better was if I dress nicer, if I put on makeup every day, if I did my hair nice everyday, he would be proud to walk down the street with me.*

*I was pregnant and sick with the flu and he made me stay in the bedroom with the door closed so he didn't have to look at me.*

### *Psychological Abuse*

Psychological abuse was present for most of the women in the study. Like other forms of abuse, psychological abuse is based on control. Women were not allowed to go places alone or had to account for their activities at all times.

*He always had to phone and if I was not there when he phoned, he'd get mad about that.*

*He always had to know where I was and what I was doing.... He would drive around where I worked, like 50 times a day. He would phone and hang up. He was constantly coming to my house.*

One woman had to take her children with her everywhere because her husband was convinced she would find somebody who would treat her better. Another husband would not allow his wife to have a bath with the door locked and he would come into the room during her bath to check on her constantly.

Women faced false accusations of having affairs. In one case, the husband accused the woman and her family of trying to put drugs in his food and coffee.

Cell phones are a new way for an abusive partner to keep track of a woman. Women are required to have their phones on at all time so they can be contacted anytime, anywhere. Women had their cell phones and long distance phone calls monitored to determine who they were talking to. Women also had their conversations listened to.

> *I could only be on the phone for a minute or two and if I told anybody how I felt, he would criticize everything that I would say to that person.*

In two cases, the husband cut the wires on the phone so women could not phone out for assistance.

Denying access to vehicles is a common means of control. One husband insisted on driving his wife everywhere she went. Lack of access to transportation is a significant problem in rural areas as it very effectively isolates women. This is accomplished in various ways.

> *He used to take the keys from the vehicles.*

> *He would take off and leave me alone with no transportation, I had my own vehicle, but I was silly enough to let him lock it up on the Quonset with the rest of his machinery.*

Another common means of control was isolating women from friends and family. One woman's family was not allowed in the yard, another woman endured so much criticism of her family and friends it was just easier not to see them.

Another means of asserting control was through fear. One woman's husband would drive recklessly to scare her, another woman was threatened with "*being locked in the granary*" if she didn't behave. Another was locked in her room until she "*saw it his way.*"

Threats were another means of creating fear and controlling a woman's behaviour. Eight of the 19 women interviewed received threats to kill them or their families.

Other research has commented on the high accessibility to guns in rural areas (Robertson). This was borne out in our study where threats and/or actions involving guns were described in eight of the 19 interviews.

Another method of psychological abuse is the threat of suicide. Nine of the men in this study threatened to kill themselves and one attempted suicide. The threat of suicide is also a means of control as the woman blames herself and feels compelled to help her husband recover.

***Physical Violence***

Physical violence was experienced by 16 of the 19 women interviewed. Physical violence usually started after verbal and psychological abuse had been occurring for years although a small number of relationships were physically violent from the beginning. One woman described the violence she experienced as:

> *It was everything ... he was physically abusive, even to himself. He would threaten to kill himself, he'd threaten to kill me, he'd threaten to kill my family. He broke things. He'd leave the house with the gun. He was mean to our dog. He did everything.*

Physical violence ranged from pushing and shoving to vicious beatings that resulted in women being hospitalized. In one incident the woman's IUD was "kicked into her stomach." Another woman described being picked up and thrown down on the carpet and choked until she couldn't see and then thrown against the wall again.

### *Sexual Abuse*

Six women reported being sexually abused. Five were sexually abused by their partners and one by other family members. This abuse involved being repeatedly forced to perform sexual acts the woman did not want to engage in, violent sex that left the woman bruised, or being physically abused if she declined to have sex. Two women described being sexually abused as children by family friends. In addition, one was raped as a teenager and another as an adult.

### *Economic Abuse*

Eight women described economic abuse in their relationships. This included being denied money for basic needs and their spouses removing all the family money from the bank account. Husbands attempted, and in one case a husband succeeded, in having his wife fired from her job. One woman was denied health care after childbirth.

> *When I had to go and buy groceries ... he would only give me $50 or $60. I couldn't even buy a bra. He would follow me into town to make sure [that was were I was going].*

> *When I left, he ripped up all my [credit/bank] cards and cleaned out the bank account. I was left with no money at all.*

> *He was trying to get me fired at work ... there were times where I just had to leave and go home because he was phoning me 15, 16 times a day.*

### *Spiritual Abuse*

One woman reported having her spiritual beliefs constantly ridiculed by her husband and her husband's family. However, she refused to let that diminish her faith and credits her beliefs with saving her life.

*Spiritual abuse brings the violence to another level ... the woman is demeaned, and so is her whole belief system. Not only do you believe you are stupid, but so is God. The result is very devastating as doubt seeps into body, soul and spirit.*

### *Abuse After Separation*

After separation, the majority of the women interviewed faced harassment from their husbands. Often, the harassment extended to their children and their extended families. This abuse included harassing phone calls, stalking, threats to them and their family, stealing personal belongings, breaking into their homes, verbal abuse, laying charges, and reporting women to Social Services.

## Coping With Domestic Violence

Women were asked how they coped with the abuse they received. Their replies indicated that coping takes place both within the relationship and in the woman's interaction with the people around them. Women used coping strategies to deal with their partners, their children, their extended family and the outside world.

Many women took years to admit they were being abused. Most did not label their experiences as abuse until they had been exposed to outside information. As a result many women did not seek support while they were in their abusive relationship.

*I didn't even let on that there was a problem, because at the time, I didn't even realize there was a problem. I accepted the way that life was as the way it should be and if there were problems, I felt they were mine to deal with.*

Not wanting to admit that abuse is happening can be very isolating. Women may choose not to see family and friends because they don't want to deal with questions and comments. Many women did not let anyone know about their situation and this made it difficult for them to receive support. One woman was afraid to admit that the situation was real...

*I never really told anybody what was going on because then it would seem real and I would have to do something about it.*

### *Embarrassment*

Women attempted to cover up the situation because of the potential embarrassment for themselves, their children, their partners, or their families.

*I guess I never let anyone know because I was embarrassed, ashamed for him ... I was too ashamed to even let my own parents know.*

*You really keep everything to yourself because you are ashamed for one thing and you don't want people to know the mess your life is in and I guess you always hope that it will change and turn around.*

One woman was reluctant to talk to a counsellor because her upbringing had stressed,

*...keeping things secret, keeping things quiet. I'd feel like I was betraying my own family.*

Another woman commented that she,

*...probably should have gone [to the doctor] a few times.... I was always bruised, my breasts were always bruised ... but then if I did, I would have to explain to the doctor how that happened.*

### *Fear of Reprisal*

Fear of reprisal was a very real concern for women. After her husband had pointed a loaded gun at the front door and threatened to blow it off, the woman,

*...never reported the man because I was scared that he was going to come back and blow my head off and I didn't want him to hurt my kids. I wanted to protect them. And what kind of mother would I be if I had their father arrested?*

*There was a fear that it would come back at me. I was obviously the one who would let someone know because there were only two people who knew about this relationship and it was him and me. And if he hadn't told anyone then he would know that it would be me.*

Fear of reprisal also included fear of losing their children.

*I was very fearful that he would take the kids and get joint custody because he was always saying that he would take them to the States with him and that would be last I'd see of them.*

### *Disbelief*

Many women were sceptical that they would be believed if they told anyone they were being abused. This was especially true for women whose husbands occupied positions of influence in the community and was borne out by their experiences.

Many women reported that their husbands had dramatic and rapid changes in behaviour. They called it "Jekyl and Hyde" or "public behaviour and private behaviour." Their husbands could be very charming to the outside world, making it difficult for others to believe the abuse that was happening at home.

At the same time many women commented that despite their best efforts to hide the abuse, after the couple had separated, many people in the community came forward to say they knew.

## Inside the Abusive Relationship

Within the relationship, women coped with the abuse by trying to please their partners in order to reduce the risk, by ignoring the verbal abuse, by detaching from what was happening to them, with counselling and by fighting back.

### *Pleasing*

Every woman we interviewed indicated they tried to please their partner to make things as easy as possible. Many women felt that if they "*did things better, things would be okay,*" and that the abuse was their fault. They looked for ways to prevent the outbursts.

> *He would get off work at 4:30 and I would run around the house to make sure that everything was perfect so then when he came home you know, maybe he wouldn't freak out on me.*

One woman described "the dance":

> *I called it a dance 'cause when I got up on the morning, I would look (to the body language) to see what kind of a dance I was going to have to do that day to make my day better.*

However, many also stated that they eventually came to realize that,

> *you keep trying and you keep trying and you discover it doesn't matter what you do, it's not good enough. Like it's never enough.*

### *Distancing*

Another very common coping strategy was for women to distance themselves from their abusive partner, "*to stay to hell out of his way*" by taking long baths, reading, taking long walks, going to bed early and/or pretending to be asleep, laying down with the kids and encouraging their partner to go out without them.

Other important strategies for coping were praying, exercising, and reading self-help books. Many women saw various types of counsellors during their relationships, often trying to determine what was wrong with their lives. For some women, keeping busy and working were very important. One woman told us "*work was her sanctuary.*" Another woman reported that she coped with abuse by having a routine.

> *I washed my floors every night, I had white colonial doors, I washed them*

*off every night, I washed my counter tops, moved everything.... I was just busy. You could probably drink the water out of my toilet. That's how clean it was.*

#### *Disassociation*

Women also reported blocking out what was happening to them. In one interview, a woman described a night of abuse as follows:

*He rolled me over and just kept tossing me.... I knew if I made it till seven o'clock in the morning, I would survive. Before morning, I was in ... almost a semi-comatose state where I knew he was there but no matter what he did to me, he couldn't hurt me. He would punch me and he would pull me. At one point I tried to get up and get away and he grabbed me by the leg and dragged me back into the bedroom, picked me up, threw me on the bed and just kept up this crazy talking.*

#### *Fighting Back*

A few women in the study fought back verbally and less often physically, recognizing that their actions at times were also abusive.

*I just didn't know what else to do and I just fought back with the same words.*

*We abused each other ... we kicked, we swore, we hit each other, things went flying ... We were both on the same level then.*

*He tried to put soap in my mouth and I think I was searching for something on the counter and there was a paring knife ... and I got hold of that. When he seen that he backed off and I said, "You get out of here." So he's down the steps and he's hollering: "I'm still the boss, I'm still the boss."*

#### *Suicide*

Three of the women in our study reported they had contemplated suicide. One as a child in an abusive home and two while they were in their abusive marriage.

*I had actually stood in my bathroom several times with pills in my hand and thought I was going to take them because I didn't know what else to do and not that I wanted to die because I didn't—you sometimes just didn't know what to do anymore.*

### Alcohol and Domestic Violence

There was a strong relationship between alcohol and abuse in this study. Alcohol abuse by the husband was present in nine of the relationships. Three women reported that they used alcohol as a means of coping with abuse.

Alcohol has been linked to spousal abuse in many studies. Some studies suggest that abusers feel violent behaviour is excused because the individual is drunk and therefore not accountable for their actions. In other words, some men drink to justify the fact they beat their wives. Other theories suggest alcohol releases inhibitions and alters judgment thereby increasing the likelihood of violent behaviour.

Although there is a relationship between alcohol abuse and domestic violence, researchers do not consider alcohol a cause of domestic violence, because the vast majority of people who abuse alcohol do not abuse their partners (DeKeseredy and MacLeod).

## Pregnancy and Domestic Violence

Six of the nineteen women reported that violence began or escalated when she was pregnant or after children were born. Many women reported that their husbands did not want to "grow up." Pregnancy and childbirth represented a loss of control for the husband as he must share the women's time and attention with another human being who has bonded more closely to his wife than he has. The pregnancy and resulting child represents a significant threat to his control. Women who are pregnant are also more vulnerable and this vulnerability may lead to violence.

## Intergenerational Abuse

Seventeen of the 19 women interviewed reported that their husbands had grown up in abusive homes in which their mothers and siblings were abused verbally and physically. A number of the women had also been raised in abusive households, abused not only by their fathers but also, in two cases, by their mothers.

This finding gives support to the theory that violence and aggression are learned behaviours (DeKeseredy and MacLeod). Witnessing the abuse of their mothers is a powerful way to reinforce traditional values of male dominance in children. Children may adopt parental beliefs that violence is an acceptable way to solve conflict and fail to develop alternate means of conflict resolutions (Barnett, Miller-Perrin and Perrin).

Growing up in an abusive household does not necessarily make a person abusive. Research shows that many people who grow up in abusive households are not violent adults (DeKeseredy and MacLeod; Barnett *et al.*; Canadian Panel on Violence Against Women). However the very high level of intergenerational violence in the lives of the women who participated in this study as well as the significant impacts this violence has on the emotional and physical health of the family indicates a critical need for effective strategies to be developed to address family violence in this region.

Children are victims of domestic violence. Dealing with the impact of domestic violence on their children was critical to the women who participated in this research.

Children who witness domestic violence fear for themselves and for their mothers. They may blame themselves for not preventing the violence or for causing it and they are more likely to experience neglect, injury or abuse.

These children exhibit many more health and behaviour problems than children who do not witness violence. These effects can be longterm, lasting into adulthood. Reported effects include anxiety, low self-esteem, shyness, depression, suicide attempts, self-blame and physical problems. These problems affect school competence, as children show poor problem-solving and conflict-resolution skills. They are also more likely to externalize behaviour problems through aggression and alcohol and drug use. Children who observe domestic violence and who are themselves abused have more behaviour problems than children who only observe the violence (Barnett *et al.*).

In this study, women reported that their children were very often caught up in the abuse. Children heard the verbal and psychological abuse and witnessed the physical violence.

> *I think now what they had to see and listen to was awful, it was a screaming match constantly and vulgar.*

At times they tried to protect their mothers from the violence even at an early age.

> *[My husband] literally had me on the floor and [our four-year-old son] was on top of [his Dad] pulling on his hair, trying to pull him off of me.*

> *On the way to town all [my husband] did was scream and yell at me. I was no good. He drove at an outrageous speed. He reached over to open the truck door and push me out ... the kids in the back seat grabbed hold of my shirt and pulled me in.*

Fathers harassed their children by phoning them to blame them for the separation or to tell them derogatory stories about their mothers. One woman reported that her children were stalked by their father.

The psychological and verbal abuse that women suffered was often directed at their children as well and some children were also physically abused. In two cases women reported verbally abusing their children and in one case verbally and physically abusing her oldest child.

Children were impacted by the violent situations they were living in. One woman reported her daughter's severe stomach-aches going away after she separated from her husband. Another reported significant improvement in her son's vision apparently due to the removal of the stress of living in an abusive household. In two cases, children (sons) were verbally and physically abusing their mothers.

> *[My ten year old son] literally kicked the living hell out of me because I*

*wouldn't let him do what he wanted to do ... I said you kicked me, I could charge you with abuse. And he said if you let me do what I wanted, I wouldn't have to hurt you ... Spoken right out of his father's mouth.*

Some women tried to protect their children from abuse by going to great lengths to ensure their children did not irritate their partners and keeping quiet during physical violence so their children would not wake up in the middle of a violent episode and be in danger.

## Support while in the Relationship

Most of the women turned to friends and family for support while they were still in the relationship. Friends and family members listened to their fears, intervened to calm down the abusive husband, sheltered women, helped them leave, took them to hospitals, and accompanied them and advocated for them with the police and other services.

Many women commented that friends and family who had experienced similar situations were especially helpful. One woman described the support she received from friends.

*She had been through a similar relationship and it was nice that we could talk because she understood where I was coming from, she understood why I was still there even though I shouldn't be.*

Some women preferred to seek support from their siblings, rather than from their parents. Often the women found it difficult to "admit to their parents what was going on," some didn't want to burden their parents because they felt their parents couldn't do anything for them anyway.

A number of women found support through various types of counselling including Al Anon, which offers programming for families of alcohol abusers and Alcoholics Anonymous.

One woman's doctor was very supportive, he believed her story when others did not and he and his wife lent a helping hand. Another woman received support from her pastor at a critical time. Women were also in contact with school counsellors.

## Leaving

Leaving an abusive or violent relationship is tremendously difficult. Fifteen of the nineteen women interviewed were not living with their abusive partner. Two couples were trying to rebuild a healthy relationship. In the third case the woman was in the process of leaving and in the fourth, the outcome was still in question.

Women often left many times before they made a complete and final break. Most women noted that the time they needed the most support was when they were trying to leave. Some women planned to leave over a long period of time, gathering information and waiting for the right time, such as when their children had graduated from high school. Other women made a very rapid decision to leave, often in situations of extreme risk.

### *Triggers To Leave*

The two main factors that caused women to leave were episodes of escalated violence and a heightened need to protect their children. At times these events coincided as children began to become involved in the violence by protecting their mothers, the violence started to focus on the children or when women realized that the violence was affecting their children.

One woman reflected:

> *If he would have killed me that night what about my boys, who's going to look after my boys?*

Another left when:

> *He threatened to kill me in front of the kids.*

Over one third of the women left after episodes of escalated violence. One put it very bluntly when she responded to the question as to what had triggered her decision to leave. She stated: "*When he broke my ribs.*"

For three women, infidelity was important in their consideration to leave. In these cases, infidelity was a form of psychological abuse in which the women were embarrassed, made to feel inadequate and at times publicly humiliated by their husbands' affairs. Two left because the abuse was affecting their emotional and mental state. One stated:

> *It was him or me, I had to leave first or he was going to die.*

### *Problems Leaving*

Women reported a number of factors that presented problems for them when they were thinking about leaving and when they actually left. The most common problem cited was the feeling that noone believed them:

> *They wouldn't believe what was going on because in all circumstances we did look happy together.*

> *Anytime I went to seek help to prepare or to do something about feeling safe, people would almost laugh at me, you know, that I was exaggerating and those kinds of things.*

Economic factors contribute to women's difficulties in leaving. Leaving an abusive relationship means living in poverty for many women and their children. Some women return to abusive relationships or refuse to leave because they can't afford to, or they don't want to lose the economic investment they have made in a marriage. Two women stayed in the same house as their abusive partners until they could sell their house. Another went back because if she left she would lose everything.

*He came into the marriage with nothing, just a bag in his car. I had all the furniture cause I'd been on my own for a long time, so he's sitting in the house with everything, I mean everything and I had nothing except my son.*

Some women also found it very difficult to deal with being alone. For some it was their first experience alone and they felt that it was easier to deal with the abusive situation than to deal with the unknown, not knowing whether or not they could handle the new situation of living on their own.

Women were also very fearful of the repercussions of leaving, that their husbands would find them, and the abuse would be even worse. Most women tried to find a safe time when their husband was not at home and the majority left when their husband was at work or away for some other reason.

Finding transportation to leave is often problematic in rural areas where there may be no close neighbours, there are no buses or taxis, and the abusive partner controls access to vehicles and communications. Women had to rely on family members or friends to provide transportation. One woman flagged down a passing car on a country road after hiding in the bush from her violent husband.

For some women, leaving was against their beliefs:

*I felt like I was doing something terribly wrong.*

*Marriage was for better or for worse,' til death do you part.*

Others were concerned that if they left and involved other people, their actions would endanger others.

*One reason I would never go anywhere else is because I never wanted to endanger anyone else.*

Leaving their homes and uprooting their children was very difficult for many:

*I am maybe more attached to the farm than most people are, but my whole life is involved in it and I loved it and my son would always [talk about our] home, his school and his friends. When he had to start school in [another town], that was the hardest thing, to watch your kid walk to school with his head down and come back from school with his head down.... He made some friends, but he said, "Mom, it's not the same."*

The most commonly reported problem for women when they were trying to leave their abusive situation was the police. Eight of the nineteen women mentioned the police played a significant positive or negative role. Many women felt the police were helpful and two especially noted the high level of support they received from female police officers. However others experienced more difficulty:

*I would say my most difficult times were with dealing with the police.*

Indeed for many women, this was their first experience dealing with the law and they were not aware of the law or of their rights.

**Services**

Half of the women in the study did not know what services were available to them when trying to deal with domestic violence or how to directly access support services.

*I had no idea there was any kind of a safe house. I had no idea what my rights were. I had no idea who to go to, you know I went kind of from one place to the other. I had absolutely no idea what was out there.*

Women who had attended alcohol abuse counselling were more aware of what services might be available. One woman found services by looking in the telephone book; another was offered some options by the police.

Although Mental Health Services is presently the focus for services for victim and survivors of domestic violence in this region, many women did not connect spousal abuse and mental health.

*Mental Health is one of the last places I would have thought to go to talk to someone when I was leaving my husband.*

As a result, women were directed to Mental Health by other government agencies such as Social Services and counselling agencies for drug and alcohol abuse. Some found the counsellors at Mental Health through word of mouth. One woman was able to find the spousal abuse support group in a newspaper ad.

The lack of awareness arises from the denial of spousal abuse as a problem in our society. People don't talk about it and resources are not directed to dealing with it. As a result, women don't realize they are not the only women who are being abused and they do not know where to turn for help.

***Counselling Services***

Every woman in the study had had contact with counsellors, most often with Mental Health. This is likely the result of our sampling methodology as Mental Health was our point of contact with survivors of spousal abuse. Most of the women interviewed were initially diagnosed as depressed or anxious by a family doctor or mental health worker. Mental Health provided women with the knowledge that the abuse was not their fault, an understanding of abuse, and information on how to get additional help.

Many women had contact with Al Anon or Alcoholics Anonymous and had tried other types of counselling including marriage counselling and self -awareness counselling. Seeking out different types of counselling often represented an attempt to find out what the women could change in their lives to stop the abuse and violence. Many of the women interviewed had attended a support group for survivors of spousal abuse.

When asked what services worked well for them, most women felt that counselling was very beneficial in helping them to realize that they had been abused, to understand the abuse and in explaining how they could access support.

The main concern voiced was the difficulty in seeing a Mental Health Therapist. Long waiting lists meant long waits to get an appointment and many women reported that the need to talk to someone was immediate. If this need was not met there was a high risk that the woman would return to the abusive relationship. Women felt that Mental Health needed to prioritize victims of abuse so they would not have to wait. Although most women found the support groups for survivors of spousal abuse very helpful, they are not suitable for everyone. One of our respondents felt the support group, *"Brought her down more than it lifted her up."* This points out the need for a variety of services to meet different needs.

### *The Legal System*

The legal system was the second most common service used. Fourteen women contacted the police and 14 women contacted a lawyer. In this study, a high proportion of women dealt with the law because the majority of the women interviewed had left their abusive relationships.

Women involved in violent or potentially violent encounters were most likely to have contact with the police. Women saw lawyers to find out what their rights were, to arrange custody, to file for divorce and to obtain restraining orders against their husbands.,

Most women leaving abusive situations must deal with the legal system. However, women felt at a serious disadvantage and experienced considerable stress when dealing with lawyers and the police. Many women stressed their need for must better information about the legal system. They also needed information about their rights; regarding safety from their partners, custody of their children, and access to their property.

Women also felt that the police and lawyers required a better understanding of family violence. In their experience the legal system needed to be sensitized about the impact of abuse and violence on women and their families.

### *The Police*

Women reported problems in dealing with the police. One woman stated:

*They were really unhelpful, they made it really difficult, they didn't explain things to me, they gave information that wasn't true, I found out later.*

The women felt that the police did not take their fears seriously, and that they did not truly comprehend the terror that women experience. One women suffered a vicious beating which resulted in a fractured face and broken ribs. After being taken to the hospital and being photographed by the police, she drove back into her yard to find her husband sitting in his car with his brother. She was under the understanding that he could return to gather up his things only if escorted by a police officer. Terrified she contacted the police who responded. "*Oh I guess we misunderstood him, we were going to meet him out there.*" Another woman recalled reporting an assault to the local police officer who said to her ...

*Well, I don't see marks, I don't see ... what did he do to you? I don't see anything ... I guess we can go out there and give him a warning but it's your word against his word.*

Another women reported that the police wanted her to move away. She felt that the police did not want to deal with the possibility that her husband might kill himself.

Another concern voiced by the women interviewed was the close relationship between the police and their husbands. This is especially problematic where the husband is a prominent member of the community. It is also a concern where the police have been long time members of the community.

In one case a woman reported that the police officer refused to come to her house when her husband tried to enter. He told the woman,

*There is nothing I can do, you should talk to your lawyer. He didn't try and hurt you ... [your husband] is not the type of person to hurt anybody.*

Some women suggested that the police tried to avoid confronting the abuser, as if they were afraid of them. Another woman reported she had a difficult time convincing the police to use the Victims of Domestic Violence Act, having to point out the relevant sections to the police officer.

Although there were a number of problems arising from women's experiences with the police, there are also a number of positive comments. Women who had dealings with the police in which the police believed them, were quick to respond, and were supportive, indicated that the police services had worked well for them. The variation in women's experiences with the police suggests that the effectiveness of the police in each case depended a great deal on the individual police officer.

### *Lawyers and Legal Aid*

Women in this study used both private lawyers and Legal Aid lawyers. Legal

Aid was only available to women in financial need. Legal Aid lawyers are available in some small communities on an intermittent basis. However, the women participating in this study who used Legal Aid reported having to travel to Saskatoon to see their lawyer. This created a difficult situation. In order to access a Legal Aid lawyer, you must have limited resources, yet at the same time you must find the money to travel.

Some women chose not to use Legal Aid because they were warned that it would take too long or that the "Legal Aid lawyers will not help you out much." However, the women using Legal Aid reported both positive and negative experiences.

Private lawyers are very costly and this creates a huge financial burden for women trying to leave an abusive relationship. Even with private lawyers, women reported both positive and negative experiences with the process and with the outcomes. Legal services that were timely, supportive, provided favorable outcomes for the women, and supplied useful information were viewed positively.

Women who had dealings with the courts all felt that the penalties given to their husbands were either inappropriate or too lenient. In their eyes, the actions of the courts did not result in adequate protection for them.

### *The Church and the Clergy*

The clergy was the third most commonly accessed set of services. Eight of the nineteen women indicated they had sought counselling and assistance from their pastor or priest. Four women felt their churches were very helpful, in one case in diffusing a threatened suicide and in the other cases, promoting the healing processes.

The Ursuline Sisters of Bruno were very important positive influences in the lives of two of our respondents, sheltering one woman and supporting another. Unfortunately this convent has closed.

Two women felt their church had let them down badly. One woman looked to her church as a backup in case her initial plan to leave her abusive husband did not work out. However, she was told by the minister that,

> *... all he could do was pray for her, he said that he couldn't do anything else.... I guess they feel that they don't have the experience and the knowledge in what to do to handle the type of situation that I was in.*

Another woman took issue with the message of her church that a marriage was for better or worse and that women had to stay in the marriage regardless of the circumstances.

### *Medical Services*

Seven of the women indicated they used medical services while they were dealing with their abusive situation. Women went to the hospital for physical injury and to doctors for counselling and medications. In two cases, doctors helped women leave their abusive situation, going beyond their medical role. One woman's doctor offered to talk to her husband about the physical violence she was receiving, but the woman declined his help out of fear of reprisal. Doctors were also active in referring women who they suspected were in abusive situations to Mental Health Services.

The high turnover rates of doctors in rural Saskatchewan precluded the development of longterm relationships with patients. These relationships were important for women to build the trust necessary to confide in their doctor.

### *Shelters*

Three women stayed in safe shelters in Saskatoon and Moose Jaw, another stayed at the YWCA in Saskatoon and one stayed in the crisis shelter in Humboldt. Lack of space in the most accessible shelter caused one woman to have to travel to Moose Jaw rather than Saskatoon and another to use the YWCA. Another woman could not access the Saskatoon shelter the first time she phoned but a space opened up for her by the time she actually left.

The crisis shelter in Humboldt was located in an apartment donated by Saskatchewan Housing Corporation. The shelter was not staffed and as a result women were reluctant to use it because they did not feel safe or supported. One woman who spent a night in the shelter in Humboldt commented.

> *I spent the night in the shelter but it was really difficult because there was nobody to talk to and it finally dawned on me that.. Oh my God ... this is a really abusive situation.... It was really scary because I felt so alone.... They didn't have any numbers for me to get of hold of anyone....*

Although this model of a crisis shelter was not effective, rural women do want to be able to access a shelter close to home.

### *Social Services*

Four women reported they contacted Social Services. Social Services provided advice, financial support and organizational support for leaving. Women's experiences with Social Services were variable, some finding them helpful, others finding it a truly demoralizing experience. One woman reflected that after talking on the telephone to a representative of Social Services, she thought to herself:

> *I have to fight at home to survive and now I have to fight with you.*

One woman got much better service from the Social Services office after her sister e-mailed the Minister of Social Services.

Women experienced difficulties arising from the location of boundaries for the provision of health and social services in this area. One woman accessed health services in a town ten kilometers away, but was expected to access social services in a town 90 kilometers away. This was very costly even for a woman who had access to a vehicle. She also felt she was being forced to leave her supportive community.

Difficulties with Social Services may arise from the lack of understanding by Social Services personnel of the situation these women were in. Women leaving abusive relationships often leave with no money and need cash immediately. Another obstacle was the reluctance of women to fully discuss with Social Services personnel the extent of their abusive situation. This may contribute to a lack of understanding by Social Services of the seriousness of the situation.

**Services for Children**

All of the women interviewed indicated a need for counselling and therapy sessions for children of all ages. At the same time, few women felt there were adequate services available for their children.

In many cases, school-aged children were able to access counselling through their schools. Some children refused to go to counselling even though they were encouraged by their parents to attend.

When dealing with older children, women felt that the counselling must be confidential. In their experience, children in high school will not become involved in counselling if they are not sure it is confidential. In the case of teenagers, some women felt the parents should not be contacted if the teenagers seek counselling.

Women looked for ways to educate their children about abuse and violence. Some women reported their children were not interested in reading pamphlets and suggested other ways of communication, such as speakers and access to crisis lines. One woman put a tape in the VCR about children who had been abused and left the room. She found her children one by one sitting down to watch the tape.

Many of the women suggested one-on-one counselling and peer group counselling for their children. These women felt it was important that their children realize that they were not the only ones in this situation. Some parents found it very difficult to talk to their children themselves:

> *I never discussed it with them because I didn't know what I was supposed to be saying, but I really think they need educational stuff and I think kids need to be told that there is more to abuse than somebody beating you.*

Another woman commented that children need answers for some questions that they would not feel comfortable asking their parents:

> *They need someone to help them understand why their father is doing this.*

A number of women would have also liked to see family therapy available to them and their children.

One of the largest service gaps in both rural and urban areas is programming for young children. Women reported that there was nothing for pre-school age children in the rural areas and that waiting lists for young children in urban areas are months long.

Mothers of small children had difficulty finding information on abuse in parenting books. They needed information to help them deal with behavioural problems connected to abuse.

## Rural Problems

### *Confidentiality*

In small towns, confidentiality is difficult to preserve. Most of the women in the study commented on the lack of confidentiality in small towns.

> *In a small town, everybody knows everybody's business and sometimes that's even scarier and you stay because you are not going to leave your husband because the whole town might know [about] it and what are they going to think about me? That's the way it works, plain and simple.*

The social stigma that can result from this lack of confidentiality may mean a women stays in an abusive relationship. A lack of confidentiality can also create safety issues. If the husband hears rumours in town that he is abusing his wife, the woman could be placed in significant danger. This potential danger is one of the reasons women keep quiet about the abuse they experience. The lack of confidentiality was a greater concern at the beginning of the process of seeking help for abuse. Women reported looking over their shoulders as they went to see the Mental Health workers to make sure nobody saw them.

Lack of anonymity in a rural community may make it more difficult for women to seek help.

> *You have to be at the point where you are ready to face your problems, before you would look for help especially in a rural community .... You have to be beyond the point of caring what people think before you would do anything to help yourself.*

### *Isolation*

Abuse on farms is easier to hide than abuse in urban areas or small towns because of the privacy afforded by a farmyard with no neighbors for many kilometers. Women from farms may also not be able to safely remain on the farm regardless of the legal requirements governing the actions of their husbands.

The *Saskatchewan Victims of Domestic Violence Act*, 1995 allows a Justice of the Peace to issue an Emergency Intervention Order to:

- restrain an abuser from communicating with the victim or her family
- direct a police officer to remove the abuser

- allow the victim exclusive occupation of the home
- direct a police officer to accompany the victim or the abuser to the home to remove their personal belongings.

However, in rural areas, due to the isolation and long police response times, many women felt this *Act* had limited usefulness. One woman commented,

> *The woman ... with the children would have access to the home, he had to stay away from the home for thirty days, and he couldn't come into the home, but I thought well, big deal, on a farm, I could have had eight houses, who cares—I would not have been there by myself, unless there is going to be a policeman with me.*

The *Victims of Domestic Violence Act* was useful to two women in our study, allowing them to stay in their homes while their husbands were removed.

### *Funding and Access to Services*

A significant problem in trying to improve services to women in rural areas was funding. Some women thought the government should look more closely at the services they were willing to fund and provide more support for survivors of abuse.

Others felt that due to the smaller population in rural Saskatchewan, there would not be sufficient numbers to be able to convince the government to improve services.

Access to services and staff of Mental Health Services for counselling was a serious concern of many women. Tight budgets have meant long waits, overworked personnel, and high rates of turnover. Women would also like to see more continuity of counsellors for themselves and their children.

Women coping with abusive relationships are often living in poverty in rural Saskatchewan, women have to travel long distances to access a safe house, to see a counsellor, to attend a support group or to see a lawyer. The costs of transportation can be prohibitive. Many of these women do not have vehicles, they may not be able to afford gas, their husbands may restrict their movements, and some towns have no bus service. There are often additional costs for a babysitter.

If a woman has a job, it may be difficult to get time off to access services. Retaining a job while leaving an abusive situation depends on the understanding and good will of the employer.

Many services in Saskatchewan are delivered in boundaries that are not contiguous and do not reflect traditional travel patterns within the urban hierarchy. As a result a woman may be seeing a social worker in one centre, a school counsellor in another centre, a mental health worker in another centre and a lawyer in another centre. This creates additional financial and psychological costs for the woman trying to access services for herself and her family.

Many of the services that are needed by survivors of family violence in rural Saskatchewan have either been reduced or their mode of delivery has changed. The result of these reductions and changes is a very disorganized geography of services for rural families to attempt to access. It also frustrates the effective delivery of services as the communication between various service agencies is more difficult and complex.

### *Attitudes*

A significant area of concern for women was attitudes. This goes hand in hand with the issues of confidentiality. People in rural areas have been slow to admit that domestic violence is a serious problem. People do not access services such as Mental Health because of the stigma attached to those services. At the same time, women do not seek help for abuse because they have to admit they are being abused and so many of them feel the abuse is their fault.

## Rural Needs

The most pressing need articulated by the women was better access to counselling for all members of the family. Counselling and support were needed in an accessible and timely manner. The women reported having to wait to see counsellors. One woman reported waiting two months for an appointment, during which time she ran into additional problems.

In order to reduce waiting times, women must be willing to disclose their abusive relationship. The local Mental Health Office is now prioritizing family violence cases, but prioritizing is only possible if the violence is disclosed or personnel are trained to recognize the signs of abuse. In areas where these cases are not prioritized, immediate access to counselling may depend on a woman's ability to pay for private counselling.

All the women interviewed indicated a need for counselling and play therapy for children. A major problem exists with the lack of information and services for pre-school children in abusive situations. School age children are able to access counselling in schools, although children and teenagers may be unwilling to attend counselling at the school due to the stigma attached.

### *Support Groups*

Women also suggested they would benefit from ongoing support groups. Many of the women had already attended a support group for survivors of spousal abuse and felt another level of support group would be very beneficial to them. A similar suggestion was the development of a peer support network where women in difficult situations would be able to talk to other women with similar experiences.

### *Crisis Line*

A crisis line with a 1-800 number was also suggested to give women a source of information and support in times of crisis. A 1-800 number is needed because long distance calls listed on a phone bill may create a dangerous situation for women in abusive relationships. A crisis number for women in abusive or violent situations is now available in the study area.

One woman recounted the problems of living in an area without a 911 system. In the time it took her to dial the seven-digit phone number for the RCMP her husband was able to break through the bedroom and the bathroom door. Although parts of the province of Saskatchewan have recently obtained a 911 system, the study area and many other rural areas in Canada are still without this service. It is expected the 911 system will be available in the study area in the near future.

### *Women's Advocate*

Women suggested an advocate to guide them through the process of leaving their partners would have been a great help. A woman in the process of leaving an abusive relationship is under considerable stress and at the same time must deal with large amounts of new and complex information and many unfamiliar processes. An advocate would have information and knowledge of the legal and social services system and could act as a guide for the woman.

### *Counselling for Men*

Counselling for men was not accessible outside of major urban centres. One woman estimated it cost $160 a month for the gas for her husband to go back and forth to the nearest city to participate in the Alternatives Program for Abusive Men. This was beyond the means of many people and was a factor in one man not continuing with the program.

### *Education and Information*

Closely related to the need for more and different types of counselling and support was the need for information on domestic violence for all segments of society. Education of the general public should focus on increasing understanding of what constitutes abuse and would increase the visibility of abuse in the community. Better understanding should reduce the tolerance for abuse and increase the demand for counselling and support for women, children and men.

Introducing the topic of abuse in high school was suggested as a means of breaking the cycle. Education could be provided about healthy relationships and about what constitutes abuse. The goal would be to stop controlling and violent behaviour before it becomes a normal means of interaction in relationships.

> *My husband says we should have something in school. To say that this is domestic violence, that you don't hit anybody and you don't say these things to people. All these guys figure that if you don't beat the crap out of somebody its not abuse, if you tell them they're a dumb bitch or whatever, big deal, they're just words, it doesn't matter. He figures they should teach every young guy in school something about it, touch on it so that it's in their minds.*

Better understanding of the nature of abuse may also enable women in abusive situations to question the situation earlier, to recognize that it is not their fault, and to seek help earlier.

Women also felt that the various service professionals such as the police, lawyers, clergy, doctors and social services personnel would benefit from a greater understanding of domestic violence. Education would improve the ability of these service professionals to deliver more effective services.

A critical issue is how to package information to reach the widest possible audience. Women suggested a variety of media, including radio, television, newspapers, the internet, women's conferences, speakers, pamphlets, booklets, crisis lines and education modules in school.

Another suggestion was to expand the "peach pages" in the telephone book so services for abused women are listed with other health and emergency services. This would make the telephone numbers less obvious to an abuser who may otherwise remove the pages.

A variety of media was seen as necessary because women in abusive situations may have restricted access to many types of information such as mail, telephones, and newspapers. Using many different forms of media increases the probability that a woman would be reached.

Different types of media are also needed to teach the wide range of audiences that make up the general public. One suggested method of distributing information was to establish a store front facility that people could visit, find information and have someone to talk to not only on abuse issues but also parenting, personal growth and other issues important to rural families.

### *Safe Shelter*

A safe shelter was a need identified by eight out of 19 respondents. Until recently there was a shelter in the area that could be used by families in crisis. However, the shelter had no staff and no garage to hide a vehicle. Few women took up the opportunity to stay there. Those that did use the shelter did not feel safe or supported. Women are adamant that any shelter must be staffed:

> *Oh definitely, it has to be staffed. If you're in an abusive situation and you've left it, you're terrified, you're absolutely terrified. The last thing you want to do is be in some strange building by yourself ... and you need some counselling right now.*

Women also felt strongly that a shelter had to be close to the community.

> *This person has already lost the roof over their head and the floor under their feet. You can't take them away from their supports, you know like their friends, their family, their relatives.... Most people in these small towns have lived here* for *ever and they grew up here and ... their families are here, their relatives are here and you can't be hauling them 200 miles away.*

*I want to be able to know that there is a place that I can go to where I am going to be safe but yet I'm still within close radius of my family.... When you leave, your life changes, your children's life shouldn't have to change. They shouldn't have to worry about not going to school ... their lives shouldn't be uprooted because they have already gone through enough, you want to keep things normal. They need a sanctuary, where it's a safe place for them to be.*

### *Other Needs*

Women indicated they needed more support and information on their legal rights and better access to lawyers. They needed help with housing, subsidized daycare, dealing with Social Services, and provision for safe transportation to a safe house. They also felt there should be more help for women who do not have a job.

### *Responsibility for Services*

When asked who should provide the funding for services for survivors of domestic violence, three quarters of the women felt the provincial government had a major responsibility. They felt that this responsibility arose because domestic violence is a significant social problem and the government has a vested interest in the longterm health of the population.

*I think it should come out of provincial coffers. It's always been such a hush hush kind of thing, not only for the women who have lived through it but for everybody, you just don't talk about it. It's been going on forever and it's a social problem and I think that there should be more funding.*

The women felt strongly that the provincial government was the appropriate body to provide services to families free of charge. These services must be free as many women in abusive situations are impoverished when they leave the relationship so that services must be available and widely accessible at no charge.

Women also suggested that the government should be involved because children are often directly involved in the abuse as it happens. Children who grow up with problems arising out of the exposure to abuse may place a higher cost on the system as the cycle of abuse continues into their adult years.

The health care system is important in identifying women who have been abused and referring them to other services. Women suggested health districts should be involved in the provision of services because,

*...they represent the community and should know how rural communities work.*

Mental Health is the focal point of services for victims and survivors of domestic violence and is one of the services offered by the Health District.

The women felt that the community itself must play a role in the provision of services. Women suggested a number of sources of support in the community such as volunteer organizations, the clergy, businesses, corporations and survivors.

## Conclusions

The results of this study show that women in East Central Saskatchewan encounter serious situations of domestic violence in significant numbers. Many women stayed in abusive situations for years because they had come to accept the abuse as normal. They had been convinced that the abuse was their fault.

Lack of knowledge, embarrassment, fear of reprisal and fear of not being believed caused women to remain silent about the abuse. Women coped with the abuse by trying to reduce the risk through pleasing their partner or distancing themselves from him.

A few women fought back verbally and physically. A small number turned to alcohol or suicidal thoughts. Others prayed, exercised, worked, or read self help books.

Alcohol was a factor in almost half of the abusive relationships. Pregnancy and childbirth were related to the onset and escalation of violence in almost one third of the cases.

Intergenerational abuse was present in 90 per cent of the cases in this study. Abusers came from households in which their fathers abused the rest of the family. In keeping with the intergenerational trend, women reported their children witnessed their abuse and in most cases were also verbally abused. This is a significant finding and calls for immediate actions and solutions. It is a particular cause for concern in rural areas because there is little counselling for children outside of the limited resources of the school system.

In rural areas, friends and family provided the main source of support for women in abusive relationships.

Women usually made the decision to leave their abusive partners when the violence began to escalate and the need to protect their children intensified. They faced many problems in leaving including economic loss and poverty, fear of added violence, the loss of their homes and communities, and fear of being alone.

Many women were unaware of the services available to them and their children when they left. Due to the sampling technique of this study and the fact that most of the women had left their abusive relationship, most of the women saw counsellors and many had interacted with the police and lawyers. In smaller numbers, women used the services of the clergy, doctors, safe houses, and social services. None of these services was adequate to meet all their needs.

Women had difficulty accessing counselling in a timely fashion. The responses of the police, lawyers, clergy, doctors and social services personnel were variable, depending on which individual the woman dealt with. This reflects a serious lack of understanding of the situation of the victims and survivors of domestic violence. It also illustrates the need for these professions and organizations to develop and utilize protocols to deal with domestic violence. In that way, the treatment of a woman and her children will not depend on the knowledge and empathy of a particular individual and some consistency of service would be achieved. In Saskatchewan, the development of services for domestic violence arose out of the safe shelter movement (Turner). These shelters are all located in Saskatchewan cities and as a result the majority of specialized services for domestic abuse are also located in cities and have not been available to rural areas. This urban bias for specialized services, combined with the centralization of more generalized services such as Social Services, Legal Aid, and some aspects of the police service creates a serious issue of access to services for rural women and their families.

As a result, rural people must either find the resources to travel for these services or forego them. Women who leave abusive situations are often impoverished and may not be able to afford the time or the money to travel to the larger urban centre. Women in rural areas are also disadvantaged by the lack of subsidized daycare, adequate employment opportunities and access to affordable housing.

There is a tremendous lack of knowledge about domestic violence, for both survivors of abuse and the general public. Women suggested more information may have reduced the years they lived with abuse and may have enabled them to save their relationships.

Information on domestic violence is a critical need. Information is needed to break the cycle of abuse, to teach children and adults what abuse is, and how to deal with conflict in constructive ways. The development of information packages suitable for many different audiences will demand considerable creativity and innovation.

Rural women in abusive situations need information to deal with the complex issues of the impact of domestic violence on them and their children. They also need information on their legal rights and on financial issues. Rural women would benefit from the development of information packages and the designation of an advocate to assist women in making agencies and agency professionals work for them.

Building on the positive aspects of community cohesion and cooperative spirit that are attributed to rural areas, rural people must develop rural solutions to the delivery of services. This will necessitate investment of time and money from government, health districts, and the community.

*This research was supported by the Prairie Women's Health Centre of Excellence in Winnipeg, and the Women's Health Bureau of Health Canada.*

## Notes

[1]See Appendix 1 for list of questions.

## References

Barnett, Ola W., Cindy Miller-Perrin and Robin D. Perrin. *Family Violence Across the Lifespan: An Introduction*. Thousand Oaks, CA: Sage Publications Ltd., 1997.

Canadian Panel on Violence Against Women. *Changing the Landscape: Ending Violence—Achieving Equality*. Ottawa: Minister of Supply and Services, 1993.

DeKeseredy, Walter S. and Linda MacLeod. *Women Abuse: A Sociological Story*. Toronto: Harcourt Brace and Co, Ltd., 1997.

Kirkwood, Catherine. *Leaving Abusive Partners*. London: Sage Publications Ltd., 1993.

Klein, Ethel, Jacqueline Campbell, Esta Soler and Marissa Ghez. *Ending Domestic Violence: Changing Public Perceptions / Halting the Epidemic*. Thousand Oaks, CA: Sage Publications Ltd., 1997.

McLaughlin, Kathleen and Sylvia Church. *Cultivating Courage: The Needs and Concerns of Rural Women Who are Abused by Their Partners*. Woodstock: 1992.

McLeod, Linda. *Preventing Wife Battering: Towards a New Understanding*. Ottawa: Canadian Advisory Council on the Status of Women, 1989.

Robertson, Audrey L. *Violence Against Women in Rural Areas: A Search for Understanding*. Master Thesis submitted to the Sociology Department, University of Saskatchewan, 1998.

Turner, Jan. "Saskatchewan Responds to Family Violence: The Victims of Domestic Violence Act, 1995." *Wife Assault and the Canadian Criminal Justice System: Issues and Policies*. Eds. Mariana Valverde, Linda MacLeod and Kirsten Johnson. Toronto: University of Toronto Centre of Criminology, 1995. 183-197.

UNICEF. *Domestic Violence Against Women and Girls*. Florence: Innocenti Research Centre, 2000.

Wallace, Harvey. *Family Violence: Legal, Medical and Social Perspectives*. Boston: Allyn and Bacon, 1999.

Weber, Martha. *She Stands Alone: A Review of the Recent Literature on Women and Social Support*. Winnipeg Prairie Women's Health Centre of Excellence, 1998.

## Appendix 1

## Domestic Violence and the Experiences of Rural Women in East Central Saskatchewan

### *Interview Questions*

Would you describe the abuse you experienced?

What things did you do to cope with your abusive situation?
Who supported you at this time?

What triggered your decision to leave the relationship?
When did you first identify your situation as abusive?
How did you leave? (What process did you go through when leaving?)
What are some of the problems you ran in to when trying to leave?
Were there times when you had a greater need for support?

Did you know what services/supports were available for abused women?
Did you try to contact any services for women who are abused?
(Lawyers, police, mental health, social services, clergy, schools hospitals, family doctors)
What services worked for you?
What services didn't work?
What services should you have had access to?

Did you know what services/supports were available for children from abusive situations?
Did you try to contact any services for your children?
What services worked for you and your children?
What services didn't work for you and your children?
What services should you and your children have had access to?

What services/supports/resources should be available to women and children in rural Saskatchewan?
Who should provide those services?
What problems do you anticipate in providing these services in rural areas?

# In the Matter of "X"

## Building "Race" into Sexual Harassment

Himani Bannerji

In the summer of 1992, I received a call from a law firm to work as an expert witness for a complaint of sexual harassment of a woman. There was a problem, however, to consider and to accommodate. She was not just a "woman" undergoing the usual sexual harassment common in workplaces, but she was a "black woman." How could we build that fact of blackness in to the case so that we could say that racism was in integral part of the sexual harassment which she underwent? We knew that there were three oppressions (among others) at work in Canadian society—namely, racism, sexism and classism—and that X's experience included all; but how were we to think of these oppressions in such a way that we could show her harassment as a composite or a crystallized form of both?

I decided to work on the case because X's oppression enraged me; it also offered a political and an analytical challenge. How to think of gender; "race," and class in terms of what is called "intersectionality," that is, in terms of their interactiveness, their ways of mutually constructing or reinforcing each other, is a project that is still in the process of being worked out. Somehow, we know almost instinctively that these oppressions, separately named as sexism, racism, and class exploitation, are intimately connected. But when it comes to showing how, it is always difficult, and strains the capacity of our conventional ways of speaking on such matters. And, if abstract theorization is partially possible, the concrete uncovering of how they actually work continues to have an elusive quality to it. The case of X is one of innumerable experiences of its kind, in varying degrees of intensity and complexity, which mark lives of black women in the West. Here the West means the U.S. and Canada, but it includes Britain and other European countries as well. For that reason also, it was a challenge to think through a problem which exists within such a wide scope.

## A Brief Outline of the Case

(outline provided by the firm of Cornish and Roland)

It is useful at the outset to specify who X is, though very briefly and mainly in terms of her work trajectory. But this offers some of the particulars with regard to which I tried to understand how she was specifically sexually harassed as a black woman. The following are some of the facts put forward as a part of the submissions of the claimant X.

Job Progression:

1. X is a 45-year-old black woman and sole-support mother.
2. X began working for Y company in 1980 on the assembly lines, first as a packer for detergent, then shampoo, then toothpaste, and finally soap. These jobs were classified as "light" and were predominately female.
3. The work force at Y was predominately white; also, to the best of X's knowledge, she was one of only two black female employees in the production area of the factory.
4. Towards the end of 1983 or the beginning of 1984, X applied for and was promoted to the position of packer "heavy-duty" in the soap department. "Heavy" jobs were historically performed exclusively by men and were performed in an area that was physically separated from the area in which X had previously been working. X was the only woman employed in that area. She was also one of the very few visible minority employees in the area.
5. In mid-1984, X was again promoted—this time to "utility," a job demanding greater skill. She was required to learn how to trouble-shoot on the line and replace the operator for breaks and lunch. This job was also within the "heavy" tasks area and had been exclusively performed by men; X was the only woman employed in this capacity.
6. X was next transferred to "mills" as a prerequisite for promotion to the "operator" position within the heavy tasks area. In this area she mainly worked alone mixing soap for the assembly lines.
7. As an operator, X was responsible for overseeing a packing line operation. This included the requirement to work in a "lead hand" type of relationship with the utility and packer. The position required her to follow written instructions, document mechanical problems, and master the new vocabulary specific to the job. In addition, X was required to have a more in-depth knowledge of the operation and equipment on the line in order to adjust and trouble shoot its operation. Her performance would essentially be judged by the rate at which her line could maintain production; to do so, X required a high level of cooperation from her male co-workers who filled the packer and utility positions on her line. (Submissions of the Claimant "X", nos.1-7)

X's experience of harassment at the workplace was extensive and ranged from job sabotages to being subjected to various obscenities. They may be summed up as:

> a. active sabotage of the work for which she was responsible,
> b. discriminatory treatment with respect to training and work assistance by senior co-workers,
> c. forced exposure to hostile material which denigrated both her race and sex, placed at and near her work station,
> d. social isolation and ostracism by co-workers,
> e. public pejorative name-calling and sexually and racially derogatory remarks. (Submissions 2)

Particular details of this conduct, randomly selected by me, include the following:

> 11. ...X was subjected to adverse treatment: the white female lead hands would run the line she was packing at an unusually high speed, would damage her locker and referred to her publicly as a "fucking bitch."
> 12. Although X complained to management, the behaviour was allowed to continue. Further, when her co-workers threatened to have her fired and complained about her to the foreman, she was transferred out of the area to the soap department.
> 19. Co-workers created an environment that was hostile to her gender and race. Pictures of "Sunshine Girls" (barely-clothed women consistently featured on the third page of *The Toronto Sun*) were displayed in her work area. When X complained, the co-workers were told to remove them, but they refused. Despite the workers' insubordination, no action was taken against them. Note, however, that when white women walked through the area, the posters were taken down and hidden. X also heard racially derogatory comments directed at a Filipino male worker. She herself was repeatedly referred to as a "bitch."
> 20. ...Obscene pictures were left at her work station and in her toolbox. One was a hand drawn sketch in which a black woman was giving a "blow job" to a white man. Another was a picture also hand drawn of a black woman giving a white man a "hand job" while a gang of white men stood in line for their turn. X was repeatedly referred to as "a fucking bitch" and "cunt." One worker went so far as to throw a bar of soap at her which hit her on her head; though her foreman was nearby, he did nothing. On one occasion, she when out to lunch with a male co-worker, the co-worker was asked on his return whether X had "fucked" him in the parking lot. (Submissions, nos. 11, 12, 19, 21)

Though X remains anonymous in terms of her personal identity, these details allow us to imagine her more concretely.

## A Reflexive Perspective

Upon some reflection it became clear to me that we have to develop a critical understanding of how "sexual harassment" is constructed with regard to women. By this I mean the need to consider two key issues, one being the conceptualization of the term "sexual," the other the category "woman" or "women" that is consistently, if contingently, linked to the complaint. The latter is perhaps the best starting point for beginning to examine the former. So let us start with the categories "woman"/"black woman." For after all, it is the need to make a transition from "woman" to "black woman" that needed my expertise.

Why is there a problem in making this shift? What changes if we do? If we keep these questions in mind and reflect on the category "woman" as conventionally used in Canada (or in other Western countries) in legal or ordinary parlance, we come to feel the fact that this category is simultaneously empty and full of social content. It both erases *and* asserts the society's history, social organization and prevalent ideologies, values and symbolic cultures. It both validates and denies powered relations of difference. What I mean by these statements is that when we use this term "woman" non-adjectivally in any given situation, we don't actually mean an *abstract*, a *general* or an *essential* entity. What we mean or refer to is a woman whose life conditions are most in keeping with the prevailing social, legal, and cultural structures, institutions and beliefs. That is, it is a woman whose life lies squarely in the middle of the dominant social organization of the masculine and the feminine, or is most normalized within its gender organization. It is so normalized as to have become a sort of code—this "woman" needs no specifying adjective or adjunct signifier. In societies based on class and "race," she is neither classed nor "raced." Who on earth could this woman be?

In answering this question while sitting in Canada or the U.S., conducting a relatively uncomplicated case of sexual harassment, the actual subject emerges. The "woman" in question, serving as the base type for sexual complaints, is a *white* woman. She demands *this* specific adjective, if we are to stretch the law beyond her to other women. Otherwise, though we can deal with her case, we cannot even begin to address the wrongs of her sister, the *black* woman, specifically here an Afro-Canadian woman, whose difference enters into the peculiar type of sexual harassment meted out to her. And yet, *normally*, daily, why is this category "woman" non-adjectivized for a white woman, while others have their differences "raced" or "coloured?"

The erasure of the fact of a white woman's whiteness which elevates her into a universal category is proof of the racist nature of Canadian/Western social organization, moral regulation, and cultural practices. Silence or absence does not always, or here, mean powerlessness. Here the silence or erasure amounts to a reference to the fact of an all-pervasive presence. About this we say—"it goes without saying.... " When a subject becomes so central as to be an icon or a typology for what goes on everyday, situating devices such as adjectives become unnecessary.

So the racism that X encounters during her sexual harassment begins in this undifferentiated notion of the "woman." In the Canadian context, it is an unspoken example of a social organization based on "race," where some are typologically "woman" and "others" are its variants, such as, black woman or woman of colour. What this abstraction both encodes and conceals is that no one is spared. The whole of the socio-legal apparatus and environment are, in practice, in social relations and values, "raced." It is *because* white women are implicitly but fundamentally "raced" as white and thus as members of the "master race," that they don't need to be named as such. This leaves us with a dilemma of either naming them in terms of the overall racist social organization to get some actual insight into equality, or of not naming them while "other" named women suffer injustices based on their difference. These are the options before us, and it is not a surprise then that the shift is hard to make from sexual harassment of "women" to that of "black women." It pulls at deep roots and calls for a shift at other levels of perception and politics.

Now, if we can accept that women are differently "sexed" in a "raced" society, we can then begin to combine sexism with racism. Others before us have done so—Pratibha Parmar, for example, uses the term "sexist racism," which can be easily reversed into "racist sexism." This composite concept codes a gender-"race" organization of the western societies in general and the society X lives in, and this society is historically connected to colonialism and slavery, and presently to an imperialist form of capital. So the central sociological issue which arises out of the case of X is that of "racist sexism" and its various ramifications, which have had an overwhelmingly negative impact on her economic and personal life. These are the issues which need to be understood and through which the notion of "sexual harassment" needs to be considered. They involve a broader analysis of Canadian society in terms of history, political economy, culture which are structured through social organization of gender, "race," and class.

I see X's life as an existential whole which is constituted by a diverse set of social relations which cannot be separated out in actuality. Racism is after all a concrete social formation. It cannot be independent of other social relations of power and ruling which organize the society, such as those of gender and class. Similarly, gender and class, in a society organized through practices and ideologies of "race" and ethnicity, are structurally and ideologically inseparable from them. As such, one can only think of racism, sexism, and class as interconstitutive social relations of organized and administered domination. It is their constantly mediating totality which shapes people's perception of each other, and as such, X's co-workers cannot see her as three separate social entities—"raced," gendered, and classed. They see her as a *black woman*, in the entirety of that construction, about whom there are existing social practices and cultural stereotypes, with which they are all familiar. One can see how gender matters within the "raced" groups and between them. Both black men and black women are subject to racism, but there is a distinct gender-appropriate difference in "raced" stereotypes regarding them. Similarly, though white and black women both suffer from sexism, there is a "raced" difference in cultural common sense regarding how they are to be gendered. Stereotypes regarding all Canadian women share a common element of patriarchal or gender organization, but this patriarchy operates through radically different significations and expectations of their social presences and functions.

I shall also use the term "racist sexualism" to convey the female/male or heterosexual dynamic of racist sexism, as I shall also claim that racist sexism is wholly possible between white and black women (or women of colour) not just between white men and black women. I shall endeavour to show in my reading of the case that racist sexual harassment is erected and that this occurs in the case of X and all other women who are non-white. I hope that by pointing out this simultaneous, formative and dynamic interrelation between racism, sexism, and implicitly of class, since race and class coincide in North America, I shall help to avoid a pointless and time-consuming debate about which is primary.

## Reading X's Case

> When the packer and utility finally returned, X attempted, for the second time, to start up the line. When she moved around in position to see whether the packer and utility were at work, she saw a group of white male employees standing around the line looking toward her. At that point she noticed that someone had placed a twelve-inch long, bright green, *Irish Spring* soap carving of a penis with white foam at its tip, on the assembly line where X would be forced to see it.
>
> The carving remained on the line for 30-45 minutes in full view of X and the group of white male co-workers who hovered around jeering and staring at X.... X recognized the incident to be not only humiliating and isolating, but a threat. (Submissions, nos. 29, 30)

My reading of the case of X begins with this incident of the carved penis. In a history of incidents, all of which amounted to small or big acts of harassment, this marks the culmination point. This event and her reaction to it must be seen as both a personal experience and a social moment, neither of which can be understood without an examination of her workplace. Her workplace, similar to others, cannot be seen only as a place of economic production, but must also be understood as a coherent social and cultural environment which is organized through known and predictable social relations, practices, cultural norms and expectations. What happens in this environment, which is daily and highly regulated, cannot just be treated as random or unpredictable behaviour. As we shall see from the general pattern of her harassment (as submitted in X's complaint) there was nothing random about the carved penis incident.

This incident marked the moment of X's ultimate humiliation, where not only was she forced to see this repugnant object but also to provide a spectacle for others in doing so. As we see from the submissions, X felt this to be not a joke but rather an act of violence against her and a threat. In a manner of speaking it is in its intensity and singularity an archetypal experience, and it highlights for the reader the real quality of her six-year work life in this company. The perspective which I have introduced in the beginning of this article is the lens through which we can now view X's work life and her workplace.

Let us begin with the organization and "race" composition of her workplace. It is significant for our purpose that X worked in an almost all-white workplace. When she worked in the women's section there was, to the best of her knowledge, only one other non-white woman working on the same floor with her. There were approximately fifty white women working with her. When she moved into the men's section not only where there no women, but the one or two non-white men who existed, appeared or disappeared among a male white work force of about a dozen. This workplace (as in other industrial concerns) was divided in men's and women's, "heavy" and "light" labour sections, respectively. As a whole, then, the "normal" atmosphere was white, where the absence or exclusion of non-white people was nothing out of the ordinary.

This recognition of the "normal" character of her workplace allows us to treat her experience there as a piece of everyday life, which then needs to be broken down or deconstructed to reveal a whole range of socio-cultural forces which play themselves out through forms of behaviour which can be called "harassment" (sexual or not). This deconstructive analytical method which takes daily incidents apart, at the same time helps to situate or locate an event within its social space, within a matrix of social relations. Feminist sociology has often taken recourse to it. The work of Dorothy E. Smith, for example, may be especially looked into for a clear idea of how such a situating critique may be put together. In this framework, a worker's or any person's experience is not seen just as her own but as a possible experience with particular variations of all similar workers or persons within that setting and context. Similarly, the social and cultural relations of any particular workplace can be assessed as ongoing and unfolding social and cultural processes, practices and values present in the society as a whole. This is to treat "power" as a "concrete" social form and relation with a specific history and locale—not as an abstract concept, and this is the only way to point out the systemic socio-structural and historical aspects of sexism or racism. This moves our understanding of oppression from intentionality (good/bad people story) to a more fundamental notion of social organization, where such experiences are routinely possible because they are intrinsic to the properties of certain organizations.

This helps us to take the next step, to locate the characteristics of the workplace within the broader Canadian society. We need to show that the workplace displays characteristics which exist in the everyday Canadian world. Therefore, *individual* behaviour, workplace relations, daily life within its precincts all come within purview of *social behaviour* and greater social and economic forces. Thus, X's work life, for example, cannot be fully understood outside of the general pattern of Canadian labour importation, labour market, labour process, and workplace. We have to consider which community works where, how, at what, and the reasons for doing so. A comparative study of work and workplaces brings this out clearly, as do cases brought to the labour and management mediating bodies, or peer behaviour brought to the personnel offices or the unions.

The socialization and organization of behaviour and social pattern and organization of workplaces and so on in terms of "race," gender, and class, require an understanding of Canadian history. Issues of colonialism, indentured labour and ethnicized immigration history need to be brought into view. Numerous studies in state or class formation in Canada provide an understanding for who become the working class, who is allowed to work here, at what jobs and wages, and what are the general socio-economic expectations from non-white immigrants. This paper will refer to this historical dimension only in so far as it speaks to this particular case and the present time in Canadian labour organization and economy. This means a broad overview of non-white, especially non-white women's, labour in Canada, and a study of the role played by the Canadian state (immigration policies and so on), which has constructed and manipulated notions such as "race" and ethnicity through its policy making and administrative procedures. Sometimes, more than others, the state has been explicit about this.

Finally, we must address daily cultural practices and everyday common sense perceptions of groups of people living in Canada regarding each other. They are connected with a historical popular consciousness and the creation of social meanings regarding different types of people. This extends to both their physical and cultural characteristics, giving rise to normative conventions and stereotypes which have powerful and daily socio-economic and political consequences. These stereotypes indicate something about the expected physical presences and absences of certain groups of people within any given social space. Sexual division of labour or gender roles express precisely this meaningful location of bodies and their physical functions within assigned social spaces or boundaries. Thus, for example, the female body is stereotypically conceived within a so-called private space (home) and the male in a public one (workplace). The former (supposedly) belongs to the worlds of reproduction (social and biological), the latter to that of production (economic and intellectual). The factual and actual presences of women in the public sphere have always been undercut by this ideological construction of the "two spheres" and cultural and moral assumptions and behaviour appropriate to that division. This has had dire personal and economic consequences for all women and has been the centre of debates regarding women in "non-traditional" jobs or the value of housework.

Similar to this binary organization, and in fact grounded in it, there has been a stereotypical, though often contradictory, set of spatial perceptions and "normal" expectations of the presence of black bodies in gender and class terms. Thus a society which is historically founded on colonialism, slavery, or the formation of class and culture on the ground of "race" and ethnicity, provides a further cultural twist to the social meanings of bodies and their appropriate location within a social space. There is not only a general administration of social space, including work space, which is so-called gender divided, but it is organized through silent practices of "race" and its attendant stereotypes. This is evident in the social map of occupations and workplaces, where men and women in general are expected to hold to two spheres, but within that, that is, within the public sphere or workplace with their own internal gender organization, black men and black women are expected to hold subordinate and inferior and further segregated positions.

An examination of Canadian immigration policy and economic history will show that certain jobs are reserved areas of the minority communities. We can practically predict that the lowest-paying, possibly piece-working, most unhealthy and unclean jobs will be the preserves of the non-white communities will hold the most dead-end, vulnerable, worst-paid positions. The expected and permissible presences and absences of black people in general, and black women in particular, will be drastically different and marginalized as compare to whites. Stereotypically, a black male or female will not be expected to fill the professional social space but that of manual and industrial labour or the lower levels of white-collar jobs. The world of high culture and intellect will neither expect them nor will they be found there in significant numbers. Thus, in a society based in the ethics of upward mobility, the non-white population will be mainly expected to reproduce the working class, making class formation a "raced" affair. In keeping with that dominant culture, including the media, cultural and educational administration, and other aspects of the state, such as welfare, all participate in creating and maintaining the appropriate socio-economic and cultural boundaries. The presence of black women in unexpected areas, i.e. in places which are contrary to ongoing conventional practices and expectations of both all women or black men, will signal a major *transgression*, and call for responses which will enforce prohibition and segregation. Racist or sexist or racist-sexist responses in the workplace can thus be interpreted also as attempts to re-establish the so called "norm"—whereby norms of gender and "race" and "raced" gender are, perhaps unconsciously even, sought to be reasserted. From this standpoint, X's story can be read as a textbook case of reassertion of racist/sexist social norms through an exercise of common-sense racism.

A further note regarding the concept of "common-sense racism." This term is useful for expanding the meaning of racism from something that this articulate, aggressive, and blatant, or a clearly thought out ideological position (for example, of the Ku Klux Klan, or that of an "apartheid" government) to the level of everyday life and popular culture. Here racism takes on a seemingly benign form of what "we" "know" about "them," meaning a collection of conventional treatment, decorum, and common cultural stereotypes, and myths regarding certain social groups. For example, we can refer to the apparently harmless notion of "blacks have an innate sense of rhythm," or the myth propagated by Philip Rushton and others that some "races" are more civilized or modern and intellectual than others due to having better genes. Furthermore, these "race"-based stereotypes commonly inform our daily life, though they originate from a long history of, and presently organized, racist practices which imply white supremacy. In sociological texts produced in Britain such as *The Empire Strikes Back*, Peter Freyer's *Staying Power, Not In Our Genes*, edited by Steven Rose and others, or Sandra Harding's edited collection *The Racial Economy of Science,* we find excellent analyses of this seemingly harmless everyday racism, which also reveal racism to be an intrinsic aspect of Western economies and culture. Given this, common-sense racism in conjunction with a more organized, practical and ideologically violent version can together provide a better explanation for understanding X's experiences. The staging of the penis incident shortly before her departure from the workplace would have certainly done credit to even the KKK.

## A Breakdown and a Breaking Down—A Deconstructive Description

When asked to describe her multiple experiences of harassment, including that of the carved penis, X said:

> Everybody apparently denied everything that I said or seen and that nothing was going to be done about it. And I don't—like I said, I started at my feet this here shaking and all of a sudden I started hollering and the guys were standing behind the union steward as he was telling me that it was all in my head, nobody seen anything and these guys were standing behind him laughing and all of a sudden the body just started going out of control, and that's when I had to eventually leave my line because it moved up to my knees. I never experienced anything like this before. (Submissions)

What is striking about this description is how personal and social it is simultaneously. In fact its traumatic character, which is intensely individually experienced, is essentially dependent upon the social environment of the workplace, a particularly organized and motivated presence of other workers, who are both male and white, and intent upon producing a humiliation and terror in a black woman has strayed into their work domain. Her presence, it seems, has disturbed their sense of territory and violated the pre-established convention of the "normalcy" of their workplace. After all the "normal" atmosphere of this place as in many industrial concerns is "white," i.e. exclusive of blacks or non-white people whose physical presences therefore would be exceptions rather than a rule. The social relations of "race" and gender here express or contain a "normalcy" which cannot be anticipatory or positive toward the presence of non-whites, especially of a female black worker. This silent organization of labour on the grounds of "race" and gender has an implicit racist-sexism embedded in it, though presumably no one has explicitly instructed these white male (and female) workers in an ideology and explicit administration of racism, as in apartheid South Africa or in certain southern states of the U.S. The norm has been diffused in the place, among other things, through a convention in hiring, through a systematic physical absence, which has incrementally created the white workers' sense of their "normal" space or territory. The question that confronts us then is how these white workers, who are used to their white "normalcy," cope or deal with this abnormal or unusual presence of non-white (and female) co-workers in their midst? What appears from X's testimony is that a general atmosphere of exceptionality regarding her presence pervades right through the workplace. X herself states that she had the option of adjusting to this very hostile environment, to the degraded demands and expectations that white men and women had of her, or to be expelled from it. Therefore, if we do not understand that her troubles began much earlier than that of working in the men's section and while among white women, we will not get a clear view of her experiences in the workplace. It is here that the analytical category of racist-sexism provides us with the basis for the later phase of "sexual harassment" that she undergoes.

"Sexual harassment," which conventionally implies a heterosexist male/female dynamic, becomes a limited concept for understanding the fundamental nature of X's experience, unless we expand it to include racist-sexism, which also exists between white and black or non-white women. This racist-sexism is endemic to the everyday world of her workplace, and to miss this by seeing her as "just another woman among women" is to gloss over the actual social relations of her workplace. It is important to note that these other women among whom X worked were white and thus brought up in a general culture of racism. We should also note that women internalize patriarchy as much as men do and can be profoundly sexist towards themselves and others. In X's case, though they could not or did not assault her "sexually," they assaulted her by calling her names, ordered her around and in general by leveling against her stereotypes common in the dominant (Anglo Canadian) culture about black women and women of colour. They had the power and numerical strength to do so as they were never prevented by the union or personnel management. The specificity of details of X's work life indicate one important truth, that though a white woman worker could have been harassed by her female or male co-workers, she would not have undergone this precise type of aggression, this intensity of humiliation and surplus domination which is expressive of racist-sexist practices and attitudes towards black women.

As I began by saying, there is a danger of reproducing racism in treating X's blackness as a given and therefore of omitting the words "black" and "white" as adjectives or indicators of meaningful social presences. Through the omissions of these adjectives the concrete nature of the workplace becomes visible to us. If we want to uncover the actual social relations present from the very beginning of her work life, we have to show how the organization of the workplace holds the same ongoing racist relations which are strengthened by the overall lack of non-white presence. The details of the submission show how "white" assumptions, meaning racist notions regarding her "black womanness," came out in a persistent aggression upon her consistent refusal to comply to illegitimate orders and expectations. Strong, hard working, often unresponsive to their insults, persistent, she seems to have violated a whole set of norms the white women workers, for example, held as basic to "women." And her very moral and physical strength and persistence when under adversity became a negative quality, some sort of an "uppity-nigger" syndrome. The condition under which she would have been seen as "normal" or tolerated was that of subservience. When she refused to do this and excelled at her job, she was not only considered a misfit but downright intolerable. They complained about her frequently and finally forced her out of the women's section. As she was a "good worker" she was promoted but also segregated from the (white) "women's world." She was in relative isolation in different stages of her work, both pushed into a choosing isolation for reasons of self-protection. Both white women and white men may have seen her as "unfeminine," but she also fell squarely within the stereotype of black women as hard labourers, beasts of burden—a construction of common-sense racism dating all the way back to slavery.

It has to be noted that though the white men's "sexual harassment" is what ostensibly drove her out of her job, both white women and men united in creating a situation that forced X out of this workplace. The extent, persistence, and scope of this is so large and long lasting that it cannot at all be explained in terms of an interpersonal dynamic, her personal temperament, or psychological problems. It is clear that the subsequent "sexual harassment" itself had a wide basis of social, i.e. environmental, support. She did not fit a "woman's place" in the workplace in terms of the ideology of the feminine and even less so a black woman's place. An aura of "masculinity" was attributed to her. After all, she was not demoted to more menial jobs but instead promoted to eventually handle that male symbol, industrial technology. This earned her more pay, at a higher risk, and a greater isolation.

X with her ability to stand up to pressures and to persist in her work and her goal of working for a better life, violated stereotypes of femininity that white women may have had about themselves and certainly regarding the competence of black women. This display of her strength may have unified them against her, as she did not cry, appeal, or withdraw ("feminine" behaviour) upon persecution but kept to herself and did her job efficiently. White men also might have found her ability to surmount obstacles and improve her skills equally intolerable and wanted her "out." In the end, after six long years of struggle, she "broke down." That is, they succeeded in "breaking her down." This occasion was therefore much less an outcome of her own psychological predisposition, than the achievement of her co-workers in keeping with social relations of power which intrinsically structured her workplace. It is this fact that gets obscured when we attempt to understand her experience solely in terms of "race"-gender neutral notion of "core" workers versus "others," or in terms of personal psychological problems. Even "sexual harassment" obscures more than it reveals.

It is interesting that white women's view of her as "unwomanly" is echoed by the psychiatrist's report which portrays X's behaviour as "unfeminine," relying on a model of gendered behaviour. When female patients display what they call more than a "normal" amount of (for women) persistence and independence, they are masculinized or become denatured women. How internalized must sexism be among women to have become so transparently mixed with professional assessment, whereby perseverance, independence, hard work etc. are seen as typically "male" behaviour and dependence, and weakness "female." Thus it was "male" or "unnatural" of X to have kept going on so long in the face of adversity. She disproved the assumption of the white women on the shop floor that X would quit if pressure were kept up. In fact, X presented them with both an anomaly and a challenge, and both the white women and white men tested out the full range of their sense of normalcy regarding how much she could tolerate. The situation was obviously unequal, with no supporters on her side since anyone who was sympathetic to her was intimidated. Her expulsion then was a question of time. She had challenged too many stereotypes, too much of the established forms of "race"/gender labour organization of workplaces in Canada by being a persistent black female worker in a "non-traditional" job, among white females and males.

If these white women wished to make sure that she did not stay where she did not belong, X felt the full weight of this state of not belonging and unwantedness. But she needed the job and, moreover, desired an improvement in her job situation. She also recognized that in her "light" job among women she would have to put up with all kinds of harassment without any more money to provide compensation. So if she were going to have to work hard in an unpleasant workplace, she wanted to be elsewhere, where she could actually make more money and possibly be left alone. Here no interaction would be expected of her either because she was alone or because she was a woman among men. What she wanted basically was to learn more about machinery and to advance in her career.

These are, according to X, the reasons for which she left behind a so-called woman's job to go into a so-called man's job. There was a period in "the mill" where she worked by herself, between her transition from "light" job to "heavy." That was a period when she re-organized herself for a new phase in her work life. This was a phase of isolation both in terms of work and environment. She was not quite anywhere, neither in a "man's job" nor in a "woman's job." But soon an opportunity came for a promotion and she was chosen to become an operator as her work had been considered extremely good by the foreman. He decided to give her a try. It is possible that he did not know where else to send her with her good work record and the continuous complaints of the white women. In a manner of speaking he neutralized her in gender terms and treated her as an abstraction, as a production facility, as "a hand." And it is through this neutralization of her gender, brought about by her anomalous status, a de-feminization, that X was put into men's work.

By the same characteristic which de-feminized X she created another threat or a challenge to male workers. She was a "superworker." She worked too hard and capably, and workplace studies show that there has always been resentment of superworkers both among time and piece workers. Superworkers provide an object of resentment and threat for two reasons. One, by being an unbeatable competition for others, which calls for this worker's elimination. The competition and intolerance become even more intense if this worker is of an undesirable "race" or gender, for example, a black woman who makes a substantial wage in overtime. As we know X was working even harder during her breaks, partly because she feared being harassed, and partly because she wanted to make money. This produced an animosity that is typical to organization of class, which in actuality is neither "race" nor gender neutral. Class is after all a competitive phenomenon, and this competition provided the reasons for resenting her, as both a superworker and a black woman superworker in a white workplace. It was intolerable that she should show up others as comparatively lazy and unenterprising. She was never seen as somebody who deserved the money she made. Everything that X did was seen as a transgression on her part and thus was utterly unacceptable to the working community which surrounded her.

So if somebody who should not be there in the first place is seen as the cause of so many "problems," why should the other workers not try to get rid of her? This is precisely what they did. At this point all the norms and forms of racism, patriarchy and class came to work and were leveled towards this woman who violated the whole working community's sense of what is owing to a black woman and the conduct required of her. A sense of outrage and nonacceptance accounts largely for the passion and intensity, which is otherwise inexplicable, with which for six years they pursued her until they drove her out. By breaking her down they reasserted on the shop floor all the norms of a racist-sexist and class-bound society.

The expectations from X obviously were that she should fit some common notion of her "natural" inferiority as a black woman and should also "know her place." Her ascribed role was to serve (in all senses), both in social and sexual terms, the white women and men, i.e. members of the dominant culture, and this is what she failed to do.

X's presence in the "heavy" task area or the men's section received much legal attention because the language of "sexual harassment," which relies essentially on heterosexuality as the offending motive, can easily attach itself to what is found within that domain. Since this area involves a direct male/female interaction, "sexual harassment" becomes obviously more actionable here. The violations here are also the most gross and blatant. I would like to point out that "sexual harassment" here has to be read as "racist sexual harassment." The fact of her "race" provides the differential, the specificity of both the type of sexism and sexual harassment which she encounters. This section of the shop floor is not only a separate section physically removed from the women's area but also a section which is the sole preserve of white male workers. We have to imagine a group of white males, with the spattering of one or two non-white males among them, who are getting progressively frustrated with a black woman's ability to learn technological skills and withstand pressures. We also heard that there was the odd non-white person who wanted to help X but were intimidated or possibly fired, for doing this.

Here, in this social space of the men's section, the racist sexism which prevailed generally in the workplace became "racist (hetero)sexualism." It becomes obvious quite early in the stage of her transfer that these men want her out of their world and they use various racist (hetero)sexual strategies to drive her out of their space. This is substantiated in terms of the pornographic pictures placed in her tool box, frequent name calling such as "cunt" or "bitch," displays of "Sunshine Girls" in her work area, frequent work sabotage and uncooperative behaviour and finally the display of the green penis with its tip of foam on it. This penis and all other incidents encode not only the sexual but the overall social relations of power, in the shape of assumptions and stereotypes which structure the workplace. X is put at all times in the most problematic situation. Everywhere she goes she is unwanted, everywhere she is expected to fail. She is promoted and simultaneously set up to fail by lack of co-operation from others. The job of an operator, as we see from the submission, entails cooperation with co-workers, but they refuse to provide it. They not only use the verbal threats and insults but also stage repeated and extensive sabotage of the machinery, work places, and her training. Her punishment for the transgression is to be situated at the intersection of winning and losing. This persistent sabotage and hostility of fellow workers indicate that X violated some basic norms of the environment, not the least of which was that blacks are not supposed to command whites and are mostly in positions to do so. Furthermore, a woman is not supposed to tell a man what to do. Nor is a woman supposed to be working with heavy machinery and a man is not supposed to be a woman's cleaner or helper in a technological work process even where "race" is not an issue. The problem further compounds in the case of a woman who is black, who demands these facilities as a routine part of her job, which in the first place should have been a white man's prerogative. What "self-respecting" white man would take orders from a black woman? Or help her to rise above himself in the hierarchy of either the workplace or society at large?

Studies have shown that white women are harassed by white men in a comparable situation on gender grounds, because a white man will not take orders from a white woman. In a workplace as elsewhere there is a continuum of set gender expectations or cultural norms. In this case, sexist harassment is doubly compounded and intensified with racist modulations. There is a difference in the nature of sexual harassment that X undergoes. Sexual harassment of white women by white men often involves an element of direct personal body contact or direct sexual solicitations, which is pornographic but not always or immediately brutal. That is, sexual overtures are directly made—for example bottoms and breasts are pinched, various simultaneously lucrative and degrading offers and innuendos are directly made. In short, there is a personal harassment that points to the particular signification of white women's bodies for white men. This signification, which is implicitly "raced," takes on a very specific racist sense in the case of a black woman's body as perceived by white men. It is important to note that none of X's recorded harassments actually involves direct personal sexual contact or conventional sexual innuendos. Her oppressors do not seek sexual favours from her or offer career related favours, such as a promotion for sexual bribes. Her sexual harassment is mediated through pornographic images of black women *servicing* white males by performing oral sex. The degradation and the objectification essential to this type of image involving black women have a tone of racist sexual violence. They compound elements of rape and evoke threats of gang rape, as well as inflicting public humiliation in a grotesque form. Studies on pornography and sexual representation of black women show similar forms which are degrading, servile, and objectifying. In these images of racist sexual servitude, various racist representations of black women, including of animality, coalesce into one synthetic image.

These images of sexual servitude and animality depicting black women are old; they are historical. They hold memories of slavery and a long history of racism in the context of class domination. Indentured labour, degrading immigration practices and immigrant labour fuse with practices of rape of black women on the plantations, their present-day humiliation in domestic labour and welfare offices, and their association with supersexed behaviour. In short, everything that we can attach racism to as a social and historical phenomenon. They represent a woman compositely, as a woman and a black woman, who is a member of a sub-working class or a sub-serving class from which subservience can be demanded by whites. This specificity of "raced" gender involves a development of an everyday racist-sexism into a stage of racial (hetero)sexual harassment.

Finally, we have to make sense of the green soap carving of a penis with its tip of white foam. This image, and its display to a captive X, marks a violation of any woman's sense of self and symbolizes a gross male sexual aggression, though not performed directly on X's body. Though the word "rape" has not been used in the submission, that this is a symbolic or a ritual reenactment of a gang-rape should not escape any sensitive observer. However, to say this is not to say enough. The character of this symbolic gang rape needs to be contextualized. In X's case it encodes centuries of master-slave relations which may have been limited as economic practice to certain countries but were culturally and socially generalized throughout the West. The practice of lynching black men and some black women is conveyed by the same gesture, in the associative contextualization of its meaning. I would like to combine the violence of both lynching and rape and call it a "lynch rape." The symbolic enactment of a gang rape is also infused here with the spirit of a spectacle which lynching entails because of its collective and public nature. Unlike the pornographic pictures that her co-workers put in her tool box, which X could see privately, by displaying the soap penis in the public space and having a number of men view her viewing the penis, there is an enactment of a ritual. It then becomes a spectacular symbolic action signifying a ritual degradation and a sort of a punishment. The moment marks X's progression—from the women's section in "light" work, to the men's section in the workplace which she left shortly after this incident. The time in between was one of a continuous struggle for self respect, survival, and self improvement. It is this struggle, unequal as it was, which culminated in this horrifying spectacle of a symbolic/ritualized gang rape which was tantamount to lynching in being an exemplary form of punishment. This is the trajectory of the work life of X and Y company. And not any moment of it is explicable without an account of the dominant social relations and forms of consciousness which structured her workplace and the society in which it existed.

In order to understand the systemic or structural dimension of this racist sexism, we must examine the behaviour of the company's administrators and its union. First, we should look at the union's response. X complained to the union on various occasions. On what ground, we may ask, did the union as workers' organ of self-representation not defend its own member? Throughout the six years, not a single action was taken by the union against the harassing peer group. Only towards the end of her stay the union responds minimally to the pressure of the personnel office to secure an apology from one of the workers. While this indicates a basic acknowledgement of X's situation, on most occasions the union representatives ignored her complaints and tore them up and threw them away. So we cannot but infer from this that the union had no room for any redress specially regarding racist peer behaviour. The executive members and shop staff of the union were all white males and the general membership was mostly white. As the union did not concede X's accusations of racism and sexism it is obvious that they had no interest in restructuring the workplace, so that it would become a safe workplace for X or other non-whites or white women workers, for that matter.

If broken machinery in the workplace creates accidents and therefore must be changed, then a bad set of social relations in a workplace are equally dangerous and productive of injury. It must also be the responsibility of the workplace to change them. This is a question of both emotional and physical safety. The kind of mechanical problem that the white male workers created through their uncooperative behaviour resulted in the lack of X's physical safety, it also resulted in reducing her productivity. But the company and the workers were so fully acculturated to sexism and racism and worker harassment that they refused to recognize these as legitimate grounds for initiating changes or redress. In spite of the fact that their job was to facilitate management at all levels of the factory, the employers took no responsibility, notwithstanding the presence of due process which exist in all workplaces. One of these officials even went so far to threaten her, by saying "If you think this is bad, wait 'till you come back and see what happens to you." It is important to note that threats are directed at the very person who is the victim rather than at the aggressors. All this not only shows poor management, but most of all, structured and normalized racist sexism within the workplace, of which I have spoken before. It is evident that the workplace takes for granted what they may call a "normal" amount of abuse on these grounds. It is not until after the penis incident that the foreman actually noted a complaint of X in his log book. There is no written record of sabotages by X's co-workers, who did not show up to put the bins under the soap shoot, for example, or did not help her with her machine breakdowns and even actively damaged them. Not only was nothing ever noted by the union or recognized by the management, but X was continuously denied the truth of her own work experience. She was always silenced and ignored. This can only be seen both as an intentional attempt to confuse and debilitate her as well as an unconscious attitude of contempt and hostility towards her. The frustration produced by this situation created a deep disturbance within X which resulted in a nervous collapse.

It is interesting that the physical symptoms of her "nervous breakdown" came precisely when they disacknowledged the reality of her experiences. Obviously this conduct of negligence and silencing in the part of the workplace is indicative of normalization of daily abuse. This notion of an acceptable amount of abuse or racism and sexism in the workplace is similar to discussions of an acceptable degree of radiation. It ignores what any radiation at all does to a human body, but arbitrarily decides that it is acceptable to expose humans to this or that degree of it. Similarly this normalization of sexism and racism poisons the whole work environment and serves as a kind of encouragement rather than as a disincentive to those who are racist-sexist. It provides a signal for workers to continue the harassment. It seems that in this normalization of sexism and racism male workers and male management overcome the traditional division between them and unite in their racism and sexism and share the same fund of stereotypes about "others."

We have already talked about assumptions and expectations in countries such as Canada about non-white people which are racist-sexist. These notions and images are cultural codes of common sense in the very day life of Canada. They are not self-conscious projections and practices of people. Nobody needs to read a book to learn them. They are handed down or are absorbed from daily living in the general social environment. Among these we have to look at specific stereotypes and see how they fit with the way X was treated by her co-workers. The conventional racist wisdom in North America is that black women will put up with a large amount of abuse, or that black working-class women are particularly without a claim to social respect. Other representations or stereotypes involve an equation between black people and physicality. A racist discourse denies black women any intellect or rationality but, instead, attributes to them merely a body for sex, reproduction, and labour. It is considered her "natural" role in life to meet the white society's needs for physical services. This "beast of burden" image of black women is prevalent from the times of slavery to now, and it has repeatedly provided the common-sense basis for how she is to be seen or treated. The other image, which in a way contrasts with the above, is that of a superwoman, of a dominant, abrasive, and castrating woman and mother. This myth claims that black women are so strong that they can endure any hardship. Michelle Wallace in her book, *Black Macho and the Myth of the Superwoman*, talks about how this mythic black woman figure is constructed. This myth, even if it seemingly aggrandizes the black woman, is essentially dehumanizing and debilitating. Reading between the lines, we find the presence of all of the above assumptions or stereotypes at work regarding X in her workplace.

It should be mentioned in this context that black women's sexuality as depicted in the West, from advertisements to the music industry to pornography, has been degrading and often portrayed in animal terms. This is consistent with the pornographic racialized sexualization which confronted X. The photographs which were out in her tool box are consistent with the degraded idea that a black woman can mainly serve an organ or a part of a white male, and with the inference that she is herself no more than a sexual organ (e.g. a "cunt").

It has been pointed out in literature on pornography that sexual violence against women reduces all women to mere genitalia and secondary sexual characteristics—to objects. But in X's case, the use of a dildo or the carved penis expresses more sharply the profound violence of pornography when racism is mixed with sexism. Racist-sexist pornography when racism is mixed with sexism. Racist-sexist pornographic stereotypes are common and powerful. In softer forms they exist in advertisements, for example, which frequently depict a black woman as an exotic body comparable to a powerful horse or panther. A more social and mundane version of this is to be found in Daniel Moynihan's study of the black family where black women as mothers and wives are shown as matriarchs who castrate black men. Moynihan's report, criticized as being racist, has still been extremely influential in subsequent reports and research dealing with poor black women and black families. The other related but inverse image is one of servitude and physical nurture. Aunt Jemima, for example, is a popular version of this servant mother, where the black woman is reduced to a single physical and social function intended mainly for white consumption. This total mother figure denoted nothing but serving, physical motherhood. There is no intellectual, moral, or even sentimental dimensions to it. Nowhere, either in the luxurious, ebony images in the advertisement or in this supermother figure or in the notion of a super woman rising above all adversity, do we ever find an association of black women with mind, soul, heart, emotion, intelligence, and creativity. What we know about X's work experience makes everything fit like a copybook exercise to all this literature on black women and racist-sexism.

Now that we have looked at X's case with regard to racist-sexist cultural common sense and internal social organization and relations of her workplace, we need to locate this workplace within today's greater Canadian society. We need to ask who works where and at what jobs, in what conditions, and at what wages in Canada? Studies show that Canadian immigration and labour history and labour management patterns consist of different stages, each of which immigrants were brought in for the precise purpose of creating the working class. Immigrant groups were and are to fit into certain slots of labour requirement and those slots were/are not in the area of developing professions. Often they are not even in highly skilled trades but rather in the most menial services and unskilled manufacturing. There is an overwhelming presence of immigrant women within these sectors, for example, in the textile industry or in service sectors, such as office or domestic work. In other skilled industrial sectors which are non-textile, very few white women drift in, and almost no black women. X was a rare exception.

We saw through her case the predictable difficulties of an untypical worker in an environment of skilled work. Women both black and white are typically to be found in the less skilled or manual areas of the work world, and black women even more so. Research on women, work and technology has told us that technology drives women out of work both in the first world and the Third World.

In the general spectrum of labour very particular kinds of work are performed by black women or by women of colour. If one wants to find out where women of colour work within the industries, one does not go to the front of the factory, which is its public profile, but rather into its basement, into the least ventilated, the darkest and the most oppressive areas in the workplace. Even in the non-industrial sector they work in areas which are always unpleasant and risky. It can be farm work, for example—growing mushrooms or picking strawberries while living in barracks or being bussed in with their children from cities. There are many cases of children falling into pits and dying. They can also be at home "homeworking" for the garment industry in oppressive conditions and underpaid, as Laura Johnson describes in *Seam Allowance*, where Chinese women sit inside closets all day with sewing machines. In the factories these women inhabit segmented corners where they endlessly swallow lint or other pollutants from the air and perform the task of sewing on half a thousand buttons a day or perform some other mindless and repetitive work.

This situation is expected, not an exception. It is the norm of organization of labour and labour market in Canada with the active help of Immigration Canada. The state is the main agency through which soul labour has been sought, brought in and employed in this country. Immigration histories point out how, with other imported workers, the immigrant non-white worker was brought to Canada in order to fill certain productive requirements. The worse the job, the more the so-called "open door" policy is adopted towards Third World countries, giving rise to the existing local black communities. They are also blamed, once they have come, for all the economic problems that pre-existed their arrival. Canadian companies in Latin America, for example, put up advertisements promising a good life upon arrival to Canada. They project many incentives and once the immigrants are in Canada, they provide a vulnerable labour force and are often considered undesirable by the white population. This produces a captive body of extremely insecure workers who can neither go back or go forward and which can be kept as a "flexible labour force" for when the labour is needed and pushed out when not. This labour has to be continuously kept in reserve. Most of all, it is to be understood that this part of the labour force is meant to be unskilled and kept as lower status members of the working class. They are called "newcomers" or "immigrants" even after they acquire citizenship and are made to feel like "guest workers," eternally labelled and marginalized as "migrants," "aliens," and "outsiders." This is evident in what the white workers think of X, even though she, unlike many of them, is a many-generations Canadian. The prevailing racist attitude creates the feeling that non-white immigrants in particular are always on sufferance. They are often in jobs and sectors which are non-unionized. Canadian labour is as a whole under-unionized, and to attempt to create a union is a "kiss of death" because the involved workers face the possibility of being fired and are usually never reemployed either by the firm that fired them or by most other firms. And where there is a union, as we saw with X, it does not necessarily protect these workers as they are not seen as equal (with whites) members within the union. X knew all of this, so she decided to learn to live with it all, to rise above it and to fight it as best she could. That is why she did not quit her job. The next place she would go to, as she told me, would be no better necessarily, in this company at least she was making $16.00 an hour. It was worth the trouble of learning to live with the problems, she told me, rather than being at a place which pays the minimum wage and offers the same harassments.

So when we examine the social and stereotypes which structure Canadian society and work, we can see how non-white people form sub-groups within the Canadian working class as a whole. The black community thus belongs to the lower part of the ladder and within that community, women hold a place which is even lower. This is systemic racism since the economy pervasively organizes a labour market on the basis of "race" and ethnicity and it is systemically impossible to profit without having workers who can be paid little and made to work much. After all, the less it puts out for production costs, including the wage of the workers, the more profit the company makes. Judging by this, women's work, especially of non-white women, is the cheapest to purchase. We should remember that the wage differential between men and women in Canada has increased rather than decreased in the last decades. This is not an atmosphere of challenging discrimination.

The problem of racist-sexist organization of labour is not only that of Canada and the United States. Writers such as Pratibha Parmar or Errol Lawrence from England have pointed out the power or pre-existing stereotypes for determining the nature of employment that non-white women or men hold in Western countries. Ranging from Turkish and other "guest workers" in Europe, to Bagladeshi women "homeworking" in Britain, to black women such as X, all non-white, immigrant workers fall within pre-existing gender-"race" slots of work and stereotypes which define the dominant culture's expectations and views of them.

These images and stereotypes of inferiority of black or non-white women are obviously economically profitable to the business community. If the worth of women's labour is low, then non-white women's labour value is even lower. Racist-sexism propagates these stereotypes and keeps this value low, and the workers vulnerable. That is why we have to relate the present situation of X to the economy of Canada, while pointing out the complicity of the Canadian state in her domination. In studies on domestic labour in Canada (for example, *Silenced* by Makeda Silvera) we see how the state is engaged in procuring domestic workers for the upper-middle class, who are almost invariably white. This work force is mostly non-white, consisting mainly of Filippinos (currently) and women from the Caribbean. We can see the material basis of racist-sexist stereotypes when we go, for example, to the airports in Britain or Canada, where South Asian women provide the cleaning workforce.

Racist-sexist cultural representations are integral to the organization of the economy. Much has been written on images of South Asian women as submissive, docile and unresisting to patriarchal abuse. In Canada, books such as *Seam Allowance*, speaking to the myth of Chinese women's "nimble fingers," and *Silenced*, about superexploitation of Black and South Asian women as domestic workers, often bring into play certain stereotypes of sexual laxity and affinity with gross physical labour. Angela Davis in *Women, Race and Class*, or bell hooks in *Ain't I a Woman,* among many others, discuss the racist-sexist perception of black women in North America from slavery to "free labour." One only needs a periodic look at the *Toronto Sun*, for example, or the television, to see what images and assumptions are circulated by the popular media among masses of people, both black and white. Stereotypes range from "yellow peril" to "black (now Asian) criminality" and are cultural lenses through which communities are viewed and introduced to each other literally *via media*. Mis- or disinformation crowd the news and other television programs, while the fashion industry, sports and music equate black people with the body and a natural gift for rhythm, and the Chinese with an innate propensity to do well in mathematics. The quintessence of all this was in the geneticist theories of social scientists such as Phillip Rushton which have found a lethal expression in Murray and Hernstein's current work.

## Conclusion

Far removed as these themes may seem from the case of X, upon deeper reflection it should become clear from the above that they are intimately related. These greater social forces in their interaction fundamentally construct X's experience, where she and her co-workers become actors in a social drama of sexist-racism and sexual harassment. This drama however is not restricted to this company and selected "bad" individuals. Culture to education, child socialization to the greater workings of the economy, media and the state, all combine openly and insidiously to acculturate members of society in racist-sexism. Jokes about "Pakis," nursery rhymes about "catching a nigger by the toe," to serious physical assaults, sexual and otherwise, (including regular police shootings of male black youth and of Sophia Cook—a black woman shot in Toronto by a police officer while she sat in a parked car), all constitute our present day social environment and its "normalcy." In such a situation, what befell X cannot be seen in any way as her own doing. Millions of white women, and black and non-white women (and men), living in the West, have to deal with different types of sexual harassment. It is not X who needs to change, as her employers suggested, but the society in which she lives. She should not be paying economic and emotional prices for wrongs that have been historically and are presently being done to her people, on the grounds of being a black working-class woman. Just as the women engineering students killed in Montreal by Marc Lepine had a right to be where they were and learning subjects hitherto kept at a distance from women in most countries, so did X have a right to her dignity and her presence in the industrial section of this multinational pharmaceutical company operating in Canada.

## References

Aggarwal, Arjun. "Characteristics of Sexual Harassment." In *Sexual Harassment in the Workplace*. Toronto: Butterworths, 1972.

Armstrong, Frederick. "Ethnicity and the Formation of the Ontario Establishment." *Ethnic Canada: Identities and Inequalities*. Ed. L. Driedger. Toronto: Copp Clark Pitman, 1987.

Armstrong, Pat and Hugh. *The Double Ghetto: Canadian Women and their Segregated Work*. Toronto: McClelland and Stewart, 1984.

Bannerji, Himani. Ed. *Returning the Gaze: Essays on Racism, Feminisim and Politics*. Toronto: Sister Vision Press, 1993.

Brand, Dionne, and Krisantha Sri Bhaggiyadatta. *Rivers Have Sources, Trees Have Roots: Speaking of Racism*. Toronto: Cross Cultural Communications Centre, 1986.

Brittan, Arthur, and Mary Maynard. *Sexism, Racism and Oppression*. Oxford: Blackwell, 1984.

Centre for Contemporary Cultural Studies at Birmingham University. *The Empire Strikes Back: Race and Racism in '70s Britain*. London: Hutchinson, 1982.

Chan, Anthony. *The Gold Mountain: The Chinese in the New World*. Vancouver: New Star Books, 1983.

Connelly, Patricia. *Last Hired, First Fired: Women and the Canadian Work Force*. Toronto: Women's Press, 1978.

Coverdale-Sumrall, Amber, and Dena Taylor. Eds. *Sexual Harassment: Women Speak Out*. Freedom, CA: The Crossing Press, 1992.

Crenshaw, Kimberle. "Demarginalizing the Intersection of Race and Sex: A Black Feminist Critique of Antidiscrimination Doctrine, Feminist Theory and Antiracist Politics." *The University of Chicago Legal Forum* (1989).

Davis, Angela Y. *Women, Race and Class*. New York: Vintage, 1983.

Estable, Alma. "Immigrant Women in Canada, Current Issues." A background paper prepared for the Canadian Advisory Council on the Status of Women, March 1986.

Gaskell, Jane. "Conceptions of Skill and the Work of Women: Some Historical and Political Issues." *The Politics of Diversity*. Eds. Roberta Hamilton and Michele Barrett. Montreal: Book Centre, 1986.

Gates, Henry Louis, Jr. Ed. *"Race," Writing and Difference*. Chicago: University of Chicago Press, 1986.

Government of Canada. *From Awareness to Action: Strategies to Stop Sexual Harassment in the Workplace*. Compiled and edited by Linda Geller-Schwartz. Ottawa: Women's Bureau of Human Resources Development Canada, 1994.

hooks, bell. *Ain't I A Woman: Black Women and Feminism.* Boston: South End Press, 1981.

Hurtado, Aida. "Relating to Privilege: Seduction and Rejection in the Subordination of White Women and Women of Color." *Signs: Journal of Women in Culture and Society* 14 (1989).

Juteau-Lee, Danielle, and Barbara Roberts. "Ethnicity and Femininity: (d')après nos experiences." *Canadian Ethnic Studies* 13 (1) (1981).

Law Union of Ontario. *The Immigrant's Handbook: A Critical Guide.* Montreal: Black Rose Books, 1981.

Mitter, Swasti. *Common Fate, Common Bond: Women in the Global Economy.* London: Pluto Press, 1986.

Nain, Gemma Tang. "Black Women, Sexism and Racism: Black or Antiracist Feminism?" *Feminist Review* 37 (1991).

Ng, Roxana. "Immigrant Women and Instutionalized Racism. In *Changing Patterns: Women in Canada.* Eds. Sandra Burt *et al.* Toronto: McClelland and Stewart, 1988.

Ng, Roxana. "*similar similar* The Social Construction of "Immigrant Women" in Canada." *The Politics of Diversity.* Eds. Roberta Hamilton and Michele Barrett. Montreal: Book Centre, 1986.

Ontario Human Rights Commission. "Racial Slurs, Jokes and Harassment–Policy Statement and Guideline." Reprinted in *Currents: Readings in Race Relations* 6 (1) (1990).

Silvera, Makeda. *Silenced.* Toronto: Williams-Wallace, 1983.

Singh, B., and Peter Li. *Racial Oppression in Canada.* Toronto: Garamond Press, 1985.

Smith, Althea, and Abigail Stewart. "Approaches to Studying Racism and Sexism in Black Women's Lives." *Journal of Social Issues* 39 (1983).

Smith, Dorothy, E. "Feminist Reflections on Political Economy." Paper presented at the Annual Meeting of Political Science and Political Economy, Learned Societies Meetings, Hamilton, June 1987.

Submissions of the Claimant "X," prepared by the office of Cornish and Associates, on behalf of the worker, to the Workers' Compensation Board, Claim # B15878672T.

Wallace, Michele. *Black Macho and the Myth of the Superwoman.* New York: Dial Press, 1979.

# II. VIOLENCE AND WOMEN'S HEALTH

# Race, Gender, Violence and Health Care

Yasmin Jiwani

Immigrant women have been the focus of numerous scholarly investigations from diverse disciplinary traditions. Yet, although constructed as a group, the needs, realities and lives of immigrant women are not homogenous nor are they a monolithic group. "Race" and class are major factors influencing immigrant women's choices and degree of access to shelter, employment, and services (Anderson, Blue, Hollbrook and Ng; Bolaria and Bolaria; Lee with Harrison; Ng). Immigrant women of colour are racialized in terms of their construction as "others" as well as their subordinate status within Canadian society (Iyer; Ocran; Thobani 1998). Legislation and policies concerning immigration have a tremendous impact on settlement and access to services. Hence, whether a woman immigrates as an "independent," a "sponsored dependent" in the family class, a convention refugee, or has received "landed status" after serving time as a domestic worker or live-in caregiver determines her subsequent status and access to services (Thobani 1998).[1] The same situation applies to undocumented women, migrant workers, and foreign students whose access to services may be further impaired by the degree of legality ascribed to their status.

Even prior to immigrating, applicants have to demonstrate that they are in good health and will not pose a risk to public health, or impose a burden on the health care system. Should they fail the medical exam on either one of these conditions, they will not be admitted into the country. According to the "excessive demands" clause, an applicant will not be admitted if their health demands "exceed that of the average Canadian (evaluated as $2,500 per year); if their admission may displace a Canadian resident from obtaining services; or if the required services are not available and/or accessible" (Laroche 53). The popular perception of immigrants as a drain on the health care system or as endangering public safety has a long history (Beiser).[2] Historically, the threat of people of colour bringing over strange diseases was used to rationalize their exclusion as citizens and immigrants (Anderson and Kirkham). That fear still remains and continues to inform policy decisions around screening mechanisms for the detection of diseases among potential immigrants (Beiser; Shroff).

Many immigrant women come to Canada as dependents of their spouses or as "sponsored" individuals who are sponsored by families or spouses (Abu-Laban). In either case, their dependency on the sponsoring spouse is underscored by the legislation (Ng). As dependents, they have little access to services. The sponsoring spouse or family has to demonstrate they are economically able to support the sponsored person for a period of ten years. If the sponsorship agreement breaks down, the woman involved can obtain hardship assistance, but she would have to verify her changed circumstances and inform the authorities (see Janoviek). Her status would then be reviewed, and she could potentially risk deportation (Dosanjh, Deo and Sidhu). Even if the sponsorship agreement is intact, should the woman's spouse be deported, she will be deported as well. The situation is often complicated by the reality that women are involved in the joint sponsorship of their own and their spouse's extended family members. The coercive pressure to keep the family together compels women to remain in abusive relationships.

## The Racialization of Women

According to Citizenship and Immigration Canada, immigrants constitute 17.4 per cent of the population, totaling 4,971,070 individuals. One out of every six Canadians is an immigrant (Kinnon). Asia and the Pacific constitute the source of 54 per cent of all recent immigrants, followed by Africa and the Middle East (18 per cent), Europe and the UK(18 per cent), and the U.S., Caribbean, South and Central America (ten per cent). Thus, it is safe to assume that most of the recent immigrants are people of colour or in the terminology of the government, "visible minorities." According to Statistics Canada, the "visible minority" population in Canada totals 3,197,480 and in BC, the figure is 660,545, constituting approximately 18 per cent of the total provincial population (Statistics Canada 1996).

The identity of groups that are racialized varies according to the particular society being examined and is reflective of a group's social status in a given historical period (Miles, 1989). Within Canada, Aboriginal peoples, people of colour, the Jewish, Irish and Ukrainian peoples have been racialized at various times in the history of the nation. Today, Aboriginal people and people of colour still remain on the outskirts of Canadian society as racialized groups who are visibly identifiable and subject to racism, exploitation, marginalization and criminalization (Bannerji; Das Gupta; Henry, Tator, Mattis, and Rees; Jiwani 2000).[3] Racialization refers to the "processes by which meanings are attributed to particular objects, features, and processes, in such a way that the latter are given a special significance and carry or are embodied with a set of additional meanings" (Miles 70). Women of colour are racialized in the sense that their skin colour serves to demarcate them and imbues their representation with negative valuations. These meanings are grounded in an ideology of racism which Bulhan defines as:

> the generalization, institutionalization, and assignment of values to real and imaginary differences between people in order to justify a state of privilege, aggression and/or violence. Involving more than the cognitive or affective content of prejudice, racism is expressed behaviourally, institutionally, and culturally. The ideas or actions of a person, the goals or practices of an institution and the symbols, myths or structure of a society are racist if (a) imaginary or real differences of race are accentuated; (b) these differences are assumed as absolute and considered in terms of superior, inferior; and (c) these are used to justify inequity, exclusion or domination. (13)

As Bulhan notes, racism can be communicated in a variety of ways and can take different forms in different historical periods. Thus, there may be many "racisms," and the task at hand is to "[understand] racisms as modes of exclusion, inferiorization, subordination and exploitation that present specific and different characters in different social and historical contexts" (Anthias and Yuval-Davis 2). The discourse of immigration itself has become racialized. Hence, the term "immigrant" is popularly constructed as referring to a person of colour (Henry *et al.*). This point is echoed by Ng who states:

> ... technically, the term, "immigrant women," refers to women who are landed immigrants in Canada. In everyday life, however, women who are white, educated, and English-speaking are rarely considered to be immigrant women. The term conjures up the image of a woman who does not speak English or who speaks English with an accent; who is from the Third World or a member of a visible minority group; and who has a certain type of job (e.g., a sewing machine operator or a cleaning lady). (cited in Lee with Harrison 16)[4]

Canadian society has long been described by scholars as a vertical mosaic (Hamilton, R.; Porter). The description highlights the stratified nature of the society and the ranking of groups within it on the basis of their class and race, as well as the particular structures of domination exerted on the basis of sexuality and ability to maintain the hegemonic power of the elite and reinforce the normative glue of social cohesion. Within this structure, women constitute a subordinated group. Their inequality is defined on the basis of institutionalized economic, socio-cultural and political devaluation, all of which are underpinned by historical and contemporary social forces. Similarly, people of colour are subordinated by institutionalized racism and largely occupy the lower rungs of the society (Henry *et al.*). Thus, the very institutions that women look to for protection and services are themselves structured on hierarchies based on race, class, gender, sexuality, age, and ability. These forces are evident also in the organization and structure of the formal health care system in Canada (see, for example, Varcoe).

However, within the category of "women," a similar hierarchy exists. Class, race, sexuality, and ability engender a ranked order and influence women's autonomy, access to services and economic mobility. As Elizabeth Spelman argues, there is no "universal woman" (Bannerji; Spelman). To submit to an essentialist notion of woman is to negate the differences between women and erase the power and privilege exercised by some women over others (Razack).[5] It is to erase the impact of racism, classism, heterosexism, and ableism in the lives of women.

Immigrant women of colour who have experienced violence are positioned at the juncture of multiple and intersecting systems of domination. Not only are they located in the lower echelons of the social stratification system of the wider society because of their race and gender, but they are also located at in the bottom of the hierarchy of preferred clients of the health care system. Compounding this situation is the reality of their subordinate status within their own communities as a result of patriarchal forces that are heightened by state policies of immigration. As women who are classed and raced, their needs and realities have and continue to remain invisible, and their voices confined to the realm of advocacy and survival.

## The Immigrant Experience: Resilience and Survival in a High Risk Context

Immigrants come to Canada for a variety of reasons. Principal among these is to secure a better future for themselves and their children. Coming to a western country from a developing nation has always carried connotations of upward mobility, economic betterment, and a more secure future. Certainly, the picture that western countries have advanced, through various channels, to the developing worlds of the South is framed in the racially inscribed language of colonialism where the south is constructed as backward, traditional and in need of modernization (read westernization) and the North, by contrast, is presented as the realm of democracy, economic prosperity, individual freedom and equality. Implicit in this language is the promise of acceptance, integration, and equality for those groups migrating to the north. Hence, many immigrants of colour come to Canada expecting that they will be able to participate fully and enjoy the fruits of their labour in economic and social terms. They bring with them their social, cultural and in many cases, economic capital.

## The Reality of Racism

Since 1976, many immigrants who were selected on the basis of their qualifications and skill-sets (as determined by the Canadian immigration point system), find themselves, upon arrival, deskilled and devalued (Ervin; Ng). Their qualifications are not recognized and they are required to obtain "Canadian experience" in order to qualify for jobs more suited to their abilities. Not having any Canadian experience because of the lack of accreditation and the reluctance of employers to hire them, they experience downward mobility. For racial minorities, this factor is compounded by the pervasive racism in Canadian society (Billingsley and Muszynski; Bolaria and Li; Boyd; Henry and Ginzberg; Henry *et al.*). The overt and covert nature of racism in Canada has been documented extensively by advocates and academics. As Frances Henry and Carol Tator confirm: "In a white dominated society, the colour of your skin is the single most important factor in determining life chances, as well as your dignity, identity, and self-esteem" (cited in Fleras and Elliot 35). In a context of intense and prevalent anti-immigrant sentiments, the reality of immigrants of colour is one of constant negotiation, adjustment, and retreat into the cultural community. And in the Canadian context where racism is more "polite" and insidious, the processes of negotiation are more nuanced and confounding leaving many people of colour doubting their own realities. This situation of being a perpetual "other" exacts its toll on the mental health of immigrants of colour. As one immigrant woman interviewed by Marion MacKinnon and Laura Lee Howard put it:

> We are living in the community but it's just like water and oil, you shake the bottle, they mix together, you cannot tell the difference and I say "Hello, hi Joe, how are you?" and then the bottle settles down, oil and water separates. We don't feel we are really mixed with the neighbours, with the community. (28)

Franz Fanon and Albert Memmi have poignantly described the psychological impact of being a perpetual outsider and being "othered." Additionally, Black feminist scholars have further elucidated on the psychological and sociological impact of racism (e.g., Davis 1990; hook; Williams, P.). As people of colour who are also immigrants, the trauma of migration combined with the experience of being "othered" contributes to a greater sense of alienation and marginalization.

## The Impact of Migration

In his study of the Southeast Asian boat people, Morton Beiser observes that immigrants go through three distinct stages during their process of resettlement in Canada. Initially, they experience a period of euphoria. This is followed by a period of disillusionment during which depression is common. Finally, a period of adaptation follows. These periods accentuate the stresses of migration that mark the lives of all immigrants resulting in a sense of loss, helplessness and alienation (Choi; Moussa 1994; Schneller; Vega, Kolody, and Valle; Zulman). MacKinnon and Howard state that, "Immigration itself is associated with increased morbidity.... These factors include: language difficulties, multiple responsibilities; financial and employment stressors; lack of acceptance by their host communities; culture conflict; and a perceived lack of social support" (25).

For refugees, these stresses are more intense as a result of witnessing or being victimized by violence. However, in the case of immigrants of colour, the harsh reality of racism and its constancy make the settlement process more difficult, if not traumatizing. American studies have underscored the negative health impact of racism (e.g., David and Collins cited in Cameron, Wells and Hobfoll). Combined with the poverty resulting from deskilling, under-employment and unemployment, the disruption of social ties and the lack of immediate supportive networks, the health impact of migration is more severe for immigrants of colour (Brice-Baker). A Canadian study indicates a high suicide rate among Asian women (Kinnon). Anderson (1987) notes that for the immigrant women in her study, loneliness and depression were a daily feature of life.

## Multiple Roles

Immigrant women have been identified as a high risk population (Meleis). Afaf Meleis defines their vulnerability as stemming from the multiple roles they are required to play within the home and the external society, as well as the constant negotiation of competing demands that results from their bi-cultural existence. The notion of "role overload" has been documented in the U.S., UK, and Canadian literature as one of the defining stressors in the lives of immigrant women (Anderson 1987; Choi; Li and May; MacKinnon with Howard; MacLeod and Shin; Rhee). Some authors have detailed the multiple work that immigrant women do in terms of constructing a transnational community, transmitting cultural knowledge, and providing support to their immediate and extended kin (Alicea; Lutz; Ng). This is in addition to the double load that most women carry with respect to working outside the home and childrearing and house work. However, the negotiation of multiple roles occurs within a larger social context, and it is the responsiveness of the receiving society which plays a critical role in exacerbating role overload. Part of this responsiveness lies in the kinds of services and programs that are available to immigrant women to facilitate their integration into the economic and cultural spheres. Yet another part deals with the attitudes that are directed at immigrant groups in general and racialized groups in particular (Bald; Henry *et al.*). Exclusion from the larger society as a result of racism increases immigrant women's role overload in terms of their responsibilities as nurturers providing a space within the home that is affirming and that provides a sense of belonging through cultural continuity.

## Racism and Sexism: Economic Exploitation and Ghettoization

Canadian social policy has tended to view immigrant women as dependents of their spouses or families and to erase their social, economic and cultural contribution to the economy (Thobani 1999). Despite having higher qualifications, immigrant women are unable to practice in their fields because of language barriers and the lack of accreditation of their qualifications. Further, they are often diverted from language instruction and economic integration programs on the assumption that they are not the principal breadwinners of the family (Ng; Roberts). As an evaluation report conducted by the Windsor Occupational Health Information Service (1995) demonstrates, immigrant women are not provided language instruction or education in terms of their employment rights. This renders them a pliant and cheap labour force, which can be easily exploited. B. Singh Bolaria and Rosemary Bolaria note that immigrant women tend to work in occupational areas that are dangerous and hazardous to health. Further, many of these sectors are unprotected by unions, rife with economic exploitation, seasonal or part-time in the kind of work they offer, and render women working within them vulnerable to all forms of violence (Anderson 1985; 1987; Jiwani 1994; MacLeod and Shin with Hum, Samra-Jawanda, Rai, Minna and Wasilewska; Philippine Women Centre; Savary). Lack of dominant language skills serves to stream women into low paying, low mobility and seasonal jobs (Ng; Ocran). This has a direct bearing on the kinds of stresses they experience, their vulnerability to violence, and their ability/inability to access adequate services.

Ghettoized in particular jobs (Iyer; Ocran), many of these women also experience gender role dislocation in the family. The deskilling and unemployment of men combined with more rapid employment of women in low paying jobs (Ng), e.g. domestic work, create additional tensions in the family. In a series of focus groups convened by the MOSAIC immigrant settlement society, women from the Kurdish, Somali, Vietnamese, Polish, and Latin American communities in Vancouver discussed the gender shifts in their family and the potential for violence. The focus group participants, "felt that immigration and the resulting changes in the family roles and expectations, appear to increase men's insecurity in the relationship, and that insecurity, in turn, resulted in dysfunctional behaviour" (4-5).

## Legal Status

By far the most common thread cited in the literature dealing with immigrant women who have experienced violence centres on the implications of the legality of their status (e.g., Abraham; Brice-Baker; Calvo; Choi; Choudry; Dosanjh *et al.*; MacLeod and Shin; MacLeod *et al.*; Narayan; Rasche; Rhee). As indicated previously, most immigrant women enter Canada as sponsored spouses. Their dependency on their spouses is underscored by the sponsorship requirements and reinforced by the state. Sponsorship obligations are often used as instruments of power and control by abusive spouses to reinforce their authority within the family (MacLeod and Shin; Moussa 1998). In essence, the dependent designation subordinates women in the relationship and accentuates their dependency on sponsors to meet basic needs (Ng). For women, this translates into a feeling of indebtedness (NAWL), a fear of deportation, fear of having their children taken away from them, and fear of poverty and destitution should they leave the abusive relationship.

In British Columbia, social assistance policies known as BC Benefits exacerbate the situation by holding the sponsoring spouses accountable for any social assistance given to women. This contributes to a continual harassment of immigrant women by their abusive spouses, who use it to threaten women not to disclose abuse and/or leave the relationship. For many women, the situation is compounded by their lack of knowledge regarding their legal rights. Language barriers, dependency and lack of dominant cultural knowledge, contribute to their inability to access information about their rights or the resources that may be available. Studies focusing on "mail order" brides are illustrative of the impact of isolation, lack of knowledge of the dominant language and systems, and dependent status as factors contributing to violence (Choi; Narayan; Philippine Women Centre and GAATW).

In addition to their legal and economic dependency, the lack of accreditation of skills and qualifications for both themselves and their spouses contribute to immigrant women being streamed into specific jobs which are "dead end" (Ng 289). The decline in their spouse's status leads to the use of other means by which spouses attempt to exert power and control within the home.

### Isolation

In describing the situation of immigrant women in the U.S., Vivian Pinn and Mary Chunko identify isolation as a key risk factor for domestic violence. Social, structural and cultural isolation contribute to women's marginalization and vulnerability to violence. Lack of dominant language skills can in effect make women more dependent on their families and communities to negotiate their survival. The lack of cultural knowledge and frameworks of meaning within the dominant society increases the sense of isolation experienced by many immigrant women (Wiik). Exclusion from the dominant culture as a function of racism exacerbates the isolation and sense of loneliness they experience (MacLeod *et al.*; Rasche; Sidhu). Many women don't know where to turn when they are victims of violence.

### Accessing Services

Existing studies indicate that lack of dominant language skills is a key barrier exacerbating the situation of immigrant women (Calvo; Chin, 1994; Choudry; Dyck; Easteal; MacLeod and Shin; MOSAIC; Perilla, Bakeman and Norris). Inability to communicate in the dominant language permeates interactions with service providers leading to feelings of frustration and heightened dependency on those who can translate. Too often, the interpreters are other immediate members of the family. This serves to compromise confidentiality and can engender feelings of shame and embarrassment (MacLeod *et al.*; Sasso). Lack of adequate and appropriate interpretation can lead to misdiagnosis thereby endangering the lives of immigrant women (Sasso).

However, language barriers are only one of many issues impeding immigrant women's access to services (Anderson and Kirkham). Given immigrant women's concentration in the lower, unprotected echelons of the labour force and the piecemeal nature of work they are required to perform, women cannot afford to take time off to access services. Should they take the time off, they often have to find transportation and accompaniment by someone who can interpret their request. And further, inability to communicate in the dominant language compounds the difficulties of negotiating with government and health care and social service bureaucracies (Gany and Thiel de Bocanegra). Thus, aside from language, other barriers also influence immigrant women's access to health care. In her study of immigrant communities and their access to health care, Christensen found that the inability to speak in the dominant language was mentioned by only 27 per cent of the individuals she surveyed. Similarly, Anderson (1987) found that immigrant women of colour who speak English fluently experienced barriers to services based on the stereotypes that health care providers had of their particular cultural groups.

## Silencing Violence

Immigrant women's marginalization in the social, cultural, political and economic spheres of society also contributes to their sense of "otherness" and lack of belonging. The retreat into their cultural communities exacts a price for immigrant women of colour who experience violence. When the community becomes the only site for a sense of belonging and self-esteem, jeopardizing one's reputation incurs social costs which could amount to stigmatization and exclusion (Dasgupta; Health Canada; Huisman; MacLeod and Shin; Rasche; Rhee; Wiik). In this sense, the plight of immigrant women who experience violence parallels that of rural women whose only choice in leaving a violent relationship is to leave their community (Jiwani with Kachuk and Moore). However, in a racist milieu where men of colour are increasingly criminalized, reporting violence can in effect be construed as "race treason" (Flynn and Crawford; see also Davis 2000; Razack). Communities are labeled and constructed as being inherently violent resulting in negative social implications for other members and children. Fear of deportation and criminalization leads many immigrant women of colour to avoid authorities and any form of official documentation that could potentially jeopardize their legal status.

The subordinate status of immigrant women as dependents, combined with their streaming into occupational ghettos that are hazardous, underpaid, and unprotected and their diversion from language classes (and concomitantly from occupational and economic mobility), contributes to their inferiorization, isolation and marginalization. Given the racism and sexism they face from the broader society, and the sexism they face from within their own communities into which they retreat in order to maintain a sense of self, immigrant women of colour are indeed in a high risk category. However, as a vulnerable population, their access to services is limited. Their gender, race, and class form a juncture where multiple forces of domination intersect. The negative health effects emanating from the stresses of migration, economic exploitation, stigmatization and marginalization worsen the situation. The negative health effects emanating from spousal abuse are further accentuated by the institutionalized racism and sexism that immigrant women of colour encounter in the formalized health care system, namely at the hands of medical professionals.

## Women, Violence and the Medical System

As a social institution, the health care system is stratified. The system is "raced, classed, and gendered" in the way in which services and labour are organized. While the janitorial, kitchen, and laundry staff occupy the bottom echelons of the system, nurses are located above them, and physicians along with hospital administrators account for the elite. The concentration of people of colour occurs at the lower end of the hierarchy, namely in the cleaning sector. Within this tiered context, there are varying levels of violence perpetrated against those who have relatively little power and control (Varcoe).

The medical professions' response to women who have been abused has been described as inadequate (Kinnon and Hanvey). According to studies cited by Dianne Kinnon and Louise Hanvey, "medical personnel identify one battered woman in 25." The absence of an effective response to the screening and treatment of battered women has been attributed to a lack of knowledge about violence among medical personnel, their unease with dealing with issues of violence, the implications of violence in terms of their own experiences of abuse, stereotypes about women, and preconceived notions about woman abuse. Further, identification of abuse tends to depend on the visibility of symptoms and the lack of alternative explanations by which to understand the injuries. For women whose symptoms are not visible, the possibility of effective identification and intervention is further reduced. The political economy of medical care is also undoubtedly an influential variable, given that physicians are paid on the basis of the number of patients they treat. The time required to deal with woman abuse is greater than the time taken to simply prescribe medication.

## Health Care Costs of Violence

It has been estimated that the medical and health related costs attributed to violence against women amount to $408,357,042 nationally (Greaves, Hankivsky and Kingston-Riechers). These include the costs of emergency visits, consultations with doctors, ambulance services, psychiatric ward care, and some treatments. They do not include the costs to patients, e.g., transportation, prescription drugs, time-off from work, child-minding, or anything else that is required to obtain medical services. Nor do they include the entire spectrum of health issues associated with the psychological forms of abuse which may result in self-harm.

In the 1999 General Social Survey on Spousal Abuse conducted by Statistics Canada (Canadian Centre for Justice Statistics), 40 per cent of the women who had experienced violence reported being physically injured and requiring medical attention. The 1993 Statistics Canada Survey on Violence against Women revealed that 45 per cent of the victims of spousal violence had been physically injured (Johnson). Further, in 21 per cent of the cases, the abuse took place during pregnancy (Varcoe). Injuries among women who had been abused included burns, cuts and scratches in 33 per cent of the cases, and miscarriages and internal injuries in ten per cent of the cases (Wilson). According to Archer, "70 per cent to 80 per cent of women who are psychiatric inpatients have a history of physical or sexual abuse. Fifteen to 30 per cent of women presenting to emergency rooms have a history of current abuse" (975). The Domestic Violence Program at the Vancouver General Hospital reported a 15 per cent disclosure rate among women presenting to the emergency department (Chambers). As Chambers notes, most women do not disclose the violence to the police or other authorities. Rather, they tend to confide in friends and family. Nevertheless, the health impact of chronic stress and violence compels many women to seek medical attention.

For women who are experiencing violence, the doctor's office may be the only place they can go unaccompanied, as medical visits tend to be more sanctioned and normalized. It may also be the only place in which they can disclose abuse if asked by a concerned physician. Yet, as a study by Barry Trute, Peter Sarsfield and Dale MacKenzie of general practitioners in Manitoba revealed, most physicians do not ask questions about violence. Trute *et al.* found that physicians who are male and who have been in practice for a long time period were less likely to detect abuse. The 1993 Violence against Women Survey found that 23 per cent of the women who had been injured by a male partner had approached a doctor. Linda Bullock, Judith McFarlane, Louise Bateman and Virginia Miller found that 8.2 per cent of the women who had visited the four planned parenthood sites in their study were victims of physical battering. While hospitals are the sites which women turn to in emergencies, the chances of the family physician being the first line of refuge for an abused immigrant women is much higher. Community-based research underscores this point (e.g. Sidhu). The role physicians can play in detecting abuse and providing referrals is therefore critical, as is the role of nurses working within clinics and hospitals (Henderson and Eriksen; Varcoe). Nevertheless, even in this context, anecdotal and community research suggests that disclosures are not given serious consideration.

## Health Effects of Violence

The health effects of violence are manifold and complex. They include Post-Traumatic Stress syndrome which groups a range of symptoms (Abbot, Johnson, Mc-Lain and Lowenstein; Archer; Argüelles and Rivero; Chuly, 1996; Ristock and Health Canada); bronchitis and upper respiratory infections (Abbott *et al.*); depression, anxiety, fear, mood swings and dissociative states (Argüelles and

Rivero); chronic pain, fibromyalgia, chronic pelvic pain, headaches, gastrointestinal disorders, irritable bowel syndrome, and pelvic inflammatory disease (Radomsky), to name just a few of the more common symptoms. Other mental health issues arising from being victimized by violence include sleep disorders, sexual dysfunction, anxiety disorders, alcohol and substance abuse, low self-esteem, suicide ideation and obsessive-compulsive disorders. Archer notes that in a study of women who had attempted suicide, 83 per cent had experienced intimate violence. Kurz and Stark found that women who had experienced intimate violence were five times more at risk of committing suicide. Women who are sexually assaulted are eight times more likely to commit suicide, six times more likely to attempt suicide, and five times more likely to have a nervous breakdown (Boychuk Duchscher).

While this list identifies some of the longer term health sequelae of violence, it does not locate these within a socio-ecological model (Perilla *et al.*) that outlines the intersections and compounding factors of race, class, sexuality, and ability/disability, as well as the larger and more immediate social context of the individual and group (Stark, Flitcraft and Frasier). To this end, Janice Ristock and Health Canada note that factors such as "racism, isolation, lack of services, language barriers, geographical barriers, and religious beliefs" can amplify the impact of violence (9). This observation is echoed in other literature focusing on immigrant women in the U.S. (e.g., Bohn; Brice-Baker; Champion; O'Keefe).

## The Medicalization of Violence: Systemic Sexism

As an institution, the health care system reproduces social inequalities by privileging those who have power and subordinating others. In so doing, the health care system draws upon the dominant language of biomedicine to categorize, manage, and process patients. Symptoms become the categorical referents which are then organized to generate the "appropriate" prescriptions. As a system of thought, western biomedicine embraces a Cartesian dualism focusing on the physical manifestation rather than the social, psychological, and economic reality of the patient. To some degree, this dualism has been tempered by recent discoveries that point to the links between "mind" and "body." However, in the case of woman abuse, the incorporation of a socio-ecological model which begins with a recognition of patriarchal power and the systemic violence of racism and classism has yet to occur. While Health Canada's population framework model signifies a beginning in its recognition of gender and class as determinants, it has not permeated the dominant medical discourse of the health care system.

In an insightful analysis of the treatment of woman abuse by the health care system, Ahluwalia and MacLean note that the medical encounter is a hierarchical one in which power inequalities between the patient and the physician are asserted and reinforced. The physician assumes the role of the expert, deciphers the symptoms of the patient, and prescribes an antidote to eliminate or control the symptoms. In keeping with the dominant ideology of capitalism and liberalism, the patient is seen as being responsible for her/his ailment and, hence, compliance becomes a way for the patient to assume responsibility. This kind of processing of patients and the commodification of their symptoms within the economic arrangements underpinning the health care system result in a management of the health effects of violence that render the patient—in this case the woman who has been abused—as being responsible for her abuse. Post-Traumatic Stress Syndrome, the Battered Women's Syndrome and psychiatric classifications become an avenue by which symptoms are managed and controlled. The labelling also serves another purpose—namely to negate the social dimensions of violence against women and to reformulate them as an "individual problem of self-abuse" (Ahluwalia and MacLean 190).

Studies by Demi Kurz and Evan Stark, Evan Stark, Anne Flitcraft, and William Fraser, Colleen Marie Varcoe, and Carole Warshaw, identify the specific ways in which women who are abused become labeled and their symptoms used to generate prescriptive interventions in the form of referrals to psychiatric services and antidepressants. In a study of the treatment of abused women in one hospital, Warshaw found that the very practices of the medical profession have a detrimental impact on the diagnosis of symptoms associated with gender-based violence. As she observes:

> ... using the standard medical shorthand, which is an important shaper of how physicians learn to organize their thinking, we see how the subject becomes a mere descriptor. What are foregrounded are the symptoms: swelling and pain on the mouth. The physician's note uses the passive voice and focuses on the physical trauma. Even the additional statement, "hit by a fist," is structured to give information relevant to the mechanism of the injury and what damage might have been done to the body. It removes the fist from the person attached to it. In doing so, the physician, although perhaps not consciously, makes a choice that obscures both the etiology and meaning of the woman's symptoms. (141)

Varcoe points to the ideology of scarcity as expressed in discourses of limited resources and inadequate funding for health care that are used to rationalize the rapid processing and turnout of emergency patients. She also notes that patients are assessed on the basis of their appearance and class and that the treatment provided by nurses varies accordingly. In her study, the nurses' perceptions of violence hinged on signs of physical abuse manifested by the women they saw. Thus, their estimates regarding the prevalence of abuse in the women presenting at emergency were much lower than indicated by the statistical evidence.

In the case of battered women, it becomes evident that societal pressures and institutional discourses and practices combine to generate treatment that perpetuates violence against women, but in ways where the agency (will) of these women is harnessed toward their own self- and intimate abuse. Hence, rather than acknowledge that the violence women are experiencing is a function of the patriarchal power of the family as embodied in the power of the male partner—a power which is supported and sanctioned by society as a whole—the women are prescribed antidepressants or diverted to psychiatrists or social workers in order to patch them up so that they can go back to their homes (Ahluwalia and MacLean; Stark *et al.*). The outcome of such interventions is "misdiagnosis; repeated, and often inappropriate treatment of symptoms rather than the root problem; lack of empathy leading to greater trauma and poor collection of forensic evidence" (Kinnon and Hanvey).

Critical analyses of the failure of the medical system to properly address the widespread and systemic issues of violence against women have resulted in a range of interventions spanning from the introduction of screening protocols in hospitals to educational measures aimed at physicians and nurses, and the insertion of violence-related curricula in medical and dental schools (Berman and McLaren; Coeling and Harman; Grunfeld, Hotch and MacKay; Hamilton, J; Henderson and Eriksen; Hotch, Grunfeld, MacKay and Cowan).[6]

The health care system is an integral part of society, and as a social institution, it reproduces the larger social forces of sexism, racism and classism that underpin and shape the status of women within the wider society. Violence against women is pervasive and remains a painful reality despite the decades of activism from the women's movement, reforms in social policy, and educational initiatives. The elimination of violence rests on the eradication of social inequalities. The health care system is predicated on these inequalities as evidenced by the tiered structures that are operative within it and the differential power and privilege accorded to individuals occupying the different levels of the hierarchy. Patients are accountable to nurses and physicians; nurses are accountable to physicians; and physicians may be accountable to hospital administrators. These categories are permeable to some extent but what they reflect is a presence and entrenchment of a hierarchy. Within this hierarchy, the woman who has experienced violence has virtually no power. If she is presenting in an emergency context, her power and agency are further reduced. As a victim of intimate violence, she embodies the brutality of patriarchal power within the home. Her power is further erased by the discourses and practice of western biomedicine which regard her as a constellation of symptoms to be categorized, managed, and processed. Class, gender, and race enter the already unequal encounter between the abused woman and the physician/health care worker. Depending on her class, she may be treated better or worse, and, depending on her racial features, she may be treated in a worse manner or have her concerns overlooked and her problems attributed to some innate cultural traits.

## Institutionalized Racism

As with sexism, the formal medical establishment and the health care it offers is not immune to racism. In fact, the traditional power and authority of physicians is maintained by ideological beliefs grounded in the perception of the superiority of western medicine and the inferiority of other, indigenous forms of health care.

Overt racism in the medical system has been observed in the unequal practices of hiring whites over people of colour, the ghettoization of people of colour in certain jobs, and their lack of advancement and absence in decision-making positions. The reluctance to accredit medical practitioners trained in other parts of the world is another manifestation of the exclusive structure of power and privilege inherent in the medical system. This latter point is an obvious indicator of systemic racism given the Canadian government's concern and preoccupation with the "brain drain" of qualified health personnel to the U.S.

In a study focusing on Black nurses in a Toronto hospital, Tania Das Gupta observed that their work was more heavily scrutinized, the demands and expectations placed on them were greater than those placed on white nurses, and Black nurses were often sidelined for advancement. These findings corroborate an earlier study by Wilson Head of racial minority nurses in Toronto hospitals. Head found that racial minority nurses were significantly underrepresented in decision-making positions in hospitals, and further were not promoted at the same rate as white nurses, despite having the same or superior qualifications (cited in Henry *et al.*).

In a series of focus groups with patients and physicians, Andrew Cave, Usha Maharaj, Nancy Gibson and Eileen Jackson found that physicians tended to stereotype patients according to their cultural groups. They also observed that patients acquiesced to the authority of the doctor and regarded western medicine as superior. Beiser's overview of the literature indicates that minority status influences the kind of health care one receives. Blacks were more likely to be diagnosed with schizophrenia than whites, and "family doctors are less likely to refer non-English clientele to specialists than their English-speaking counterparts, and surgeons are less likely to perform procedures such as cardiac bypass surgery, or kidney replacement on minority, than on majority group patients" (29). A recent American study found that Black patients were not only less likely to seek emotional assistance from professionals but were also more likely to be underdiagnosed for psychiatric disorders (Kosch, Burg and Podikiju). It is not clear whether this finding is equally applicable to physicians of colour.

In an interesting study on patient-physician pairing, Gray and Stoddard found that after controlling for socio-economic factors, minority patients tended to choose minority physicians. While there are methodological shortcomings to their analysis, the preference for physicians from the same racial or ethnic group is observable among Canadian immigrants and may be predicated on issues concerning language barriers, social networks, and cultural comfort.

## Erasure, Trivialization and Silencing

Studies of immigrant women's access to, and encounters with, medical professionals consistently point to the erasure and trivialization of their health concerns. The MOSAIC consultation with immigrant women from various ethnocultural communities revealed that women felt they could not communicate with their physicians and further, that the physicians' focus on the physical aspects of their health negated the root causes of their illness and erased the totality of their being (see also Anderson 1987). In other words, physicians did not employ a socio-ecological analysis that would situate the woman in the context of her experiences and lived reality. Given the stresses and impact of migration combined with the dislocation of traditional roles, the role overload identified by Gil Choi and Afaf Meleis, as well as the streaming of women into dangerous and unprotected jobs, it is surprising that physicians negate these vital aspects of immigrant women's health.

Anderson notes that the Indo-Canadian women in her study, "continually repeated that health professionals did not understand their concerns, so in other words, there was no point in trying to communicate with them" (1987: 426). This lack of response serves to communicate to immigrant women of colour that their concerns are not worthwhile. Consequently, many immigrant women feel silenced. Abraham found that health professionals' insensitivity and apathy toward immigrant women stems from their racist stereotypes and perceptions about particular ethnic groups. Research conducted by Linda MacLeod and Maria Shin, MacLeod *et al.*, and Surjeet Sidhu with immigrant women in Canada confirms this observation.

Sidhu's study of 22 immigrant women who had experienced abuse highlights the structural dependency of these women on their spouses. As sponsored immigrants, many of the women relied on the same physician as their abusive partners. The family physician is thus in a position of conflict serving the abuser and victim at the same time and may be more likely to believe the abuser's account of the violence. As Sidhu argues,

> This made it awkward for the women to discuss marital issues. Due to the physician-patient confidentiality, the physicians would not suggest a joint consultation between patients. It was up to the individual to approach the doctor. If the partners were unwilling to cooperate or expressed anger at the women for raising "their" family problem in the public arena, the women risked more abuse from their partners. (33)

Sexism combined with racist stereotypes contribute to immigrant women's vulnerability and erasure. The longterm health impact of dealing with these forms of oppression is exacerbated by the weight of "enduring racism in silence" (Jackson and Inglehart cited in Cameron *et al.* 201).

### "The Undeserving Patient"

The prevalence of racist stereotypes about people of colour among health care professionals has been documented extensively by Varcoe in her participant-observation study of nurses in several emergency departments. Varcoe observed that nurses had definite notions of deserving versus non-deserving patients. Non-white, poor, and intoxicated or overdosed women were usually seen as non-deserving patients. Varcoe maintains that the health care system is organized around discourses of scarcity, deservedness, and violence. She further argues that violence is understood within two frameworks of meaning—that of pauperization and racialization. The two obviously intersect in situations where patients are both poor and of colour. However, in the case of women of colour, violence was more readily associated with their culture. This culturalization of violence or cultural racism (Razack) prevalent among many nurses is reflective of the dominant Canadian discourse on race and racism that pervades mainstream services (MacLeod and Shin). As Varcoe notes, nurses' perceptions of women of colour who had been abused was to attribute their abuse to their culture. This leads to a situation of heightened visibility and scrutiny on the one hand, and on the other hand, a dismissal of the woman's experience in terms of her cultural membership. As one nurse in her study stated:

> Culturally, because I have had a lot to do with a [certain group of] people in the last [few] years, I would say overall, that as a group of nurses [at this hospital] people are more suspicious of abuse in a multicultural type of patient situation than they are in an actually Caucasian situation. (215)[7]

The immigrant women of colour interviewed by Anderson noted the prevalence of similar stereotypes which impacted on their ability to access appropriate health care. Anderson suggests that:

> One could argue that non-white women's experiences are shaped by the history of imperialism and oppression, and are not only the result of their immigrant status. Instead, these experiences have to be understood in terms of their status as non-white immigrant women from a Third World nation. So, not only must non-white immigrant women contend with ideologies about women's roles, but they must also contend with stereotypes that are entrenched within the mainstream culture, which determine the ways they are perceived. (1987: 433)

For the immigrant woman of colour who has experienced intimate violence, the encounter with the health care system is fraught with risks of being further revictimized. Not only may she be faced with language barriers, isolation, and fears about her legal status, but her whole personhood is reduced to racial stereotypes about the particular cultural group to which she belongs. Her positioning at the juncture of societal racism and sexism, institutional racism and sexism, and her own experiences of patriarchal violence in the home place her in a high-risk situation. Her dependency on the state in terms of immigration status, on the medical system in terms of health services, and on her sponsoring spouse serve to drastically limit her choices and her agency. Yet, immigrant women of colour survive.

## Toward Equity and Recognition

In addressing the specific barriers that immigrant women face, the existing literature advances several recommendations which are noted below. Many studies argue for the implementation of culturally sensitive services (e.g., MacLeod *et al.*; Majumdar and Roberts; Perilla *et al.*; Sanchez, Plawecki and Plawecki; Schwager, Mawhiney and Lewko). Siyon Rhee argues for culturally appropriate services, and Williams and Becker (1994) indicate a need for culturally competent or culturally congruent services. Within these models, cultural issues tend to become foregrounded, and the influence of structural issues tend to be muted. However, as Helene Moussa points out:

> The phrase "cultural sensitivity" is often used in Canada for relating in a positive manner to the cultural background of refugee and immigrant women. I would like to suggest that "sensitivity" is a very passive, if not a patronizing term. One of the most important approaches for anyone working with refugee and immigrant women is first and foremost to *respect* differences in values and decision-making style. And secondly to recognize that refugee and immigrant women are not in a position of power in Canada because of pervasive racism, the class structure, gender inequality, and because of their uncertain legal status. An assumption behind "cultural sensitivity" can also be that refugee and immigrant women have nothing to offer Canadian society let alone having ways they can solve their own issues. (1994: 66)

In part, the appeal of the "cultural sensitivity" approach is that it enables service providers and health care personnel to deal with the tangibles—the manifest attributes of the patient—and address these with cultural prescriptions. Structural issues such as racism, lack of employment, deskilling, marginalization and ghettoization, which contribute to vulnerability to violence are expressions of structural inequalities and require political and social action. Health care, like other institutions in society, is predicated on a capitalist-commodity model despite the rhetoric of universalism and compassion. Thus, as patients are moved through the system, their illnesses are translated into units of time and concomitantly, dollars and cents. While the culturally-specific approach advocated by some studies is untenable in a milieu of immense racial and cultural diversity, it still functions as a remedy and to some small extent, actually facilitates service provision to marginalized groups (Agnew).[8] However, it is impossible for health care providers to know every culture in detail, and similarly impossible to apply culturally specific knowledge in ways that account for diasporic, relational, and generational manifestations of cultural formations. Nevertheless, as existing studies demonstrate, there is a need to take into consideration the various factors impacting on a person's life and find ways to address the ensuing dis-ease stemming from their social, structural, and cultural location.

## Finding Ways Out

Some of the strategies identified in the existing literature cohere around the following: creating social networks of support (Emmott); advocating critical analyses of structural issues and self-reflection (Brice-Baker; Hamilton, J.; Legault; Lynam; Varcoe); empowering women (Varcoe; Yam); taking a historical approach to understand the social location of the women (Bohn), and employing a holistic approach (Sanchez *et al.*). These strategies are not mutually exclusive but rather overlap in practice. When employed in concert, they work toward empowering the immigrant woman of colour, viewing her in context and as a person and working with her to develop viable strategies. Underpinning all these strategies is the issue of respect and dignity—respecting different social locations, histories and realities without inferiorizing or trivializing their import.

## Moving from Risk to Safety

Irihapeti Ramsden (1990, 1993), offers a model of "cultural safety" which neatly encapsulates both the practical strategies that can be employed as well as a conceptual framework by which to understand, appreciate, and address the power inequalities and imbalances that structure the medical encounter between indigenous peoples and the white medical professionals who serve them. While Ramsden's model is grounded in the Maori reality and relationship with the white settler community in New Zealand, her observations and findings echo the lived realities of Aboriginal people and people of colour in Canada. Hence, when she states that "we are not a perspective" (1990: 2), she challenges the dominant normative model of multiculturalism which identifies other cultures as perspectives with the dominant culture as the central organizing principle—what Hall refers to as the "white eye"—gazes out on.

In referring to cultural safety, Ramsden discusses "cultural risk" and argues from the perspective of the Maori woman who is presenting to a white health professional. She defines cultural risk as "a process whereby people from one culture believe that they are demeaned, diminished and disempowered by the actions and delivery systems of people from another culture" (Wood and Schwass cited in Ramsden 1993: 7). The Maori woman is thus at risk of being erased or having her concerns trivialized by a white, dominating establishment.

Although speaking in the context of nursing, Ramsden's recommendations on reducing cultural risk are appropriate to the kinds of changes that health care professionals in Canada can implement in order to ensure access and equitable treatment. Her recommendations pivot on and incorporate many of the strategies identified above but underscore the recognition of the differential power relations between the dominant and subordinate groups. For instance, she notes that self-reflexivity and value interrogation are necessary steps but that in order to implement structural change, nurses (or other health care professionals) need to be made aware of the impact of poverty, historical, and social processes, and to have this understanding inserted in the training of other health professionals so that in the longterm, cultural risk is reduced. As Polaschek elaborates, the concept of cultural safety,

> ... makes clear the structural dimension of health care provision, that care is not simply provided for individuals but for members of groups whose care inevitably reflects the position of their groups as a whole within general society. It shows that such group interrelationships which influence health care provisions are unequal. It highlights the power dimension of ethnic relationships, from social disadvantage to explicit racism, which affect the provision of services such as health. It critiques the assumption of social consensus.... (456)

The notion of power differentials is underscored in Ramsden's work as well as Polaschek's elaboration of it. Polaschek notes that "culture" as used in this conceptual framework is not the same as the anthropological definition of culture which when popularized is susceptible to being static and reified. Rather, the framework is grounded in the wide diversity of Maori culture, reflecting the power relations that have subordinated that indigenous community.

## Translating Cultural Safety into Reality

The eradication of racism and sexism within health care constitutes a necessary point of departure for implementing structural change and thereby reducing the power inequalities that contribute to the disadvantage of particular groups and most especially, to the risks faced by immigrant women of colour. Implicit in this endeavour is the necessity of dismantling stereotypes and negative perceptions through such means as power sharing and value-based self-interrogation (Hamilton, J.; Lynam). Recognizing the differential and unequal impact of legislation and other policies on immigrant women of colour is also vital. Immigrant women of colour's dependency on the state in terms of immigration policies (Brice-Baker; Dosanjh *et al.*), the medical system, social welfare agencies, and the increased scrutiny of these women must be acknowledged and apprehended. Using a socio-ecological approach that takes into account the structural, social, and economic variables impacting on a woman's life is also a necessity.

Additional mechanisms that are identified in the literature that would make health care more equitable include the following:

1. Informing women about their rights, services that are available, and the particular procedures that are necessary to ameliorate their health condition

(Cave *et al.*). This can be achieved through outreach (Williams and Becker), partnerships with the communities, and the inclusion of community members in training and administration of services. It can also be achieved by relaying necessary health information on violence to diverse groups through the use of local, ethnic and mainstream media (MOSAIC).

2. Listening to immigrant women's voices is critical (Shroff; Varcoe) and can be undertaken by ensuring the representation of these voices in policy and program consultations, partnerships in projects, delivery of services, and inclusion of immigrant women of colour in decision-making bodies within the health care system. Majumdar and Roberts identify a successful model for the delivery of AIDS education that involved the training of women from different communities who then went back to their communities with the knowledge and information they had received.

3. Implementing support groups that are within geographic proximity to women's homes would help reduce isolation, which is a key risk factor, and also allow immigrant women of colour to develop social networks of support that are equally critical for their well-being (Dyck).

4. Implementing a coordinated health care approach that integrates diverse health professionals would not only help to reduce isolation but also reduce risks stemming from other factors such as language barriers, unfamiliarity with the bureaucracy, and a sense of helplessness (MOSAIC).

5. Increasing the availability of alternative models of health care and validating indigenous or cultural models of health care would also help in empowering immigrant women of colour.

For immigrant women of colour who have experienced violence, the most serious needs are interpretation, advocacy, and support. Advocacy and support for victims have been described as essential in the literature dealing with violence (Kurz and Stark). However, their importance and implications for the safety of immigrant women of colour are accentuated because of issues of legal status, dependency on the sponsor, as well as racism and sexism within the system. Kurz and Stark observed that in the hospital setting where one physician acted as an advocate for battered women, the treatment that the women received was not only more appropriate but actually facilitated their situation. The physician-advocate helped to transform "problem patients" into "patients with problems" (263).

It is apparent that to meet the needs of racialized immigrant women who have experienced violence, health providers have to take into consideration the totality of a woman's location, as well as recognize the multiple forms of institutional, societal and individual levels of violence that are impacting on her. Such an approach involves embracing a socio-ecological perspective. It involves assessing the risks that render immigrant women of colour vulnerable to violence, and eliminating these risks in order to enhance their level of safety. To this end, a conceptual reframing is necessary so that, rather than centering the analysis on the needs of health care institutions, immigrant women's needs become the focal point of analysis and intervention. In-house advocates, social support networks and groups, and other practical measures are necessary in order to balance the current unequal power relations between immigrant women of colour and all health care providers.

## Conclusion

This review of the literature outlines the major factors impacting on immigrant women of colour who have experienced violence in terms of their access to health care. Key factors that impact on immigrant women and that increase their risk to violence include: the dependency on their spouses as underscored by immigration legislation; isolation; lack of the dominant language skills and knowledge about the dominant cultural norms; ghettoization and exploitation in underpaid, hazardous and unprotected jobs; marginalization and alienation combined with the lack of social support networks; and the combination of sexism from within their communities and the dominant society, as well as the racism of the external society including health care professionals. Inferiorization, trivialization, and erasure of the concerns and realities of immigrant women of colour are some of the ways in which immigrant women of colour are treated. The racism they encounter serves to categorize them in terms of their culture and often results in their social construction as "undeserving" patients. Within a health care context where the discourses of scarcity, commodification, and racialization operate, immigrant women of colour who have experienced violence are triply jeopardized—by their race, class, and gender.

Existing studies identify a number of avenues whereby immigrant women and disadvantaged peoples can be better served by the health care system. Underpinning many of these recommendations is the recognition of the necessity to incorporate a socio-ecological model. The latter incorporates an examination of the structural location of the individual patient, a socio-historical analysis of the group and the stresses it has encountered, and an analysis of the social, economic, and political reality of the group. The individual is seen within the context of larger and immediate social forces impacting on her lived reality. Ramsden's model of cultural risk incorporates these variables and offers a conceptual rethinking of the directions that health care workers can pursue. Within this model, health care providers are encouraged to critically reflect on and interrogate their beliefs and to treat other groups and individuals in more respectful ways. More importantly, the model suggests ways in which to implement structural changes which can work to reduce the risk of disadvantaged groups both immediately and in the longterm.

The literature also identifies practical measures that health care providers can implement to better serve the needs of immigrant women of colour who have experienced violence. These include avenues by which to reduce the isolation immigrant women experience, ways to empower them, and vehicles by which to reach out and inform diverse communities about the services that are available and about their rights to adequate and appropriate health care.

In conclusion, the barriers faced by immigrant women of colour in accessing the health care system are substantial. The system's response, as outlined in this review, is one of inferiorization, trivialization, and erasure—*whakam* or the emotional white-out that Ramsden describes (1990, 1993). These responses are predicated on and, in turn, reproduce the dominant discourses of racism and sexism. In order to redress the inequalities, the system requires structural change. However, the point of departure for such change has to be situated in a broader and more complex definition of violence. As Chezia Carraway argues:

> Our societal definition of violence must include the direct results of poor medical care, economic inferiority, oppressive legislation, and cultural invisibility. By broadening our definition of violence, we combat the minimalization of our experiences as women of colour by the dominant culture. We must name the violence, or we will not be able to address it. (1302)

## Notes

[1]According to 1976 Immigration legislation, there are three categories under which immigrants can come into the country: independent, family class, or refugee. The independent category is applicable to those who have the necessary skills, or who are willing to invest, and/or those who can show their economic self-sufficiency. The family class refers to those individuals who are sponsored by a family member or who are dependent on the independent applicant.

[2]This perceived threat has, in recent times, generated considerable empirical analysis focusing on the health expenditures of immigrants. Chen, Ng, and Wilkins found that immigrants tend not to suffer from chronic illnesses or diseases and, further, have lower levels of physician visits. The exceptions occurred for those who were in the low income brackets and for women who reported more frequent physician contacts (Dunn and Dyck).

[3]See also Reitz and Sklar for an examination of the impact of exclusion experienced by "visible minorities" in terms of their economic mobility.

[4]While it is true that immigrant women of European background are an increasingly significant presence in the Canada, the stereotype of the immigrant woman as a woman of colour prevails in the media and the public imagination.

[5]The history of slavery and colonialism are quintessential reminders of the very real differences among women and how these differences were used by the governments of the time to maintain patriarchal power (Mohanty; Strobel).

[6]These interventions have produced valuable tools for medical practitioners by which to ameliorate the treatment of women who have experienced violence and who are presenting at emergency departments, clinics, and doctors offices.

[7]One can assess from this quote just how far the language of multiculturalism has

permeated the thought and talk of members of the dominant society. That a "multicultural" type of patient exists seems rather illogical and can only be understood as a euphemism for a person of colour or as someone from a different cultural background, but even here, bicultural would be a more accurate term. Nevertheless, the designation presupposes the existence of a monocultural person as the norm.

[8]Agnew notes that advocating for "culturally sensitive" services has been one of the few ways in which women of colour from immigrant communities have been able to ensure the provision of services to their communities.

## References


Abbott, Jean, Robin Johnson, Koziol McLain and Steven R. Lowenstein. "Domestic Violence Against Women: Incidence and Prevalence in an Emergency Department." *Population Journal of the American Medical Association* 273 (22) (1995): 1763-1767.

Abraham, Margaret. "Ethnicity, Gender, and Marital Violence: South Asian Women's Organizations in the United States." *Gender and Society* 9 (4) (August 1995): 450-468.

Abu-Laban, Yasmeen. "Keeping 'Em Out: Gender, Race, and Class Biases in Canadian Immigration Policy." *Painting the Maple: Essays on Race, Gender, and the Construction of Canada.* Eds. Veronica Strong-Boag, Sherrill Grace, Abigail Eisenberg and Joan Anderson. Vancouver: University of British Columbia Press, 1998. 69-82.

Agnew, Vijay. *In Search of a Safer Place: Abused Women and Culturally Sensitive Services.* Toronto: University of Toronto Press, 1998.

Ahluwalia, Seema and Brian D. MacLean. "The Medicalization of Domestic Violence." *Sociology of Health Care in Canada.* Ed. B. Singh Bolaria and Harley D. Dickinson. Toronto: Harcourt Brace Jovanovich, 1988. 183-197.

Alicea, Marixsa. "'A Chambered Nautilus': The Contradictory Nature of Puerto Rican Women's Role in the Social Construction of a Transnational Community." *Gender and Society* 11 (5) (October 1997): 597-626.

Anderson, Joan. "Migration and Health: Perspectives on Immigrant Women." *Sociology of Health and Illness* 9 (4) (1987): 410-438.

Anderson, Joan. "Perspectives on the Health of Immigrant Women: A Feminist Analysis." *Advances in Nursing Science* 8 (1) (1985): 61-76.

Anderson, Joan, Connie Blue, Angela Hollbrook and Mirian Ng. "On Chronic Illness: Immigrant Women in Canada's Work Force—A Feminist Perspective." *Canadian Journal of Nursing Research* 25 (2) (1993): 7-22.

Anderson, Joan and Sheryl Reimer Kirkham. "Constructing Nation: The Gendering and Racializing of the Canadian Health Care System." *Painting the Maple: Essays on Race, Gender, and the Construction of Canada.* Eds. Veronica Strong-Boag, Sherrill Grace, Abigail Eisenberg and Joan Anderson. Vancouver: University of British Columbia Press, 1998. 242-261.

Anthias, Floya and Nira Yuval-Davis. *Racialized Boundaries, Race, Nation, Gender, Colour and Class and the Anti-Racist Struggle*. London: Routledge, 1992.

Archer, Lynda A. "Empowering Women in a Violent Society, Role of the Family Physician." *Canadian Family Physician* 40 (May 1994): 974-985.

Argüelles, Lourdes and Anne M. Rivero. "Gender/Sexual Orientation, Violence and Transnational Migration: Conversations with some Latinas We Think We Know." *Urban Anthropology and Studies* 22 (3-4) (1993): 259-275.

Bald, S. R. "Coping with Marginality: South Asian Women Migrants in Britain." *Feminism/Postmodernism/Development*. Ed. M.H. Marchand and J. L. Parpart. London: Routledge, 1995. 119-126.

Bannerji, Himani. "Returning the Gaze: An Introduction." *Returning the Gaze: Essays on Racism, Feminism and Politics*. Ed. H. Bannerji. Toronto: Sister Vision Press, 1993. ix-xxix.

Beiser, Morton. "Towards a Research Framework for Immigrant Health." Presented at the Metropolis Health Domain Seminar, December 12-13, 1996. *Metropolis Health Domain Seminar, Final Report*. Ottawa: Minister of Public Works and Government Services Canada, 1998. 23-32.

Berman, Sandra and Norma-Jean McLaren. *Multicultural Change in Health Service Delivery. Resource Manual, 1 and 2*. Vancouver: Chara Health Care Society and Multiculturalism British Columbia, March 1997.

Billingsley, Brenda and Leon Muszynski. *No Discrimination Here? Toronto Employers and the Multi-Racial Workforce*. Toronto: Social Planning Council of Metropolitan Toronto and the Urban Alliance on Race Relations, May 1985.

Bohn, Dianne K. "Nursing Care of Native American Battered Women." *AWHONNS Clinical Issues Perinatal Women's Health Nursing* 4 (3) (1993): 424-436.

Bolaria, B. Singh and Rosemary Bolaria. "Immigrant Status and Health Status: Women and Racial Minority Immigrant Workers." *Racial Minorities, Medicine and Health*. Eds. B. Singh Bolaria and Rosemary Bolaria..Halifax: Fernwood, 1994. 149-168.

Bolaria, B. Singh and Peter S. Li. *Racial Oppression in Canada*. Toronto: Garamond Press, 1988.

Boychuk Duchscher, Judy E. "Acting on Violence Against Women." *The Canadian Nurse* 90 (6) (June 1994): 21-25.

Boyd, Monica. "Family and Personal Networks in International Migration: Recent Developments and New Agendas." *International Migration Review* 23 (3) (1989): 638-670.

Brice-Baker, Janet R. "Domestic Violence in African-American and African-Caribbean Families." *Journal of Social Distress and the Homeless* 3 (1) (1994): 23-38.

Bulhan, Hussein Abdilahi. *Frantz Fanon and the Psychology of Oppression*. New York: Plenum Press, 1985.

Bullock, Linda, Judith McFarlane, Louise H. Bateman and Virginia Miller. "The

Prevalence and Characteristics of Battered Women in a Primary Care Setting." *Nurse Practitioner* 14 (June 1989): 47-56.

Calvo, Janet M. "Health Care Access for Immigrant Women." *Man-Made Medicine: Women's Health, Public Policy, and Reform*. Ed. Kary L. Moss. Durham, NC: Drake University Press, 1996. 161-181.

Cameron, Rebecca P., Jennifer D. Wells and Stevan E. Hobfoll. "Stress, Social Support and Coping in Pregnancy." *Journal of Health Psychology* 1 (2) (1996): 195-208.

Canadian Centre for Justice Statistics. *Family Violence in Canada: A Statistical Profile, 2000*. Ottawa: Statistics Canada, 2000.

Carraway, Chezia G. "Violence Against Women of Colour." *Stanford Law Review* 43 (July 1991): 1301-1309.

Cave, Andrew, Usha Maharaj, Nancy Gibson and Eileen Jackson. "Physicians and Immigrant Patients." *Canadian Family Physician* 41 (October 1995): 1685-1690.

Chambers, Susan D. *An Analysis of Trends Concerning Violence against Women: A Preliminary Case Study of Vancouver*. Vancouver: FREDA Centre, 1998.

Champion, Jane Dimmitt. "Woman Abuse, Assimilation, and Self-Concept in a Rural Mexican American Community." *Hispanic Journal of Behavioural Science* 18 (4) (November, 1996): 508-521.

Christensen, Carol. Presentation at Ending Violence Against Women: Setting the Agenda for the Next Millennium—10th International Nursing Conference, June 1-3, 2000, Vancouver, British Columbia.

Chen, Jianjian, Edward Ng and Russell Wilkins. "The Health of Canada's Immigrants in 1994-5." *Health Reports* 7 (4) (Spring, 1996): 33-45.

Chin, Ko-Lin. "Out of Town Brides: International Marriage and Wife Abuse Among Chinese Immigrants." *Journal of Comparative Family Studies* 25 (1) (Spring 1994): 53-69.

Choi, Gil. "Acculturative Stress, Social Support, and Depression in Korean American Families." *Journal of Family Social Work* 2 (1) (1997): 81-97.

Choudry, Salma. "Pakistani Women's Experiences of Domestic Violence in Great Britain." Research Findings, 43. London: Home Office Research and Statistics Directorate, n.d.

Coeling, Harriet V. and Gloria Harman. "Learning to Ask about Domestic Violence." *Women's Health Issues* (1997): 263-268.

Das Gupta, Tania. *Racism and Paid Work*. Toronto: Garamond Press, 1996.

Dasgupta, Das Shamita. "In the Footsteps of 'Arundhati': Asian Indian Women's Experience of Domestic Violence in the United States." *Violence Against Women* 2 (3) (September, 1996): 238-259.

Davis, Angela. "The Color of Violence Against Women." *ColorLines* 3 (3) (Fall, 2000). Available online: http://www.arc.org/C_Lines/CLArchive/story3_3_02.html

Davis, Angela. *Women, Culture and Politics*. New York: Vintage Books, 1990.

Dosanjh, Raminder, S. Deo and Surjeet Sidhu. *Spousal Abuse in the South Asian*

*Community*. Vancouver: FREDA Centre, 1994.

Dunn, James and Isabel Dyck. "Social Determinants of Health in Canada's Immigrant Population: Results from the National Population Health Survey." *Working Paper Series, #98-20*. Vancouver: Vancouver Centre of Excellence for Research on Immigration and Integration in the Metropolis (RIMM), October, 1998.

Dyck, Isabel. "Managing Chronic Illness: An Immigrant Woman's Acquisition and Use of Health Care Knowledge." *American Journal of Occupational Therapy* 46 (8) (1992): 696-705.

Easteal, Patricia. "Double Jeopardy, Violence Against Immigrant Women in the Home." *Family Matters, Newsletter of the Australian Institute of Family Studies* 45 (Spring/Summer, 1996).

Emmott, Sue. "'Dislocation,' Shelter and Crisis: Afghanistan's Refugees and Notions of Home." *Gender and Development* 4 (1) (1996): 31-38.

Ervin, Alexander M. "Service Providers' Perceptions of Immigrant Well-Being and Implications for Health Promotion and Delivery." *Racial Minorities, Medicine and Health*. Ed. B. Singh Bolaria and Rosemary Bolaria. Halifax: Fernwood, 1994. 225-243

Fanon, Frantz. *Black Skin, White Masks*. Translated by Charles Lam Markmann. New York: Grove Press, 1967.

Fleras, Augie and Jean Leonard Elliot. *Unequal Relations: An Introduction to Race, Ethnic and Aboriginal Dynamics in Canada*. Second Edition. Scarborough, Ont.: Prentice Hall, 1996.

Flynn, Karen and Charmaine Crawford. "Committing 'Race Treason': Battered Women and Mandatory Arrest in Toronto's Caribbean Community." *Unsettling Truths: Battered Women, Policy, Politics, and Contemporary Research in Canada*. Eds. K. D. Bonnycastle and G. S. Rigakos. Vancouver: Collective Press, 1998. 91-102.

Gany, Franscesca and Heike Thiel de Bocanegra. "Overcoming Barriers to Improving the Health of Immigrant Women." *Journal of the American Medical Women's Association* 51 (1996): 155-160.

Gray, Bradley and Jeffrey J. Stoddard. "Patient-Physician Pairing: Does Racial and Ethnic Congruity Influence Selection of a Regular Physician?" *Journal of Community Health* 22 (4) (August 1997): 247-259.

Greaves, L., O. Hankivsky, and J. Kingston-Riechers. *Selected Estimates of the Costs of Violence Against Women*. London: Centre for Research on Violence Against Women and Children, University of Western Ontario, 1995.

Grunfeld, Anton, Deborah Hotch, and Kathleen MacKay. *Identification, Assessment, Care Referral and Follow-up of Women Experiencing Domestic Violence Who Come to the Emergency Department for Treatment. Final Report.* Vancouver: Vancouver Hospital and Health Sciences Centre, 1995.

Hall, Stuart. "The Whites of Their Eyes." *The Media Reader*. Eds. Manuel Alvarado and John O. Thompson. London: British Film Institute, 1990.

Hamilton, Janice. "Multicultural Health Care Requires Adjustments by Doctors and Patients." *Canadian Medical Association Journal* 155 (5) (September 1,

1996): 585-587.

Hamilton, Roberta. *Gendering the Vertical Mosaic: Feminist Perspectives on Canadian Society*. Toronto: Copp Clark, 1996.

Health Canada. *Report on an Information Session with Ethnocultural Communities on Family Violence*. Ottawa: Health Canada, March 19-20, 1994.

Henderson, Angela D. and Janet R. Ericksen. "Enhancing Nurses' Effectiveness with Abused Women: Awareness, Reframing, Support, Education." *Journal of Psychosocial Nursing* 32 (6) (1994): 11-15.

Henry, Frances and Effie Ginzberg. *"Who Gets the Work?" A Test of Racial Discrimination in Employment*. Toronto: Social Planning Council of Metropolitan Toronto and the Urban Alliance on Race Relations, January 1985.

Henry, Fances, Carol Tator, Winston Mattis, and Tim Rees. *The Colour of Democracy: Racism in Canadian Society*. Toronto: Harcourt Brace Canada, 1995.

hooks, bell. *Killing Rage, Ending Racism*. New York: Henry Holt and Co., 1995.

Hotch, Deborah, Anton Grunfeld, Kathleen MacKay, and Leigh Cowan. *Domestic Violence Intervention by Emergency Department Staff*. Vancouver: Vancouver Hospital and Health Sciences Centre, 1995.

Huisman, Kimberly. "Wife Battering in Asian American Communities." *Violence Against Women* 2 (3) (September 1996): 260-283.

Iyer, Nitya. "Some Mothers are Better than Others: A Re-examination of Maternity Benefits." *Challenging the Public/Private Divide, Feminism, Law and Public Policy*. Ed. S. B. Boyd. Toronto: University of Toronto Press, 1997. 168-194.

Janoviek, Nancy. *On the Margins of a Fraying Safety Net: Aboriginal and Immigrant Women's Access to Welfare*. Vancouver: FREDA Centre, 2000.

Jiwani, Yasmin. "The Criminalization of Race/The Racialization of Crime." *Erasing Connections*. Eds. W. Chan and K. Mirchandana. Toronto: Broadview Press, 2000.

Jiwani, Yasmin. "Women of Colour and Poverty." *Occasional Working Papers in Women's Studies and Gender Relations* 3 (1) (1994): 1-15.

Jiwani, Yasmin with Patricia Kachuk and Shelley Moore. *Rural Women and Violence: A Study of Two Communities in British Columbia*. Vancouver: FREDA Centre, 1998.

Johnson, Holly. *Dangerous Domains: Violence Against Women in Canada*. Scarborough, Ont.: Nelson Canada, 1996.

Kinnon, Dianne. *Canadian Research on Immigration and Health: An Overview*. Ottawa: Health Canada, 1999.

Kinnon, Dianne and Louise Hanvey. "Health Aspects of Violence Against Women: A Canadian Perspective." 1996. Available online at http:/hwcweb.hwc.ca/canusa/papers/canada/english/violenab.htm

Kosch, Shae Graham, Mary Ann Burg, and Shifa Podikiju. "Patient Ethnicity and Diagnosis of Emotional Disorders in Women." *Family Medicine* 30 (3) (1998): 215-219.

Kurz, Demie and Evan Stark. "No-So-Benign Neglect: The Medical Response to Battering." *Feminist Perspectives on Wife Abuse*. Eds. K. Yllö and M. Bograd. New York: Sage Publications, 1988. 249-266.

Laroche, Mireille. "Health Status and Health Services Utilization of Canada's Immigrant and Non-Immigrant Populations." *Canadian Public Policy* 26 (1) (2000): 51-73.

Lee, Jo-Anne, with the assistance of Cheryl Harrison. *Immigrant Settlement and Multiculturalism Programs for Immigrant, Refugee and Visible Minority Women: A Study of Outcomes, Best Practices and Issues*. Victoria: Ministry Responsible for Multiculturalism and Immigration, June 1999.

Legault, Gisèle. "Social Work Practice in Situations of Intercultural Misunderstandings." *Journal of Multicultural Social Work* 4 (4) (1996): 49-66.

Li, Nancy and Patrick May. "A Tale of Two Communities—HIV/AIDS Education in Asian Women." Unpublished report prepared for the Asian Society for the Intervention of AIDS. Vancouver: March 1997.

Lutz, Helma. "The Legacy of Migration: Immigrant Mothers and Daughters and the Process of Intergenerational Transmission." *Comenius* 15 (3) (Fall 1995): 304-317.

Lynam, Judith. "Towards the Goal of Providing Culturally Sensitive Care: Principles upon which to Build Nursing Curricula." *Journal of Advanced Nursing* 17 (1992): 149-157.

MacKinnon, Marion with Laura Lee Howard. *Affirming Immigrant Women's Health: Building Inclusive Health Policy. Final Report*. Halifax: The Maritime Centre of Excellence for Women's Health, May 2000.

MacLeod, Linda and Maria Y. Shin. *Isolated, Afraid and Forgotten: The Service Delivery Needs and Realities of Immigrant and Refugee Women Who Are Battered*. Prepared for the National Clearinghouse on Family Violence. Ottawa: Health and Welfare Canada, December 1990.

MacLeod, Linda and Maria Y. Shin in collaboration with Queenie Hum, Jagrup Samra-Jawanda, Shalen Rai, Maria Minna and Eva Wasilewska. *Like a Wingless Bird: A Tribute to the Survival and Courage of Women Who Are Abused and Who Speak Neither English Nor French*. Ottawa: National Clearinghouse on Family Violence, 1994.

Majumdar, B. and J. Roberts. "Culturally Sensitive AIDS Education for Hamilton-Wentworth Immigrant Women." System-Linked Research Unit, Working Paper Series, April 1995.

Meleis, Afaf, I. "Between Two Cultures: Identity, Roles and Health." *Health Care for Women International* 12 (1991): 365-377.

Memmi, Albert. *The Colonizer and the Colonized*. Boston: Beacon Press, 1965.

Miles, Robert. *Racism*. London: Routledge, Key Idea Series, 1989.

Mohanty, Chandra. "Under Western Eyes: Feminist Scholarship and Colonial Discourses." *Third World Women and the Politics of Feminism*. Eds. C. T. Mohanty, A. Russo, and L. Torres. Bloomington: Indiana University Press, 1991. 51-80.

MOSAIC. *Immigrant Women's Health: A Community Consultation Project.* Vancouver, BC: MOSAIC, January 1996.

Moussa, Helene. "Violence Against Refugee Women: Gender Oppression, Canadian Policy, and the International Struggle for Human Rights." *Resources for Feminist Research* 26 (3/4) (1998): 79-111.

Moussa, Helene. *Challenging Myths and Claiming Power Together: A Handbook to Set Up and Assess Support Groups for and with Immigrant and Refugee Women.* Toronto: Education Wife Assault, 1994.

Narayan, Uma. "Male-Order Brides: Immigrant Women, Domestic Violence and Immigration Law." *Hypatia* 10 (1) (1995): 104-119.

National Association of Women and the Law (NAWL). "Gender Analysis of Immigration and Refugee Protection Legislation and Policy." NAWL Ad Hoc Committee on Gender Analysis of the Immigration Act, Submission to Citizenship and Immigration Canada, March 1999.

Ng, Roxana. "Racism, Sexism, and Immigrant Women." *Changing Patterns: Women in Canada.* Eds. S. Burt, L. Code, and L. Dorney. Toronto: McClelland and Stewart, 1993. 279-301.

Ocran, Amanda Araba. "Across the Home/Work Divide: Homework in Garment Manufacture and the Failure of Employment Regulation." *Challenging the Public/Private Divide: Feminism, Law and Public Policy.* Ed. S. B. Boyd. Toronto: University of Toronto Press, 1997. 144-167.

O'Keefe, Maura. "Racial/Ethnic Differences Among Battered Women and Their Children." *Journal of Child and Family Studies* 3 (3) (1994): 283-305.

Perilla, Julia L., Roger Bakeman, and Fran H. Norris. "Culture and Domestic Violence: The Ecology of Abused Latinas." *Violence and Victims* 9 (4) (1994): 325-339.

Philippine Women Centre. *Trapped: Holding on to the Knife's Edge—Economic Violence against Filipino Migrant/Immigrant Women.* Vancouver: FREDA Centre, 1997.

Philippine Women Centre and the Global Alliance Against Traffic in Women Canada (GAATW). *Echoes: Cries for Freedom, Justice and Equality, Filipino Women Speak.* Vancouver: GAATW Canada and the PhilippineWomen Centre, 1999.

Pinn, Vivian W. and Mary T. Chunko. "The Diverse Faces of Violence: Minority Women and Domestic Abuse." *Academic Medicine* 72 (1) (Supplement, January 1997): S65-S71.

Polaschek, N. R. "Cultural Safety: A New Concept in Nursing People of Different Ethnicities." *Journal of Advanced Nursing* 27 (1998): 452-457.

Porter, John. *The Vertical Mosaic: An Analysis of Social Class and Power in Canada.* Toronto: University of Toronto Press, 1965.

Radomsky, Nellie A. *Lost Voices: Women, Chronic Pain, and Abuse.* Binghampton, NY: Haworth Press, 1995.

Ramsden, Irihapeti. "Kawa Whakaruruhau: Cultural Safety in Nursing Education in Aotearoa (New Zealand)." *Nursing Praxis in New Zealand* 8 (3)

(1993): 4-10.

Ramsden, Irihapeti. "Cultural Safety." *The New Zealand Nursing Journal, Kai tiaki* 83, (110) (1990): 18-19.

Rasche, Christine E. "Minority Women and Domestic Violence: The Unique Dilemmas of Battered Women of Color." *Journal of Contemporary Criminal Justice* 4/3 (1988): 150-171.

Razack, Sherene. *Looking White People in the Eye, Gender, Race, and Culture in Courtrooms and Classrooms*. Toronto: University of Toronto Press, 1998.

Reitz, Jeffrey G. and Sherrilyn M. Sklar. "Culture, Race, and the Economic Assimilation of Immigrants." *Sociological Forum* 12 (2) (1997): 233-277.

Rhee, Siyon. "Domestic Violence in the Korean Immigrant Family." *Journal of Sociology and Social Welfare* 24 (1) (March 1977): 63-77.

Ristock, Janice L. and the Mental Health Division, Health Promotion and Programs Branch, Health Canada. "The Impact of Violence on Mental Health: A Guide to the Literature." *Discussion Papers on Health/Family Violence Issues, 3*. Ottawa: Minister of Supplies and Services, 1995.

Roberts, Barbara. "Immigrant Women: Triple Oppression, Triple Jeopardy." Presentation given at the opening meeting of the Simone de Beauvoir Institute Research Seminar (1987-1988): *Immigrant Women/La femme immigrante. Collection 'Working Papers/Inedits' 3*. Montreal: Publication of the Simone De Beauvoir Institute, 1990.

Sanchez, Tony R., Judith A. Plawecki, and Henry M. Plawecki. "The Delivery of Culturally Sensitive Health Care to Native Americans." *Journal of Holistic Nursing* 14 (4) (1996): 295-307.

Sasso, Angela. *Interpreter Services in Health Care: A Call for Provincial Standards and Services*. Report prepared for the Multicultural Health Committee, Affiliation of Multicultural Societies and Service Agencies of British Columbia. Vancouver: January 2000.

Savary, Rosalind. *What Does Gender Have to Do with It? An Environmental Scan on Women's Health Issues*. Prepared for the Adult Health team, Health Promotions and Programs Branch, Health Canada, British Columbia /Yukon Regional Office, 1998.

Schneller, Debora Podolsky. "The Immigrant's Challenge: Mourning the Loss of Homeland and Adapting to the New World." *Studies in Social Work* 51 (2) (March 1981): 95-125.

Schwager, K. Walter, Anne-Marie Mawhiney and John Lewko. "Cultural Aspects of Prevention Programs." *Canadian Social Work Review* 8 (2) (Summer 1991): 246-254.

Shroff, Farah M. "Walking the Diversity Talk: Curriculum within First Year Midwifery Education." *Health and Canadian Society* 4 (2) (1996/97): 389-446.

Sidhu, Surjeet. *Perspectives of Women Who have Experienced Violence in Relationships and Their Children*. Research initiated and conducted by the Richmond Coordinating Response Committee to End Violence Against Women.

Richmond, British Columbia: November 13, 1996.
Spelman, Elizabeth V. *Inessential Woman: Problems of Exclusion in Feminist Thought.* Boston, MA: Beacon, 1988.
Stark, Evan, Anne Flitcraft, and William Frasier. "Medicine and Patriarchal Violence: The Social Construction of a 'Private' Event." *International Journal of Health Services* 9 (3) (1979): 461-493.
Statistics Canada. *Canadian Statistics: The People—Population.* 1996. Available at http://www.statcan.ca/english/Pgdb/People/Population/demo40c.htm
Strobel, Margaret. "Gender, Sex, and Empire." *Essays on Global and Comparative History.* Washington: American Historical Association, 1993.
Thobani, Sunera. "Sponsoring Immigrant Women's Inequalities." *Canadian Woman Studies/les cahiers de la femme* 19 (3) (1999): 11-16.
Thobani, Sunera. "Nationalizing Citizens, Bordering Immigrant Women: Globalization and the Racialization of Women's Citizenship in Late 20th Century Canada." Doctoral Dissertation, Department of Sociology and Anthropology, Simon Fraser University, British Columbia, 1998.
Trute, Barry, Peter Sarsfield and Dale A. MacKenzie. "Medical Response to Wife Abuse: A Survey of Physicians' Attitudes and Practice." *Canadian Journal of Community Mental Health* 7 (2) (1988): (no page numbers).
Varcoe, Colleen Marie. "Untying Our Hands: The Social Context of Nursing in Relation to Violence against Women." Doctoral Dissertation, School of Nursing, University of British Columbia, 1997.
Vega, W. A., B. Kolody, J. R. Valle. "Migration and Mental Health: An Empirical Test of Depression Risk Factors among Immigrant Mexican Women." *International Migration Review* 21 (3) (1987): 512-529.
Warshaw, Carole. "Limitations of the Medical Model in the Care of Battered Women." *Violence Against Women: The Bloody Footprints.* Eds. Pauline B. Bart and Eileen Geil Moran. Newbury Park, CA: Sage, 1993. 134-146.
Wiik, Maija-Liisa. "Immigrant Women and Wife Abuse: A Phenomenological Exploration." Masters Thesis, Department of Counselling Psychology, University of British Columbia, 1995.
Williams, Oliver J. and R. Lance Becker. "Domestic Partner Abuse Treatment Programs and Cultural Competence: The Results of a National Survey." *Violence and Victims* 9 (3) (1994): 287-296.
Williams, Patricia J. *The Alchemy of Race and Rights.* Cambridge: Harvard University Press, 1991.
Wilson, Laurene J. "Patient Satisfaction and Quality of Life: A Study of Women with Abusive Male Partners Treated in an Emergency Department." Doctoral Dissertation, School of Criminology, Simon Fraser University, 1998.
Yam, Marylou. "Wife Abuse: Strategies for a Therapeutic Response." *Scholarly Inquiry for Nursing Practice: An International Journal* 9 (2) (1995): (no page numbers).
Zulman, Arthur. "The Hidden Trauma of Immigration." *Australian Family Physician* 25 (11) (November 1996): 1707-1710.

# Remembrance of Things Past

## The Legacy of Childhood Sexual Abuse in Midlife Women

Sari Tudiver, Lynn McClure, Tuula Heinonen, Christine Kreklewitz and Carol Scurfield

The prevalence of childhood sexual abuse (CSA) has been described as "shockingly frequent" in both Canada and the United States, with estimates ranging from 12-38 per cent in the female population (Finkelhor, Hotaling, and Smith; Roberts).[1] Some have sought help to come to terms with the traumas they experienced, others have not.

From statistics and personal narratives, we know that a significant number of women in their menopausal years have experienced such abuse. Yet, almost nothing has been written about the possible effects of childhood sexual abuse on women in the menopausal years and beyond. Other life cycle changes, such as pregnancy and childbirth, raise or trigger associations to past abuse (Courtois and Riley; Kreklewitz). The transitions of menopause may do so as well. This article looks at some possible implications a CSA history may have for women experiencing menopause and for their heath care providers.

Researchers are uncovering some of the emotional, psychological, and physical consequences of these experiences. Yet, the implications of these findings are not considered by most health care providers who have not been trained to address the needs of survivors and who do not routinely ask about abuse in a medical history. Ignoring the issue may influence whether a woman receives appropriate diagnosis and treatment. Conditions which may have their origins in a past history of abuse may be missed or misunderstood by a care provider and by the patient, who never discuss the possible deeper causes of, for example, certain respiratory problems or chronic pain. Some survivors may be fearful of seeking health care because it involves being touched, often in ways that are invasive or confining. Many survivors avoid routine and preventive services, such as PAP smear testing, manual breast examination, mammograms, and preventive dental care. Others seek help for their complaints and suffer in silence when they receive care.

Since 1996, our research team has explored the experiences of some women survivors of childhood sexual abuse in their use of health services (Heinonen, Merrett-Hiley, McClure, Tudiver and Kreklewetz.). The women discussed difficulties they experienced with invasive examinations and tests and recommended specific improvements in the organization and quality of care provided by health practitioners. In a study of 25 health care providers including physicians, nurses, mammographers and sonographers, dentists and dental hygienists, we explored the professionals' views on and education about CSA; their experiences with CSA patients; and how prepared they felt for such encounters (Tudiver, McClure, Heinonen, Scurfield andKreklewetz.). When asked for recommendations, care providers offered insights into the limitations and barriers to change that they experience and discussed realistic options. Our aim is to encourage appropriate professional bodies and individuals to consider developing new structures (e.g., referral networks), relevant curriculum, and to formulate policies and practice guidelines that would more sensitively meet the needs of women survivors of childhood sexual abuse. Addressing these issues has the potential to improve the quality of care for all women and men.

## Impact of Childhood Sexual Abuse

Childhood sexual abuse is broadly defined as "any sexual activity between a child less than age 18 and a person of power, usually two or more years older, and who has authority over the child"(Holz 13). Although the specific behaviours involved in CSA may vary, abuse situations commonly elicit fear in the victim by the perpetrator, whether psychologically through verbal threats, or less often, by physical force, to coerce the vulnerable victim into sexual acts.

Profound, longterm effects may result from such abuse (see, for example, Bala).[2] Several authors link the effects to symptoms of post-traumatic stress syndrome, the abuse being the source of the traumatic stress. Women may experience one or more symptoms including: hyper-arousal, flashbacks, insomnia, nightmares, and anger control problems. Some survivors describe intricate sleeping rituals with unusual sleep patterns and feelings of fear, anxiety, feeling dissociated from one's body, nausea, and shame. Often symptoms developed as coping strategies that helped the patient survive the abusive situation but may have become maladaptive.

Relationship or interpersonal problems may be reflected in sexual dysfunction, difficulty with intimacy, parenting problems, or social isolation. Survivors have had repeated violations of their physical and emotional boundaries and often encounter "boundary confusion," reflected in inappropriate closeness and familiarity, or as perpetual avoidance of any closeness. Concerns of trust and safety are especially sensitive for CSA survivors, who fear losing control. Some survivors experience depression, low self-esteem, and panic attacks. There may also be patterns of self-abuse, such as alcohol or drug abuse, eating disorders, and self-injuries, suicidal gestures or attempts, personality and disassociative disorders.

Ranjan Roy's excellent study of the complex relationship between childhood abuse (including CSA) and chronic pain examines the literature on short-term and longterm health consequences of childhood abuse and the limitations of the research. He argues that practitioners need to recognize the relevance of childhood abuse to pain complaints, such as chronic pelvic pain and gastrointestinal disorders. "Somatic complaints without organic cause" are also frequently cited in women with a history of CSA. Common somatic (body) complaints include chronic pelvic pain, chronic headache, abdominal pain, and gastro-intestinal complaints. Chest pain, throat pain, respiratory symptoms, musculoskeletal, and neurological symptoms are also cited, but less frequently, by CSA survivors. Several studies have revealed the association between a history of CSA and multiple somatic complaints.

Kendall-Tackett and Marshall studied the association between diabetes and abuse history (sexual or physical abuse) after noting higher rates of health problems in adult survivors of abuse than in the general population. The link between diabetes and CSA survivors was chosen because chronic stress, which is a component of abuse, can lead to an elevation in blood levels of triglycerides, free fatty acids, cholesterol, glucose, and insulin. Their study revealed that patients with abuse histories were significantly more likely to have diabetes than their non-abused counterparts. Further research needs to be done in these areas.

Survivors of CSA describe how invasive tests or procedures may lead memories or unresolved anxieties to resurface. For example, PAP smear tests, use of vaginal probes in ultrasound examinations, touching and compressing the breast in mammograms, or dental care can evoke feelings of powerlessness and depersonalization reminiscent of previous abuse. One sonographer we interviewed identified possible signs of past sexual abuse:

> Body language and how they react to the way you touch them, how they pull away, how they look away, sheets clenched up to their neck, the legs not spreading open. I don't know if they feel bad, they feel dirty, I'm not sure what's going through their mind when they don't want to do that ... how they look at you, how they don't look at you, how they are very evasive on answers. I think those are a lot of the keys—and you have to learn to read people's reactions.

Reactions such as these may puzzle and frustrate care providers who are unaware of the causes of such fears and intent on getting the job done. Patients may be blamed or labelled "uncooperative," adding to victimization. Feelings of anxiety and fear—and the lack of understanding from care providers—may lead some women to avoid needed tests and preventive care.

## CSA and Menopausal Changes

Midlife women with a CSA history, like other menopausal women, may experience a variety of symptoms and complaints, some of which are directly attributable to the hormonal changes of menopause, while causes of other symptoms may be less clear. We don't know whether survivors perceive the normal changes of menopause differently from women without a history of CSA or whether hormonal changes and the process of aging may trigger or exacerbate other symptoms or conditions associated with a history of abuse.

We do know that all aspects of the physical self may be affected by CSA. Sue Blume poignantly wrote that many women with a history of CSA are "at war with their bodies," a description much like the way many women without such a history say they feel about peri-menopausal changes. Negative attitudes about their bodies resulting from CSA (e.g., shame, disgust) and feelings of powerlessness, sexual victimization, violation, and secrecy often result in a woman feeling disconnected or dissociated from her body. Heavy bleeding and other changes in menstrual patterns, hot flashes, and issues of sexuality and perceived body image may be difficult to cope with. Some women survivors may have avoided pregnancy or parenting due to concerns about their own abilities to parent and menopause may be the first time that hormonal changes force them to seek medical care. We can surmise that some CSA survivors are challenged—more so than other women—to see their bodies positively, as "normal," and healthy during menopause.

Midlife women often find themselves facing invasive exams (eg. PAP tests and vaginal ultrasounds, mammograms, colonoscopies, and rectal exams) for screening or diagnosis of diseases or conditions associated with advancing age. As noted earlier, these experiences may be particularly unsettling for CSA survivors. Another sonographer we interviewed described a midlife woman's disclosure:

> One lady ... the doctor had palpated a mass and there was a history of cancer in her family so there was a strong concern for ... ovarian cancer. So he really wanted the internal done and she was one of the ones that was climbing off the back of the table—and I said, "I really want to do this scan to see what's wrong because the doctor has some really strong suspicions and you have a really strong history. Could you help me? What can I do to make you more comfortable? What can I do to make it easier for you? Do you want to touch the probe yourself while I'm scanning?"... She says, "You know what? I've been married 25 years, I have three children, I haven't had sex with my husband for 20 years because I can't stand it anymore because my dad used to rape me constantly." ... So yes, she just told me all these things. I said, "I understand." And she put her hand on the probe and I said, "I promise I'll go as fast as I can." And she sort of laughed and she said "Okay." It was a good thing we did it because there was a suspicious mass, she ended up having surgery and it was removed.... She even came back later and thanked me.

Many women undergo hysterectomy and surgical menopause in the perimenopausal years, experiences that may prove traumatic for women with a

CSA history. As Ruth Wukasch notes, a hysterectomy might generate memories associated with past abuse.

> The parallels between a hysterectomy and abusive experience could stir up unresolved feelings from a prior sexual assault; incestual sexual contact is often achieved without force and often there are no outward signs of physical abuse, creating psychic pain and dark secrets. Women with long repressed memories of an abusive experience might have a poor surgical adjustment that includes episodes of depression, panic attacks and/or multiple physical complaints. Such problems might be blamed on the surgery alone, especially if the woman has never disclosed the history of CSA to the physician or resolved it with counselling.... The experience from this study indicates women need to be asked specifically about a history of negative sexual experience because information this sensitive is rarely volunteered. (53-54)

Midlife is also a time of personal reassessment and changing relationships. Partners retire or separate, children leave home, parents become dependent or die. In addition to the physiological/hormonal changes of menopause, unresolved issues and memories may emerge without warning (Courtois).

Not all women with a history of childhood sexual abuse will experience unusual difficulties during menopause. Counselling or therapy has helped many women come to terms with their past and acknowledge the strengths of being a survivor. However, it is the responsibility of the care provider to be aware of possible long-term effects and alert to signs of distress which women may show.

## Are We Opening "Pandora's Box?"

Some care providers fear that asking about past abuse might open a "Pandora's Box" or "can of worms" which they have neither the time nor skills to address. They worry that patients may feel distressed or offended by such questioning or that it is inappropriate in some medical situations, such as when a patient is seen once. In addition to lacking education about CSA, practitioners we spoke with identified other obstacles to disclosure, including lack of privacy in health care settings, lack of time, and limited resources for referral.

The general consensus among practitioners and patients, however, is that some form of routine screening for CSA is appropriate and necessary. Evidence shows that failing to ask empowers the abuse situation, contributes to feelings of isolation, and conveys the impression that it is irrelevant to current issues or symptoms (Seng and Petersen 13) As one woman commented, "If your doctor is afraid to talk about it [sexual abuse] then what are you going to feel?"

Researchers suggest that sensitive questions be asked when the patient is fully dressed and sitting, and recommend a task-oriented question such as, "Is there anything about your past experiences that makes this exam particularly difficult for you?" with a follow-up question such as "What can I do to make it easier for you?" This gives the patient control over whether they wish to disclose further details and/or offer practical suggestions to ease their care.

How deeply issues of CSA are explored and addressed depends on the nature of the practitioner's scope of practice. Open-ended questions may be appropriate for nurse practitioners or physicians trying to treat a 50-year-old woman experiencing chronic pelvic pain or gastrointestinal problems with no other determined causes. Understanding how a childhood trauma might affect a woman in midlife may be crucial to accurately diagnosing and treating somatic and psychosomatic complaints. They are in a position to build rapport and trust, laying a basis for dis-closure and willingness to engage in appropriate treatment, including counselling.

Mammographers, sonographers, and others who perform diagnostic tests and screening, however, usually see a patient only once and have almost no information beyond what is on a requisition form. As our interviews indicated, they regularly encounter patients with severe anxieties that make it difficult to secure an accurate mammogram or ultrasound. Their challenge is to make the patient feel more relaxed in a short period of time.

Dentists and dental hygienists may see patients regularly or irregularly, with some potential to develop rapport and trust. Yet, oral care is not structured to encourage much discussion between patient and practitioner. The work dentists and hygienists perform is invasive, and for patients who may have experienced oral sexual abuse, preventative or restorative dentistry may create acute anxiety.

Patients highly anxious about invasive tests or procedures benefit from health care providers who acknowledge anxieties and seek ways to make examinations more comfortable. Based on survivors' recommendations, this can be done by increasing the patient's sense of control during exams where touch is required, particularly where a woman feels especially vulnerable. Clinicians are asked to have a respectful, calm, accepting approach, to listen carefully, be sensitive to individual needs, offer choices wherever possible, respect privacy, and examine gently, asking permission before touching. Careful and thorough explanations of procedures, warning about pain, encouraging questions, and confirming that the patient can stop the procedure at any time, has been shown to improve experiences of survivors with the health care system. It may help empower women to assert themselves in other areas of their lives and regain some sense of control about what happens to their bodies (Friedman, Samet, Roberts, Hudlin and Hans; Teram, Schachter, and Stalker).

Rather than a "Pandora's Box," asking questions may lead to new insights for patient and practitioner and, hopefully, appropriate treatment. All patients—including those without a history of CSA—have fears and anxieties and will benefit from sensitive clinical practices.

## Some Practical Suggestions

There is an urgent need for health care providers to be educated about issues related to childhood sexual abuse, in ways appropriate to their practice. This can be done through curriculum development, continuing education programs, development of practice guidelines, informal education, and establishing referral networks. Having childhood sexual abuse survivors involved in these initiatives was suggested as a way to provide powerful, collaborative learning opportunities.

Addressing survivors' needs presupposes an environment in which women feel safe to speak about their past. This requires some flexibility in appointment time, staffing and in how medical settings are structured. Currently, most medical environments are intimidating, rather than accommodating to patients. Women with disabilities, a large proportion of whom have CSA histories, and immigrant and refugee women who may be fearful to speak about their past, encounter particular obstacles in accessing services. Private space for taking histories or for invasive tests should be accommodated in the design and structure of health services. Small changes (artwork, music, appropriate health information) can help ensure that an environment feels safe and welcoming. In a time of corporate pressures on health services, even small patient-centered changes are hard won.

There is also a crucial need for research that will help women and care providers understand the possible impacts a CSA history may have on a woman's experiences of menopause and midlife. Do menopausal changes and midlife transitions heighten certain somatic complaints, feelings and emotions rooted in past traumas? Does a CSA history affect the progression of other conditions of aging? Might remembrance of past traumas also lead ultimately to positive re-assessments and new insights about oneself and others? Midlife is a time for taking stock of one's life, venturing into new activities and relationships, taking risks. A woman with a CSA history may, at such a time, begin a process of reflection (or re-reflection) which others can support.

Alternately, health practitioners and women survivors must not assume a CSA history is the dominant factor in the complex changes associated with menopause. More likely, its significance is subtly woven into the fabric of a woman's life and may emerge in unexpected ways, or at times, not at all. Long hidden from view, CSA and its implications must be acknowledged within diagnosis and therapy, so it does not receive too much or not enough attention.

*Thanks to Lore Calimente, M.Nsg, for help with the literature review and to the Prairie Women's Health Centre of Excellence for funding the research.*

## Notes

[1]Women consistently show a higher prevalence of CSA than men, but the consequences for both sexes are profound and require more attention and research.

[2]The full research report on which this article is based, an extensive bibliography and related resources for women survivors and for their health care providers are available at www.cwhn.ca/resources/csa/index.html.

## References

Bala, M. "Caring for Adult Survivors of Child Sexual Abuse." *Canadian Family Physician* 40 (1994): 925-931.

Blume, E. S. *Secret Survivors: Uncovering Incest and Its After-Effects in Women.* New York: Ballantine Books, 1990.

Courtois, C. "Adult Survivors and Sexual Abuse." *Family Violence and Abusive Relationships* 20 (2): 443-446.

Courtois, C., and C. Riley. "Pregnancy and Childbirth as Triggers for Abuse Memories: Implications for Care." *BIRTH* 19 (4) (1992): 222-223.

Finkelhor, D. G. Hotaling, I. Lewis, and C. Smith. "Sexual Abuse in a National Survey of Adult Men and Women: Prevalence, Characteristics, and Risk Factors." *Child Abuse and Neglect* (14) (1990): 19-28.

Friedman, L., J. Samet, M. Roberts, M. Hudlin, and P. Hans. "Inquiry About Victimization Experiences: A Survey of Patient Preferences and Physician Practices." *Archives of Internal Medicine* 152 (1992): 1186-1190.

Heinonen T, A. Merrett-Hiley, L. McClure, S. Tudiver, and C. Kreklewetz. "Perception and Utilization of Health Care Services by Women Survivors of Childhood Sexual Abuse: A Preliminary Study." Report of research for the Manitoba Research Centre on Family Violence and Violence Against Women. Winnipeg: University of Manitoba, 1997.

Holz, K. "A Practical Approach to Clients Who Are Survivors of Childhood Sexual Abuse." *Journal of Nurse-Midwifery* 39 (1) (1994): 13-18.

Kendall-Tackett, K. and R. Marshall. "Victimization and Diabetes: An Exploratory Study." *Child Abuse and Neglect* 23 (6) (1999): 593-596.

Kreklewitz, C. "Parenting Themes for Incest Survivor Mothers and Daughters." Unpublished M.A. thesis. Winnipeg: University of Manitoba, 1995.

Roberts, S. "The Sequelae of Childhood Sexual Abuse: A Primary Care Focus for Adult Female Survivors." *The Nurse Practitioner* 21 (12) (1996): 42-52.

Roy, R. *Childhood Abuse and Chronic Pain: A Curious Relationship?* Toronto: University of Toronto Press: 1998.

Seng, J., and B. Petersen. "Incorporating Routine Screening for History of Childhood Sexual Abuse into Well-Woman and Maternity Care." *Journal of Nurse-Midwifery* 1 (40) (1995): 26-30.

Teram, E., C. Schachter, and C. Stalker. "Opening the Doors to Disclosure: Childhood Sexual Abuse Survivors Reflect on Telling Physical Therapists About Their Trauma." *Physiotherapy* 85 (2)(1999): 88-97.

Tudiver, S., L. McClure, T. Heinonen, C. Scurfield, and C. Kreklewetz. *Education and Preparation of Health Care Providers for Meeting the Needs of Women Survivors of Childhood Sexual Abuse.* Winnipeg: Prairie Women's Health Centre of Excellence, 2000.

Wukasch, R. "The Impact of a History of Rape and Incest on the Post Hysterectomy Experience." *Health Care for Women International* (17) (1996): 53-54.

# Literacy Learning for Survivors of Trauma

## Acting "Normal"

Jenny Horsman

In this article I explore one aspect of the findings of a research study which examined the impacts of abuse on women's literacy learning.[1] The research study was sponsored by the Canadian Congress for Learning Opportunities for Women (CCLOW) and funded by the National Literacy Secretariat. I interviewed literacy workers, learners, counsellors, and therapists who were interested in reflecting on their concerns and experiences in relation to issues of violence and adult literacy learning.[2] I had two central questions for interviewees: what impacts of abuse do you see in your literacy program/your work? How can/should literacy programs address these impacts of violence? As I talked to learners and workers during the research process, I heard over and over again about their frustration—learners feeling that their failure to learn must prove they are stupid and workers struggling with feeling incompetent as they question what they could do better. This frustration confirmed the need for the research, and for changes to literacy work to follow from it.

### The Deficit Model

There is a common tendency in literacy work to slide into an approach where the deficit is seen as residing in the learners. In societies where literacy is highly valued and taught during compulsory schooling, it is easy for literacy work to frame the learner as the "problem," with a deficit of skills, and to lose awareness of the learners' strengths and knowledge, and of the socially-framed nature of the problem. In the deficit model, only the individual literacy learner needs to change, society can be left unaltered.

Learnings from the therapeutic field offer reframings of old problems to help us to work differently in literacy. However, this discourse can easily be a slippery slope to new deficit models for literacy work with those who have experienced violence. A therapeutic focus simply on individual "healing," implies that the person is sick and can be well. Sandra Butler eloquently critiques "individualized, de-contextualized, and de-politicized healing." "Healing" should not be seen as an individual problem. It may not even be "abnormal" in this society for women to have experienced trauma and so to have learned crucial survival strategies which they continue to bring to all future situations. The goal of literacy work with those who have experienced trauma should not be simply to support their individualized "healing" or to help them to become well, or "normal." Trauma survivors should not be seen as "poor souls" in need of healing. It is, however, the responsibility of literacy workers, funders, and others in the field to recognize that all literacy learning must be carried out in recognition of the needs of survivors of trauma. Those needs should be "normalized" as an everyday part of the literacy program. What some of those "needs"[3] look like and how they could influence literacy work will be examined in the rest of this article.

## Exploring Violence and Trauma

In my interviews I heard about an enormous range of violence. I was told about childhood violence in the home and in school, about adult violence in relationships and in the classroom, and about the ways in which the current and past violence impinged on learners' and workers' safety and on women's learning as adults. Workers frequently talked of how isolated they felt with the stories of violence, of their knowledge of the absence of safety for students, and of their own fears that they, too, were not safe. I was disturbed by the prevalence of the stories and by the statistics about women and girls' experience of violence, which suggest that the experience of violence, rather than freedom from it, is "normal."

During the study, I shifted from speaking about "violence" to using the term "trauma." I preferred the term trauma, as the emphasis of the term is on the reaction of the person and draws the focus away from the degree or amount of violence experienced. Judith Herman provides a clear definition of trauma:

> Traumatic events overwhelm the ordinary systems of care that give people a sense of control, connection and meaning. Traumatic events are extraordinary, not because they occur rarely, but because they overwhelm the ordinary human adaptations to life.... They confront human beings with the extremities of helplessness and terror and evoke the responses of catastrophe. (33)

Although this therapeutic term creates new problems by taking attention away from the agent that causes the trauma, it does draw attention to the impact of trauma, which leads a person to experience subsequent violence as also traumatic:

> They have an elevated baseline of arousal: their bodies are always on the alert for danger. They also have an extreme startle response to unexpected stimuli,

> as well as an intense reaction to specific stimuli associated with the traumatic event. (Herman 36)

This awareness seems valuable to help workers realize, for example, that loud and aggressive talk in the classroom might evoke extreme terror in some learners, or to notice that learners may experience government pressure to get into the workforce as controlling and terrifying. Many learners described how the pressure brought back earlier experiences of being abusively controlled.

The therapeutic literature suggests that the sensitivity of the trauma survivor is abnormal, in comparison with some assumed "normal" level of arousal. Events which provoke a reaction are described as "minor stimuli" (van der Kolk, McFarlane and Weisaeth 3). The perspective on how major the stimuli "really" are, is that of someone who has not experienced trauma. The survivor would not describe the stimuli as "minor." I think it is crucial to be able to understand major reactions to levels of violence (that some might see as minor), *and* to question the implication that "healing" from trauma is a process of no longer reacting "unreasonably," and of moving from abnormal to normal.

Several survivors I interviewed described the sensitivity they felt they had gained from experiencing trauma as a valuable asset. They spoke, for example, of their ability to sense the danger in a situation or to sense someone's intentions. Some suggested that their experience would be different if their sensitivity were valued and sought out, rather than feeling they must hide it and act "normal," disguising their discomfort.

In the literacy field, as in the rest of society, there seems to be little focus on the extent of women's experiences of violence. This silence allows the preservation of the implication that a "normal" life is one in which violence is not experienced.

## Responding to Impacts of Violence in Literacy and the Issue of Presence

One literacy worker wrote to me about the experience of a student in her class:

> She thought she pretty much had sorted out her childhood but Math has brought it back *big time*. She is going to keep a journal—she's very articulate and observing. We are talking a lot as she struggles but the struggle is really extreme and I'm worried.... Yesterday she managed to blank completely for an hour so that she arrived too late to write a make-up test—now she's wondering if she really needed to miss the original test. She made arrangements the night before to get here at a particular time, she ate a particularly soothing breakfast—her partner knew this was *the plan* for the day—then all of a sudden it was an hour later and she hadn't left. Later she remembered a conversation with herself about what time class really started and so when she really needed to get here! When she arrived she couldn't feel her lower extremities at all. A couple of times through the test she was having trouble

> breathing. I did everything I could—let her talk about it—gave her help with the questions to make it more like a class and not a test, etc., etc. but she was determined to go on with it. Finally she quit and left—she was okay I think—I urged her to figure out how to care for herself in the afternoon.

Therapists and counsellors I interviewed often spoke of experiences of trauma leading to dissociation. Therapists use this term to refer to a process whereby a person who is experiencing unbearable trauma distances herself from it. This strategy, learned at the time of the initial trauma, becomes an ongoing process which a survivor may unconsciously slip into when something triggers memory.

One caution I have about the concept of dissociation, and particularly some of the more medical interpretations of it as "disorder" or ailment, is the way in which it suggests that "normal" is to be present, and "abnormal" to be dissociated. This either/or approach can easily erase the complexity of degrees of presence and the wide range of factors which could lead to greater or lesser presence in any particular situation. As I stated earlier, it is important to avoid sliding into pathologizing learners as "ill" if they dissociate, and diagnosing who is dissociating and who is merely "daydreaming." I chose to use the word "presence" in order to focus on the nuances of presence, and to create a positive way of speaking about the challenge for learners to explore what hinders and supports their presence, rather than focussing learners' attention negatively on dissociation, or "not paying attention," as a problem.

Literacy workers are very familiar with the idea that many learners have difficulty paying attention for any stretch of time, and that many often appear to be daydreaming or bored. This discourse of "inattention" can lead some literacy workers to identify those who are not paying attention as not serious students or not motivated. Others might think about learning disabilities, intellectual disabilities, fetal alcohol, or attention deficit disorders. Still others might judge their own teaching as not interesting enough and be continually looking for ways to make the class more stimulating or interesting in order to hold the learners' attention better. Whatever the judgment as to the cause, the result is likely to be frustration for workers and learners alike.

Greater efforts at stimulation may even be counterproductive to creating a relaxed learning environment. One instructor told me that she worked with many students who, although they were in the class regularly, frequently were so spaced out that they did not even recognize work that they had done as their own. She said that, just as missing schooling as children had meant that they did not get a good grasp of the material overall, as adults they were also missing class, even though they were physically in the classroom. So again, they were having trouble making meaning for themselves and understanding the whole. As a consequence, students often told her that they must be stupid because, if they were in class and still had not "got it," then there was no other explanation. This learner frustration makes it crucial to search for explanations which lead to new possibilities for learning.

Recognition by programs, that many learners have difficulty staying present for a variety of reasons, could become part of the everyday discourse in the programs. The difficulty of staying present could be mentioned when a student enters a program. It could become part of the talk about what will be happening in the class or group and part of staff and volunteer training.

The concept could be normalized and space created for learners to notice when they are less present and what is contributing to it. Do they have crises happening in their life? Are they having nightmares and trouble sleeping? Are they uncomfortable? What do they think or feel about the topic of the class? Are they anxious and panicked? Has something triggered them and connected them to an earlier trauma (a tone of voice, the sound of chalk, the ringing of a bell, a quality of light...)? If spacing out is named as something many learners struggle with as they seek to learn literacy, and the classroom is made into a place which is accepting and supportive of the variety of challenges learners will be facing, then, rather than repeating the childhood shame and covering up, learners can work at becoming more aware and conscious of what is happening for them.

Learners should be encouraged to strengthen their awareness of their degree of presence, to build knowledge about what they need to stay present and what they learn from leaving, and learn to ask for what they need to support their learning processes.

### "All or Nothing": Living with Crises

Several therapists talked about survivors as frequently showing opposing patterns at the same time. For example, they spoke about women moving between taking complete control and abdicating control; complete trust and no trust at all; a defended self and no boundaries or self-protection at all. They spoke of women switching between extremes and having enormous difficulty with ambiguity. They suggested that it would be healing for women to learn to find middle ground. One therapist stressed that if one pattern is present you could expect to see the opposite also there.

Another aspect of "all or nothing" that therapists spoke about was a tendency for survivors to make enormous, "heroic" effort, but to be less likely to carry out daily ongoing work. I was told that the idea of daily effort gradually leading to change was often unusual to survivors. Those who grew up in violent and chaotic homes may have had little experience of seeing regular effort lead to results. As children, such learners are unlikely to have been given the support or space to work at learning something regularly or to do homework regularly and see the results of their own persistence. One therapist said survivors are often amazed that what they need to do is consistent daily activity. She said they are aghast that it is something so boring and routine that is required.

Several literacy workers who work in full-time community college programs said that many of their students who come in at the beginning of the year ready to make an enormous effort, convinced that this time they will just "do it," drop out soon after, when they are not doing brilliantly. Instructors are often frustrated, wondering how to help the students stay in for the long haul. The insight that such students may not have had practice with the concept of daily work leading to change, or have knowledge of "middle-ground," suggests new ways to think about approaches to help them to stay in a program and learn successfully.

Counsellors also spoke of another dimension, of the "all or nothing" concept as "totalizing." This is explained as a tendency to move instantly from experiencing one example to concluding "it is always this way." For example, one mistake means "I always make mistakes, I am stupid and nothing will change it." Or, "You let me down once I can never rely on you, you always let me down, I will never trust you again over anything." Small failures are complete failures. Clearly this could be very problematic for literacy learning, undermining any possibility of seeing mistakes as part of learning and of continuing to practise writing or reading regularly.

Curriculum which could help to make "middle-ground" visible, and included more exploration of what leads to successful learning, would be useful to all learners. One literacy worker suggested that another way of characterizing and making "middle-ground" visible, is to think in terms of "good enough." Perhaps a variety of modes of helping learners to see their gradual progress would be useful. Portfolios of work, for example, could be used to help learners see the shifts in their own work for themselves. Mentors and role models might also be able to support learners, by describing times when they have continued in the face of frustration and failures and revealing that although daily work may be boring, it is part of the process of reaching a goal.

"All or nothing" ways of relating to the world can mean that trauma survivors live with regular crises. Instructors talked a lot about the crises in learners' lives and the energy they consume. Therapists and the therapeutic literature talk about how scary it can be for someone who is used to living in a state of crisis to live without crises. A group of workers described crises as a way of "putting off success and change." One learner said that after living with crisis all her life she had no sense of who she would be if she were not in crisis.

## Trust and Boundaries

Trust, or the attention required to assess whether it is safe to trust, is another of the issues which workers and counsellors spoke about as taking up energy and impeding the learners' presence in the program. A survivor described the problem as profound: "The first thing I learned, in a long list of strategies to survive my childhood, was not to trust anybody. The second thing I learned was not to trust myself" (Danica 17).

Many ways of working to help to build learners' trust in their own knowledge, trust in their ability to judge the safety of a situation, and the trustworthiness of others, could be developed and used more consciously in literacy programming.

Many processes which are already used by some teachers, such as journal writing, timed writing, followed by reading aloud and group work, might help to build such skill.

To be trustworthy, workers have to learn to respect their own boundaries and the boundaries of others, as well as support those who do not have good boundaries to learn to create them. Counsellors spoke about the importance of workers coming to recognize when their own boundaries have been crossed, noticing their own anger as a guide to that, and learning to put back in place the clear limits that are necessary to avoid feeling burnt-out, "used," and angry at those who make demands. The ability to reinstate boundaries when they have slipped is an important skill to model for women who may not have learned even the simple right to keep boundaries. In contrast, literacy workers often spoke about how hard they found it to create any limits and boundaries for themselves. A typical example of workers' ambivalence was one worker's account of closing her door after class and trying to ignore when students knocked. When we talked about it, she realized that she had never given herself permission to tell students when she was and was not available to them and to ask them to respect her "boundary." Instead, she said she felt angry that they hammered on her door when she needed to get office work done. Perhaps more often, workers talked about not even setting such basic limits, feeling they had to stretch to meet their students' needs, which were too critical to be denied.

Much therapeutic literature describes the connection between trauma and difficulties creating boundaries.

> This impaired ability to trust one's perceptions and act on them also extends to setting appropriate boundaries. The essence of sexual abuse is having one's most intimate boundary—the skin on one's body—violated. (Mitten and Dutton 134)

Some literacy workers spoke of trauma leading to building a "wall" or being completely exposed and saw problems created from being over-defended or under-defended. Counsellors and therapists stressed that to be trustworthy was to avoid "rescuing" even when asked, as to do so is to collude in the suggestion that the survivor cannot act on her own behalf and can only be "saved" by someone else taking over.

An obvious aspect of boundaries must be clarity about touching and the negotiation of touch. A hand on the shoulder, a pat on the back, or a hug that may seem a supportive gesture for some, could be invasive and traumatic for others. That basic respect for the boundary between one person's body and another's is important if the classroom is to be a place where a survivor can relax and feel safe. Alternative ways—words and looks of encouragement—to show support and encouragement or sympathy need to be found. The classroom offers quite a challenge for those who are not comfortable being too close to others, or close to men in particular. Working together at a computer or in a group at a table could be extremely threatening for some students. The proximity of an instructor coming up behind a student to help, or towering over a student who is sitting, could be a trigger. A male instructor would need to be especially sensitive to what might trigger students and take particular care around issues such as touch, closeness, and relative height.

## Safety and Telling Stories

Much good literacy practice includes learners writing about their own lives. Learners are often asked to keep "response" or "dialogue" journals where the instructor or facilitator writes a reply or reaction after each journal entry. Beginning literacy students are asked to tell a "language experience" story, where an incident from their own lives becomes the basis for their own reading.

I want to draw attention to the energy that learners have to put into deciding what they will say or write and into worrying about whether they will be shamed. This tension and fear is another distraction from the task of developing the ability to read and write with ease. One therapist suggested that learners may be continually asking themselves "If I tell this, can you hear, or will I have to take care of you?" and "If I tell this, can you hear, or will you shame me?" That doubt takes us back to the question of trust. When learners have built some trust that the classroom is a safe place to take risks in learning, they may be tempted to be more open with the stories of their lives. Disclosures make a demand on the instructor and on other learners to be able to "hear." But, safety, in the literacy program, is a complicated concept. Some learners will want the program to be a safe place to tell their stories, others will want it to be a place where they are safe from violence or hearing disturbing accounts of violence in the lives of others.

Several therapists stressed that if the focus of the literacy program is only on pain, a crucial opportunity to create a space for hope, for belief in the possibility of change, and for discovering joy in learning is lost. Several therapists and literacy workers stressed the importance of knowing when to shift the energy in the classroom from pain to pleasure and make space for fun and humour. One literacy worker drew on her own experience when she observed that children in violent or alcoholic families are often not allowed to be frivolous, to laugh and play, and that the humour in such homes is often hurtful teasing, where those with less power are exposed to put-downs and made the butt of the humour. This literacy worker thought that it was very healing to create possibilities for humour, joy, and laughter that is not at anyone's expense. In her practice, she integrated a range of playfulness and fun with a non-judgmental atmosphere where learners could also speak about their pain. Finding an appropriate balance between a space for the telling of pain and for experiencing pleasure and joy would be creative and extremely challenging for literacy workers.

Many literacy workers talked about the challenge to create a safe space in their programs. This was especially true where racism between groups created tensions and where participants had connections and relationships outside the classroom.

In such circumstances, the power of the instructor to create a respectful and safe environment for all is often limited. Yet program workers spoke of how stressful and active a role they played to try to create a safer space.

In programs serving people on the street, the commitment to create a place that is safe for all learners requires an active "policing" role on the part of workers, to make sure learners do not bring weapons into the program and to remove anyone who is violent or abusive from the program. Although workers spoke of the importance of the safer space they were creating, they also spoke of the exhausting task of enforcing it and the tension of being the recipients of anger unleashed when they barred students from the program. They stressed that creating a safer space is an ongoing challenge which forces them to recognize the power dynamic in which they impose limits and struggle continually to maintain them, in the face of the threat of violence.

## Conclusion

Seeing the complexity of awareness needed for both workers and learners around such issues as presence, trust, boundaries, and crises, adds awareness to the question of why learning to read is such a difficult and lengthy process. Where the struggles around each of these issues are ones which a literacy learner has to carry out in private—to reveal her difficulties in these areas is to have herself judged as "abnormal"—then energy is required not only to struggle with the difficulties, but also to hide this struggle.

It is crucial that, within the literacy program (and perhaps also more broadly in education), the range of what is "normal" be broadened and the discourse opened up to include awareness of the struggles that many learners, whether survivors or not, have in a broad range of areas. If the challenges learners face are made an active part of the curriculum, then all learners can benefit from exploring what it takes to be fully present in the classroom and from the knowledge gained from the times of less presence; from discovering a deeper understanding of ambiguity and middle ground rather than staying with the stark contrasts of "all or nothing"; from considering crises and how to live both in and out of crisis; from examining questions of trust in terms of the possibility of trusting their own knowledge and trusting others in the class not to judge and put them down; from learning to set boundaries and respect the boundaries of others; from deciding which stories to tell when; and from creating a safer place to learn.

The silence about the widespread experience of violence, and the impacts of such experiences on learning, limit the possibilities for literacy learning. The funding constraints and bureaucratic structures which shape literacy work are blocking the recognition that a whole range of learning is integral to the literacy learning process. Unless the challenges many learners experience are recognized, the accessibility of literacy will be limited to those who can learn fast and easily. The pressure for survivors of violence to learn, while "acting normal" and disguising the impacts of experiences of violence on their learning will slow, or even block, learning for many women. This silence must be challenged and new practices and policies developed to enhance women's learning.

*This is a small extract only from the findings of a much larger research study. The study formed the basis of a book:* Too Scared to Learn: Women, Violence and Education, *published in Canada by McGilligan Books, Toronto, 1999 and internationally by Lawrence Erlbaum, Mahwah, New Jersey, 2000. Various articles based on this research and subsequent research, as well as materials focussing on practical implementation, are available at www.jennyhorsman.com. For further information on the impact of violence on learning contact the author at feedback@jennyhorsman.com.*

## Notes

[1]This study focused on women literacy learners' experience of violence. Further studies are needed to explore the particularities of men's experience and women's experience in other educational settings. However, many of the implications for literacy programming for women emerging from this research would strengthen literacy learning and other educational programming for *all* students.

[2]I identified key contacts in five regions (British Columbia, Prairies, Central Canada, Atlantic, and North) who each identified women interested in talking to me. Overall, I talked to approximately 150 people, mostly women, in focus group sessions, individual interviews, and through computer networks.

[3]I want also to recognize that not only learners, but also literacy workers, are survivors of trauma. Such experience will have impact on their work and teaching, just as learners' experiences have impact on their learning.

## References

Butler, S. Notes from lectures and workshops. OISE/UT, March 1992.

Danica, E. *Beyond Don't. Dreaming Past the Dark.* Charlottetown: Gynergy, 1996.

Herman, J. *Trauma and Recovery: The Aftermath of Violence—From Domestic Abuse to Political Terror.* New York: Basic Books, 1992.

Mitten, D., and R. Dutton. "Outdoor Leadership Considerations with Women Survivors of Sexual Abuse." *Women's Voices in Experiential Education.* Ed. Karen Warren. Dubuque, Iowa: Kendall/Hunt, 1996. 130–140.

Van der Kolk, B. A., A. C. McFarlane, and L. Weisaeth. *Traumatic Stress: The Effects of Overwhelming Experience on Mind, Body, And Society.* New York: The Guilford Press, 1996.

# Struck Dumb

Mary Nyquist

No one would guess it, but she's not really here. Behind her desk with her feet on the floor, she's arranged herself, as usual, to appear tidy, concentrated, and at ease. Once again, though, nothing's being registered. Those marks on the blackboard, what are they supposed to mean? How can anyone understand when there are so many words missing? The few that do get spoken refer to numbers already there, chalked up, formed blankly in relation to themselves, an abstract, invisibly disciplined brigade, moving in and out of formation only in order to reform. There are no commands, no one is barking orders or threatening punishment. But it's not hard to figure out they're expected to take his direction, to reproduce exactly the moves he makes, to do just what he does. The slightest deviation leads to trouble. Even when it seems to be working, an alternate route meets with disapproval. What counts, obviously, is making sure there's no messing up along the way.

Everyone else seems willing to go along with this or at least give it a try. So why can't she fall into line? For weeks it's been getting harder and, recently, it's not even been an option. Maybe she's just too far behind from not having done any homework lately. Somehow, it doesn't seem only a question of catching up, though. It's more like her ability to grasp what's being done is going. There are moves her mind would ordinarily be making but can't. Understanding what's going on doesn't just elude her; it's actually made impossible, prevented. The figures appear, disappear, reform, reappear, without entering any zone of meaning. It's as if the blackboard, a huge video screen, is displaying a game with symbols in perpetual, ordered motion, while controls, mobile figures, and score signals are all mysteriously withheld. Not from everyone, though. This flotilla of figures really seems to mean something to other people here. Or at least to be of some use. What stops their thoughts from spiralling outwards, upwards, she wonders? A special energy source to which she's lost access? Or an invisible store of counting beans, neatly compartmentalized? Perhaps they've a kind of internal abacus that keeps their mental hands occupied, busy manipulating tangible, workable things keeping all these airy numbers open to the touch of thought, even to silent speech.

For her, though, all that's happening is a dizzying sort of deafness. It won't be long before she won't be able to hear a thing. Already his voice sounds as if it's coming from far, far away. It has such a distance to travel that by the time it reaches her ears it's barely audible. He, too, is receding, though she can still see his mouth moving as he lip-synchs faint, unintelligible sounds. Ever so slowly the volume gets turned lower and lower, finally diminishing to a low-toned, buzzing hum. The buzz is so soft now that the sound of her own breathing is all that can be heard. Not that listening to it has a calming effect. The air is coming in more and more uneven intervals. There are irregular gaps between breaths but also within each one, where tiny, jagged gasps lurch toward a sudden, desperate gulp in the wildly arhythmical beat of a ball bouncing down the stairs, with three quick short taps on one step followed by a high twist up and down. Better not to think about it, though, for the more she does the more difficult it is to get enough air. Even when trying to breathe deeply she can't seem to get enough. But she keeps forgetting to make the effort. And now her heart is racing. It's pounding so hard that someone else will surely soon hear it. If she doesn't keep her mind away from all this strange, crazy fear things will get worse, as they did last week. Oh, why is it happening again so soon? What's wrong, why can't she stop it? It's already so bad that she's no longer even pretending to take things down. The paper has only a few, fragmentary formulae, and now her pen has stopped writing altogether. Her hand probably wouldn't move even if she wanted to scribble something. Besides, she can't really focus her vision any more, at least in this room. Everything's getting blurry except her hands, which lie there cold and lifeless on the desk, and her bag, which she'll have to pick up if she gets away. If she doesn't move soon even her breathing will come to a halt. What if she passes out, suddenly, right now? What if she loses the power of moving altogether, and remains stationery, a seated statue, when everyone else gets up to leave?

That she appears to be here makes it feel even more that she's not. If only she could disappear completely. If her not being here were the simple, literal truth, this wouldn't be so hard to bear. At least she wouldn't have to worry about what to say if someone were to notice she's not paying any attention. Or watched her slumping to the floor, which is what she's afraid will happen soon. It would be such a tremendous relief to feel no eyes could possibly reach out to touch her. Invisibility would cover her gently, like a shawl, protecting her from shame. But would it, really? There's nothing she wants more, nothing, and yet such a lot is already absent that it's hard to imagine how going all the way would ease the pain. Here she is, not really here, yet overwhelmingly present to herself, all the more horribly present because so much else is slipping away. Barely able to hear, see, or move, she's here in tiny particles of stress-specked pain, which pervade the space around and within, making it pulsate with a deadly, life-assaulting energy. The more lethal it becomes, the more it absorbs everything else into it, obliterating restless, outstretched legs, pencils, plaits, the scent of cologne mixed with the stench of pinkish eraser peelings. Could she disappear so completely that it would go, too? If her breathing stops, might not it all, at the same time, stop, too? If she stays absolutely still for long enough, maybe she'll be able to drop into a quieter, less chaotic space, where there won't be awareness of any kind.

To be able to leave it behind is what she wants. The movement away has already started, and it would be so easy just to let it go. But stop. Remember where you are, you idiot. This isn't either the time or the place for such foolishness. For all you know, you've already given yourself away. Is that what you want, to become a laughingstock? To be singled out as a basket case, looney, crackers? You can't expect to keep carrying on like this. And if you faint dead away again? Is that what you want? Imagine having to be carried out by who knows who, with all sorts of remarks being passed back and forth over your body, and everyone hanging around while the calls get made. Never, ever knowing exactly what's happened. The longer you stay here, without doing anything, the more you're likely to bring all this on. And this time it's certain to be worse afterwards. There'll be more questions, more half-suppressed sniggers, more eyes avoiding you in the halls. If this is what you want, just keep it up. You're already doing a great job, so just keep it up. If you really don't want to create a scene, then you'd better get away, right now. This very moment. Either get out of here quietly, or shape up and get to work.

But can she? However much she wants to, she may not be able to get away. It might not be possible to break through this paralysis. Everything that could move seems immobilized. Let's see if she can lift her hand up a bit. No, not even her little finger will cooperate. What about shifting her left foot over a ways? No, not that, either. How this happens, she doesn't know. It's as if a transparent casing, moulded exactly to the shape of her body, encloses her tightly, holding her in place. Holding her so she can barely breathe. Or as if her movements are being directed by an unknown operator, who's decided that for the time being she will have no choice but to stay put. Paralysis by remote control. But there must be a way of wresting the control panel away, of taking it back. She can't stupidly remain here, doing nothing, motionless. It's too humiliating. If she can't break out of this cycle soon, she'll have to hurl herself to the very bottom of the despair that has hollowed her out, hurl herself with so much force that there will be no chance of recovery. Stop this, then. Stop thinking, stop noticing. That would be a way of breaking free. You must leave, right now. This has gone on long enough. Just get a move on. Get out, now. If you don't get up right now, this very second, it will be too late. Just get up. Remember your bag, and walk quickly, as if you know what you're doing. Now. Right now. Or it will be too late.

***

It looks as if nobody's been in since the last time she was here. That old mop hasn't moved an inch and has the very same, mousy dustball sitting on it. No one's bothered to whisk away the cobwebs that stretch over the sink, and across the window, too. That large one over there is sagging, maybe even tearing a bit. Perhaps the motes of dust that are always drifting about in here danced a little bit too long on its ladders. This room must not be used at all anymore. When were those cans of paint last opened, she wonders. That pale yellow, her favourite, could it actually ever have been used? Why is that hideous green everywhere instead? Including on every one of those brush handles, which even the strongest turpentine will never see clean. It's such a relief to find that nothing's changed. Everything is so much always the same it must mean they're using the other room all the time now. So this is still untouched, still unused, still hers. And no one knows it. If her luck would just continue to hold. If only people wouldn't get it into their heads to look for her here.

It's almost comfortable on the floor, now that these old boxes are getting less rigid and sharp edged. The cement is cold with the retentive, deep-held cold of those stones along the creek. But at least it's not damp the way the cellar at home is. No one will think of coming in here, she hopes. "She had to run off to the washroom again," is probably what they'll think. If she can get just a few moments of peace, with no one to listen to, no one expecting her to attend, no one looking at her to see how she is. If only she could stay here. If only this room could be her home. She would miss Pal, that's all. His warm and happy softness. Otherwise, she wouldn't mind a bit. Even going without food wouldn't bother her.

Those tears seem finally not to be stinging her eyes any more. Good thing it didn't start up because if it hadn't stopped someone might have been able to tell. No matter what she does, he always knows. There are only a few minutes before the next bell rings. If no one comes, there'll be enough time to become presentable, to knit this quiet into the frayed, unravelled threads of her everyday self. The next class probably won't be so bad. There's going to be a guest speaker, which means a lot of talking and commotion. And then there's choir, which everyone likes. The piece they're doing now, something baroque, she thinks, has so many different voices and so much movement there's no chance of drifting away. Tomorrow there's a special presentation of some sort. At least she didn't pass out today. Or get caught. If this doesn't come undone, there's maybe a good chance of making it through the rest of the week.

# Do We Need to Syndromize Women's Experiences?

## The Limitations of the "Battered Woman Syndrome"

Elizabeth Comack

In May of 1990, the Supreme Court of Canada rendered its decision in the case of Angelique Lyn Lavallee, a Winnipeg woman charged in the shooting death of her common-law partner, Kevin Rust. In its decision, the Court accepted the testimony of an expert witness, psychiatrist Fred Shane, as to the "Battered Woman Syndrome" (BSW) and its applicability for establishing self-defence in Lavallee's case. The net result of the Supreme Court ruling was to acquit Lavallee on the charge of second degree murder. *R.* v *Lavallee* stands as a landmark judgement in Canadian jurisprudence in that it marks the legal recognition of the BSW in cases involving women who kill their abusive partners. For this reason, the case has generated considerable interest and debate. A key concern has been whether the decision constitutes a benefit for women. How one approaches this issue depends very much on the standpoint adopted. The Supreme Court's decision could be said to represent a benefit for Angelique Lavallee.[1]

The decision has also had an impact on cases similar to hers. In February of 1991, for example, a BC court dropped a second-degree murder charge against a woman who had shot her abusive partner. The court cited the legal recognition of the BSW as the basis for its decision (*Vancouver Sun* March 1, 1991). More recently, after intense lobbying efforts by groups like the National Association of Elizabeth Fry Societies, the Justice Minister announced in 1995 that there would be a review of cases of women serving prison sentences for killing their abusive partners. Ninety-one women—most of who were sentenced pre-*Lavallee*—have asked that their cases be reviewed (*Globe and Mail* February 2, 1996).

While there appears to be grounds for optimism, I want to argue the case for a more cautious reading of the *R.* v *Lavallee* decision. This involves situating the case in a broader context, one which starts from the knowledge that violence against women in our society is widespread and pervasive (Johnson). Indeed, women are much more likely to be killed by their abusive partners than to kill them. Historically, the law has played a role in rationalizing, condoning, and legitimating the violence. Law, in other words, has been *part of the problem* in our efforts to respond to the violence that women encounter form their male partners. It is this recognition that has led to the feminist movement to challenge the male-centeredness of law. This movement has involved not only the naming of the ways in which law reproduces the male standpoint but determining strategies by which a female standpoint could be incorporated in law to move it in a more "gender-inclusive" direction. From this perspective, a key question in evaluating *R.* v *Lavallee* becomes: Does the syndromization of women's experiences offer a viable strategy for realizing a more women-centred perspective in law? While the strategy to force a legal acceptance of BSW is a consequence of the good intentions of some feminists, the way in which BSW makes sense of women's experiences—and the easy fit between the "psy" discourse in which it is situated and legal discourse—leads one to be very skeptical about its potential for challenging the male-centeredness of law.

## Gender Bias in the Law on Self-Defence

The BWS is not technically a defence on its own but is used to substantiate one of the legal defences which, if accepted by the court, would either absolve or mitigate the criminal liability of the accused. Here lies the crux of the problem: those legal defences, and the concepts of criminal liability generally, are coloured by a distinct *male bias*. This bias is especially evident in regard to self-defence.

In order for self-defence to apply to a particular case, a number of legal requirements must be met. First, it must *reasonably* appear to the accused that a threatened assault was *imminent*. Self-defence is not justified if it is used in retaliation of a past assault or in anticipation of a future assault that is not imminent or immediate. Second, the force used in self-defence must be *in proportion* to that used by the assailant. It cannot be excessive force, beyond the amount necessary to repel the attack. Finally, the use of force is a *last resort*. The courts presume that the accused has reasonable grounds to believe that s/he could not otherwise preserve her/himself.

When these requirements are applied to cases involving an abused woman who has retaliated, several problems emerge. For one, defences within the criminal law are predicated on ideal types that provide the frame of reference when interpreting the accused's actions. In the case of self-defence, the "typical persons" and "typical situation" envisioned reflect a distinct male bias. Self-defence has been developed to apply to assaults between male strangers where the person attacked was assumed to be the physical equal of the attacker and where both were able and willing to fight back in the course of the attack.[2] When applied to assaults between partners (that is, one male and one female who are not strangers), the question is whether the defence can offer equal protection to the female who retaliates against the male. The woman is not only unlikely to be equal in size and physical strength , but her ability and willingness to fight back are conditioned by her gendered socialization.

Another problem surfaces with the objective standard used by the courts to determine the applicability of self-defence. This is the model of the "reasonable man" (Naffine 1987, 1990). Given the male-centeredness of this standard, the question is whether the law can appreciate that what a woman might reasonably perceive to be a life-threatening situation may be quite different from male perceptions.

Problems are also encountered with the notion of "imminent danger." In several cases before the courts, a women who suffered a history of abuse retaliated when their attackers were sleeping (*R* v. *Lavallee*). Similarly, use of deadly force is justified only after the accused has exhausted all other reasonable measures. If an abused woman is presumed by the court to have other courses of action to follow (such as leaving the relationship or securing protection in the community), her use of force will not conform to the criteria required to establish self-defence.

Given its male-centeredness, feminist writers have argued that the law on self-defence is unable to reflect or incorporate the experience of abused women (Russell; Sheehy). Indeed, it was largely in response to such limitations that the BWS was introduced in the courts.

## The "Battered Woman Syndrome"

The BWS is a psychological construct made popular by Lenore Walker (1979, 1984, 1989). The syndrome is premised on two theories: the cycle of violence and learned helplessness. It is designed to explain the cyclical and patterned nature of the violence that occurs in abusive relationships and the psychological effects on the woman (such as feelings of guilt, a sense of helplessness, and low self-esteem) which, over time, produce a "psychological paralysis" that prevents her, despite the constant beatings, from terminating the relationship.

When introduced in court through the testimony of an expert witness (usually a clinical psychologist like Walker), the BWS is aimed at addressing issues relevant to the substantiation of self-defence. With regard to the notion of "imminent danger," the recognition of the patterned nature of the violence is designed to demonstrate that a battered woman may be very familiar with the signals of "imminent" violence from her batterer. The syndrome also addresses the issue of "reasonable fear." Given the regular and persistent patterns of abuse that a woman typically endures, the syndrome suggests that her fears of a life-threatening assault or serious bodily injury are reasonable. Finally, in terms of the criterion of "last resort," the psychological effects on the battered woman (particularly her sense of "learned helplessness") are aimed at underscoring the psychological consequences of the relationship that prevent her from escaping the situation.

## Evaluating the "Battered Woman Syndrome"

At first glance, it would appear that a status defence like the BWS is capable of rectifying the male bias in the law on self-defence. It does call attention to the nature of domestic violence, and it does shed light on the emotional and psychological effects experienced by women who suffer a history of abuse. Indeed, the syndrome has been juxtaposed with accounts that either interpret a woman's experience as a result of her masochistic tendencies (she "enjoys" the abuse) or view the failure of a woman to leave as evidence that the violence was not as severe as she would have us believe. Nevertheless, while the intent behind the BWS may be to challenge the prevailing stereotypes and misconceptions about abused women, the particular account offered in their place is fraught with difficulties.

The syndrome is designed to answer the question: why doesn't she just leave? In defining the parameters of the problem, this question presumes that the normative expectation is for a woman who encounters abuse to terminate the relationship. Therefore, if she does stay, she is deviant, and it is this deviance that is seen to require explanation. The explanation we are offered is learned helplessness.[3] According to Walker, learned helplessness provides "a psychological rationale for why the battered woman becomes a victim, and how the process of victimization further entraps her, resulting in psychological paralysis to leave the relationship" (1977/78: 525). Consequently, women such as Angelique Lavallee are described as "feeling trapped," "helpless," "powerless," "worthless," and "vulnerable." They "lack motivation" and possess a "damaged self-esteem" (*R.* v *Lavallee*). In essence, the BWS locates the source of the problem in the *psychological inability* of the woman to take control of her life—to exercise the "right" choice—to leave the relationship. What are the consequences of this account?

One consequence is a failure to *contextualize* the violence in terms of both the behaviour of violent men and the social, political, and economic conditions that promote the violence. For instance, although the cycle of violence theory would suggest that the behaviour of the abusive male is a significant factor in explaining the abusive relationship, little attention is actually devoted to the *dynamics of male power and control.* Instead, the cycle of violence merely repeats itself, "unaltered by time and circumstances" (Dobash and Dobash 224), until the woman's victimization becomes complete.

Not only is the behaviour of the male abuser placed on the sidelines, there is also no sense of negotiation, of resistance, or of help-seeking behaviour (and the results of that effort) on the part of the abused woman. For instance, the abused woman is often confronted with inadequate financial means to support herself and her children, limited social support networks that would facilitate leaving, the fear (often instilled by her abusive partner) of losing custody of her children, and threats (made against her, her children, and others) in the event she does leave. Under such conditions, an abused woman may "choose" to remain in the relationship. The "reasonableness" of her choice may be reinforced by the knowledge that, even if she were to leave, there is no guarantee that the violence would stop—it may well escalate.

Another consequence of this account is that, in defining the woman as deviant, possible behavioural and experiential similarities between an abused women and other persons are overlooked. As Donileen Loseke and Spencer Cahill have noted, the sociological literature on marital stability and instability would suggest that, "at least in regard to their reluctance to leave their mates, battered women are quite similar to both other women and to men" (304). What this suggests, therefore, is that women who remain in violent relationships are not as deviant as the BWS presumes.

In sum, the BWS offers an account that serves to *individualize, medicalize,* and *depoliticize* an abused woman's experiences (Ahluwalia and MacLean; Comack 1987, 1993). In the process, abused women are transformed into victims—not so much of their male abusers as of their own dysfunctional personalities.

## The "Easy Fit" Between the Law and the Expert's Account

It is important to note that, during her trial, Angelique Lavellee's voice was never heard in the Winnipeg courtroom.[4] It was the psychiatrist's voice that the court was listening to—his account of her experience, her perception, and her "state of mind." Indeed, the main points of concentration in the Supreme Court decision were the admissibility of the psychiatrist's expert testimony and the trial judge's instruction to the jury regarding that testimony. Both were affirmed by the Court.

There is an easy fit between a psychological construct like the BWS and the individualized, case-by-case decision-making approach used by the courts in resolving legal conflicts. Walker, for instance, defines forensic psychology as the "translation of the psychological principles into the language and principles of the legal process" (Walker 1989: 270). Moreover, she perceives her role as expert witness in court to be that of "telling the battered woman's story ... in a more *male approved way*" (Walker 1989: 258) [emphasis added].[5]

But the fit between the expert's account and the law goes much deeper than mere appearances. In addressing the criteria of the "reasonableness" of an accused's belief that deadly force was necessary to protect herself, expert testimony sets up an "exceptional" standard for certain women—those who conform to the dictates of the BWS. As Isabel Grant notes:

> The focus in on the irrationality of a woman's response and on the need for terminology to transform that irrational response into a reasonable one for a "battered woman." She must either be reasonable "like a man" or reasonable "like a battered woman." Trapped in this dichotomy, the "reasonable woman" may disappear. (cited in Martinson, MacCrimmon, Grant, and Boyle 52)

The syndrome provides a stereotype of how the abused woman not only *does* behave but how she *should* behave. What happens, then, when a woman fails to conform to the criteria laid down by the syndrome? What if she has left the relationship in the past or is not found to be totally dependent on her partner? Not all women will be successful in their attempts at conformity.[6]

In contrast to the expert's account, rather than casting women who are abused in the role of deviant, I would argue that abused women share many of the experiences of women-as-a-group in a male-dominated society. Instead of succumbing to their "dysfunctional" personalities, abused women are caught—economically, socially, politically, and often quite literally—in a "dysfunctional" social relation. From this perspective, rather than helpless or passive victims, abused women are very much active *survivors* (Comack 1996). Caught in an "insane" situation, a woman's choices will invariably be limited and constrained, sometimes to the point where defending herself with deadly force may well be a "reasonable" survival strategy. In these terms, there are a number of valid, plausible, and rational explanations for why a woman might not leave an abusive relationship and why her perceptions and fears may be reasonable ones that do not require reliance on a syndrome to uncover or to understand.

## Concluding Remarks

My reading of the *R.* v *Lavallee* decision suggests that we need to think twice before embracing the legal recognition of the BWS. To the extent that the Supreme Court decision affirmed the expert's account as valid, it empowers the "psy" profession to speak for abused women, to tell their "truth" (Smart). But that "truth" is one that individualizes, medicalizes, and depoliticizes the experiences of abused women. In the process, other factors—like the actions of the abusive male or the structural constraints that limit the woman's choices—go unacknowledged. The net effect is that, rather than challenging the male-centeredness of law, the BWS offers a compatible discourse that presents women's lives in a "male approved way."

While the focus of the discussion has been on the limitations of the BWS for realizing a more gender-inclusive law, there are other elements in *R.* v *Lavallee* that feminists would do well to support. In particular, the Supreme Court decision succeeds in naming the gender bias in the law on self-defense.[7] It also acknowledges the historical role of law in promoting violence against women,[8] the prevailing cultural myths and stereotypes about abused women that invade the practice of law,[9] and the fact that women's perceptions are often very different from men's.[10] Rather than the syndromization of women's experiences, it is *these* elements that feminists should promote in their continuing struggle to challenge the power of law to define women's lives.

## Notes

[1]Although, admittedly, this was at some cost in terms of privacy, money, self-esteem, and four years of her life. As Laureen Snider has noted: "It did what criminal 'victories' always do, that is, save her from an even worse alternativeß—that of being put in prison for the next 20 years" (personal communication, 29 January 1992).

[2]The paradigmatic case used by the courts has been the one-time "bar-room brawl."

[3]"Learned helplessness" derives from the work of psychologist Martin Seligman. Seligman placed dogs in cages and administered electric shocks at random and variable times. Over time, the dogs ceased all voluntary escape activity and instead developed coping skills to minimize the pain (such as lying in their feces). This learned helplessness response was said to consist of trading the unpredictability of escape for the more predictable coping strategies. According to Walker (1989: 50-51), abused women—like Seligman's laboratory animals—develop coping strategies rather than escape responses to the violence they encounter.

[4]Only Lavallee's statement to the police about the events on the night of the shooting were entered as evidence (*R.* v *Lavallee* 101).

[5]To this end, the expert witness is advised to dress appropriately (for example, by wearing non-prescription glasses to portray a scholarly appearance or by appearing a little "extra" feminine to counteract attacks on her feminist beliefs) and to use a variety of ploys when appearing on the witness stand: "She might give a slightly bemused smile or else put her hand gently to mouth, as if to stifle a giggle" (Walker 1989: 313, 316). Women defendants are similarly coached on how to act and how to dress, so as to conform to the law's image of woman.

[6]Indeed, expert testimony on the BWS may be catering to other socially—constructed ideas about women and victimization, particularly those myths based on racialized understandings of who the women are. For instance, Walker (1989: 206) notes that black women do no benefit as often from expert witness testimony on the BWS; they appear "too angry" in court (1989: 217).

[7]In addressing the imminence rule, the Court rejected both the paradigmatic case of the bar-room brawl and the decision in *Whynot* that a physical assault must actually be in progress before self-defence can apply. Such a requirement, according to the Court, would be tantamount to sentencing a woman to "murder by instalment" (*R.* v *Lavallee* 120).

[8]The Court states: "Far from protecting women from it, the law historically sanctioned the abuse of women within marriage as an aspect of the husband's ownership of his wife and his "right" to chastise her. One need only recall the centuries-old law that a man is entitled to beat his wife with a stick "no thicker than his thumb" (*R.* v *Lavallee* 112).

[9]On the question of "alternatives to self-help," the Court noted that popular misconceptions and mythology have interpreted a woman's failure to leave an abusive relationship as either a sign of masochism or a disclaimer to the severity of the abuse she encountered. The Court further maintained that it was not for the jury to pass judgement on the fact that an accused woman stayed in an abusive relationship and that the self-defence doctrine does not require a person to retreat from her home instead of defending herself: "A man's home may be his castle but it is also the woman's home even if it seems to her more like a prison in the circumstances" (*Lavallee* 124).

[10]In approaching the legal requirements of self-defence, the Court noted that these elements were premised on what the "reasonable man" would do under the circumstances, and stated that: "If is strains credibility to imagine what the 'ordinary

man' would do in the position of a battered spouse, it is probably because men do not typically find themselves in that situation" (*R.* v *Lavallee* 114).

## References

Ahluwalia, S., and Brian D. MacLean. "The Medicalization of Domestic Violence." *Sociology of Health Care in Canada.* Eds. B. S. Bolaria and H. D. Dickinson. Toronto: Harcourt Brace Jovanovich, 1988. 183-197.

Comack, Elizabeth. *Women in Trouble: Connecting Women's Law Violations to Their Histories of Abuse.* Halifax: Fernwood Publishing, 1996.

Comack, Elizabeth. "The Feminist Engagement with the Law: The Legal Recognition of the Battered Woman Syndrome." *The CRIAW Papers, 31.* Ottawa: Canadian Research Institute for the Advancement of Women, 1993.

Comack, Elizabeth. "Women Defendant and the "Battered Wife Syndrome:" A Plea for the Sociological Imagination." *Crown Counsel's Review* 5 (11) (1987): 6-10; 5 (12) (1988): 5-16.

Dobash, R. Emerson, and Russell Dobash. *Women, Violence and Social Change.* London: Routledge, 1992.

Johnson, Holly. *Dangerous Domains: Violence Against Women in Canada.* Toronto: Nelson Canada, 1996.

Loseke, Donileen R., and Spencer E. Cahill. "The Social Construction of Deviance: Experts on Battered Women." *Social Problems* 31 (3) (1984): 296-310.

Martinson, Donna, Marilyn MacCrimmon, Isabel Grant, and Christine Boyle. "A Forum on *Lavallee* v. *R*: Women and Self-Defence." *University of British Columbia Law Review* 25 (1) (1991): 23-68.

Naffine, Ngaire. *Law and the Sexes: Explorations in Feminist Jurisprudence.* Sydney: Allen and Unwin, 1990.

Naffine, Ngaire. *Female Crime: The Construction of Women in Crimonology.* Sydney: Allen and Unwin, 1987.

*R* v. *Lavallee.* 1990. 55 C.C.C. (3d) 97 (S.C.C.).

Russell, Stuart. Ed. *Feminist Review of Criminal Law.* Ottawa: Ministry of Supply and Services, 1985.

Seligman, M. E. *Learned Helplessness.* San Francisco: Wiley, 1975.

Sheehy, Elizabeth. *Personal Autonomy and the Criminal Law: Emerging Issues for Women.* Ottawa: Canadian Advisory Council on the Status of Women, 1987.

Smart, Carol. *Feminism and the Power of Law.* London: Routledge, 1989.

Wallee, Brian. *Life with Billy.* Toronto: Seal Books, 1986.

Walker, Lenore. "Battered Women and learned Helplessness." *Victimology* 2 (3/4) (1977-78): 535-544.

Walker, Lenore. *The Battered Woman.* New York: Harper and Row, 1979.

Walker, Lenore. *The Battered Woman Syndrome.* New York: Springer, 1984.

Walker, Lenore. *Terrifying Love: Why Battered Women Kill and How Society Responds.* New York: Harper Collins, 1989.

# Mapping the Politics of a Research Journey

## Violence Against Women as a Public Health Issue

Katherine M. J. McKenna and Dawn G. Blessing

This article sets out to map a journey, to tell a story that is not often told. We hear about the research of our colleagues normally only in the final stages and then, we see only the product. The treatment of the research process is usually limited to explaining the methodological or theoretical framework within which the work has been placed. We believe, and in fact have come through our research practice to be convinced, that the means and ends of scholarly work are difficult to distinguish, and have a relationship that is complex and shifting. This goes far beyond any straightforward causal or even dialectical relationship. It's not just that the means one uses—that is, one's research design and process—affects the outcome, but that the process, even the original intent, is changed along the way. The means not only enter into the end and change it: the end, rather than being a fixed point, is a process that constantly transforms the means. All of us begin the research process with a plan. How many of us follow through with that plan exactly as pre-thought, towards a pre-visioned, predictable finite end?

We are of the opinion that feminist researchers should address what we all know to be true in a forthright open manner. That is that the systems we function within and interact with, be they institutions, funding bodies or community groups, operate dynamically with research intentions, process, and outcome. How we reconcile feminist politics, community activism, academic credibility, and the imperative of seeking and gaining funding for research is often problematic and complex. Although an examination of where any of us as feminist researchers might be in this process is not simple, and may be personally disconcerting, it is extremely important. This is especially the case when dealing with a topic like violence, which has such critical importance for the actual lives of so many women, whatever their position on the social matrix. What we have to say about this issue has real-life consequences that have to be carefully considered at each stage of the research journey. Each time that a shift in research direction, process or intent is undertaken, all the locations on the route change relative to each other. The imagery of mapping is useful to adopt here: we are not talking about moving in a straight causal line from point A to point B. We offer our own research story here as a modest attempt to open a dialogue, in the hope that it may encourage others to examine their own research journeys and reflect upon the implications, even moral consequences, of their locations relative to where they have been or might be in the future.

## Background

This article is the story of the "research journey" undertaken by four researchers affiliated with Queen's University. Dawn Blessing, who was the originator of our project, was at the time a faculty member with the School of Nursing at Queen's University and has a Masters degree in Nursing. She was also a research associate with the local Health Unit in the city of Kingston, and the counties of Frontenac, Lennox and Addington (KFL&A) in eastern Ontario. Her many years of work in the health field and her concern as a feminist with the issue of violence against women led her to question why there was so little connection between these two important interests. She wondered why there has been traditionally little interest on the part of Health Units in the issue of violence in general, and especially toward women. Impressed by the dramatic findings produced by such studies as the Canadian Panel on Violence Against Women, the Toronto-based Women's Safety Project (Haskell and Randall) and The Violence Against Women Survey conducted by Statistics Canada, she sought to place the issue on the public health agenda.

Her initial exploratory probes amongst some colleagues met with mixed results. Although she received some support at the Health Unit (which gave her two seed grants totalling $4,000 in 1994-95), she encountered a general dismissal of the Statistics Canada findings and ignorance about the other Canadian studies. There was a sense that the data on the prevalence of violence against women, if it was to be believed at all, only applied to larger urban areas with multiple social problems—not to our peaceful small-town and rural community. She decided then to do a local study, placing the issue of violence against women within a totally different, public-health perspective, moving beyond documentation of prevalence to an assessment of the health costs and implications of violence against women. This, she optimistically hoped, would form the basis for policy decisions that would provide the justification for moving new funds into the prevention of violence against women. If Health Units are concerned with bicycle safety, AIDS prevention, injury avoidance and tobacco use, why not also with preventing violence against women?

## The Medical Versus the Public Health Models

Central to Dawn Blessing's approach to this project was her concern with putting violence against women on the public health agenda. Typically, the effects of violence have been seen within the framework of a medical model of injury treatment, rather that from the contextual perspective that public health mandates. The medical perspective is that of disease treatment of individuals by "the credentialed practitioner's expert application of medical arts and skills. Foremost among these arts are diagnosis, prognosis and treatment" (Koss and Harvey 248). The failure of the medical profession to adequately address the issue of violence against women is related to this focus on effect rather than cause. Study after study has found that health care professionals routinely ignore the obvious causes of women's injuries, treating only the symptoms (Canadian Public Health Association, 1994; Canadian Panel on Violence Against Women; Hanvey and Kinnon; Heise 1993; Innes, Ratner, Finlayson, Bray and Giovanetti; Sorenson and Saftlas; Warshaw). They avoid facing the full social reality of violence against women, especially that which occurs within the private sphere and is inflicted by the men with whom women have intimate relations. Doing so would challenge a dogma of medical treatment that looks at the body as a biological machine to be treated, separated out of any other social or political context.

This is, of course, an arbitrary separation for the sake of convenience and effectively reproduces a doctor-patient relationship which can be especially problematic for female survivors of domestic assault, "in which the unacknowledged need to maintain control and power reproduces an abusive dynamic antithetical to the care a battered woman most needs" (Warshaw 144). Added to this is the difficulty many women who have come from locations of double or multiple oppression face in dealing with officials who represent powerful professions and institutions that are not accommodating of difference. Doctors, in particular, as part of the culture in which they live and typically from powerful class, race and gender locations, often share the social prejudices of the dominant culture at large. At times they blame the women, stigmatizing them as "repeaters" who collaborate in their own abuse if they return with frequent multiple injuries (Kurz and Stark 256). All too often, if action is taken to address the root cause of the violence, it is seen as a mental health issue, to be resolved by the victim's treatment, not the perpetrator's (Jones 223).

In a discussion paper for the Family Violence Prevention Division of Health Canada, it was recently conceded that, despite initiatives taken by professional groups such as the Ontario Medical Association to educate their members, there is still "valid concern that hospitals (that is, the physicians working in them) are not identifying abuse among women patients and that ongoing training is required to increase the detection rate and to ensure that all women receive appropriate and sensitive care" (Hanvey and Kinnon 19). Recently, efforts have been made to reform health curricula to include violence against women for both doctors and nurses (Holt and Ross; Hoff; Hotch, Grunfield, Mackay and Cowan). In Vancouver, a pilot study has been undertaken to establish and improve protocols in hospital emergency rooms for recognizing and treating women and children who have been victims of abuse (Grunfield, Hotch and Mackay). However, even where these initiatives draw upon a feminist systemic analysis of gendered power relations, they still focus on treatment by the medical expert rather than solutions that might be empowering to the woman who is the patient. This is where the public health model can be of great service in addressing the issue of violence against women.

The major difference between the medical and the public health approaches to health is that where the former treats the individual after illness has appeared, the latter looks at whole populations to find the causes and takes a "determinants of health" approach. It can be argued that the greatest advances that have been made in the actual eradication of ill health are due to public health initiatives such as inoculation, sanitation, and public education on how to prevent contagion. The most common, not the most exotic, diseases are of concern, and the environment in which they occur is important. This ecological concern lends itself to prevention and easily adapts to a contextual approach to the health of the population. If children are getting scurvy because their mothers cannot afford to buy fresh fruit and vegetables, a doctor would prescribe vitamin supplements but a public health official could legitimately examine the poverty that is the cause of the population's being at risk. This does not always happen, of course, but it is clear that violence against women, as a systemic health problem affecting a significant population, should be a legitimate public health issue. The contextual approach lends itself very well to an examination of different realities in which women experience violence, depending on their race, class, ethnicity, ability or other social location. And because public health goes to the community and addresses a problem within the context in which it occurs, it can be an approach that can be used to reach whole groups of individuals who would not reveal the full story of their injuries to their physicians or to a hospital staff member.

Surprisingly, it is only recently that public health education has begun to recognize the issue of violence, let alone gender specific violence, as a legitimate health concern. In 1991, a report on the delivery of community health services relating to woman abuse concluded that, with the exception of one pilot project in New Brunswick, "no formal programs have been reported in community health units to address the treatment or prevention of woman abuse" (Innes *et al.* 20). From 1988 to 1991, of more than 80 projects funded under the Family Violence Initiative and reported by the National Clearinghouse on Family Violence, only one involved the participation of a local health unit; another involved an epidemiological study of risk factors in family violence. A recent Issue Paper published by the Canadian Public Health Association, entitled "Violence in Society: A Public Health Perspective" breaks new ground in recommending that violence eradication should be a top government priority in the health sector. However, even though many of the results of research on violence against women are reproduced in the body of the report, they are ultimately rendered invisible by the carefully-worded gender-neutral nature of the final recommendations which focus on violence done by "perpetrators" to "victims" and "adults" to "children." It is encouraging, then to see a World Bank Discussion Paper "Violence

Against Women: The Hidden Health Burden" (Heise, Pitanuuy and Germain), forthrightly acknowledge that the vast majority of violence committed on women is perpetrated by men. But such an analysis is not placed specifically within the North American context. Perhaps the authors found it more acceptable to acknowledge this fact within a global context, to see it in "other" countries rather than to acknowledge it as a pressing health issue in our own Health Unit District backyard. Dawn Blessing's project aimed at bringing these public health concerns home and at locating violence against women as a major health concern within our own community. She decided that the best way to proceed with her project was to undertake a survey which would first document local prevalence and then connect it to a variety of health effects and behaviours.

## Methodological Issues

In the North American context, the individual who pioneered feminist survey research on violence against women was Diana Russell, who conducted a large-scale survey which produced statistics that were then shocking in what they indicated about its prevalence (1986, 1990). In Canada, her work was both carried on and improved upon by the Women's Safety Project, which as yet has a large part of its findings still unpublished (Randall and Haskell). It was a major study of a random sample of 420 women in Toronto which looked at all aspects of women's safety and experiences of sexual and physical assault. Its ambitiousness lay in the fact that it was also an in-depth survey, involving a face to face interview that took an average of two hours to administer and looked at multiple incidents over a woman's entire life. It brought together the quantitative and qualitative by being both a numbers count and an opportunity to study women's own expressed perceptions of their experiences. Lori Haskell and Melanie Randall's preliminary findings were first published with the results of the Canadian Panel on Violence Against Women and have since appeared in a journal article (Randall and Haskell). Sections of the questionnaire developed by Haskell and Randall for the Women's Safety Project were also used in the Statistics Canada Survey on Violence Against Women.

We were tremendously impressed with the work of the Women's Safety Project, especially with its innovative combination of the collection of quantitative data with intensive personal interviews. We planned to follow this work by incorporating some of the same method of interviewing with the use of a modified version of the Conflict Tactics Scale (CTS). The prime advantage to the CTS is that it allows for a complex and graduated measure of violence, ranging from behaviours such as name-calling to the extremes of severe physical assault. The scale has been used to good effect in the Statistics Canada Survey on Violence Against Women and by studies such as that of Walter DeKeseredy and Katharine Kelly on dating relationships among college and university students. But the CTS, despite its many advantages, has also been used by some scholars in an anti-feminist manner, to diminish or trivialize the issue of violence against women. The patriarch of them all is Murray Straus, the original designer of the Conflict Tactics Scale, which he used in his investigation of "troubled families." His bias is clear in his framing of the issue as one of "family violence." The original CTS took as its starting point the premise that there were families with poor conflict resolution skills and that the inability to negotiate difficulties could lead to an escalation of confrontation to the point where violence would erupt. His famous 1980 study hit the Canadian and U.S. press dramatically. It claimed that, contrary to what feminists in the battered women's movement had been saying all along, in fact women were just as violent as men, and that this was by their own admission in response to his survey. Since that time he has continued to write in this vein, undeterred by an avalanche of criticism. As recently as 1993, he asserted that there was "a near equality between husbands and wives in domestic assaults" (Straus 76).

The debate about the CTS has been so extensive and been held over such a long period of time that we can only sketch its outlines here. Russell P. Dobash and Rebecca Emerson Dobash have written at length on this, and one would think that they would have finally closed the debate in their comprehensive article with Margo Wilson and Martin Daly, "The Myth of Sexual Symmetry in Marital Violence." As Leonore Walker has pointed out, the ways in which Straus and his followers used the CTS did "not account for the difference in gender response styles, particularly women's tendency to over-report their own aggressive acts and men's tendency to underreport theirs" (696). Rather, Straus's scale asks the same questions of men and women, not differentiating between the realities of violence experienced by men and women. It does not count sexual violence, nor does it adequately deal with what is retaliatory and what is aggressive violence. It often does not distinguish among acts such as biting and hitting with a fist. It also does not count the total number of incidents. If a woman throws a plate once, that is considered to be as serious as an assault as repeated beatings. One 1994 study (Cantos, Neidig and O'Leary) has shown that even where both partners suffer injury, women's are more severe and the result of much more extreme violence. What this all adds up to is expressed perceptively by Kersti Yllö. She observes that, "these findings" by Straus and his followers, "have no relation to the experience of practitioners who are overwhelmed by the needs of abused women." "Critiques," she complains:

> appear "nonscientific." The fact that most social scientists are men, and that abused wives and their advocates are women, accentuates the divisions and status differences. The challenges offered by feminist researchers, shelter workers, and battered women, themselves, are defined as subjective. Their way of "knowing" about the topic has not been gleaned through the scientific method, which, supposedly, enables an "objective" analysis. Rather, their understanding is grounded in body and feeling as well as mind. The fusion of thought and feeling is regarded as diminishing rather than enhancing knowledge. (1988: 41)

The Statistics Canada Survey and studies such as that of DeKeseredy and Kelly have used the CTS in ways that both challenge Straus on his own ground and use the scale in a modified form, exploiting its advantages while removing its liabilities. This work, in its identification of violence in all its forms, has also led to much controversy but in the form of anti-feminist backlash. Recently right-wing extremist, John Fekete dedicated a whole book to a virulent attack on everyone in Canada and beyond who had done any feminist or socially progressive work on violence, sexual harassment and related issues. The constant refrain from him and other critics is that researchers have gone "too far," and have classed the trivial with the serious in terms of sexual harassment and other forms of violence. DeKeseredy and Kelly, for example, are accused of counting seemingly innocuous acts, such as verbal attempts at seduction, as equivalent to attempted rape. The Statistics Canada survey is equally criticized for including women's assertion that they are "somewhat afraid" to go out after dark in with women who say that they are "quite afraid" (Fekete). The argument is that the seriousness of violence and harassment is overstated because the boundaries are blurred between mild and severe incidents. The irony of this accusation is that it is a twisted form of the criticism that was aimed by feminists at researchers like Straus, whose work polemicists like Fekete most admire.

We were aware of the minefield surrounding the use of the CTS, but decided that because one of our key goals in the design of a local study on violence was to duplicate and compare our results to the Statistics Canada survey, its use was to our advantage. We decided to blend a carefully modified CTS with the interview techniques of the Women's Safety Project by developing and conducting a questionnaire in our own community. But we considered it even more important to go beyond this local survey on prevalence to link it to issues of violence to public health and to include community groups in the project from the earliest planning stages. Perhaps we were naïve in thinking that the generation of local data would sway the KFL&A Health Unit in our favour and that we could at the same time do more qualitative research designed by and for our community that could be a model for other communities. But that is exactly what we set out to do.

## Embarking on the Research Journey

Once she had decided to undertake the project on violence against women, Dawn Blessing began to gather together a research team. She was already familiar with a colleague who she knew shared her interest in violence against women, Tina Pranger, a professor of Rehabilitation Therapy at Queen's University who was then in the final stages of completing a Ph.D. dissertation. Together they approached Katherine McKenna, an adjunct faculty member in Women's Studies at Queen's who had a doctorate in history and taught feminist theory. Will Pickett, a research associate with the KFL&A Health Unit and a member of the Department of Community Health and Epidemiology at Queen's, asked Dawn if he could be included in our project. We were also joined in the early stages of our work by community researcher Kate Thomas, who has a Master of Social Work, and by a research assistant, Marisa Des Mazes, who graduated in spring 1995 from Queen's School of Nursing. We mention our various credentials to give a sense of the multidisciplinary nature of our team as well as our qualifications. We were all fairly junior and at the time of our grant applications had one Ph.D. amongst us—and that was in the humanities.

Because of our status as junior scholars, the prospects for obtaining funding to conduct our research were not, realistically, all that good. We were happy with our working relationship and wanted to go it alone rather than along a more established route, that of attaching ourselves to a more senior scholar who could "front" us for the purpose of grant applications. This was primarily because we wanted to be free to be both academic and activist, and preferred to be directed by community partners in a collectivity rather than by a project leader in a hierarchically structured research team. We were not aware of any research "star" locally who would have been willing to cooperate with us in such an enterprise.

With only one Ph.D. amongst us, we decided that we didn't have much chance of obtaining a Social Sciences and Humanities Research Council (SSHRC) grant. The National Health Research Development Program (NHRDP) was a possibility, but we had heard that it was biased in favour of the medical model of "scientific" research. We were all familiar with the experience of other feminist researchers in the medical field, such as Karen Messing, who had pointed out in her work on women's occupational health that,

> proposals were more likely to be accepted [for funding] if the project involved non-humans or human cells in culture rather than live humans, if the work was done in a laboratory rather than in the field, if there was a woman on the peer review committee, and if there was no visible worker input at any level of the project.... Thus, [she concluded] studies were funded in inverse proportion to the likelihood that their results might support...social change. In particular, all our proposals specific to women were rejected. (222-3)

Although research using humans has been more favoured recently, we thought Messing's point about the difficulties of finding funding for work that supported social change for women was well taken. We decided that we would have a better chance of an NHRDP grant if we established a research track record first. Unfortunately for us, the federal Family Violence Initiative had ended, and it was well known that traditional funders such as the Ontario Women's Directorate and the Status of Women Canada were no longer in a position to give much support. Consequently, we looked to other funding sources.

Our first real prospect seemed to suit us perfectly: applying for a Healthy Community Grant (Ontario Ministry of Health). This was a new program funded by the Ontario Ministry of Health but administered through District Health Councils (DHC), so that decisions are made locally concerning grants. One of the priority areas for funding was "healthy relationships." These grants were not intended to be primarily for academic research, we were informed, but this actually suited us very well since our intent was to be a community-based project. Most of us on the team had come to the issue of violence against women as community activists. We didn't want to launch our project in isolation from our feminist roots. We wanted to start out our research by building a community coalition. There were, of course, existing umbrella organizations, at least for the City of Kingston. In particular, the local Kingston Coordinating Committee Against Domestic Assault Against Women (CCADAW) was a good place for us to start. We were all aware of the funding and resource challenges being faced by agencies such as the Sexual Assault Crisis Centre Kingston and Kingston Interval House. Over the past few years, CCADAW has struggled to survive, wounded not by indifference or neglect but by the sheer exhaustion of its members. We saw an opportunity, so we hoped, to boost the morale of hard-working feminist front-line agencies by undertaking the hard work of coalition-building and maintenance ourselves.

This would be the first phase of our project, followed by a consultative period during which we would, among other things, compile existing data collected by local agencies, and design and test a questionnaire to be administered locally with the help of our community coalition. We tried to strike a balance between the necessity of setting out a definite agenda for the funding proposal, while leaving enough flexibility to be open to input at the earliest stages of project design from our community partners. After having completed the preliminary work of consultation, coalition building, consolidation of existing community resources and project design, we hoped that we would then have sufficient track record to justify an NHRDP proposal (not to mention two more in-hand Ph.Ds by then). In the planning stages for our grant proposal we spent many hours consulting with the Women's Safety Project's co-investigators, Lori Haskell and Melanie Randall. They gave us invaluable advice and assistance in all aspects of putting together our grant proposal. It was, incidentally, during these consultations that we decided to call ourselves the Women's Safety and Health Project which was intended to be an expression of our debt to their work and our sense of carrying on what they had started in new directions.

We were optimistic about our chances of getting the grant. Our request for this first phase was modest ($25,000) and we were able to obtain the official sponsorship of KFL&A Health Unit. We set about doing the groundwork to obtain and demonstrate broad-based community willingness to participate. Over the summer of 1994, we contacted numerous community groups and conducted in-depth discussions about our project with ten of them. The explicitly feminist organizations were particularly cautious in granting their support. Despite the fact that they knew some of us through other contexts, they were justifiably concerned about our commitment to grass-roots work in addition to academic research. We were asked some searching questions about what we would be doing that would be new, that would address solutions and not only document the incidence of violence against women, and that would not direct scarce funding dollars away from direct services to women. One feminist community agency refused to even meet with us on the grounds that our work would not be worthwhile in helping women and would only duplicate what they saw as an excess of elitist academic research. We were sorry not to have been able to talk with them about these important issues, but we understood their position.

We were able to convince those with whom we spoke that our work would be worthwhile, since we shared their concerns. Our intention was for our research to provide justification for the direction of new funding from public health sources to organizations dealing with the issue of violence against women. The ten groups that we met with endorsed our project in writing. An additional 19 letters of support were received from the larger community. We thought that our final application package was impressive and presented a model of community activism combined with research that we had not seen anywhere else. Yet when we heard back about the funding (District Health Council) we found that we were only ranked fifth out of seven applicants, despite the fact that of all the projects considered and evaluated according to strengths and weaknesses in the publicly available memorandum detailing the decisions, our project had the smallest number of the weaknesses identified. We were criticized for the fact that "sponsors with multicultural representation did not appear to be included," because our project "focused attention on treatment issues rather than prevention" and, most tellingly, that we did "not address this subject in relation to men's roles in healthy relationships."

We were vulnerable to the criticism that we had minimal multicultural representation (although we certainly had some) because we had concentrated our efforts on front-line service providers in the KFL&A region, many of which had multicultural representation but were not explicitly multicultural groups. This was not recognized or perhaps even known to the District Health Council. None of the successful projects, however, involved multicultural groups either, nor were they criticized for this omission. They all fell within the priority funding area of raising healthy children and included a drug education program by Parents Against Drugs, an in-school mentoring program by Big Brothers, and a therapeutic recreation program for children sponsored by a community service group. The Big Brothers project was for boys who were identified as being at risk but who were, in fact, identified in the application and by the DHC only as "children." This suggests that, while our alleged inattention to males was a problem for the funders, the Big Brothers' project's exclusion of girls was not.

We were disappointed by this rejection, which seemed to be at least somewhat politically motivated, but we decided to move forward. Our next hope was for a grant from the Trillium Foundation. Funded by provincial lottery money, it had recently expanded its mandate to encompass projects that would "explore and document systemic barriers underlying social and economic disadvantage, leading to the generation of ideas and solutions for social change." We were encouraged by their stated commitment to support endeavours that were "community-affirming," that would "stop the cycle of disadvantage" and aid in "the development of collaborative efforts and networks" (The Trillium Foundation 1994). Admittedly we were now in a very large pool of applicants, as over 1200 proposals were put forward. Still, we were very disappointed to find that we had been unsuccessful. The reasons given verbally to us over the telephone were that there was so much research already in our area, that what we wanted to do was not different enough from what others had done, that our results might not be generalizable to other communities, and that our project was simply not compelling. Given the total lack of work on violence against women as a public health concern, we were dismayed by this response. We were glad to see, however, in Trillium's annual report (1995), that they did support many initiatives that dealt with the issue of violence. Of 167 projects funded under the new guidelines, 21 dealt with the issue of violence, and 13 specifically with violence against women, all of them extremely worthy proposals. None of them, however, looked specifically at violence against women as a public health issue.

At this point, we did not know where to turn. We considered a number of options. Perhaps we should go a more strictly research route and apply for a small grant of SSHRC money to design a questionnaire through our university Advisory Research Committee competition. We thought about doing a study of local hospital emergency room statistics, newly compiled in Kingston (1993) under the Canadian Hospitals Injury Reporting and Prevention Program (CHIRPP). This would be a much more narrowly focused epidemiological study that would draw on Will Picket's expertise and could be broadened to other hospitals across Canada generating CHIRPP data. Finally a solution presented itself to us right under our noses. Dawn Blessing was also involved in a major research endeavour, the Better Beginnings, Better Future Project funded by the Ontario Ministries of Community and Social Services, Health and Education and Training, as well as (at that time) the federal Ministry for Indian and Northern Affairs. Through her, we were able to become part of an already-funded large research project. The project's research director allowed us, within the context of an existing questionnaire, to design the section dealing with violence focusing exclusively on women's experiences. After a year and a half of broad research consultation and grant proposal writing, this seemed almost too easy. We were relieved to find a way to proceed with at least some part of our work but were acutely aware that a major component of our research vision had been shelved: our active involvement in community development and activism (except through Dawn's role with the local Kingston project). We wrote to our local supporters and informed them of how things stood. We regretted this, but what other realistic option did we have? In times of severe cutbacks, it was highly unlikely that another such opportunity would present itself.

The Better Beginnings, Better Futures Project is a 25-year primary prevention longitudinal research demonstration project. One aspect of the research will measure the impact of local primary prevention programs on children and families in designated high need areas in one native reserve and eight urban sites across Ontario. On the reserve and in each urban area the communities were consulted closely in the planning stages for this project. The research will follow all of the parents (predominantly mothers) and their children born in these areas in 1994, surveying them at regular intervals in follow-up questionnaires that ask for information on diverse issues of the parent's and the child's life including health issues. Dawn Blessing designed the portion of the questionnaire on violence issues in consultation with the communities involved as part of the standard process used in the larger study. We were not able to add a great deal to what had to be a short section of an already-approved lengthy survey. The limited nature of what we could ask was mitigated by the fact that we would be able to correlate statistics on violence among the mothers of these children with data on a myriad of other health behaviors. We would be able to track these behaviours over time, as well as the influence of prevention programs. If some women who were involved with violent men were able to leave them over the 25-year period, we would be in a position to document what factors enabled them to do so. We felt that these research benefits outweighed the limited scope of what we were permitted to add to the study. In the end, as we had earlier decided, we used a modified version of the CTS. We designed it so that the women would be asked about their experience of violence and made it a graduated scale of behaviour, ranging from name-calling to violent sexual assault. We simply asked if a women had experienced any of these within the previous year and who had been the perpetrator.

We felt that our questionnaire addition was so straightforward, even conservative, that we were quite surprised at the negative reaction of one of our fellow investigators. An academic, he claimed that he had been the only one who had to this point expressed a desire to publish findings on violence from the study data, and he accordingly wanted a say in what was asked. Following Straus's lead, he objected to our questions on the basis that they were asking only about partner-to-self violence and not self-to-partner abuse. He contended that if we were concerned about children learning violence, then we could not afford to pass up information on women's violence to men, and that if we ignored these factors, we would end up acting as though we think that the serious problem of women's violence against men did not matter. This was researcher who was quite senior to us and it caused us more than one moment of panic. Fortunately, he did not pursue the issue aggressively and we were able to convince the research director that our approach was valid.

## Conclusion

Despite our hopes for the Better Beginnings data, it seems to us that our project has run up against roadblocks at every turn. We did not have sufficient academic credentials to facilitate funding from the traditional research sources, and our cross-disciplinary focus made it difficult to place ourselves either within the SSHRC or the NHRDP frameworks. On the other hand, we were considered to be too academic and research-oriented for more community-based funders such as the DHC and Trillium. Feminist organizations have limited resources for financing research. The DHC was clearly uncomfortable with the women-centered aspects of our proposal, yet front line agencies were also suspicious of our feminist credentials as academics working within a patriarchal university structure. We had hoped to combine a commitment to our community with academically credible research, but we were unsuccessful in this because we could not obtain the requisite funding. Our final participation in the Better Beginnings, Better Futures project was a good opportunity and a reasonable compromise of these conflicting goals, but it is a far cry from the community activism we had originally envisioned. And our "ownership" of the data generated is certainly not guaranteed.

Indeed, the question that we are asking ourselves, and that we would like to open up for general discussion in the area of feminist research, in this: Is the imperative of obtaining academic status, a necessary precursor of getting jobs, grants and respect in a tough, competitive academic climate, in conflict with a feminist research agenda? One does not hear too much talk in academic circles about feminist action research these days, as one did ten or more years ago. To give an example, in the spring of 1995 our project team presented a session at the Canadian Women's Studies Association meeting on "Organizing a Community-Based Research Project: Violence Against Women as a Public Health Issue." The attendance at our session was, to say the least, sparse. Yet earlier that day some papers focusing primarily on postmodern theoretical issues were packed. The author of the densest paper of them all at that session expressed her anxiety about appearing to be academically competent and made it clear that her work was explicitly geared to validating her academic worthiness. Yet an intelligent community front-line worker would have found her presentation to be almost totally incomprehensible. In our anxiety to be taken seriously as academics in an environment that has treated feminist research as not serious, too overtly "political" or lightweight, have we erred too far to the side of the abstract, abstruse and inaccessible?

Feminism, especially radical feminism that names and challenges patriarchy, appears to be in almost complete eclipse in the brave new postmodern world we now inhabit. There are, it is true, some good reasons for rethinking some of the assumptions that feminists have tended to make in the past. As Angela Harris has tellingly observed, radical feminists have tended to generalize from white women's experience of patriarchy to all women so that, even when the oppression of others is acknowledge, it is seen as qualitatively the same. This can mean for example, "that black women are white women, only more so" (601).[1] While acknowledging the validity of this and similar charges, and not ignoring the important work on issues such as violence and poverty undertaken by socialist feminists, it is still true that it has been radical feminists who have launched the most effective challenges to violence against women, whether theoretically or in front-line work.

Feminist postmodernists like Judith Butler have, it is important to note, asserted that, "Within feminism, it seems as if there is some political necessity to speak as and for women, and I would not contest that necessity." There are times, she concedes, when we must have "recourse to identity politics." So feminists agree, Butler concludes, "that demonstrations and legislative efforts and radical movements need to make claims in the name of women" (15). In practice, though, however insightful the post-structuralist critique of dominant discourses, the fear of essentialism on the part of such theorists is so great that direct political action on behalf of "women" is rarely discussed.

Sharon Marcus, in her analysis of the discourse of rape, for example, offers us many valuable insights into "the gendered grammar of violence" (392), but she advises women who experience rape to simply fight back on an individual basis, to refuse the "script" of the rape scenario. "Rape exists" she contends, "because our experience and deployment of our bodies is the effect of interpretations, representations and fantasies which often portray us in ways amenable to the realization of the rape script: as paralyzed, as incapable of physical violence, as fearful" (400). Perhaps some women might feel powerful enough to fight back against their attackers in some situations, but Marcus assumes that there is no context to the rape and that it involves the classic and false stereotype of the surprise attack by the stranger in the alleyway. In fact, the rapist is more likely to be someone with whom the woman has an intimate relationship, such as a husband or father. Or, the victim might literally be less physically powerful or enabled, such as, for example, women who are disabled or institutionalized, or children. Not all women are even clear on how to define what is and is not rape within such contexts, let alone refuse its script.

While not denying the importance of postmodern analysis, which is not necessarily in itself apolitical, we still want to assert that the insights of radical feminism into the gendered nature of violence are crucial to understanding violence against women. Such an analysis means nothing without an activist credo that provides for separatist strategies that give women the space, safety, and time to examine how they might understand and remove themselves from the sources of violence in their and their children's lives. The Harris government in Ontario has commissioned a report which calls for limiting women's stay in shelters to one or two days until they can get a restraining order and a security system, relying on neighbours to call the police, and treating male and female rape victims in the same outpatient health clinics.[2] This dismantling of the shelter movement and compromising of women's safety and security is being proposed in the name of empowerment and equality for women.

While this certainly calls out for discourse analysis, it is not enough to point to the patriarchal subtext here. It is also important to commit to positive political action, and to undertake research that provides the "facts" to support that action. Are all such research initiatives, then, doomed to failure because of the demands of a patriarchal system that finds abstract theorizing safer and more acceptable to fund than community activism? Do we all as feminist researchers and activists end up selling our souls for the sake of academic credibility and obtaining the all-important grants? We hope not, but the distance we ourselves have moved from our original intentions certainly raises such troubling issues as a very real concern. We present this as a challenge for us all to consider, and invite other feminists to enter into this discussion.

## Postscript

Since, as often happens with academic writing, it has been more than two years since our initial paper was submitted, reviewed, revised and re-revised for publication, it has been suggested that we might want to update the route that our research journey has taken since that time. The Better Beginnings, Better Futures project has undergone some cutbacks and hard questioning by the Ontario Provincial Government, but is still, at this point, being supported. The questionnaire has been implemented, the interviews conducted and the research data gathered, entered and analyzed. Katherine McKenna has been involved in another violence-related project in Kingston, a broadly based group composed of representatives from Queen's Faculty of Education, Women's Studies and the Office of Residences along with St. Lawrence College and Kingston Interval House. Called the Violence Intervention and Education Workgroup (VIEW), it is funded by the Ontario Ministry of Education and Training to undertake educational initiatives on violence against women and girls and has so far also survived the cutbacks as well. It has been possible through the resources of VIEW for the Women's Safety and Health Project to obtain a small grant to hire a student, Priya Watson, to help with the preliminary data analysis of the Better Beginnings survey. The VIEW grant has also enabled us to return to some of our original intentions. Part of the funds are being used to write up our findings in an accessible format to be distributed back to the communities that were surveyed, and our findings were debuted at the Annual General Meeting of Kingston Interval House in the fall of 1997.

As for the original research team, many of us have now moved on to other endeavours. Kate Thomas, although in sympathy with our work, has of necessity taken full-time work as a social worker to support herself and her child and has little time to participate in research.

Dawn Blessing has had a parting of the ways with the local Health Unit. They felt that her work on violence against women was not compatible with their research goals, and she has since moved to Thunder Bay where she is now a counsellor in the Family Violence and Psycho-Social Program of Family Services. Although she remains interested in the project, she has decided that front-line service work is where she needs to be rather than in research.

Shortly after winning a prestigious university-wide teaching award, Tina Pranger decided that she too needed a break from the university environment. She now lives in Prince Edward Island, where she works with the Department of Health and Social Services as a community-based health researcher. Although she is still committed to continuing the project, the logistics of this have been difficult. She plans to complete her doctorate in the near future.

Katherine McKenna has also recently left Queen's to become the Director of the Centre for Women's Studies and Feminist Research and the Centre for Research on Violence Against Women and Children at the University of Western Ontario. Together with Will Pickett and colleagues from the Better Beginnings, Better Futures Project, she is working on a paper based on the violence survey.

Will Pickett continues in his appointment with the Health Unit and the Department of Community Health and Epidemiology at Queen's. He has successfully defended his Ph.D. dissertation and was awarded a major grant from Agriculture Canada for his work on farm injuries. He has also been named as a principal investigator with the Ontario Tobacco Research Unit. He remains committed to continuing with the project.

As a final ironic footnote, although it would appear that at long last there will be a concrete publication resulting from the violence portion of the Better Beginnings survey, despite all our initial concern about having a senior faculty member "front" our group, the same colleague who opposed our project will be one of the co-authors on the article. He "owns" some crucial data that we need to include and has agreed to let us proceed, despite our philosophical differences. Such are the realities of the politics of research!

## Notes

[1]The authors wish to thank student Cheryl Dunn for bringing this source to our attention.

[2]The report was commissioned by the Ontario Women's Directorate and entitled "Framework for Action on the Prevention of Violence Against Women in Ontario." The Ontario Government released only a four-page excerpt of the report's Executive Summary in December, 1996, in the face of the intensive feminist criticism it generated.

## References

Butler, J. "Contingent Foundations: Feminism and the Question of 'Postmodernism.'" *Feminists Theorize the Political.* Eds. J. Butler and J. W. Scott. New York: Routledge, 1992. 3-21.

Canadian Public Health Association. *Violence in Society: A Public Health Perspective*. Issue Paper, 1994.

Canadian Panel on Violence Against Women. *Changing the Landscape: Ending Violence—Achieving Equality*. Final Report. Minister of Supply and Services Canada, 1993.

Cantos, A. L., P. H. Neidig, and K. D. O'Leary. "Injuries of Women and Men in a Treatment Program for Domestic Violence." *Journal of Family Violence* 9 (1994): 113-124.

Dekeseredy, W., and K. Kelly. "The Incidence and Prevalence of Women Abuse in Canadian University and College Dating Relationships." *The Canadian Journal of Sociology* 18 (1993): 137-159.

District Health Council of Kingston, Frontenac and Lennox and Addington. *Memorandum to Sponsors of Proposals for 1994/95 Healthy Community Grants,* 1994.

Dobash, R. E., and R. P. Dobash. "The Nature and Antecedents of Violent Events." *The British Journal of Criminology* 24 (1984): 269-288.

Dobash, R. P., R. E. Dobash, M. Wilson and M. Daly. "The Myth of Sexual Symmetry in Marital Violence." *Social Problems* 39 (1992): 71-91.

Fekete, J. *Moral Panic: Biopolitics Rising.* Montreal/Toronto: Robert Davies Publishing, 1994.

Finkelhor, D., R. J. Gelles, G. T. Hotaling and M. A. Straus. Eds. *The Dark Side of Families: Current Family Violence Reserach.* Newbury Park, CA: Sage Publications, 1989.

Gelles, R. J. "Review of Abuse and Battery: Social and Legal Responses to Family Violence." *Journal of Marriage and the Family* 54 (1) (1992): 245.

Gelles, R. J. "Research and Advocacy: Can One Wear Two Hats?" *Family Process* 33 (1994): 93-96.

Grunfield, A., D. Hotch, and K. Mackay. *Identification Assessment, Care, Referral and Follow-up of Women Experiencing Domestic Violence Who Come to the Emergency Department for Treatment.* Vancouver: Domestic Violence Program, Department of Emergency Medicine, Vancouver Hospital and Health Sciences Centre, 1995.

Hanvey, L., and D. Kinnon. *The Health Care Sector's Response to Woman Abuse.* Ottawa: National Clearinghouse on Family Violence, 1993.

Haskell, L., and M. Randall. *Private Violence/Public Fear: Rethinking Women's Safety.* [Final report prepared for Solicitor General of Canada]. Unpublished manuscript, 1994.

Harris, A. "Race and Essentialism in Feminist Legal Theory." *Stanford Law Review* 42 (1990): 581-616.

Heise, L. "Violence Against Women: The Hidden Health Burden." *World Health Statistics Quarterly* 46 (1) (1993): 78-85.

Heise, L., J. Pitanuuy and A. Germain. *Violence Against Women: The Hidden Health Burden.* World Bank Discussion Paper No. 255. Washington, D.C.: World Bank, 1994.

Hoff, L. A. *Violence Issues: An Interdisciplinary Curriculum Guide for Health Professionals.* Ottawa: Health Canada, Health Services Directorate, Mental Health Division, 1994.

Hoff, L. A., and M. M. Ross. *Curriculum Guide for Nursing: Violence Against Women and Children.* Ottawa: University of Ottawa, Faculty of Health Sciences, School of Nursing, 1993.

Hotch, D., A. Grunfield, K. Mackay, and L. Cowan. *Domestic Violence Intervention by Emergency Department Staff.* Vancouver: Domestic Violence Program, Department of Emergency Medicine, Vancouver General Hospital and Health

Sciences Centre, 1995.

Innes, J. E., P. A. Ratner, P. F. Finlayson, D. Bray, and P. B. Giovannetti. *Models and Strategies of Delivering Community Health Services Related to Woman Abuse.* Edmonton: Health and Welfare Canada, Nation Health Research and Development Program and the University of Alberta, 1991.

Jones, A. *Next Time She'll be Dead: Battering and How to Stop It.* Boston: Beacon Press, 1994.

Koss, M. P., and M. R. Harvey. *The Rape Victim: Clinical and Community Interventions.* 2nd ed. Newbury Park, CA: Sage Publications, 1991.

Kurz, D., and E. Stark. "Not-so-Benign Neglect: The Medical Response to Battering." Eds. K. Yllö and M. Bograd. *Feminist Perspectives on Wife Abuse.* Newbury Park, CA: Sage Publications, 1988. 249-266.

MacLeod, L. *Understanding and Charting Our Progress Toward the Prevention of Woman Abuse.* Health Canada: Family Violence Prevention Division, 1994.

Marcus, S. "Contingent Foundations: Feminism and the Question of 'Postmodernism.'" *Feminists Theorize the Political.* Eds. J. Butler and J. W. Scott. New York: Routledge, 1992. 385-403.

Messing, K. "Don't Use a Wrench to Peel Potatoes: Biological Science Constructed on Male Model Systems is a Risk to Women Worker's Health." Eds, S. Burt and L. Code. *Changing Methods: Feminists Transforming Practice.* Peterborough: Broadview Press, 1995. 217-263.

National Clearinghouse on Family Violence. *Family Violence Initiatives: Summaries of Funded Projects (1988-1991).* Health Canada, Ottawa: National Clearinghouse on Family Violence, 1994.

Ontario Ministry of Health. *Healthy Community Grants Program: Overview.* 1994.

Ontario Women's Directorate. *Framework for Action on the Prevention of Violence Against Women in Ontario.* Toronto: Ontario Women's Directorate, December, 1996.

Peters, R. DeV., and C. C. Russell. *Better Beginnings, Better Futures Project: Model, Program and Research Overview.* Toronto, Queen's Printer for Ontario, 1994.

Randall, M. and L. Haskell. "Sexual Violence in Women's Lives: Findings From the Women's Safety Project, A Community-Based Survey." *Violence Against Women* 1 (1) (March 1995): 6-31.

Russell, D. E. "The Incidence and Prevalence of Intrafamilial and Extrafamilial Sexual Abuse of Female Children." *Child Abuse and Neglect* 7 (1983): 133-146.

Russell, D. E. and N. Howell. "The Prevalence of Rape in the United States Revisited." *Signs* 8 (1983): 688-695.

Russell, D. E. *The Secret Trauma: Incest in the Lives of Girls.* New York: Basic Books, 1986.

Russell, D. E. *Rape in Marriage.* Bloomington: Indiana University Press, 1990.

Sorenson, S. B., and A. F. Saflas. "Violence and Women's Health: The Role of

Epidemiology." *Annals of Epidemiology* 4 (2) (1994): 140-145.

Statistics Canada. *Violence Against Women Survey.* Questionnaire Package. Ottawa: Statistics Canada, 1993.

Statistics Canada. "The Violence Against Women Survey." *The Daily* November 18, 1993.

Straus, M. A. "Physical Assaults by Wives: A Major Social Problem." *Current Controversies on Family Violence.* Eds. R. J. Gelles and D. R. Loseke. Newbury Park, CA: Sage Publications, 1993. 67-87.

The Trillium Foundation. *Request for Proposals.* Toronto: Trillium Foundation, 1994.

The Trillium Foundation. *In Search of the Civil Society: The Trillium Foundation Annual Report for 1994-95.* Toronto: Trillium Foundation, 1995.

Walker, L. E. "Psychology and Violence Against Women." *American Psychologist* 44 (1989): 695-702.

Warshaw, C. "Limitations of the Medical Model in the Care of Battered Women." *Violence Against Women: The Bloody Footprints.* Eds. P. B. Bart and E.G. Moran. Newbury Park, California: Sage Publications, 1993. 134-154.

"Welcoming the Kingston and Region Injury Surveillance Program." *Health Canada CHIRRP News* 1 (March 1994): 6-7.

Yllö, K. "Political and Methodological Debates in Woman Abuse Research." *Feminist Perspectives on Wife Abuse.* Eds. Kersti Yllö and Michele Bograd. Newbury Park, California: Sage Publications, 1988. 28-50.

# WOMEN, POVERTY AND HIV INFECTION

JUNE LARKIN

I was introduced to the gendered face of AIDS/HIV through my work with South African teachers and learners. As a collaborator on violence prevention programs for South African schools, I was confronted with the force of the AIDS epidemic and the gendered impact of the disease. The HIV incidence rate among South African girls is three to four times higher than boys (Brown) and, worldwide, four-fifths of all infected women are African (UNAIDS 1999).

In South Africa, the legacy of violence that underpinned the apartheid state has led to extremely high levels of violence across the country. A history of oppressive political practices has embedded violence as a normal part of gendered relations (Human Rights Watch). The high incidence of rape in South Africa has been linked to the rapid spread of the HIV virus, particularly in females. Our program on gendered violence had to highlight this crucial link. Dealing with sexual violence is considered a key factor in the fight against AIDS.

The connection between AIDS and gender violence is not limited to the African context. Sexual violence is a problem for women worldwide although women's vulnerability to HIV infection varies. The disease has struck most severely in countries struggling with a crumbling infrastructure inherited from colonial rule. In the developing world, the collapse of local economies has resulted in conditions that increase the risk of HIV infections such as landlessness, an increasingly migratory labour force and rapid urbanization (Simmons, Farmer and Schoepf). In these harsh conditions, women have suffered disproportionately through their exclusion from the formal cash economy. The reduction of health care services through the imposition of austere structural adjustment programs has off-loaded the burden of AIDS care to women for whom economic survival is already a full-time job (Abrahamsen).

With the rate of female HIV infection on the rise in Canada, it seems that we have much to learn from the African situation. A focus on local factors, however, has limited a broader understanding of the global forces that shape women's vulnerability to HIV infection (Farmer, Connors, Fox and Furin). Although the developing regions account for 90 per cent of the worldwide incidence of HIV/AIDS (Sewpaul and Mahlalela), the transnational nature of sex tourism, the growing drug trade and international business and recreational travel have made AIDS a global moving target. For women worldwide, the practices of drug use and transactional sex are often a direct consequence of trying to cope with limited economic resources (Connors).

The particular social and economic conditions that affect women vary across the world. More and more, however, women are linked by their subordination within a global economy that has created conditions of female impoverishment (Farmer and Kim). In Canada, the erosion of the social safety net has heightened the HIV risk for women. Cuts to social assistance and the essential services of child care, subsidized housing, legal aid and family violence programs are forcing women into situations conducive to HIV infection. The threat of AIDS may seem remote to women who are facing homelessness, unemployment, prostitution, and domestic abuse due to scarce economic resources, but these are the women most at risk.

Murli Sinha uses the term "structural violence" to refer to the social forces that create conditions of HIV risk and he identifies poverty as one of the primary forces. Within AIDS research and commentary, however, economic factors are given scant attention in the discussion of HIV vulnerability. In this paper I want to examine poverty as a form of structural violence that operates as a conduit for the gender transmission of AIDS.

## Women and HIV/AIDS

Although the first reported case of a woman testing HIV+ occurred as early as 1981, women with HIV/AIDS have been an understudied population (Leenerts; Farmer *et al.*). The fact that nine out of ten infected women live in a developing country may be one reason the HIV risks for women have received minimal attention in Canada. Racist and essentialist notions of Third World populations as vectors of disease have operated to frame female infection as a disease of the "other." A focus on Africa and the stereotypes of sexually promiscuous Black women have deflected attention from the role of industrial countries in the spread of the virus worldwide. In the Caribbean, for example, socio-epidemiological researchers have demonstrated that AIDS is a North American import:

> ...the virus came to Haiti, the Dominican Republic, Jamaica, Trinidad and Tobago and the Bahamas from the United States, probably though tourism and transnationals returning home from abroad.... In a country as poor as Haiti ... AIDS might be thought of as an occupational hazard for workers in the tourist industry. (Simmons *et al.* 76)

In the popular commentary of AIDS, there is little mention of sex tourism and the men who travel to Asia for the services of commercial sex workers. In the North American context, myths around HIV/AIDS as a "gay" disease have further limited the exploration of gender factors that contribute to HIV vulnerability (Kalichman *et al.*).

Across the world, AIDS is a disease that feeds on the social inequalities of gender, social status, race, and sexuality. In societies where the epidemic is heterosexually driven, women are contracting the disease at a higher rate than men (UNAIDS 2000). Worldwide, women are the fastest-growing group of AIDS sufferers. In 1996, women accounted for 42 per cent of the over 21 million adults living with HIV infection (Connors; UNAIDS 1999). In Canada, despite an overall decrease in reported AIDS cases, the proportion of reported AIDS cases among women is increasing. Between the period 1985-1994 and the year 1999, the percentage of positive HIV test reports among females rose sharply from 9.8 per cent to 24.8 per cent (Health Canada 2000b). Aboriginal women are a particularly vulnerable group. The proportion of women among reported Aboriginal AIDS cases (49.6 per cent) is much higher than the proportion of women among non-Aboriginal cases (20 per cent) (Health Canada 2000a).

Given the stark increases in incidence among women in both the industrialized and the developing world, women are now considered to be the population most at risk for HIV infection. In every country, poor women are the most highly affected group and women of colour are, by far, the most economically impoverished women (Farmer).

A focus on behaviour modification as the route to AIDS prevention, has lifted the epidemic out of the broader contexts of women's lives. Enormous power is granted to women's knowledge and behavioural practices while the social and economic constraints on women's agency are ignored. The attempt to fight HIV at the individual level has deflected attention from the social processes that shape the dynamics of HIV transmission (Farmer). The way Connors sees it: "Structural factors—social class and economic status—far more then individual decisions and aspirations, explain why HIV increasingly affects women in the United States and elsewhere" (92).

The real sources of women's risk have been obscured by the failure to link poverty and sexual oppression to the spread of the disease. In the following sections, I consider the relevance of economic factors in issues related to women and the HIV/AIDS epidemic.

## Women and HIV Risk

A male bias in AIDS diagnosis has resulted in women being considered at low risk for HIV infection. Even after the Centre for Disease Control (CDC) recognized that women were contracting the HIV virus, the definition of AIDS continued to be based on opportunistic illnesses registered in men (Simmons *et al.*). The initial case definition did not include gynaecological infections, cervical cancer, or other disease manifestations unique to women. When invasive cervical cancer was recognized as an indicator disease for women, the number of reported female AIDS cases in the United States doubled in a single year (Farmer).

The overall method of tracking HIV transmissions has led to a miscalculation and under-reporting of female HIV/AIDS cases. The delay in identifying female opportunistic illnesses means that a woman diagnosed with HIV may have been living with the virus for several years (Edelson; Jaffer and Pang). Without a formal AIDS diagnosis, Canadian women have been unable to access treatment, disability benefits, specialized housing and other services that can ease the management of the disease. Low income women, who are particularly vulnerable to the financial stress of AIDS, suffer additional hardships when AIDS-related services are unattainable due to a misdiagnosis of their illness.

Women's greatest risk for HIV infection is through forced or consensual intercourse with men. More than four-fifths of all HIV infected women contract the virus through heterosexual transmission. The risk of HIV infection during unprotected vaginal intercourse is as much as two to four times higher for women (UNAIDS 1999). During heterosexual sex, the exposed surface area of the vagina and labia women is larger than the vulnerable penile surface area (Simmons *et al.*). Semen infected with HIV contains a higher concentration of the virus than female sexual secretions. In general, the male-female transmission of HIV is much more efficient than female-male transmission. A single episode of unprotected intercourse is risky for women who may be receiving infected semen from a male partner. Young women are particularly vulnerable to infection through intercourse prior to menstruation when the lower reproductive tract is still developing (UNAIDS 1999).

The presence of an untreated STD can increase the risk of HIV transmission. Women are more likely than men to have an undetected STD because the sores and symptoms may be mild or difficult to recognize (UNAIDS 1999). Poor women worldwide have less access to seek medical services because they lack the financial resources for quality health care. The imposition of user-fees through structural adjustment programs imposed by the World Bank has contributed to the precarious health condition of women in developing countries. In Canada, the erosion of Medicare and the threat of a two-tier health care system pose grave concerns for the future health status of low-income women (Maher and Riutort).

Women's biological susceptibility to AIDS is increased when their sexual autonomy is compromised by poor socio-economic circumstances. A lack of economic resources can force women into survival sex where condom use is difficult to negotiate. When women are economically dependent on a male partner a demand for safe sex practices can result in abandonment or violence. The tearing and bleeding that can result from forced sex multiplies the risk of HIV infection (UNAIDS 1999). Abused women may not recognize HIV-related symptoms they believe to be a consequence of physical violence such as skin lesions or abdominal pain. Compared with men, HIV-infected women have a significantly lower rate of survival. Domestic violence has been proposed as one factor that may explain the gender difference in AIDS mortality (Stevens and Richards).

## Women as Carriers of AIDS

The lack of concern for the personal impact of HIV infection for women calls into question the perceived value of female bodies in AIDS-related research. For the most part, AIDS research and commentary targeting women have been focused on women as carriers of the disease. Women entered the AIDS discourse when the growing rate of heterosexual HIV infection raised concerns about women transmitting the virus through sex work or pregnancy (Tallis). The focal point was centred around encouraging changes in women's behaviour that would reduce the AIDS risks for unborn children and sexual clients. Notably absent from the discussion of mothers and prostitutes as AIDS transmitters was the role of men as vectors of the disease. One of the first AIDS textbooks, published in 1984, limited the cover-age of women to a single chapter on prostitutes and children with no mention of men as "johns," fathers, or paying sexual customers who are implicated in the spread of the HIV virus (Rodriguez).

The western dichotomy of women as mother or whore has informed international AIDS prevention programs that are focused on the regulation of women's sexual behaviour. Female bodies are viewed as potential AIDS contaminators with little concern about the personal impact of the disease on HIV infected women. The transmission of maternal AIDS is considered a threat to nation building because the production of healthy offspring is at risk (Booth). Proposed strategies for controlling maternally-transmitted AIDS include the spacing of pregnancies, improved sex education, and easier access to contraception. Curbing the reproductive power of poor and racialized women has been a strong focus in nation building and this practice is continuing under the guise of AIDS prevention. Such practices are primarily targeted at Third World and immigrant women considered too ignorant to understand the complexities of AIDS and poor women worldwide who are regarded as undeserving of children they may be unable to support.

The threat of the global whore stretches beyond the boundaries of the nation state. Sex workers are constructed as international contaminators responsible for the spread of the disease through sexual transactions with foreign customers. The hysteria about prostitutes as a source *of* risk means the possibility of HIV transmission from client to sex worker is seldom considered (Patton).

While some women may choose a career in the sex trade, many women turn to prostitution as an alternative to dire poverty. As reported by UNAIDS (1999), for many girls and women, "sex is the currency in which they are expected to pay for life's opportunities, from a passing grade in school to a trading licence or permission to cross a border" (3). The growing demand for low-risk sexual partners has led to increased child sexual exploitation and a growing rate of HIV infected girls. Most vulnerable are girls from developing countries who are sold into the international flesh trade to service male sex tourists.

The scapegoating of prostitutes and mothers in the AIDS/HIV epidemic obscures the larger array of economic factors that contribute to the global spread of the disease. Farmer sums it up this way:

> Dominant readings are likely to foster images of women with AIDS that suggest they have large numbers of sexual partners, but less likely to show how girls ... are abducted into the flesh trade, and even less likely to reveal how political and structural violence—for example, the increasing landlessness among the rural poor and the gearing of economies to favor export—come to be important in the AIDS pandemic today. (330)

**Cultural Difference**

Although indices of social inequalities are neglected in much of the research on HIV/AIDS, culture is often a dominant theme. Cultural factors are granted etiological power that shift attention from poverty, racism and other forms of structural violence that create HIV risk conditions for women from various cultural groups (Farmer). The promotion of "culturally sensitive AIDS education programs" for women is based on the theory that ignorance is the key factor in the disproportionately high HIV rate in racial minority women. Standard conclusions about education as the key to AIDS prevention in various cultural groups are often at odds with the data collected in research studies. In their analysis of a questionnaire administered to 1,173 high risk African American/ Latino women in the United States, the researchers found that ignorance about AIDS was not a general problem but went on to recommended "culturally sensitive education" as a primary prevention strategy (Farmer).

In many epidemiological studies, "race" is viewed as an explanatory variable, rather than a factor of risk. The rush to impose narrow culturalist explanations of the higher HIV rate in racial minority women reinforces racist constructions of women's sexuality that are divorced from larger systems of power and domination. What gets masked in cultural explanations of AIDS is the female face of poverty that cuts across racialized groups.

Women of colour do not share a common culture or set of origins. But, as Simmons, Farmer and Schoepf point out, "what they do share is a low social position within a context rife with economic and gender inequality" (62). In their stance against cultural explanations in the fight against AIDS, Farmer *et al.* insist that,

> ... we ... have something more to offer. For example, we can do the important work of showing how structural violence and cultural difference are conflated. Too often, poverty and violence against the poor are collapsed into an all-accommodating concept of culture. We can show how "culturally sensitive" explorations have served to undermine explorations that have shaped the lives of others. (201)

## Conclusion

With the increasing rate of HIV infection in Canadian women we cannot afford to ignore the lessons of the developing world—"namely, that AIDS explodes in contexts characterized by social inequalities and dislocations" (Simmons *et al.* 66). Poverty and gender inequality are two reasons women are the fastest growing group of AIDS victims worldwide. For women living in poverty, AIDS is just one more risk on a long list of dangers that are part of everyday survival.

If we are to develop a meaningful response to AIDS we need to consider the way local and global economies are putting women at risk. The success of AIDS prevention programs will depend on our ability to minimize women's struggle against poverty and other forms of structural violence.

## References

Abrahamsen, R. "Gender Dimensions of AIDS in Zambia." *Journal of Gender Studies* 6 (2) (1997): 177-189.

Booth, K. "National Mother, Global Whore, and Transnational Femocrats: The Politics of AIDS and the Construction of Women at the World Health Organization." *Feminist Studies* 24 (1) (1998): 115-135.

Brown, M. "United Nations Development Program." *The New York Times* 11 January 2000.

Connors, M. "Sex, Drugs, and Structural Violence: Unravelling the Epidemic Among Poor Women in the United States." *Women, Poverty and Aids: Sex, Drugs and Structural Violence*. Eds. P. Farmer, M. Connors and J. Simmons. Maine: Common Courage Press, 1996. 91-123.

Edelson, N. "Lesbians and AIDS: Low Risk Identity, High Risk Behaviour?" *The Optimist* 11 September 1999: 11.

Farmer, P. and Yong Kim. "Introduction." *Women, Poverty and Aids: Sex, Drugs and Structural Violence*. Eds. P. Farmer, M. Connors and J. Simmons. Maine: Common Courage Press, 1996. xiii-xxi

Farmer, P., M. Connors, K. Fox, and J. Furin, eds., with D. Devine, S. Lamola, J. Millen, and J. Simmons. "Rereading Social Science." *Women, Poverty and AIDS: Sex, Drugs and Structural Violence* Eds. P. Farmer, M. Connors and J. Simmons. Maine: Common Courage Press, 1996. 147-205.

Farmer, P. "Women, Poverty and AIDS." *Women, Poverty and Aids: Sex, Drugs and Structural Violence*. Eds. P. Farmer, M. Connors and J. Simmons. Maine: Common Courage Press, 1996. 3-38.

Health Canada. "HIV and AIDS Among Aboriginal People in Canada." 2000a. Online. Retrieved August 16, 2000. http://www.hc-sc.gc.ca/hpb/lcdc/bah/epi/aborig_e.html.

Health Canada. "AIDS and HIV in Canada." 2000b. Retrieved 27 July 2000. http://www.hc-sc.gc.ca/hpb/lcdc/bah/epi/ahcan_e.html

Human Rights Watch. *Violence Against Women in South Africa: The State Response to Domestic Violence and Rape.* New York: Human Rights Watch, 1995.

Jaffer, F. and N. Pang. "Women and HIV/AIDS: Taking on Myths." *Kinesis* 6 (July/August 1996): 6.

Kalichman, S., Williams, E., Cherry, C., Belcher, L. and Nachimson, D. "Sexual Coercion, Domestic Violence, and Negotiating Condom Use Among Low-Income African American Women." *Journal of Women's Health* 7 (3) (1998): 371-378.

Leenerts, M. H. "The Disconnected Self: Consequences of Abuse in a Cohort of Low-Income White Women Living with AIDS." *Health Care for Women International* 20 (1999): 381-400.

Maher, J, and M. Riutort. "Canadian Health Care: A System in Peril." *Confronting the Cuts: A Sourcebook for Women in Ontario.* Eds. L. Ricciutelli, J. Larkin, and E. O'Neill. Toronto: Inanna Publication and Education Inc., 1997. 69-76.

Patton, C. *Last Served?: Gendering the HIV Pandemic.* Bristol, PA: Taylor and Francis, 1994.

Rodriguez, B. "Biomedical Models of HIV And Women." *The Gender Politics of HIV/AIDS in Women.* Eds. N. Goldstein and J. Manlowe. New York: New York University Press, 1997. 25-42.

Sewpaul, V. and Mahlalela, T. "The Power of the Small Group: From Crisis to Disclosure." *Agenda* 39 (1998): 34-43.

Simmons, J., P. Farmer, and B. Schoepf. "A Global Perspective." *Women, Poverty and Aids: Sex, Drugs and Structural Violence.* Eds. P. Farmer, M. Connors and J. Simmons. Maine: Common Courage Press, 1996. 39-90.

Sinha, M. "Sex, Structural Violence, and AIDS: Case Studies of Indian Prostitutes." *Women's Studies Quarterly* 1&2 (1999): 65-72.

Stevens, P. and D. Richards. "Narrative Case Analysis of HIV Infection in a Battered Woman." *Health Care for Women International* 19 (1998): 9-22.

Tallis, V. "Introduction: AIDS is a Crisis for Women." *Agenda* 39 (1998): 6-14.

UNAIDS. "Global Strategy Framework on Young People with HIV/AIDS." UNAIDS March 2000.

UNAIDS. "Women, HIV and AIDS." 1999. Online. Retrieved 12 July 2000. http://www.avert.org/womenaid.html

# The Health-Related Economic Costs of Violence Against Women in Canada

## The Tip of the Iceberg

Tanis Day and Katherine M. J. McKenna

Violence against women is a major cause of pain and suffering in Canadian society. Not only are the acts abhorrent in themselves, but a large part of our economy exists because violence against women exists. Those of us who work to end violence often think of it in terms of very real, yet qualitative and intangible social costs. These might include the injustice of the abuse of male power, the despair of being trapped in a home where your husband or father is a tyrant, the devastating effects of witnessing abuse on the next generations of children, the everyday fear of murder and rape experienced by all women, or the unrealized potential of those women and girls whose lives are blighted by male violence the world over. Yet there also are costs to society that are very concrete and can be measured in a more quantitative manner.

If we attach a dollar value to these costs, it is not because we think they are the only factors that are important. There are those who might feel that translating a woman's or girl's pain into a dollar value does not support a sensitive understanding of the issue. We recognize that many aspects of violence can never be measured in any way. Suffering has no price tag, the loss of self-worth and joy has no yardstick. However, if there were no violence against women in our society, we would spend much less in many areas—medical, judicial/legal, social services and personal costs, not to mention lost employment and educational opportunities. We feel that to have a complete description of violence against women in Canada, it is important to know what the ultimate cost is to society. This is not intended to replace other ways of studying the problem of male violence against women in our society but to add to and expand our knowledge of this issue.

Expressing the costs of violence with a conservative dollar estimate provides us with a better understanding of the social impact of abuse and gives information on its current status in society. It supports and develops existing research in the field. The high costs to society can be used as a means of persuading politicians and policy makers that it is time to act on the problem, and show them that it is ultimately false economy to treat the consequences rather than the causes. The economic costing of violence against women can establish a baseline for improvement of services to victims, and measure long-term cost reduction to society. Economic costing studies are of use to a broad spectrum of individuals. Activists and workers with survivors of abuse find that the cost estimates are a powerful publicity tool, as do fundraisers who are raising money for private services that work to end violence. Policy makers and government service providers can employ the results to justify new programs, and researchers who work to better understand the problem are provided with new information. An interesting aspect of economic costing is that it often provides a middle ground on which both fiscal conservatives and anti-violence activists can meet. Both can agree that something that affects society so strongly must be brought to an end.

In a recent review article on the economic costs of violence against women, Carrie Yodanis and her colleagues observed:

> Certainly, all business and government decisions do not come solely from cost/benefit analyses. Increasingly more businesses and agencies are looking to alternate means of management and decision-making. Yet, in these times of increased global competition and down-scaling at business and state levels, economic costs and benefits unquestionably remain central to the decision making process. (Yodandis, Godenzi and Stanko 274)

While our work is not a cost/benefit analysis, this quotation demonstrates the importance of determining the economic costs of violence. With these factors in mind, this paper begins to measure the enormous economic apparatus that exists in relation to the pain and suffering of Canadian women victims of violence. The costs are public and private, covered by the individual women, their families, employers, communities, and the taxpaying public. However, it must be recognized at the outset that any collective statistics reflect only a proportion of the impact of violence, as most acts and effects of violence are kept private. Any recorded numbers, therefore, are gross underestimates of the full magnitude of the costs of violence against women in society. In addition, much violence against women is not physical in nature. Women may be abused emotionally, spiritually, verbally, psychologically, financially, or through intimidation, isolation and control. Almost all data collected relate to visible physical or sexual violence only. In this, the calculations of this paper show an incomplete picture. The true costs are much higher. In other words, those costs that we can report represent only "the tip of the iceberg."

The inspiration for this work came from the final report of the Canadian Panel on Violence Against Women and Children. Published in 1993, it called for research on the costs of violence, but did not produce any estimates itself (12). In the same year, the groundbreaking Canadian Violence Against Women Survey was conducted by Statistics Canada (1993) which for the first time gave the data needed for a national costing exercise. Although economic costing has been widely used in many other contexts, Tanis Day was the first economist to develop a comprehensive methodology for estimating the costs of violence against women. Funded by the Canadian Advisory Council on the Status of Women before it was closed by the federal government in 1995, she developed a template which included six major categories of costs to both the individual and society: Judicial, Social Services, Health, Employment, Education, and Personal. (See Figure 1) This method uses a straightforward accounting methodology and looks at both short-term and long-term costs, both direct and indirect. Direct costs are costs resulting from the actual incidence of violence, both short and long term. For example, direct costs of violence to the individual might involve damaged property, missed days from work or legal fees. Direct costs to society might include social services, the cost of the police, jail and the health care system dealing with the immediate aftermath and long-term effects of the incident of abuse. Indirect costs also result from the violence but reflect secondary consequences. They involve making more assumptions, and consequently are more difficult to measure. Examples might be associated secondary health effects such as depression, behavioral problems in child witnesses to violence, and reduced educational and employment opportunities. For society, indirect costs might be felt in mental health services, child welfare services, and lost productivity and thus foregone tax revenue. Some of these costs can be assessed, and some may not be possible to determine. This creates another underestimate of the total economic cost of violence to society.

To date, there has not been a study which has been able to undertake a comprehensive national examination of the full range of costs as outlined by Day. This study, which was first released in 1995, only looks at one possible branch of the model, that of health costs. This path breaking research was followed by Greaves, Hankivsky, and Kingston-Reichers, who used the same methodology and expanded the economic costs to include selected aspects of three additional social categories: Social Services/Education, Criminal Justice and Labour/Employment. It provides only a partial overview and the numerical analysis is not done to the level of accuracy neccesary for reliable results (Greaves *et al.*). Also building upon the Day methodology, Kerr and McLean estimated the partial costs of violence against women in the judicial/legal, social service, health and employment sectors for the province of British Columbia. Additional studies costing violence against women have been conducted in Australia, New Zealand, Holland, Chile, Nicaragua, Switzerland, and the United States, using a variety of methodological approaches.[1] Many of them interview small samples of abused women to document their personal costs and usage of various social and legal services. Others confine themselves to the costs of domestic violence only. All of these studies are hampered by the lack of national prevalence figures. As Yodanis *et al.* observe, "For the most part, however, we do not know the prevalence or

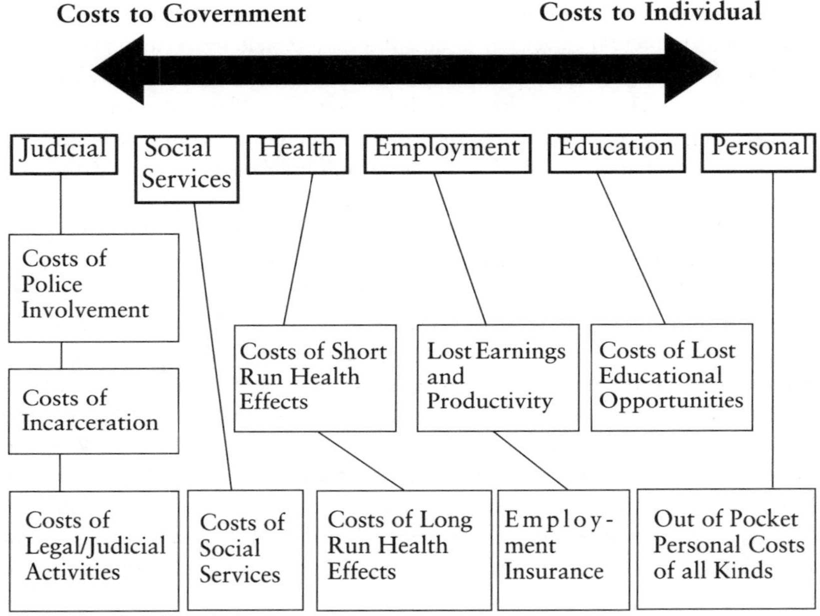


**Figure 1**

impact of violence against women on society" (266). In this respect, Canada is fortunate to have the 1993 Statistics Canada Violence Against Women Survey, the first such exercise in determining the prevalence of all kinds of violence against women across an entire nation.

Canada shares with all other countries of the world, however, the problem of missing or incomplete data. Yodanis *et al.* outline this problem.

> The majority of costs of violence studies rely predominantly on existing data, generally those gathered by government agencies. This data can be an important starting point for estimating the costs of violence. Yet, relying too heavily on the existing data creates problems, not due to inadequate researchers, but because of the inadequate data. Since the existing data are always incomplete, the cost estimates based on this data, likewise, suffer from shortcomings which limit their benefits. (266)

One way of compensating for the inevitable inaccuracies and the assumptions that often must be made to determine the economic costs of violence is to always use the most conservative estimate possible. Thus the costs that are reported in this study are most certainly underestimates. They also do not take into consideration that for many sectors of society, such as those who suffer from discrimination based on race or ethnicity, the disabled, and those living in poverty, the costs are likely to be multiplied many times more than for women without these characteristics. This must always be kept in mind, although these factors cannot be costed adequately.

The data used for this project were drawn from a variety of sources including the Statistics Canada Violence Against Women Survey (1993) and other surveys undertaken by Statistics Canada, made public through agencies such as the Canadian Centre for Justice Statistics and the Canadian Centre for Health Information. If national data were not available, data from Canadian studies that offered a large sample size were used. For example, the Canadian Urban Victimization Survey covered the population of seven major cities. Its sample size was taken to be big enough to accurately represent urban Canadians. Another source was the Quebec health survey which covered the entire provincial population. Small-size samples were not used, unless there were a large number of such studies that all demonstrated the same result. An example of this was the proportion of women patients admitted to psychiatric hospitals who are known to be abuse sufferers. Studies on this topic showed the number was at least 50 per cent regardless of the location or date of the research.

Base data for studies on violence are difficult to collect because of issues of privacy and self-identification. Most victims of violence do not identify themselves as such to the system. A woman may visit her family physician many times without ever saying that she is suffering from abuse. Data on violent acts against women were not available from hospital statistics. Staff do not consistently record which patients are being treated for the results of violent acts. Therefore, data on some of the most substantial costs, such as hospital admissions, are not available. Fortunately, the professional associations of medical service providers are starting to realize that they need to collect this type of information and appropriate steps are being taken. This is further reason why the total amount estimated is truly "the tip of the iceberg."

Finally, a group of eight survivors of violence across Canada were interviewed in order to enlarge our understanding of personal costs and to add a human, qualitative dimension to the quantitative results of the costing exercise. The interviews were conducted face to face or over the telephone, on more than one occasion. The women were invited to tell their stories. They were also asked to go through their personal financial records to estimate the dollar amounts they had spent on various personal costs. The results were not tabulated or analyzed, but only reported as examples. Space does not permit a complete summary of the results of these interviews, but three samples are included here in Appendix 1 to give a sample of the stories that were gathered.

This article focuses on the health-related costs of violence against women as a first attempt at a comprehensive economic costing using the Day model. Health has been chosen out of the conviction that it is the most fundamental and comprehensive aspect of violence against women in our society. Since this paper was first released in 1995, numerous studies have reinforced the importance of viewing violence against women as a health issue, particularly from a public and community wellness perspective (Ascencio; Heise *et al.*; Jiwani; Kinnon and Hanvey; McKenna and Blessing; Plichta; Sutherland, Sullivan and Bybee; Thurston; Wisner, Gilmore, Salxman and Zink).

The remainder of this article shows the calculations of immediate and longer term costs that are possible to estimate. It also includes discussions of various costs that are not currently possible to measure. All costs are calculated in Canadian dollars, for a total of all costs incurred in 1993, the year coinciding with the Canadian Violence Against Women Survey.[2]

## Cost Calculations

The Statistics Canada national survey on violence against women gives a comprehensive view of violence in Canadian women's lives. The survey measures only attacks that would be consistent with legal definitions of these offenses, and that could be acted upon by a police officer (Statistics Canada 1993a: 2). For the total population of women 18 years of age, and over, the annual rate of all violent acts for the twelve-month period preceding the survey in 1993 was ten per cent. The total number of affected women was 1,016,000 (Statistics Canada 1993b: 2). Because of multiple assaults against individual women in the year, the total number of incidents of sexual, physical or partner assaults was 2,635,000 (Statistics Canada 1993: Table 3).

From the time of an incident of violence, a woman will experience immediate repercussions. These can include physical injury, distress, and fear. She may seek medical attention. Of sexual assaults measured in the Canadian Urban Victimization Survey in 1982, victims were injured in 61 per cent of cases, with 20 per cent of them receiving medical attention (Solicitor General Canada 1985: 5). The injured woman may contact a dentist because of damage to her face and teeth. She may also take time off work to recuperate from the incident. The Statistics Canada (1993) survey found that almost one-third of wife-assault incidents led to time off from regular activities, and 50 per cent of wives who were injured ended up missing days of work.

## Medical

Over the lifetime of the women surveyed in the Violence Against Women Survey, 45 per cent of wife assaults resulted in injuries, and of the injured women, 40 per cent saw a doctor or nurse (Rodgers 1994a: 8-9). The Statistics Canada survey figures show that for injuries over a woman's lifetime resulting from all types of assaults, 28 per cent of injured women received medical attention. It is known that

272,000 incidents resulted in injury in 1992 (Statistics Canada 1993c). The Statistics Canada violence survey 12-month data are too small to make reliable estimates of the numbers of women seeking medical help in 1992. However, based on the lifetime data, an assumption is made that of the women who were injured, 28 per cent of them sought medical attention. This amounts to 76,160 Canadian women in 1992 seeking medical attention as a result of acts of violence.

A list of the most common injuries sustained from physical assault in a partner situation include serious bleeding, multiple bruising, bleeding of internal organs, injuries to the face and head, perforated eardrums, burns from stoves, appliances or acids, dental damage, broken bones, and injuries to the breasts, chest and abdomen, especially if the woman is pregnant (see Jaffe, Wolf, Wilson and Zak; Ontario Medical Association; Current Concepts in Emergency Medicine; Rounsaville and Weisman; Taylor and Campbell). Over the lifetime, the most frequent types of injuries reported to the Statistics Canada survey were bruises in 90 per cent of injuries, cuts, scratches and burns in 3.3 per cent, broken bones in 12 per cent, fractures in eleven per cent and internal injuries and miscarriages in ten per cent of spousal assaults (Rodgers 1994a: 8). Women may go to the emergency ward of a hospital or to a family physician. A study which reviewed hospital emergency room records found that only one in 25 cases of wife assault was identified as such (Stark, Flitcrat and Zuckerman). The average cost of a hospital emergency visit in Canada in 1992 was $32.62 (Statistics Canada 1994a, Part 2: 11). Each consultation with the physician-on-duty in the emergency ward costs $75.80 in Ontario (Ontario Ministry of Health).

A premium of $13.20 is charged for visits between midnight and 8 a.m., and for Saturdays, Sundays and holidays there is an additional $7.80 charged per consultation. It is known that most acts of violence against women occur on the weekend and in the evening or night (Lupri 18). Therefore, there would be an additional charge for some proportion of the women receiving attention at the emergency ward of their hospital. For the sexually assaulted women in Ontario who receive treatment using a medical kit provided by the provincial Ministries of the Attorney-General and the Solicitor-General, the charge for the examination and documentation is $282.60. A consultation with a family doctor costs $51.40. There is no information to judge whether women more commonly use the emergency ward or a doctor's office. However, one study estimates that 53.8 per cent of sexual assault victims are treated in Ontario using the kit (MacDonald).

Each of these consultations probably includes such additional costs as x-rays and laboratory charges. For example, a set of four skull x-rays costs $50.80. Putting a cast on a broken bone costs between $9.40 and $89.60, depending on the body part and when the cast is applied. Laboratory charges depend on the test conducted, with costs ranging from $1 to $250, with most charges in the $5 to $50 range. Suture costs depend on the length and depth of the wound and where it is on the body, with higher charges for injuries to the face. Costs range from about $13.60 to $93.30. Surgical procedures required to stop internal bleeding cost hundreds of dollars. Given all of the above figures relating to costs of medical attention, an arbitrary figure of $100 per visit is assumed. Using a figure of $100 per victim is certainly a gross underestimate since the costs of hospital and doctors' services alone amount to more than this. However, it can be accepted with certainty that this is not an overestimate. Using the $100 per patient cost figure, the total cost for initial medical assistance resulting from acts of violence against women in 1992 is $7,616,000.

There is no figure for the cost of admitting women to overnight or longer-term stays in hospitals. These figures are only for the initial consultation resulting from the act of violence. The average cost of a short-term unit in hospitals in 1992 was $142.78 per day (Statistics Canada 1994a, Part 1: 71), and the average length of stay was 8.11 days (Statistics Canada 1994a, Part 1: 67). The average cost per day of all long-term units was $75.38 (Statistics Canada 1994a, Part 1: 103) with an average length of stay of 215.06 days. It is not known what proportion of injured women were admitted for stays in hospitals, which presents a serious barrier to measuring medical service costs to victims of violence against women.

## Dental

Immediate trauma to the woman can include damage to her teeth and mouth.[3] There may be fractured, missing or displaced teeth, lacerations in the mouth, fractures of the bones in the jaw, or bruised or scarred lips. Since the dental community has only recently become aware of its role in the treatment of victims of violence, little work has yet been done to document effects of abuse among dental patients. The Mayer and Galan survey examined the number of elderly dental patients who were recognized to be suffering from elder abuse. There was approximately one such patient per dentist across the country. Since there are no other data on victims of violence, this number will be used, even though it includes male elderly and excludes non-elderly females. There are 13,477 dentists in Canada and 2,635,000 incidents of violence. This means there were 195.5 potential assault cases per dentist in the country. However, not all victims of assault suffer dental damage. Assuming that only one client per dentist is a victim of assault, it follows there are about 13,477 dental patients per year visiting dentists because of assault. This is probably a gross underestimate.

Repairing damaged teeth can range from $32 for a simple filling to $604 for a back molar with root damage, according to the Ontario Dental Fee Guidelines. For a victim of violence, the repair work may be more significant than the work involved in a standard filling. It is likely an underestimate that each woman would spend only $100 on dental work related to the act of violence. Using this figure, a rough approximation of the dental costs to non-sexually assaulted women is $1,347,700.

## Workplace

When a woman is assaulted, she frequently needs to take time off from her regular activities to recover. If she works in the labour force, as do 62.2 per cent of Canadian women (Statistics Canada 1992: Table 3 B-8),[4] she will miss time at work. Consequently the economy loses the contribution she would make in paid productive effort during those days, and she loses the income unless she is protected by a benefits package with sick leave coverage. If she works in her home at unpaid work, the economy loses the contribution she would make in producing goods and services for consumption in the home. The Statistics Canada survey shows that 335,000 assaulted women took time off as a result of an act of violence in the year being researched (1993c). The average annual income for women in 1992 for full-time, full-year workers was $27,202 (Cross 66)[5] or $108.38 a day. Multiplying the number of women in the paid work force and at home who took one day off equals $36.3 million. (For a breakdown of this calculation, see Appendix 2.) Adding this figure to $7.6 million in immediate medical costs and $1.3 million in dental work yields $45.2 million.

## Long-Term Health Effects

After the initial violent incident, a woman may never suffer another actual assault, or she may suffer many more. Shelter workers estimate that, on average, women suffer 35 to 40 incidents of abuse before they turn to a shelter for help. There may be many repercussions for the woman as the abuse continues. She may suffer psychiatric disorders, turn to drug or alcohol abuse, or suffer from long-standing physical disorders. She is very likely to have her productivity at work seriously reduced. The consequences of living in a violent atmosphere are also tragic for her children. Unfortunately, the data required to be able to cost out most of these effects do not exist. Where it is possible to do so, cost estimates are made.

Women who sustain long periods of violence often end up with long-term health problems. Where the injury itself might have been bruises or broken bones, the longer term effects are more systemic. All women living with violence show long-term systemic symptoms, not just those experiencing physical or sexual abuse. Emotional, psychological, and spiritual violence rob women of their well-being regardless of the level of physical assault. There is a recognized Battered Women's Syndrome which is described as a prolonged pattern of depression and a general sense of helplessness, fear, and social withdrawal (Jaffe *et al.*).

The most common symptoms include ulcers, heart disease, genital problems, anemia, asthma or bronchitis or emphysema, skin allergies, hypertension, digestive disorders, vision problems, backaches, arthritis, rheumatism and headaches. There are also severe psychological problems including extreme nervousness or irritability, depression, acute anxiety attacks, suicidal thoughts or attempts, confusion, memory loss, insomnia, fatigue and eating disorders (Jaffe *et al.*; see also, Ontario Medical Association; Chenard, Cadrin and Loiselle). In a Quebec study of a population of women who had lived in a shelter one year earlier, only two per cent reported no health problems at all, compared with 30 per cent of women in a matched sample of the general population. The average number of problems for the ex-sheltered women was 4.1 while the number was only 1.8 for the matched women. Of the ex-sheltered women, 46.3 per cent had at least one consultation with a health care professional during a two-week period (Chenard *et al.* 51) prior to the survey. This was 1.81 times the rate for socio-economically matched women in the total population. The average number of consultations for the ex-shelter women was 0.6, compared with 0.4 consultations for the matched women. Multiplying these averages by 26 to get an annual figure yields an average of 15.6 consultations for the ex-shelter women and 10.4 consultations for the women in the matched sample. The difference between the two is 5.2. This represents the additional consultations taken by the women who had lived with violence.

The service providers include general practitioners, medical specialists, social workers, nurses, dentists, chiropractors, psychologists, pharmacists, optometrists, and opticians. The costs for a consultation with these professionals vary from $15 an hour for a nurse to more than $100 an hour for a therapist. An arbitrary figure of $40 was chosen to cost these consultations as it is at the low end of the hourly fees.

It is assumed that all women victims of violence use health care professionals, not just those who stayed in shelters. However, since not all victimized women will have long-term symptoms, the 46.3 per cent figure is used as a proportion of all victims with long-term effects requiring care. Due to data limitations, an assumption must be made that the remaining victims never consult a professional as a result of the violence. This will make the final figure an underestimate compared to the actual number of visits resulting from violence.

There is another twist in calculating a cost for these long-term effects. The victims from the Statistics Canada survey in 1992 would not yet have accessed all long-term services. Instead, it is all the women who suffered violence in all previous years aggregated who would have been using these services in 1992. Therefore, it is appropriate to use the lifetime figure from the survey rather than the annual figure. The survey shows that 5,377,000 women in Canada have suffered from violence over their lifetimes. Of these, 2,652,000 women suffered from wife assault (Statistics Canada, 1993b: Table 3).

While it is certainly true that many of the women who were sexually assaulted or physically assaulted by a non-partner man would also need long-term health care, the proportion of 46.3 per cent comes from a survey of wife assault survivors. Therefore, it cannot be assumed that the same proportion would apply to victims of sexual assault or non-partner assaults by males. These women have been left out of the calculation entirely. The measured cost underestimates by only considering the long-term health consequences for some wife assault victims. Multiplying 46.3 per cent times the lifetime population of wife assault victims yields a total of 1,227,876 women. Multiplying this number by the 5.2 additional visits per year yields 6,384,955 additional consultations per year. This amounts to $255.4 million at $40 a consultation. Adding this figure to the costs of immediate services yields a total of nearly $300.7 million.

This figure may still be an underestimate as it does not include such things as costs of physiotherapy or other treatments, nor admissions to various types of clinics such as alcohol recovery or eating disorder clinics. Some survivors may continue to consult with these service providers for the rest of their lives.

**Psychiatric Effects**

One aspect of the tragedy surrounding women victims of violence is the long-term psychiatric results. Studies show that of women admitted to psychiatric hospitals or psychiatric units in other hospitals, 50 per cent are victims of violence and of them, 90 per cent have been violated by a family member (see Carmen, Reiker and Mills; Hoffman and Tober; Ontario Medical Association). In one study, 93 per cent of female psychiatric in-patients reported at least one severe incident of physical or sexual abuse by a male partner (Firsten). The average number of patients per incident of physical or sexual abuse by a male partner. The average number of patients per day for psychiatric hospitals and units in all hospitals in 1992 was 35.07 (Statistics Canada 1994a, Part 1: 43). Supposing that half were women (which may be an underestimate since women tend to suffer more psychiatric problems than men), then almost 8.77 patients per day would be women victims of violence. In 1992 there were 1,210 hospitals in Canada (Statistics Canada 1994a, Part 1: 2). This means there were 10,611.7 women victims admitted. The average cost in 1990 of one patient-day in psychiatric wards was $127.86 (Statistics Canada 1994a, Part 1: 51). This is $1,356,811.9 per day for the victims. Multiplying by 365 days to get the annual figure yields $495,236,344.

An additional 52.71 victims per day visited long-term psychiatric hospital emergency wards as ambulatory patients (Statistics Canada 1994a, Part 2: 7). There were 21 of these hospitals (Statistics Canada 1994a, Part 2: 2) and the cost per visit was $34.03 (Statistics Canada 1994a, Part 2: 11). Again assuming that 25 per cent of the patients are women victims of violence, the annual cost is $3,437,869. Another 11.42 ambulatory patients used emergency wards in short-term psychiatric hospitals (Statistics Canada 1994a, Part 2: 7) at a cost of $91.83 per visit (Statistics Canada 1994a, Part 2: 11). The total cost for the proportion of abused women patients was $1,432,891. Additionally, 51.74 patients (Statistics Canada 1994a, Part 2: 13) visited long-term psychiatric hospital clinics per day at a cost per visit of $67.20 (Statistics Canada 1994a, Part 2: 15). The cost for caring for women abuse survivors is almost $6.67 million a year.[6]

The total for these patients is $506,772,343 a year. Physicians' services, billed directly to the provincial health systems, cost more, but cannot be measured here due to lack of information about number of physician services per patient. The running total is now $807 million.

## Drug and Alcohol Abuse

Many women victims of violence turn to alcohol and/or drugs to cope. A study by the Addiction Research Foundation found that women who are assaulted by their male partners are 74 per cent more likely to rely on sedatives, and 40 per cent more likely to take sleeping pills than women who are not assaulted (Groeneveld and Shane). This is especially true for long-term victims. The drugs may include both illegal drugs and prescribed drugs. Only a small proportion of the actual costs of these addictions can be measured. First, there is the loss of life experience and joy that accompanies the physical condition of drug dependency. There is the additional loss of productive capacity, both for the woman and her family. Her performance in the paid work force is also affected. The costs to the woman of purchasing the alcohol or drugs are the only costs that could be measured financially, and the quantities are unrecorded. Only women's own stories can give a glimpse of what these out-of-pocket costs are for the victims. There are also the longer-term societal costs of supporting and helping these women to recover from their addictions.

The Statistics Canada (1993) national survey indicates that approximately 25 per cent of all ever-married women who have lived with violence had used alcohol, drugs or medication to help themselves cope. Sustaining emotional abuse or physical injury raised the rates to 31 per cent and 41 per cent respectively. The rates were higher for women who suffered the violence in a previous relationship than women currently living with violence. This indicates the longer-term effects of living with violence, compared to the immediate effects of specific episodes of violence.

The Quebec study of ex-shelter women, shows that these women had a higher rate of use of medications and that they took more types of medications than women in the whole population. In the two days prior to the survey interview, 43.6 per cent of the ex-sheltered women compared to 31.7 per cent of all women had taken three or more types of medication. The main difference was in the use of tranquillizers, sedatives, or sleeping pills, and vitamin and mineral supplements. Of the ex-sheltered women, 18.2 per cent used some form of tranquillizer, compared to 9.9 per cent of the women in the matched population. There were also higher levels of analgesics, skin ointments, heart or blood pressure medications, laxatives, cough or cold remedies, stimulants, and other medications. The average number of all types of medications taken by all ex-sheltered women was 3.4 per day, compared to 2.4 for the matched female population (Chenard *et al.* 53-55). Without more detailed information on how many women consume drugs or alcohol as a result of violence in their lives, it is not possible to attempt to measure an aggregate cost.

## Second-Generation Effects

One of the most serious aspects of violence against women is how it affects the next generation, either through child abuse or through children witnessing attacks on their mother. In British Columbia, witnessing violence is classified as child abuse. In one-third of families in which wife assault takes place, the children are also directly abused. In families where violence exists, it is estimated that 68 per cent to 80 per cent of children witness the attacks (Canadian Council on Social Development 1). Witnessing such violence in one's own home can lead to severe long-term problems. How the children deal with the horrors of their lives depends on many factors of their own personality and environment (Moore, Peplar, Weinberg, Hammond, Wadell and Weiser). For many, the violence becomes a way of life which they pass on to others when they are old enough. One study indicates that of young offenders charged with a violent offense, half have witnessed their fathers attacking their mothers (House of Commons).

Many of the children grow up expecting their own relationships with partners to be violent. The Statistics Canada survey shows the male partners in marriages involving violence were three times more likely to have grown up in a family with violence and twice as likely to have witnessed their fathers assaulting their mothers compared to the population at large. The violence in these second-generation families was also more severe and ongoing. Women with violent fathers-in-law suffered injuries in 29 per cent of cases, compared to 16 per cent in all other violent marriages (Rodgers 1994a: 13-14).

Children who witness violence at home suffer many psychological effects including low self-esteem, insecurity, anxiety, guilt, nightmares, sleep disturbances, bed-wetting, and feelings of fear and vulnerability. These children often display abnormal social behaviours, including either externalized aggressive acts or internalized depression and withdrawal. All of these consequences of the father's violent behaviour affect the children's education. Such things as their inability to concentrate, disturbing other children, or disruption and conflict with authorities all lead to poor academic performance. If their mothers leave the abusive situation, the children face a relocation to a new home, sometimes stopping along the way in transition housing or staying with friends or relatives. There is then a further adjustment to a new school. Furthermore, the mothers almost certainly face a severe drop in the family income, so the children may also face the difficulties of poverty. The children also have to learn new ways of living without violence.

Children who come from violent homes often end up being labelled by the system as problem children. The end result for some adolescents may be running away, becoming involved in drug and alcohol abuse, or even committing suicide. The problems resulting from the violence are not solved but passed on to the next generation. The personal costs to these children of lost opportunities for health and well-being in their lives cannot be measured. It is difficult to estimate the costs to them as individuals or to the whole of society for such things as special needs in the schools, medical consequences, truancy, homelessness, policing, legal and penal consequences, probation, social work or lost productivity in the workforce. Society pours vast amounts of money into after-the-fact help and control for children from violent homes. A more effective approach would be to put money directly into reducing the tolerance for violence against women and children in the home.

## Long-Term Workplace Issues

The immediate workplace costs for women who took time off work due to an assault are close to $22 million. (See Appendix 2 for calculations.) This amount assumes only one day off per year for each individual who was affected. Unfortunately, many women are injured to such an extent that they require longer absences from work than one day only. Furthermore, many women undergo more than one incident of abuse per year, and therefore show repeated patterns of days missed. Therefore, the $22 million figure grossly underestimates the extent of lost output at work. The Statistics Canada survey shows that over their lifetimes, 35 per cent of assaulted married women suffered a single attack, 22 per cent percent suffered two to five attacks; nine per cent suffered six to ten attacks, and 32 per cent suffered eleven or more attacks in total (Statistics Canada 1993b: Table 2).

Information from the Ontario Criminal Injuries Compensation Board shows some examples of how much time women spent out of their place of employment due to acts of violence. One file reports a 30-year-old woman, recently married, who was beaten severely in the face, requiring extensive surgical repair. She was unable to work for 35 weeks because of her injuries and surgery. In a study conducted for the Family Violence Program of the Canadian Council on Social Development, 21 Canadian women were surveyed about how their abusive relationships affected their paid employment. Over half said the violence affected their attendance. One woman used up 500 hours of sick leave over the last year of her relationship. One woman said she often missed Mondays because the beatings took place on the weekends. However, the authors report that overall, the women missed very few days, given the levels of violence in their lives. They were usually determined to get to work, no matter what. In all cases, however, the end result was a significant negative effect on their ability to do a good job (Denham and Gillespie 7-9).

The 1982 Canadian Urban Victimization Survey (CUVS) includes all victims of violent acts. This is not limited to violence in the home or sexual abuse but includes violence during robberies and other stranger violence. For these victims, 52 per cent of the women who were injured lost time away from their normal daily activities. This is in accord with the lifetime figure of 50 per cent of wives who took time off their daily activities reported in the Statistics Canada survey. Of the victims in the CUVS, 15 per cent were away for up to five days, 19 per cent for six to twenty days, and 18 per cent for three weeks or more (Solicitor General Canada 1985: 6).

To use these proportions for a calculation, the assumption is made that the rate of injury and time taken from daily activities has not changed since 1982. Using formulae spelled out in Appendix 2, the cost of extra days off is $335.3 million for women in the paid workforce and $203.7 million for women who work in the home. The combined total of $539 million pushes the annual cost of violence against women to nearly $1.35 billion.

The second cost in the workplace to the women and to society is this lower level of productivity during all their time at work. The women have to function at work under the stress and fear generated by their home life. They may be preoccupied with their family troubles, or they may be fatigued, and consequently may have reduced ability to concentrate. In manufacturing positions, this may lead to lower safety levels for them and their co-workers. Women may fear losing their jobs, or being judged unsympathetically by bosses and coworkers. They may also have to deal with sudden appearances or phone calls from their abusive partners while at work. The possibility of promotion declines and, in one case reported in the CCSD report, the abusive husband prevented the woman from attending interviews for promotions by "marking" her (Denham and Gillespie 9). All of these consequences reduce the productivity of the women and others in their workplaces. This decline in output and efficiency is not possible to fully measure.

## Costs to the Victims and Society

There are many other ways in which women and all of society pay the costs of violence against women. Some are measurable and some are not. What follows is a brief look at a few more costs of violence against women. Most of the numbers are anecdotal, or too imprecise to be able to add to the total, but they demonstrate the wide range of social costs.

*Transition Homes:* The term "transition home" stands for any safe shelter for women and their children escaping from a violent home situation. For the women and children who have no other options, the shelters become an essential link in their protection. In 1993, there were 371 shelters operating across Canada, providing 1,088,335 resident days of service. The shelters offer a variety of services other than housing, depending on the needs of the women and availability of services within the community. Included are crisis counselling, crisis phone lines, support groups for both the women and children, counselling for both women and children, legal information and assistance, educational services, housing referral and referral to outside professionals. The average annual cost per shelter for all expenditures was $364,000 (Statistics Canada 1993d), or just over $135 million in total. That figure does not include the value of volunteer hours or the costs assumed by women who used other housing alternatives such as hotels.

*Rape Crisis/Sexual Assault Centres:* Crisis centres are agencies that provide crisis intervention and on-going intervention for victims of sexual assault or any other women who choose to access them, through 24-hour phone lines and through face-to-face support. The centres provide counselling services for both the short-run and longer-term, including both individual and group support. Public information and education is made available by these centres. They also act as advocates for the women if they need support with the legal system. Volunteer labour is an integral component of the centres' operations because of underfunding. The total value of volunteer labour in 85 crisis centres in Canada funded by provincial governments is $8,460,207.[7] Adding this amount to the value of the funding gives a total of $29,381,878 to operate the centres. In addition, the centres regularly apply for funding from other sources such as municipalities and foundations, as well as organizing fund-raising projects, as regular funding is grossly inadequate. The centres run programs that serve the needs of the women victims immediately and after-the-fact. When trauma is handled well at first, the long-term consequences are far less devastating. Every dollar spent in preventing long-term consequences helps women and is a significant saving in the long run.

*Other Prevention and Treatment Initiatives:* A telephone survey of the provincial governments provided information on prevention initiatives, funding of crisis centres, and other programs for women victims of violence. The cost of prevention and treatment initiatives, which include public education, community outreach and counselling, is $28,790,275 (but this is a conservative estimate, not including all provinces and based on figures available in the early 1990s).

*Welfare:* One direct societal cost is when women flee violent situations and need to access public welfare for survival. They may or may not be able to find paying work and stop receiving assistance. Anecdotal evidence suggests that possibly ten per cent of the caseload is made up of these women and children fleeing violence. Further, if women are owed child or spousal support from estranged husbands, but are afraid to contact the men because of risking exposure to more violence, the social assistance system often ends up paying to support the children. Some welfare workers perceive this as a way that abusive men are reinforced for violence against their wives as the threat effect can be used as a way to avoid paying support.[8]

*Support Groups and Networks:* Another place where human effort and money is spent to support the victims of violence is through women's support groups. The groups may be organized through an agency such as a transition home, in which case they would be measured already, but other groups are organized through agencies such as the YWCA, local churches, universities, or organizations created for this purpose. Women pay out-of pocket for the support they receive to heal from the effects of violence in their lives. Women who do not have organized support groups may have a special friend or a sister or another relative in whom they can confide. Often these people do not live locally and the woman must bear the cost of long-distance telephone calls.

*Transportation:* Women may need to travel to the hospital, or to doctors' appointments, or even to another city for special services. They may travel by ambulance, taxi, bus, airplane, or their own vehicle. No matter how long or short the distance, there are costs associated with this transportation.

*Childcare and Eldercare:* When women spend time attending doctor appointments, therapy sessions, women's support groups, or in longer-term admissions to hospitals or clinics, they are often faced with having to find and pay for childcare or eldercare. This is especially critical if the father of the children is present and the mother fears he may harm the children in her absence. Sometimes the need for childcare prevents women from seeking the help they would otherwise access.

*Repairs:* Another personal cost to victims of violence is physical repair to their homes if the violence caused damage to walls, windows, etc. They may also need to repair or replace furnishings or personal belongings such as torn or bloodied clothing, smashed furniture or household goods, and other possessions including eyeglasses, dentures, or other prosthetic devices. If the woman leaves a violent home situation, she will be faced with furnishing a new home for herself and her children. Estimates of such costs can easily run into the tens of thousands per woman.

*Research:* Another way society pays for the existence of violence is through funding research into various aspects of the problem. The Canadian Panel on Violence against Women is one example, with a $10-million cost. Research projects such as the one producing this report are widespread. Documents, surveys, videos, newsletters, and fact sheets have costs attached which, cumulatively, can amount to many millions of dollars.

*Effects on Workers:* It is a gruelling process to face violence every day, even if it is not happening directly to you. Women who work in the shelters and crisis centres, spend their days helping women escape from extreme violence. While the women themselves move on, the workers stay to continue to give support to the never-ceasing flow of victims. This often causes burn-out among the workers, and puts stress on their own families and friends. This is also true for front-line medical workers. There is a similar but less intense effect for the researchers who work at bringing the facts of violence against women and children into the public eye. Working with the individuals or the data and stories, and presenting the information, can also be a very demanding process requiring support from family and friends.

*School-based Violence:* Another cost to individuals and society is due to violence directed against girls in their school environments. For the girls and young women facing gendered violence in this setting, the results can be debilitating. Such attitudes can be internalized, self-esteem lowered and abuse may appear more acceptable. These problems may contribute to increasing violence in the intimate relationships between teens.

*Deaths:* The loss of women's lives at the hands of their partners or ex-partners, or at their own hands if they commit suicide, is impossible to quantify economically. There is no way that the women or their families and friends could ever be compensated for the loss of happiness, contribution to family and community, and productivity. The effect on children who grow up without their mothers because of acts of violence, often carried out by their own fathers, is terrible and unpredictable. Such acts affect everyone, creating an escalation in the level of fear all live with daily. About 80 women a year in Canada are killed by their partners or ex-partners, a rate nine times higher than the risk of being killed by a stranger. Women are shot, stabbed, beaten, strangled, poisoned, and burned to death. Of all spousal deaths in 1991, police recorded that 52 per cent could be attributed to an argument and a further 24 per cent to jealousy. There was a history of domestic violence known to the police in 51 per cent of the killings of wives and in 68 per cent of the 25 killings of husbands each year (Wilson and Daly). This means that for the majority of women incarcerated for killing their husbands, the final act was probably one of self-protection resulting from long-term abuse in the relationship. The loss of liberty these women face, and their loss as mothers and members of their communities, is a resulting cost of the abuse they withstood.

From all the available evidence, the conclusion is clear: violence against women is a very expensive problem in our society. The total of the measurable costs relating to health and well-being alone amounts to **$1,539,730,387** per year. This is just the tip of the iceberg, representing but one branch of the six detailed in Figure 1. If all of these were costed, the total would certainly be many times greater than this, and for each year that we do not dedicate the necessary resources to end the problem of violence against women, they will continue to rise. Since these results were initially released, there were indications in many sectors that the problem of violence against women was being taken as a priority issue. Recently, however, there have been sweeping government cuts across Canada to services and programs aimed at reducing or ending male violence. From our point of view, this is a particularly striking example of bad planning, poor policy, and false economy, not to mention moral evasion of a pressing issue of social justice. As a society, we must realize that investing today in ending violence will reap significant social dividends for all as we move toward a violence-free future.

*This paper was originally commissioned by the Canadian Advisory Council on the Status of Women in Ottawa, which was subsequently closed by the federal government in 1995. An earlier version was printed and distributed by the Centre for Research on Violence Against Women and Children of The University of*

*Western Ontario. The authors would like to thank the research assistants who worked on this project: Deborah Campbell, Peggy Mahon, Beth McCauley, Melanie Samson, Astrid Stark, Barb Smith, Joan Vance and Sandy Wellman. In particular, our deepest thanks go to the women who shared their stories for the purposes of this research.*

## Notes

[1]See, for example, Blumo, Gibb, Innis, Justo and Wilson; Friedman and Couper; Kerr and McLean; Korf, Meulenbeck, Mot, and van der Brandt ; KPMG Management Consulting 1996, 1994; Laurence and Spalter-Roth; Leonard and Cox; Morrison and Orlando; Snively; Stanko, Crisp, Hale and Lucraft; Wisner, Gilmore, Salzman and Zink .

[2]This survey still stands as the only comprehensive data source for violence against women in Canada. A subsequent survey conducted as part of the Crime Victimization Survey of the General Social Survey in 1999 looked at only domestic violence rates for both men and women.

[3]The dental community of Canada had recently realized that it is often the first service provider to see the results of violence, and it is beginning to take some responsibility for patients in this respect. (See Mayer and Gala; Podenieks; Wilson; Vaughn.)

[4]The labour force participation rate is calculated to exclude widows.

[5]The average earnings for women working full-time, full-year in 1991 were $26,800. Using the CPI for the rate of growth in annual earnings to 1992 of 1.5 per cent, the annual figure for 1992 becomes $27,202. CPI from Statistics Canada, *The Consumer Price Index*, July 1994, Table 3, 21.

[6]Note that the figures for ambulatory patients are given daily averages calculated on an annual basis. Therefore, if the ambulatory clinics are only open five days per week, this is already accounted for in the annual averages, and it is appropriate to multiply by 365 rather than 251.

[7]The total number of volunteer hours in Ontario was measured by a telephone survey conducted by Tanis Day.

[8]Information courtesy of Policy Analysis, Social Assistance Programs Branch, Ministry of Community and Social Services, Ontario.

## References

Agudelo, Saul Franco. "Violence and Health: Preliminary Elements for Thought and Action." *International Journal of Health Services* 22(2) (1992): 365-376.

Ascencio, R.L. "The Health Impact of Domestic Violence: Mexico City." *Too Close to Home: Domestic Violence in the Americas.* Eds. A. R. Morrison and M. B. Orlando. New York: Inter-American Development Bank, 1999: 81-101.

Berish, Marlene. *Family Violence Through EAP Project: Report on Phase 1.*

National Clearinghouse on Family Violence, June 1987.

Bishop, Joan, and Paul G. R. Patterson. "Guidelines for the Evaluation and Management of Family Violence." *Canadian Journal of Psychiatry* 37 (7) (September 1992): 458-471.

Blumel, D., G. Gibb, B. Innis, D. Justo, and D. Wilson. *Who Pays? The Economic Costs of Violence Against Women.* Queensland: Women's Policy Unit, Office of the Cabinet, 1993.

British Columbia. *The British Columbia Task Force on Family Violence: Backgrounder*, British Columbia: 1992.

British Columbia. *Is Anyone Listening? Report of the British Columbia Task Force on Family Violence.* British Columbia: February, 1992.

British Columbia. *List of Contracted Agencies and Programs.* British Columbia: Ministry of the Attorney-General, Community Justice Branch, Victim Services Division, April 1, 1993 to March 31, 1994.

Bowker, Lee H. and Lorie Maurer. "The Medical Treatment of Battered Wives." *Women and Health* 12 (1) (1987).

Calgary, Alberta. *Mayor's Task Force on Community and Family Violence: Final Report.* Alberta: March, 1991.

Canada. *Family Violence: Situation Paper.* Ottawa: Ministry of Supply and Services, 1992.

Canada. *Status Report on the Federal Response to Reaching for Solutions: Report of the Special Advisor on Child Sexual Abuse.* Ottawa, 1993.

Canada Department of Justice. *Family Violence Initiative.* Ottawa: Minister of Justice and Attorney-General of Canada, 1991-1995.

Canadian Advisory Council on the Status of Women. *Male Violence Against Women: The Brutal Face of Inequality, A Brief to the House of Commons Subcommittee on the Status of Women: Violence Against Women.* Ottawa, February 13, 1991.

Canadian Council on Social Development. "The Secret That Can't Be Left at Home: Family Violence and the Workplace." *Vis-A-Vis: A National Newsletter on Family Violence* 9 (12) (Spring 1991).

Canadian Council on Social Development. "A Violent Legacy: Exploring the Links Between Child Sexual Abuse and Wife Assault." *Vis-A-Vis: A National Newsletter on Family Violence* 9 (2) (Summer 1991a).

Canadian Council on Social Development. "November is Family Violence Prevention Month," *Vis-A-Vis: A National Newsletter on Family Violence* 9 (3) (Fall 1991b).

Canadian Council on Social Development. "Dating Violence: Not an Isolated Phenomenon." *Vis-A-Vis: A National Newsletter on Family Violence* 9 (2) (Winter 1992).

Canadian Council on Social Development. "Social Action: First Mourn ...Then Work For Action." *Vis-A-Vis: A National Newsletter on Family Violence* 1(2) (Fall 1993).

Canadian Council on Social Development. "Support Groups for Women: What

They Are, and What They Can Do." *Vis-A-Vis: A National Newsletter on Family Violence* 11 (3) (Winter 1994).

Canadian Council on Social Development. "Wife Assault and the Criminal Justice System: Can Women Find Fairness in a System Built for Men?" *Vis-A-Vis: A National Newsletter on Family Violence* 8 (1) (Spring 1990).

Canadian Panel on Violence Against Women. *Changing the Landscape: Ending-Violence Achieving Equality. Final Report.* Ottawa: Canadian Panel on Violence Against Women, 1993.

Carlile, John Batchin. "Spouse Assault on Mentally Disordered Wives." *Canadian Journal of Psychiatry* 36 (4) (May 1991): 265-269.

Carmen, Elaine, Reiker, Patricia Perri and Trudy Mills. "Victims of Violence and Psychiatric Illness." *American Journal of Psychiatry* 141 (3) (March 1984): 378-383.

Chenard, Lucie, Helene Cadrin, and Josette Loiselle. *State of Health of Women and Children Victims of Violence: Research Report.* Quebec: Direction de la santé publique Régie régionale de la santé et des services sociaux Bas-Saint-Laurent, Rimouski, September, 1993.

Crawford, Ralph. "Violence—Our Shame." *Journal of the Canadian Dental Association* 59 (11) (1993): 873.

Cross, Philip. "Statistics Canada, Perspectives in Labour and Income." *The Labour Market Year-End Review* (Spring 1993).

"Current Concepts in Emergency Medicine: General and Family Practice" *Ontario Medical Review* (August 1984).

Day, Tanis. *The Health Related Costs of Violence Against Women: The Tip of the Iceberg.* London, Ontario: Centre for Research on Violence Against Women and Children Publication Series, The University Of Western Ontario, 1995.

DeKeseredy, Walter S. *Four Variations of Family Violence: A Review of Sociological Research.* Ottawa: Family Violence Prevention Division, Health Canada, October, 1993.

Denham, Donna and Joan Gillespie. *Wife Abuse: A Workplace Issue. A Guide for Change.* Ottawa: Family Violence Program, Canadian Council on Social Development, 1992.

Epstein, Rachel, Roxanna Ng, and Maggi Trebble. *The Social Organization of Family Violence: An Ethnography of Immigrant Experience In Vancouver, A Report to the Non-Medical Use of Drugs Directorate.* Ottawa: Health and Welfare Canada, 1978.

Flanzer, Jerry P. "Alcohol and Family Violence: Then to Now—Who Owns the Problem?" *Journal of Chemical Dependency Treatment* 3 (1) (1989): 61-79.

Friedman, L. and S. Couper. *The Costs of Domestic Violence: A Preliminary Investigation of the Financial Costs of Domestic Violence.* New York: Victim Services Agency, 1987.

Firsten, Temi. *An Exploration of the Role of Physical and Sexual Abuse for Psychiatrically-Institutionalized Women.* Toronto: Ontario Women's Directorate, 1990.

Greaves, L., O. Hankivsky, and J. Kingston-Riechers. *Selected Estimates of the Costs of Violence Against Women.* London, Ontario: Centre for Research on Violence Against Women and Children Publication Series, The University of Western Ontario, 1995.

Godenzi, A. and C. Yodanis. "Male Violence: The Economic Costs, a Methodological Review." Council of Europe, 1999. Available online at: http://www.eurowrc.org/13.institutions/3.coe/en-violence-coe-oct99.htm

Groeneveld, Judith and Martin Shane . *Drug Use Among Victims of Physical and Sexual Abuse: A Preliminary Report.* Toronto: Addiction Research Foundation, July, 1989.

Health and Welfare Canada. *National Health Expenditures in Canada.* Ottawa: Heatlh and Welfare Canada, 1990.

Health and Welfare Canada. *Wife Abuse: The Impact on Children.* Ottawa: Information from the National Clearinghouse on Family Violence, 1991.

Heise, Lori. "Gender Violence: A Statistics for Action Fact Sheet." New York: International Women's Tribune Centre, UNIFEM Resource Centre, October, 1992.

Heise, Lori. "Violence Against Women: The Hidden Health Burden." World Bank Discussion Paper No. 255. Washington, DC: World Bank, 1994.

Heise, Lori, Marry Ellsberg, Megan Gottemoeller. "Ending Violence Against Women." *Population Reports* Series L (11) Baltimore: Johns Hopkins University School of Public Health, Population Information Program, 1999. Available online at: http://www.jhuccp.org/pr/111/111creds.stm

Helton, Anne Stowart. *Protocol of Care for the Battered Woman.* Denton: Texas Woman's University, June, 1986.

Hilberman, E. "The Battered Woman." *Emergency Medicine* 2 (4) (1979).

Hoffman, B. F. and B. B. Toner. "The Prevalence of Spousal Abuse in Psychiatric In-Patients: A Preliminary Study." *Canadian Journal of Community Mental Health* 7 (2) (1988): 53-59.

House of Commons. *Crime Prevention in Canada: Toward a National Strategy, Twelfth Report of the Standing Committee on Justice and the Solicitor General.* Issue no. 87, Tuesday, February 23, 1993.

House of Commons. *The War Against Women: Report of the Standing Committee on Health and Welfare, Social Affairs, Seniors and the Status of Women.* Ottawa: Sub-Committee on the Status of Women. June 1991.

"How is Violence Measured?" Inter-American Development Bank, Technical Note 2. Available online at: www.iadb.org/sds/SOC/site910e.htm

Hutchinson, Bonnie Enterprises. *Breaking the Cycle of Family Violence: A Resource Handbook Prepared for the Staff of Correctional Services Canada.* Ottawa: Correctional Services Canada, 1988.

Jaffe, Peter, David A. Wolfe, Susan Wilson, and Lydia Zak. "Emotional and Physical Health Problems of Battered Women." *Canadian Journal of Psychiatry* 31 (7) (1986): 625-628.

Jiwani, Yasmin. *Intersecting Inequalities: Immigrant Women of Colour, Violence and Health Care*. Vancouver: FREDA Centre for Research on Violence Against Women, 2000. Available online at http://www.harbour.sfu.ca/freda/articles/hlth03 .

Johnson, Holly and Peter Chisholm. "Family Homicide." *Canadian Social Trends*. Ottawa: Statistics Canada, Autumn 1989.

Kennedy, Leslie W., Robert A. Silverman, and David R. Forde. "Homicide in Urban Canada: Testing the Impact of Economic Inequality and Social Disorganization." *Canadian Journal of Sociology* 6(4) (1991): 397-410.

Kerr, R. and J. McLean. *Paying for Violence: Some Costs of Violence Against Women in B.C.* Victoria: Ministry of Women's Equality, Government of British Columbia, 1996.

Kinnon, D. and L. Hanvey. "Health Aspects of Violence Against Women: A Canadian Perspective." Paper presented at the Canada-U.S. Women's Health Forum, 1996. Available online at http://www.hc-sc.gc/canusa/papers/violence.htm.

Korf, D. J., H. Meulenbeck, E. Mot, and T. van den Brandt. *Economic Costs of Violence Against Women*. Utrecht, Netherlands: Dutch Foundation of Women's Shelters, 1997.

KPMG Management Consulting for Office of Women's Policy. *The Financial and Economic Costs of Violence in the Northern Territory*. Darwin, Northern Territory, Australia: Office of Women's Policy, 1996.

KPMG Management Consulting. *Tasmanian Domestic Violence Advisory Committee: Economic Costs of Domestic Violence in Tasmania*. Melbourne: KPMG Management Consulting, 1994.

Krugman, Richard. "Child Abuse and Neglect." *World Health* 46 (1) 22 (January-February 1993).

Kurz, D., and E. Stark. "Not-So-Benign Neglect: The Medical Response to Battering." *Feminist Perspectives on Wife Abuse*. Eds. K. Yllo and M. Bograd. New York: Sage Publications, 1988: 249-266.

Laurence, L. and R. Spalter-Roth. *Measuring the Costs of Domestic Violence Against Women and the Cost-Effectiveness of Intervention: An Initial Assessment and Proposals for Further Research*. Washington, D.C.: Institute for Women's Policy Research, 1996.

Leighton, Barry. *Spousal Abuse in Metropolitan Toronto: Research Report on the Response of the Criminal Justice System*. Ottawa: Solicitor-General of Canada, Police Research and Demonstration Division, no. 1989-02.

Lent, Barbara. "Wife Assault: A Medical Perspective." *Reports on Wife Assault*. Toronto: Ontario Medical Association, Committee on Wife Assault, January, 1991.

Lent, Barbara. "Approaches to Treatment of the Male Batterer and His Family." In Reports on Wife Assault." Toronto: Ontario Medical Association, Committee on Wife Assault, January 1991.

Leonard, Helen and Eva Cox (Distaff Associates). *Costs of Domestic Violence*. Haymarket, New South Wales: New South Wales Women's Co-ordination

Unit, 1991.

Lupri, Eugene. "Male Violence in the Home." *Canadian Social Trends*. Ottawa: Statistics Canada, Autumn 1989.

MacDonald, Gary and Lorraine Touchette. "Profile of Transition Homes/ Shelters for Victims of Family Violence." *Health Reports* 5 (2) (1993).

MacDonald, Sheila. Personal communication, 1994.

MacLeod, Linda. *Wife Battering and the Web of Hope: Progress, Dilemmas and Visions of Prevention*. Ottawa: Family Violence Prevention Division, Health and Welfare Canada, May, 1989.

Manitoba. *Family Dispute Services: Orientation Package*. Manitoba: Department of Family Services, Child and Family Services Division, October, 1993.

Mayer, Laureen and Douglas Galan, "Elder Abuse and the Dentists' Awareness of the Problem: A National Survey." *Journal of the Canadian Dental Association* 59 (11) (1993): 921 –926.

McKenna, K. M. J., and D. Blessing. "Mapping the Politics of a Research Journey: Violence Against Women as a Public Health Issue." *Resources for Feminist Research* 26 (1/2) (1998): 77-96.

Miller, Ted, R. "Costs of Juvenile Violence: Policy Implications." *Pediatrics* 107 (1) (2001): 1-7.

Moore, Timothy, Debra Peplar, Brenda Weinberg, Liz Hammond, Janice Waddell, and Liza Weiser. "Research on Children from Violent Families." *Canada's Mental Health* 38 (2/3) (July/September 1990).

Morrison, Andrew R. and María Beatriz Orlando. "Social and Economic Costs of Domestic Violence: Chile and Nicaragua." *Too Close to Home: Domestic Violence in the Americas*. Eds. A. R. Morrison and M. B. Orlando. New York: Inter-American Development Bank, 1999: 51-80.

National Clearinghouse on Family Violence. "Point of Contact: Family Violence and Health Care Professionals." *Vis-A-Vis: Newsletter of the National Clearinghouse on Family Violence* 3(2) (Spring 1985): 1-3.

New Brunswick Advisory Council on the Status of Women. *Services to Women Living in Rural Areas: A First Look*. Moncton: New Brunswick Advisory Council on the Status of Women, February, 1987.

New Brunswick. *Woman Abuse Consultation: A Report on Concerns About the Legal System's Response to Woman Abuse*. Fredericton: Public Legal Education and Information Service of New Brunswick, November, 1992.

Newfoundland and Labrador. *Report of the Consultations on Building a Provincial Strategy to Address Violence*. St John's: Women's Policy Office, March, 1994.

Newfoundland and Labrador. *Beyond Reasonable Doubt: The Influence of Victim Stereotypes and Social Biases on Police Response to Women's Complaints of Sexual Assault*. St. John's: The Provincial Advisory Council on the Status of Women, Newfoundland and Labrador, September, 1991.

Northwest Territories. *Report by the Task Force on Spousal Assault*. Yellowknife: Spousal Assault Task Force reporting to the Minister responsible for the Status of Women, May 15, 1985.

Ontario. *Compensation for Victims of Crime Act.* March, 1987.

Ontario. *Sexual Assault Prevention Initiative.* Toronto, 1990-1994.

Ontario Criminal Injuries Compensation Board. *21st Report of the Criminal Injuries Compensation Board, 1989 to 1992.* Toronto: The Criminal Injuries Compensation Board, 1993.

Ontario Medical Association. *Reports on Wife Assault.* Toronto: Ontario Medical Associaton January, 1991.

Ontario Ministry of Health. *Schedule of Benefits: Physician Services under the Health Insurance Act.* Toronto: Ministry of Health, 1992.

Ontario Ministry of the Solicitor-General and Correctional Services. *Law Enforcement Activity in Relation to Spousal Assault in Ontario, 1986-1991.* Toronto: Ministry of the Solicitor-General and Correctional Services, May, 1994.

Ontario Women's Directorate. *Wife Assault.* Toronto: Women's Directorate, September 1992.

Plichta, S. "The Effects of Women Abuse on Health Care Utilisation and Health Status: A Literature Review." *Women's Health Issues* 2 (3) (1992): 154-161.

Podnieks, Elizabeth. "Elder Abuse and Neglect: A Concern for the Dental Profession." *Journal of the Canadian Dental Association* 59 (11) (1993): 915-920.

Post, Robin D., Allan B. Willett, Ronald D. Franks, Robert M. House, Susan M. Back, Michael P. Weissberg. "A Preliminary Report on the Prevalence of Domestic Violence Among Psychiatric Inpatients." *American Journal of Psychiatry* 137(8) (August 1980): 974- 975.

Quebec. *General Practitioners Manual.* 1993.

Quebec. *Medical Specialists Manual, Costs of Psychiatric Treatment.* 1993.

Roberts, Julian V. "Criminal Justice Processing of Sexual Assault Cases." *Juristat: Service Bulletin* Statistics Canada, Canadian Centre for Justice Statistics 14 (7) (March 1994).

Rodgers, Karen. "Wife Assault in Canada." *Canadian Social Trends.* Ottawa: Statistics Canada, Autumn 1994: 3-8.

Rodgers, Karen. "Wife Assault: The Findings of a National Survey," *Juristat: Service Bulletin* [Statistics Canada, Canadian Centre for Justice Statistics] 14 (9) (March 1994a).

Rodgers, Karen and Gary MacDonald. "Canada's Shelters for Abused Women." *Canadian Social Trends.* Ottawa: Statistics Canada, Autumn 1994: 10-14.

Ross, Colin A. and Vikram Dua. "Psychiatric Health Care Costs of Multiple Personality Disorder." *American Journal of Psychotherapy* 47 (1) (Winter 1993): 103-111.

Rounsaville, Bruce and Myrna M. Weisman. "Battered Women: A Medical Problem Requiring Detection." *International Journal of Psychiatry in Medicine* 8 (2) (1978): 191-201.

Sandroff, R. "Sexual Harassment in the Fortune 500." *Working Woman* (December 1988).

Saskatchewan. *Provincial Medical Fee Schedule.* 1993.

Schuler, Margaret. Ed. *Freedom from Violence: Women's Strategies from Around the World.* New York: UNIFEM, United Nations Development Fund for Women, 1992.

Shrader, Elizabeth. *Methodologies to Measure the Gender Dimensions of Crime and Violence.* Gender Unit, Poverty Reduction and Economic Management, Latin America and Caribbean Region, The World Bank, July 2001.

Sibbald, Patricia and Clive S. Friedman. "Child Abuse: Implications for the Dental Health Professional." *Journal of the Canadian Dental Association* 59 (11) (1993): 909-912.

Snively, S. *The New Zealand Economic Costs of Family Violence.* Auckland: Coopers and Lybrand, 1994.

Solicitor-General Canada. "Female Victims of Crime." *Canadian Urban Victimization Survey Bulletin* 4 (1985).

Solicitor-General Canada. "Cost of Crime to Victims." *The Canadian Urban Victimization Survey Bulletin* 5 (1985a).

Solicitor-General Canada. "Patterns in Violent Crime." *The Canadian Urban Victimization Survey Bulletin* 8 (1987).

Southwest Safe Shelter. *A Brief for the Canadian Panel on Violence Against Women.* Swift Current, Saskatchewan: Southwest Safe Shelter, undated.

Stanko, E., D. Crisp, C. Hale, and H. Lucraft. *Counting the Costs: Estimating the Impact of Domestic Violence in the London Borough of Hackney.* Swindon, Wiltshire, UK: Crime Concern, 1998.

Stark, E., Flitcraft, A. and W. Frazier. "Medicine and Patriarchal Violence: The Social Construction of a 'Private' Event," *International Journal of Health Services* 9(3) (1979).

Stark, E., A. Flitcraft, and D. Zuckerman. "Wife Abuse in the Medical Setting: An Introduction for Health Personnel." *Domestic Violence Monograph* 7 (April 1981).

Stark, M. A. "Medical Costs of Intra-family Assault and Homicide." *Bulletin of the New York Academy of Medicine* 62(1986): 556-561.

Statistics Canada. *The Consumer Price Index.* July, 1994.

Statistics Canada. *Hospital Indicators 1991-92: Part 1 and Part 2 Diagnostic and Therapeutic.* Ottawa: Statistics Canada, Health Statistics Division, November, 1994a.

Statistics Canada. "The Violence Against Women Survey: Highlights." *The Daily* Thursday, November 18, 1993a.

Statistics Canada. *Violence Against Women Survey, 1993. Shelf Tables 1–25.* Ottawa: Statistics Canada, November, 1993b.

Statistics Canada. *Violence Against Women Survey, 1993.* Special data run, Karen Rodgers. Ottawa: Statistics Canada, November, 1993c.

Statistics Canada. Health Statistics Division. "Transition Home Survey, 1992-93." *Health Reports* 5 (4) (1993d).

Statistics Canada. *Labour Force Annual Averages.* 1992. Ottawa: Statistics Canada, 1992.

Statistics Canada. Canadian Centre for Health Information. "Quarterly Hospital Information System." *Health Reports* Supplement 3(4) (1991).

Stephenson, June. *Men Are Not Cost-Effective.* Napa: Diemer, Smith, 1991.

Straus, M. and R. J. Gelles. "The Costs of Family Violence." *Public Health Reports* 102 (6) (1987): 638-641.

Sutherland, C. A., C. M. Sullivan, and D. I. Bybee. "Effects of Intimate Partner Violence Versus Poverty on Women's Health." *Violence Against Women* 7 (10) (2001): 1122-1143.

Taylor, Wendy K. and Jacqueline C. Campbell. "Treatment Protocol for Battered Women." *Response Nursing Network on Violence Against Women* 81 14 (4) (1991).

Thurston, W. E. "Health Promotion from a Feminst Perspective: A Framework for an Effective Health System Response to Woman Abuse." *Resources for Feminist Research* 26(3/4) (1998/9): 175-202.

Toronto Rape Crisis Centre. *Application and Final Report to Ministry of the Solicitor-General and Correctional Services.* Toronto: Community Sexual Assault/Rape Crisis Centre Funding Grants Program, 1993/94, 1993.

Vaughn, Martha. *Family Violence Resource Materials for the Dental Community: An Annotated Bibliography.* Ottawa: Health Canada, May, 1993.

Wilson, Margo. "Family Violence: A Problem with Relevance for the Dental Hygienist." *Probe: Journal of the Canadian Dental Hygienists Association* 27(5) (1993): 173-175.

Wilson, Margo and Martin Daly. "Spousal Homicide." *Juristat: Service Bulletin* [Statistics Canada, Canadian Centre for Justice Statistics] 14 (8) (March, 1994).

Wine, Shelley and Marlene Berish. *Domestic Violence and the Workplace: An Annotated Bibliography.* Ottawa: National Clearinghouse on Family Violence, June, 1987.

Wisner, C. L., T. P. Gilmore, L. E. Salzman, and T. M. Zink. "Intimate Partner Violence Against Women: Do Victims Cost Health Plans More?" *The Journal of Family Practice* 48 (6) (1999): 439-443.

Women's Health Centre. "What is Women's Health?" *Focus on Women* 1(4) (October 1993).

Yodanis, Carrie, Alberto Godenzi and Elizabeth A. Stanko, "The Benefits of Studying Costs: A Review and Agenda for Studies on the Economic Costs of Violence Against Women." *Policy Studies* 21 (3) (2000): 263-276.

Zorza, Joan. "Woman Battering: High Costs and the State of the Law," *Clearinghouse Review,* Special Issue (1994).

## Appendix 1: Women's Stories

The following three stories are from women who shared them in hopes of benefiting other women. Their names have been changed.

### *Camille's Story*

Camille is 25 years old. Raised as an only child in a comfortable home, she grew up to be strong and independent. Two years ago, after completing university, she met Daniel. Three years younger than Camille, and raised in a severely dysfunctional family where violence was present, Daniel had been on his own since he was 15. Daniel's mother had left his father twenty years ago after he broke her jaw in a drunken rage. Camille and Daniel were a strange match perhaps, but she was entranced by him. "I was aware of the dangers of imbalance," says Camille. "Perhaps I saw a role for myself as saviour. I did not realize how deeply his insecurity and self-hatred flowed."

They moved into an apartment together in Montreal. Searching for jobs, and running out of money, they spent most of their time together. They began having recurring verbal fights. Although Camille's dissatisfaction was with her own life, Daniel took it personally. The aggression escalated. Daniel began accusing Camille of seeing other men behind his back, of still loving her previous boyfriend more than him, and of being in love with her best girlfriend who lived in another city. He could not believe that Camille had any love for him. She expended a great deal of energy trying to convince him that she did truly love him. After a two-week Christmas holiday with her parents, she returned to Montreal to discover that Daniel had had two affairs while she was away. Convinced that she had been "cheating" on him, he thought that if he confessed, she would as well. But she had nothing to confess. "The idea of him believing I was an 'evil, lying, horny bitch who opens her legs to everyone' broke my heart. I thought of the crack of his father's fist into his mother's jaw filed away in his two-year-old subconscious, and tried to convince him to get therapy. He wavered between hatred and love, screaming obscenities at me one minute and weeping in misery the next."

After a period of this crisis-level interaction, Daniel moved out. Camille decided she couldn't help him and would have to forget him. However, he began harassing her, phoning many times daily, and coming over to the apartment. One night at 4:00 a.m., he pounded on the door. When she didn't answer immediately, he smashed the window and crawled through it. Camille woke to the sound of shattering glass and found him sitting soberly in the living room, smoking a cigarette. After he refused to leave, Camille called the police. He was put in jail for several days, then issued a restraining order. He ignored the order and continued trying to see Camille. "I was terrified by the intensity of his anger, and my friends convinced me that I had to remove myself from his life. I would have to disappear." Camille had to break her lease and find replacement tenants. She had to pay to have the window repaired. She spent two weeks finding an affordable apartment and got an unlisted telephone number. She also went to court over Daniel on two occasions. She met with a social worker and sought group therapy. She eventually moved away from Montreal. The immediate financial costs to her were the time lost from looking for work, repairing the windows, the costs of moving, and acquiring an unlisted telephone number. The costs to society were her time spent with the social worker, as well as police and court time. "The greatest costs to me were psychological. My morale and self-assurance had plummeted and I wasn't quite sure how to regain the magic I had felt prior to this relationship, only eight months previous. I had physically freed myself of the relationship, I had no dependents and I was young and educated. On a scale of domestic violence, my case was not an extreme one, yet it has left deep imprints on me."

### *Grace's Story*

Grace is an Aboriginal professional woman living in the Prairies. Early in her marriage, she suffered a nervous breakdown and was hospitalized for anxiety and depression. At that point she called on friends and family to help. This was the beginning of her power to heal. Eventually she left her husband after discovering his violence toward her extended to their children. He was given supervised visitation rights to see the children. When Grace left the marriage, she was forced to relocate and get an unlisted telephone number. She lost many personal possessions as a result of relocation and was also forced to take over all mortgage payments, car payments. and payments on a loan the couple had taken out jointly. With very restricted income, she couldn't meet these payments, and her credit card company garnished her bank account.

She now faces the costs of single parenting: no rest-time, no contact with the father or the grandparents, no one with whom to share the responsibilities and demands of child raising. Grace must also be aware of the effects of her ex-husband's behaviour on her children. She knows that mothers are the primary therapists for their children. She is also faced with the racism endemic in Canadian society against Aboriginal women, especially single Aboriginal mothers. She feels dismissed, ignored and undermined when she has to make contact with social services. Grace is thankful for her caring women friends and her own family.

Grace estimates her financial costs, including to loss of deductibles in insurance coverage, car, loan and mortgage payments, counselling services, relocation costs, rental of a car, prescriptions and legal fees, at $20,150. This does not include the psychological, emotional, or physical costs to her or her children.

### *Anne's Story*

Anne was raised in a financially successful but severely dysfunctional family. Her father was alcoholic, and emotional abuse was rampant. "I grew up in Father's late stages of alcoholism so I experienced his blackouts, physical and verbal abuse, setting the couch on fire, legal, moral and ethical problems and eventually his final stages of body rot. Because of Father's mood swings, friends could not safely and freely come to visit so I began to isolate a lot in order to hide the family secret of chemical dependency. Isolation became a coping mechanism for me."

At age 13, Anne was violently sexually assaulted by a stranger in a park. She chose not to tell her family because of fear of further violence at home if she told. This secret made Anne very sick. She hid her insecurities in over-achievement. Her high school years were spent fighting anorexia, bulimia, migraines, and irritable bowel syndrome. When she was 16, Anne was admitted to hospital for two weeks for irritable bowel syndrome.

After high school, Anne went on to become a registered nurse and opened a business. During these years she drank excessively, including binge drinking. She also used drugs to cope, and her eating disorder was out of control. She faced constant health crises and visited the emergency ward approximately once a month, totalling close to 50 visits. She had constant migraines as well. She used drugs including tranquilizers, Demerol and over-the-counter pain relievers. She was admitted to hospital for two weeks at age 21. During these years she estimates that she spent approximately $800 on prescription drugs per year.

At age 25 Anne eloped with a man who subsequently began abusing her. During her first pregnancy, she was able to stop her addictive behaviours. After her daughter was born, however, she returned to her earlier ways. She continued visiting the hospital frequently and was abusing both alcohol and drugs. She had two, two-week admissions to hospital for colitis and irritable bowel syndrome during these years and began monthly visits to a psychologist. The marriage ended in separation, with her eating disorder and her abuse of alcohol both active. She sold her business and returned to live with her parents, where she found her father in the ravaging late stages of alcoholism. "Life was very unpredictable. On one occasion he sexually assaulted me and I did not know how to tell anyone. I returned to nursing and started abusing prescription drugs and injecting Demerol. When usage interfered with my work, I resigned without telling anyone the real reason."

During the next three years Anne went from nursing to bartending, from social drinking to alcoholism, and experienced date rape from a casual acquaintance. She nursed her father through his final days and consoled her mother who was falling apart due to her husband's drunken rages. Standing over her father one day, Anne suddenly saw where her behaviour would take her. She admitted herself to an in-patient alcohol treatment clinic. The cost (in 1984) was approximately $3,500. At the clinic, with new-found self-awareness and sobriety, she met the man who became her second husband. Together they started a successful business and had two children. "I lived every day to meet the needs of my husband, his children, my child, our children, his father, and the people who worked for us in the business. This was my purpose in life."

Unfortunately, this husband also returned to alcoholism and drug abuse. He, too, was physically and emotionally violent. Anne's behaviour patterns did not change, nor did her health improve. Eventually she had major surgery including a complete hysterectomy, rectocell repair, urethra dilatation, and panulectomy. She continued to need the emergency ward approximately monthly and had as many as three hospital admissions annually over many years.

When her mother died, something changed inside Anne. "I stood at the fork in the road to destiny and with a broken heart and a confused and battered mind and a debilitating physical condition, I prayed and sought help in recovery." She entered a rehabilitation recovery centre and a women's recovery home. Her thoughts were for her children, knowing that to be healthy for them she needed to be healthy herself. She joined a variety of women's groups and self-help groups. With seven to 14 meetings per week including counselling, she finally came through her dark days to a new life. She writes, "My life is in balance ... I know there are still strengths and frailties, challenges and triumphs to be faced with my work, my custody battle for my children, family, friends and community ... I claim ownership of my freed self ... I suffered from the seeds of oppression, humiliation, disappointment and repression ... The seeds are slowly being replaced by freedom, justice, independence, life, liberty, achievements and dreams, and the pursuit of happiness."

Anne has estimated her financial costs over the last five years alone to be approximately $140,000.

## Appendix 2: Calculations of the Costs

### Medical Costs

Incidents resulting in injury = 272,000
Assumption: 28 per cent sought medical help, based on lifetime data.
Therefore, total number of women seeking medical attention = 0.28 multiplied by 272,000 is 76,160.
Arbitrary $100 cost per visit, based on information about costs of various services.

Therefore, estimated total annual cost of immediate medical attention = $7,616, 000

(Does not include ambulance, drugs or other treatments, or admissions to hospitals.)

### Dental Costs

Number of dentists in Canada = 13,477
Assumption that one client per dentist per year seeks dental assistance due to violence, based on information about violence against elderly.
Arbitrary cost per visit to dentist for repair work = $100.

Therefore, estimated total annual cost for dental care = $100 multiplied by 13,477 = $1,347,700

### Workplace Costs

#### *Paid Work*

Number of women who took time off from their regular daily activities = 335,000
Labour force participation rate for women = 62.2 per cent or .622
Therefore, women taking at least one day off paid work = 0.622 multiplied by 335,000 = 208,370
Average annual salary for women = $27,202
Average daily wage for women = $27,202 divided by 251 working days per year = $108.38

Therefore, total cost for each woman to take one day off paid work = $108.38 multiplied by 208,370 = $22,583,140

***Unpaid Work***
Number of women who took time off from regular activities = 335,000
Number in labour force = 208,370

Therefore, average number at home = 335,000 - 208,370 = 126,630
Average daily wage = $108.38

Therefore, the total cost for each woman to take one day off unpaid work multiplied by 126,630 = $13,724,159

Therefore, total cost of lost output from paid and unpaid work
= $22,583,140 + $13,724,159 = $36,307,299.

(Does not include value for lost household output of women working in paid labour force.)

**Long-Term Effects**

Percentage of ex-shelter women who had at least one consultation with medical service provider during two-week period preceding survey = 46.3 per cent

Average number of consultations of all ex-shelter women in two-week period = 0.6
Average number of consultations of all other women (matched sample) in two-week period = 0.4
Average number of consultations per year = 26 multiplied by (two-week level)

Therefore, the average number of consultations per year for all ex-shelter women = 26 multiplied by 0.6 = 15.6

Average number of consultations per year for other women = 26 multiplied by 0.4 = 10.4
Difference in the number of consultations between ex-shelter and other women = 15.6 - 10.4 = 5.2

Number of women experiencing violence in a lifetime = 5,377,000
Number experiencing spousal abuse = 2,652,000
Proportion from above of percentage of ex-shelter women with at least one consultation 46.3 per cent
Due to lack of information, must assume all other victims never consult after the initial incident, including remain 53.7 per cent of spousal assault victims, and 100 per cent of victims of sexual and common assaults by non-partner males.

Therefore, estimable number of women seeking long-term treatment of additional 5.2 consultations per year = 0.463 multiplied by 2,652,000 = 1,227,876

Therefore, total number of consultations resulting from violence that can be estimated = 5.2 multiplied by 1,227,876 = 6,384,955.2

Arbitrary cost per consultation = $40

Therefore, total cost per year of additional consultations for wife-abuse victims = $40
multiplied by 6,384,955 = $255,398,200

(Does not include consultations for sexual assault victims, non-partner male assault victims, or over half of all wife-assault victims.)

**Psychiatric Effects**

***Inpatients, All hospitals***
Number of patients per day per hospital = 35.07
Proportion of women psychiatric patients who are known victims of violence = 50 per cent
Must assume men and women are patients in equal proportions.

Therefore, percentage of all patients who are women victims of violence = 0.5 multiplied by 0.5 = 0.25

Therefore, number of all patients who are women victims of violence = 0.25 multiplied by 35.07 = 8.77

Number hospitals = 1,210

Therefore, women-victims in-patients in all hospitals per day = 8.77 multiplied by 1,210 = 10,611.7

Average cost per patient day = $127.86
Total cost per day $127.86 multiplied by 10,611.7 = $1,356,811.90
Total cost per year = 365 multiplied by $1,356,811.90 = $495,236,344

***Ambulatory Patients***
Long-term psychiatric hospitals, emergency wards
Number of patients per day = 52.71
Percentage of women victims of violence = 0.25 multiplied by 52.71 = 13.18

Number of hospitals = 21
Therefore, women victim patients in all hospitals = 21 multiplied by 13.18 = 276.78
Cost per visit = $34.03
Total cost per day = $34.03 multiplied by 276.78 = $9,418.82
Total cost per year = 365 multiplied by $9,418.82 = $3,437,869

***Short-term psychiatric hospitals, emergency wards***
Number of patients per day = 11.42
Percentage of women victims of violence = 0.25 multiplied by 11.42 = 2.85
Number of hospitals = 15

Therefore, women-victim patients in all hospitals = 15 multiplied by 2.85 = 42.75
Cost per visit = $91.83

Total cost per day = $3,925.73
Total cost per year = 365 multiplied by $3,925.73 = $1,432,891

***Long-term hospitals, Psychiatric clinics***
Patients per day = 51.74
Percentage of women victims of violence = 0.25 multiplied by 51.74 = 12.94
Number of hospitals = 21

Therefore, women victim patients in all hospitals = 21 multiplied by 12.94 = 271.74
Cost per visit = $67.20

Total cost per day 271.74 multiplied by $67.20 = $18,260.93 Total annual cost 365 multiplied by $18,260.93 = $6,665,239

Total annual cost of women-victims' psychiatric hospital stays all types = $506,772,343.

(Does not include physician services or drugs.)

**Long-term Workplace Effects**

Proportion of all injured women taking time off work = 52 per cent

Lengths of time injured women were away from work as a result of violence:
15 per cent for one to five days (mid-point of 2.5 days)
19 per cent for six to 20 days (mid-point of 13 days)

18 per cent for 21 days or more (arbitrary choice of 30 days)
Therefore, proportions of all women who take time off work taking this many days:

15/52 = 28.9 per cent take one to five days
19/52 = 36.5 per cent take six to twenty days
18/52 = 34.6 per cent take twenty-one days or more
Number of women taking time off work = 335,000

Total days lost = (0.289 multiplied by 335,000 multiplied by 2.5)
+ (0.365 multiplied by 335,000 multiplied by 13)
+ (0.346 multiplied by 335,000 multiplied by 30)
= 242,038 + 1,589,575 + 3,477,300
= 5,308,913.

***Cost of Lost Time from Paid Work***
Labour force participation rate = 62.2 per cent
Total number of days lost from paid work = 0.622 multiplied by 5,308,913 = 3,302,144
Average daily wage = $108.38

Therefore, total cost of lost days of paid work = $108.38 multiplied by 3,302,144 $357,886,367

Subtract the cost of the first day already calculated = $35 7,886,367 - $22,583,140 = $335,303,227

***Cost of Lost Time from Unpaid Work***
Total number of days lost from regular activities = 5,308,913
Number of days lost from paid work = 3,302,144

Therefore, number of days lost from unpaid activities = 5,308,913 - 3,302,144 = 2,006,769

Therefore, total cost of lost days of unpaid work = $108.38 multiplied by 2,006,769 = $217,493,624

Subtract the cost of the first day already calculated = $217,493,624 - $13,724,159 = $203,769,465.

Therefore, estimated total cost of paid and unpaid lost work = $335,303,227 + 203,769,465 = $539,072,692.

(Does not include productivity losses, quits, lack of promotions, etc.)

**Existing Community Responses**

***Transition Homes***
Number of transition homes = 371
Average annual cost per shelter, not including volunteer hours = $364,000
Therefore, total annual cost = 371 multiplied by $364, 000 = $135,044, 000.

(Does not include value of volunteer labour.)

***Crisis Centres***
Number of centres in Ontario = 28
Total volunteer hours in Ontario = 205,708

Therefore, total number of 8-hour days of labour = 205,708 divided by 8 = 25,714. Average wage per day = $108.38

Therefore, value of volunteer days in Ontario = $108.38 multiplied by 25,714 = $2,786,883

Therefore, value of volunteer days per centre = $2,786,883 divided by 28 = $99,532

**Other provinces' crisis centres and amount of funding**
(believed to be incomplete information):

British Columbia= 23 crisis centres, total 53 agencies, $3,990,383
Alberta = 0
Saskatchewan = 4 centres, $621,190
Manitoba = 29 agencies including crisis centres and transition homes, $4,862,400 total
Northwest Territories = 0
Yukon = 1, funding unknown
Ontario = 28, $9,368,398
Quebec = 23, $1,766,000
New Brunswick = 2, funding unknown
Nova Scotia = 1, $230,000
Prince Edward Island = 1, $79,300
Newfoundland = 1, $3,500

Total = 57 crisis centres in other provinces similar to Ontario crisis centres. Assume same average number of volunteer hours across all provinces.

Therefore, total value of volunteer days in crisis centres only = $99,532 multiplied by 57 = $5,673,324

Total amount of funding = \$20,921,671
Therefore, total cost of operating crisis centres = \$2,786,883 + \$5,673,324 + \$20,921,671 = \$29,381,878.

(Does not include agencies operated without provincial funding. Does double count some costs of transition homes in Manitoba.)

**Provincial and Territorial Prevention and Treatment Initiatives**

Total costs of prevention and treatment initiatives = \$28,790,275
(Does not include all provinces and territories.)

***Estimate of annual health-related costs of violence against women in Canada:* \$1,539,730,387**

# III. STRUCTURAL FORMS OF VIOLENCE AGAINST WOMEN

# A Question of Silence

## Reflections on Violence Against Women in Communities of Colour

Himani Bannerji

**Calcutta, November 15, 1997**

Dear Ena and Angela,

*Breaking with scholarly protocols, I am writing this piece as a letter to you because what I want to say needs an embodied reader. The topic is too close to our everyday life and politics to come wrapped in a package of academic or theoretical abstractions. Thank you for asking me to write and for accepting a piece that is more reflection than definitive research. Thank you also for being my ideal readers through whom I can speak to others.*

### I

Issues of patriarchy and violence against women are disturbing in general, but they become even more so when considered in relation to our so-called own communities. I am speaking of South Asian communities about which I know most, but what I have to say may apply to "other" Canadian communities which are non-white.[1] I know that violence against women is a pervasively present phenomenon among us, in spite of much talk about honour and respect for women, including deification of the feminine principle as claimed by the hindus. I also know that not only I but large numbers of women, have been in a position to know of instances of violence of various degrees and have not known what to do or where to speak about it. We have often spoken among ourselves in a private or personal capacity, and sometimes we have expressed our concerns publicly. I have been haunted by the story of a Sri Lankan woman who killed her two daughters and attempted suicide. These events are not, as far as I can understand, a matter of personal pathology—they have to be informed with a consideration of her migration, her isolation, her lack of economic and social support, an extremely abusive marriage, and a sexist and racist host society, where hospitals continue to neglect signs of violence against women. On a lesser scale, we worry about women who leave the temporary refuge of the shelters for their "homes," returning to the same partners whose violence drove them out in the first place. But in spite of our general concern and common knowledge, I have not read anything extensive or substantial on the phenomenon of violence against women within their so-called communities—communities which are constituted by outside forces with (rather than by) "people of colour." Perhaps there is writing coming out of the United Kingdom or United States, but it has not gained enough prominence to attract public attention.

So, as things stand now, a direct critical assessment, social analysis, or political project on this issue has not been undertaken. We seem to have left this task mainly to poets and fiction writers, whose business we think it is to deal with experience. And as you know, as social scientists we have been taught to regard experience with extreme suspicion as a source for reliable social knowledge. Even though certain types of feminist theorists have sought to valorize experience, the current discursivism of feminist theories has put a big question mark against experience, against actual lives as they are lived by women. But rendered into literary or cultural artifacts and relegated to the borderlands of fact and fiction, what we know and say about community violence against women does not create the same pressure for address or redress as it would if we had to admit that this violence is a direct part of our diasporic reality. We would then have to speak to and act on patriarchal violence within our homes, within the moral or social regulation of the very modalities of constituting "the community." As things are, we maintain a public silence, even if we know it only rebounds on us negatively. We need to explore this silence, to ask what our investment in it might be. This is precisely what I am trying to do in this letter, as well as to speak to the nature of patriarchal violence within the terrain of our domestic lives.

We cannot even begin to plumb the depth of this silence unless we recognize its complex character. As you know, silence is highly telling—it can mean anything from complicity to resistance. Its presence, in the shape of an absence in public discourse about violence against women in South Asian or other non-white communities, speaks volumes about our political and sociocultural organization and stance. And even though this silence creates large holes in the fabric of our public political culture, that which we have not addressed directly seeps out, is displaced, or slips into other concerns or issues. The repressed returns, as it were, in court cases, in refugee and immigration hearings, in women's shelters, changing individual and private instances into examples of public and collective lives.

One of the reasons for this paradoxical silence may be that public utterance puts us in a situation of responsibility—it makes us accountable to and for others and ourselves. After all, what we say in print, in any public medium, is fixed in form, content, and time. It becomes part of an acknowledged, even official reality, liable to be seen as a distinct political position. We are no longer just overheard or peeped into. The doors of the community open as we speak "out." So, obviously, we are wary, not only about what we say in public, but where and how we say it. We want to assess the location and reception of our public statements, our disclosures and discussions in the arena of social communication.We are, if anything, overly sensitive towards the ideological strands or networks into which they will be woven, how our statements will be received by those who are not "us," particularly those "others" who consider us not as people but as "ethnic communities." These are not unimportant considerations for those who hold not only "minority" but "visible minority" status in a white and christian majoritarian nation state. But then we are in a situation of double jeopardy, since speaking and not speaking both entail problems. In fact, we may be better off breaking this silence, since this articulation itself is a political act giving rise to other political possibilities. But going public in this matter requires that we are able to expose and critique the patriarchal constitution of our communities, which is the same as all other communities, without too much squeamishness about our dirty laundry.

## II

To put forward our critique regarding violence against women in our communities, we cannot begin by taking the concept of "community" for granted. We need to remember that it is a political and cultural-ideological formation reliant upon social relations that are the base of social life and not a spontaneous or natural association of people. This constructed and contingent nature of the concept of community is important to keep in mind, since it is becoming increasingly common in social sciences to treat this concept, along with a definite article or an adjective, as a natural, almost an instinctive, form of social and cultural association. Cultural anthropology, with its various types of relativism, seems to have been an important source for this practice of considering "community" as a self-contained and natural formation, a social given, which may be interchangeable with the concept of civil society.

But if, instead of naturalizing "community," we see it as a formation, an ideological, that is, cultural and political practice, it becomes possible for us to develop a critique of the social organization, social relations, and moral regulations which go into the making of it. We can then begin to see that a group of people with a language, a religion, or an interest in common may only become an identifiable and stable social and political structure—in spite of the presence of power relations among them—through a combination of internal and external factors. It is in their interaction of contradiction and convergence that a so-called community is formed. This community, as in the case of women and issues of gender and patriarchy, can only hold itself together by maintaining a silence about issues of power. A community is also formed both on grounds of difference and commonness. The difference is obviously from those who lack features in common, and therefore are "others" to the collective "self" of the community, usually a smaller group marked out as different by the majority. This makes the community into a minoritarian concept, one whose political and social roots fit in being collectively marked out as different from the hegemonic group. It is not difficult to understand this process of community formation when we see the different ways in which the Canadian state and hegemonic common sense mark out their social "others." This othering implies racism, ethnicization (with a "race" component), and homogenization. People who are thus mothered also bond together vis à vis these designatory processes in a defensive move, while being penned within a political and cultural boundary. Silence regarding malpractices within these stereotypically constructed and defensively self-constituted communities is therefore not unexpected.

Inscribed and instituted politically from the outside, the communities themselves also suppress internal sources of division and seek to present themselves, at least in their representational endeavours, as seamless realities. Silence, therefore, regarding class, gender, and other power relations, characterizes this voluntary aspect of community-making as well. And as we shall see later, the technology for constructing differences relies on the concept of tradition, which is implicated in both aspects of community formation. This is what characterizes these communities as traditional, in contradistinction to the "modernity" of the "Canadians," the second half of this binary paradigm. This construction of traditionality is then fleshed out with the invention of particular traditions—relevant for different nationalities and cultural groups. Needless to say the notion of a traditional community rests explicitly on patriarchy and on severely gendered social organization and ideology. These are legitimated as an essence of the identity of these communities. This traditional (patriarchal) identity, then, is equally the result of an othering from powerful outside forces and an internalized Orientalism and a gendered class organization.

Keeping these processes of community formation in view disputing its natural and synonymous status as and with civil society—we can begin our critique by invoking our general membership as women of these communities. We need to remember that we are the "others" of white women in the Canadian national imaginary, and this is connected with the fact that we are an integral part of the peoples who were brought as indentured workers or migrated to Canada from former colonies under severe economic conditions created by post-colonial imperialism. Unlike European or white women, we present "Canada" with the problem of inassimilation. We are simultaneously essentialized into homogenized, yet racialized and ethnicized subjects, whose actual differences are drowned in the multicultural discourse of diversity. We are worried, understandably, to speak of "our" brutalities and shortcomings, because of not being even minimally in control of the public and political domains of speech or ideological construction. The pre-existence of a colonial/racist/Orientalist perception and stereotypes of us, embedded in official and everyday structural and cultural practices and meanings, have been powerful sources of distortion and misrepresentation of our subjectivities and politics. This, of course, is not only true of Canada but of elsewhere in the West as well. This sexist-racist common sense, with its pervasive presence in the political economy and dominant culture of Canada, is rooted in a history of colonial conquests, genocides and ongoing projects of profit and rule. This is productive of an ethos of European or white supremacy that provides the political conscious or unconscious of Canada's nation state and political-cultural space. We are simultaneously present and absent in these spaces and in the apparatus of the state. It is this paradox of presence and absence, of difference and sameness (as some sort of members of this Canadian nation), that multiculturalism both constructs and augments. Our political and social identities are contingent upon this. We might say that the reasons both for our presence in Canada and for the official discourse of multiculturalism are connected to our actual absence in and abdication of public space and speech regarding ourselves and our communities' horrendous treatment of women.

The situation is complicated. But how can it be any different, when we come from colonial and imperialist histories and presents and find ourselves in the midst of a white-settler colony struggling to transform itself into a liberal democracy? Canada's participation in imperialism on the coat tails of the United States is not hidden from public view. Inhabiting this terrain, our refugee and immigrant statuses mark us as second-class citizens, if citizens at all. We stand, both men and women, uncertainly at the edge of "Canada," the nation. Comprehended in this political economy, a racialized class organization which is as much about whiteness as blackness, we step back in time. We are recolonized directly—and that isn't just speaking metaphorically. Coming from countries that have seen anti-colonial struggles in one form or another and shaken off direct colonial rule, we put ourselves back into socio-political spaces closely resembling a colony—at least where we are concerned. Here we are marked by a difference which has less to say about us—our histories and cultures—than about a mode of socio-political interpretation within a pre-established symbolic and practical schema of a racialized or ethnicized colonial and slave-owning discourse.

It is at the receiving end of this proliferation of denigrating differences and homogenization that the incoming "others" go through their community formation. Of course, at the same time they are going through a process of class formation as well, which is creating a difference among themselves, as much as between them and "Canadians." But the discourse of community cannot and is not meant to express or accommodate that. In the ideological discourse of "the community" it was made to appear that when people migrated, they did so as communities, not as responses to national and international political economy.

We can say, therefore, that there is nothing natural about communities. In fact they are contested grounds of socio-cultural definitions and political agencies. Contradictory processes of creating "us" and "them" are at work in them, and we have here a situation of mini-hegemonies confronting and conforming to a national ideological hegemony. Form and content of communities reflect this, and we continue to be constructed and excluded by the same overarching hegemony. This becomes evident when we look at the discourse and workings of official multiculturalism, in which where we are from, as nationalities and cultures—Jamaica, Vietnam, or India—matters very little when we are being distinguished from "Canadians," while our specific differences provide the stepping stones for this general difference. We know very quickly that we are not "them" or "Canadians," while our "us" can cross national boundaries, and sometimes it does. Racism, Eurocentrism, or ethnocentrism, which impacts on all non-whites in this way, generates a space for a broader community among us, creating a ground for anti-racism. But this again is not a given or a foregone conclusion, since internalized racism or community boundaries generally help create a closed in sociocultural space and a highly fragmented political agency. So while there is in this mechanism of mass exclusion, called multicultural community, room for the excluded to unite irrespective of their different regional and individual histories, languages, and religions, the unity in actuality has not been more than that of region, religion, and perhaps language. In fact, regional and linguistic communities seem to be in the process of fast alternation on the ground of religion—thus being "hindus" and "muslims" has currently become alarmingly relevant. This deepening of traditionality has not boded well for women among these communities.

So, possibilities for a community of the excluded notwithstanding, we have been docile with regard to the political economy of Canada. We have, by and large, uncritically inhabited the socio-economic zones, grids, or boxes created for us by Manpower and Immigration or Employment and Immigration Canada. We have been legally bonded and bounded. This boundary, invisible though inexorable, is the outer wall of the community—whatever that may be—and it not only keeps others "out," but us "in." From this point of view community is not only an ideological and social category but also a category of the state. This becomes evident if we reflect on the role of this category in the mode of administering the civil society, for example, in electoral politics, in organizing the labour market, in social assistance, or cultural funding.

You might at this point object to this non-cultural way of reading the sociogenetics of the concept of community, which goes against the grain of conventional use of the term. You might refer to the role that our own ethnocultural varieties and differences play in the making of communities. You might want to speak of religions, languages, social customs—the semiotic and moral constructions and regulations that we identify ourselves by. Are we not as communities in these terms, making "us" distinct from others? These would be, or should be, our questions if we were to read "community" as an equivalent for civil society. But as I have pointed out, communities are formed through the pressure of external forces far more than for reasons of cultural expression. There is no reason for the inhabitants of any region to engage in an exercise of collective self-identification unless there is the presence of a dominant group which is ascribing certain definitions and identity markers onto them. This process of complex and contradictory interactions between external and internal forces, which I have already spoken to, makes it evident that "community" is a very specific way of politicizing and organizing cultural particularities of social groups. In this it is no different from the use of the concept of caste or religion with which the colonial powers created administrative and ruling regimes in the colonies.

Questioning the status of the community as a natural, social formation does not automatically imply a dismissal of points of commonality among peoples of different regions, cultural habits, nationalities, and histories, or, for that matter, among religious groups from those regions. It is true that such people often tend to seek each other out, to speak the same language, eat the same food, or display fashions. Very often in the earlier part of their existence in Canada it is a survival necessity for learning the ropes in the new country, getting employment or business contacts, and so on. But if the Canadian society into which they come were non-threatening and non-exclusive, if racism were not a daily reality, this stage of cultural bonding would be short and more fluid than it is at present. In that case cultural practices would not harden into "identities" or ethnic typologies, but would be temporary stages of social becoming, both at individual and collective levels. Such elective affinities or cultural associations cannot be called communities, which imply organization and institutionalization—a mechanism for a rigid cultural reproduction. Voluntary cultural associations are both temporary and much less organized, and often a very small part of the existence of people. This is evident if we observe the European or white immigrants who may live in ethnic networks, for example the Italians or Ukrainians, but who did not ossify into permanent communities with fixed and branded identities.

Things are different with us, that is, non-white immigrants—even if we are conversant in English or French, which people from South Asia, Africa, and the Caribbean generally are. With them the process is reversed, since they come as individual migrants and slowly harden into the institutional form of the community. The reason for this, I am afraid, is not what is inside of them but rather in their skin. Their skin is written upon with colonial discourse—which is Orientalist and racist. Thus memories, experiences, customs, languages, and religions of such peoples become interpreted into reificatory and often negative cultural types or identities. The political process of minoritization accompanies this interpretive exercise, and together they lead to the formation of communities. When we speak of "diversity" it is this set of reified and politicized differences that we are invoking, and they provide the basis for ethnocultural identity and politics of representation.

That communities are not simple self-projections of cultural groups but, rather, inherently political formations, is something we need to keep in mind. This is particularly important in the last two decades, when a discourse of community and cultural diversity has been engraved into the Canadian body politic. This is not just at the level of society at large, but in the official formulation and implementation of multiculturalism. Though it may strike one as curious that any "ism" can be made out of culture (we don't, after all, talk of "culturalism" as state policy), we do live in an era when political and ideological stances are created and institutionalized out of features of everyday life or cultures (especially of non-white people). Entire administrative apparatuses are alerted to cultural characteristics of non-white/non-European "others," extending from law and policing to mental health and labour. Such cultural "isms" and their practicalization in the context of ruling and administration cannot but need and create essentialist characteristics in the interests of stability and predictability. If the groups were not to be seen as homogeneous in terms of possessing these essential traits, no administration could be put in place. Difference and diversity would not then be effective categories for deployment in ruling but indeed contrary to it.

We might ask at this point a question or two regarding the content of these putative differences and diversities. Is this content entirely invented? Are they simply baseless, imagined essentialities? The answer to this question points us toward the epistemology implied in the creation of all ideological categories, as elaborated by Marx, and best discussed in *The Gerinan Ideology*. It is not that ideology invents particular sociocultural features, found among many, but rather it centres some and erases others which might contradict the centrality of the selected ones. These selected features do not exist as discrete or floating pieces but rather assume a categorical status by an extraneous connection which is established among them, often in a causal or positive mode. In other words, a discursive mode is established which creates falsehood, we might say, by a particular arrangement of existing characteristics. It is the whole discursive organization that is distortive or untrue, not particular features as such, and it is in their establishment as "essential" that the harm is most palpable. This ideological activity of consciousness has been called power/knowledge when particularly annexed to the project of ruling. Critique of colonial discourse, now so frequently practised, provides us with more than ample examples of this. It is there we see that paradigms, such as that of civilization and savagery or tradition and modernity, offer the discursive terrain or interpretive schema for understanding or representing cultural traits of colonized or enslaved peoples. It is from this source that the content of difference and diversity of official multiculturalism evolves. This reduces non-Europeans the world over into pre-modern, traditional, or even downright savage peoples, while equating Europeans with modernity, progress, and civilization. The social ethos and cultural identities of the "others" of Europe are presumed to be religious, their conduct ritualistic, and their temperament emotional and unruly. They are at once civilizationally ancient (and therefore in decay) and primitive (therefore undeveloped). These are the ideological underpinnings of the not so benign discourse of multicultural diversity. This is difference and representation as constructed through historical and social relations of power, and it leads to the making of a selective constellation of cultural attributes and ideological packages which contour and control the multicultural community.

This, then, is the ascriptive or normative process through which multicultural communities come to life and into political play in relation to state repression and conditional or limited rewards. Furthermore, we have a situation here of double reification, which combines communitization from above (state and dominant ideology or hegemonic common sense) and from below (from the subject populations themselves). These reified collectivities of difference create a situation of unofficial apartheid, a general culture of apartheid in the overall socio-cultural terrain of the country. Essentialized cultural identities already in place are rigidly maintained, while the general culture of apartheid proliferates fragmented and enclosed cultural territories which are both officially and voluntarily maintained. Political participation of non-white immigrants or their political subjectivities or agencies are increasingly conceived and conducted on these bases. The concept of community and its organization, then, provide the articulating bases between people and the state.[2]

## III

These complexities of community formation provide us the problematic within which patriarchal violence, in its various manifestations, has to be grounded. We must remind ourselves here of the pervasive presence of patriarchy and specific forms of gender organization in all societies of our present day world and of their long historical presence. Both general social organization and specific forms of ruling, of creating hegemonies, require this gendering and patriarchy as ideological and moral regulation. Whether this patriarchy is intrinsic and biologically based or contingent need not detain us here. What is important is that they have been historically in place for a very long time. The incoming peoples about whom we have been speaking come from spaces as deeply patriarchal and gender organized as the social space they enter into in Canada. They do not learn patriarchal violence after coming here. They also come from a social organization and politics of class, from national hegemonic systems, all of which are organized by gender and patriarchy. Class and gender, seemingly two distinct systems of oppression, are only so in theory—in practice they constitute and mediate each other in a network of overall social relations of power. White or not, immigrants and "Canadians" all live in this gendered and classed social reality. So violence against women, latent or blatant, is not surprising among communities which have, like all other social groups, all the social conditions for this and other patriarchal forms of violence such as homophobia. Misogyny, an extreme form of patriarchy, cannot be discussed here in detail—but it should suffice to point out that the homosexual male has long been feminized and the lesbian seen as a masculinist, female aberration. The hatred for both contains, on the one hand, a displaced hatred for women and, on the other, an anger or even hatred for those who invert the patriarchal social norm of heterosexuality. Unlike the artificial divide instituted between the West and the rest, there is in fact a deep commonality between them in matters pertaining to these hegemonic norms and regarding practices and ideologies of property and class. What, then, is the specificity of violence against women within the confines of the community?

The answer to this question refers us back to the point I made about recolonization, which occurs when people of former colonies return to direct white rule by coming to the West. Class and gender organization and normative behaviour undergo a peculiar twist in this situation. On the one hand the process of internalization of colonial values, such as of racism, is intensified and projected through self-hatred and anti-Black racism; on the other hand, this submission gesture is refuted or compensated by gestures of resistance. They revive and develop further a certain kind of nationalism, with some features in common with the nationalism of formerly colonized countries. This can happen very easily as these non-white, non-European communities function like mini-cultural nationalities in this recolonizing context. They seize upon the mainstream's and the state's tendencies and rules to differentiate them, and adopt these cultural differences. They proclaim these differences to be substantive and inherent, and proclaim their cultural autonomy in the face of an ethics of assimilationism while seeking to become political agents within the same framework of ideologies and institutions. Their resistance, what there is of it, is mostly cultural, and typically minority, politics, which cannot and does not aspire to state formation, unlike anti-colonial nationalisms.

In this surrender-submission dialectic they rely mainly on colonial discourse, especially as they are from "the East." The main idea that they carry over with themselves and deepen on the Western soil is their self-characterization as "traditional." From this stance they engage in self-reification as a collective group and develop logically their self-projection as religious, anti- and pre-modern peoples. They evoke mythical pasts or histories to support their current ideological stances and create a politics internal to their definition of community that relies extensively on patriarchal moral regulations. This invention of tradition legitimizes and institutionalizes them as clients of the state, while the essentialist logic of community formation homogenizes all into one, and a few can represent the rest to the state and the world at large.

The community, as we can see, is a very modern formation, as is cultural nationalism. Its appeal to tradition, i.e. religion and antiquity, are its passwords into some limited space in the realms of power. To speak authoritatively in a representational capacity it is therefore imperative to speak in moral terms. This is most effectively done through a religious discourse and related practices of moral regulation. It requires in particular an absolute subscription to feudal or semi-feudal patriarchies, as well as the erasure of class, as this leads to social conflicts. All this provides a situation of surplus repression for women, sexual "others," as well as for people of lower-class standing—all in the way of creating communities. Hierarchy and patriarchy as natural or divinely ordained conduct allows for a peculiar situation where class and gender power are both vindicated and occluded at once. Domination of women, of sexual "others," and subordination of children take on here the character of duties that each male head of the family and the male leaders of the community, who may also be religious heads, must perform. Patriarchal social violence is thus daily and spiritually normalized in these walled towns of communities or religious and cultural ghettoes.

What is put forward by the communities as assertion of difference, as resistance, often turns out to be colonial discourse with reversed valuations. In this context, tradition is considered in a highly positive light, while modernity, rationalism, and social criticism are negatively valorized. Religious fundamentalism is considered a particularly authentic sign of our Easternness. This is mini-cultural nationalism writ small, within a larger national imaginary, putting up its barricades and political signs with a neo-colonial inflection. This situation is not new. In the context of development of one strand of nationalism in India, among the hindu petty bourgeoisie, we have already seen this situation on a much larger scale. Many scholars and critics, feminists and others, have remarked on the peculiar importance of the sign of woman, as mother in particular, and of the feminization of the land or country as mother-goddess. These ideological manoeuvres have little to do with women, except to indicate their property or service role to the nation. The same could be said of the use of women and familial regulations pertaining to the ideological positioning of the community.

## IV

The vested interests of upwardly mobile males, with religious patriarchal power in their hands, either in these types of communities or in nationalist projects, makes it difficult to question the imputed homogeneity or unity of the community. "Divisive" issues of gender and class, or for that matter of internalized colonial discourse or racism, cannot therefore be broached without enormous resistance and silencing from within. In formulating the interest of women and the causes of their oppression, no matter how aware of and informed with other social relations of power, we thus need to step back from the ideological and political schema of the community. Furthermore, we need to speak about patriarchy in inter- and intra- class terms, even at the risk of being misunderstood as separatist feminists, because it involves being "disloyal" to our so-called civilizations or national cultures.

If we do take this "disloyal" stance, which is the only real critical stance we can take, we can see that a cognisance of patriarchy and gender is also a cognisance of class and property relations in general. It is this that patriarchal or male perception cannot see or tolerate. Their resistance to colonial or national domination has never been questioning of either property or patriarchy. This is where their male and petty bourgeois or bourgeois class character is fully visible. This does not mean that mini-cultural nationalities or political collectives do not engage in class politics, but they do so, fully though implicitly, with the purpose of upward mobility rather than in the interest of social and economic equality. They are part of the phenomenon of class formation and display the same characteristics as did the bourgeoisie in their earliest years of state formation, when they spoke in the name of all. It is then that they created theories of democracy and liberalism, which they were unable to actualize due to their class interests. In this commitment to an ethics of possession and politics of property, where property includes labour power and physical or reproductive capacities, the "others" of metropolitan capitalist democracies are in no way different from the mainstream, though their operational modalities may be highly situation specific.

In this erasure of class and gender, in protecting property and its proprieties, the "traditional" communities and the "modern" Canadian state show a remarkable similarity and practical convergence. Through the state's need to create an apparatus of political interpellation of "others," official multiculturalism came into being. This could then create political agencies through the various modalities of development of multiculturalism, whose ideology is refracted in the language and practices of diversity and implementation of institutional projects. Neither class nor gender, which are differences created through social relations of power, nor "race," another of these excruciating constructs of power, could be raised as issues within this discourse of diversity and redressed. In fact, what counted as difference were so-called cultural differences, and the project was aimed at preaching "tolerance' to the majority while leaving relations of power unchallenged either among them or among the objects of their tolerance. An intensification of class, gender, and patriarchy was encouraged through multicultural identifications, since the "others" were deemed "traditional" (i.e., patriarchal, hierarchical, and religious) and thus "natural" practitioners of these inequalities. Criticisms of abuse of women in the community, even when brought into the court, fell prey to "cultural" or "religious" legal arguments.

This continues to be the case. Definitional boundaries that are vital for legal and social jurisdiction of the Canadian state, which is as thoroughly "traditional" in these matters as the immigrants, rest on these essentialization gestures. It suits the Canadian state just as much as it suits the elite in the communities to leave intact these traditions and rituals of power. That the community is a political-ideological construct, particular to history and a politics, and therefore ignores the real diversities among people migrating from "other" countries, can have no place in this scheme of things. Progressive and critical people among these immigrants are thus dubbed atypical, Westernized, and inauthentic to their culture, both by the leading conservative elements among them and by their progenitor protector, the Canadian state. Violence against women or sexual "others," aggressive and hateful attitudes towards the religion of others, especially towards islam, become the bedrock of normal community identity. Oppression of women and feudal (rather than bourgeois) patriarchy thus become "our" social being, and such behaviour earns or maintains a colonial or racist contempt for us, while being treated permissively by the state. This deprives women of legal and political recourse and social assistance. On the other hand, the same type of characterization also deprives muslim males in Canada, particularly from Arab countries, of legal justice, since the community as a whole is tarred with the brush of fanaticism.

Communities, or the elite of these mini-nationalities, of course play their card of cultural difference according to dictates. They too, in spite of their anti-liberal stance, separate culture from all other social moments, such as that of economy. Equating "culture" with religion, and making a particularly elite brand of that religion the fountainhead of all ethical and customary values, they too assert the master script and make no fundamental socio-economic demands. Through the mask of pre-modernity and anti-materialism they participate most effectively in a capitalist state of a highly modern nature. In return for proclaiming a primordial traditionality they are left alone as rulers of their own communities, to rule over women, sexual "others," the economically dispossessed, and children. The social space of countries they migrate from or flee as refugees becomes a state of mind rather than a place in history.

The political and cultural conflicts raging in South Asia, Egypt, Algeria or Latin America, for example, where secularism and religious fundamentalism are in struggle, are altogether erased. A totalizing myth of tradition engrosses entire land masses, in fact two-thirds of the world, which foundationally rests on patriarchy. This is the imputed and self-proclaimed organic unity or wholeness of communities!

When we look at the status of women in the communities, we find it to be one of "property," of belonging to individual male heads of families as well as to the institutions called the family and the community. The morality of a collective organic nature seems to apply to them, whereas males are encouraged to individualism and entrepreneurialism in their very definition of masculinity. This control over women as a community's property, the object of patriarchal command, is not only traditional or god-given, but this sacred authority is actualized and reinforced by the secular construction and sanction of the Canadian state. The legal category of "the head of the family," with all the prerogatives and responsibilities pertaining to it, is entirely a category of state-delegated power to men. It is a category that extends from "immigrants" to "Canadians," and offers men who hold this position practically a life-and-death power over women and children. This has been discussed especially with regard to "sponsored immigrants," generally wives, who are held at the mercy of their husbands since they have no legal rights in Canada independent of their relationship with their husbands. The threat of deportation that hangs over their head—the loss of livelihood, displacement, separation from children, and social disgrace that might result from a breakdown of sponsorship—is a violent and volatile one. This is what makes innumerable women stay with their husbands in dangerous and humiliating situations, or to return to their so-called homes. Any challenge to the cultural identity of being "traditional," which means questioning religious and patriarchal injunctions, cannot be very effectively mounted from such a vulnerable socio-economic location. If this law were to have been amended, and wives of immigrating husbands could be seen as independent political and legal adults, not as their dependants, we might have seen something quite different from "traditional" behaviour. It is then that we would have known whether muslim women veil themselves because they want to or because they are made to under conditions of subtle and overt duress. As it is we have no way of knowing their real will, since they are subject to what is called "multiple" but also converging patriarchies of the community male elite and the Canadian state. Facile anti-racism or cultural nationalism simply offers a window-dressing of legitimation.

To return to a theme introduced earlier, we might say that women's status as a "sign" or even a symbol for "our" cultural autonomy amounts to no more than being handmaidens of god, priest, and husband. This subordination or domination is mediated and regulated through the patriarchal family code and anchored to the moral regulations of honour and shame. Any deviance from the domestic patriarchy of family (extended into wider kinship networks), from strict heterosexist codes, is a pathway to shame and punishment. This may range from censure to physical violence to social ostracism by the community. Women, and involved men, who help to bring about sexual disgrace may even be killed. The cases of killings of "deviant" women in Vancouver—for example, a woman who left her community by developing an emotional and sexual attachment outside of it—may be extreme but not out of line with this moral regulation. The irony, therefore, of a situation where the most powerless member of the community is exalted to the status of goddess or an embodiment of honour of the community, should not be lost on anyone. In fact, if she were not powerless, she could not have been pushed into the mould of a symbol or disembodied into a metaphor. This metaphoric or symbolic exaltation is simultaneously an objectification of women and of "our" difference from "the West." Disembodiment and objectification are the foundation of violence against women, which cannot happen without a material or social base of domination. It is not an accident that the honour of this symbolic investiture is not conferred upon men and that women have no choice about being chosen as symbolic or significatory objects.

The dehumanization involved in converting a person, an embodied socio-historical being, into a sign or symbol implies much more than an epistemological violence. It is based on the same principles that enabled a physical, social, and symbolic violence to be visited upon Jews in pogroms and the holocaust, on various indigenous peoples in colonial genocides, and on Africans in slavery. Thus patriarchy, anti-Semitism, or racism, with or without fusing into each other, provide an overall social organization of relations of domination which extends from everyday-life repressions to extermination. The symbol is a formalization of actual, violent, social relations that organize the society as a whole. It is a way of encoding, naming, and perpetuating them. This reality is evident in widow immolations in India, stoning of adulterous women in Pakistan, or female genital mutilation among some groups in Africa, to give a few examples. Discursivities entailed in these symbolic expressions mediate and stabilize violent social relations through various forms of textualization. They make room for elite males to be exonerated from responsibility as perpetrators of such social violence.

The significational figurations of women have been used as objects of hegemony by colonizers, nationalist elites, and their analogues in Canada—the communities of non-white immigrants and by the state. Women have become objects for creating history but are given no role of their own to play in the making of it, except as victims of wars. The organization of societies in terms of gender has identified women with the private sphere, except at a symbolic level. This means an identification with "home," domesticity, and the family, which come into being through their activities and end up by being their enclosures.

The most prominent of the women signs in the contexts of nations and communities is that of the mother, the ultimate incarnation of the "good woman." The "goodness" of women in this extreme patriarchal incarnation, but in others as well, is manifested in a nurturing and sacrificing conduct at the service of the patriarchal family and equally patriarchal causes of larger collectivities, such as the nation or the community. Fear of disruption of this normative design comes chiefly from a fear of women's sexuality, which is, therefore, demonized and punished. The somewhat lesser disruptive source is the life of reason, which would put women in public spaces. Any move made by women in these directions is therefore considered to be "Western," "white," or "colonial," that is, treasonable to the greater "national" or community causes. But it is also "abnormal," as it would upset the sign of difference with which "our" co-opted male elite make political deals in multicultural terms or create attempts at cultural national resistance. It is important to note that both female sexuality and interest in rationality or education become threatening because they confer on women active roles which transgress the normative public-private divide. Containment and control of women through the normative mechanism of femininity underpin both proscriptions. In situations where such fully religious fundamentalist conduct cannot be enjoined, the proscriptive moral regulations still hold in a somewhat compromised or "modernized" manner. But it is not an exaggeration to say that the more women belonging to the community could be forced into its organizing religio-patriarchal norms and forms, the more the community could proclaim its definitively authentic status. Straying from these laid-down paths would call for censures of betrayal of a nature similar to those extended towards white women by white supremacist groups for betraying the empire, the "race," or the nation through miscegenation.

When we examine issues of patriarchal violence against women, it becomes apparent that the traditional community's social organization does not serve the greater good of the collectivity. Neither women nor less privileged men have their interests represented in it. The real benefit that it confers on males of all classes is great power over women and children, even men who are excluded or marginalized by the host society. This is not unlike national governments that cannot face up to international financial powers but rule as dictators within national boundaries. In fact, the international or the multicultural national state's approval of them is dependent upon how well they can control these internal forces and their potential for opposition.

By a perverted extension of this logic the men of these communities are excused, even by anti-racist or otherwise feminist activists, for their generally sexist or even violent misconduct against women. Racism and class discrimination are held responsible for the rage that men vent on women, children, or homosexual members of their communities. This tolerance can extend to severe abuse or even murder. Locking up women without their clothes, severe beating, mutilating or burning them with cigarette stubs are some of the violences we have heard of. It is extraordinary how infrequently it is noted, if at all, that women too are subjects of colonialism and racism, and these oppressions are intensified by sexism or gross forms of patriarchy. It is a known fact that non-white women mostly work at worse paying and more menial jobs than their husbands, keep a double day of work inside and outside the home, and suffer from particularly humiliating forms of sexual harassment. In spite of all this, a woman does not often take out her frustration on her husband and children, as a man does. And certainly her mistreatment of them is never explained in the same terms, nor extenuated by the community and others for the same reasons, with which even the Canadian justice system credits abusive men. Whereas compromised and reduced masculinity of such men is noted sympathetically by scholars of colonialism and slavery, the compromised humanity of women, their punishment through hyper-femininity, rarely draws equal attention. If anything, a woman who wants to go beyond such roles and ascriptions, who is critical of patriarchy within the community, is often blamed for aiding and abetting in the colonial project of emasculation. Meanwhile, police and other forms of state and daily racist, social violence are directed against non-white women. The police murder of the sons of black women (and men) is as much a violence against their mothers (and fathers) as is the shooting of Sophia Cook or the strip search of Audrey Smith.[3]

## V

I have outlined so far, and quite extensively, some salient aspects of the social problematic and certain specificities regarding violence against women in the community. Obviously a lot more remains to be said. But this is an attempt to break the silence I referred to at the beginning of my letter. I have tried to point towards a politics that, I hope, addresses the multiple social relations of power which organize our society. I have tried to show that a simplistic binary politics of self and other, of essentialist identities pitted against each other in a politics of cultural nationalism, is not a viable option for women. This reflection of cultural nationalism, of so-called multicultural community politics, does not erase racism or colonial oppression. In fact, the real struggle against the socially hegemonic forces and their expression in the Canadian state requires the perspective that I have offered. We cannot allow ourselves to be blackmailed in the name of cultural authenticity, identity, and community, any more than we can be duped by the mythologies of social democracy proffered by a racist and imperialist bourgeois state.

What awaits us is the political task of forging a real anti-racist feminism informed by a class analysis, with a critique of imperialism exposing the hoax of globalization. This politics cannot be brought to life if we stop only at a critique of patriarchal and gendered social organization. Such a critique, without an awareness and theorization of women as historical and social agents, would fall into the trap of showing women as victims of men and society. We must remember, then, that because women are also subjects of colonialism, racism, and class organization, because they also inhabit the same social relations as men, they too are part of the dynamics of resistance and domination. They have the same political needs, rights, and potentials as men—to be full citizens or members of nation states and to become agents in revolutionary politics.

It will not serve women to look for enclosed and co-opted identities in the name of family, god, nation, or the multicultural state—to live for their approbation. Our politics will have to be indifferent to special pleadings of arguments of spurious difference but concentrate instead on the workings of the construction of difference through social relations of power, on the instruments of ruling. Developing a critical perception of sexist-racist social and cultural common sense and of the apparatus of the state, questioning laws that position "immigrants" in vulnerable roles within the political economy, questioning "multiculturalism" which co-opts and distorts popular political agency—these are our immediate tasks. Obviously they are not easy tasks, nor are results to be achieved instantly. Nor can they be carried on within the locked doors of community or identity politics. We, non-white women, women of "communities," must claim various political movements in Canada as our own. This means the women's movement and movements of resistance against state and class power, against pervasive and insidious racism and homophobia. Though it may sound like a tall order, it is possible to enter our politics through the door of particular "women's issues," for example, and come into the arena of a general political resistance. It is only in doing this that one can shape one's politics in ways that are nuanced by other struggles, where what comes out is the convergence of various politics against oppression, and not their separate directions. I don't think we need to fear a loss of specificity, of our selves, in a vast sea of abstractions or generalities, controlled by others. If we can frame our critique and create organizations that challenge patriarchy, heterosexism, class, and "race" with even a semblance of integrity, we will create the bases for an embodied, social revolution. Needless to say, in this process we will have to redefine our friends and enemies, our notions of insiders and outsiders, and to whom, when, how, and about what we can talk. This open letter about our silence is only a very small experiment at that talk.

With love and solidarity,
Himani

## Notes

[1]I am aware that calling people "non-white" is a debatable practice. I would not do so if I were to use it as a term denoting identity—namely, as a signification for *who we are.* I use this term as a political signifier, not an ontological one, to point out the hegemonic cause of our woes, namely racism. In this matter where we come from, our national cultures, are less significant than the fact that whoever is not "white" will fall within the purview of racialization and discrimination. For this purpose I prefer to use the expression "non-white," since the conventional terms "women of colour," "immigrants," etc. do not always do the job at hand.
[2]Here we might, following Althusser, speak of being interpellated by the ideological apparatuses of the state, the state being understood as both an institution and

a general political body. The political subjectivities and agencies of communities constructed through these processes are both conditional and subcontracted to current hegemonies.

[3] See notes 20 and 21 in Chapter 2, "Geography Lessons" in my book, *The Dark Side of the Nation: Essays on Multiculturalism and Gender.*

## References

Bannerji, Himani. *The Dark Side of the Nation: Essays on Multiculturalism and Gender*. Toronto: Canadian Scholars' Press, 2000.

# Violence Against Refugee Women

## Gender Oppression, Canadian Policy, and The International Struggle For Human Rights

Helene Moussa

Since the 1985 United Nations Women's Decade Conference in Nairobi, international women's groups, particularly those from the South, have been organizing women at the grassroots and national levels to raise public consciousness on the issue of gender oppression, and lobbying governments to recognize violence against women as both a form of gender oppression and a human rights issue. In 1990, when the United Nations announced that its World Conference on Human Rights would be held in Vienna in June 1993,women's organizations were quick to note that women's issues were not even named on the agenda. By the time of the conference, women's organizations had a petition with half a million names from 124 countries demanding that gender violence be recognized as a violation of human rights. Even though the 150 governments represented at the conference had been lobbied at home, it was not until the conference took place that the international women's organizations succeeded in winning their demand that the government delegates address women's rights at every level of their debates. In addition, women, including refugee women, testified at the Global Tribunal on Violations of Human Rights, held in conjunction with the conference. Based on their testimonies, the following types of violence and violations of human rights that women around the world suffer were identified: persecution for political participation; violation of social and economic rights; sexual violence committed against women in war-torn countries; violence against women in the family; and violation of women's bodily integrity (Reilly 2-3)

Another accomplishment of the conference, which was a direct result of the intensive feminist networking and lobbying between 1985 and 1993, was the adoption of principles and actions to eradicate gender oppression. Paragraph 19 of the final Vienna Declaration and Program of Action affirmed that,

> The human rights of women and the girl-child are an inalienable, integral and indivisible part of human rights...Gender-based violence and all forms of sexual harassment and exploitation, including those resulting from cultural prejudice and international trafficking, are incompatible with the dignity and worth of the human person, and must be eliminated. (cited in Bauer 73).

While it is not within the United Nations' mandate to enforce international conventions, it is within its purview to promote and encourage the application of these decisions. International instruments also play the important role of setting standards. One of the strengths of the Vienna Declaration is that it can be "translated" to the reality of refugee women and children who, in effect, do not have rights as citizens but in the context of the Declaration do have rights as "human persons."

Despite the numerous criticisms about the organization of the 4th World Conference on Women in Beijing (1995) and the parallel NGO Forum in Huairou, the more than 25,000 women who gathered at the Forum once again demonstrated women's ability to overcome obstacles that prevent their full participation in decisions directly affecting their lives. The women came organized and prepared with their agendas for action. They were determined to be heard. Particularly striking was the participation of refugee women and women living in conflict areas in Africa, Asia, Central America, Europe, and the Middle East. Peace-making and peace-building were the predominant themes of their workshops. They elaborated on the strategies they were implementing that would lead the conflicting/warring parties in their countries to negotiate for peace and that would create a democratic and a peaceful culture inclusive of women after formal agreements were signed.

International NGO networks and their allies in the UN system also succeeded in having the following demands included in the Beijing Declaration and Platform of Action: that governments address the root causes of forced displacement; the redress of economic marginalization of refugee women; inclusion of refugee women in decision-making that affects them; greater access to education and training for refugee women, including training and education about their human rights; the application of a gender perspective to legal instruments and practices that affect refugee women; the prevention and elimination of violence against women and the recognition of refugee women's human rights; and the adequate gender-sensitive training for the judiciary, police, border guards, and refugee camp personnel.

Women's lobbying efforts to have gender oppression recognized have made some governments respond. In March 1993, three months before the Vienna Conference, the Canadian Immigration and Refugee Board issued "Guidelines on Women Refugee Claimants Fearing Gender-Related Persecution." This recognition that women can experience persecution primarily because they are women is a landmark decision in Canadian and International legal jurisprudence. In May 1995, the United States Naturalization and Immigration Service issued guidelines entitled "Consideration for Officers Adjudicating Asylum Claims for Women" and in 1996, the Australian government indicated that they were studying comparative practices domestically and internationally with the objective of establishing gender guidelines for decision-makers in the asylum process.

These policies are important because they signal that governments are beginning to acknowledge the role violence and gender oppression play in the lives of refugee women. These acts of violence can take different forms: economic exploitation, including the feminization of poverty and the commoditization of women in the media; sexual violence, including sexual assault, wife assault and psychological abuse, genital mutilation and sexual slavery/trafficking; dowry death; and the abortion of female fetuses after sex-determination tests. To understand how this violence is perpetrated against refugee women and how it restricts their freedom and mobility, security and well-being, one must understand how gender relations inform the social, economic, cultural, and political realities in the countries of origin and in the countries where they seek asylum.

In this article, I attempt to develop this understanding by looking at the systems that contribute to the gender-related violence and oppression perpetrated against refugee women. I provide an overview of the context in which refugee women experience sexual violence and oppression in their countries of origin—experiences which may cause them to flee. Their vulnerability during flight and in asylum countries is briefly touched on, while an extensive discussion of international and Canadian refugee policy reveals how such policies can both hinder and protect refugee women's interests in their struggle to find safety in a receiving country. Finally, using Canada as the example country, I provide an overview of the options available to refugee women who face violence in the home and how racism and gender barriers hinder their attempts to find refuge inside their receiving country.

Refugee women are, of course, a diverse group of women. They come from different racial, ethnic and class backgrounds, represent a wide range of ages, have varying levels of education, and come from different political orientations.[1] While recognizing that the experience of refugee women is not homogeneous, in this article I will nonetheless focus on the similarities and patterns in their experience to underscore how violence and gender oppression affect all refugee women regardless of their background. Patriarchal culture not only legitimates and perpetuates the domination of women but also tolerates violence against women as a justification of their "place" in gender relations. As Roxana Carrillo states, "Women experience violence as a form of control that limits their ability to pursue options in almost every area of life from the home to the schools, workplaces, and most public spaces. Violence is used to control women's labour in both productive and reproductive capacities" (27).

The underlying assumption in this article is that sexual, racial, and economic oppression are inextricably interrelated. A gender, race, and class analysis is therefore central to a sustained analysis of the refugee experience. Critical theorist Iris Young argues that oppression consists of systemic institutional processes that require people to follow the rules of others and prevent them from participating in society to their fullest capacity (38). Woven into my analysis of the experience of refugee women are the "five faces of oppression" identified by Young—exploitation, marginalization, powerlessness, cultural imperialism, and violence (39-65).

In addition to the analysis of literature and statistics, I have drawn on several other resources to develop this study. I have gathered material and knowledge from my participation in international committees and networks and from working in national and community boards and committees in Canada whose purpose is to influence refugee policy and service in first asylum countries and in Canada. Qualitative material has come from interviews and conversations I have had with refugee women from a wide range of countries and, in particular, from Ethiopia and Eritrea. These interviews were conducted over a number of years (1988 to 1994) and complement the in-depth research I have conducted with and about refugee women to document their experience (Moussa 1993, 1995).

## The Global Refugee Situation

Today about 80 to 90 per cent of the world's refugees are women and their dependents and 50 per cent of these are children (Forbes Martin 1). The numbers of refugees since the Second World War have increased dramatically. For example, immediately following the Second World War the number of refugees in the world was estimated at 2 million, and they were predominantly located in Europe. By 1995, the estimated number of refugees under the protection of the United Nations High Commission for Refugees (UNHCR) was estimated at 27.5 million (UNHCR 1995a: 19). These figures do not include the 2.4 million Palestinians refugees who are under the care of the United Nations Relief Works Agency for Palestinian Refugees (Bannenbring 6).[2] If the total refugee number approximates 29.5 million people, then there about 22 million to 25 million refugee women and their dependents in the world today.

Where do these refugees go? Over 80 per cent of the world's refugees registered by United Nations agencies are in the Third World.[3] In 1992 African countries alone hosted 5.7 million refugees (U.S. Committee for Refugees). Twenty-seven of the 36 poorest countries of the world (that is, those countries with less than $400 per capita GNP both "produce" and "receive" refugees (Stein 49). [Appendix 1 provides a statistical overview of the numbers of refugees resettled in Canada between 1986 and 1993. Appendix 4 indicates the number of refugee claimants accepted (from the 1989 Backlog) between 1986 and 1993. The number of refugees resettled in Canada is a fraction of the global refugee population.]

What has generated this enormous movement of displaced women, children and men? Ruth Sivard's 1987 study on world militarism documented that, since the Second World War, 119 of the 120 wars have been waged in the Third World. Many of these wars occurred in the process of decolonization and the establishment of neo-colonial policies. Between 1960 and 1986 there were 144 successful coups d'état and 50 per cent of all Third World governments were controlled by the military (Sivard 1987). In 1990, 64 Third World countries were under military control, and 28 of the 37 armed conflicts were in the Third World (Sivard 1991). Amnesty International's 1993 Annual Report revealed that 161 countries (out of 181 member nations of the United Nations) exercised "gruesome" methods to control dissent and to humiliate and force people to sign false confessions (Amnesty International 1993). The lack of democracy and the flagrant violation of human rights by many Third World governments are major causes for the flow of refugees. In 1994 alone, four million people fled their countries because of armed conflict and human rights violations.

By 1995, the total number of wars had reached 130 (Kane) and with the collapse of the Soviet Union, these wars were no longer restricted to the Third World. The most dramatic exclusion and expulsion of people in the mid-1990s took place in the Caucuses region, the former Yugoslavia, and Rwanda. Violence and persecution motivated by ethnic, racial, and religious differences is destructive of the social fabric and economic structures of entire nation states. The destruction of community and resulting human rights violations of human dignity remain the most dramatic causes for forced displacement.

While the human rights record of refugee-producing countries is inextricably related to global militarization, the developed countries are complicit in this escalating trend of violence. For example, Sivard documents that in 1990 developed countries provided $56 billion (U.S.) in economic aid to developing countries and exported $35 billion (U.S.) in arms. Furthermore developed countries spend as much on military power in one year as the poorest two billion people earn in total income (Sivard 1993). Between 1984 and 1990, 56 per cent of arms sent to the Third World went to countries with highly repressive governments (Sivard 1991). Regehr's study, *Arms Canada*, documents that 60 per cent of the countries purchasing Canada's military commodities have been reported by Amnesty International and the United Nations Commission on Human Rights as regular violators of human rights. While Canadian arms sales to the U.S. and Europe declined in 1992, Third World sales "leaped ahead" irrespective of human rights abuses in those countries receiving arms (Regehr).

Economic inequalities between the North and the South is another causal factor of forced displacement of people. These inequalities have not only placed constraints on the development of Third World countries but have also aggravated the "tensions that are inherent to major economic and political transformations" (Zolberg 158). Structural adjustment policies introduced by the World Bank and the International Monetary Fund (IMF) since the 1970s have further aggravated the processes of democratization and the gap between the rich and poor within Third World countries and on a global scale. Today, many Third World governments face a situation whereby half of their export earnings must go to pay the servicing of debt (the interest and fees) while the principal, the original amount borrowed, remains untouched. Thus governments borrow more money to pay debt while trying to implement the conditions imposed by lenders. Typically the IMF requires the imposition of structural adjustment policies that include devaluation of national currency (thus making imports more expensive), reduction of public sector spending, stimulus to exports and easing restriction on foreign investment. These policies may lead to displacement of people for political reasons. As governments are forced to implement unpopular policies to meet conditions imposed by the World Bank and the IMF, they often implement more repressive measures against their dissenting population. Spending on the police and military forces is justified as a way of maintaining public order in the face of popular opposition to government policies.

The end of the Cold War brought the announcement of the triumph of the "universalized" global market economy. Perhaps the most disturbing aspect of this global system is that the formidable power and mobility of global corporations is (directly or indirectly) undercutting the effectiveness of national governments to carry out essential policies on behalf of the people. Leaders of nation states are losing substantial control of their own territory. They conform to the demands of the corporations who in the new world economy have unrestricted ability to cross national boundaries.

According to the International Labour Office (ILO) the poor and most vulnerable groups (usually women, children and the elderly) bear the heaviest debt burden (Fromont). Widespread unemployment and marginalization have been a significant cause of social and civil strife in many countries. The risk of war is most likely to occur in countries experiencing difficult financial circumstances: for example, 24 out of 27 countries involved in war in the past ten years are heavily indebted. The total indebtedness of Third World countries rose from $250 billion (U.S.) in 1970 to $1,900 billion (U.S.) in 1995 (George).

The refugee situation today is no longer ad hoc or temporary. It is a continuous phenomenon, and for many refugees a permanent life situation. In the post-Cold War era, the growing number of refugees and internally displaced peoples is no longer caused by ideological conflict between the Capitalist West and Communist East. Rather, it is caused primarily by armed conflict and militarization of governments, as well as economic and political instability often created by western intervention.[4] Refugee women and men with whom I have had personal conversations, interviewed or heard speak at meetings always underscore that they never considered living anywhere else before the circumstances that led them to make the decision to flee their countries of origin.

## Sexual Violence in the Countries of Origin

In situations of war and repression, men, women, and children are equally vulnerable to human rights abuses, including sexual violence and torture. Women and girls, however, are particularly vulnerable to sexual violence under repressive regimes and especially during civil strife and wars. Not all refugee women and girls are tortured or sexually violated in their countries of origin; many, however, will flee their countries of origin to escape such violence.

As I have noted, repressive regimes exist in 161 out of 181 countries today (Amnesty International 1993). In most of these countries women are arrested and sexually tortured because of their political actions, the political actions of other family members, or for belonging to certain social, ethnic, religious or political groups. Once in prison, women are at great risk of being raped by prison guards and in the torture chamber. Women are raped with such objects as sticks and bottles. In some countries dogs have been trained to sexually violate women. They can be raped in front of their husbands, partners, parents or children; they can be made to witness the rape and torture of their sisters, mothers and grandmothers and the torture of male members of their family or political group. Women, too, are often victims of sexual torture at the hands of the police and military (Amnesty International 1990, 1995).

Sexual torture of women is designed to destroy their identity as women. It can be inflicted upon women as a "punishment" for not conforming to cultural norms and it is used as a form of intimidation that forces women to reveal information about political activities of family members, individuals and groups allegedly involved in political activities against the state. Sexual torture relates political activity with sexual activity (Agger 1989). In the case of women, it is usually men who torture women. The reverse is not the case for men.

Under repressive conditions and because of the stigma associated with women's sexuality, women have very little recourse. Obviously, they cannot seek the protection of the police, let alone the law. Indeed, the police and the military may themselves be the perpetrators of sexual violence "on behalf" of the state. In many cases women cannot count on the support of their family and community since a woman's loss of virginity is perceived as a shame to the family in some cultures. Survivors of sexual violence will often choose to remain silent about such experiences. In addition to the trauma of being raped, these women will often become pregnant and not be able to abort the fetus of their rapist because abortion is either not available to them or it is illegal (Amnesty International 1990; Allodi and Stiasny; Agger, 1989, 1987; Dutch Refugee Association; *Manvi Newsletter*; Mollica and Son). Having to carry the child of their rapist is the epitome of patriarchal control over women's reproductive power.

In times of war, women are even more vulnerable to rape. Women's bodies become the site of combat when they are raped as a vengeance to the "enemy" (Enloe; Korac; Moussa 1993; *Women's World*). Often, they are "captured" by fighting armies on either side and forced to serve as maids and housekeepers, as well as forced to render sexual services.

The sexual violation of women and girls intensifies during "ethnic" conflicts. The 1990s have witnessed the beginning of an era of widespread "ethnic" conflicts which have result in civil wars, "ethnic cleansing" and brutal expulsion of peoples. These in turn have become major causes of forced human displacement. Political leaders in countries where "ethnic" battles rage—for example, the former Yugoslavia—use religion and ethnicity to uphold narrow nationalistic control of populations to maintain their grip on power. A central strategy of "ethnic cleansing" is to rape women and girls.

As revealed in the "ethnic" wars of the former Yugoslavia, and Rwanda, women and girls are victimized by all sides involved in the conflict. They are subjected to the sexual violence of rape and torture in the name of "ethnic cleansing," often they are ostracized by their own families, friends and neighbours, and their pain and suffering are used for political purposes. Javanka Stojsavljevic, OXFAM UK Regional representative for former Yugoslavia, reveals how these violations of women's rights are used as propaganda by the political powers involved in the conflict:

> The reason why the issue of rape has a public profile in former Yugoslavia is only because of its use as a weapon of propaganda; it suits a number of political agendas, which concern both national and international communities; namely, geographic boundaries, territorial rights, and sovereign states. It seems that it is not the right of women to protection from sexual violation that is important, but the wider political battles that can be fought through their experiences of violation...the use of rape in conflict to further these agendas results in further violations of a woman's dignity and integrity. (Stojsavljevic 40)

In other words, rape in war as in peace deprives women of their fundamental rights and should not be attached to honour or reputation.

Victims of "ethnic cleansing" in Rwanda and the former Yugoslavia have sought refuge in countries bordering their own or in camps within their own borders. Even in these temporary asylums, women and girls are not safe, but are the victims of rape by the men who are military and camp officials. Similarly, women who flee their homes and country of origin to escape repression or war are most often at risk whether they travel alone or in groups, by land or by sea. While crossing the border to the country of asylum, women may once again experience intimidation, sexual harassment and rape—this time in "exchange" for "safe passage." Once in the asylum country, they are equally vulnerable to sexual violence in the refugee camps and settlements, in urban areas, and when they seek to register their status with the police, other state organs or the staff of the United Nations High Commission on Refugees (UNCHR). State officials whose role it is to protect refugees and members of society are often perpetrators of violence against refugee women. Male (refugee) members of their families are also powerless and unable to protect women. Refugee women may also be raped by members of their own refugee male population (Agger 1993; Forbes Martin; Mollica and Son; Moussa 1993; Tu Khuong). The double bind for refugee women is that the word "refugee," in effect, signifies powerlessness and subjection while ostensibly conveying protection. But, refugees have no rights. It is the prerogative of states to grant them asylum, refugee status and immigrant status, or to deport them. To become a refugee is a lived experience, marked by sharp, if not violent discontinuities of identities, social and economic status, culture, family, and community relationships.

During my research with refugee women in Canada, I asked them what it was like to be a refugee in the countries of first and second asylum. They responded by offering the following metaphors: "it is like living in the air," " it is like living in a desert with people," and "it is like being a nothing." They also felt that "anyone can do anything to you." The gender differences within the limited protection refugees have in asylum were very clear to the women (Moussa 1993). A refugee woman from Eritrea identified this difference in her own experience in the Sudan:

> I was walking with [my husband] when a man stopped us and started touching my arms and shoulders. [My husband] wanted to fight him but I stopped him because we have no rights as refugees. [My husband] would be jailed and then I would not have any protection [from rape] (Moussa 1993: 188)

## International Policy and the Protection of Refugee Women

From asylum countries, refugee women may apply to the receiving countries, such as Canada, for refugee status. Not only do refugee women have to contend with sexual harassment and violence in camps or settlements, they must also deal with the policies that throw up difficult barriers in their struggle to find refuge.

Law on determination of refugee status is governed principally by the 1951 United Nations Convention and Protocol Relating to the Status of Refugees. Refugee is defined in the convention as a person who,

> Owing to well-founded fear of being persecuted for reasons of race, religion, nationality, membership in a particular group or political opinion, is outside the country of his nationality and is unable or, owing to such fear, is unwilling to avail himself of the protection of that country; who, not having a nationality and being outside the country of his former habitual residence, is unable to, or owing to such fear, is unwilling to return to it (United Nations, "Convention and Protocol Relating To the Status of Refugees," 1983, Article 1(2), pp. 12 and 39).

This definition of "refugee" has been incorporated in Canada's *Immigration Act*.

Although the definition uses gender-exclusive language, women who are deprived of protection from the state—for such specified reasons as persecution based on race, religion, nationality, political opinion, and membership in a social group—may make a successful refugee claim (Hathaway; Paul). However, an examination of the socio-political realities in the situations of refugee women suggests that the definition is, in fact, discriminatory in its impact on women. To imply that refugee women are equal under the law (that is, the same as men) because they are not explicitly excluded from the international definition of refugee, fails to recognize that the inequalities that exist between men and women will exacerbate pre-existing inequalities between them, since they do not enjoy substantive equality in society.

Refugee women are also more likely than men to migrate with other members of their community to refugee camps or to refugee settlements where, if they are among the few to meet selection criteria, they may be resettled in countries like Canada. In general, women have less education and work experience than men and are responsible for their children and dependents. These factors are perceived by resettlement countries as a barrier to speedy economic self-sufficiency (Kelly). An additional structural barrier, not often mentioned, is the location of Canadian visa offices. In 1993 in the continent of Africa, for instance, there were only five such permanent offices—in Cairo (Egypt), Tunis (Tunisia), Nairobi (Kenya), Johannesburg (South Africa) and Abidjan (Ivory Coast). While visa officers will travel to a selected number of other capital cities in Africa, their scheduled arrival is not announced. Since the majority of refugee women are in refugee camps or settlements (in some parts of Asia they may be in detention centres), they very likely do not have the funds to travel to the capital city. In addition, the likelihood that they would leave their dependents and take further personal risks by travelling alone once again is very slim. In fact, in many cases they will not be allowed to leave their camps, settlements or detention centres, let alone travel to other parts of the country without government authorization.

A major feminist criticism of the UN and consequently of current Canadian policies is that their definition of "refugee" does not include gender oppression and does not provide for the special protection refugee women need because of gender inequality in the countries producing and receiving refugees. In practice, for instance, "women are much less likely to be involved in politics (as it has been traditionally defined) or the publicly active religious, racial, nationalistic, or social groups whose persecution is well known" (Stairs and Pope 162). Women, however, suffer just as much from institutional oppression. As a result, the omission of gender as a ground for persecution in the international definition of refugee may preclude many women from making successful refugee claims (Castel; Foote; Indra; Macklin; Meijer; van Willigen).

As early as 1984, the European Parliament called on states to recognize women who experience gender-based persecution as a "social group" for the purpose of the definition of "refugee." Unfortunately, this interpretation has not been universally accepted. When the issue was discussed at the UNHCR Executive Committee meetings in 1985, several states refused to consider women as a particular social group on the ground that such consideration could interfere with state culture or religious practice (Johnson; UNHCR Executive Committee Conclusions, 39th session, 1989). As a compromise, the following resolution was passed by the Executive Committee, in which it was:

*Recognized that states, in the exercise of their sovereignty, are free to adopt*

> *the interpretation* that women asylum-seekers who face harsh and inhuman treatment due to their having transgressed social mores of the society in which they live may be considered as a "particular social group" within the meaning of Article 1A(2) of the 1951 United Nations Refugee Convention (UNHCR Executive Committee, 1985:85). [emphasis added]

The rationale for holding that women form a social group is based on their lack of power rather than on any real or perceived threat they pose to the state. Felicite Stairs and Lori Pope observe that: [the] state does not reflect the reality of many women's lives. It is women's general lack of power and the improbability of women posing a threat to the state that makes it possible for the state and private citizens whose actions are sanctioned by the state to pay women less for their work, to limit their participation in academic, cultural and political life, to harm them physically, and to discriminate against or persecute women in other ways (Stairs and Pope).

Those who oppose recognizing women as a "social group" fear that this could open the door for too many claims for refugee status. The claim on the basis of persecution, however, has to be based on the eligibility and protection needs of each case and not the number of other persons who might be subjected to similar persecution. In addition, women seeking refugee status under the "social group" would still have to meet part of the refugee definition that they have a well-founded fear of persecution based on the UN Convention definition (Castel).

## Perceptions of Refugee Women

Portraying refugee women as vulnerable and victims of aggression reveals their special circumstances as refugee women. However, such a depiction also tends to portray them as being unable to successfully survive, cope and even adapt. This perception of women in turn hinders their chances for resettlement in countries such as Canada, because the expectation of immigration criteria is that refugees, like immigrants, will become economically independent in a short period of time. Focussing only on their vulnerability places the problem on women rather than on the aggression and discrimination perpetrated against them because they are women. Such a focus overlooks that refugee women can make positive contributions to the society in which they live.

This negative perception of refugee women was radically challenged in the mid-1985 gender and development debate that emerged in feminist literature. As the debate developed, women of the North and South revealed that women are in fact actively involved in development and clearly pointed out the problematic denial of the important contribution of women's work in the home and in the public domain in the gendered division of labour. One of the debate's outcomes has been the changing understanding of women's position in development plans and implementations of these plans. The analysis that emerged from the women from the South shifted the focus from the concept of women in development (WID), which implied integrating women in existing unequal societal structures, to gender and development (GAD), whereby women are seen as agents and beneficiaries of development, as well as having the "right to new ideas" about their role in society (Antrobus; Sen and Grown).

Not surprisingly, the contributions of refugee women to agricultural work often go unreported because of the gendered views of what is seen as productive labour of the host countries. The following commentary was made by the Jordanian government with respect to Palestinian refugees:

> The traditional social attitude of the people considers the wife who is helping her husband in agricultural work as being economically non-active and leads, therefore, to her exclusion from members of the labour force in agriculture. The same applies to all female family members helping men in agriculture. (Sudha Hindiych cited in Waring 75)

And yet Gaim Kibreab noted in his study of Eritrean refugees in the Sudan, that women were more informed about the social and economic issues that affected the members of the refugee community because they were much more directly involved in these concerns than were men. Hanne Christensen also observes that in the case of Afghan refugee women, in Pakistan,

> [i]t is not so much women's work that is regarded as a violation of the norms. The women have always worked in and for the household in unpaid form, and that is recognized. It is the income obtained from the work that is regarded as objectionable because it affects the man's obligations to keep his family and supply his wife's material needs. Women's work income is regarded as dangerous to the established social order. (Christensen 56)

In many refugee receiving countries, employment opportunities for women are strictly and narrowly defined along gender lines. Women have to go through considerable difficulties to support themselves and their dependents economically if the male head of household abandons them in refugee camps or if they are separated from their husbands when they are uprooted (Dutch Refugee Association; Krumel; Forbes Martin; United Nations Economic Commission for Africa; Wiesinger). Intimidation harassment and assault are once again ways in which women may be further victimized. Refugee women are therefore doubly marginalized because they are refugees and because they are women.

For some refugee women, prostitution can become the only source of economic survival. In countries where prostitution is illegal, refugee women are at greater risk regardless of the fact that the male customers may be citizens of the host country, including such state officials as the police and refugee camp guards. Prostitution may lead to imprisonment and often women will be violated by prison guards. Sometimes refugee women are forced to engage in prostitution by pimps (male refugees) and by their refugee spouses (Demeke; Moussa 1993).

The shift in international assistance to refugees has slowly adapted the gender and development approaches to the refugee situation. For example, a very significant thrust of the UNHCR "Guidelines on the Protection of Refugee Women" is that refugee women should be involved in all levels of decision-making that affect their social and economic lives (UNHCR Guidelines). Forbes Martin illustrates specific examples where this approach has successfully occurred. In Mexico, Guatemalan refugee women carried out a needs assessment survey of the refugee population in their area which led to specific recommendations to the Mexican Government, the UNHCR and NGO representatives. Refugee women coordinators in a settlement in Zaire are responsible for the distribution process to residents, as well as for specific health and education needs of refugee women. The Khmer Women's Association in the camps along the Thai-Cambodian borders employed social workers and teachers for literacy, sewing/weaving classes, as well as day-care teachers while women are in classes. And, in a settlement in Zambia, women were represented in all levels of the structure of a development-planning management committee.

The strength, determination and resilience of refugee women have been observed by all those who have worked with them. My own research has lead me to recognize that refugee women are not just satisfied with surviving. Indeed, their decision to flee their homes and countries of origin is in defiance of state violence and patriarchy. Their actions are clearly aimed at changing their circumstances and, as such, are forms of resistance. Refugee women must be seen as *victimized* but not as passive victims. They should also be recognized as active shapers of their personal and collective lives (Moussa 1993).

## Canadian Policy and Refugee Women

There are two ways refugees can apply for resettlement in Canada. The first is to apply at a visa office abroad. This is called the "overseas determination process." The second is to arrive at the Canadian border by land, air or sea and claim refugee status. This is called the "refugee claimant process."

In the overseas determination process, women and men who are applying outside Canada have to meet two criteria: they have to be eligible according to the United Nation's Convention and Protocol as stated in Canada's Immigration Act, and they have to meet Canadian immigration admissibility criteria designated to ensure that they can successfully (that is, economically) establish themselves in Canadian society. Since such criteria are based on skills and the employability of refugees/immigrants, refugee women will often be at a disadvantage. Women are seen as dependents. Their skills and strengths are not seen as "assets" in the family or the public sphere. This bias is clearly evident in statistics on the immigration status of refugees (see Appendices 1 to 4). For these reasons, it is not surprising that male refugees are by far the largest number of "principal applicants" landed between 1986 and 1993. In the case of refugees selected in the overseas process (Appendix 1), 76 per cent to 79 per cent of the "principal applicants" were male refugees. In the case of refugee claimants in the 1989 backlog (Appendix 4), 81 per cent to 82 per cent of the "principal applicants" were male refugees. Conversely, a significantly higher percentage of the refugee women were landed during the same period in the "spouse" category—94 per cent to 96 per cent among the overseas selected refugees (Appendix 1) and 81 per cent to 85 per cent for refugee claimants in the backlog (Appendix 4). This disproportionate gender distribution of male and female refugee is also evident in the breakdown of landings by the ten highest countries of refugee origin (Appendices 2 and 3). The percentage of refugee women entering Canada as "principal applicants" is clearly not a reflection of the overall global refugee population.

It is interesting to not that in Canada in 1993 the percentage of female refugee claimants accepted in the "principal applicant" category increased to 33 per cent compared with 20 per cent in 1990, 19 per cent in 1991 and 18 per cent in 1992 (see Appendix 4). The implementation of the Canadian "Guidelines on Women Refugee Claimants Fearing Gender-Related Persecution" in 1993 could explain this higher acceptance rate of female refugee claimants. At the same time, the patterns of overseas selection in 1993 remained similar to previous years (Appendix 1). This unchanged pattern could be explained by the fact that guidelines are not applied to the overseas determination process.

The irony of the "employability" criteria is that highly qualified refugee women (and men) will, as do immigrants, have to start at the bottom of the job market. As compared with Canadian-born women, immigrant and refugee women are heavily concentrated in factory occupations (Boyd 1986; Ng and Das Gupta). Refugee women are also at a disadvantage because the Canadian job market is gendered both in the kind of jobs that are available for women and because women do not receive equal pay for equal work. In addition, media stories and images of refugees do not portray them as contributing to the economy, culture (beyond "exotic" food and music) and history of Canada. Rather, they are portrayed as abusers of the Canadian refugee and welfare systems, as well as criminals and drug-dealers. In contrast, many studies in Canada, Europe and the U.S. have shown that refugees and migrants make significant economic and cultural contributions to their host countries (for example: Beiser; Richmond; Spencer; Stalker). While the categories of "principal applicant" and "spouse" are gender neutral, in reality the landing statistics (Appendices 1 to 4) not only reflect the stereotype that women are dependent but also reinforce the role of women in the home, that is, non-productive labourers. The home-care skills and efforts of refugee women to hold their families together in the adjustment process are not only invisible but also are not recognized in economic terms. Furthermore the refugee determination process totally ignores the critical role refugee women play in the survival of family members in asylum countries and in Canada.

The UNHCR responded to the special protection and resettlement needs of refugee women by establishing the Women at Risk Program. In 1988, Canada was the first country to participate in this program. Many advocacy groups hoped that it would remedy the gender imbalance in the number of refugees admitted.

The UNHCR "Women at Risk—Procedures and Guidelines" identifies the two categories of eligibility for refugee women under this program. The first category defines women who "will be in precarious situations where the local authorities cannot ensure safety." The second category defines women at risk as "applicants who are not under immediate peril but who are existing in permanently unstable circumstances which allow for no other remedy." While it was "accepted that the integration of such women into Canadian society can be expected to be difficult," it was assumed that with special assistance from the Canadian Government and sponsoring groups these women would eventually adjust successfully (Employment and Immigration Canada 2). "Risk" in the second category therefore refers to the assumed length of time these women would need to become economically independent in Canada. When we consider that 80 to 90 per cent of the world refugee populations is women and their dependants, the 290 refugee women over seven years who have been admitted through this program is miniscule (Marching Centre, Settlement Branch, Employment and Immigration Canada, 1995). The drop in acceptance rate between 1993 (46 women) and 1994 (26 women) is a further indication that protection of refugee women is not a priority of the Canadian Government.

It has become clear that because of the length of time (sometimes as long as eight months) that it takes to process refugees overseas, only women in the second category "not under immediate peril," can be considered for resettlement in Canada. In contrast, European countries which do not officially subscribe to the Women at Risk Program follow through with the required procedures (for example, medical examinations) once the women and their dependants arrive in Europe. In such circumstances, a woman who is at risk could be admitted within 48 hours. It is also important to note that the UNHCR definition of a woman at risk does not have resettlement "admissibility" as one of the criteria.

In 1993, the first review of the Canadian Women at Risk Program was carried out by the International Strategy Research Analysis and Information Branch, Immigration and Citizenship Canada. While the findings of this study clearly point to the contradictions of the "admissibility" criteria, no changes were recommended. A major gap in this study's data is the omission of women who were rejected in the Canadian overseas process or were not recommended by the UNHCR because of the long time it takes for Canadian authorities to process these women's applications.

As a result, the Canadian Council for Refugees (CCR), at its biannual consultation (May 1994, Ottawa), passed a resolution requesting that the Minister of Citizenship and Immigration together with NGOs implement a five-year (1995-2000) gender quota action plan to ensure that a minimum of 50 per cent of "principal applicants" in the overseas selection process are women. In addition, the CCR resolution requested a minimum 20 per cent increase access to the Women at Risk Program.

In 1989 Canada established the refugee claimant process for people who apply for refugee status when they reach Canadian borders (by sea, land or air). Their refugee status is determined at a hearing of the Immigration and Refugee Board (IRB), a quasi-judicial administrative tribunal which operates independently of the Federal Ministry of Human Resources. Today these hearings are held in Halifax, St. John's, Ottawa, Montreal, Toronto, Winnipeg, Calgary, and Vancouver. Two IRB members take part in the hearing. Only one member needs to make a positive assessment for a claim to be accepted. Refugee claimants have the right to be represented by counsel and the right to an interpreter. In addition, an IRB refugee hearing officer brings our additional information by questioning the claimant. The 1951 United Nations Convention Relating to the Status of Refugees and Protocol as incorporated in Canada's Immigration Act is applied to each claim. Unlike the overseas determination process, the immigration admissibility criteria is not applied when considering refugee claimant cases.

On March 8, 1993, Nurjehan Mawani, the Chairperson of the IRB, officially issued the IRB Guidelines on "Women Refugee Claimants Fearing Gender-Related Persecution" at a special International Women's Day educational event for IRB members and for guests from NGOs and women's groups. In 1992, the draft guidelines were circulated internally within the IRB for comments, to legal scholars and to such groups as the Canadian Council for Refugees' Working Group on Refugee Women's Issues, the Canadian Advisory Council on the Status of Women, and some Canadian churches. The establishment of the Guidelines is also the result of the efforts and the concerns raised by NGOs and refugee networks such as the Working Group on Refugee Women's Issues (Toronto), feminist lawyers, members of the IRB, in particular the IRB Working Group on Refugee Women. In 1992-1993, refugee advocacy groups such as the National Action Committee on the Status of Women and the Canadian Council for Refugees, the International Centre for Human Rights and Development and the media played a strong role in bringing to the attention of the public and the Minister of Immigration clear cases of gender persecution that were rejected by the IRB.

The Guidelines do not add gender persecution to the enumerated grounds of admissible forms of persecution. Instead, the Guidelines aim to assist IRB members in establishing the link between gender persecution and one or more of the grounds as accepted by the UN Convention—race, religion, nationality, membership in a particular social group, and political opinion. The Guidelines outline forms of persecution that can be primarily directed towards women. These include, for example, persecution due to political views or activities of a relative, transgression of religious beliefs, social mores, legal and cultural norms, or violence exerted by someone in public authority or in private life. They provide IRB members with procedures and methods for evaluating whether individual claims of gender persecution meet the refugee standard as established by the Convention (for example, it must be established that state policies or law are basically persecutory). The Guidelines are being used along with other international instruments, such as the Universal Declaration of Human Rights, The Convention on the Elimination of All Forms of Discrimination Against Women, the Convention on the Nationality of Married Women, to set standards as to what constitutes a violation of human rights. Since the Guidelines were issued, claims relating to sexual assault, wife abuse, enforced sterilization, female genital mutilation among other oppressive actions solely directed towards women have been linked to the persecution of refugee women.

While on the one hand policies such as the gender Guidelines are established to offer refugee women fearing gender-based persecution an opportunity to find safe haven in Canada, on the other hand policies are established that make it particularly difficult for refugee women to remain in Canada. The "Right to Landing Fee" (commonly referred to as the "Head Tax") established in February 1995 by the Minister of Immigration is a specific example. Before permanent status in Canada can be granted, a fee of $975 is now imposed on all immigrants and refugees (each individual member of a family are charged this fee). The fee has been justified by the Minister of Immigration as a measure to reduce the national deficit. Not only will this fee reduce the chances for refugee women to come to Canada but those who are in Canada will undoubtedly find it very difficult to pay the fee in order to remain in this country.

## Violence As A Barrier In The Reconstruction Of Refugee Women's Lives

Once in Canada, refugee women encounter a new set of barriers in their attempts to reconstruct their lives, for example in seeking services (language, legal, etc.) and paid employment. These barriers are rooted in the pervasiveness of racism, sexism and classism in Canadian society. The pressures on arrival in Canada are generally extensive for all refugees. Refugee claimants under the "refugee claimant process," for example, are in limbo until they are granted refugee and landed immigrant status. The stress of "waiting" further intensifies the fear of deportation, which is a prevalent feeling among all refugees.

Keeping the family together has particular significance for refugee women. Members of a family can arrive separately, children may have been separated from parents in flight or even in the country of origin. Whether it is the male or female spouse who arrived first, the family will never be the same as it was in their country of origin. Renegotiating relationships and identities is critical for the well-being of all family members. Separation from the extended family,[5] in addition to concern about their family's safety in the war-torn countries of origin or in countries under repressive regimes, add to the accumulation of stress. The pressures to find housing, work, schooling, and so on, let alone not knowing how institutions function and dealing with pervasive racism, leave very little space to process the grief of the personal and material losses since fleeing their homes and country. Refugee women will often defer and suppress their own emotional needs to hold the family together.

The alienation which is part of North American life affects refugees in a much more drastic way because they experience multiple losses of the structures that under normal circumstances sustain their identities. For example, they lose their home and country, their network of family, friends, and acquaintances, the familiarity of their neighbourhood and religious institutions, the security of work, their cultural food and language, their health and education benefits and their citizenship. Racism and hostility towards refugees create additional layers of alienation for refugees during and after the initial settlement process.

An abused refugee woman claimant may be in a particularly precarious position if her status is dependent on her partner's refugee claim. In some cases, if the woman arrives before her spouse, she may have developed a sense of her own autonomy and familiarity with Canadian society and institutions. While she may look forward to the arrival of her spouse, once he rejoins his wife and children, the process of adaptation as a family in a new country is stressful on relationships.

An understanding (though not legitimation) of the particularity of male violence in refugee families requires a consideration of two essential components in their life histories. First, is the intersection of gender ideology and masculinity in their countries of origin with Canadian patriarchal, race and class ideologies. Second are the effects of the violence men experience and witness under the repressive regimes from which they fled and how this experience can reinforce (or dispel) their notions of and need for control.

While the lives of refugee women, not unlike immigrant women, will be shaped by race, gender, class and ethnicity in Canadian society, it is their lived experience as refugees and the barriers to taking action or speaking out against violence which are rooted in the gender ideology and experience of their countries of origin that affect the ways they respond to violence against them in the family.

The support and advice of elders in their countries of origin are often named by refugee women as a possible source of restraint on men's abuse of their female partners. While the intervention of elders does not preclude the possibility of sexist decisions, women can sometimes find a family member to give them support and refuge. Lacking the extended family and not knowing where to seek support in Canadian society, newly-arrived refugee women are more likely to suffer in silence. Furthermore, racism and hostility towards refugees makes it even harder to break the silence. A community worker in an "ethnic" agency, for instance, informed me that battered refugee women will choose solidarity with their community rather than seek personal safety. These refugee women believe that revealing male violence will only exacerbate the "violent," "terrorist" image the media portrays and that many Canadians believe about their people.

Family members and friends (in Canada and at home) may also collude to prevent reporting male violence and may even blame the woman. Some refugee male abusers have also been known to threaten relatives and even friends as a means of silencing them and withdrawing their support from the wife. Whatever the "reason," community denial rather than sanctions against male violence inevitably reinforces the isolation of the woman, if not the continuation of violence perpetrated against her in her own home. It is for this reason and because the leadership in most "ethnic" community centres is predominantly male that women will most often seek the assistance from multi-ethnic centres rather than their own "ethnic" community centre. Increasingly, however, women's committees are being established by women in "ethnic" community centres. Their ability to influence services provided to abused women depends on the level of autonomy and power they are able to develop within the centre and the community. The growing number of immigrant, refugee and visible minority women's coalitions is another potential place of safety where abused refugee women can voice their issues and receive support.

Fear of further reprisals from their abusive partner is another reason why refugee women may remain silent. Since the majority of refugee women enter Canada as a sponsored "spouse" (See Appendices 1 to 4), abused refugee women fear that they will lose their sponsorship and be deported and separated from their children, or that the abuser (or in-laws who may have sponsored the couple or the woman) will use the sponsorship support as a threat to silence them. Nor will an abused refugee woman consider the option of divorce. Not only do they fear that divorce will result in their loss of sponsorship and subsequent deportation, religious beliefs, such as those of Catholics and Muslims, as well as gendered cultural traditions, make it difficult for refugee women to perceive that they have a "right" to seek divorce. It is particularly difficult for women who come from cultures where decisions of the group and particularly the extended family take priority over the individual. Extended family ties, whereby two families are in effect joined in a new extended family as a result of the marriage, will make it difficult for a women to recognize that she has the "right" as an individual to decide to terminate the marriage. Chinese family counsellors in Toronto have found ways of easing the barriers to divorce in their culture(s) by replacing the concept of "divorce" as an individual right with culturally valued concepts of the importance of "restoring the children's mental health" and leaving the home to "preserve the family" (Chan 24). A lack of knowledge of and misconceptions about Canadian family, immigration and refugee law can be serious barriers to taking action and speaking out about the violence in their lives.

Abused refugee women need assistance in making the transition from the way family problems were mediated in their countries of origin to the Canadian context where institutions exist to serve the needs of abused women. It takes time for refugee women to become aware of such services. Often there were either no such services to their country of origin, or they had no reason to seek the assistance of these services. In addition, the stress of having to repeat their story of abuse to service providers, including the police, is aggravated when they are not fluent in English or French. In addition, a refugee woman will find it very difficult to report her spouse to the police. The image of the police as "protector" is not a part of their lived experience. Refugees generally distrust state officials such as the police, the military and the judiciary. This distrust is strongly embedded in their experience under dictatorships and in war situations. In Canada, racism and the negative attitudes towards refugees by members of the police force add to this distrust of authority figures. Refugee women, therefore, find it very difficult to be the ones to "send" their spouse to prison. In the world view of many refugee women, violence of refugee men is perceived as the result of systemic oppression rather than individualistic behaviour. In their view, there have to be effective community-based approaches which would make male batterers accountable while at the same time protecting women (Moussa 1993, 1995).

Sexual assault counselling and assistance to abused refugee women also requires different approaches. Sometimes sexual assault in the family becomes entangled with the way women have dealt or not dealt with their past. Sexual abuse can very likely become the catalyst to remembering premigration and migration experiences of torture (sexual or otherwise); witnessing torture; sexual assault in flight; or sexual assault in the asylum countries. The support and counselling needs of refugee women who are abused by their spouse but who escaped the above violations will still necessitate recognition of their refugee experience.

It is therefore important that service providers distinguish between the needs of abused refugee women who have been in Canada for several years, those who are recent arrivals, and those who are claimants under the "refugee claimant process." Difference in ages of abused refugee women must also be taken into account. To date, there is no research that documents how differences in time of arrival, refugee status and age influence and affect their actions when they are abused by their partner.

Research and reports on violence against immigrant and refugee women in Canada do underscore the fact that analysis and solutions from the experience of the mainstream women's movement cannot be transplanted (Moussa 1995). The battered women's shelter movement is an example of an institution which was developed to meet mainstream women's needs. For many abused refugee women a shelter is not necessarily a viable option. Moving out of their homes is once again an uprooting experience and re-experiencing of refugee "homelessness" and "poverty." Conditions of confinement and sharing limited space can be a reminder of a prison or a refugee camp (Moussa 1995).

It is essential to encourage and support refugee and immigrant women who are actively exploring and testing models of intervention that work to protect and assist refugee women living with violent men (Moussa 1995). Ethno-specific communities also have to deconstruct ideologies and practices which condone male power and superiority over women.

## Conclusion

While Canada is the first country to have established a set of guidelines that specifically addresses gender-related persecution, the application of these guidelines may not consistently benefit all refugee women. Ongoing assessment of the Guidelines needs to be undertaken to determine their effectiveness and the implication of their interpretation.[6]

There are two key processes that particularly need to be assessed. The first of these are the decisions made about refugees by the senior immigration officers at Canadian border stations. These crucial first decisions determine whether a refugee is eligible to pursue a claim for refugee status or is turned back and not allowed to enter Canada. The second is the consistency or lack of consistency in the reasons which determine which refugee claims are accepted or rejected.

In addition, there are several improvements that should be made to strengthen the application of the Guidelines. The application of the Guidelines should be mandatory and not be left to the choice of individual IRB members. Canadian policy should be consistent in its application. The Guidelines should also be applied in the overseas selection process and not limited to the refugee claimant process. IRB members should be interviewed and screened prior to their appointment to determine their position on sexism, racism, classism and other forms of discrimination. Anti-racist and anti-sexist education of all IRB members and cultural interpreters should be mandatory. These educational activities should be monitored to ensure that anti-racist and anti-sexist behaviours and actions are integrated into the IRB. Women refugee claimants should be informed that they can choose legal counsel to assist them and should be assisted in finding counsel. They must be informed that they can apply independently of their spouse in case of death or if the relationship breaks down before the hearing. Refugee women need to be well prepared by their lawyers and the lawyers should understand the political context of the refugee woman's experience. It may be easier for a refugee woman to share her experience with a female lawyer; however, in many cultures, it is taboo for women to discuss sex and the private parts of their bodies with anyone else. Lawyers must respect these cultural norms and listen carefully to refugee women when discussing their experiences.

Despite these applications and efforts to improve the Guidelines, however, we will still look at refugee women and their cultures through the lens of our own history, culture, and ideology unless we undertake a deeper analysis of our perceptions. The difficult question is: How can we cross this bridge to be able to listen to what refugee women are saying? The highly legal discourse of the Guidelines assumes that "fairness" and "objectivity" are in place in the process of determining a refugee claim. The implications of ideological perspective(s) towards women from other cultures, social classes and races are assumed to be dealt with when IRB members attend educational workshops to improve their "gender/cultural sensitivity." But is it enough to be "culturally sensitive" or "gender sensitive"? These concepts are often used in Canada as a way of relating in a positive manner to the cultural background of refugee women. "Sensitivity" is a psychological response and as such is only a partial strategy. Moreover, this approach can inadvertently pathlogize other cultures. To truly hear refugee women's stories, the listener has to deconstruct her or his own sexist and racist assumptions.

Sherene Razack, human rights and feminist scholar, argues that one has to consider how women's stories of violence are heard in the legal system. Razack posits that one has to recognize and overcome the power relations created by patriarchal and racist constructs which will directly affect the relationship between the "teller and the listener, between the telling and the hearing" (1993: 56), in this case, between the refugee woman and the IRB member, interpreter or lawyer. Storytelling, Razack maintains, is not always empowering because we do not recognize "the complex ways we construct meaning," and we have not developed "an ethical vision based on our differences" (1993: 62).

In a trenchant analysis of IRB transcripts of refugee hearings on claims based on domestic violence and transgression of cultural norms, Razack argues that women's claims for asylum are most likely to succeed when they are presented as "victims of dysfunctional and exceptionally patriarchal cultures" (1995: 46). Razack argues for a shift in the current refugee discourse which she asserts is based on pity to a discourse based on justice and responsibility (1995: 85). In such a discourse, women would not have "to speak of their realities of sexual violence at the expense of their realties as colonized people" (1995: 48). Quoting feminist scholar Homa Hoodfar, she emphasizes that we must not fight sexism with racism (1995: 72).

Refugee women themselves may find it difficult to recognize the political nature of their experience. It is therefore important for those working with refugee women who have been sexually violated or tortured to understand the interrelationship of the historical and political realities in the countries of origin of these women. In their counselling of refugee women, Richard Mollica and Linda Son clearly describe the interactive cultural, political and historical dimensions of sexual trauma. While their focus is geared to psychoanalytic "treatment" of sexually tortured or raped refugee women, the concepts and approaches could very well be adapted in the refugee determination process and by refugee women's legal counsel in preparation for hearings. The psychoanalytic treatment used by Inger Agger and Soren Buus Jensen also enables women to analyze the political context of the violence exerted on them (for example, rape in time war, sexual torture in prison). Similar to Mollica and Son, this analysis enables women to understand their disclosures of violence as being a testimony about or a "witnessing" of a political context of violence which leads to becoming a refugee rather as opposed to a "confession" from a victim. In this approach, sexual violence is perceived as political rather than a private experience.

Violence against refugee women is gender oppression and a crime against human rights. We must address the root causes to put a halt to the economic and social forces that create refugees. At the same time, Canada must continue to ensure that services provided to refugee women respect their human rights and that they have access to education and employment that will enable them to fulfil their potential. We must continue to lobby for changes in refugee policy and practice that are responsible and just. Finally, we must ensure that refugee determination personnel and officers of the courts receive appropriate education and the tools to analyze gender-based refugee claims, as they are, in the end, the final gatekeepers or refugee women's safety and well-being.

*Although the issues facing refugee women remain the same, this paper was originally written in 1994 and subsequently revised.*

## Notes

[1]A study of the social construction of refugee women from Ethiopia and Eritrea revealed differences because of their family and school experiences, their ethnic or national, cultural, religious, class and educational backgrounds, their rural and urban camps, urban and rural settlements, as well as a wide and diverse range of personal experiences (see Moussa 1993).

[2]According to Francis Deng, Representative of the United Nations General Secretary on internally displaced people, in 1995 there were 30 million internally displaced people world-wide. These people flee refugee-like situations of war, abuses of human rights and civil strife but remain *within* national borders. There are no international instruments that extend protection for their human rights as a distinct category of forcibly displaced persons. The majority of internally displaced people are also women and their dependents. United Nations Economic Social Council, "Human Rights, Mass Exoduses and Displaced Persons—internally displaced persons." (Report of the Representative of the Secretary-General, Mr. Francis M. Deng, submitted pursuant to Commission on Human Rights resolution 1993/95 and 1994/68. E/CN.4/1995/50, 2 February, 1995).

[3]I use the terms "Third World," "developing countries" and countries in the "South" interchangeably to connote countries in Africa, Asia, the Caribbean, Latin America, the Middle East and the Pacific that have been colonized and are still under the domination of the global cultural/economic/military system today. Conversely, "developed," "first world" and countries in the "North" refer to Canada, the U.S., Australia and European countries that are part of this colonial and post-cultural/economic/military colonial domination of "Third World" countries.

[4]For a more expansive discussion of the root causes and consequences of forced displacement see Moussa and Taran.

[5]Unfortunately, the debate on Canada's family reunification policies is problematic because of ideological differences as to what constitutes a "family." Increasingly restrictive definitions (that is, the immediate and the nuclear family) are often rationalized because of economic pressures on the state.

[6]For critiques of the Canadian Guidelines, see Foote; Macklin; Razack 1995; and the Minutes of the Canadian Council for Refugees Consultations, May 12, 1993 (Toronto) and November 11-13 (Calgary): "Agenda Setting Meeting National Consultation on Immigration and Refugee Protection," June 28, 1993, hosted by the Refugee Law Research Unit, York University Centre for Refugee Studies under the sponsorship of the Minister of Employment and Immigration Canada.

## References

Agger, Inger. *The Blue Room: Trauma and Testimony among Refugee Women a Psychosocial Experience.* London: Zed Press, 1993.

Agger, Inger. "Sexual Torture of Political Prisoners: An Overview." *Journal of Traumatic Stress* 2 (3) (1989): 305-317.

Agger, Inger. "The Female Political Prisoner: A Victim of Sexual Torture." Paper presented at the Eighth World Congress on Sexology, Heidelberg, June 14-20, 1987.

Agger, Inger and Soren Buus Jensen. *Trauma and Healing Under State Terrorism.* London: Zed Press, 1996.

Agger, Inger and Soren Buus Jensen "Testimony as Ritual and Evidence in Psychotherapy for Political Refugees." *Journal of Traumatic Stress* 3 (1) (1990): 115-130.

Allodi, F., and S. Stiasny. "Women as Torture Victims." *Canadian Journal of Psychiatry* 35 (1990): 144-148.

Amnesty International. *Amnesty International 1993 Report.* New York: Amnesty International, 1993.

Amnesty International. *Amnesty International 1995 Report.* New York: Amnesty International, 1995.

Amnesty International. *Women in the Front Line: Human Rights Violations Against Women.* New York: Amnesty International, 1990.

Antrobus, Peggy. "Women in Development." *Changing Perceptions: Writings on Gender and Development.* Eds. Tina Wallace and Candida March. Oxford: OXFAM, 1991. 311-314.

Bannenbring, Fredo. "Refugees: A New Challenge to Foreign and Development Policy." *Development and Cooperation* 1 (1991): 6.

Bauer, Jan, "Report on UN Conference on Human Rights. June 14-25, 1993," Prepared by Article 19(UK) and Canadian Network on International Human Rights, Ottawa, 31, October 1993.

Beiser, Morton *et al.* "The Mental Health of South East Asian Refugees Resettling in Canada." Final Report to Canada Health and Welfare NHRDL, 1995.

Boyd, Monica. "Immigrant Women in Canada." *International Migration: The Female Experience.* Eds. Rita J. Simon and Caroline Bretell. Totowa, New Jersey: Rowman and Allanheld, 1986. 45-61.

Boyd, Monica. "At a Disadvantage. The Occupational Attainments of Foreign Born Women in Canada." *International Migration Review* 18 (4) (1984): 109-119.

Canada. *An Act to Amend the Immigration Act, 1976 and to Amend other Acts in Consequence Thereof.* 21 July, 1988. Ottawa.

Canadian Council for Refugees Bi-annual Consultation. Resolutions. Ottawa, May 1994.

Carrillo, Roxana. "Violence Against Women: An Obstacle for Development." *Gender Violence: A Development and Human Rights Issues.* Eds. Charlotte

Bunch and Roxana Carrillo.New Jersey: Center for Women's Global Leadership, 1991.

Castel, Jacqueline R. "Rape, Sexual Assault and the Meaning of Persecution." *International Journal of Refugee Law* 4 (1) (1992): 39-56.

Chan, Sui-lin Lisa. *Wife Assault: The Chinese Family Life Services Experience.* Toronto: Chinese Family Life Services, 1989.

Christensen, Hanne. *The Reconstruction of Afghanistan: A Chance for Afghan Women.* Geneva: UN Research Institute for Social Development, 1990.

Demeke, Tadele. "Refugee Women's Survival Strategies and Prostitution in Eastern Sudan." *Refugee Participatory Network* 7 (1990): 26-28.

Dutch Refugee Association. *International Seminar on Refugee Women.* Amsterdam: Dutch Refugee Council, 1985.

Employment and Immigration Canada. "New Immigrant Language Training Policy." *Immigration Policy and Development.* Ottawa: Employment and Immigration Canada. 1992. 1-6.

Enloe, Cynthia. *Does Khaki Become You? The Militarisation of Women's Lives.* London: Pandora Press, 1988.

Foote, Victoria. "Refugee Women as Particular Social Group: A Reconsideration." *Refuge* 14 (7) (1994): 8-12.

Forbes Martin, Susan. *Women Refugees.* London & New Jersey: Zed Press, 1991.

Fromont Michel. "Poverty and Exclusion: The Infernal Duo." *The World of Work.* Geneva: International Labour Organization, 1995.

George, Susan. "Le danger d'un chaos financier generalise." *Le Monde Diplomatique* (July 1995): 23-24.

"Global Tribunal on Violations of Women's Human Rights: Existing Practices Provide Inadequate Protection." *Libertas Newsletter* 3 (3) (June 1993): 2-3.

Hathaway James. "Gender-Specific Claims to Refugee Status and Membership in a Particular Social Group." Workshop Organized by the Toronto CRDD Working Group on Women Refugee Claimants, December 5, 1990.

Heise, Lori L. with Jacqueline Pitanguy and Adrienne Germain. *Violence Against Women: The Hidden Health Burden.* Washington DC: The World Bank, 1994.

Hindiyeh, Sudha. "Social Change and Agriculture in the West Bank 1950-1967: Aspects of Sharecropping and Communalization." *If Women Counted: New Feminist Economics.* Ed. Marilyn Waring. San Francisco: Harper, 1990.

Immigration and Citizenship Canada. "Woman at Risk Program Review." Study conducted for International Refugee and Migration Policy Branch by Strategic Research, Analysis and Information Branch, June 1994. 1-31.

Immigration and Refugee Board. "Guidelines Issued by the Chairperson Pursuant to Section 65(3) of the *Immigration Act.* Guidelines on Women Refugee Claimants Fearing Gender-Related Persecution." Ottawa, March 9, 1993.

Indra, Doreen. "Gender: A Key Dimension of the Refugee Experience." *Refugee* 7 (1987): 3-4.

Johnson, Anders B. "The International Protection of Women Refugees." *International Journal of Refugee Law* 1 (2) (1989): 221-224.

Kane, Hal. *The Hour of Departure: Forces that Create Refugees and Migrants.* Washington DC: World Watch Institute, 1995.

Kelly, Ninette. "Working with Refugee Women: A Practical Guide." International NGO Working Group on Refugee Women. Report from the International Consultation on Refugee Women. Geneva, November 1988.

Kibreab, Gaim. *Refugees and Development in Africa: The Case of Eritrea.* Trenton, New Jersey: The Red Sea Press, 1987.

Korac, Maya. "Women's Groups in the Former Yugoslavia: Working with Refugees." *Refuge* 4 (8) (1995): 12-15.

Krummel, Charon. *Women Refugees and the Experience of Cultural Uprooting.* Geneva: World Council of Churches, 1986.

Macklin, Audrey. *Opening the Door: First Crack.* Proceedings of the Gender Issues and Refugees: Development Implications Conference held at York University, May 9-11, 1993. Toronto: Centre for Refugee Studies.

*Manavi Newsletter.* 3 (2) (1991). Special issue on violence against women.

Marching Centre, Settlement Branch, Employment and Immigration Canada, 1995.

Meijer, Marijke. "Oppression of Women and Refugee Status." *International Seminar on Women Refugees.* Amsterdam: Dutch Refugee Association, 1985.

Mollica, Richard F. and Linda Son. "Cultural Dimensions in the Evaluation of Treatment of Sexual Trauma." *Psychiatric Clinics of North America* 12 (2) (1989): 378-363.

Moussa, Helene and Patrick Taran. *A Moment to Choose: Risking to Be with Uprooted People.* Geneva: World Council of Churches, 1996.

Moussa, Helene. *Women Claiming Power Together: A Handbook to Set Up and Access Support Groups for/with Immigrant andRefugee Women.* Toronto: Education Wife Assault, 1995.

Moussa, Helene. *Storm and Sanctuary: The Journey of Ethiopian and Eritrean Women Refugees.* Dundas, Ontario: Artemis Enterprises, 1993.

Ng, Roxana and Tania Das Gupta. "Nation Builder: The Captive Labour Force of Non-English Speaking Immigrant women." *Canadian Woman Studies/les cahiers de la femme* 3 (1) (1981): 83-89.

Omvedt, Gail. *Violence Against Women: New Movement and New Theories in India.* New Delhi: Kali for Women, 1990.

Paul, Karola. "Granting Refugee Status for Gender-Based Persecution and Attitudes and Behaviour in the Hearing Room." Presentation by Karola Paul, Chief, Promotion of Refugee Law Unit, Division of International Protection, UNHCR, Geneva. IRD/CRDD Workshop of the Working Group on Women Refugee Claimants Determination Issues in Refugee Claims made by Women. Toronto, March 19, 1992.

Razack, Sherene. " Domestic Violence as Gender Persecution: Policing Borders of Nation, Race and Gender." *Canadian Journal of Women and the Law* 8 (1) (1995): 45-88.

Razack, Sherene. "Story-Telling for Social Change." *Gender and Education* 5 (1) (1993): 55-70.

Regehr, Ernie. "Key Canadian Components Missing: UN Reports First Arms Trade Register." *The Ploughshares Monitor* 14 (4) (1993): 10,19.

Reilly, Niamh. *Testimonies of the Global Tribunal on Violations of Women's Rights, Vienna 1993*. New Jersey: Center for Women's Global Leadership, 1994.

Richmond, Anthony. *Global Apartheid: Refugees, Racism and the New World Order*. Oxford: Oxford University Press, 1994.

Schuller, Margaret, Ed. *Freedom from Violence: Women's Strategies from Around the World*. New York: UNIFEM, 1992.

Sen, Gita and Caren Grown. *Developments, Crisis and Alternative Visions: Third World Women's Perspectives*. New York: Monthly Review Press, 1987.

Sivard, Ruth Leger. *World Military and Social Expenditure, 1991*. Washington, DC: World Priorities, 1993.

Sivard, Ruth Leger. *World Military Expenditure*. Washington, DC: World Priorities, 1991.

Sivard, Ruth Leger. *World Military Expenditure*. Washington, DC: World Priorities, 1987.

Spencer, Sarah. Ed. *Immigration as an Economic Assistance: The German Experience*. London: Tretham Books, 1994.

Stalker, Peter. *The World of Strangers: A Survey of Immigrant Labour Migration*. Geneva: International Labour Organization, 1994.

Stairs, Felicite and Lori Pope. "No Place Like Home: Assaulted Humanitarian and Compassionate Grounds." *Journal of Law and Social Policy* 5 (1990): 148-225.

Stein, Barry N. "The Nature of the Refugee Problems." *Human Rights and the Protection of Refugees under International Law: Proceedings of a Conference held in Montreal, November 29 - December 2, 1987*. Ed. Alan E. Nash. Halifax: The Institute for Research on Public Policy, 1988. 47-72.

Stojsavljevic, Jovanka, "Women, Conflict, and Culture in Former Yugoslavia." *Gender and Development* 3 (1) (1995).

Tomasevski, Katarina. *Women and Human Rights*. London: Zed Books, 1993.

Tu Khuong, Dao. "Victims of Violence: South China Sea." *Refugees: The Trauma of Exile*. Ed. Diana Miserez. Boston: Martinus Nijhof Publishers, 1988. 13-17.

United Nations. Convention and Protocol Relating to the Status of Refugees, Final Act of the United Nations Conference of Plenipotentiaries on the Status of Refugees and Stateless Persons and the Text of the 1951 Convention Relating to Refugees, Resolution 2198 adopted by the General Assembly and the Text of the 1967 Protocol Relating to the Status of Refugees, United Nations, 1983, Article 1 A (2): 12 and 39.

United Nations Economic Commission for Africa (UN/ECA). Africa Training and Research Centre for Women, "Refugee Women and Displaced Women in Independent Africa." (E/ECA/ATRCW/86/06).

United Nations Economic and Social Council, Commission of Human Rights, Fifty-first session: "Human Rights, Mass Exoduses and Displaced Persons–

Internally Dsplaced Persons." Report of the Representative of the Secretary-General, Mr. Francis Deng. Submitted pursuant to Commission on Human Rights Resolutions 1993/95 and 1994/68. E/CN.4/1995/50. 2 February 1995.

United Nations High Commission for Refugees (UNHCR). *The State of the World's Refugees: In Search of Solutions.* Oxford: Oxford University Press. 1995.

United Nations High Commission for Refugees (UNHCR). *Sexual Violence Against Refugees: Guidelines on Prevention and Response.* Geneva: UNHCR, 1995.

United Nations High Commission for Refugees(UNHCR). "Guidelines on the Protection of Refugee Women." Geneva, 1991. Prepared by Mary A. Anderson and the UNHCR Senior Coordinator for Refugee Women.

United Nations High Commission for Refugees (UNHCR) Executive Committee Conclusions, 39th Session, October 1989. "Refugee Women." *International Journal of Refugee Law* 1 (3) (1989): 253-254.

United Nations High Commission on Refugees (UNHCR) Executive Committee 36th Session. "Refugee Women and International Protection." *Conclusions of the International Protection of Refugees adopted by the /Executive Committee of the UNHCR. Program.* Geneva: UNHCR, 1985. 84-85.

van Willigen, Loes. "Women Refugees and Sexual Violence." *International Seminar on Women Refugees.* Amsterdam: Dutch Refugee Association, 1985. 20-24.

United States Committee for Refugees. *1993 World Survey.* Washington, DC: American Council for Nationalities Services, 1993.

United States Naturalization and Immigration Service. "Consideration for Officers Adjudicating Asylum Claims for Women." Washington, DC, May 26, 1995. Memorandum to all INS Asylum Officers and HQASM Coordinators. From Phyllis Coven, Office of International Affairs. 1-19.

Wiesinger, Rita. "Identity and Personality of Refugee Women." *A WR Bulletin* 2 (1) (1984): 9-14.

*Women's World* 24 (1990/91). Special issue of ISIS-WICCE on Poverty and Prostitution.

Young, Iris. *Justice and the Politics of Difference.* New Jersey: Princeton University Press, 1990.

Zolberg, Aristides *et al.* "International Factors in the Formation of Refugee Movements." *International Migration Review* 20 (2) (1986): 151-169.

# APPENDIX 1

## Convention Refugees and Designated Class, 19 years of Age and Above Family Status by Gender and Year of Landing (1986-1993)

| | 1986 | | 1987 | | 1988 | | 1989 | | 1990 | | 1991 | | 1992 | | 1993 | | Total | |
|---|---|---|---|---|---|---|---|---|---|---|---|---|---|---|---|---|---|---|
| | F | M | F | M | F | M | F | M | F | M | F | M | F | M | F | M | F | M |
| Principal Applicant | 2,161 | 7,974 | 2,685 | 9,117 | 3,272 | 11,264 | 4,750 | 15,287 | 4,797 | 17,180 | 7,497 | 24,524 | 7,877 | 23,942 | 5,280 | 12,328 | 38,319 | 121,616 |
| % by year | 21% | 79% | 23% | 77% | 22% | 78% | 24% | 76% | 22% | 78% | 23% | 77% | 25% | 75% | 24% | 76% | 24% | 76% |
| Spouse | 2,745 | 106 | 2,963 | 162 | 3,809 | 151 | 5,134 | 343 | 5,706 | 373 | 6,284 | 712 | 5,496 | 652 | 3,185 | 426 | 35,386 | 2,925 |
| % by year | 96% | 4% | 95% | 5% | 96% | 4% | 94% | 6% | 94% | 6% | 90% | 10% | 89% | 11% | 88% | 12% | 92% | 8% |
| Dependants | 159 | 175 | 179 | 185 | 217 | 271 | 488 | 773 | 383 | 487 | 621 | 641 | 722 | 534 | 375 | 292 | 3,144 | 3,368 |
| % by year | 48% | 52% | 49% | 51% | 44% | 56% | 39% | 61% | 44% | 56% | 49% | 51% | 58% | 42% | 56% | 44% | 48% | 52% |
| Total | 5,065 | 8,255 | 5,827 | 9,464 | 7,298 | 11,686 | 10,444 | 16,419 | 10,900 | 18,064 | 14,435 | 25,915 | 14,095 | 25,528 | 8,840 | 12,746 | 76,500 | 128,077 |
| | 38% | 62% | 38% | 62% | 38% | 62% | 38% | 62% | 38% | 62% | 36% | 64% | 39% | 61% | 41% | 59% | 37% | 63% |

Source: Employment and Immigration Canada, Immigration Statistics

# APPENDIX 2

## Convention Refugees and Designated Class, "Principal Applicants" 19 years of Age and Above Ten Highest Countries of Origin by Gender and Year of Landing (1986-1991)*

| | 1986 | | 1987 | | 1988 | | 1989 | | 1990 | | 1991 | | Total | |
|---|---|---|---|---|---|---|---|---|---|---|---|---|---|---|
| | F | M | F | M | F | M | F | M | F | M | F | M | F | M |
| 1. Afghanistan | 29 | 237 | 50 | 342 | 78 | 342 | 83 | 302 | 73 | 290 | 84 | 369 | 397 | 1,882 |
| Percent by year | 10% | 90% | 13% | 87% | 19% | 81% | 22% | 78% | 20% | 80% | 19% | 81% | 17% | 83% |
| 2. El Salvador | 298 | 670 | 298 | 619 | 260 | 533 | 251 | 544 | 542 | 1,203 | 944 | 2,020 | 2,593 | 5,593 |
| Percent by year | 30% | 70% | 82% | 68% | 33% | 67% | 32% | 68% | 31% | 69% | 32% | 68% | 32% | 68% |
| 3. Ethiopa | 159 | 526 | 181 | 507 | 289 | 777 | 496 | 1,120 | 516 | 1,082 | 469 | 1,115 | 2,110 | 5,127 |
| Percent by year | 23% | 77% | 26% | 74% | 27% | 73% | 30% | 70% | 32% | 68% | 30% | 70% | 29% | 71% |
| 4. Iran | 113 | 491 | 126 | 520 | 177 | 1,035 | 193 | 896 | 214 | 904 | 494 | 1,787 | 1,317 | 5,633 |
| Percent by year | 19% | 81% | 20% | 80% | 17% | 83% | 18% | 82% | 19% | 81% | 21% | 79% | 20% | 80% |
| 5. Kampuchea, Dem. Rep. | 129 | 412 | 205 | 436 | 181 | 425 | 191 | 499 | 70 | 181 | 45 | 78 | 821 | 2,031 |
| Percent by year | 24% | 76% | 31% | 79% | 30% | 70% | 28% | 72% | 28% | 72% | 37% | 63% | 29% | 71% |
| 6. Poland | 500 | 1,752 | 744 | 2,119 | 1,013 | 3,158 | 1,653 | 5,763 | 1,418 | 5,459 | 1,796 | 5,262 | 7,124 | 23,513 |
| Percent by year | 22% | 78% | 26% | 74% | 22% | 78% | 23% | 77% | 21% | 79% | 26% | 74% | 23% | 77% |
| 7. Romania | 392 | 61 | 63 | 485 | 65 | 450 | 63 | 505 | 84 | 535 | 75 | 232 | 389 | 2,468 |
| Percent by year | 13% | 87% | 11% | 89% | 14% | 86% | 12% | 88% | 16% | 84% | 24% | 76% | 14% | 86% |
| 8. Somali, Republic of | 4 | 18 | 3 | 50 | 32 | 127 | 63 | 260 | 185 | 608 | 592 | 1,443 | 879 | 2,506 |
| Percent by year | 18% | 82% | 6% | 94% | 20% | 80% | 20% | 80% | 23% | 77% | 29% | 71% | 26% | 74% |
| 9. Sri Lanka | 13 | 163 | 38 | 381 | 20 | 112 | 26 | 128 | 157 | 781 | 493 | 2,461 | 747 | 4,026 |
| Percent by year | 8% | 92% | 9% | 91% | 15% | 85% | 17% | 83% | 17% | 83% | 17% | 83% | 16% | 84% |
| 10. Vietnam, Soc. Rep. | 508 | 1,772 | 541 | 1,859 | 674 | 2,063 | 1,147 | 2,799 | 723 | 2,380 | 321 | 1,076 | 3,914 | 11,949 |
| Percent by year | 22% | 78% | 23% | 77% | 25% | 75% | 29% | 71% | 23% | 77% | 23% | 77% | 25% | 75% |

Source: Employment and Immigration Canada *As a result of new and emerging conflict situations, the ten highest countries of origin differed after 1992. The gender patterns remain the same.

# APPENDIX 3

## Convention Refugees and Designated Class, "Spouse" 19 years of Age and Above Ten Highest Countries of Origin by Gender and Year of Landing (1986-1991)*

| | 1986 | | 1987 | | 1988 | | 1989 | | 1990 | | 1991 | | Total | |
|---|---|---|---|---|---|---|---|---|---|---|---|---|---|---|
| | F | M | F | M | F | M | F | M | F | M | F | M | F | M |
| 1. Afghanistan | 78 | 1 | 117 | 2 | 144 | 5 | 137 | 14 | 139 | 15 | 181 | 14 | 796 | 51 |
| Percent by year | 99% | 1% | 96% | 2% | 97% | 3% | 91% | 9% | 90% | 10% | 93% | 7% | 94% | 6% |
| 2. El Salvador | 314 | 30 | 327 | 58 | 276 | 40 | 302 | 49 | 433 | 84 | 593 | 113 | 2,245 | 374 |
| Percent by year | 91% | 9% | 85% | 15% | 87% | 13% | 86% | 14% | 84% | 16% | 84% | 16% | 86% | 14% |
| 3. Ethiopa | 98 | 13 | 70 | 8 | 129 | 11 | 181 | 17 | 205 | 25 | 198 | 31 | 881 | 105 |
| Percent by year | 88% | 12% | 90% | 10% | 92% | 8% | 91% | 9% | 89% | 1% | 86% | 14% | 89% | 11% |
| 4. Iran | 110 | 3 | 129 | 7 | 268 | 6 | 315 | 28 | 283 | 42 | 511 | 78 | 1,616 | 164 |
| Percent by year | 97% | 3% | 95% | 5% | 98% | 2% | 92% | 8% | 87% | 13% | 87% | 13% | 91% | 9% |
| 5. Kampuchea, Dem. Rep. | 322 | 3 | 236 | 13 | 233 | 4 | 314 | 4 | 106 | 2 | 44 | 2 | 1,255 | 28 |
| Percent by year | 99% | 1% | 95% | 5% | 98% | 2% | 99% | 1% | 98% | 2% | 96% | 4% | 98% | 2% |
| 6. Poland | 602 | 17 | 708 | 15 | 1,114 | 32 | 2,052 | 108 | 2,165 | 78 | 1,378 | 77 | 8,019 | 327 |
| Percent by year | 97% | 3% | 98% | 2% | 97% | 3% | 95% | 5% | 97% | 3% | 95% | 5% | 96% | 4% |
| 7. Romania | 68 | 3 | 130 | 3 | 96 | 5 | 107 | 15 | 176 | 6 | 93 | 4 | 670 | 36 |
| Percent by year | 96% | 4% | 98% | 2% | 95% | 5% | 88% | 12% | 97% | 3% | 96% | 4% | 95% | 5% |
| 8. Somali, Republic of | 3 | 0 | 5 | 0 | 12 | 0 | 15 | 3 | 65 | 6 | 143 | 16 | 243 | 25 |
| Percent by year | 100% | 0% | 100% | 0% | 100% | 0% | 83% | 17% | 92% | 8% | 90% | 10% | 91% | 9% |
| 9. Sri Lanka | 49 | 1 | 89 | 3 | 29 | 1 | 24 | 3 | 117 | 16 | 443 | 79 | 751 | 103 |
| Percent by year | 98% | 2% | 97% | 3% | 97% | 3% | 89% | 11% | 88% | 12% | 83% | 17% | 88% | 12% |
| 10. Vietnam, Soc. Rep. | 350 | 11 | 318 | 12 | 435 | 12 | 578 | 25 | 572 | 7 | 504 | 9 | 2,757 | 78 |
| Percent by year | 97% | 3% | 91% | 9% | 97% | 3% | 96% | 4% | 99% | 1% | 98% | 2% | 97% | 3% |

Source: Employment and Immigration Canada *As a result of new and emerging conflict situations, the ten highest countries of origin differed after 1992. The gender patterns remain the same.

## APPENDIX 4

### Refugee Claimants in the Backlog before 1989, 19 years of Age and Above Family Status by Gender and Year of Landing (1990-1993)

| | 1990 | | 1991 | | 1992 | | 1993 | | Total | |
|---|---|---|---|---|---|---|---|---|---|---|
| | F | M | F | M | F | M | F | M | F | M |
| Principal Applicants | 549 | 2,170 | 2,143 | 9,046 | 867 | 3,996 | 3,080 | 6,347 | 6,639 | 21,559 |
| Percent by year | 20% | 80% | 19% | 81% | 18% | 82% | 33% | 67% | 24% | 76% |
| Spouse | 412 | 92 | 1,943 | 381 | 920 | 168 | 1,426 | 345 | 4,701 | 986 |
| Percent by year | 81% | 19% | 85% | 15% | 85% | 15% | 80% | 20% | 81% | 19% |
| Dependents | 21 | 28 | 251 | 198 | 275 | 137 | 1,921 | 1,769 | 2,465 | 2,132 |
| Percent by year | 43% | 57% | 56% | 44% | 67% | 33% | 52% | 48% | 54% | 46% |
| TOTAL | 982 | 2,290 | 4,337 | 9,620 | 2,062 | 4,301 | 4,882 | 6,910 | 12,263 | 13,126 |
| | 30% | 70% | 31% | 69% | 32% | 68% | 41% | 59% | 48% | 52% |

Source: Employment and Immigration Canada, Immigration Statistics

# Living on the Edge

## Women, Poverty and Homelessness in Canada

Suzanne Lenon

In 1998, the mayors of Canada's large urban centres declared homelessness a national disaster. Who the homeless are and what measures should be taken to alleviate this crisis are currently the subjects of much public attention. Traditionally, homelessness has been constructed and viewed as a male experience. Our predominant understanding of what constitutes homelessness (and therefore who is homeless) is based on those who are visibly without shelter and who use emergency shelters. Generally, women are not as prevalent as men among shelter users and hence make up only a small percentage of research samples. Women's homelessness is often "invisible" as women rely on their domestic and sexual roles as a strategy to avoid shelters, such as taking up temporary residences in short-term sexual relationships. Recent reports suggest, however, that the visible face of homelessness in Canada is changing: youth, families, and women are the fastest growing groups in the visibly homeless and at-risk population. In 1996, for example, families represented 46 per cent of the people using hostels in Toronto; ("Taking Responsibility for Homelessness") in Montreal it is estimated that 4,000 to 5,000 youth are homeless and that 30 to 40 per cent of homeless people are women (Santé Québec).

In grappling with how, as a nation, we have arrived at this state of emergency, one which the United Nations has condemned as a violation of human rights, the public gaze is more often than not intensely focused on the issue of provision of shelter, both as cause and solution to the homelessness crisis. Although the severe lack of affordable housing in Canada is a pressing issue, with tangible and material consequences, paring down the meaning of homelessness to simply one of physical housing obscures the relations of power that contribute to housing insecurity. Homelessness in Canada is one manifestation of a wider structure of disadvantage and exclusion based on classism, sexism, and racism. These tools of exclusion offer useful explanatory and analytical accounts of the processes which structure women's vulnerability to homelessness.

Canada is experiencing widening economic and social inequity as government and business interests merge in the interests of making our economy more globally competitive and facilitating increased wealth accumulation by the rich. This inequality is evident in the following indicators:

- the poorest 20 per cent of all families brought in 5.0 per cent of all income in 1989, but by 1998, their share had dropped to 4.3 per cent. At the same time, the richest 20 per cent of Canadian families' share of all income increased from 42.8 per cent to 45.5 per cent (Statistics Canada); and
- the average income gap increased over the last decade from $7,616 in 1989 to $8,219 in 1998. In other words, the average poor Canadian family had to get by on $8,219 *less than* the poverty line (Statistics Canada).

The process of globalization exerts a downward pressure on our social safety net by prioritizing the reduction of deficits and debt, and the lowering of taxes as key objectives of state policy. The unquenchable corporate thirst for massive wealth accumulation is undermining national solidarity and legitimates inequality of rewards. Decades of deficit-reduction hysteria have diminished our collective expectations of what we can afford to provide for each other and what we believe possible for a just, caring, and compassionate society.

As such Canadians have witnessed an unprecedented dismantling and restructuring of our social welfare state. Health, education, and social services are increasingly privatized and income support programs have been dramatically and drastically scaled back. The shift from Unemployment Insurance (UI) to Employment Insurance (EI) in 1996, for example, reduced payments to people working in temporary, contract, and seasonal jobs. It also replaced the number of weeks with the number of hours worked as the indicator for entitlement. This change means individuals must work for longer periods of time before qualifying for benefits. Benefit levels and duration of benefits have also been significantly reduced. The proportion of unemployed people receiving EI benefits has declined significantly from 87 per cent in 1990 to 36 per cent by 1998. This drastic reduction undermines the program's ability to insure against unemployment and increases the incidence of poverty.

As fewer people are eligible for EI they must turn to provincial social assistance programs for basic economic support. These too have undergone dramatic reductions. In response to significant reductions of federal transfers under the Canada Assistance Plan (CAP) in 1989 and, subsequently under the Canada Health and Social Transfer (CHST) in 1996, the efforts of provincial governments have coalesced around one key objective: to reduce social assistance budgets in favour of continuing to provide funding for health care and education. This has involved linking income support more firmly to employment through mandatory work provisions (workfare); redefining eligibility and entitlement to benefits; and reducing or freezing benefit levels. There is no longer any requirement for provincial governments to spend money on social assistance programs nor to maintain minimal national standards.

Social assistance benefit rates have always been far below the poverty line, not reflecting even the basic costs of living. For example, a single parent with one child receiving welfare in Alberta received $11,088 in 1998, only 50 per cent of the poverty line. The average income for a single employable person in Newfoundland in 1998 was nine per cent of the poverty line, that is, only $1,323 (National Council of Welfare). Furthermore, the lack of inflation protection has meant that the value of welfare benefits continues to decline in relation to the cost of living. Cutbacks to social assistance and other social programs have had a disproportionate impact on women as women experience higher rates of poverty than men. Fifty-seven per cent of single parent families headed by women are poor; and almost 19 per cent of adult women in Canada are poor—the highest rate of women's poverty in two decades (Statistics Canada).

The erosion of the income of low-income households and the economic insecurity of women are a significant factor shaping women's vulnerability to homelessness and ability to access housing once homeless. In Canada, housing is primarily a commodity that is allocated by market forces. As with anything else that depends upon market allocation, one's economic and social power determines the extent of its rewards. Market-dominated housing policies disadvantage women, particularly female-led households, given their unequal position within the labour market, their lower average income levels, and their higher rates of dependency on income supports. As such, women-led households face severe housing affordability problems.

A single parent earning minimum wage devotes an inordinate amount of her income to shelter, paying more than 50 per cent of her income on rent in cities like Toronto, Ottawa, or Windsor. The shelter component of social assistance has fallen and no longer covers the average market rent in a given area, leaving little left for other basic needs such as food and clothes (Centre for Equity Rights in Accomodation). In Vancouver, a single person receiving social assistance pays more than two times her welfare income (that is, 128.5 per cent) towards rent for a one-bedroom apartment (Canadian Association of Food Banks). According to an April 2000 study, people who use food banks in Toronto have, on average, $4.95 a day to spend on all their needs other than rent—food, transportation, utilities, laundry, school supplies, personal toiletries, etc. In 1995, the average amount was $7.40 (Food and Hunger Committee). That food bank use in Canada has more than doubled in a decade is testimony to increasing depths of poverty and material deprivation, which impinge directly on women's ability access to adequate housing.

Along with income and class inequality, inequitable gender relations also structure women's homelessness. Women are vulnerable to homelessness through different mechanisms of the patriarchal family structure. Women's unpaid work in the reproductive economy, that is, the household, limits their ability to achieve and sustain economic autonomy. While paid employment is clearly one route to economic independence, the issue of autonomy within households is also critical.

As noted above, women are more vulnerable to poverty; escaping this poverty hangs on access to the income of other family members. The link between economic security and dependency on marital or other personal relationships is problematic, particularly as a contributing factor to homelessness. Residing in the same house does not mean that everyone shares equally its resources or that there are consensual relations within it. Women are much more likely to experience housing insecurity and become homeless through the breakdown of marital or other personal relationships in which they are either materially or financially dependent.

Feminist theorists and activists have unveiled a gendered imbalance of power within households, and a blatant indicator of this is the extent of violence by men against women and children. Women's homelessness is frequently the result of male violence such as wife assault, sexual abuse of children and youth, and sexual harassment of tenants. In 1996, for example, 8,450 women and children in Toronto turned to a women's shelter or the general hostel system because of domestic violence ("Taking Responsibility for Homelessness"). In Calgary in 1996, 2,587 women-led households faced a housing crisis, of which 971 were absolutely homeless (Calgary Homelessness Study). Conversely, when a woman has limited personal and financial resources, limited access to subsidized child care, and is faced with extremely low rates of social assistance, she may feel that she cannot afford to leave an abusive situation.

The dynamics of violence in women's lives and the various means by which they cope with it challenge conventional notions of "homeless." While current formulations suggest that homelessness is a deficiency and a condition to be remedied (with housing the solution) it has been suggested that housing is the problem to which homelessness may well be a solution (Tomas and Dittmar). While the meanings attributed to "home" include various social and psychological dimensions beyond physical shelter, homeless women with histories of family disruption and abuse distinguish being housed from being safe, so that homelessness is a problem for women, but it is *also* a strategy for escaping violence. Defining homelessness as a housing issue exclusively neglects the experiences of "home" for women. For women, homelessness is not resolved by simply having a roof over her head unless it is accompanied by a sense of safety and security.

Experiences of sexual harassment and sexual assault are common for women living on the street or in hostels. Homelessness is a much more dangerous condition to be in for women. The results of a study of homeless people in Toronto, for example, demonstrate this risk of sexual violence. It found that 43.3 per cent of the women sampled had received unwelcome sexual advances as compared to 14.1 per cent of men. More than one in five women interviewed reported being raped in the past year (Ambrosio).

Public discussions on homelessness are disturbingly silent on issues of race as a determinant of homelessness despite the reality that racial minority and immigrant women comprise a disproportionate share of homeless women and shelter users. Aboriginal people also are over-represented in the homeless population in Canada as they also experience disproportionate rates of poverty. The Royal Commission on Aboriginal Peoples found that between 40 and 76 per cent of Aboriginal households in large urban areas fall below the poverty line. The situation is even more serious for female-headed single-parent households, of which 80 to 90 per cent fall below the poverty line ("Taking Responsibility for Homelessness").

Racial minority women experience the effects of both sexism and racism within a predominantly profit-driven housing system, particularly in terms of access. Their lower incomes and diminished housing options contribute to greater affordability problems and increase the likelihood that their housing conditions will be unsuitable or inadequate. A recent study of housing conditions among immigrant and racial minority women found that while their experiences of housing insecurity reflect the general pattern of class and gender based disadvantage, they also included acute instances of housing related crisis exacerbated by racism (Novac). Landlords have long discriminated against people of colour based on their race and low income. While Canada has a reputation of being more tolerant and less overtly racist than the United States, Aboriginal women and women of colour consistently tell us and articulate quite clearly that skin colour matters in Canadian society and, in this instance, within the housing market. Yet relations of power based on race are rarely put forth as a factor structuring homelessness in Canada. This silence works to exclude the experiences and lived realities of a significant portion of the homeless population from the public discourse on homelessness, and ultimately hinders strategies to effectively and holistically deal with the homelessness crisis.

Women experience vulnerability to homelessness in a variety of ways as they occupy a range of different and shifting positions in relation to a wide variety of power structures. They can become homeless for a variety of reasons including the breakdown of family relationships; sexual or racial harassment; the loss of employment; inadequate income supports such as social assistance; the high rental costs of a market dominated housing system. Women's ability to negotiate through discrimination based on class, race, and gender shifts as the patterns of their lives change over time. The social and economic policy choices made by governments in response to corporate forces, however, create an increasingly precarious existence for low-income women. The dismantling of the welfare state is eroding their economic, social, housing, food, and overall personal security. Their ability to make claims to social and economic justice is undermined by popular images of the poor as lazy and hence less deserving of basic economic and social rights.

Homelessness is a feminist issue. It is directly linked to fundamental inequities of power and privilege. Conceptualizing the causes of and solutions to homelessness simply in terms of physical housing cloaks the relations of power by which those women marginalized and excluded by global capitalism become homeless. Investigating all women's experiences of housing insecurity and their journey into homelessness will offer more satisfying explanatory accounts and perhaps more challenging and engaging public discussions about the meanings of home and homelessness.

## References

Ambrosio Eileen, Dilin Baker, Cathy Crowe, and Kathy Hardill. "The Street Health Report: A Study of the Health Status and Barriers to Health Care of Homeless Women and Men in the City of Toronto." Toronto: May 1992.

"Calgary Homelessness Study." J. Arboleda-Florez and H. L. Holley, Co-Principal Investigators. Calgary, 1997.

Canadian Association of Food Banks. "Hunger Count 1999." Toronto: Canadian Association of Food Banks, 1999.

Centre for Equality Rights in Accomodation (CERA). "Homelessness in Ontario: The Case for a Needs-Based Shelter Supplement." Toronto: Centre for Equality Rights and Accomodation, 2000.

Food and Hunger Action Committee. "Planting the Seeds: Phase 1 Report." Toronto: May 2000.

National Council of Welfare *Welfare Incomes 1997 and 1998*. Ottawa: Minister of Public Works, and Government Services of Canada. Winter 1999-2000.

Novac, Sylvia. *A Place to Call One's Own: New Voices of Dislocation and Dispossession.* Ottawa: Status of Women Canada, 1996.

Santé Québec. "Dénombrement de la clientèle itinérante ... de Montréal et de Québec." Ville de Québec, 1998.

Statistics Canada. *Income in Canada.* Ottawa: Statistics Canada, 1998.

"Taking Responsibility for Homelessness: An Action Plan for Toronto. Report of the Mayor's Homelessness Action Task Force." Toronto: January 1999.

Tomas, Annabel and Helga Dittmar. "The Experience of Homeless Women: An Exploration of Housing Histories and the Meaning of Home." *Housing Studies* 10 (4) (1995): 493-515.

# Before and After

## A Woman's Story with Two Endings ...

Woman Abuse Council of Toronto

### June 1995: Before the Cutbacks

A woman, who has immigrated to Canada from South America has three adolescent children and is living in downtown Toronto. She speaks limited English and has never worked outside of the home in Canada.

The woman goes to the doctor after receiving serious injuries from her husband. He has been increasingly abusive to her, both emotionally and physically, over the last ten years.

By attending training sessions at the Centre for Spanish Speaking Peoples, the doctor has learned how best to detect and deal with women patients who are being abused by their partners. The doctor discusses the woman's situation with her and reinforces that abuse is a crime. He discusses various options for her protection and safety, including referring her to a woman's shelter. He also urges her to visit the Centre for Spanish Speaking Peoples, which offers counselling programs for Spanish speaking women. The doctor schedules a follow-up appointment to check her injuries and continues to encourage her to take some action to protect herself and her children.

The mother and children go to the Centre for Spanish Speaking Peoples, and, by attending counselling sessions and a support group, she gains the strength and information to make the decision to leave her husband. She has learned what she needs to do to end years of emotional and physical abuse. Once she has made the decision to leave, a staff person provided through the Multilingual Access to Social Assistance Program (MASAP) helps her with the welfare application process, which would otherwise be difficult given her limited knowledge of English.

*The MASAP Program was completely eliminated in the first rounds of massive cuts to social spending in October 1995.*

The mother and her children go to a shelter, where they receive support, referrals, advocacy, and information. They all attend counselling groups, where they each continue to gain the strength and self-confidence to legally leave an abusing husband and father.

*Due to cutbacks in funding and changes in agency mandates, shelters are now being told to focus on food and housing needs only. Emotional needs, including counselling, are seen as luxuries.*

The mother is referred to Legal Aid, where she qualifies for a legal aid certificate and is able to get a lawyer to start divorce proceedings. At the same time, the mother and children get on the Battered Women's Priority List for Metro Toronto Housing, and they are offered housing within three to four months.

The mother attends English as a Second Language classes at the Centre for Spanish Speaking Peoples, where she also continues to get support and information. Once her English has improved, the centre refers the mother to Dixon Hall for employment retraining. She completes a six-week course and has two job interviews as she prepares for the next stage of her independence—a job.

*The Legal Aid system is currently in a state of upheaval. Women are being given legal aid certificates, but lawyers are refusing to honour them because payments are not assured.*

*Every one of the 4,000 hostel beds in Toronto was occupied on October 20, 1995. This was unprecedented at this time of year, before the winter weather. Over the past year, the number of single mothers using hostels has increased by 53 per cent—from 639 to 965. Hostel use by single mothers and their families rose faster than any other homeless group.*

*The job retraining program offered through Dixon Hall, like others across the province, was closed down due to cuts in social spending.*

## January 1996: After the Cutbacks

A mother with three adolescent children speaks limited English and has never worked outside the home. The woman goes to her doctor after her abusive husband has seriously injured her.

Her doctor has been a participant in the community education project at the Centre for Spanish Speaking Peoples. Through this project, physicians were trained in how to detect and respond effectively to women patients who are experiencing abuse at the hands of their partners. However, the project at the centre took place over a year ago and was not funded for a second year. There has been no follow-up, and the doctor does not remember much of the information, only the basic principles.

## The Statistical Story

*Several studies of hospital emergency room patients have demonstrated that 25 to 35 per cent of all women attending emergency rooms are there because of injuries/illness resulting from domestic violence. Physicians often estimate that one or two per cent of their female patients are assaulted by their partners, but conservative estimates indicate that at least one in eight women in Canada are assaulted by their partners. In one Ontario hospital, the number of reported wife assault cases increased 1,500 per cent after policies and procedures were implemented to deal with women abuse.*

The doctor treats the wounds, gives the mother the number of the Centre for Spanish Speaking Peoples, and suggests that she contact them. In the meantime, the doctor urges her to do whatever is necessary not to antagonize her husband and to keep him happy so that her wounds can heal that she will not be hurt further.

The woman does not call immediately, fearing what will happen if her husband finds out that she has talked to someone about the abuse. However, after much consideration, and after seeing how upset her children are, she does call the centre. The Centre for Spanish Speaking Peoples has reduced staff as a result of cuts to community service agencies, and the woman is put on a waiting list. The centre used to get Purchase of Service funding to provide counselling to low-income people, but this program has been cut entirely. She is mailed brochures in Spanish about social assistance, shelters, subsidized housing, and the Legal Aid system. Because of budget cuts, there is not much more the centre can do.

Two weeks later, after the woman has received the brochures, her husband finds them and assaults her again for daring to take "family problems to a stranger."

After the second assault within one month, the woman begins to feel desperate enough to take action. She phones the Metro Toronto Housing Authority and, with great difficulty given her limited English, she gets the message that there is a three-year waiting list for subsidized housing. She then phones four shelters and discovers that there is no room—two shelters have started up a waiting list and say she could call back in a month, while the other two shelters suggest she contact a housing co-op. At this point, the woman tries to call welfare but can't get through on the general number. This is especially hard for her, because she is limited in when she can use the phone safely.

*On October 6, 1995, the provincial government announced the cancellation of the Multilingual Access to Social Assistance Program (MASAP) along with massive cuts to ethno-specific, multi-service community agencies, and support services battered women.*

Still unable to talk to someone on the phone, she hears on the radio about the massive cuts to welfare. The woman fears that even if she gets through on the phone line she still won't be eligible, so she makes no further attempts to call.

Almost two-thirds of separated or divorced women have suffered sexual, physical, or emotional abuse. Many of these women end up on social assistance.

The 21.6 per cent cut to social assistance means that a single parent with one child will receive $7.76 a day per person. Two adults with two children receive

$5.01 a day per person.

Children represent 40 per cent of all people receiving social assistance.

People on social assistance (40 per cent of whom are children), will be required to subsist on income that are more than 40 per cent below Statistics Canada's low-income cutoff (Ontario Social Safety Network).

The mother leaves with her three children to stay with her sister. The living situation is crowded and gets difficult very quickly with two families sharing an apartment. Tensions between the sisters emerge, as do tensions between the children. The husband knows where the mother is living. The mother and her children have no income and can only look forward to continuing to live in these crowded conditions. In fact, they will wait up to three years for subsidized housing. The mother tries to find a job but with few work skills and limited English, she is unable to find work.

The JobsOntario Training program has been cut by $86 million, and the program is being terminated.

In the end, the mother and her children return to the violent home. The children avoid being home as much as possible as the tension increases daily. They feel helpless to support their mother, yet are angry at her for returning to such an abusive man. The mother is further isolated, given that the husband flaunts the fact that she tried to leave and could not "make it on her own"—and has come "crawling back" to him. The father's violence escalates and is directed towards the children as well.

In a Canada-wide study of assaulted women, significant numbers of women reported that their partners had abused their children physically (26 per cent), psychologically (48 per cent), and sexually (7 per cent) (OWD 1994). In some studies, up to 50 per cent of young offenders charged with crimes against people were found to have been exposed to domestic violence as children (OWD 1994a). It has been shown that there are more serious child adjustment problems related to witnessing domestic violence than to the separation, divorce, or loss of parents.

The two stories in this article have offered a glimpse of the life of one woman and her family, and their first-hand experience with abuse. More and more women and families across Ontario could tell similar tales. Amid the stories of cost-cutting and reducing deficits, we must also consider the social deficit and take steps now so our society won't be paying in the years to come.

## References

Ontario Social Safety Network. "Welfare Rate Cuts: Backgrounder # 2." Toronto: Ontario Social Safety Network, 1995.

Ontario Women's Directorate (OWD). "Wife Assault." Toronto: Ontario Women's Directorate, 1994.

Ontario Women's Directorate (OWD). "Dispelling the Myths." Toronto: Ontario Women's Directorate, 1994a.

# Locked In, Left Out

## Impacts of the Budget Cuts on Abused Women and their Children

Ontario Association of
Interval and Transition Houses

Violence against women is a complex form of oppression. It touches every aspect of life for women and their children. Government cuts to women's shelters, while they highlight the impact of social program reduction on abused women, are only one part of a web of cuts to the supports women need to escape danger. To be free, survivors of violence—both women and child witnesses—literally need a safety net of programs and policies protecting their right to safety and equality.

### Cuts to Direct Services for Abused Women and their Children

*These cuts of the government have affected my family profoundly. I seem to be caught in a crack, as I hear so many others are. My abusive and controlling ex-husband has the ultimate control over us now.*

—-Dorothy, a survivor.

The first blow to abused women was the cut to services that directly work with survivors and their children—those services that, historically, have been the strongest advocates against violence. These services have supported countless numbers of survivors, often being credited with saving their lives. Women's grassroots services have educated the community, changed the policies and practices of systems, and provided the expertise needed to effectively pursue and end violence against women. All of these services have been imperiled, where they haven't already been eliminated entirely.

*Emergency Women's Shelters:* On October 1, 1995, emergency shelters that provide front-line crisis intervention to women experiencing violence had a 2.5 per cent provincial funding cut; and in April 1996 another cut of 2.5 per cent.

Shelters have been chronically underfunded since their inception almost 20 years ago. A five per cent overall cut, therefore, has had dramatic consequences on services that shelters are able to provide. Furthermore, cuts to women's shelters must be examined in the context of provincial government requirements that services fundraise 20 per cent of their cost for basic core services.

*Second stage women's shelters:* On December 31, 1995, the government eliminated all provincial funding for programs in second stage shelters for abused women and their children. Services reduced or eliminated included counselling for women and children, advocacy, language interpretation, and other programs. Second stages provide temporary housing for three months to a year. They are used by women who have been unable to secure permanent housing, have multiple barriers to escaping abuse, or need additional support. Since women in second stage shelters have decided to separate permanently from abusive partners, they may be particularly vulnerable. Survivors in second stage shelters use the service during the first few months after leaving an abusive relationship, a time when women are often stalked, harassed, assaulted, and murdered by former partners.

*Crisis lines:* Cuts were made to provincial funding of 24-hour crisis intervention phone lines in Ontario, including The Assaulted Women's Helpline in Toronto and SOS Femmes, the only crisis phone line assisting Francophone women in distress. These crisis intervention lines are front-line services, and are often the first contact with assistance for women fleeing from violence.

*Community counselling:* The five per cent overall cut to community programs included cuts to those counselling programs specifically addressing violence. Largely, delivered by family and children's service agencies in Ontario, these programs provide individual and group support for both women and children witnesses experiencing violence.

*Child protection:* Children's Aid Societies had budget reductions as a result of provincial cuts. These services provide supports to children experiencing violence, including support to child survivors of incest.

*Culturally specific services:* First Nations and Aboriginal social service programs were also reduced. Community counselling groups for specific racial and cultural communities as well as services specifically for Francophone women also received severe cuts. Many of these services gave direct counselling and advocacy support to abused women and their children on addressing issues of violence.

*Community advocacy:* Services providing housing and legal advocacy were cut along with other front-line agencies. Agencies such as housing help centres, free legal clinics and so on, have been used frequently by abused women attempting to find safe, affordable housing, or to explore their legal rights. Provincial cuts also affected provision of necessities such as food and clothing for abused women starting anew.

## Cuts to Other Essential Supports for Abused Women

It is important that the public and all partners in the justice system understand the implication cuts to legal aid will have on the administration of justice in Ontario.

—Susan Elliott, Head of the Law Society of Upper Canada, in "Changes to Ontario's Legal Aid Plan, a Guide for Legal Aid Lawyers."

Most critical among the supports survivors use to leave an abusive situation are those programs and supports women and children need to provide basic needs (such as food and shelter), address legal issues, become financially independent, and ensure the health and safety of themselves and their children. All women leaving an abusive relationship, whether or not they use or have access to direct shelter and counselling services, will find fewer supports as a result of funding cuts.

*Legal Aid:* In October 1995, the Ontario Legal Aid Plan, managed by the Law Society of Upper Canada, was cut by $153 million. In response, the Law Society made drastic changes to both the eligibility criteria for legal aid and to the fees Ontario lawyers may charge for providing legal services to clients receiving legal aid assistance. The eligibility changes included making "spouse or child at risk" a priority for assistance, but the definition of "at risk" has still not been determined, other than to restrict it to physical injury. (Subsequently, the Plan included "very serious psychological harm" as part of its first priority definition.) Guidelines for assistance in family law matters, already underfunded by the Plan, cut the hours lawyers can bill for divorce, child custody and access, support, and property settlements dramatically, sometimes by half.

Other changes affecting abused women included the introduction of fees for applications to the Plan, a lower limit on certificates issued per year, restrictions on legal aid recipients changing lawyers, and restrictions on eligibility for immigration and landlord/tenant matters. A program offering one free two-hour legal consultation for abused women, initiated in conjunction with the Ontario Women's Directorate, has also been limited.

*Criminal and family courts:* Reductions in the number of court officials and prosecutors has resulted in chief judges in Ontario predicting "chaos" for criminal court proceedings (Tyler). For abused women, who must testify as "victim witnesses" in assault trials, the chaos caused by cuts will only increase the pressures of a justice system chronically unresponsive to their needs.

*Social Assistance:* On October 1, 1995, welfare recipients received a 21.6 per cent cut to their monthly assistance cheque from the provincial government. These cuts drove recipients further below the poverty line (Monsebraaten). On a monthly basis, a sole support parent with one child currently receives a *maximum* of $511 for rent and $446 for food, clothing, transportation, and other basic necessities.

*Housing:* Along with social assistance shelter allowances, housing subsidies to tenants whose rent exceeds social assistance guidelines were cut by 21.6 per cent. In some cases, social assistance recipients were threatened with termination of benefits unless they moved into less expensive housing (Morrison). Funding for creating new co-operative housing has been frozen, and the government is strictly adhering to full-market rent geared to income ratios within co-op housing.

*Child care:* Changes to child care delivery and subsidies for low-income women in Ontario have reduced crucial support for women escaping violence. In August 1996, the government released the results of a child care "review" suggesting 15,000 new child care spaces could be created by a number of changes to child care delivery, including recommending lower wages for staff, subsidies for space in unlicensed, unregulated child care arrangements, increases in child to staff ratios, and decreases in government inspections. But according to the Ontario Coalition for Better Child Care, subsidies for child care spaces have already been reduced by 9,000 spaces and most municipalities in Ontario are not accepting any new applicants for subsidized daycare (McCuaig).

*Language interpretation services:* Cuts were made to interpretation services for women whose first language is not English or French. The cultural interpreter service for multilingual access to social assistance was eliminated, cutting off this important option for abused women needing to seek financial assistance to leave abuse situations.

*Services for people with disabilities:* Abused women with disabilities will encounter increased barriers to escaping danger or using what services remain for addressing violence. For example, funding for Wheel-Trans, public transit for persons with disabilities in Toronto, was reduced, and eligibility for use of the service restricted by a new definition of "disability." Persons that are approved to access this service must now pay a user fee when applying for registration. Doctors' forms that confirmed eligibility for the pay-per-use service are no longer acceptable as "proof" that the service is needed.

## Cuts that Compound

Women's lives are not defined only by abuse they suffer at the hands of intimate partners. Nor can their experiences of violence be narrowly defined within their personal relationships. Destroying services in the following areas further prevents women and their children from gaining freedom from all forms of violence against women.

*Anti-racism and anti-discrimination work:* Severe cuts and changes have been made to programs and policies that specifically work to end racism, create or ensure the rights of First Nations and Aboriginal Peoples, and assist persons with disabilities. This area includes anti-racism education, advocacy, and legal protection from disenfranchised communities (Ontario Social Safety Network 4).

*Education and training:* Women have seen large increases in their tuition fees for post-secondary education and cuts to training programs as a result of provincial budget reductions of 20 per cent. Further cuts and increases are expected in these areas. Women who are recipients of welfare are no longer able to attend school (Toughill), thus post-secondary education is a prerogative only for those who are well-off.

*Pay equity:* The provincial government has frozen funding to support pay equity implementation guidelines required of women's workplaces in the broader public sector. Pay equity by "proxy comparator," the method used to bring equity to over 80,000 women working in poorly paid workplaces, such as women's shelters, has been eliminated. The current government favours a voluntary pay equity policy which requires women to launch—and win—a public complaint against their employer before equity is assured.

*Employment equity:* Also eliminated was the provincial employment equity legislation that ensured protection for women, people of colour, First Nation and Aboriginal Peoples, and people with disabilities, in hiring and promotion practices. To replace employment equity in Ontario, the provincial government has proposed an Equal Opportunity Plan which would again put the onus on victims of discrimination to challenge unfair practices in a public complaints process.

**Impacts**

In our August 1996 survey of OAITH members, we asked shelters to report the impact of the cuts on women's decisions about remaining with, or returning to, abusive partners. Our results clearly show that a significant number of women in Ontario are now making decisions to remain in, or return to, abusive situations based primarily on barriers created by budget and service cuts. Moreover, more than half of the shelters answering our surveys say women are now forced to use the shelter more as a temporary respite from violence, rather than as an avenue of escape.

*Social assistance:* One hundred percent of shelters responding to our surveys reported that the cuts to social assistance had a severe impact on survivors. Shelters continued to report that as women struggle to survive on General Welfare Assistance and Family Benefits (GWA/FBA), they are being forced to make choices between food and rent or clothing and prescription medication and so on. More women are coming to the shelter with large debts as a result of desperate struggles against poverty. Women who still have credit cards are using them to the limit to provide basic essentials for their children. Some women, even after struggling for years to win custody of their children, have returned children to abusive partners who have money to feed and shelter them.

Abused women, many of whom have been prevented by violence from receiving training or education, have been cut off welfare as a result of the provincial government decision to deny assistance to students. Staying in school has become very difficult, often impossible, for survivors with children. This has been devastating to women who have planned to improve their future by recreating their lives.

Women are waiting longer before receiving their benefits after applying for GWA/FBA and many of the procedures now instituted in social assistance offices, such as home visits and checks on adults living in the same residence, demean women and make them feel blamed for leaving the violence. Shelters reported that women are having child and spousal support payments deducted from their GWA/FBA allowance, even though they are not actually receiving the court-ordered support payments from their ex-partner.

Welfare workers tell survivors to find part-time or casual work to supplement their assistance, but with a slight increase in income, they may no longer qualify for General Welfare or Family Benefits (GWA/FBA). Women who are receiving Unemployment Insurance from the federal government also struggle because they cannot obtain a drug card, moving allowance, or other minor support for the General Welfare system.

Elimination or reduction of these additional supports under GWA or FBA have also affected the supports to abused women starting over with nothing. Before cutbacks, women were eligible for community "start-up" funds to purchase beds and other very basic furniture and supplies. Shelters report these funds have decreased, or become inaccessible, depending on the discretion of the social assistance caseworker. Transportation costs, dental coverage, and repairs have all been eliminated or reduced for women. Ontario Drug Benefit user fees on prescriptions for GWA/FBA recipients mean that women unable to afford the user fees go without proper health care or use the personal needs supplement for other basic needs to pay for the increase in costs.

> *It is becoming increasingly more difficult for women to even retain a lawyer as the tariff set out by Legal Aid really restricts hours of service on any issue. A women in our program spoke with 25 firms before she found someone to take her on a (legal aid) certificate.*
>
> —Second stage shelter worker, southern Ontario, October 1996.

*Legal Aid:* Since cuts to the Ontario Legal Aid Plan came into effect, many abused women have been denied legal aid or legal representation for family law matters in Ontario. Again, 100 per cent of shelters responding to us reported women having problems either with accessing legal aid itself, or with finding a lawyer who would accept a legal aid certificate. This, in spite of Legal Aid Plan eligibility guidelines designating "spouse or child at risk" (Law Society of Upper Canada) as a priority for assistance.

It would appear that in the absence of any clear definition of abuse, other than it *must* be physical, local Legal Aid Plan offices are using their discretion on deciding which abused women are "deserving." One shelter survey respondent reported: "Legal aid is only issued with physical abuse, *and* police involvement *and* if a woman is only requesting custody and support, *and* is not a property owner (even jointly). Therefore, most women don't qualify. " Other local Legal Aid offices have given similarly incorrect information; for example, that legal aid is available only if the father has actually threatened to abduct the children, or only if the abused is *convicted* of assault. One woman was told, wrongly, that there is no legal aid for family law matters.

Some shelters find that lawyers who still take some legal aid cases will not take *family* law cases, arguing that restrictions in hours for family law legal aid certificates will not allow them to recover costs from time and expenses involved in representing abused women. Also, as a result of Legal Aid Plan time restrictions for family law, shelters report that some women have been abandoned by lawyers in the middle of court cases because the maximum time allowed by Legal Aid expired. In such cases, women must either represent themselves or rely on appointed Duty Counsel who go unprepared into complex cases. Some judges have shown little tolerance for these circumstances, and women fear their lack of understanding may negatively influence cases.

To generate revenue for a cash-strapped legal aid fund, the Ontario Legal Aid Plan has introduced user fees. Women who qualify for social assistance are exempt from these fees, but there are many low-income survivors outside the social assistance system who now must pay a $25 application fee to *apply* for a legal aid certificate. Women whose applications are rejected must pay user fees to appeal Legal Aid Plan decisions. All of this delays and hinders their chance to escape violence. Shelters report longer delays in processing applications and issuing certificates (one shelter reports the wait at a minimum of six week). In some cases, women are being asked to apply to legal aid before making an appointment under the two-hour free consultation policy in order to establish that they are "deserving" of free assistance. Even if women are able to secure a certificate and a lawyer, the reduced amount of time that lawyers are paid for family law cases often means abused women must assist the lawyer with paperwork involved in the case. Some women have been told that they must personally serve legal papers *on their abuser*, or pay for a private process server, because the lawyer cannot afford the expense and court-based process service for family law has been eliminated. Clearly, such a practice puts abused women in *grave* danger and puts pressure on them to stop legal proceedings.

> *The government is putting out that shelters are still open and this is true, but all supports have been cut or eliminated, making it impossible for us to provide referrals for women to get on with their lives. This means women are staying (at the shelter) much longer and, therefore, we are serving fewer women.*
>
> —Shelter director, Metro Toronto, September 1996.

*Housing:* Abused women may still apply for priority for subsidized units, but many of the shelters noted there is an increased pressure on women to prove they "really are abused" and that their safety is at risk. Other new criteria reported for priority status included: a requirement by one office that women apply within three months of assault; loss of priority status for women who move into an area close to the abuser; and a requirement for co-signers to obtain public housing.

Shelters also reported that waiting lists for subsidized housing were too long to be of any assistance and there were no units becoming available, perhaps as a result of resident reluctance to move in an insecure economy. Other women have been told that there is no longer any rent geared to income (RGI) units available. Due to cutbacks in the funding of co-operative housing, market rent units are replacing the RGI housing in areas when these units become available. Since market rents are not affordable for low-income women, most abused women in shelters cannot consider them. The government's decision not to build new co-operative housing is problematic to abused women, since there are no new options for finding the safe, low-income housing they need.

## The "Human Cost"

For abused women, the emotional costs of the cutbacks are terrible: depression, despair, and hopelessness. Survivors live with the increased fear and stress that comes from the inability to act on positive change in their lives. Even if they successfully leave an abuser's control, they find other forces directing their destiny. Many remain powerless and afraid, with few options for building a new life. As a result of extreme emotional demands placed on abused women, overall personal health decreases and illness increases (Day).

Clearly, women in violent relationships face a "no-win" situation. With little support or assistance to return to a life free from violence, women are locked in with abusers who endanger the lives of themselves and their children. When they try to get away, they discover they cannot financially support themselves and their children. Lack of safe, affordable child care or child care subsidy prevents many women from seeking what few jobs exist.

Women who are trapped with, or forced to return to an abuser, will certainly be subjected to further abuse. Already, far too many women die because they lack options and support for escape. Shelters have already noted increases in the number of women talking about suicide, in the level of fear of death from the abuser, and in the amount of time women need before they feel strong enough to try to escape permanently.

## The Impacts of Cuts on Children

> *Miraculously, my sister-in-law sent me some money in the mail. The boys came home from school to find me cooking a big supper. They were so happy! One of them said, "Mom, we were just talking about how hungry we were and how great it would be if we came home to find you making mashed potatoes and gravy and meat!" I suddenly felt so sad and worthless.*
>
> —Phyllis, a survivor.

By far the most devastating effect of the cuts for violence survivors is the impact on their children. Testimonies by women about the impact of government cuts show how heartbreaking the effects of poverty, created by the cuts, can be on women and children's daily lives. When women speak about the future of their children, they see only lost hopes and tragic consequences.

When women are trapped in violent homes, their children are trapped with them. The effects of witnessing violence, coupled with the impacts of severe poverty, suggest a bleak, insecure future for children. Often, children are used by abusive fathers to control and coerce women, at the expense of the children. Often, they are sexually and physically abused by those same men. Children living with an abuser learn the value of power and control over others—a value that has been devastating to themselves and their mothers. Often, they learn that they are worthless. To consign children to continuing violent experiences consigns them to a high risk of bringing the violence into their adult lives.

Legal Aid Plan changes and cutbacks may play a critical part in entrenching the difficulty abused women have always had in protecting their children from abuse. Women who have sought to win custody from an abuser, may more and more lose custody to abusive fathers because they cannot afford legal representation, child assessments, and so on. Children may, therefore, be more often forced to live with, or spend increasing amount of time with, abusive fathers.

## Cumulative Effects

All of the cuts together create an environment that, in effect, revictimizes abused women and reinforces, or rewards, male violence. With little help, support, or assistance, abused women are left to fend for themselves and their children. With the knowledge that the women they abuse have no where to run, abusers can and do increase their control and power over women with little or no consequence.

For women attempting to escape violence, erosion of already inadequate supports has a devastating effect. The "bottom line" is more than an exercise in fiscal "efficiencies." It is the blocking of escape routes abused women and women's advocates have struggled to open for over 20 years. We are moving back to a time when survivors had "no place to go." Violence will continue unchallenged, unless we take action to move forward again.

## References

Day, T. *The Health Related Costs of Violence Against Women in Canada: The Tip of the Iceberg*. London: Centre for Research on Violence Against Women and Children, 1995.

Law Society of Upper Canada. "Changes to the Ontario Legal Aid Plan: A Guide for Legal Aid Lawyers." Toronto: Law Society of Upper Canada.

McCuaig, Kerry. Ontario Coalition for Better Child Care. Personal communication. October 8, 1996.

Monsebraaten, Laurie. "Welfare's Boogeyman." *Toronto Star* Aug.12, 1995: C1.

Morrison, Ian. "Welfare Rate Cuts Anniversary Report." Toronto: Steering Committee on Social Assistance, Ontario Social Safety Network, October 1996.

OAITH. "Survey of Membership" Toronto: OAITH, August 1996.

Ontario Social Safety Network. *Social Safety News* 11 (November 1995).

Toughill, Kelly. "University Students to be Cut Off Welfare." *Toronto Star* April,12, 1996: A14.

Tyler, Tracey. "Cuts Mean Justice Chaos Top Judges Warn." *Toronto Star* January 31, 1996.

# Men at Work to End Wife Abuse in Quebec

## A Case Study in Claims Making

Juergen Dankwort and Rudolf Rausch

We examine men responding to violence against women in this article by focusing on projects developed by domestic violence offender programs in Quebec. Two reasons turned our attention in this direction, which regard both the prevalence of this violence and what remedies are proposed to end it.

First, estimates of domestic violence in the province place violence against women well within North American rates, bearing grim testimony that we face a major social problem worthy of study. Almost 30 per cent of Canadian women at some point in their lifetime in relationships with male partners were assaulted by them (Canadian Center for Justice Statistics; Johnson and Sacco). In response over the past two decades Canadian regions, including Quebec made important strides in recognizing and combatting the problem. At last count, Canada's National Clearing House on Family Violence listed 200 programs for domestically violent partners and 432 transition houses and shelters for abused women, 42 and 100 respectively in Quebec (Health Canada 1996, 1998).

Second, the authors see social problems as more than objective conditions and reified social arrangements, viewing phenomena such as violence against women as socially constructed, individually willed, and profoundly influenced by those who develop a stake or make claims in relation to it. As Blumer puts it, a social problem is in fact "the product of a process of collective definition" (917). We reason that examining responses to the problem through domestic violence program leaders working with men who abuse their partners may further our understanding of how this type of abuse is actually defined and affected by the activities of groups making assertions of grievances and claims in relation to it. Seen in this light, work largely carried out by men for men on violence against women has strategic potential in furthering or hindering the efforts begun by the battered women's movement and, by extension, social justice.

## History of Quebec Wife Abuse Offender Programs

Reflecting a trend begun in other parts of North America in the late 1970s, Quebec saw its first three programs specifically designed for domestic violence offenders between 1983 and 1984 in Montreal, Laval, and Sherbrooke. These programs were developed and implemented mostly by men who shared ideological and social ties with a growing "men's liberation movement" venerated in the men's gender magazine, *Homme-Info* (Dulac 1984, 1990). Occupational and educational links of the program founders were essentially in mental health disciplines and in academia (both clinical psychology and social work). Two of those three programs seeded several others in subsequent years based on similar androcentric cultural references. By dividing and multiplying, and through rudimentary training and mentoring work, similar ideas and practices with abusive men soon spread to other areas of the province by the spring of 1988. This, coupled with sparse information provided in the literature on the subject, accounted for the relative homogeneity of most of the first 16 programs.

Fifteen programs consisted of varying cognitive-behavioral formulations, whereas one, having become quite critical of earlier pathology and stress conceptualizations of wife abuse, underwent a transformation, adopting a "profeminist perspective which centered on men's power and control over women" (Rondeau). Only two of the programs were developed in collaboration with shelters for battered women. The others functioned through autonomous boards of directors and without any formal or direct accountability to victims' resources or the criminal justice system.

The growth of these programs was detailed in the first provincial overview of such programs through a descriptive study commissioned by the Quebec Ministry of Health and Social Services in 1989 (Rondeau, Gauvin, and Dankwort 1988). Although recommendations for government funding of the programs were not included in the report, it nevertheless served as a lynchpin for the state to take on an increasing role in matters regarding violence against women generally and funding wife abuse programs in particular.

Whereas domestic violence offender programs were developed in many other areas of North America jointly, with coalitions comprised of collateral resources such as victims' services, probation and law enforcement units, a majority of Quebec's programs created instead a provincial association for themselves in June of 1988. Known as l'Association des ressources intervenant auprès des hommes violents (ARIHV), it identified the primary objectives of promoting its affiliated member programs, including their funding base, and enhancing communication among programs as a way of overcoming their perceived isolation from one another (L'Arihv en bref). This ardent organizing effort represented an important milestone in the claims-making activities of wife abuse programs in Quebec—a new addition to the existing activities of battered women's shelters, the criminal justice system, and other victims' services.

Not long after ARIHV's entrance into the political arena, the Quebec Ministry of Health and Social Services, equipped with the Rondeau Report, established task forces to develop Government policy regarding (a) program guidelines, (b) a framework for funding them, (c) program evaluation, and (d) staff training requirements. Importantly, these ministerial task forces provided for the first time an opportunity for input on interventions with abusive men from claimsmakers other than the abusive men's programs themselves. The invited included representatives of Quebec's two associations of battered women's shelters, as well as victims' advocates from the public (government) section.

The outcome of this exchange was the bilingual publication of two documents respectively titled *Les Orientations*, and *Dealing with Violent Spouses: Guidelines* (Ministère de la Santé et des Services Sociaux). Though the texts provided voluntary guidelines for wife abuse programs calling for greater coordinated and cooperative work with others, their primary impact was to give them the official recognition deserving of public support and institute the funding policy adopted through a parallel task force. For the first time, state funding was allocated to wife abuse programs on a continuous basis. Guidelines identified battering as a criminal act, the need for batterers to take responsibility for their violent behavior, the need for programs to implement preventive measures that "go beyond personalized therapies," and the need to give priority to victim safety. However, no means of monitoring any of these principles or activities was mentioned, and, to the best of our knowledge, no mechanism was established to evaluate the programs or to hold them accountable in any way to the guidelines. Furthermore, the task force on training requirements for counsellors working with batters aborted when ARIHV representatives withdrew from the process, invoking the desire to wait until the guidelines task force had concluded its work. To our knowledge, no documents delineating training or evaluation of standards were ever produced either.

Aware of the growing need for a coherent response to domestic violence with the increasing number of offenders now being charged for assault, the Quebec Government mandated an interministerial steering committee in April of 1993 to develop government policy regarding spouse abuse and its effects on children. The committee was composed of representatives from the Ministries of Justice, Public Security, Education, Health, and Social Services, as well as from the Secretariats of the Family and of the Status of Women. The resulting provincial consultation and the establishment of an enlarged consultative committee provided a second formal opportunity for input to grassroots victims' resources, including the battered women's shelter associations as well as the native women's association and advocates for women with disabilities. Police, academics, mental health professionals, ARIHV, and other pivotal actors now met around the same table.

About 18 months later, this enlarged consultative committee with diverse interests remarkably arrived at a policy by consensus. Known as the Politique d'intervention en matière de violence conjugale (Québec), it set out official provincial government policy in partner abuse that would even apply to any nongovernmental agencies or community groups receiving public funding. Administratively, it endorsed the view that the elimination of partner abuse rested in a multifaceted, coordinated community response. Ideologically, it bolstered the view that the principle of equality for men and women, the safety of women and children, and the accountability of batterers must be a priority in an intervention. Though this represented another important step forward in addressing the problem of violence against women, the means for implementing accountability and evaluating wife abuse programs were again not mentioned.

## Concerns Over the Rise of Wife Abuse Offender Programs

During their rapid growth, the utility and desirability of offering psychosocial intervention to wife abusers became a contested site for discursive engagements in Quebec as elsewhere (Berliner; Dankwort 1988, 1991; Francis and Tsang; Walker). Controversy embodied both the hopes and limitations of abusive men's services, especially for those promoting the safety and welfare of battered women. Though these concerns have been discussed previously (see aforementioned references), we highlight several below relevant to the focus of our study.

One concern was about the public perception of wife abuse with the increasing number of domestic violence cases managed by law enforcement and mental health institutions. As more batterers were charged and prosecuted, overburdened courts increasingly came to refer or even divert them to rehabilitation programs, some operating as autonomous clinics, and others located in mainstream mental health agencies, hospitals, and family service agencies. This alarmed those who felt that focusing on men's psychological deficiencies through "treatment" rather than their willful and assaultive behavior through legal sanction would constitute a setback for hard-won recognition that beating a woman in the privacy of her home demanded safety for her and punishment for her partner (Dobash and Dobash 1992; Hart; Storrie and Poon; Walker).

Critics of domestic violence offender programs were also apprehensive about their aims and objectives. The program's underlying philosophy (its modality) affected a wide range of program components such as counselling methods or techniques and relationships it had, if any, with collateral resources in the community. For example, alternative explanations for violent behavior, ranging from combinations of childhood experiences, improper socialization, and overbearing stress (connected with role conflict, low self-esteem, poor impulse control, and myriad other social or economic tensions) conveniently served to externalize and obscure individual responsibility. Understanding violence as a result of personal deficiencies, ego impairment, or other disorders conveyed a very different "loss of control" meaning than viewing violence as the use of force or threats to reinforce power and control over one's partner (Adams; Gondolf and Russell; Pence and Paymar; Placek). Testimony from the directors of Ontario and Quebec associations of transition houses and rape crisis centres before a House of Commons subcommittee on the status of women disclosed their grave misgivings over how the underlying sociopolitical causes for violence against women were being redefined through interventions with batterers, which contributed to a mystification of moral responsibility, reduced such acts to individualized medical or psychological problems, and served to exonerate the batterer.

Ramifications of these issues were profound and anecdotal concerns from women's advocates found support in the literature. As James C. Overholser and Sarah H. Moll observed, treatment that obscures the logical and behavioral consistency of an aggressor can hinder his partner's ability to evaluate her safety and to make informed decisions about her own future if she attributes cause for the abuse beyond her spouse's control. Moreover practice experience and research showed how persistent invitations from batterers to support their accounts of violent incidents (male bonding) combined with nondirective, client-centered psychotherapy might actually strengthen unwanted attitudes that underpin violence against women, especially if vague personal/emotional problems and self-esteem are the focus of treatment (Adams; Andrews, Zinger, Hoge, Donald, Gendreau and Cullen; DeKeseredy; Hart; U.S. Department of Justice).

Modality, in turn, would determine what methods a program would employ. Prevailing perceptions that battering was caused by stress, pathology, and sex-role socialization, and that batterers were burdened with psychological deficiencies, resulted in the widespread use of relaxation training, social skills, anger management, and cognitive behaviorist therapy over the span of weekly group counselling sessions. There was concern over how such methods highlighting expressive behaviors failed to challenge men's beliefs of entitlement to control women or their personal complicity in intentional, instrumental acts of violence. Thus, any positive changes achieved through a program were feared to be, at best, cosmetic and temporary, teaching a man cues about imminent outbursts without connecting his anger with his chosen means (abuse) and his selected target (spouse). At worst, a man's participation in counselling could teach him refined ways of manipulation and lure his partner back into an abusive and dangerous relationship while she underestimates his lethality and hopes that he will change (Austin and Dankwort 1999a; Gondolf; Hart).

A final concern regarded issues about program structure and interservice protocol with collateral services. For example, in some cases, the length and means of intervention became an issue where batterers in some U.S. jurisdictions were meeting court-mandated treatment requirements by simply speaking with a counsellor on the telephone, spending a weekend retreat with a program offering an experiential human growth agenda, or taking a correspondence course that simplistically reviewed the costs of battering and even provided the answers to test questions. If not operating as autonomous service providers, counsellors working with batterers were often under contact with mainstream social service agencies that similarly functioned separately and at a distance from women's shelters (Browning; Currie; Jennings). Protocol also regarded issues about confidentiality, including decisions to warn potential victims about perceived dangers and reporting reassault to probation and/or police. Victims' resources, such as shelters for battered women, anticipated information about perpetrators from wife abuse programs, whereas the latter invoked client confidentiality and in some cases eschewed collaborating with the criminal justice system so as to maximize trusting, therapeutic conditions for the men. In short, such divergent interests widely influenced everything from the nature and frequency of contacts with the men's partners or collateral resources (such as probation and shelters), to policies for excluding men from treatment or obliging them to repeat counselling sessions.

## Orientation and Practice of Quebec Abusive Men's Programs

Based on a review of the literature and unpublished program documents, most of Quebec's abusive men's services appear to use hybrids of cognitive-behavior group therapy, including "a psychiatric perspective about men's low self-esteem and emotional dependence" and a view that "social-cultural and environmental factors contribute to constrained masculine roles" with the primary goal of rehabilitating participants (D'Amours; Ouellet, Linday, and Saint-Jacques; Ouellet, Lindsay, Beaudoin, and Saint-Jacques; Presentey and Letarte; Rondeau *et al.*).

Several have also undertaken more innovative primary and secondary prevention projects on a macro level, that is, activities promoting social change within their respective communities that extend beyond offering a curative counselling service to a relatively limited number of persons. The most common were dating violence prevention projects in local high schools, which in two instances (Accord Mauricie and Vivre Sans Violence) were undertaken in concert with the programs' local shelters for battered women. Other innovative projects included media watches to counter violence, sexism, and misogyny in newspapers and editorial cartoons. The antipornography project of Vivre Sans Violence was a partnership with the local sexual assault prevention center. Another program (Après Coup) worked in partnership with the Carfour pour Elle women's shelter to provide intervention to children of battered women.

Although such collaborative projects in the province between wife abuse programs and victims were encouraging for those concerned with the issues raised above, they were not typical. More often, strained or distant relations between offenders' and victims' services appeared to be common, not the least of which regarded tensions as related to the offender programs failing to inform victims' services about what they were doing and maintaining a policy of strict client confidentiality that reduced interservice contacts (Lacombe; Regroupement provincial de maisons d'hébergement et de transition pour femmes victime de violence conjugale).

## Emergence of Standards for Wife Abuse Offender Programs

It was against this background of proliferating wife abuse treatment for offenders and attending concerns that the idea to create program standards first took hold in the United States and then in Canada. A survey and analysis of standards for wife abuse programs has recently been published elsewhere (Austin and Dankwort

1999b; Dankwort and Austin). It will suffice to mention that at the end of 1997 a clear trend for bringing some uniformity to batterer intervention became evident in that 24 states had developed such guidelines, seven more had these in draft form, and 13 plus the District of Columbia were in the process of developing them. Similarly, three provinces, including Quebec, had developed standards in Canada, and two other provinces and one territory had these in draft form. Correction Service Canada also had a set of guidelines for all programs within their jurisdiction. Elements of standards typically included directives on general program goals, the protocol and procedures programs should follow (including counselling format), and program staff ethics and qualifications. Programs were to insure that the abuse of power and control of offenders be central in their work, that programs prioritize the safety and well-being of victims (including support and collaboration with victims' services and other collateral resources such as law enforcement), and that group intervention be the principal format used.

## Quebec's Association of Wife Abuse Offender Programs

Perhaps the most elaborate and unusual proposal vigorously promoted the ARIHV calls for the creation of a province-wide, integrated, generic service network for "men in difficulty" (ARIHV). The client target population consists of men presenting various high-risk situations, including wife abuse, drug and/or alcohol abuse, marital and family crisis, depression or suicidal ideation, and occupational or professional crisis. The two cornerstones of these integrated services are described as being a 24-hour provincial hotline for men "in difficulty" and a series of regional "preventive men's hostels or shelters" (Delangis). Other projected components include 24-hour regional crisis intervention services, referral to existing and additional regional or local "specialized spousal and family violence therapy services," and, finally a proposed "preventive risk-intervention service" (ARIHV).

The basic framework of this project was summarily outlined by ARIHV in a working paper presented to a government ministerial committee charged to study the implementation of their domestic violence hotline at the end of May 1997. Even before it had been approved by ARIHV's membership in early December of the same year, the lobby group rapidly presented a document titled *Preventive Hostels for Violent Spouses and Men in Difficulty Within a Domestic or Family Context* (Delangis) to a provincial meeting of regional health council members delegated to oversee funding and service delivery. Although the stated purpose of this document and its submission was to "stimulate reflection and commentary," its immediate impact was to legitimate men's hostels or shelters that were either on the drawing board or already in operation.

## The Claims-Making Process

What is instructive about this proposed network of men's services is the history and process through which the scheme evolved by using media-publicized, dramatic cases of violence against women as political leverage. Moreover, gaining acceptance for the network was accomplished in virtual absence of supporting evidence for its feasibility and with little or no public scrutiny or debate. In November 1998, ARIHV's news bulletin announced to its members that they and their collaborating organizations were awaiting the approval for the 24-hour hotline component from the Cabinet of the Minister to proceed to the stage of "calling for tenders" (L'Arihv en bref). Astonishingly, this signified that the Government of Quebec was ready to both endorse and invest in the first stages of this network. A more detailed examination of the origin and step-by-step development of the proposed men's network helps to explain why the project was successfully advanced to this stage of imminent approval and funding.

The first hostel project for batterers in the Province appeared on the drawing board in 1987, when a committee, composed of a judge, two criminologists, two advocates from battered women's shelters, a youth protection worker, and lawyers, proposed creation of La maison d'hébergement l'emprise (Delangis). Though the hostel never opened because funding was not furnished, the initiative introduced the idea that resources for shelters should no longer be exclusively for victimized women. The fact that at least one of the women's shelter advocates left the project when it became apparent the hostel would likely be used as an alternative (diversion) to criminal sanction for domestic assaults was telling of growing differences among key actors in this field.

Referring back to this hostel endeavor, both ARIHV and Delangis then reported years later that the hostel project, hotline and crisis services were recommended in a coroner's inquest into the murder of a wife by her husband and his subsequent suicide, which occurred in Montreal in 1992 (David). The following were among the 17 recommendations of Coroner David: training for police and other intervenors in domestic violence cases, improved tracking and detection measures via criminal justice records, and more rigorous procedures for firearms seizures. The testimony given at the inquest by l'Emprise and ARIHV also produced a series of recommendations advancing the agendas of these two organizations. Duly noted were stable financing for wife abuse offender programs, the establishment of presentencing and postsentencing shelters for domestic violence offenders, as well as a hotline and crisis service for both domestic violence offenders and victims.

The stage was now set to promote several men's hostels. They ranged in diversity from Le Passant in Granby, which is basically a generic refuge for temporarily or chronically homeless men, to a specific intensive residential therapy program for wife and child abusers. The latter program was run by Apres-Coup and was financed through their operating budget to nonresidential therapy for perpetrators and by a fee-for-service from residential clients. It closed its doors in the spring of 1999, partly because it was underused and partly because it lacked funding. Although this residential initiative was not evaluated as far as is known to the present authors, the organization's batterer program did undergo one of the rare qualitative evaluations in the province (Presentey and Letarte).[1]

The next milestone in promoting a men's service network was provided by another murder-suicide. Here a batterer with adjunct histories of substance abuse and mental health problems tracked down his estranged wife, who had escaped to another city. The man caught up with her, killing her and their son before taking his own life. This tragedy occurred even though the batterer had been receiving medical treatment at a hospital and a concerned neighbor had gone to both the hospital and the police to warn of the man's death threats. The subject was already on file in the police computer, indicating he was under conditional release after uttering death threats two months prior to the murders. Police had released the man to hospital, which in turn also promptly released him after preliminary psycho-medical intervention (Bérubé).

ARIHV officials once again presented testimony, this time before Coroner Bérubé, promoting their project and citing the previous 1993 coroner's report to support their position. As might be expected, Berube's report, appearing in the spring of 1997 and consisting of ten recommendations, included a service with a 24-hour hotline and psychosocial support (including temporary residential services, if necessary) for violent spouses in crisis or for men experiencing conjugal or family difficulties. A few weeks later, ARIHV officials presented their proposal on their integrated homosocial project to government officials (ARIHV) and, in December, the Delangis document on preventive men's hostels was presented to the regional health boards.

## Discussion

The above domestic violence murder/suicide cases illustrate a number of serious systemic problems and questionable individual decisions taken at crucial moments in the escalation of abuse. Lack of training and communication among police and medical practitioners and failure to charge and incarcerate the perpetrator for breach of prior release conditions appear to stand out and provide compelling grounds to do more to prevent, reduce or stop wife abuse. Cases involving revictimization or worse (i.e., homicide) underscore the importance of a coordinated, functional, multiservice intervention project. Lessons to be drawn from these attacks on women and children regard the need for additional staff training in professions likely to have contact with domestic violence cases, and a truly coordinated intervention plan with systematic reviews and community audits to assess its strengths and weaknesses.

In reviewing the rise of programs for abusive men, this article has detailed how the government increasingly became a key play in the role of arbiter between offender and victims' service providers. At times, such initiatives seemed progressive, encouraging wider community participation in facilitating a more prominent place for victims and affirming the willful and criminal nature of battering. Coroners David and Bérubé critiqued existing interventions as too limited, inadequate, and inconsistent, recommending structural changes. Yet, beyond existing criminal prosecution of offenders, government initiatives were paradoxical, falling short of completing and implementing policies that could monitor the compliance of abusive men's services with such recommendations and assess their results.

Although the ARIHV project may appear to be promising from the viewpoint of early detection or prevention and is certainly holistic in its scope of proposed services, it also raises cause for concern. It is axiomatic that help for men in the domestic violence field must be developed in conjunction with, not separate from, victims' services. Indeed, guidelines or standards, which delineate intervention with batterers, are near unanimous in calling for such a coordinated and multi-faceted approach. Yet, the founding programs that make up ARIHV's leadership evolved, as we noted above, in relative isolation of victims' services in the province. What is more, there is no evidence that a major transformation toward prioritizing collaborative work with victims' services and victims' advocates had become a major objective for the organization in its ongoing promotional work.

It is significant that battered women's resources and advocates have been woefully absent from the developmental process of the men's project by all accounts. With the exception of the original l'emprise project where two battered women shelter advocates briefly participated on their own behalf in 1988 (and not in the capacity of delegated representatives), there has been neither systematic consultation with nor accountability to victims' advocates until May of 1998. Moreover, this later inclusion of the battered women's shelters only resulted because one of the Provinces' two shelter associations wrote to Quebec government officials (Ministère de la santé et des services sociaux) on March 30, 1998, requesting the men's hotline proposal to be tabled until the impact of such a distinct service on battered women's safety could first be assessed. Furthermore, deploring the conceptual juxtaposing of "violent" and "men in difficulty," both provincial shelter associations thereafter requested that means be found to promote a common understanding of these projects, including their approaches to intervention (L'Arihv en bref). The battered women's hotline (S.O.S. Violence Conjugale), in operation since 1992, has yet to be invited to participate in the consultation process over the integrated men's services in spite of their expertise.

It is equally significant that the ideological framework or rationale for the ARIHV project lacks a rigorous and critical foundation with regard to violence perpetrators. It notably fails to take into account a full spectrum of generally accepted elements in wife abuse dynamics. By all evidence, only two publications by Quebec sociologist Dulac serve as the project's supporting references, and a critical analysis of these works reveals that they are limited to generalizations over crippling male sex-role conditions, with barely a mention of men's power and control derived from institutional privileges, in patriarchal society.

In Dulac's (1999) generic proposal for working with men "in difficulty," the primary directives are for counsellors to understand the "masculine condition," and based on that, to create a "climate of confidence with the men," to insure confidentiality, to promote intimate rapport in groups and self-reliance, to explore men's pain and other emotions, and to provide social skills and training (including ways for men to relate other than through competition). Confrontation, a widely regarded centerpiece of batterer intervention, is implied to be appropriate only inasmuch as it is genial and comfortable for the offenders. Its only mention is found in a telling quote where a man recalls his first group encounter where, after experiencing confrontation, he found it innovate and so enjoyable ("j'ai trouvé ca l'fun") that he was very eager for the next group session. The only place where power is even suggested is in the words "homophobia," "sexism," and "men's strategies to adapt and resolve conflict." However, nothing is said about them other than listing them as themes for the psychoeducational facet of group encounters. Making abuse of power and control central to any curriculum with batterers is regarded as crucial and, for that reason, again delineated in most batterer guidelines. For those reading Dulac's material the "fundamental and essential" directive to counsellors is to "access men's suffering wherein one will locate certain trauma because of male socialization" (1999: 43).

Indicative of a narrow vision generated through men's identity politics, Dulac described a situation where a potentially suicidal and verbally aggressive focus group participant relates, with a litany of coarse language (swearing), how police were called when he was told by a receptionist he had to wait to see a counsellor at a local community service centre. Dulac interprets this vignette to illustrate how men are not "passive, dependent, and submissive" in their requests for help and that "a cultural bias acts against men who express their request for service in a more virile manner" (Dulac 1997: 20).

In a similar vein, the ARIHV document, which describes the actual men's project states that the lack of appreciation of "masculine needs" in regard to intervention portended a high risk for conjugal and family violence clientele in the absence of services which should be "unique, anonymous, easily and rapidly accessible" (20). ARIHV notes that consciousness has been raised with regard to women's issues, resulting in a network of services for them and laments this absence with regard to men and the "masculine condition." This is then followed by a denunciation of prejudicial and stereotypical views allegedly held by service providers who believe that "men have no emotions, men want to control everything, and that men possess adequate personal resources"(10).

It would hardly be surprising if victims' advocates found it difficult to accept how a man's verbal abuse in the above example is so readily normalized by proponents of a new and comprehensive men's network in Quebec that purports, among other things, to be effective in responding to wife abuse. A more critical account of this incident would certainly have queried how aggressive the man was the day the police were called to the centre, the receptionist's version, and if the subject was as violent at home. It may well be that some service providers hold some of the stereotypes Dulac and ARIHV describe, and thus require further training. However, it may also be true, as reported in the wife abuse literature, that some of the therapists participating in the focus groups from where the narratives were drawn are collusive with batterers and require training for that reason.

ARIHV's proposition to optimally counter wife abuse from within a generic network of homosocial services for men burdened with difficulties appears seriously flawed. Dulac's position that men who underuse mental health services would be more inclined to seek help from an androcentric, homosocial network is purely speculative. As reported by ARIHV itself between 1992 and 1997, the number of wife abusers who annually contacted the existing domestic violence hotline in the province (S.O.S. Violence Conjugale) to help them stop their abuse increased from 330 to 447—and this without the women's hotline even undertaking any public education efforts to target male abusers.

The publications (Dulac 1997, 1999) that appear to serve as the principal theoretical and methodological reference for the ARIHV project are informative inasmuch as they explore some aspects of the social construction of gender. They are remarkably short-sighted, however, in that the willful exploitation of power inequity is limited to a consideration of the "costs" of masculinity. On one hand, mental health perspectives are generously infused, which is telling of the organizations involved in the production of the documents.[2] We do not dispute that this has merit. A strong case can certainly be made for the price men pay in myriad ways to reap the benefits of a hierarchical system that has bestowed advantages based on gender. Indeed, the literature on masculinity for decades has developed, albeit not always critically, this dimension of "male conditioning." In the area of mental health, this would appropriately include attention to a wide range of issues such as men's experiences of shallow relationships, poor health, and early death, not to mention the unequal ways men share the benefits of patriarchy based on their differences within gender signified by race, sexual orientation, social class, and ability. It is clear that space and time for men to explore their own encounters with oppression (i.e., their own dehumanization) can arguably serve to actually raise empathy for those they have hurt or might victimize. This therefore becomes a useful strategy in stopping abuse. However, it hardly represents a balanced curriculum for effective intervention with offenders.

In his explorations of male social movements to find an optimal political terrain for men engaging in progressive social justice work, sociologist Michael A. Messner, among others, emphasizes the requirement in any project or activity to highlight the institutional privileges men enjoy as a group. This recognition (not surprisingly, also a cornerstone of the feminist paradigm in the woman abuse field) compels one to examine accountability of the batterer to his victim(s), program facilitators to the victim and her advocates, and the program's accountability to all of these plus the wider community (Adams; Hart, 1988; Storrie and Poon; Pence and Paymar).

Those advantages or entitlements that men enjoy in patriarchy are not mentioned in Dulac's recent works, which inform ARIHV's proposals. Dulac constructs deterministic-laden text that not only obscures intention in human behavior through his sex-role reification but also conceptually turns meaning on its head. Empowerment, for example, usually associated with the goal of moving a battered woman from victim to survivor, is prescribed by Dulac (1999: 8) as the goal for batterers to achieve responsibility for self. Abused women and children virtually vanish from the text, presumably to avoid evoking guilt in batterers, simplistically seen as a therapeutically counterproductive emotion. There is neither mention of the existence of practice standards with wife abusers nor an account of how shame as an aspect of remorse can move an offender from denial and minimization to owning his own abusive behaviours.

The bibliography of these texts underpinning the ARIHV proposal is generous with references to men's liberation and men's rights, whereas specialists who have focused on wife abuse research and interventions are conspicuously wanting. Reading them reminds one of controversial men's and women's liberation authors of the 1970s who challenged the very idea that men are privileged over women because everyone had been socialized into oppressive conditions through sex-role socialization.[3] This represents, moreover, a significant shift for a writer and researcher who, only a decade earlier, published persuasive critiques of the same strand of the men's liberation movement in Quebec because of its minimization or denial of institutionalized male power and privilege.[4] The "about-face" begs the question if men in the province have evolved to such an extent—if they have divested themselves of their privilege and shared power so generously over just one decade—that these themes are now passé. Regrettably, we find little evidence that such a transformation has occurred in either the public or private domain in English or French Canada.

## Conclusion

In an era of competing claims for diminishing family violence funding, Quebec's provincial association of wife abuse offender programs strategically make political use of coroners' inquests to construct a rationale for legitimacy and funding for a greatly expanded network of men's services. Through timely and selective repetitious lobbying, the project to develop hostels and a 24-hour hotline, as well as to encourage the attendance of psychosocial services by domestic violence offenders, took on a life of its own and materialized as a claim that may soon see the light of day. Although there is an unquestionable need to enhance wife abuse interventions, especially more coordinated community projects with all key actors from law enforcement to victims' services and offender programs, the current project and how it was promoted by ARIHV give reason for serious concern. We find convincing the requests of battered women advocates in the province who are saying that public scrutiny and debate is long overdue in regard to what must be considered the most far-reaching proposal on wife abuse intervention that has yet been brought forward for government support.

Because standards now exist for batterer interventions and can be developed further, it would seem prudent to abide by them, monitor their compliance, and fund only those programs that follow them. In any event, support for homosocial men's projects should always be contingent on whether the project's content or curriculum, its structure, and its protocol incorporate those major themes in the politics of masculinities that would give such works a balanced foundation for achieving progressive and collaborative social change. Messner has fully reviewed these conditions as comprising three themes, all of which we agree must be in evidence: (a) making prominent the institutionalized privileges that men derive by virtue of their position in society and in the family; (b) considering the disadvantages that come with maintaining and reinforcing privilege; and (c) factoring in the differences and inequalities that exist among men and that amount to other (besides gender) signifiers of power differentials such as race, social class, sexual orientation, and ability.

This account of men's programs mobilizing to stop domestic violence has demonstrated how the issue of violence against women continues to be a site of conflicting ideology and practice. The literature in Canada as elsewhere has extensively discussed how the political dimension of this violence was gradually reformulated into individualistic, deviant acts, thus distancing the phenomenon from wider social and institutional practices of oppression (e.g, De Keseredy and MacLeod; Dobash and Dobash 1979; Walker). The lobbying efforts of a liberal reformist men's organization to promote itself by utilizing a branch of the judiciary (coroners) and a government department eager to adopt its homosocial network illustrate hegemonic practice for the control of a profoundly sociopolitical issue. It brings to mind Currie's recollection of how it has been a lot easier to get recognition for women as victims and to mobilize support for the notion of male violence as an individual, criminal matter than it has been to get recognition for how interpersonal violence in women's everyday lives is linked to and inseparable from larger economic and political demands for social justice. In our view, those working to combat violence against women must be mindful, as Walter DeKeseredy and Linda MacLeod have argued, that our responses to woman abuse do not unwittingly replicate the same values, attitudes, and structures that contribute to woman abuse.

## Notes

[1]It is interesting to read that the study, not widely distributed yet financed by the Solicitor General of Canada, found that Apres Coup had limitations that included conceptualizing batterer accountability solely in terms of self-control and male empowerment, whereas the effects of the men's violence on women and children was not in view during the observed intervention sessions.

[2]The same organizations collaborated in the production of both Dulac Texts: Action Intersectorielle pour le Development et la Recherche sur l'Aide aux Hommes (AIDRAH), Association des Ressources Intervenant aupres des Hommes Violents (ARIHV), Association Quebecoise de Suicidologie (AQS), and the Federation des Organismes Benevoles et communsulaties d'Aide et de Southen aux Toxicomanas (FOBAST)

[3]A thorough review of men in movements in America was published by Carrigan, Connell, and Lee. They discuss how some in the men's movement dismissed the

power structure and the nature of its dynamics by which men in particular benefit as a group. By highlighting only the unfair burden men bear, which includes the masculine qualities required to own everything and run everything, an abstractism simply referred to as "society" is identified as responsible for denying both men and women their autonomy, sexuality and self-respect, resulting in a plethora of uncommunicative, sexually impoverished relationship between the sexes. Through crude oversimplifications about gender in which any serious look at utilitarian power is avoided, the struggle therefore became, in the words of Goldberg "surviving the myths of male privilege" because of the "hazards of being male."

[4]See, for example, Dulac's (1989) critical discussion of the emerging strand of men's homosocial organization through the father's rights movement. He notes that the central preoccupations around divorce and custody unequivocally regard issues of men's maintaining or reinforcing their perceived loss of power and control. In an article published a year later (Dulac 1990), the author explores varying attitudes of men toward the emergence of feminism and highlights the power inequity between men and women in patriarchy, even cautioning how the development of the field of men's studies may chiefly serve to contest the place of and the claims by woman's studies. Exemplary is Quebec author Chabot who wrote that benefits derived from patriarchy are illusory and that no sound strategy that can serve to bring men and women out of their respective alienation should stem from clarifying who among the sexes is better and worse off (Chabot 45).

## References

Adams, D. "Treatment Models for Men Who Batter: A Profeminist Analysis." *Feminist Perspectives on Wife Abuse*. Eds. K. Yllö and M. Bograd. Newbury Park, CA: Sage, 1988. 176-199.

Andrews, D.A., L. Zinger, R. D. Hoge, L. Donald, P. Gendreau, and F. T. Cullen. "Does Correctional Treatment Work? A Clinically Relevant And Psychologically Informed Male Analysis." *Criminology* 28 (1990): 369-404.

Arihv en bref. *Association des Ressources Intervenant aupres des Hommes Violents newsletter* 7 (5) (1998).

Association des Ressources Intervenant aupres des Hommes (ARIHV). "Projets intégrés d'intervention auprès des hommes pour prévenir et enrayer la violence conjugale et familiale pour hommes en difficultés dans un contexte conjugale et familiale." Unpublished document. Montreal: Association des Ressources Intervenant auprés des Hommes Violents. May, 1997.

Austin, J., and J. Dankwort. "Standards for Batterer Programs: A Review and Analysis." *Journal of Interpersonal Violence* 14 (1999a): 152-168.

Austin, J., and J. Dankwort. "Domestic Violence: A Humanist or Feminist Issue." *Journal of Interpersonal Violence* 5 (1999b): 218-229.

Berube, J. *Rapport D'Enquête Du Coroner décès Françoise Lirette #88811 A-114729, Loren Gaumont-Lirette #88810 A-11470, et René Gaumont #88812 A-114728*. Le Coroner en chef, Governement du Québec. April, 1997.

Blummer, H. 1971. "Social Problems as Collective Behavior." *Social Problems* 18: 198-206.

Browning, J. 1984. *Stopping the violence: Canadian Programmes for Assaultive Men.* Ottawa: National Clearinghouse on Family Violence, Health Canada.

Canadian Center for Justice Statistics. *Family Violence in Canada.* Ottawa: Statistics Canada, 1994.

Carrigan, T., B. Connell, and J. Lee. "Hard and Heavy: Toward a New Sociology of Masculinity." *Beyond Patriarchy: Essays by Men on Pleasure, Power and Change.* ED. M. Kaufman. Toronto: Oxford University Press, 1987. 139-192.

Chabot, M. *Des hommes et de l'intimidé*. Montreal: Editions Saint-Martin, 1987.

Currie, D. "Group Model for Men Who Assault Their Partners." *Understanding Wife Assault.* Ed. D. Sinclair. Toronto: Publications Ontario, 1985. 120-143.

Currie, D. "The Criminalization of Violence Against Women: Feminist Demands and Patriarchal Accommodations." *Unsettling Truths: Battered Women, Policy, Politics, and Contemporary Research in Canada.* Eds. K. D. Bonnycastle and G. S. Rigkoe. Vancouver: Collective Press, 1985. 41-51.

D'Amour, M. "Les thérapies pour conjoints violents: Utils mais pas magiques." *La Gazette des femmes* 15 (1991): 24-26.

Dankwort, J. "Une conception alternative de la violence conjugale." *Service Social* 37 (1988): 83-119.

Dankwort, J. "Intervention with Wife Abusers: Conceptual Trends and Practice Dilemmas." *Canadian Review of Social Policy* 28 (1991): 59-84.

Dankwort, J. and J. Austin. "Standards for Batterer Intervention Programs in Canada: A History and Review." *Canadian Journal of Community Mental Health* 18 (1999): 19-38.

David, A. M. *Rapport d'Enquête du Coroner décès Pierre Lepage, A-59951 et Rhéa Landry, A-72786.* Le Coroner en chef, Gouvernment du Quebec. February,1993.

De Keseredy W. S. "Woman Abuse in Dating Relationships: The Relevance of Social Support Theory." *Journal of Family Violence* 3 (1988 ): 1-18.

DeKeseredy, W. S. and L. MacLeod. *Women Abuse: A Sociological Story.* Toronto: Harcourt Brace, 1997.

Délangis, S. "Hébergement préventif pour conjoints violente en hommes en difficulté dans une contexte conjugale ou familiale." Unpublished document. Quebec: ARIHV, December, 1997.

Dobash, R. H., and R. P. Dobash. *Violence against Wives: A Case Against the Patriarchy.* New York: Free Press, 1979.

Dobash, R. H., and R. P. Dobash. *Women, Violence and Social Change.* London: Routledge, 1992.

Dulac, G. "Les masculinistes et la pornographie." *Les Cahiers du Socialisme* 16 (1984): 126-134.

Dulac, G. "Le lobby des pères, divorcé et paternité." *Canadian Journal of Women and the Law* 3 (1989): 45-68.

Dulac, G. "Les hommes et les études féministes." *Nouvelles Practique Sociales*

3 (1990): 85-97.

Dulac, G. *Les demandes d'aide des hommes.* Monorail: Center for Applied Family Studies, McGill University, 1997.

Dulac, G. *Intervenir auprès des clientèles masculines. Théories et pratiques.* Montreal: Center for Applied Family Studies, McGill University, 1999.

Francis, B., and A. Ka Tat Tsang. "War of Words / Words of War. A Dossier on Men's Treatment Groups in Ontario." *Canadian Social Work Review* 14 (1997): 201-220.

Goldberg, H. *The Hazards of Being Male: Surviving the Myth of Male Privilege.* New York: Signet, 1976.

Gondolf, B. W. "The Effect of Batterer Counselling on Shelter Outcome." *Journal of Interpersonal Violence* 3 (1988): 275-290.

Gondolf, B. W., and D. Russell. "The Case Against Anger Control Treatment Programs for Batterers." *Response* 93 (1986): 2-6.

Hart, U. *Safety for Women: Monitoring Batterers' Programs.* Harrisburg, PA: Pennsylvania Coalition Against Domestic Violence,1988.

Health Canada. *Transition Houses and Shelters for Abused Women in Canada.* Ottawa: National Clearinghouse on Family Violence, 1996.

Health Canada. *Canada's Treatment Programme for Men Who Abuse their Partners.* Ottawa: National Clearinghouse on Family Violence, 1998.

House of Commons. "Hearings Before the Sub-Committee on the Status of Women." Ottawa: Government of Canada, 1991.

Jennings, J. L. "History and Issues in the Treatment of Battering Men: A case for Unstructured Group Therapy." *Journal of Family Violence* 2 (1987): 193-211.

Johnson, H., and V. de Sacco. "Researching Violence Against Women: Statistics Canada's National Surveys." *Canadian Journal of Criminology* 37 (1995): 281-306.

Lacombe, M. Ed. *Au grand jour.* Montreal: Les Editions des Revenue-Menage, 1990.

Messner, M. *Politics of Masculinities: Men in Movements.* Thousand Oaks, CA: Sage, 1997.

Ministère de la Santé et des Services sociaux. *Les orientations.* Quebec: Author,1992.

Ouellet, P., J. Lindsay, G. Beaudoin, and M-C. Saint-Jacques. *L'intervention de groups auprés des conjoints violents: Quant l'évaluation s'allie à la pratique.* Montreal: Cri-Viff. Collection Outils, No.1. September,1995.

Ouellet, P., J. Lindsay, and M-C. Saint-Jacques. *Evaluation de l'éfficité de programme de traitement pour conjoints violents.* Quebec: Centre de recherche sur les services communautaires, École de service social, Université de Laval, 1993.

Overholser, J. C., and S. H. Moll. "Who's to Blame? Attributions Regarding Causality in Spouse Abuse." *Behavioral Sciences and the Law* 8 (1990): 107-120.

Pence, H., and M. Paymar. *Education Groups for Men who Batter.* New York: Springer, 1993.

Presenley, R., and I. Letarte. *Rapport final: Recherche-action avec le programme d'intervention masculine Aprés-Coup*. Ottawa: Solicitor General, Government of Canada, March,1995.

Placek, J. "Why do Men Batter their Wives?" *Feminist Perspectives on Wife Abuse*. Eds. K. Yllo and M. Bograd. Newbury Park, CA: Sage,1988. 133-157.

Québec. 1995 *Politique d'intervention en matière de violence conjugale.*

Regroupement provincial de maisons d'hébergement et de transition pour femmes victime de violence conjugale. "Les groupes pour hommes agresseurs: une panacée?".*Avalanche* 3 (9) (1988).

Regroupement provincial de maisons d'hébergement et de transition pour femmes victime de violence conjugale. "Quand les theories frôle l'impertinence! Veux-tu savoir la dernière?" *Avalanche* 4 (12) (1989).

Rondeau, G. "Bilan des programmes." Eds. J. Broue and C. Guèvremont. *Quand l'amour fait mal.* Montreal: Editions Saint-Martin, 1989.126-141.

Rondeau, G. , M. Gauvin, and J. Dankwort. *Les programmes québécois d'aide aux conjoints violents. Étude sur les programmes québécois* . Québec: Ministère de la Santé et des Services sociaux, Direction générale de la planification et de l'évaluation, 1988.

Storrie, K., and N. Poon. "Programs for Abusive Men: A Socialist Feminist Perspective." *Criminal Justice: Sentencing Issues and Reform.* Eds. L. Samuelson and B. Schissel. Toronto: Garamond Press, 1991. 329-350.

U.S. Department of Justice. *Preventing Crime: What Works, What Doesn't, What's Promising*. Washington, DC: Author, 1998.

Walker. G. A. *Family Violence and the Women's Movement: The Conceptual Politics of Struggle.* Toronto: University of Toronto Press, 1990.

# Erasing Race

## The Story of Reena Virk

Yasmin Jiwani

On November 14, 1997, 14-year-old Reena Virk, a girl of South Asian origin, was brutally murdered in a suburb of Victoria, British Columbia. Reena was first beaten by a group of seven girls and one boy between the ages of 14 and 16. She was accused of stealing one of the girl's boyfriends and of spreading rumours. Her beating was framed as retaliation to these alleged actions. According to journalistic accounts, the attack began when one of the girls attempted to stub out a cigarette on her forehead. As she tried to flee, the group swarmed her, kicked her in the head and body numerous times, attempted to set her hair on fire, and brutalized her to the point where she was severely injured and bruised. During the beating, Reena reportedly cried out "I'm sorry" (*The Vancouver Sun* 1999a: A10). Battered, Reena staggered across a bridge trying to flee her abusers but was followed by two of them—Warren Glowatski and Kelly Ellard. The two then continued to beat her, smashing her head against a tree and kicking her to the point where she became unconscious. They then allegedly dragged her body into the water and forcibly drowned her. Reena's body was found eight days later on November 22, 1997, with very little clothing on it. The pathologist who conducted the autopsy noted that Virk had been kicked 18 times in the head and her internal injuries were so severe as to result in tissues being crushed between the abdomen and backbone. She also noted that the injuries were similar to those that would result from a car being driven over a body. The pathologist concluded that Reena would likely have died even if she had not drowned.[1]

This chilling murder of a 14-year-old girl was singled out by the news media and heavily reported in the local, national, and international press. The media's initial framing of the murder focused largely on "girl-on-girl" violence. The issue of racism, sexism, pressures of assimilation, and the social construction of Reena Virk as an outcast were rarely addressed. When they were addressed, it was always in the language of appearance—that she weighed 200 pounds and was five feet, eight inches tall. According to media accounts, her heaviness and height precluded her from being accepted. The assumptions regarding the validity of normative standards of beauty and appearance were significantly absent in all accounts of the story. Rather, as with dominant frameworks of meaning that are utilized to cover stories of racialized immigrant and refugees communities—Reena's difference was underscored and inferiorized.

This article focuses on the framing of the Reena Virk murder in media accounts. The aim is to draw attention to the lack of coverage and critical analysis of racism as a form of violence communicated by exclusion, scapegoating, and targetting of "others," and underpinned by the inferiorization of difference as well as its framing as deviance. Additionally, this article argues that the absence of any discussion of racism as a motivating factor in the murder is symbolic of the denial of racism as a systemic phenomenon in Canada. The absence of any mention of racism in the judicial decision concerning the murder is echoed in the news coverage of the decision, thereby privileging a particular interpretation of the case as one involving physical gang violence. Finally, the erasure of race in the discourse of the news media is made evident by the complete denial of the Virk's appearance and racialized identity and its significance in terms of her vulnerability to violence. By not referencing "race" in this context, the media were able to negate and omit any substantive discussion of racism, and at the same time, to reinforce hegemonic notions of racism—as behaviour which is simply confined to hate groups.

## Racialized Girls and their Vulnerability to Violence

A recent study conducted by the Alliance of Five Research Centres on Violence underscores the vulnerability of girls and young women to male violence. It has been found, for instance, that girls comprise 84 per cent of the reported victims of sexual abuse, 60 per cent of the physical child abuse cases, and 52 per cent of cases of reported neglect (Department of Justice). Girls are also victims in 80 per cent of the cases of sexual assaults reported to police (Fitzgerald). Many flee abusive homes and end up on the streets where they are subjected to further abuse (Alliance). The situation is compounded for marginalized girls who have to deal with the interlocking effects of racism, homophobia, classism, ableism, and sexism (Jiwani 1998b; Razack).

The Working Groups on Girls (WGG) noted in its report that immigrant and refugee girls experience higher rates of violence because of dislocation, racism, and sexism from both within their own communities and the external society (Friedman). Caught between two cultures, where their own is devalued and constructed as inferior, and where cultural scripts in both worlds encode patriarchal values, these girls face a tremendous struggle in trying to "fit." When they don't, they suffer intense backlash. In effect, what these girls experience is a double dose of patriarchy—the patriarchal values encoded in the dominant society which resonates with the patriarchal values encoded in their own cultural backgrounds.

At the core of the diversity of experiences that shape the lives and realities of girls from marginalized groups is the intensity of rejection and exclusion mediated by the mainstream of society. Faced by racism, and the double dose of sexism, girls from racialized immigrant and refugee communities have few avenues of recourse available to them.[2] The obverse side of this rejection is the overwhelming pressure to conform and assimilate into the dominant normative framework and thereby strive for at least conditional acceptance. However, the internalization of the dominant culture often leads to an inferiorization, negation, and hatred of the self and their communities.

## Cultural Identity and Conflict

Rather than focusing on girls' experiences of racism and sexism, many studies have tended to concentrate on issues of cultural and intergenerational conflict within racialized immigrant communities. To some extent, these studies have emerged in response to prevailing occupations in the area of ethnicity and identity retention, cohering around the debate of whether such identity is primordially rooted (Geertz; Isaacs) or situationally constructed (Keyes; Lyman and Douglass). Further, the prevalence of these identity-oriented studies suggests a greater degree of comfort in looking at "cultural" issues of co-existence, conflict, and exchange, or assimilation and acculturation (Drury; Jabbra; Kim; Rosenthal, Raieri, and Klimidis), although more recently, this trend has shifted (see, for example, Matthews).

Despite the use of culture as the focal point of inquiry, many of these studies reveal that girls within racialized immigrant cultures experience a greater degree of dissatisfaction and strain with the normative values imposed by their own culture (Hutnik; Miller; Onder; Rosenthal *et al.*). The contextual factors influencing and shaping this dissatisfaction tend not to be examined in structural terms, i.e., as emanating from the subordinate position of the cultural group in relation to the dominant society, and the construction of racialized immigrant communities as deviant Others (Bannerji 1993; Thobani; Tsolidas as cited in Turnbull 163). Nor has the complex interaction of sexism and racism shaping the lives and choices of young women been examined in great detail in Canadian studies (see Bourne, McCoy, and Smith; Vertinsky, Batth, and Naidu). Thus, rather than focusing on how racialized girls are inferiorized and how they internalize dominant values which embody a rejection of the self and their cultural communities, many of the existing studies tend to frame these "Other" communities as being problematic insofar as clinging to traditional, non-liberatory, and patriarchal cultures (Alicea).

Within the context of the violence of racism, girls from marginalized communities are often faced with systemic barriers around which they must negotiate their survival. They may choose to try to conform and assimilate, although this choice is often not available to them due to the exclusionary impact of racism and/or homophobia. On the other hand, the deviant characterization of their communities by the mainstream often forces them into silence as they are afraid to report experiences of violence for the fear of betraying their own communities (Burns; Razack). As Burns notes,

> Our abuse has been hidden in our communities' refusal to acknowledge the pervasiveness of violence in our lives. This refusal is not maliciousness but a protective measure born of the legitimate fear that such information would be used as a weapon by the dominant culture. Our abuse has been hidden behind bravado and denials. The result is the creation of a climate of tolerance. (4)

Yet, it is critical to form a space whereby the specific kinds of violence that racialized girls experience can be discussed and analyzed. It is not enough to universalize their experiences within the category of "girls" or "women" (Tipper; Russell), or alternatively "youth" and "children." At the same time, focusing on culture fails to capture the structural forces of oppression that shape the lives of racialized and marginalized girls. A central issue here is the subtlety with which racism is communicated and naturalized, and how it intersects with sexism to influence the lived reality and strategies of survival of racialized girls. As Kimberle Crenshaw notes, "Race and gender are two of the primary sites for the particular distribution of social resources that ends up with observable class differences" (97).

An analysis of how racism interlocks with other systems of domination to influence the life chances and reality of racialized girls requires acknowledging racism as a form of violence that is endemic and pervasive. Nevertheless, while it has become increasingly common to accept the structured inequality produced and reproduced by sexism, the same does not hold true for racism. Thus, rather than accepting racism as a structure of domination, similar to sexism, and as arising from a legacy of colonialism, the reality of racism has to be "proven" continually (Bannerji 1987; 1993). In part, this denial of racism is formed and informed by the dominant mediated discourses on race and racism which are powerfully communicated through the mass media.

## The Mass Media, "Race," and Racism

The media play a critical role in communicating notions of "race" and racism. In effect, they help define these terms and locate them within the public imagination (Hall 1990; van Dijk, 1993). In the production and reproduction of social knowledge, the mainstream mass media are crucial vehicles in reinforcing hegemonic interpretations and interests (Cottle). Thus, how they frame race and racism is both derived from and informed by social life and reproduced in everyday talk and thought (Smitherman-Donaldson and van Dijk; van Dijk 1987).

Previous research has documented the ways in which Canadian mainstream media communicate notions of "race" and forward particular definitions of racism (Bannerji, 1986; Indra; Jiwani, 1993; Scanlon). These definitions explain racism as arising from ignorance, increasing immigration, and economic downturns (Jiwani 1993; see also van Dijk 1993). Such explanations are privileged through various discursive means so that they appear to be meaningful and resonate with everyday social reality. "Racists" are then defined as ignorant, uneducated, and usually rural-based individuals who at times are organized into hate groups (Jiwani, 1993). At the same time, "race" is represented by allusions to cultural differences and phenotypic differences where these can be readily observed (i.e., through film footage and pictures), and through Manichean oppositions which underscore these differences within the footage itself or in the presentation of the story (see also JanMohamed; Jiwani, 1998). It has been argued that the Canadian news media communicate race and racism by "omission and commission"—at times in a deliberate manner, and at other times, through strategic absence (Jiwani 1993).

## Media Frames—The Erasure of Race/Racism

As the events leading to Virk's murder unfolded in the daily papers and television newscasts, the horror of what "girls do to other girls" was highlighted and quickly overshadowed the issue of male violence. In contrast to the numerous deaths of women by their spouses and ex-spouses, Reena's death was held up as symbol of how girls are not immune to committing acts of violence. Story after story in the daily papers covered the issue of teen girl violence, quoting research to support the main contention that girls are just as dangerous as boys.[3] Even though existing research clearly links the issue of teen girl violence to the *internalization* of a dominant, patriarchal culture which values sex and power, this connection was trivialized if not side-stepped altogether (Artz; Joe and Chesney Lind). Additionally, counter-evidence which demonstrates that only 3.83 per cent of violent crimes are committed by girls (Schramm) failed to hit the headlines in the same manner or intensity.

Headlines from *The Vancouver Sun* during this early period (November, 1997) framed the story in the following way: "Teenage girls and violence: The B.C. reality"; "Girls fighting marked by insults, rumours, gangs"; "Bullies: Dealing with threats in a child's life"; "Girls killing girls a sign of angry, empty lives." This last headline suggests that had girls followed a traditional (gender-based) lifestyle, their lives would not be so empty and frustrating. Throughout the coverage, the media dwelt with puzzlement on the increasing violence of teenage girls at a time when they were supposedly enjoying greater equality. Statistics indicating the growing number of girls graduating with honours, as compared to boys, were used to demonstrate this perplexing contradiction. Implicit throughout the news coverage was the sense that girls do not deserve to be violent because of the privileges they are now enjoying, and further, that girls are not used to the demands inherent in these privileges and therefore, can not cope, a disturbing echo of late nineteenth-century ideology.

At no time did the media provide any in-depth analysis of the violent nature of the dominant culture or examine ways in which violent behaviour is internalized as a function of coping with a violent society. Nor did the media report on the kinds of violence to which girls are generally subjected to, or the differential impact of violence on girls and boys from different backgrounds. In fact, this kind of coverage only surfaced with the school murders in Littleton, U.S.A., and the subsequent copy-cat murder in Taber, Alberta (see for instance, *The Vancouver Sun* 1999b), where suddenly, boys who were considered marginalized became the objects of public sympathy and reporting.

While the dominant filter became one of girl-on-girl violence, this subsequently shifted, albeit slightly, towards a sustained coverage of schoolyard bullies, sprinkled with some sympathetic coverage of children who are marginalized in school because they do not fit peer-group normative standards. Aside from opinion pieces written by individuals, mostly South Asian, none of the news articles discussed the issue of racialization as it impacts on girls who are physically different by virtue of their skin colour or the pressures of assimilation that racialized girls experience in attempting to fit within their peer group culture. Interestingly, in contrast to previous patterns of coverage observed in the news accounts of the stories of young racialized women, accounts which tended to focus on issues of cultural and intergenerational conflict (Jiwani 1992), the coverage of the Reena Virk murder did neither. Instead, the coverage continued to focus on girl-on-girl violence in the immediate aftermath of the murder.

Subsequent coverage of the court appearances and sentencing of the six girls who were charged, focused on Virk's inability to find acceptance in her peer culture, and once again, emphasized her weight and height as the major contributing factors. Despite her physical difference—as a racialized girl—there was no mention, save one, of the possible motive being racism. Instead, the stories repeatedly stressed her lack of "fit" and her overweight appearance. The implication was that had Reena Virk fit the normative standards, she would have been acceptable. Normative standards in this society imply a body which is thin, white, (or exotic and beautiful), able-bodied, heterosexual, and which conforms to accepted notions of female teenage behaviour.[4] In essence, the victim is held responsible for her own fate. The issue of racism as a motive is significantly absent in early media coverage and only surfaced two years later in the coverage of the trial of one of her attackers (Hall 1999a).

A brief interlude in the construction of the story occurred with the revelation that Virk had allegedly been sexual abused by a close family member. This underlined once again, her lack of "fit"—both within her familial culture and the external, dominant culture of her peers. The allegations were immediately denied in the detailed coverage of the eulogy delivered by an elder of the Jehovah's Witness church at her funeral. The denial was underscored by her mother's comments to reporters suggesting that Reena had been a troubled child. Journalistic accounts which stressed her inability to conform to her family's ethnic values, combined with the strict beliefs of the Jehovah Witness Church, reinforced her mother's statements and helped locate the issue as one of intergenerational conflict, youth rebellion, and cultural conflict (Beatty and Pemberton; Dirk). However, despite this obvious location and familiar terrain, these lines of inquiry were never investigated in subsequent stories. The allegations were reported again in a subsequent article which focused on a friend's disclosure of Virk's sexual abuse by a family member but were not contextualized in reference to existing statistics on child sexual abuse and the links between violence in the home and running away from home (Kinnon and Hanvey).[5] Aside from these subdominant motifs, the framework of the story remained that of the escalating girl-on-girl violence.

Not only was Virk's racialized identity erased, but there was a significant lack of attention paid to even the *possibility* that her death was racially motivated. Almost two years later, at the trial of one of her alleged murderers, Warren Glowatski, the issue of racism was brought up by one witness—Syreeta Hartley, his girlfriend (Hall 1999a). However, aside from the brief reporting of her testimony in the daily coverage of the trial, the issue itself was neither investigated by the media nor considered to be of importance by Justice Macaulay in his decision (*R.* v *Warren Paul Glowatski*, 1999). This absence occurred despite the hate crimes legislation available to the courts; existing documentation of the activity of hate groups in schools and colleges campuses (Prutzman; Sidel); existing studies which highlight the vulnerability of racialized girls to violence; or the racial connotations imbuing the acts of brutality to which Virk was subjected, as for example, the stubbing of a cigarette on her forehead—the place usually used to put a *bindi* which is a common practice among various South Asian cultures.

The significant absence of any discussion or investigation of racism as a motive reflects not only a minimization of the violence of racism but also its sheer taken-for-granted character as a non-problematic and unrecognizable element. As Neal Hall (1990) and Philomena Essed point out, everyday racism is ingrained in the daily interactions of people of colour with the dominant society—it structures common-sense reality and is thereby naturalized in an insidious way. Part of its naturalization arises from its taken-for-granted nature and embeddedness. The media's denial of racism corresponds with hegemonic definitions of racism as an activity confined to extreme hate groups, rather than as a system and structure of domination inherent in the very fabric of society and its institutions. Thus, even though Syreeta Hartley's testimony was explicit in highlighting the racial motivations of the murder, its import was minimized both by the media and the judge. As one journalist stated, "Syreeta Hartley said her former boyfriend told her that his involvement was partly motivated by racism. Virk was Indo-Canadian" (Hall 1999a: A5). The media also reported that Glowatski did not know Reena Virk and had never spoken to her.

At no time did the local or national media dwell upon or investigate the fact that

Warren Glowatski had first bragged about picking a fight with a Native man (Hall 1999b). The issue of why he would first select a Native man as the target for his aggression remained unexamined and yet suggests the vulnerability of marginalized groups and the hierarchy in which they are positioned. The reporting implies that it is much easier to beat a Native man and get away with it, than it is to beat up a white male. The value of difference is thus communicated by allusion and association.

The dominant framing of "other" cultures as deviant is naturalized and taken for granted by the dominant media, and tends to be used strategically to underline the "unassimilable character" of immigrant communities (Jiwani 1992). However, in the case of Reena Virk, there was a significant absence of any kind of cultural framing. It could be argued that the dominant media have become more sensitized to issues of cultural representations. Alternatively, the media's reluctance to use a cultural frame may be derived from the possibility that some of the girls involved in the first fight were themselves of South Asian origin. This in itself does not negate the reality that many members of a racialized community internalize the normative values and behaviours of the dominant society and reject identifiers and people of their communities. In fact, the cultural frame would have allowed the media to continue a noted tradition—that of portraying racialized communities as being sites of conflict and disturbance created by their own members (Entman; Indra). It can be argued that in this particular instance, the construction of girl-on-girl violence became a dominant filter as it better served masculinist hegemonic interests within a contextual climate of backlash against women. For the media to have focused on culture at this point would, by necessity, have involved an examination of racism as predicated on Virk's exclusion from and marginalization by her peer group, as well as the defining characteristics which resulted in her "lack of fit." Organizing and translating information within this frame would thus have resulted in a confrontation with the reality of racism and its prevalence in Canadian society, as well as the vulnerability of racialized people to racially motivated violence.

As an elite institution, the media reproduces hegemonic values and often does so by reporting on the decisions and perspectives of other elites (van Dijk 1993). In the case of Reena Virk, the accounts which were reported on a sustained basis—each story referenced the other thereby resulting in a cumulative stock of knowledge—tended to be based on the reports or announcements of other elites. These included academics, police, and judges. Alternative interpretations based on the views of advocates were significantly absent, the exception being those cases where individuals wrote opinion pieces which were subsequently published. Thus, the complete absence of any mention of racism in Judge Macaulay's sentencing decision was echoed in the news coverage and served to secure his view of the case as the dominant and preferred interpretation—that the murder was the result of violent intent but an intent that was unconnected to racism, sexism, or a combination thereof.

## Conclusion

From the above analysis, it can be seen that the Canadian print media continue to favour and forward interpretations of race and racism which resonate with elite definitions and which reinforce hegemonic interests. In the case of Reena Virk, the critical issues facing racialized girls were never examined by the media, nor was the issue of racism dealt with in any substantive manner. Rather, as with issues concerning child abuse, racism was relegated to the background and overshadowed by stories regarding the increasing levels of girl-on-girl violence and the inability of Reena Virk to "fit." Thus, the issue of racism was erased from the dominant discourse; Reena Virk's identity as a racialized young woman has been similarly erased in terms of its significance and contribution to her vulnerability and marginality. As a young woman of colour, she was visibly different, yet her difference was only understood in terms of her weight and height and her general "inability to fit." The issue of what she needed to "fit into" was never explored, nor were the assumptions underlying normative standards of beauty and behaviour for teenage girls interrogated. Yet these issues are central to highlighting the particular ways in which racism and sexism interact in shaping the lives of racialized girls, and in contributing to their marginalization and vulnerability to violence—both as girls and as racialized others. The erasure of race and racism in this story reinforced the accepted stock of knowledge that racism is confined to the acts of organized hate groups. Thus, the structured nature of racism as a system of domination which informs everyday life and constrains the life chances of racialized peoples remains outside the dominant discourse, relegated to the margins.

## Notes

[1]This composite is derived from the accounts presented in various newspapers and magazines over a two-year period (1997-1999).
[2]For a discussion of racism and sexism within the school system, see Bourne *et al.*
[3]This analysis of news coverage is based on articles on the story of Reena Virk which were published in *The Vancouver Sun* during November and December in 1997. In addition, an electronic search of all articles appearing in Canadian newspapers pertaining to the decision in the Warren Glowatski trial were also examined.
[4]In their examination of girls' critique of schooling, Bourne *et al.* note that the South Asian girls in their focus groups commented on how their appearance is exoticized suggesting that this is one of the ways in which they are considered acceptable.
[5]In their review of the literature on violence against women, Kinnon and Hanvey note that, "60 to 70 per cent of runaways and 98 per cent of child prostitutes have a history of child abuse" (7).

## References

Alicea, Marixsa. "'A Chambered Nautilus,' The Contradictory Nature of Puerto Rican Women's Role in the Social Construction of a Transnational Community." *Gender and Society* 11 (5) (1997): 597-626.

Alliance of Five Research Centres on Violence. *Final Report on Phase I, Violence Prevention and the Girl Child.* 1998. Research funded by the Status of Women Canada. Available online: http://www.harbour.sfu.ca/freda/

Artz, Sibylle. *Sex, Power, and the Violent School Girl.* Toronto: Trifolium Books, 1998.

Bannerji, Himani. "Now You See Us/Now You Don't." *Video Guide* 8 (40) (1986): 5.

Bannerji, Himani. "Introducing Racism: Notes Towards an Anti-Racist Feminism," *Resources for Feminist Research* 16 (1) (May 1987): 10-12.

Bannerji, Himani, ed. *Returning the Gaze: Essays on Racism, Feminism and Politics.* Toronto: Sister Vision Press, 1993.

Beatty, Jim and Kim Pemberton. "Teen Recanted Claims Of Abuse Says Church Elder." *The Vancouver Sun.* November 29, 1997. A3.

Bourne, Paula, Liza McCoy and Dorothy Smith. "Girls and Schooling: Their Own Critique." *Resources for Feminist Research* 26 (1/2) (Spring 1998): 55-68.

Burns, Mary Violet C., ed. *The Speaking Profits Us: Violence in the Lives of Women of Colour.* Seattle, WA: Centre for the Prevention of Sexual and Domestic Violence, 1986.

Cottle, Simon. "'Race,' Racialization and the Media: a Review and Update of Research." *Sage Race Relations Abstracts* 17:2 (1992): 3-57.

Crenshaw, Kimberle Williams. "Mapping the Margins: Intersectionality, Identity Politics, and Violence Against Women of Color." *The Public Nature of Private Violence, The Discovery of Domestic Abuse.* Eds. Martha Fineman and Roxanne Mykitiuk. New York: Routledge, 1994. 93-118.

Drury, Beatrice. "Sikh Girls and the Maintenance of an Ethnic Culture." *New Community* 17 (3) (1991): 387-399.

Entman, Robert M. "Modern Racism and the Images of Blacks in Local Television News." *Critical Studies in Mass Communication* 7 (1990): 332-345.

Essed, Philomena. *Everyday Racism. Reports from Women of Two Cultures.* Translated by Cynthia Jaffe. Claremont, CA: Hunter House, 1990.

Fitzgerald, Robin. "Assaults against Children and Youth in the Family, 1996." *Juristat* 17 (11) Ottawa: Canadian Centre for Justice Statistics, Statistics Canada, November 1997.

Friedman, Sara Ann with Courtney Cook. *Girls, A Presence at Beijing.* New York: NGO WGG (Working Groups on Girls), 1995.

Geertz, Clifford. "The Integrative Revolution: Primordial Sentiments and Civil Politics in New States." *Old Societies and New States.* Ed. Clifford Geertz. New York: Free Press, 1963. 105-57.

Hall, Neal. "Virk's Killing Motivated by Racism, Witness Says," *The Vancouver Sun* April 15, 1999a: A5.

Hall, Neal. "Accused Changed Bloody Clothes on the Night Virk Dies, Court Told." *The Vancouver Sun.* Tuesday April 20, 1999b: A6c.

Hall, Stuart. "The Whites of Their Eyes." *The Media Reader.* Eds. Manuel Alvarado and John O. Thompson. London: British Film Institute, 1990.

Hutnik, Nimmi. "Patterns of Ethnic Minority Identification and Modes of Adaptation." *Ethnic and Racial Studies* 9 (2) (April 1986): 150-167.

Indra, Doreen. "South Asian Stereotypes in the Vancouver Press." *Ethnic and Racial Studies* 2 (2) (1979): 166-189.

Isaacs, Harold. *Idols of the Tribe, Group Identity and Political Change.* New York: Harper and Row, 1975.

Jabbra, Nancy. "Assimilation and Acculturation of Lebanese Extended Families in Nova Scotia." *Canadian Ethnic Studies* 15 (1) (1983): 54-72.

Jan Mohamed, Abdul R. "The Economy of Manichean Allegory: The Function of Racial Difference in Colonialist Literature." *Critical Inquiry* 12 (1) (1985): 59-87.

Jiwani, Yasmin. "To Be or Not to Be: South Asians as Victims and Oppressors in the *Vancouver Sun.*" *Sanvad* 5 (45) (1992): 13-15.

Jiwani, Yasmin. "By Omission and Commission: Race and Representation in Canadian Television News." Unpublished doctoral dissertation, School of Communications, Simon Fraser University, 1993.

Jiwani, Yasmin. "On the Outskirts of Empire: Race and Gender in Canadian Television News." *Painting the Maple: Essays on Race, Gender, and the Construction of Canada.* Eds. V. Strong-Boag, S. Grave, A. Eisenberg, and J. Anderson. Vancouver: University of British Columbia Press, 1998. 53-68.

Jiwani, Yasmin. *Violence Against Marginalized Girls: A Review of the Literature.* Vancouver: FREDA, 1998b.

Joe, Karen A. and Meda Chesney-Lind. "'Just Every Mother's Angel': An Analysis of Gender and Ethnic Variations in Youth Gang Membership." *Gender and Society* 9 (4) (August 1995): 408-431.

Keyes, Charles F. "The Dialectics of Ethnic Change." *Ethnic Change.* Ed. Charles F. Keyes. Seattle: University of Washington Press, 1981. 4-30.

Kim, Jin K. "Explaining Acculturation in a Communication Framework: An Empirical Test." *Communication Monographs* 47 (August 1980): 155-179.

Kinnon, Diane and Louise Hanvey. "Health Aspects of Violence Against Women." Available online: http://hwcweb.hwc.ca/canusa/papers/english/violent.htm.

Lyman, Stanford M. and William A. Douglass. "Ethnicity: Strategies of Collective and Individual Impression Management." *Social Research* 40 (1973): 344-365.

Macaulay, J. "Reasons for Judgment in *R v. Warren Paul Glowatski.*" Supreme Court of British Columbia, Docket 95773. June 2, 1999.

Matthews, Julie Mariko. "A Vietnamese Flag and a Bowl of Australian Flowers: Recomposing Racism and Sexism." *Gender, Place and Culture* 4 (1) (March 1997): 5-18.

Meissner, Dirk. "Murdered Girl Was Turning Her Life Around, Mother Says" *The Vancouver Sun*. Monday April 19, 1999. B6C

Miller, Barbara D. "Precepts and Practices: Researching Identity Formation among Indian Hindu Adolescents in the United States." *New Directions for Child Development* 67 (1995): 71-85.

Onder, Zehra. "Muslim-Turkish Children in Germany: Socio-cultural Problems." *Migration World Magazine* 24 (5) (1996):18-24.

Prutzman, Priscilla. "Bias-Related Incidents, Hate Crimes, and Conflict Resolution." *Education and Urban Society*. 27 (1) (November 1994): 71-81.

Razack, Sherene H. *Looking White People in the Eye, Gender, Race, and Culture in Courtrooms and Classrooms*. Toronto: University of Toronto Press, 1998.

Rosenthal, Doreen, Nadia Ranieri, and Steven Klimidis. "Vietnamese Adolescents in Australia: Relationships between Perceptions of Self and Parental Values, Intergenerational Conflict, and Gender Dissatisfaction." *International Journal of Psychology*. 31 (2) (April 1996): 81-91.

Russell, Susan with the Canadian Federation of University Women. *Take Action for Equality, Development and Peace: A Canadian Follow-up Guide to Beijing '95*. Eds. Linda Souter and Betty Bayless. Ottawa: CRIAW, Canadian Beijing Facilitating Committee, 1996.

Scanlon, Joseph. "The Sikhs of Vancouver." *Ethnicity and the Media*. Paris: Unesco, 1977.

Schramm, Heather. *Young Women Who Use Violence: Myths and Facts*. Calgary: Elizabeth Fry Society of Calgary, 1998.

Sidel, Ruth. "Battling Bias: College Students Speak Out." *Educational Record* 76 (2,3) (Spring-Summer 1995): 45-52.

Smitherman-Donaldson, Geneva and Teun van Dijk. *Discourse and Discrimination*. Detroit: Wayne State University Press, 1988.

Thobani, Sunera. "Culture isn't the Cause of Violence." *Vancouver Sun* September 26, 1992: A12.

Tipper, Jennifer. *The Canadian Girl Child: Determinants of the Health and Well-Being of Girls and Young Women*. Ottawa: Canadian Institute of Child Health, September 1997.

Turnbull, Sue. "The Media: Moral Lessons and Moral Careers." *Australian Journal of Education* 37 (2) (1993): 153-168.

Van Dijk, Teun A. *Communicating Racism, Ethnic Prejudice in Thought and Talk*. United States: Sage, 1987.

Van Dijk, Teun A. *Elite Discourse and Racism*. Sage series on Race and Ethnic Relations, Volume 6. California: Sage, 1993.

*The Vancouver Sun* May 8, 1999a: A10

*The Vancouver Sun* Special issue on Teen Violence May 14, 1999b.

Vertinsky, Patricia, Indy Batth and Mita Naidu. "Racism in Motion: Sport, Physical Activity and the Indo-Canadian Female." *Avante* 2 (3) (1996): 1-23.

# Labelling Young Women as Violent

## Vilification of the Most Vulnerable

Kim Pate

Violent crime committed by young people has decreased in recent years. At the same time, calls for harsher punishment of youth mount. The resulting tension of competing interests and objectives generated by misinformation and media coverage of high profile, violent crime involving youth is embodied in the proposed *Youth Criminal Justice Act* (YCJA). The legislation incorporates the punitive and progressive criminal justice agenda. While providing more regressive sentencing options for young people convicted of the most serious offences, the YCJA also embodies the commitment of the federal government to reduce reliance on incarceration as exemplified by the emphasis on extra-judicial measures.

Against this backdrop of current juvenile justice reform measures, this paper explores the factors contributing to the reality that poor, young, racialized women and girls are among the fastest growing prison populations world-wide. The so-called "War on Drugs," evisceration of education, health and other social support services, and "gender-neutral" zero tolerance policies have contributed significantly to this phenomenon. Furthermore, too many imprisoned women and girls are over-classified in terms of their security risks to the general public.

Around the world, we are seeing that women and girls with cognitive and/or mental disabilities are more likely to be criminalized, jailed, and then classified as maximum security prisoners. Many of them were previously institutionalized in psychiatric hospitals and/or involved in other mental health services. Many are criminalized as a result of their disability-induced behaviour in institutions and/or the community.

We enter this century and millennium with the ever-present and persistent challenge of ensuring that women and girls behind prison walls have access to justice. As the economic, social, and political climates within our provinces and territories continue to produce ever more daunting challenges to the survival of the most marginalized, we also struggle to resist the rush to vilify women and girls. This paper will highlight the key issues, research, and approaches recommended to address these matters and strengthen commitment to equality and justice for women and girls.

## Background

There is a pressing need to counter misinformation about the nature and extent of young women's violence. A few years ago, I was alerted to this as a result of a call I received from a reporter. He asked me whether I would be prepared to do an interview about the increase in violent offending by young women. "What increase?" was my response. He said his local police source had advised him that their community had seen a 200 per cent increase in robbery offences alone over the past decade. When I asked him how many actual cases those figures represented, he was not certain.

Further investigation revealed that two young women had been charged with robbery—one happened about ten years earlier, the other had just occurred. Prior to that, there were apparently no charges or convictions of girls or young women on record. Technically, then, the statistic was correct. The impression of young women erupting into violent behaviour created by the 200 per cent figure and the accompanying media hype was, however, incredibly skewed and inaccurate. The reality was that the violent behaviour perceived to be "erupting" was non-existent and the actual risk posed to the public by the two young women in question was extremely low.

I still receive many calls from reporters, students, and other members of the public requesting information about the increasing number of violent girls, especially about those who are involved with gangs. Sensationalized media accounts of youth crime, especially any involving young women perpetrating violence, attract a disproportionate amount of "air time." As Yasmin Jiwani points out in, *Violence Prevention and the Girl Child: The Final Report,* while girl gang violence may be prominent in the public imagination, the reality is that only 3.83 per cent of violent crimes are committed by young women.

## Factors Contributing to the Increased Criminalization of Women and Girls

In Canada, and internationally, we are also seeing the feminization and criminalization of poverty. Most single parents are women, the majority of whom live below the poverty line. As social programs have been dismantled, women, especially sole support mothers, are faced with the reality of having to make ends meet within the context of a shrinking social welfare system. In order to survive and support their families with insufficient resources, many are forced to work under the table, prostitute themselves, and, occasionally, some even carry packages across international borders for money.

All too often, and increasingly so, these survival approaches result in the criminalization of women and girls for fraud, soliciting for the purposes of prostitution, trafficking, and/or importation charges. Think of the comparative savings in terms of both human and fiscal costs if the monies required to jail them, as well as the expenses of state-provided child-welfare services and support for those who have children seized by the state, were invested in our communities instead. This re-investment of ever-shrinking resources would undoubtedly benefit the women and girls currently being criminalized, as well as many others who are marginalized in their communities. Ultimately, such social and community development is beneficial to all of us.

Another result of funding cutbacks to services over the past decades is the obliteration of progressive policy developments to de-institutionalize those labelled as mentally handicapped and/or mentally ill. These trends to normalize and integrate services for those with cognitive and mental disabilities have been seriously compromised by funding cuts. This has resulted in more people—particularly women and girls who have traditionally been over-represented in these sectors—literally being dumped into the streets and, ultimately, into the wider, deeper, and stickier social control net of our criminal justice system. Although the criminal justice system is the least effective and most expensive system that could be used to respond to cognitive and mental disabilities, it is a system that cannot refuse to "service" anyone who is criminalized, regardless of their disability.

Once in prison, the practical reality is that mental health needs have been equated with risk. Mental-health concerns that are disabling undoubtedly create very real needs for those who have them and for those who try to control prisons. But, equating mental and cognitive disabilities with risks only serves to perpetuate the social construction of persons with mental disabilities as dangerous.

Although this is precisely the kind of stereotyping prohibited by the equality provisions of the section 15 of the *Canadian Charter of Rights and Freedoms,* most such young women end up isolated in segregated and/or maximum security units in juvenile and adult jails. Most of these women and girls pose the greatest risk to themselves and their own well-being. They are, however, perceived as difficult to "manage" in prison settings, especially if they resist restraint, lock-up, or medications, slash and carve their bodies, burn themselves, swallow items, try to smash in their own skulls, gouge out their eyes, try to kill themselves, et cetera.

The inability of correctional systems to address cognitive challenges and mental health needs has thus been used as a reason to classify women and girls with cognitive or mental disabilities as risks to the community. As a result, they are imprisoned in high security settings where they are subjected to harsh, often inhumane and illegal treatment. Since this kind of treatment occurs directly as a result of these women prisoners' cognitive and mental disabilities, it is clearly discriminatory and thus contravenes human rights as well as s. 15(1) of our constitutionally enshrined *Charter of Rights and Freedoms.*

We must continue to pursue opportunities to challenge the increasing criminalization of those with cognitive and mental disabilities. In addition, we must focus upon the development of community-based services. Where we have not been able prevent women or girls with cognitive or mental disabilities from being criminalized in the first place, we need to work to have these women and girls taken out of the prisons on passes and/or released into the community so that they may access the community-based services they need. It would be folly of the most profound and irresponsible proportions to focus on the development of institutionally-based services alone.

Another significant factor in the increasing trend to criminalize women and girls is the adoption and application of so-called "gender neutral" zero-tolerance policies. As will be discussed in more detail below, part of the backlash to increased attempts to hold violent men accountable has been the application of zero-tolerance policies to charge and/or counter charge women and girls. While eliminating violence is an important objective and violence should never be condoned, the state should not counter-charge women and girls involved in relatively minor altercations in school yards, or those who defend themselves or others from violence perpetrated against them by abusive men.

## Impact of Stereotypes of Young Women and Violence

The notion of criminality has evolved from such outdated labels as "immorality." Women and children have traditionally been seen as inherently morally "pure." They have also been perceived as property and, therefore, subject to the control of the men who fathered them or married them. Any woman who dared to step outside of her designated role as a "good" mother, wife, daughter, et cetera, was likely to be judged immoral. If she deigned to commit violent acts, regardless of the circumstances (i.e., whether reactive or even defensive), or if she engaged in sexual acts outside of marriage (regardless of whether she was raped or otherwise the subject of unwanted sexual advances); and, worse still, if she voluntarily engaged in sexual activity because she enjoyed it, she would be deemed an aberration and relegated to the margins of her gender.

The more outside of the male-based norms and stereotypes a woman or girl strayed, the more likely she was to be assessed as either "mad" or "bad"—the former pathologized the woman and thus slightly alleviated her degree of personal responsibility and blame for the immorality. The latter label, on the other hand, clearly placed full blame and responsibility on the woman. One might well inquire as to what has really changed. The same processes are still used by the media, by too many authors (e.g., Pearson, CSC research, etc.), and by the regressive forces of the right, albeit with new labels and sometimes convoluted commentary.

Christie Barron points out that:

> [The media] often decontextualizes the acts of crime for public consumption. When youth crime is presented in a social, economic and political vacuum, it appears as if nothing else is occurring in society except kids doing bad

> things.... Most of the establishment authorities agree that there were ever-increasing numbers of girls involved in violent crimes.

One of the psychiatric social workers asserted: "I've been working with kids since the late '60s and I've seen more females involved in violent acts, more involved in gangs; it may be a wannabe type of situation." One of the probation officers stated that girls became involved in violence because of " trivial stuff" such as someone making a bad comment. She also stated that the number girls involved in violent crime has increased but not necessarily to the level of violence of the boys.

The youth I talked with provided a context for any increase in female violence. "...There should be recognition of circumstances in the youth world relative to their own existence and experience, as opposed to circumstances important to the criminal justice system situated in the adult world." In commenting about the media depiction of young women as violent, one of the young women interviewed by Barron indicated: "I think media looked at the wrong thing; they looked at what [the girls] do but not why. They don't care; they just want to make money" (84-85). Moreover, as she astutely pointed out, the media consistently failed to focus on how degrading and violent prostitution is for the girls involved.

Barron further states that:

> violent youths have become "folk devils," to whom are attributed characteristics that feed societal panic but clash with the youths' perceptions of self. Youths are pathologized within professional discourse and portrayed as unremorseful monsters in need of medical treatment. Explaining youth crime as an individual problem denies the structural and cultural barriers that youths say contribute to their actions. These professional stereotypes are reproduced and confirmed as 'truths' through such powerful institutions as the media. (67)

## The Differences Between Men's and Women's Violence

The manner in which young women and girls behave "violently" has been largely ignored or minimized historically. Where and when it is addressed, violence by women and girls tends to either be seen as a function of masculinity or a lack of femininity, or as an indication of extreme behaviour often characterized as madness. Perhaps the greatest difficulty in terms of addressing violence perpetrated by young women is that most of the "research" in this area is, in fact, the postulating of theory by academics that often does not include the voices and/or experiences of women and girls themselves. Some notable exceptions are Christie Barron's research, Justice for Girls in Vancouver, and the National Youth in Care Network, as well as that of a group of researchers who work out of the University of Glasgow in Scotland under the name of Girls and Violence.

It is interesting to note that up until the 1970s, the occasional violent acts committed by women were generally ignored by law enforcement authorities world-wide. During the '70s a new mythology emerged that linked the women's movement to a new wave of violent offending by women. White, adult women, as leaders of the women's emancipation movement, were identified as causing the surge in serious criminal offending by women. Although the facts clearly do not support such contentions, many have concluded that more women and girls are committing offences because of the influence of some women's desires to be equal to men. Furthermore, the breakdown of the family (also perceived to be a consequence of women's desire for emancipation) is believed to have resulted in girls not having their fathers around to help socialize them. The juvenile justice system has a long history of paternalism, such that young women who defy authority, particularly if they defy parental authority and run away from home, tend to be sanctioned more harshly than their male counterparts.

American author Meda Chesney-Lind calls this the "liberation" hypothesis. She furthermore states that in the 1990s we were in the midst of a second wave that causally links women's equality with girls'—especially poor, minority girls—participation in gangs. Nevertheless, throughout both "waves" of the women's movement, there have been no substantiated significant changes in the levels and patterns of girls' violent and aggressive behaviour in Canada, the United States, and the United Kingdom (Chesney-Lind 1998). There are, however, marked differences in external responses to violent or aggressive actions, especially those perpetrated by youth.

The development of so-called zero-tolerance policies has resulted in increased policing and prosecuting of all forms of violence committed by boys and girls. Proportionately, because the overall number of young women charged with violent offences remains relatively low, the increased numbers create more substantial percentage increases in the statistics for girls than they do for boys.

In addition, there has been an increased criminalization of young women's survival skills. In the past, it was relatively easy to institutionalize or enforce social controls on young women if they ran away, missed curfew, engaged in sexual activity or displayed behaviour that might be defined as "unfeminine" or, worse yet, unmanageable. Under the old *Juvenile Delinquents Act*, a young woman could be imprisoned in a juvenile home for such activities. The introduction of the *Young Offenders Act* (YOA) in 1982 was supposed to end the arbitrary detention of young women for such activities. However, the way the YOA is being implemented by police and judges belies its legislative intent. We fear that the new *Youth Criminal Justice Act* will not rectify this situation if only the law, and not the practices, change.

Indeed, Ann Campbell and others have challenged us to consider whether it is morally or ethically appropriate for women and girls who need to use violence and aggression as a means to survive should relinquish these tools. She maintains, that:

> Secure in our relationships and relatively protected from physical harm, most women do not need to use aggression as a tool to keep the world at bay. But

> when the ties that bring women close to others are destroyed, what do they have to fear in aggression? They cannot fear the loss of what they do not have. And the indisputable law on the street is fight or get beaten.... Where ever women face lives of brutal exploitation that destroys their faith in the value of trust and intimacy, they will be driven to it. We cannot demand that women desist from its use when their survival requires it. (1993: 140).

As Megan Stephens further points out:

> Instead of making it a priority to lock up youth, society must begin to try to deal with the environmental factors that compel these young women to behave violently. If the young women that I spoke with were victims, they are victims of a system that has dismissed them as 'bad girls' instead of trying to understand why they think they are driven to act violently.... Any attempt to 'eliminate' youth violence will need to take into consideration the social contexts from which these children come and we need to understand how these contexts seem to make the use of violence not only legitimate but, at least in the minds of these young women, sometimes even necessary. (169-170)

Finally, Mark Totten confirms that,

> the literature suggests that women's use of violence is qualitatively different from that of men: whereas male violence tends to be more frequent, serious, and utilitarian, female violence is more often contextualized in significant factors related to self-defence, anticipation of an upcoming physical or sexual assault, and prior victimization by physical and sexual abuse. (51)

## Purpose of the Youth Justice System

It is now more than 17 years since the *Young Offenders Act* was proclaimed into law and paraded internationally as one of the most innovative and progressive legislative responses to juvenile justice. Since its inception, however, the legislation has had its most progressive elements gradually chiselled away.

The YOA was based on youth-positive principles and it is distressing to observe continued attempts to erode its fundamental tenets and guiding principles. Regressive changes have failed youth and further marginalized many youth with special needs, particularly young women. The YOA called for the least restrictive interventions possible for young people. In fact, it called for an examination of all other youth-serving systems (such as education, child welfare, and children's mental health) prior to invoking its provisions. Alternative or diversionary options are entrenched in the *Act*. Paradoxically, the past decade has seen just the opposite result. In many schools or group homes, for instance, matters that would previously have been dealt with by an internal administrative authority are increasingly likely to be referred to the juvenile justice system.

As Kim Brooks, Vincent Shiradeli, and Jason Ziedenberg reveal in their report on school violence, the larger threat to young people comes not from school violence,

> but recent attempts to turn the schools into funnels for the juvenile justice system. Nearly every state has recently changed their laws to require that schools share information with the courts—watering down the confidentiality laws that were the hallmark of the juvenile court's rehabilitative model. Teachers and principals are referring students to police, settling trivial matters in the courts rather than in the classrooms. And if you can't find real evidence of a threat, you can always turn to the Federal Bureau of Investigation's new 'profiling' software that pretends to know all tell-tail signs for potential school shooters, including having parental troubles, disliking popular students, experiencing a failed romance, and listening to songs with violent lyrics. (4)

Consider, for a moment just how many young people experiencing adolescence might have this profile.

Rather than adopt a "zero violence" approach, zero-tolerance policies have resulted in ever increasing numbers of disenfranchised youth being jettisoned out of schools and communities, usually through, rather than into, a thinning social safety net. Rather than nurturing our youth, we are increasingly scapegoating and disposing of them as though they are expendable human refuse. Statistics reveal that there has been an overall reduction in youth crime generally, as well as a relatively low incidence of violent and repeat youth crime more specifically.

These figures notwithstanding, police, reporters, and communities continue to blame the youth justice system, especially the YOA, for crime, quickly and too easily criminalize the behaviour of young people, and throw them to the wide, expensive, and ineffective net of the juvenile justice system.

Young people are best served by supportive and proactive interventions, as opposed to the punitive and reactive approaches characterized by, and endemic to, criminal justice responses. Indeed, there is more than sufficient evidence that preventative approaches to crime are far more cost-effective than current criminal justice approaches. Accordingly, we should focus on developing and enhancing high quality supportive services for children, youth, and adults alike—from universal and enriched health care, child care, and educational opportunities to effective gender, anti-poverty, anti-racism, and conflict-resolution programs. Recognizing the current stresses of fiscal restraint and downsizing, schools might redirect efforts to consolidating creative energies and encouraging an empowered student body to provide peer and mentoring support, for example.

Professional training on the developmental, educational, as well as psychosocial attributes of young people should be a prerequisite for those working in the youth justice system. In addition, the high number of young offenders who have been abused must be recognized and reflected in the professional training of those who come in contact with young offenders. It has been reported that at least 50 per cent of the youth serving time in British Columbia had previously been sexually abused. In addition, even higher percentages have been reported in Alberta and Manitoba studies. Similarly, a 1994 Ontario study conducted by Margaret Shaw revealed that of the young women in custody, 63 per cent had been physically abused and 58 per cent had been sexually abused. Given these statistics, it seems obvious that specialized training for dealing with abuse victims is crucial.

In order to ensure significant short- and long-term change, proactive education and training programs are required for judges, lawyers, probation officers, police officers, and all other youth justice personnel. The reorientation of those involved with young people is a prerequisite component to the development of positive and effective change within the youth justice and all other youth-serving systems. And young people themselves, as well as front-line workers, should be involved in the development of professional training, as well as in services and programs designed to address the needs of youth.

Providing supportive and empowering services to young people at the time of their first contact with the youth justice system generally reduces the likelihood of future "criminal" involvement. Nevertheless, these services should not exist *only* within the youth justice system because that would result in criminalizing youth who are simply in need of some supportive services. Preventative and proactive approaches must be emphasized within the child welfare, educational, medical, and mental health systems as well.

## Custody Must Really be the Last Resort

In terms of custodial sanctions, the YOA stipulates that such dispositions must only be used as a last resort. Further, when custody is resorted to, "open" custody should be considered before "secure" or "closed" custody. Secure custody was intended as the absolute last resort in terms of sentencing under the *Young Offenders Act*. Moreover, open custody was envisioned as easily distinguishable from secure custody, for example a group-home type of setting as opposed to an institution. In most provinces, however, the two forms of custody are virtually indistinguishable and provincial authorities have been the most vocal opponents of the two tiers of custody in the juvenile justice system. It comes as no surprise, therefore, that where both still exist, most open custody settings are now institutional and rather secure in nature.

The provisions of the new *Youth Criminal Justice Act* (YCJA) are even more clear and stringent in their direction. The focus on extra-judicial measures will hopefully help reduce the current reliance upon custody. Without resources to enable communities to develop meaningful community-based options, however, it remains to be seen whether this objective will be realized. Indeed, as we have also seen in the adult system, each time a new reform is introduced which aims to reduce reliance on prison, adequate resources are more often than not usually the key element that will determine their success or demise.

The introduction of conditional sentences probably provides the most recent example of this phenomenon. Initially embraced and utilized by the judiciary as a bona fide alternative to jail for many, after several years of resource deficient implementation, the scheme has now largely fallen into disrepute. Essentially, as Carol LaPrairie and others within the Department of Justice have chronicled, too many people were granted conditional sentences. Inadequate supports and supervision, coupled with stringent and often onerous conditions, resulted in many breaches of the conditions and subsequent jail terms—often for longer periods than if those concerned had received a prison sentence in the first place. Without sufficient resources for implementation, we fear that the progressive provisions of the YCJA may suffer a similar fate.

Where existing programs and services do not address the needs of young people, or the protection of society, the first priority must be to address these service or programming deficits. Rather than resorting to the "adult" criminal justice context at ever earlier ages, the federal and provincial authorities should focus on redistributing the $170 million spent annually on federal transfers for youth justice to the development and enhancement of youth-positive community-based dispositional options. This would result in improved educational and psycho-social programs and services in both community and institutional settings.

There is a paucity of community-based and therapeutic alternatives for young people in general and young women in particular. The federal Minister of Justice could address some of these issues through cost-sharing agreements with the provinces, rather than proposing legislative amendments. Such moves unfortunately also have the tendency to be simplistic, diminishing the pressure to create more proactive and preventative means of addressing complex issues and concerns. The federal government could reduce justice transfers for custody beds with a corresponding increase in community resource development for young people. Furthermore, provinces should be encouraged to develop gender-specific and culturally-appropriate services and programs for young people. Too frequently, the services and programs that do exist are ill-equipped to deal with issues such as gender, race, class, and sexual orientation.

## Institutional Abuse Issues

The emerging picture of the extent of institutional abuse of young people is grotesque (Standing Committee on Justice and Legal Affairs; CAEFS). Young people who have already been labelled as behaviour or management problems are especially vulnerable to abuse at the hands of institutional staff. It is extremely important that victims of abuse can take action and be heard and responded to in supportive ways. Audits and investigations into abuse allegations in residential schools, group homes, orphanages, and custodial centres provide horrendous examples of how and why youth are inadequately protected from abusive conduct. Institutional mechanisms for dealing with internal and external abuse are overwhelmingly inadequate. Reports generally place specific emphasis on the particular needs of young women, who have often been victims of abuse prior to their institutionalization.

It is frightening that children placed under the control of the Canadian government are experiencing physical, sexual, verbal, and emotional abuse. We know that such abuse can have an irreparable and debilitating impact on the lives and psyches of our youth. The fact that abuse is perpetrated by the very systems established to assist them only underscores the reasonableness of youth rejection of the values and authority that do harm to them.

Women are increasingly being charged in circumstances where they have called the police in relation to assault and/or threats directed at them by abusive men, especially if they have managed to defend themselves or otherwise reacted to the violence perpetrated against them. This is especially true for Aboriginal and other racialized women. The increasing numbers of younger women in the provincial and federal prison systems in Canada are also of particular concern to CAEFS. Unless we resist the calls for more punitive and regressive scapegoating of youth, and instead embark upon a public education campaign to inform the public about the excessive penalizing and incarceration of youth, we are not likely to see much change in the current slide away from justice for young people.

First Nations and Aboriginal youth are disproportionately jailed. For eight of the nine most common offences tracked in Canada, youth serve longer prison sentences than do adults. In addition, we jail youth at four times the rate we jail adults, and many times the rate in most states in the U.S. and European countries.

To make matters worse, young women usually end up being jailed in mixed youth centres. This results in many incidents of sexual harassment and rape, most of which go unreported. When we conducted research on young women in custody we found two rather shocking results. First, we discovered that many young women do not define what they experience as sexual harassment or rape. Instead, they talk about it as being flirting or fooling around, or their "turn in the closet." Secondly, for those who do identify what they experience as sexual harassment or rape, most claim that they would not report such assaults (CAEFS).

Too many young women explained their reluctance to report sexual and non-sexual assaults as a consequence of their fear that there would be repercussions, such as being held in more isolated conditions. This fear has been reinforced by experience. Not only are young women and girls often all mixed together, whether they are remanded in custody, or serving a disposition of open or secure custody, they are often isolated and have more limited access to services and programs than their male counterparts (CAEFS).

When a young woman reports a rape or has suddenly ended up impregnated while in custody, the institutional response is rarely to address the issues. Instead, what generally happens is that the young women are subjected to more restrictive and isolated conditions of confinement. This reinforces the adage that women, especially racialized young women, are too few to count. This reality has important implications for women in prison generally.

As the Amnesty International reports on the situation of male staff in women's prisons in the United States, and Madam Justice Arbour's *Commission of Inquiry into Certain Events at the Prison for Women*, have amply illustrated, strip-searching and male staff in women's prisons is an on-going issue. This is particularly the case when one considers the disincentives for women and girls to report harassment and sexual assault.

> Within the institutional environment, the young women were taught they were individually responsible for their past and its shortcomings, and if they wanted to have a chance to succeed in the future they would need to change both themselves and their sense of self and accept the values of mainstream society that "many, if not most acts of aggression are taboo." ... [These are] institutional attempts to place the sole responsibility for a resident's "problems" on the individual, forcing him or her to accept the institutional definition of the situation. (Stephens 164-165)

In addition, Stephens concluded that, "that young women can be, and are, violent, and that violent young women are not crazy or irrational but actually offer coherent explanations of how and why they choose to use violence" (167).

## Women and Girls: Still Considered Too Few to Count

All young people suffer as a result of the lack of adequate support services and other systems-based deficiencies. Those who work with young people will be all too familiar with the erosion of resources and support for our community-based support systems for youth. The relatively small numbers of young women who are criminalized and enter the system, as compared to young men, result in even fewer services for young offenders in any community.

Young women are disproportionately disadvantaged as a result of a lack of gender-focussed community and institutional programming and services, and extremely limited access to open custody settings. The majority of young women who receive open custody dispositions must serve their sentences in secure custody and/or co-ed correctional facilities. Girls and young women also tend to have limited access to the services and programs, both in the community and in institutions. In many young offender centres across the country, incidences of sexual assault and/or pregnancies during custody have led to the further segregation of young women in correctional facilities. Young women are in real need of women-centred approaches in the youth justice system, as their needs are often ignored, or at best subsumed, by those of young men.

As Joan Sangster has identified in her historical review of young women in the juvenile justice system, female juvenile delinquency is a "social construction." Indeed, when they looked at who was actually in custody, Raymond Corrado, Candice Odgers and Irwin Cohen found that the majority of the young women who were sentenced to custody were there essentially for "protective" reasons and the offences for which they were convicted were relatively minor. They identify the lack of community-based, non-custodial placement options as the primary reason for what they refer to as "administrative-based incarceration." They also talk about the fact that the resistance of young women to authority and the resistance of the community to allow young women to return to their "street lives" is also a key factor in predisposing juvenile justice authorities to locking young women up in treatment and custodial programs.

Staff also cite a complete lack of resources for young women in terms of job training (in the community or institutions), education with day care for teenage mothers, or parenting programs. In addition, there are no provisions for pregnant teens within the institutions. Lack of medical staff also places limitations on the movement of pregnant youth to camps or open custody facilities.

The over-representation of young women in custody for administrative breaches (such as the non-payment of fines) and child-welfare type concerns (such as child neglect) are further indicators of systemic bias. Canadian, American, British, and Australian studies of youth court charges and sentencing reveal that young women are disproportionately and overwhelmingly charged and imprisoned for administrative breaches, non-criminal behaviour, and non-status offences (such as traffic violations) (Howard League; Standing Committee on Justice and Legal Affairs; Chesney-Lind 1986).

Of the very few who are arrested for crimes of violence, most involve young women reacting to violence perpetrated against them, or offences previously labelled as status offences that have been reclassified as serious offences as a result of "zero tolerance" (CAEFS; Chesney-Lind 1986). Obviously, we all wish to see a decrease in the use of violence in our communities. However, criminalizing youth does not diminish violence, it merely legitimizes it in the hands of the state.

Young women appearing before the courts tend to have fewer charges against them than males. Systemic bias and discriminatory practices undergo a multiplier effect where gender, race, class, ethnicity, and/or sexual orientation converge. The stereotype of girls becoming gun-toting gang-robbers is simply not supported by statistics. That does not mean that there are not specific and egregious examples of young women committing violent offences. It does mean, however, that every time one such incident occurs, journalists and talk show hosts beat the bushes for other examples to support extreme interpretations of the event. Police officers, teachers, social workers, criminologists, and others asked to supply "expert" opinions have a responsibility to present an accurate picture when they choose to comment in such circumstances.

In a discussion of the current focus on girls as gang members and gang leaders, Meda Chesney-Lind succinctly frames the issues and our challenges:

> As young women are demonized by the media, their genuine problems can be marginalized and ignored. Indeed, the girls have become the problem. The challenge to those concerned about girls is, then, twofold. First, responsible work on girls in gangs must make the dynamics of this victim blaming clear.

> Second, it must continue to develop an understanding of girls' gangs that is sensitive to the context in which they arise. In an era that is increasingly concerned about the intersections of class, race, and gender, such work seems long overdue. (1998: 57)

Much is already known about effective and empowering ways to meet the needs of young women. This information, combined with adequate funding for existing and innovative support services and networks, will result in more effective interventions, increased prevention, and decreased recidivism.

## Lisa Neve and Lessons Learned

In Canada and the United States, we are also facing another backlash. Every time women take one step forward, efforts to shove us backwards abound. With respect to women's involvement in the youth justice and adult corrections system, an excellent, albeit odious, example of this trend is the treatment received by a young First Nations woman, diagnosed as suffering from fetal alcohol syndrome. In November 1994, Lisa Neve became the second woman in Canada to be labelled a dangerous offender and sentenced to an indeterminate sentence.

Although the designation was ultimately overturned on appeal, as a result of that designation, Lisa Neve was classified as a maximum security prisoner and spent six years in prison, most of it in segregated, maximum security units in two different men's prisons.

I first met Lisa when she was twelve years old. She had been dragged into secure "treatment," followed fairly quickly by secure custody. The system was not impressed by her assertive and confident manner. Unlike so many other young women her age, she was clearly a respected and undisputed leader. These qualities are not ones that are generally accepted, much less encouraged or nurtured, in our social control systems—be they child welfare or criminal justice in orientation. They are seen as particularly unacceptable when embodied by a young woman. Sexism, racism, heterosexism, and class biases intersect to provide an incredibly discriminatory lens through which women like Lisa are viewed and judged.

As a result, it did not take long for the adults in authority to label Lisa as a "problem" in need of "correction." Once the labels were applied, they not only stuck, but they also attracted other labels that built upon and expanded those prior. Consequently, although Lisa had started out as "mischievous," or "a brat," she was later labelled an instigator, negative, and eventually, aggressive, sociopathic and finally, a dangerous offender. Largely based upon accounts of her institutional behaviour in young offender centres, as well as her "unfeminine" renegade behaviour while working the street, Lisa was characterized as the most dangerous woman in Canada by Justice Murray in 1994 and then as a maximum security prisoner by the Correctional Service of Canada for more than four years.

Including her pre-trial detention, Lisa spent approximately six years in jail for an offence which the Court of Appeal eventually determined warranted a three-year sentence, as opposed to the indeterminate one that had been imposed. To make matters worse, she spent most of her time living in some of the most severe and limiting prison conditions in Canada. Nobody should ever have to face the tortuous ordeal that Lisa was forced to endure.

Our hope was that the Court of Appeal's decision would result in broader systemic changes to the administration of justice for women across Canada. Unfortunately, although the court challenged such sexist interpretations of the law as acceptance in the lower courts of a psychological assessment of Lisa that "effectively implies ... that a woman's thoughts about murder can somehow be equated with a man's commission of a murder," it stopped short of calling for the much needed broader systemic reforms that Lisa's case exemplified.

The court did note, however, the typical nature of this young woman's "violent" offences, in that "every offence which Neve committed was entangled in some way with her life as a prostitute." They also pointed out that while it was not to be condoned, Lisa's violent offences were generally characterized as attempts to avenge wrongs done to others. Furthermore, they characterized Lisa as "a young woman with a relatively short criminal record for violence, [who was] disposed to telling shocking stories of violence."

Finally, in determining if and when the dangerous offender provisions should apply, the Court of Appeal determined that,

> the question is whether, relatively speaking compared to *all* other offenders in Canada—male and female, young and old, advantaged and disadvantaged—Neve falls into that small group of offenders clustered at or near the extreme end of offenders in this country.

They also found that Lisa Neve did not fit into that group at all.

Within two days, Lisa went from facing the rest of her life in prison to being released from prison. Uncharacteristic of most young Aboriginal people adopted out to white families at birth, Lisa's adoptive family remains extremely supportive. Despite such support, Lisa still has to work extremely hard to overcome the impact of her imprisonment as she plans for the future. Her mental-health challenges since exiting prison are legion and have been life-threatening, as she struggles to combat the feelings of despair and thoughts of self-destruction and suicide that at times still envelope her. The biggest danger for Lisa remains, however, the reaction of others to her infamous dangerous offender label.

## Concluding Comments and Observations

There is sufficient evidence that a preventative approach to addressing crime within the context of socio-economic, gender, racial, and ethno-cultural realities is far more cost-effective than current criminal justice approaches. Rather than placing young people in either the adult or the juvenile justice system, most people would prefer to see better services for youth in community settings. While popular in the short term, "quick fix" criminal justice responses cannot address what are fundamentally social justice and equality issues. It is far too simplistic and short-sighted to presume that the off-loading of scapegoated youth onto the criminal justice system will solve youth crime. Nor will youthful offending be eliminated by the mere enactment of the *Youth Criminal Justice Act* in isolation. Broader-based social reform is fundamental.

As was discussed earlier, the Minister of Justice recently re-introduced, as Bill C-7, the replacement for the *Young Offenders Act*. The proposed *Youth Criminal Justice Act* aims to divert more youth from the youth justice system via extra-judicial means. It also proposes more stringent measures for youth convicted of serious and/or multiple offences. Unfortunately, so far there do not appear to be sufficient resources allocated, or national standards developed, to ensure that life will be breathed into the more progressive amendments. Yet again we are left to rely on the provinces and territories to implement progressive elements of the Bill. Without new resources there is faint hope that some of the provinces will do much to change the administration of juvenile justice in their respective jurisdictions. Hence, unless the government links its cost-sharing agreements with the provinces to the implementation of the progressive portions of the proposed new Act, the *Youth Criminal Justice Act* could end up being a mere rhetorical reframing of vitally important and unresolved issues pertaining to criminalized youth in Canada.

The legal system reinforces sexist, racist, and classist stereotypes of women while simultaneously legitimizing patriarchal notions of the need to socially control women. We must commit to transforming the social and economic position of girls and women and adamantly challenge attempts to further subjugate women if we are truly interested in addressing violence in our communities. We must also refuse to fuel panic with exaggerated and inaccurate claims about increased violent offending by women and girls. Refusing to address the issues raised by the involvement of women and girls in our criminal justice system will continue to cost us much more than money.

## References

Adler, F. *Sisters in Crime: The Rise of the New Female Criminal.* New York: McGraw-Hill, 1975.

Alvi, Shahid. *Youth and the Canadian Criminal Justice System.* Cincinnati, Ohio: Anderson Publishing Co., 2000.

American Correctional Association. "Female Offenders." *Corrections Today Magazine* 63 (1) (February 2001).

Arbour, The Honourable Louise. *Commission of Inquiry into Certain Events at the Prison for Women in Kingston.* Ottawa: Public Works and Government Services, 1996.

Artz, Sybille. *Sex, Power, and the Violent School Girl.* Toronto: Trifolium Books,

1998.

Barron, Christie L. *Giving Youth a Voice: A Basis for Rethinking Adolescent Violence*. Halifax: Fernwood Publishing, 2000.

Batacharya, Sheila. Racism, "Girl Violence and the Murder of Reena Virk." Unpublished M.A. Thesis. Department of Sociology and Equity Studies in Education, Ontario Institute for Studies in Education of the University of Toronto, 2000.

Borum, R. "Assessing Violence Risk Among Youth." *Journal of Clinical Psychology* 56 (10) (2000): 263-268.

Brennan, Tim and James Austin. *Women in Jail: Classification Issues*. Washington, DC: U.S. Department of Justice, National Institute of Corrections, 1997.

Brooks, Kim, Vincent Schiraldi, and Jason Ziedenberg. *Schoolhouse Hype: Two Years Later*. Washington DC: Justice Policy Institute, April 2000.

Butts, Jeffrey A. *Update on Statistics: Offenders in Juvenile Court, 1992*. Washington, DC: Office of Juvenile Justice and Delinquency Prevention, October 1994.

Campbell, A. *Girl Delinquents*. Oxford: Basil Blackwell Publishers Ltd., 1981.

Campbell, A. "Girls' Talk: The Social Representation of Aggression by Female Gang Members." *Criminal Justice and Behavior* 11 (2) (1984): 139-156.

Campbell, A. *Men, Women and Aggression*. London: Pandora, 1993.

Canadian Association of Elizabeth Fry Societies (CAEFS). "Submission of the Canadian Association of Elizabeth Fry Societies to the Standing Committee on Justice and Legal Affairs Regarding the Comprehensive Review of the Young Offenders Act–Phase II." Ottawa: April 1996.

Canadian Centre for Justice Statistics. *Juristat Service Bulletin* 14 (8) (1994): 10.

Canadian Centre for Justice Statistics. *Youth Court Statistics: 1991-92*. Ottawa: Statistics Canada, 1992.

Carrington, Peter and Sharon Moyer. *The Statistical Profile of Female Young Offenders*. Ottawa: Department of Justice Canada, 1997.

Chesney-Lind, Meda. *What to Do About Girls? Promising Perspectives and Effective Stategies*. Arlington, Virginia: ICCA Conference, 1998.

Chesney-Lind, Meda. "Women and Crime: The Female Offender." *Signs: Journal of Women in Culture and Society* 12 (1) (1986): 78-96.

Chesney-Lind, Meda and Barbara Bloom. "Feminist Criminology: Thinking About Women and Crime." *Thinking Critically About Crime*. Vancouver: Collective Press, 1997.

Chesney-Lind, Meda and John M. MacDonald. "Gender Bias and Juvenile Justice Revisited: A Multiyear Analysis." *Crime and Delinquency* 47 (2) (April 2001): 173-195.

Comack, Elizabeth, Vanessa Chopyk, and Linda Wood. *Mean Streets? The Social Locations, Gender Dynamics and Patterns of Violent Crime in Winnipeg*. Ottawa: Centre for Policy Alternatives, December 2000.

Commission on Systemic Racism in the Ontario Criminal Justice System. *Racism Behind Bars: The Treatment of Black and Other Racial Minority Prisoners in*

*Ontario Prisons (Interim Report)*. Toronto: Queen's Printer, 1994.

Commission on Systemic Racism in the Ontario Criminal Justice System. *Report of the Commission on Systemic Racism in the Ontario Criminal Justice System*. Toronto: Queen's Printer, 1995.

Corrado, Raymond R., Candice Odgers, and Irwin M. Cohen. "The Incarceration of Female Young Offenders: Protection for Whom?" *Canadian Journal of Criminology* 42 (2) (April 2000):189-207.

Dell, Colleen and Roger Boe. "Female Young Offenders in Canada: Recent Trends." Research Brief No. 1997 B-18. Ottawa: Correctional Service of Canada, 1997.

Dell, Colleen Anne and Roger Boe. "Female Young Offenders in Canada: Revised Edition." *Research Report No. R-80*. Ottawa: Research Branch, Correctional Service of Canada, 1998.

Department of Justice Canada. *Fact Sheets: Youth Criminal Justice Act*. Ottawa: Department of Justice Canada, 1999.

Doob, Anthony and Jane B. Sprott. "Is the 'Quality' of Youth Violence Becoming More Serious?" *Canadian Journal of Criminology* (April 1998): 185-194.

Dorfman, Lori, and Vincent Schiraldi. "Off Balance: Youth, Race and Crime in the News." *Building Blocks for Youth*. Washington, DC: Youth Law Center, 2001.

Economic and Social Research Council. "A View from the Girls: Exploring Violence and Violent Behaviour." *Girls and Violence*. Scotland: University of Glasgow, 2000.

Eron, Leonard, Jacquelyn Gentry and Peggy Schlegel. Eds. *Reason to Hope: A Psychosocial Perspective on Violence and Youth*. Washington, DC: American Psychological Association, 1996. Howard League. "Imprisoning Girls." *Criminal Justice: The Magazine of the Howard League* 15 (2) (1997).

Espelage, D.L., K. Bosworth, and T.R. Simon. "Examining the Social Context of Bullying Behaviors in Early Adolescence." *Journal of Counseling and Development* 78 (3) (2000): 326-333.

Faith, Karlene. *Unruly Women: The Politics of Confinement and Resistance*. Vancouver: Press Gang, 1993.

Frank, J. "Violent Youth Crime." *Canadian Social Trends*. Ottawa: Statistics Canada, 1992. 2-9.

Hannah-Moffat, Kelly. "Creating Choices or Repeating History: Canadian Female Offenders and Correctional Reform." *Social Justice* 18 (3) (1991): 184-203.

Hannah-Moffat, Kelly. "Feminine Fortresses: Women-Centred Prisons." *The Prison Journal* 75 (2) (1995): 135-164.

Hannah-Moffat, Kelly. "From Christian Maternalism to Risk Technologies: Penal Powers and Knowledges in the Governance of Female Prisons." Unpublished Ph.D. Thesis, University of Toronto, Centre of Criminology, 1997.

Howard League for Penal Reform. "Imprisoning Girls." *Criminal Justice: The Magazine of the Howard League* 15 (2) (1997).

Gilligan, Carol. *In a Different Voice.* Cambridge, Massachusetts: Harvard University Press, 1982.

Heidensohn, Frances M. *Women and Crime: The Life of the Female Offender.* New York: New York University Press, 1985.

Jiwani, Yasmin. *Violence Prevention and the Girl Child: Final Report.* Vancouver: The Alliance of Five Research Centres. 1999.

Kershaw, Anne, and Mary Lasovich. *Rock-A-Bye Baby: A Death Behind Bars.* Toronto: Oxford University Press, 1991.

Leschied, Alan W. "Informing Young Offender Policy in Current Research: What the Future Holds." *Forum on Corrections Research* 12 (2) (May 2000): 36-39.

MacDonald, John M. and Meda Chesney-Lind. "Gender Bias and Juvenile Justice Revisited: A Multiyear Analysis." *Crime and Delinquency* 47 (2) (April 2001): 173-195.

Matthews, Fred. "Violent and Aggressive Girls." *Journal of Child and Youth Care* 11 (4) (1998): 1-23.

McDowell, J. "From Barbie Dolls to Buck Knives: Youth Violence is Rising and Girls Getting More Involved." *B.C. Report.* September 19, 1994: 36.

McGovern, C. "You've Come a Long Way, Baby. Prodded by Feminism, Today's Teenaged Girls Embrace Antisocial Male Behaviour." *Alberta Report.* July 31, 1995: 24-27.

McMahon, Maeve. "Net-Widening: Vagaries in the Use of a Concept." *British Journal of Criminology* 30 (1990): 121-149.

Pearson, Patricia. When She Was Bad: Violent Women and the Myth of Innocence. Toronto: Random House of Canada Ltd., 1997.

*R.* v. *Neve,* Court of Appeal of Alberta, June 29, 1999.

Reitsma-Street, Marge. "Canadian Youth Court Charges and Dispositions for Females Before and After the Implementation of the Young Offenders Act." *Canadian Journal of Criminology* 35 (1993): 437-458.

Reitsma-Street, Marge. "Justice for Canadian Girls: A 1990's Update." *Canadian Journal of Criminology* 41 (1999): 335-364.

Sangster, Joan. "Girls in Conflict with the Law: Exploring the Construction of Female 'Delinquency' in Ontario, 1940-60."*Canadian Journal of Women and the Law* 12 (1) (2000): 1-29.

Schramm, Heather. *Young Women Who Use Violence: Myths and Facts.* Calgary, Alberta: Elizabeth Fry Society of Calgary,1998.

Shaw, Margaret. *Survey of Federally Sentenced Women.* Ottawa: Solicitor General of Canada, Ministry Secretariat (User Report Number 1991-4), 1991.

Sprott, Jane and Anthony Doob. "Bad, Sad and Rejected: The Lives of Aggressive Children." *Canadian Journal of Criminology* 42 (2) (April 2000): 123-133.

Standing Committee on Justice and Legal Affairs. "Renewing Youth Justice: Thirteenth Report of the Standing Committee on Justice and Legal Affairs." Ottawa: House of Commons, April 1997.

Statistics Canada. *The Daily.* Ottawa: Statistics Canada, August 2000.

Statistics Canada. *The Daily.* Ottawa: Statistics Canada, August 2000.

Stephens, Megan A. "Violent Young Women: The Importance of Social Context in Making Sense of Young Women's Use of Violence." Unpublished disseration, Carleton University, Ottawa, 1997.

Suleman, Zara and Holly McLarty. *Falling Through the Gaps: Gaps in Services for Young Women Survivors of Sexual Assault.* Vancouver: Feminist Research, Education, Development and Action (FREDA) Centre, 1997.

Swern, Elisa. "Young Women as Perpetrators of Violence." Unpublished Master's Thesis, Ottawa: Carleton University, Department of Sociology and Anthropology, 1995.

Task Force on Federally Sentenced Women. *Creating Choices: The Report of the Task Force on Federally Sentenced Women.* Ottawa: Correctional Service of Canada, 1990.

Totten, Mark. *The Special Needs of Females in Canada's Youth Justice System: An Account of Some Young Women's Experiences and Views.* Ottawa: Department of Justice, 2000.

"Violent Crime by Females on the Increase." *Vancouver Sun* July 23, 1998: A1-A2.

Women and Imprisonment Group. *Women and Imprisonment.* Melbourne, Australia: Fitzroy Legal Service, 1995.

# Legal Responses to Violence Against Women in Canada

Elizabeth A. Sheehy

Any history of the development and changes in the law as it relates to women and male violence is also a chronicle of the history of the women's movement and its relationship to law.[1] All of the legislation and policy that recognizes women's rights to be free of male violence has been put in place because of the political strength and persistence of the women's movement in our country. While this movement has always articulated women's issues and rights in the context of equality, the repatriation of Canada's constitution in 1982 from Great Britain (*Constitution Act*) and, specifically, the enshrinement of women's equality rights in ss.15 and 28 of the *Canadian Charter of Rights and Freedoms*, for the first time created a specific legal tool by which to advance these claims.

In spite of our many legal advances, violence against women has not subsided in Canada because women's vulnerability to male violence and our ability to harness law are inextricably linked to women's social, economic, and political position in Canada, in relation to those who hold power. Thus, while law is an important tool in advancing women's equality rights, law alone cannot end this violence until all women's equality is fully realized.

Before I commence, I would like to define my terms. First, when I speak of feminists or the women's movement in Canada, I am speaking of women who accept and recognize the existence of women's subordination economically, socially, and politically, and who have a commitment to engage in struggle, of one sort or another, to change women's inequality. This movement is aimed at achieving equality for all women and recognizes that women do not experience uniformly the benefits or disadvantages of sex but, rather, are differentially affected by white supremacy, class privilege, the heterosexual presumption, and the "norms" of ability.

Second, when I speak of women's equality, I am referring to the idea of substantive equality. The difference between formal and substantive equality is that while formal equality merely insists on equality of treatment (and only to the extent that the decision-maker agrees that the two groups are similarly situated), substantive equality looks to the end result.[2] Are women and men in a given society equal recipients of the benefits and burdens of that society? Among women, are we equally credible when we speak in the justice system? Are we equally free of violent assault? Sometimes, the most productive route to substantive equality will be to use formal equality or equal treatment as a tool; at other times, the specific conditions of women's lives, including, for example, the threat and impact of male violence or racialized abuse experienced by African-Canadian women, will require very particular rules or practices to move us toward equality.

Third, when I speak of law, I am using the term broadly, to refer to the law as drafted by legislators, as interpreted by judges in the common law or by jurors as finders of fact in trials, and as implemented by those who enforce the law and wield a great deal of discretion, such as police and prosecutors. Thus the women's movement has recognized that the achievement of reforms in statutes or even in constitutions does not guarantee that those laws will become a lived reality, for police can refuse to take reports or can discredit women's accounts of violence; prosecutors can decide which cases to pursue, based on their perhaps discriminatory beliefs or on their prediction that the case will fail in court due to the discriminatory beliefs of others; judges can effectively nullify a law through narrow interpretations, through the creation of common law defences that uphold male supremacy,[3] through the use of constitutional doctrines, through rulings on the evidence, and through instructions to the jury; and, even if a conviction is imposed, a judge can undermine its symbolism by imposing a sentence that makes a mockery of the conviction.[4] Because of all of these ways that law works, women's advocates must be prepared for a longterm process of both political struggle and legal engagement.

## Women's Legal History

In the nineteenth century, as part of the ongoing process of colonization, England imposed British common law, including criminal law, on the inhabitants of what is now called Canada. Criminal law, in this context, must be linked to other forms of law that confer legal status, rights, and obligations, given that criminal law acts as an enforcement mechanism for many legal relations and values.

From the Middle Ages through to the mid-nineteenth century, women in England experienced a massive curtailment of their role in public life, through the exclusion of women from the church, the destruction of hereditary offices of government and their replacement by appointed office, and the growth of the universities and professions, through which women's occupations in the public sphere were superseded by male control (Atkins and Hoggett; Sachs and Wilson). Judges played a major part in this process, by creating the common law doctrine of women's "legal disabilities": women and children were declared to be the legal property of their fathers and girls, once married, became the legal property of their husbands. Women did not have separate legal identity from their fathers or husbands, such that they were severely restricted in their ability to accumulate property and wealth, to assert control over their children and their own destiny, and to protect or claim their own physical integrity. Women's lack of legal status had public law implications as well: women could not vote in elections, participate in government or make policy, enter the professions, including law, or generally participate in public life (Sachs and Wilson).

These limits on women's legal status were reflected in the criminal law's stance on violence against women such that British law did not prohibit violence against women but rather, at best, regulated its "excesses." Thus, the British law as stated by Bacon in the mid-eighteenth century was that "The husband hath, by law, power and dominion over his wife, and may keep her by force within the bounds of duty, and may beat her, but not in a violent manner" (cited in Strange 295). As a member of our Supreme Court, Justice Wilson, stated:

> [T]he law historically sanctioned the abuse of women within marriage as an aspect of the husband's ownership of his wife and his "right" to chastise her. One need only recall the centuries-old law that a man is entitled to beat his wife with a stick "no thicker than his thumb." (*R.* v. *Lavallee* 872)

Similarly, rape was criminal only to the extent that either a father or a husband held a proprietary interest in the woman's sexuality: it was a crime against the father if the girl was chaste and unmarried; it was a crime against the husband if she was monogamous and married (Clark and Lewis).

Thus, in 1892 Canada's first *Criminal Code* only punished rape if it was committed by a man other than the woman's husband; penetration was required; and the prosecutor had to prove non-consent, usually by proving violent resistance by the girl or woman. Rape was also adjudicated according to three common law rules that were unique to this offence: a rule permitting the evidence that a woman had reported the offence "at the earliest reasonable opportunity" to rebut a presumption that the complaint was false; the use of women's past sexual history evidence to demonstrate their lack of credibility; and the requirement that the jury be warned that it is dangerous to convict based solely upon the uncorroborated testimony of a woman or child.[5]

Assault upon a woman could be prosecuted in the 1892 *Code* as any other assault. An offence of indecent assault against a wife occasioning actual bodily harm was enacted in 1909 (Boyle) and remained in the *Criminal Code* until 1960 (McLeod 1989). It was punishable by two years imprisonment, which was then extremely low in comparison to punishments of execution and life imprisonment for many other offences.

Wife murder could be punished by the law prohibiting murder, but it was in no way parallel to husband murder, which was in law a form of "petit treason" (Gavigan). Additionally, numerous practices and doctrines made it difficult to say that wife murder was outright prohibited. The defence of provocation, for example, reduced murder to manslaughter on the basis that someone engorged by "passion" has lost self-control and should thereby be treated more leniently by the criminal law. Of course women's behaviour, whether it be by infidelity, insubordination, or by desertion, was (and arguably still is) more easily characterized as provocative from the standpoint of the male legislators who enacted, the male police who enforced, and the male judges and jurors who interpreted the law.[6]

Some women would have had access to remedies in civil law for rape, seduction, or breach of promise to marry, although these remedies depended on access to money to pursue them, were interpreted as essentially aimed at compensating fathers and husbands for lost value in the sexual property of women and were given generous interpretations for only chaste and "deserving" women (Backhouse 1986).

## First-Wave Feminism

At the same time that this *Criminal Code* was adopted in Canada marking women's social subordination by its narrow prohibitions, the first wave of the feminist movement was already well underway, as women in the United Kingdom, Europe, the United States, and Canada fought for the extension of the promise of liberal democratic rights to them (Mossman). Women variously made important gains in the political and legislative arenas, after long and arduous campaigns, for example, reversing women's common law disabilities with respect to holding and dispensing of property, concluding valid contracts by legislation as early as 1872 in Ontario, and achieving the right to vote in federal elections, for non-Aboriginal women, in 1918 (see, Altschul and Carron; Abell).

In spite of these and many other gains, including the admission, by special legislation in 1892, to the bar of Canada's first woman lawyer in 1897 (Backhouse 1985), the judges of the common law countries for 60 years resisted and denied women's claims to be recognized as "persons" entitled to participate fully in public life, including the practice of law. So it was that rather than lead the way in advancing women's equality, and rather than even reflecting women's changing social position, the judges, almost to a man, in countless cases, acted as "dogged defenders of male supremacy" (Sachs and Wilson 48).

At long last, in 1929, the Privy Council decided the famous "Persons" (*Edwards v. A.G. Canada*) case in women's favour, ruling that in the absence of evidence of parliamentary intent to the contrary, women should be presumed included within the legal understanding of "persons." This case constituted a sudden and dramatic reversal of six decades of legal precedent. It cannot be explained internally but only by reference to the context of the changes that had already been wrought in the legal landscape, by legislation, through the women's movement (see Mossman; Sachs and Wilson).

## Second-Wave Feminism

Although once the public sphere was opened to women and the theoretical possibility was created of women as lawyers, legislators, and judges exerting a more direct influence on the law regulating male violence against women, the formal equality of opportunity models did not yield immediate results in terms of women's access to law. While our first woman magistrate was appointed as early as 1916 (Harvey), it was not until 1926 that most provinces admitted women to the practice of law, and Québec did not do so until 1941. Women were not permitted to sit as jurors in Manitoba until 1952 and until 1971 in Québec (Harvey). By the 1950s, only four per cent of Ontario law students were women (Hagan and Kay) and by 1971, women were still greatly underrepresented in the profession at a rate of 38:1 (Hagan and Kay).

In 1970, when the Royal Commission on the Status of Women was appointed to inquire into the steps that should be taken by the federal government to ensure equal opportunities for women, violence against women was conceptualized as a formal equality issue. The Commission focused on the unfairness in the *Criminal Code* of limiting criminal responsibility for sexual offences to men as perpetrators, of not protecting boys and men from sexual offences, and of the different rules for rape depending on the female's age, marital status, and moral character.

Although these criticisms were rendered deeper and more complicated by the work of the women's movement in providing services for women who had been raped (crisis centres) and for women who were fleeing violent men (women's shelters), the law reforms subsequently passed in 1982[7] essentially used the model of formal equality employed by the Royal Commission. The new offences were gender neutral such that assaults on boys and men are punishable, as are assaults committed by women upon males. Sexual assault became a three- tiered offence, with higher sentence ceilings as the offence involves more violence and/or injury. The structure parallels that used for non-sexual assault, implying the only difference is the sexual nature of the attack. The offence can be committed by a husband against a wife; it need not include penetration; and many of the evidentiary rules unique to rape were abolished in the *Criminal Code*. Finally, a number of specific reforms have also been legislated that create new evidentiary rules for the testimony of children and abolish some of the common law rules for dealing with their evidence (Boyle).

In the area of wife assault, while one of its earliest forms had been sex-specific, a similar pattern of second-wave feminism to law reform can be discerned. An undifferentiated offence of a common assault was in the *Code* from 1960 on, but it was usually dealt with in the family rather than criminal law courts (Bonnycastle and Rigakos) and was often treated as a private matter, requiring the woman to initiate and carry the prosecution, rather than the public prosecutor. The women's movement attempted to introduce formal equality by forcing police, prosecutors, and judges to deal with wife assault as they would any other life-threatening harm. However, the demands made by the women's movement have tended to be translated by the state in punitive terms rather than as a way to protect women's lives and safety (Currie).

For example, in 1982, the Attorney General for Ontario wrote to prosecutors urging them to encourage police to lay charges of assault rather than leaving the burden of prosecution to individual women. He also suggested that such assaults be considered more serious than stranger assaults because "the victims are in a captive position socially or economically and accordingly the likelihood of a recurrence is far more substantial." In 1984 the same office designated resources to appoint 50 Crowns to deal with domestic assault matters. In 1982, the federal Solicitor General wrote to police chiefs across the country, urging them to aggressively charge in cases of spouse assault, and in 1983 guidelines were created for the RCMP and police and prosecutors in the Yukon and the North West Territories (McLeod 1989).

Some jurisdictions drafted guidelines requiring that charges be laid by police as a matter of course, to avoid discriminatory exercise of discretion (Ontario Provincial Police). Other jurisdictions adopted "no drop" guidelines for prosecutors, to curb their discretion such that they must continue with a prosecution and do not have the discretion to desist, even when the woman expresses a desire to withdraw the charges (Manitoba Department of Justice).[8]

At the same time, women in Canada became engaged in another political and legal struggle with respect to women's equality. When the government proposed to repatriate (or bring home) Canada's constitution and to attach a new bill of rights that would constitute the supreme law of the country permitting the courts to declare contrary legislation inoperative, women were not included in the negotiations over the terms of the new constitution, nor were their interests or analyses represented in the specific proposals. Women's groups across the country fought successfully for a voice in the drafting process (Hosek) and worked hard to give as full a scope as was possible to a concept of substantive, not mere formal, equality in the language of the new *Charter*, now s. 5 and 28.

With the passage of the equality guarantees in the *Charter*, feminists inside and outside of law began to reconfigure their ideas about equality and to conceptualize violence as both an expression of women's inequality and a barrier to substantive equality. That women's struggle for equality and freedom from violence was a longterm one was painfully illustrated by a notorious exchange in the House of Commons in 1982 when women Parliamentarians attempted to put the issue and statistics of wife battering on the legislative agenda and the House erupted in prolonged laughter and general derision (Bonnycastle and Rigakos). Although the next two days in the House saw resolutions and apologies by the male members, the obstacles to simple law reform as a strategy to end violence against women were illuminated all too clearly.

## Third-Wave Feminism

The achievements of the second wave of feminists and the guarantee of at least formal equality under the *Charter* have permitted the third wave of feminists to bring critical analysis and new understandings of equality to the issue of the legal treatment of violence against women.

As of the 1980s, women constituted 50 per cent of students in Ontario law schools; as of 1991, the ratio of men to women in the profession in Ontario was 2.63:1 (Hagan and Kay). Women have marked achievements in law, including three women jurists who have sat or sit at the highest level of court in Canada,[9] two of whom have explicitly articulated feminist visions of law. At the level of government, in 1992 the Federal/Provincial/Territorial Attorney Generals made a public commitment to promoting gender equality within the criminal law and stated that "legal theory, common law, and statute law must be developed equally from both male and female perspectives." Three prominent women judges have been appointed to head very important public inquiries into the treatment of women in the legal profession, federally sentenced women offenders, and women convicted of killing allegedly violent mates (see Wilson; Arbour; Ratushny). In 1995, Status of Women Canada released its "Gender Plan" outlining the commitment of the federal government to adopting policy that advances women's equality (Status of Women Canada); in 1996, the Department of Justice appointed a Senior Advisor on Gender Equality who is to ensure that women's equality issues are integrated into all of the work, policy, litigation, and legislation of the department (Bernier). As well, between 1993 and 1997, the Department of Justice invested in ongoing consultations with the women's movement on violence against women.

What kinds of new insights and legal strategies around violence against women has the third wave brought us in Canada? Again I will deal with sexual assault and wife assault in turn. Both areas of law reform have revealed to us the serious limitations of a formal equality model.

First, our experience with sexual assault indicates that the mere change in language has not shifted the underlying operative understandings of "rape." For example, although the new laws are broader in terms of definitions of prohibited conduct and protected groups of women, those who enforce and interpret these laws may still hold and wield the same beliefs and values that more explicitly underpinned the old laws. Feminist researchers such as Lorenne Clark and Debra Lewis had previously demonstrated that although the former legislation did not explicitly endorse the notion that women should be protected under the law against rape only to the extent that they constituted the sexual property of individual fathers or husbands, this was in fact the way that the law was interpreted by police, by Crown attorneys, and by judges. Many feminists assert that the new reforms have not disrupted these beliefs or the practices in which they manifested. For example, even ten years after the reforms, crisis centre workers reported that the legislative restrictions on women's sexual history were simply ignored by defence, Crown attorneys, and judges in sexual assault trials (Sheehy 1991). Feminist researchers found that the former understandings of "real rape" still underlay investigative and prosecutorial decisions, such that stereotypes continued to play a significant role (Muzychka) and the "unfounding" rate for sexual assault remains incongruously high (Roberts).

Second, the neutrality in the language describing the offence has been criticized, as it tends to hide the gendered nature of sexual assault, erroneously conveying the notion that "equality" has been achieved by suggesting that the law now recognizes that men can be raped too, and women can be sexually violent. Of course the gendered statistics have not changed in this regard,[10] but we may have lost a critical and shared social understanding of the meaning of rape for women (Cohen and Backhouse). For example, in one case, the issue of whether touching a woman's breast amounted to a sexual assault had to be litigated all the way to the highest court in the country, because lower court judges took the gender neutral approach literally, reasoning that breasts were secondary sex characteristics, like men's beards, and that since touching a man's beard was not a sexual assault, touching a woman's breast was likewise not a sexual assault.[11]

Finally, women have discovered that the *Charter*, in the hands of the same judiciary, can be used once again to doggedly defend men's rights at the expense of women's security. Thus, using the *Charter* as a weapon, a significant feature of the law, a non-discretionary ban on women's sexual history evidence in all but four fairly narrow situations, was declared unconstitutional by the Supreme Court because it allegedly violated men's rights to fair trials (*R.* v. *Seaboyer; R.* v. *Gayme*). Women's equality rights were barely mentioned by the judges, so irrelevant were they seen to be by the Supreme Court of Canada. This put women in Canada back by almost two decades and raised serious questions about whether the *Charter* would be used to roll back women's democratic gains (see Sheehy 1991).

The response of the Canadian public, and of course the women's movement, was one of disbelief and outrage with the decision of the Supreme Court. Such an outcry was raised that the Minister of Justice initiated a law reform process that ultimately was led by the women's movement and its lawyers. Feminists determined that any new law needed to name women's equality and women's rights as the legal and constitutional basis for the reform; that women's interests and perspectives needed to be incorporated into the law; that women's experiences of racism, ableism, and lesbophobia needed to be recognized in crafting the law; that the law had to be drafted so to specifically challenge the underlying beliefs about women and rape; and that mechanisms to check discretion had to be built into the law.[12]

The newest sexual assault law was passed in 1992 (*An Act to Amend the Criminal Code* 1992). The preamble to the law sets out women's *Charter* rights as the impetus for the law and specifies the particular problems that it is meant to solve as an interpretive aid for the judiciary. The law now defines consent as "voluntary agreement to engage in the activity," rather than leaving it to the judges, and specifies situations in which there can be no consent in law, such as where consent is expressed by a third party, where the woman was incapable of consenting, and where her agreement was achieved through reliance upon a position of trust or authority over the woman. It creates a new process and set of criteria by which to limit when sexual history evidence is admissible and sets out certain prohibited uses of this evidence. Finally, it imposes a new and significant limit on men's defence of "mistaken belief" regarding consent, by requiring that men take "reasonable steps" to ascertain consent.

This law is only just beginning to receive judicial interpretations at the higher levels of court, so it is difficult to assess at this early point its impact (see Sheehy 1996). It is also being challenged again under the *Charter* by men (*R.* v. *Darrach*); it remains to be seen whether the statements of legislative purpose will inspire the judges to pay deference to the democratic process and uphold the law.

In 1994, the justices of the Supreme Court again used the *Charter* to widen men's immunity from criminal liability for sexual and other violence against women by recognizing a new defence of "extreme intoxication" (*R.* v. *Daviault*). Again, feminist criticism and the women's movement's outrage reached the public domain (Sheehy 1995a), and the Department of Justice, in consultation with women's groups, amended the *Criminal Code* in response (*An Act to amend the Criminal Code* 1995; Sheehy 1995b).

In the meantime, another defence strategy has flourished, that of demanding access to women's personal records so as to dig for information that can be used to contradict her statements or to undermine her credibility (see MacCrimmon). Unfortunately, our Supreme Court has once more upheld men's rights at the expense of women's, based on the *Charter* (*R.* v. *O'Conner; R.* v. *Carosella)*. Once more, a hue and cry has been raised and broadly based consultation within the women's movement and with the Department of Justice ensued. The result is another new law, Bill C-46 (*An Act to amend the Criminal Code* 1997), which puts limits on disclosure of women's records, creates the legal possibility of women having standing in court to defend their interests in the criminal process, and again frames the law in legal and constitutional terms pursuant to women's equality rights. This law is also under attack using the *Charter*, and it remains to be seen whether this democratic gain by the women's movement will be obliterated by the Supreme Court (*R.* v. *Mills*).

The difficulties with the specific legal strategies around wife assault have been identified by both researchers and the women's movement. First, gender neutral offences and policies have furthered the criminalization of women. Thus we see new practices of counter-charging women such that women who resist the violence of their mates or who fight back can be charged as well.[13] By way of further example, our *Criminal Code* s.753 creates a process by which a prosecutor can apply to have an offender convicted of a "serious personal injury offence" declared a dangerous offender such that the sentence will be an indeterminate one. Although sex offenders have been incarcerated under this section, it had never, until 1996 (*R.* v. *Currie*), been used to deal with persistently violent men who threatened and terrorized their former mates. However, it had been used, on two notorious occasions, to declare young women who primarily posed a danger to themselves as "dangerous offenders."[14]

Second, the resistance of police, prosecutors, and judges continues to shape women's responses to criminal law (see Rigakos), and police failure to implement in any consistent fashion the various "zero tolerance" policies remains problematic. Third, mediation and diversion have been used to take these cases out of the criminal law system;[15] while the women's movement has not insisted on increased punitive sentencing in response to wife battering, it has viewed the adjudication of criminal responsibility to be critical. Finally, as long as women's external realities of poverty and male violence persist, criminal law intervention may carry more risk than benefit for women. Thus, numbers of women have refused criminal justice intervention because the costs to women, and sometimes to their mates and children, have been too high (Martin and Mosher). For example, some prosecutors and judges have proceeded with contempt charges against women who refuse to testify; some women have experienced retaliatory violence from their mates; and others have experienced abuse from the state (Snider). New sentencing laws such as Bill C-41[16] that require judges to consider specific aggravating factors such as abuse of a position of trust and responsibility and the fact that the offence was committed against the offender's spouse or child, may do little to address these structural issues because sentencing is inherently focused on the individual.

One of the more controversial responses to violence against women is a new substantive criminal offence called criminal harassment, "stalking." The impetus for this offence came not from the women's movement but from the federal government, following the lead of many states in the United States, and conceptualizing, drafting, and passing the new law in a record time of eight months (Cairns Way). Women's groups did not deny the significance and dangerousness of the behaviour of men, usually former partners, who terrorize women, but voiced many concerns: why create a new law when the old ones (assault, peace bonds) are not enforced? Women's groups participated reluctantly, tentatively, and ultimately unsuccessfully in the reform, attempting to shape a law that at least would not increase women's inequality. The problems with the law are many, including the imagery and examples that informed it, which were of the dangerous "stranger," not the angry ex-husband or former boyfriend; the use of gender neutrality in its drafting, such that women who are trying to collect child support from their mates have been charged with stalking; and the use of traditional understandings of legal culpability such that only a man who consciously intends to create fear in the mind of the woman can be found guilty (Cairns Way).

In contrast, a substantive equality model, which would take account of the inequalities in which women currently find themselves and would be directed at ending the violence rather than reinforcing it, excusing it, or further isolating the woman, has been sought by the women's movement. The subsequent interventions were more formal and directive. For example, some police departments created protocols for dealing with violence against women, to ensure professional, prompt, and safety-conscious responses by police to calls from women asking for emergency assistance (British Columbia Ministry of the Attorney General). In several provinces, new initiatives are underway that attempt to create altogether new ways of dealing with wife assault, de-emphasizing the criminal law approach and focusing on stopping male violence. In Manitoba a new family violence court has been created, which speeds the process of prosecuting these offences, but also has developed specialized sentencing practices that are arguably more attuned to ending violence (mandatory counselling for male batterers is a regular feature of over 50 per cent of the sentences) and to ensuring the safety of the woman (Ursel and Brickey). In Saskatchewan new legislation was proclaimed in 1995 that creates an interdisciplinary approach to wife assault (Turner): it provides for emergency intervention orders (EMOS), victim assistance orders (VAOS), and warrants of entry. EMOS can cover a range of actions including exclusive possession of the matrimonial home, removal of offender by police, and restraining orders. VAOS can provide monetary aid, temporary possession of property, restraining orders, and their breach can result in a criminal conviction.

The notion of substantive equality has also brought with it the idea that women need access to the resources of the state if they are to challenge violence perpetrated against them and to defend their equality rights. Thus, two Ontario legal clinics have created policies whereby they provide legal services to women only, in the context of cases involving wife assault, as a way of meeting women's greatly underserved legal needs and avoiding conflicts of interests (Carey). This practice has been challenged by defence lawyers but ultimately was upheld by the body governing the practice of law in Ontario. In the context of legal aid, women have sometimes succeeded in seeking funding to hire their own lawyers in the criminal process, given that Crown attorneys cannot and do not always act as their advocates.

Finally, legal responses to violence against women have been created outside of criminal law as well. The women's movement has created and sustained a support system of crisis centres and shelters, feminist models of counselling and support, and public education campaigns around the issues of male violence of women. Numerous initiatives have been put in place across the country. The federal government and provinces have enacted human rights codes and tribunals to adjudicate wrongs including sex discrimination, which has been held to include sexual harassment against women (*Brooks* v. *Canada Safeway Ltd.*). This behaviour may be verbal but some claims pursued are actually cases of sexual assault that have taken place in the workplace. The consequences of a human rights claim may be an order to apologize to and/or compensate a woman, or some other order aimed at rehabilitating the wrongdoer; if the claim is settled by the board without adjudication, however, any public educative value is lost as the terms are not disclosed publicly. The human rights models in place in Canada have proven to be profoundly inadequate (Faraday; Young); however, there is currently tremendous energy being invested in the re-visioning of these schemes so as to capitalize on and deal with issues of group rights and wrongs and their potential to provide justice to persons who cannot, for many reasons, pursue litigation in the criminal or civil courts.

The provinces have also created criminal injuries compensation legislation and boards, to provide some monetary compensation for those injured by the criminal acts of others. These schemes do not do much to address violence against women in a direct way, since the proceedings are not public, the decisions are not published, and the offender is not punished (the money comes out of an allocated fund) (see Sheehy 1994). However, since many women who do not pursue criminal prosecution may seek compensation, these claims can provide much more public information about the extent and consequences of male violence, for example, the sexual abuse of children. As many more women have sought compensation under these schemes, the response of the legal system has been to close this avenue down by: informing the alleged offender of his right to appear and contest the issue of whether a crime occurred; reducing compensation to the extent that the crime victim was at "fault" by invoking woman-blaming beliefs;[17] imposing stricter proof requirements upon the claimants; and limiting the kinds of financial losses for which such women can claim.

In all provinces and territories, women can also sue their assailants in civil law for assault and battery; they can sue police in negligence for failing to enforce the law in a sex discriminatory way, in violation of women's equality rights under the *Charter* (*Jane Doe* v. *Metropolitan Toronto Police*); and they can sue institutions that failed to protect them, such as Children's Aid Societies (Sheehy 1994). In all of these cases, some benefits in combatting violence against women are possible through public education and resultant changes to institutional practices of law enforcement. Certain other law reforms need to be put in place, however, including longer time limits within which women can decide whether to pursue a civil suit, especially when childhood sexual abuse is the wrong, access to legal aid to pursue these cases, and judicial education, among other reforms.

Many provinces also have disciplinary boards that hear complaints of sexual assault against professionals such as doctors (Rodgers). Some law societies have begun to define professional behaviour and misbehaviour by reference to sex discrimination and sexual harassment (Certosimo). A few judges have been held to account publicly for both their "private" behaviour (e.g. convictions for wife assault) ("Judge convicted of assaulting wife") and for their courtroom behaviour, including sexual harassment of women lawyers, inappropriate and biased statements about women, and voiced opinions on violence against women. Most have been reprimanded at best, many have been exonerated and their remarks "explained," but some have been disciplined more severely and have been removed from the bench.[18]

## Conclusion

Violence against women must be conceptualized as an issue of substantive equality, and it will be crucially important to clarify and articulate that understanding as a long-term goal. Clarity about this goal should help steer away from legal responses that frame women as passive "victims," or that feed the "law and order" agenda. A women's movement that is vital and independent of government is critical to this task. Drawing upon the knowledge generated by the women's movement, we must draft legislation that presumes women's inequality, acknowledges context, and challenges power relations and beliefs, such that public debate and social change become possible.

A government committed to ending violence against women will take its leadership and advice from the women's movement since that is where it will find the expertise and the political commitment to women's equality. We must, simultaneously, de-emphasize law as the solution, and support the women's movement; which continues to put the pressure on the state and thereby creates the political conditions for further engagement with law.

We need new standards for judging our lawyers and judges as professionals, including questions of impartiality and bias, in light of their commitment to advancing equality rights and their behaviour in the prosecution and defence of male violence against women.

The placement of feminists in law as lawyers and policy makers is also crucial to provide inside expertise as well on legal strategies and responses, as is the inclusion of women within government itself. Such women must be present in such numbers as to permit the pooling of ideas and experience and to withstand the inevitable backlash.

Mechanisms of enforcement need to be considered, giving women access to power to insist that law be followed. Statutory reviews of the operation of new legislation should be enacted as part of the statute, so as to permit ongoing monitoring and to provide women's groups with the tools with which to pursue further reform. Our hopes for our future include publicly available and enforceable guidelines for police, Crowns, and judges; legal standing for women in criminal proceedings apart from the prosecutor; access to money to hire our own lawyers; and the power to choose to avoid law altogether.

*This article was delivered as a speech in October 1996 in Ascuncion, Paraguay, to the "Seminario sobre violencia contra la Mujer," sponsored by the Canadian International Development Agency. The footnotes were added in May 1999.*

## Notes

[1]For an overview and a specific discussion of feminist theorizing about rape law reform see Boyd and Sheehy.

[2]For concrete examples of this distinction see Shrofel.

[3]A developing defence of "rage" used predominatly in femicide prosecutions is arguably one such example (see Côté).

[4]Ontario Judge Mercier disagreed with a jury's verdict in convicting a man of sexual assault against his ex-girlfriend; he gave Bernard Albert a suspended sentence with one day of probation ("Man gets day's probation in rape of ex-girlfriend").

[5]For a more nuanced discussion of the forms of the rape prohibition before and after this date see Backhouse 1983; Boyle.

[6]There is an abundant feminist literature on the use of this defence for wife murder; see Edwards.

[7]The *Criminal Law Amendment Act*. The reforms are thoroughly described in Boyle.

[8]More generally see McLeod 1993.

[9]Justice Bertha Wilson (retired); Justice Claire L'Heureux-Dubé; and Justice Beverley McLachlin.

[10]The fact that sexual assault remains a deeply gendered crime has even been acknowledged by the Supreme Court of Canada in *R.* v. *Osolin* (669).

[11]*R.* v. *Chase* (1987), 37 C.C.C. (3d) 97 (S.C.C.) reversing (1984), 55 N.B.R. 97 (C.A.). The lower court decision is analyzed in Dawson.

[12]See McIntyre for a detailed account of the consultation process as well as the women's movement's various drafts and strategies.

[13]See, for example, *R.* v. *O'Leary* wherein Mrs. O'Leary refused to sign a bond requiring her to keep the peace in circumstances where her husband had pleaded guilty to assaulting her, counter-charges against her had been dismissed, yet she was willing to enter into a mutual bond on the condition that counselling be required of her husband.

[14]The women were Marlene Moore, who committed suicide in the Prison for Women in 1988 at the age of 28 (see Kershaw and Lasovich) and Lisa Neve (see Renke).

[15]There are conflicting views about whether this a positive or negative response in terms of responding to wife assault. Compare, for example, Snider 1998 with Stubbs.

[16]*An Act to Amend the Criminal Code*, S.C. 1995, c. 22.

[17]See, in the area of sexual assault, *Re Attorney General for Ontario and Criminal Injuries Compensation Board et al.; Re Jane Doe and Criminal Injuries Compensation Board* reversing a decision of the Board. For a discussion of a woman's claim for wife assault see Wiegers.

[18]See Bourrie, who details the resignation of Judge Bienvenue of the Québec Superior Court; see also "Controversial Judge Resigns" which details the resignation of Justice Sirois from the Saskatchewan Queen's Bench.

## References


Abell, J. *Bringing It All Back Home: Feminist Struggle, Feminist Theory and Feminist Engagement With Law. The Case of Wife Battering*. LL.M. Thesis. Osgoode Hall Law School, 1991.

*An Act to Amend the Criminal Code (production of records in criminal proceedings)*, S.C. 1997, c. 30.

*An Act to Amend the Criminal Code*, S.C. 1995, c. 22.

*An Act to Amend the Criminal Code (self-induced intoxication)*. S.C. 1995, c. 32.

*An Act to Amend the Criminal Code*, S.C. 1992, c. 38.

Altschul, S., and C. Carron. "Chronology of Some Legal Landmarks in the History of Canadian Women." *McGill Law Journal* 21 (1975): 476–494.

Arbour, The Honourable Louise, Commissioner. *Commission of Inquiry into Certain Events at the Prison for Women in Kingston.* Ottawa: Public Works and Government Services, 1996.

Atkins, S., and B. Hoggett. *Women and the Law*. Oxford: Basil Blackwell, 1984.

Backhouse, C. "The Tort of Seduction: Fathers and Daughters in Nineteenth-Century Canada." *Dalhousie Law Journal* 10 (1986): 45–80.

Backhouse, C. "To Open the Way for Others of My Sex': Clara Brett Martin's Career as Canada's First Woman Lawyer." *Canadian Journal of Women and the Law* 1.1 (1985): 1–41.

Backhouse, C. "Nineteenth-Century Canadian Rape Law 1800–1892." *Essays in the History of Canadian Law, Vol. II.* Ed. D. Flaherty. Toronto: The Osgoode Society, 1983. 200–247.

Bernier, C. "Bringing a Feminist Analysis to the Department of Justice." Unpublished paper, 1996, on file at the University of Toronto Law Library.

Bonnycastle, K., and G. Rigakos. "The 'Truth' About Battered Women as Contested Terrain." *Unsettling Truths. Battered Women, Policy, Politics, and Contemporary Research in Canada.* Eds. K. Bonnycastle and G. Rigakos. Vancouver: Collective Press, 1998. 10–20.

Bourrie, M. "Disgraced Judge Resigns Before Impeachment." *Law Times* 30 September–October 1996: 1.

Boyd, S., and E. Sheehy, "Feminism and the Law in Canada: Overview." *Law and Society. A Critical Perspective.* Eds. T. C. Caputo, M. Kennedy, C. E. Reasons, and A. Brannigan. Toronto: Harcourt, Brace, Jovanovich, 1989. 255–270.

Boyle, C. *Sexual Assault.* Toronto: Carswells, 1984.

British Columbia Ministry of the Attorney General. *Policy on the Criminal Justice System Response to Violence Against Women and Children. Violence Against Women in Relationships Policy.* Victoria: British Columbia Ministry of the Attorney General, 1996.

*Brooks* v. *Canada Safeway Ltd.* [1989] 1 S.C.R. 1219.

Busby, K. "Discriminatory Uses of Personal Records in Sexual Violence Cases." *Canadian Journal of Women and the Law* 9.1 (1997): 148–177.

Cairns Way, R. "The Criminalization of Stalking: An Exercise in Media Manipulation and Political Opportunism." *McGill Law Journal* 39 (1994): 379–400.

*Canadian Charter of Rights and Freedoms,* Part I of the *Constitution Act, 1982*, being Schedule B to the *Canada Act 1982* (U.K.), 1982, c. 11.

Carey, R. "Useless (UOSLAS) v. The Bar: The Struggle of the Ottawa Student Clinic to Represent Battered Women." *Journal of Law and Society* 8 (1992): 54–81.

Certosimo, M. "A Conflict is a Conflict is a Conflict: Fiduciary Duty and Lawyer-Client Sexual Relations" *Dalhousie Law Journal* 16 (1993): 448–470.

Clark, L., and D. Lewis. *Rape: The Price of Coercive Sexuality.* Toronto:

Women's Press, 1977.

Cohen, L., and C. Backhouse. "Desexualizing Rape: Dissenting View on the Proposed Rape Amendments." *Canadian Woman Studies/les cahiers de la femme* 2.4 (1980): 99–103.

*Constitution Act, 1982,* being Schedule B to the *Canada Act 1982* (U.K.), 1982, c. 11.

"Controversial judge resigns." *The [Toronto] Globe and Mail* 28 February 1998: A10.

Côté, Andrée. *Violence Against Women and Criminal Law Reform: Recommendations for an Egalitarian Reform of the Criminal Law.* Ottawa: Action Ontarienne contre la violence faite aux femmes, 1995.

*Criminal Law Amendment Act*, S.C. 1980-81-82, c. 125.

Currie, D. "The Criminalization of Violence Against Women: Feminist Demands and Patriarchal Accomodation." *Unsettling Truths. Battered Women, Policy, Politics, and Contemporary Research in Canada.* Eds. K. Bonnycastle and G. Rigakos. Vancouver: Collective Press, 1998. 41–51.

Dawson Brettel, T. "Legal Structures: A Feminist Critique of Sexual Assault Law Reform." *Resources for Feminist Research* 14 (1985): 40–43.

Edwards, S. "Male Violence Against Women: Excusatory and Explanatory Ideologies in Law and Society." *Gender, Sex and the Law.* Ed. S. Edwards. London: Croon Helm, 1985. 183–218

*Edwards* v. *A.G. Canada*, [1930] A.C. 124 (P.C.).

Faraday, F. "Dealing with Sexual Harassment in the Workplace: The Promise and Limitations of Human Rights Discourse." *Osgoode Hall Law Journal* 32 (1994): 33–63.

Federal/Provincial/Territorial Working Group of Attorney Generals, *Gender Equality in the Canadian Justice System*. Ottawa: Department of Justice, 1992.

Gavigan, S. "Petit Treason in Eighteenth-Century England: Women's Inequality Before the Law." *Canadian Journal of Women and the Law* 3.2 (1989–90): 335–374.

Hagan, J., and F Kay. *Gender in Practice. A Study of Lawyers' Lives.* Oxford: Oxford University Press, 1995.

Harvey, C. "Women in Law in Canada." *Manitoba Law Journal* 4 (1970): 9–38.

Hosek, C. "Women and Constitutional Process." *And No One Cheered.* Eds. K. Banting and R Simeon. Toronto: Agincourt, 1983. 280–300.

*Jane Doe* v. *Metropolitan Toronto Police* (1998), 39 O.R. (3d) 487 (C.A.).

"Judge convicted of assaulting wife." *The Ottawa Citizen* (31 May 1989) A5.

Kershaw, A., and M. Lasovich. *Rock-A-Bye Baby. A Death Behind Bars.* Toronto: McClelland and Stewart, 1991.

MacCrimmon, M. "Trial by Ordeal." *Canadian Criminal Law Review* 1 (1996): 31–56.

"Man Gets Day's Probation in Rape of Ex-Girlfriend." *The Globe and Mail* 21 June 1990: A1.

Manitoba Department of Justice. *Directive of the Attorney General and Solicitor*

*General Regarding Spousal Assault.* Winnipeg: Manitoba Department of Justice, 1992.

Martin, D., and J. Mosher. "Unkept Promises: Experiences of Immigrant Women With the Neo-Criminalization of Wife Abuse." *Canadian Journal of Women and the Law* 3.1 (1995): 3–44.

McIntyre, S "Redefining Reformism: The Consultations that Shaped Bill C-49." *Confronting Sexual Assault. A Decade of Legal and Social Change.* Eds. J. Roberts and R. Mohr. Toronto: University of Toronto Press, 1994. 293–327.

McLeod, L. "Policy Decisions and Prosecutorial Dilemmas: The Unanticipated Consequences of Good Intentions." *Wife Assault and the Canadian Criminal Justice System.* Eds. M. Valverde, L. McLeod, and K. Johnson. Toronto: Centre of Criminology, 1993.

McLeod, L. *Wife Battering and the Web of Hope: Progress, Dilemmas and Visions of Prevention.* Ottawa: National Clearinghouse on Family Violence, 1989.

Mossman, M. J. "Feminism and Legal Method: The Difference it Makes." *Australian Journal of Law and Society* 30 (1986): 30–52.

Muzychka, M. *Beyond Reasonable Doubt: The Influence of Victim Stereotypes and Social Biases on Police Response to Women's Complaints of Sexual Assault.* St. John's, NF: Provincial Advisory Council on the Status of Women, 1991.

Ontario Provincial Police, *Police Standards Manual 0217.00. Police Response to Wife Assault.* Toronto: Ontario Provincial Police, 1994.

*R.* v. *Lavallee*, [1990] 1 S.C.R. 852.

*R.* v. *Carosella*, [1997] 1 S.C.R. 80.

*R.* v. *Chase,* (1987), 37 C.C.C. (3d) 97 (S.C.C.).

*R.* v. *Chase*, (1984), 55 N.B.R. 97 (C.A.).

*R.* v. *Currie,* (1996), 26 O.R. (3d) 444 (C.A.).

*R.* v. *Darrach* (1998), 38 O.R. (3d) 1 (C.A.).

*R.* v. *Daviault*, [1994] 3 S.C.R. 63.

*R.* v. *Mills*, [1997] A.J. No. 891 (Q.B.), on appeal to the Supreme Court of Canada.

*R.* v. *O'Connor*, [1995] 4 S.C.R. 411.

*R.* v. *O'Leary* (14 February 1989), (Ont. Prov. Ct.) [unreported].

*R.* v. *Osolin*, [1993] 4 S.C.R. 595 at 669.

*R.* v. *Seaboyer*; *R.* v. *Gayme*, [1991] 2 S.C.R. 577.

Ratushny, Lynn. *Self-Defence Review: Final Report.* Ottawa: Minister of Justice and Solicitor General of Canada, 1997.

*Re Attorney General for Ontario and Criminal Injuries Compensation Board et al.; Re Jane Doe and Criminal Injuries Compensation Board,* (1995), 22 O.R. (3d) 129 (Gen. Div.).

Renke, W. "Case Comment: Lisa Neve, Dangerous Offender." *Alberta Law Review* 33 (1995): 650–676.

Rigakos, G. "The Politics of Protection: Battered Women, Protection Orders, and

Police Subculture." *Women, Policy, Politics, and Contemporary Research in Canada.* Eds. K. Bonnycastle and G. Rigakos. Vancouver: Collective Press, 1998. 82–92.

Roberts, J. "Sexual Assault in Canada: Recent Statistical Trends." *Queen's Law Journal* 21 (1996): 395–421.

Rodgers, S. "Health Care Providers and Sexual Assault: Feminist Law Reform?" *Canadian Journal of Women and the Law* 8.1 (1995): 159–189.

Royal Commission on the Status of Women. *Report of the Royal Commission on the Status of Women.* Ottawa: Queen's Printer, 1970.

Sachs, A., and J. H. Wilson. *Sexism and the Law: A Study of Male Beliefs and Judicial Bias.* Oxford: Martin Roberston and Co., 1978.

Sheehy, E. "Legalizing Justice for All Women: Canadian Women's Struggle for Democratic Rape Law Reforms." *Feminist Law Journal* 6 (1996): 87–113.

Sheehy, E. *The Intoxication Defence in Canada: Why Women Should Care.* Ottawa: Canadian Advisory Council on the Status of Women, 1995a.

Sheehy, E. *A Brief on Bill C-72.* Ottawa: National Association of Women and the Law, 1995b.

Sheehy, E. "Compensation for Women Who Have Been Raped." *Confronting Sexual Assault. A Decade of Legal and Social Change.* Eds. J. Roberts and R. Mohr. Toronto: University of Toronto Press, 1994. 205–241.

Sheehy, E. "Feminist Argumentation Before the Supreme Court of Canada in *R.* v. *Seaboyer*; *R.* v. *Gayme*: The Sound of One Hand Clapping." *Melbourne University Law Review* 18 (1991): 450–468.

Shrofel, S. "Equality Rights and Law Reform in Saskatchewan: An Analysis of the Charter Compliance Process." *Canadian Journal of Women and the Law* 1.1 (1985): 108–118.

Snider, L. "Struggles for Social Justice: Criminalization and Alternatives." *Unsettling Truths: Battered Women, Policy, Politics, and Contemporary Research in Canada.* Eds. K. Bonnycastle and G. Rigakos. Vancouver: Collective Press, 1998. 145–154.

Status of Women Canada. *Setting the Stage for the Next Century: The Federal Plan for Gender Equality.* Ottawa: Status of Women Canada, 1995.

Strange, C. "Historical Perspectives on Wife Assault." *Wife Assault and the Canadian Criminal Justice System.* Eds. M. Valverde, L. MacLeod, and K. Johnson. Toronto: Centre of Criminology, 1993. 293–304.

Stubbs, J. "'Communitarian' Conferencing and Violence Against Women: A Cautionary Note." *Wife Assault and the Canadian Criminal Justice System.* Eds. M. Valverde, L. MacLeod, and K. Johnson. Toronto: Centre of Criminology, 1993. 260–289.

Turner, J. "Saskatchewan Responds to Family Violence: *The Victims of Domestic Violence Act, 1995.*" *Wife Assault and the Canadian Criminal Justice System.* Eds. M. Valverde, L. MacLeod, and K. Johnson. Toronto: Centre of Criminology, 1993. 183–197.

Ursel, J., and S. Brickey. "The Potential of Legal Reform Reconsidered: A Case

Study of the Manitoba Zero Tolerance Policy on Family Violence." *Post-Critical Criminology*. Ed. T. O'Reilly-Fleming. Scarborough: Prentice Hall, 1996. 56–77.

Wiegers, W. "Compensation for Wife Abuse: Empowering Victims?" *University of British Columbia Law Review* 28 (1994): 247–307.

Wilson, The Honourable Bertha, Commissioner. *Touchtones for Change: Equality, Diversity and Accountability. The Report on Gender Equality in the Legal Profession*. Ottawa: Canadian Bar Association, 1993.

Young, D. *The Handling of Race Discrimination Complaints at the Ontario Human Rights Commission*. Toronto: unpublished, 1992.

# Contributor Notes

***Himani Bannerji*** is an Associate Professor in the Department of Sociology at York University in Toronto. She is the author and editor of several books, including: *The Dark Side of the Nation: Essays in Multiculturalism, Nationalism and Gender; Thinking Through: Essays in Feminism, Marxism and Anti-Racism; Unsettling Relations: The University as a Site of Feminist Struggles*; *Returning the Gaze: Essays on Racism, Feminism and Politics*; and *The Writing on the Wall: Essays on Culture and Politics.*

***Dawn G. Blessing,*** RN, BSN, MSN, is currently working as a couple and family therapist with Family Services in Thunder Bay, Ontario. She has been involved with community-based programs and research in the areas of women's and children's health.

***Elizabeth Comack*** is a Professor of Sociology at the University of Manitoba where she teaches courses in feminist criminology and the sociology of law. Her recent publications include *Locating Law: Race/Class/Gender Connections* (1999, editor), and *Women in Trouble: Connecting Women's Law Violations to Their Histories of Abuse* (1996). She is currently completing a SSHRC-sponsored research project entitled, "Gendered Violence: Women, Violence and the Criminal Justice Response."

***Maria Crawford*** worked for many years in women's shelters in Ontario as well as with many grassroots anti-violence organizations across Canada, and internationally, on the issue of lethal violence against women. She is recognized as an expert witness on Intimate Femicide, and is currently the Executive Director of Eva's Initiatives, an organization in Toronto serving homeless youth.

***Juergen Dankwort***, MSW, PhD, has worked in the domestic violence field since 1986. His range of experience includes designing, implementing and facilitating groups for domestically violent persons; providing staff training to work effectively and strategically with such offenders; and serving as a resource person to both government and non-government agencies for policy and protocol development in Canada, the U.S. and overseas. He has conducted research and has published and lectured extensively on this topic. He taught at the Graduate School of Social Work, University of Houston, Texas, until recently, and has since conducted research and is teaching in British Columbia, Canada.

***Tanis Day*** taught economics at Queen's University in Kingston, Ontario before leaving to become a consulting economist in 2000. She lives in Kitchener-Waterloo where she practices advanced energy healing.

***Walter DeKeseredy*** is a Professor of Sociology at Ohio University in Athens, Ohio. He has published dozens of journal articles and book chapters on woman abuse, crime in public housing, and criminological theory. He is the author of *Woman Abuse in Dating Relationships: The Role of Male Peer Support* and *Women, Crime and the Canadian Criminal Justice System*; with Ronald Hinch, coauthor of *Woman Abuse: Sociological Perspectives*; with Desmond Ellis, coauthor of the second edition of *The Wrong Stuff: An Introduction to the Sociological Study of Deviance*; with Martin Schwartz, coauthor of *Contemporary Criminology*, *Sexual Assault on the College Campus: The Role of Male Peer Support*, and *Woman Abuse on Campus: Results from the Canadian National Survey*; with Linda MacLeod, *Woman Abuse: A Sociological Story*; and with Shahid Alvi and Desmond Ellis, *Contemporary Social Problems in North American Society*. In 1995, he received the Critical Criminologist of the Year Award from the American Society of Criminology's Division on Critical Criminology. In 1993, he received Carleton University's Research Achievement Award. Currently he serves on the Editorial Boards of *Criminal Justice*, *Women & Criminal Justice*, *Violence Against Women: An International and Interdisciplinary Journal*, and *Crime and Delinquency*.

***Myrna Dawson*** teaches in the Centre of Criminology at the University of Toronto. She specializes in criminology and the sociology of the law, researching social and legal responses to violent victimization. She is co-author, with Rose-mary Gartner and Maria Crawford, of *Woman Killing: Intimate Femicide in Ontario, 1991-1994* (1977). For her work on intimacy and the law, she received a Canadian Policy Research Award from the Government of Canada, and for her research on specialized domestic violence courts, she received (with her co-author Ronit Dinovitzer) the Gene Carte Award from the American Society of Criminology.

***Anthony N. Doob*** is a professor at the Centre of Criminology, University of

Toronto. He has been teaching at the University of Toronto since 1968 and has been associated with the Centre of Criminology since 1971. He served as Director of the Centre of Criminology from 1979 to 1989 and was one of the members of the Canadian Sentencing Commission from 1984 until 1987. He is an author of over 150 articles, books, and reports covering a wide range of topics including sentencing, the operation of the youth justice system, and public knowledge and attitudes about sentencing and other aspects of the youth and criminal justice systems.

***Rosemary Gartner*** teaches in the Centre of Criminology at the University of Toronto. An award-winning scholar, she has performed ground-breaking cross-national research into female homicide in a wide variety of contexts. She has contributed to 18 books, including two chapters in the *Encyclopedia of Sociology*. She is the co-author (with Myrna Dawson and Maria Crawford) of *Woman Killing: Intimate Femicide in Ontario, 1991-1994* (1977). Her book, *Violence and Crime in a Cross-National Perspective* (1984) (co-authored with Dane Archer) won a Distinguished Scholarship Award from the American Sociological Association and an Outstanding Scholarship Award from the Society for the Study of Social Problems. It also received the Behavioural Science Research Prize from the American Association for the Advancement of Science.

***Tuula Heinonen*** is an Associate Professor at the Faculty of Social Work, University of Manitoba. She has conducted research on women's health in the Philippines and Canada. She is also interested in immigration and cultural retention and international social development in Asia.

***Jenny Horsman*** is a community educator and researcher with a feminist perspective. She has more than two decades of experience in the adult literacy field in England, Sierra Leone and Canada. She is the author of numerous articles as well as *Something in My Mind Besides the Everyday: Women and Literacy* (Toronto, Women's Press, 1990) and *Too Scared to Learn: Women, Violence and Education* (Toronto: McGilligan Books, 1999 and internationally, Mahwah, NJ: Lawrence Erlbaum and Associates, 2000). Her current work focuses on the impact of trauma on learning. She travels widely to give lectures and workshops on this issue.

***Yasmin Jiwani*** recently joined the faculty at the Department of Communication Studies, Concordia University, Montreal. Prior to her move to Montreal, she was the Executive Coordinator of the BC/Yukon FREDA Centre for Research on Violence Agasint Women and Children. Yasmin has written extensively on violence, as well as on issues of racism and the media. Her past work includes a critical analysis of the media coverage of the murders of the Gakhal family in Vernon, BC, and more recently, the media's treatment of the story of Reena Virk. Her main interests lie in mapping the intersections of intimate and systemic forms of violence, and identifying viable points of intervention.

***Holly Johnson*** is the Chief of Research at the Canadian Centre for Justice Statistics at Statistics Canada. For many years, the primary focus of her work at Statistics Canada, and teaching at Queen's University, has been domestic violence and other crimes of violence against women. She is the author of a text and numerous other publications on this topic and was the principal investigator of Statistics Canada's national survey on violence against women. Currently, she is head of a Research Unit designed to explore Statistics Canada data sources for their application to important policy areas, including delinquency by youth, trends in crime rates, and family violence

***Christine Kreklewitz***, MSc, is an interdisciplinary PhD candidate at the University of Manitoba. She received her Master's Degree in Family Studies and her areas of research expertise include sexual abuse and violence within the family context (i.e., incest survivor mothers and parenting, the intergenerational transmission of incest, and incest offenders.) She has also completed research involving early childhood school transition, at-risk children and youth, and program evaluation. Her work focuses increasingly on qualitative research, feminist research, and the effects of sexual abuse on women's health.

***June Larkin*** is the Coordinator of the Undergraduate Program in Women's Studies, St. George Campus, for the Institute for Women's Studies and Gender Studies, University of Toronto.

***Emma D. LaRocqu***e is a Plains Cree Métis originally from northeastern Alberta. She is a writer, poet, historian, social, and literary critic, and a professor in the Department of Native Studies, University of Manitoba. For more than two decades, she has lectured both nationally and internationally on Native/White Relations, focusing on the colonial experience, identity, gender roles, and Aboriginal Literatures. LaRocque has a PhD in Interdisciplinary Studies, an MA in History, an MA in Peace Studies, and a BA in English/Communications. She is the author of *Defeathering the Indian* a study of stereotypes about "Indians" in public school.

***Suzanne Lenon*** works as a Crisis Line and Training Coordinator at the Ottawa Rape Crisis Centre.

***Diane J. Forsdick Martz*** is the Director of the Centre for Rural Studies and Enrichment at St. Peter's College in Muenster. At the Centre for Rural Studies and Enrichment, she is working on the sustainablility of rural communities, the work of farm families and the issue of domestic violence in rural communities. She has taught geography at the University of Saskatchewan since 1981 and at St. Peter's College since 1988.

*Katherine M. J. McKenna* is an Associate Professor of History and Women's Studies at the University of Western Ontario in London.

*Lynn McClure* has worked for several years as a nursepractitioner at Klinic Community Health Centre inWinnipeg. She has a Masters degree in nursing and also has certification as a Womens' Health Nurse Practitioner in the U.S. As well as providing primary health care to women, she has been interested in, and involved with, others in research that has practical application to the delivery of health care.

*Helene Moussa* is a past member of the Refugee and Migration Service World Council of Churches in Geneva, Switzerland.

*Mary Nyquist* teaches in English, Women's Studies/Gender Studies and Literary Studies at the University of Toronto. Involved in feminist and anti-racist organizations for over 20 years, she has facilitated community groups for survivors of domestic violence and has introduced a course on gendered violence into the Women's Studies/Gender Studies curriculum. She has published numerous academic essays on a wide variety of early modern, enlightenment, nineteenth- and twentieth-century literary texts, and is currently engaged in a research project on early modern European colonialist and democratic conceptions of "tyranny." She is also completing her first volume of poetry.

*The Ontario Association of Interval and Transition House*s (OAITH) is a network of women's shelters and other services which lobbies provincially and federally for change to end violence against abused women and their children. Copies of "Locked In, Left Out" are available for $10.00 each from OAITH, 2 Carlton Street, Suite 1404, Toronto, Ontario, M5B 1J3. Tel: (416) 977-6619. Fax: (416) 977-1227. Email: oaith@web.net.

*Kim Pate* is the proud mother of Michael and Madison, budding pro-feminist and feminist penal abolitionists. A teacher and lawyer by training, she is the Executive Director of the Canadian Association of Elizabeth Fry Societies (CAEFS) and the President of the National Associations Archive in Criminal Justice (NAACJ).

*Rudolf Rausch* has been licensed as a psychologist in Quebec since 1985 and listed by the Canadian Register of Health Service Providers in Psychology since 1990. In addition to his private psychotherapy practice in Vaudreuil-Dorion, he has been active in the field of wife abuse as a staff trainer, consultant, and clinical supervisor for a variety of agencies since 1987. He has taught intervention with wife abusers at the Universite de Quebec, Universite Laval, and has taught groups of clinicians, family mediators, and correctional service workers. His consultative work and training has included involvement with both federal and provincial government as well as the judiciary.

***Deborah Bryson Sarauer***, BA, BSW, RSW, is a registered social worker who works as a family therapist for Mental Health Services of the Central Plains Health District in rural Saskatchewan. Deborah believes rural mental health workers need to be able to think and work outside their own comfort zone in order to work effectively with and honour the lives of rural people. Previously, she was Dean at St. Peter's College in Muenster and continues to farm with her husband on a multi-generational family farm.

***Martin D. Schwartz*** is Professor of Sociology and Presidential Research Scholar at Ohio University, where he has twice won the College of Arts and Sciences Outstanding Teacher Award, and been named the university's Outstanding Graduate Faculty Member. He has published more than 75 articles, chapters, edited books and books on a variety of topics in such journals as *Criminology, Deviant Behavior, Violence Against Women, Justice Quarterly, Journal of Family Violence,* and *Journal of Interpersonal Violence.* Among his books he is the co-author (with Walter DeKeseredy) of *Contemporary Criminology*; *Sexual Assault on the College Campus: The Role of Male Peer Support*; and *Woman Abuse on Campus;* and (with Lawrence Travis) *Corrections: An Issues Approach,* now in its 4th edition; the editor of *Researching Sexual Violence Against Women: Methodological and Personal Perspectives,* and the co-editor (with Dragan Milovanovic) of *Race, Class and Gender in Criminology: The Intersections.* He is North American editor of *Criminal Justice: The International Journal of Policy and Practice,* and has served as deputy editor of *Justice Quarterly*, and on the editorial boards of *Criminology, Humanity & Society, Violence Against Women; Race, Class & Gender; Teaching Sociology,* and the *Journal of Criminal Justice Education.* He has received the career research achievement award of the American Society of Criminology's Division on Critical Criminology.

***Carol Scurfield*** graduated from the family practice residency at the University of Manitoba in 1983. She has practiced in rural and northern Canada. For the past 15 years she has worked at the Women's Health Clinic in Winnipeg, Manitoba. Her interests include all issues that affect the health of women but especially issues related to adolescent health and women who are marginalized by the health care system.

***Aysan Sev'er*** is a first-generation Turkish-Canadian. She teaches graduate and undergraduate courses on gender relations and sociology of the family at the University of Toronto. Her research focuses on problematic issues in women's lives, such as separation and divorce, sexual harassment, and violence by male partners. She is interested in extreme forms of violence against women in some of the developing countries, and how the local and international communities can combine forces toward the elimination of such violence. Currently, she is publishing a feminist journal on women's health called *Women's Health and Urban Life.* Her most recent book, *Fleeing the House of Horrors,* is being published by the University of Toronto Press.

***Elizabeth Sheehy*** teaches Criminal Law and Procedure and Women and the Law at the University of Ottawa, Faculty of Law, where she focuses her research and writing on the legal response to male violence against women and the legal construction of equality. She will be the Shirley Greenberg Professor of women and the Legal Profession for 2002-2004.

***Sari Tudiver*** is an Associate Editor of *A Friend Indeed: The Newsletter for Women in the Prime of Life*. She has been involved in education, research, writing, and advocacy in women's health for over 20 years. Particular interests include reproductive and genetic technologies, women and pharmaceutical use and ensuring that women have access to health information. She served as Resource Coordinator at the Women's Health Clinic in Winnipeg (1993-1998) and is the author of a number of publications and research reports on women's health. She is currently a senior policy analyst with the Women's Health Bureau at Health Canada. A founding member of the Canadian Women's Health Network, Sari served on its executive from 1993-2000.

***The Woman Abuse Council of Toronto*** is an intersectoral policy development and planning body. The goal of the council is to create a more effective community response to woman abuse that protects women and holds abusers accountable.

# Permissions

"Methods of Measurement" by Holly Johnson first appeared in *Dangerous Domains: Violence Against Women in Canada* (Toronto: Nelson Canada, 1996: 26-60). Reprinted with permission from the author.

"Understanding the Attacks on Statistics Canada's Violence Against Women Survey" by Anthony N. Doob first appeared in M. Valverde, L. MacLeod and K. Johnson (Eds.), *Wife Assault and the Canadian Criminal Justice System* (Toronto: Centre for Criminology, University of Toronto, 1995: 157-165). Reprinted with permission from the author and the publisher.

"The 1999 General Social Survey on Spousal Violence: An Analysis" by Yasmin Jiwani first appeared in *Canadian Woman Studies/les cahiers de la femme*, 20 (3) (2000): 34-40. Reprinted with permission from the author.

"Exploring the Continuum: Sexualized Violence by Men and Male Youth Against Women and Girls." by Aysan Sev'er first appeared in *Atlantis* 24 (1) (1999): 92-104. Reprinted with permission from the publisher.

"The Incidence and Prevalence of Woman Abuse in Canadian Courtship" by Walter DeKeseredy and Martin D. Schwartz first appeared in their book *Woman Abuse on Campus: Results from the Canadian National Survey* (Thousand Oaks, California: Sage Publications, 1998: 35-62). © 1998 by Sage Publications. Reprinted with permission from the publisher.

"Woman Killing: Intimate Femicide in Ontario, 1974-1994" by Rosemary Gartner, Myrna Dawson, and Maria Crawford first appeared in *Resources for*

*Feminist Research/Documentation sur la recherche féministe* 26 (3-4) (1998/99): 151-172. Reprinted with permission from the publisher.

"Violence in the Aboriginal Communities" by Emma D. LaRocque first appeared in M. Valverde, L. MacLeod and K. Johnson (Eds.), *Wife Assault and the Canadian Criminal Justice System,* (Toronto: Centre for Criminology, University of Toronto, 1995: 104-122). Reprinted with permission from the author.

"Domestic Violence and the Experiences of Rural Women in East-Central Saskatchewan" by Diane Forsdick Martz and Deborah Bryson Saraurer was commissioned by the Prairie Women's Health Centre of Excellence in Winnipeg and is available on their web site at http://www:pwhce.ca. Reprinted with permission from the Centre for Rural Studies and the Environment at St. Peter's College in Muenster, Saskatchewan and from the Prairie Women's Health Centre of Excellence.

"A Question of Silence: Reflections on Violence Against Women in Communities of Colour" by Himani Bannerji first appeared in her book, *The Dark Side of the Nation: Essays in Multiculturalism, Nationalism and Gender* (Toronto: Canadian Scholar's Press, 2000: 151-174). Himani Bannerji copyright © 2000. Reprinted with permission from Canadian Scholar's Press, Inc.

"Race, Gender, Violence and Health Care: A Review of the Literature" was excerpted from Yasmin Jiwani's article *Intersecting Inequalities: Immigrant Women of Colour, Violence and Health Care* published by the FREDA Centre for Research on Violence Against Women in Vancouver (2000). The article can be found on their website at http://www.harbour.sfu.ca/freda/articles/hlth03. Reprinted with permission from the author.

"Remembrance of Things Past: The Legacy of Childhood Sexual Abuse in Midlife Women" by Sari Tudiver, Lynn McClure, Tuula Heinonen, Christine Kreklewitz and Carol Scurfield is available on the the Canadian Women's Health Network's web site at http://www.cwhn.ca/resources/csa/article.html. The article first appeared in *A Friend Indeed: The Newsletter for Women in the Prime of Life* 18 (4) 2000. For a sample issue and subscription information please contact *A Friend Indeed* at (204) 989-8028 or visit their web site at www.afriendindeed.ca. Reprinted with permission from the authors and the publisher.

"Literacy Learning for Survivors of Trauma: Acting "Normal" by Jenny Horsman first appeared in*Canadian Woman Studies/les cahiers de la femme* 17 (4) (1998): 62-73. Reprinted with permission from the author.

"Struck Dumb" by Mary Nyquist first appeared in *Canadian Woman Studies/les cahiers de la femme* 17 (4) (1998): 69-71. Reprinted with permission from the author.

"Do We Need to Syndromize Women's Experiences? The Limitations of the 'Battered Woman Syndrome'" by Elizabeth Comack first appeared in K. D. Bonnycastle and George S. Rigakos (Eds.), *Unsettling Truths, Battered Women, Policy, Politics, and Contemporary Research in Canada* (Vancouver, BC: Collective Press, 1998: 105-111). Reprinted with permission from the author.

"Mapping the Politics of a Research Journey: Violence Against Women as a Public Health Issue" by Katherine M. J. McKenna and Dawn G. Blessing first appeared in *Resources for Feminist Research/Documentation sur la recherche féministe* 26 (1/2) (1998): 77-96. Reprinted with permission from the publisher.

"Women, Poverty and HIV Infection" by June Larkin first appeared in *Canadian Woman Studies/les cahiers de la femme* 20 (3) (2000): 137-141. Reprinted with permission from the author.

"The Health-Related Economic Costs of Violence Against Women: The Tip of the Iceberg" by Tanis Day and Katherine M. J. McKenna is published by permission of the authors. The project was originally commissioned and funded by the Canadian Advisory Council on the Status of Women. An earlier version was printed and distributed in 1995 by the Centre for Research on Violence Against Women and Children of The University of Western Ontario in London.

"In the Matter of 'X': Building Race into Sexual Harassment" by Himani Bannerji in her edited collection, *Thinking Through: Essays on Feminism, Marxism and Antiracism* (Toronto: Women's Press, 2000: 121-158). Himani Bannerji copyright © 2000. Reprinted with permission from the Women's Press.

"Violence Against Refugee Women: Gender Oppression, Canadian Policy, and the International Struggle for Human Rights" by Helene Moussa first appeared in *Resources for Feminist Research/Documentation sur la recherche féministe* 26 (3/4) (1998): 79-111. Reprinted with permission from the publisher.

"Living on the Edge: Women, Poverty and Homelessness in Canada" by Suzanne Lenon first appeared in *Canadian Woman Studies/les cahiers de la femme*. 20 (3,4) (2000): 123-126. Reprinted with permission from the author.

"Before and After: A Woman's Story with Two Endings..." by the Metro Toronto Committee Against Wife Assault & Metro Woman Abuse Council appeared in L. Ricciutelli, J. Larkin, and E. O'Neill (Eds.), *Confronting the Cuts: A Sourcebook for Women in Ontario* (Toronto: Inanna Publications and Education Inc., 1998: 103-107). Reprinted with permission from the Woman

Abuse Council of Toronto.

"Locked In, Left Out: Impacts of the Budget Cuts on Abused Women and Children" by the Ontario Association of Interval and Transition Houses appeared in L. Ricciutelli, J. Larkin, and E. O'Neill (Eds.), *Confronting the Cuts: A Sourcebook for Women in Ontario* (Toronto: Inanna Publications and Education Inc., 1998: 29-38). Excerpted and reprinted with permission from the Ontario Association of Interval and Transition Houses in Toronto.

"Men at Work to End Wife Abuse in Quebec: A Case Study in Claims Making" by Jurguen Dankwort and Rudolf Rausch first appeared in *Violence Against Women* 6 (9) (2000): 936-959. © 2000 by Sage Publications. Reprinted with permission from the publisher.

"Erasing Race: The Story of Reena Virk" by Yasmin Jiwani first appeared in *Canadian Woman Studies/les cahiers de la femme* 19 (3) (1999): 178-184. Reprinted with permission from the author.

"Labelling Young Women as Violent: Vilification of the Most Vulnerable" by Kim Pate first appeared on the web site for the Canadian Association of Elizabeth Fry Societies at http://www.elizabethfry.ca. The author recognizes the support provided by the Youth Justice, Department of Justice Canada for the development of this article. Reprinted with permission from the author.

"Legal Responses to Violence Against Women in Canada" by Elizabeth A. Sheehy first appeared in *Canadian Woman Studies/les cahiers de la femme* 19 (1/2) (1999): 62-73. Reprinted with permission from the author.